Chinese Law

I0888304

Chinese Law

Knowledge, Practice and Transformation, 1530s to 1950s

Edited by

Li Chen and Madeleine Zelin

BRILL

LEIDEN | BOSTON

This paperback was originally published in hardback as Volume 3 in the series *Brill's Series on Modern East Asia in a Global Historical Perspective.*

Cover illustration: "A legal plaint by Qu Guangming to recover the balance of his father's deposit in a farming-land lease, with reply of Magistrate Wang of Nanbu county, Sichuan, in 1888 (Gangxu 14/9/7)." Courtesy of the Nanbu County Archives now at the Nanchong Municipal Archives in Sichuan, China.

Library of Congress Cataloging-in-Publication Data

Chinese law : knowledge, practice and transformation, 1530s to 1950s / edited by Li Chen and Madeleine Zelin.
pages cm. — (Brill's series on modern East Asia in a global historical perspective ; volume 3)
Includes papers presented at the International Workshop on Chinese Legal History, Culture, and Modernity, held at Columbia University in New York City in early May 2012.—Acknowledgement
ISBN 978-90-04-28848-5 (hardback : alk. paper) — ISBN 978-90-04-28849-2 (e-book)
1. Law—China—History—Congresses. 2. China—History—Republic, 1912–1949—Congresses. 3. China—History—Qing dynasty, 1644–1912—Congresses. I. Chen, Li (Professor of History and Sociolegal Studies), editor. II. Zelin, Madeleine, editor.
KNN107.C48 2015
349.5109'03—dc23

2014041889

ISBN 978-90-04-36283-3 (paperback, 2018)
ISBN 978-90-04-28848-5 (hardback, 2015)
ISBN 978-90-04-28849-2 (e-book, 2015)

Copyright 2015 by Koninklijke Brill NV, Leiden, The Netherlands.
Koninklijke Brill NV incorporates the imprints Brill, Brill Hes & De Graaf, Brill Nijhoff, Brill Rodopi, Brill Sense and Hotei Publishing
All rights reserved. No part of this publication may be reproduced, translated, stored in a retrieval system, or transmitted in any form or by any means, electronic, mechanical, photocopying, recording or otherwise, without prior written permission from the publisher.
Authorization to photocopy items for internal or personal use is granted by Koninklijke Brill NV provided that the appropriate fees are paid directly to The Copyright Clearance Center, 222 Rosewood Drive, Suite 910, Danvers, MA 01923, USA. Fees are subject to change.

This book is printed on acid-free paper and produced in a sustainable manner.

For Jonathan Ocko†
A great friend, scholar and mentor

Contents

PART 2
Production and Application of Legal Knowledge

Acknowledgements

The editors would like to thank all the participants of the International Workshop on Chinese Legal History, Culture, and Modernity, organized by the two editors and held at Columbia University in New York City in early May 2012. They also would like to acknowledge their gratitude to the Faculty of Arts and Sciences of Columbia University for funding this workshop and to the staff of the Weatherhead East Asian Institute at Columbia University and our research assistants for helping with the logistics.

The two-day-long workshop generated very interesting and fruitful discussions among a large number of participants from different countries and multiple disciplines, including Daniel Asen, Jennifer Altehenger, Thomas Buoye, Yi-hsiang Chang, Li Chen, Pengsheng Chiu, Xiaoping Cong, Elizabeth Dale, Jianpeng Deng, Maura Dykstra, Bryna Goodman, Weiting Guo, Quinn Doyle Javers, Yonglin Jiang, Margaret Kuo, Michael Ng, Jonathan Ocko, Nancy Park, Johanna Ransmeier, Billy So, Philip Thai, Janet Theiss, Glenn Tiffert, Margaret Wan, Yanhong Wu, Taisu Zhang, Ting Zhang, and Madeleine Zelin. With one exception, all the chapters of this volume developed from the papers originally presented at the workshop. In the last one and a half years since the workshop, the editors have been working with the authors, reviewers, series editors and editors at Brill to revise the chapters and move this project through the various stages of revision. We regret that we have been unable to include more papers in this volume but the comments and participation of all the scholars who attended the workshop at Columbia University benefited the analysis of this volume in different ways. We greatly appreciate their input and participation. We are also grateful to the anonymous reviewers for their feedback and to the series editors, Madeleine Zelin and Billy So, and the editors and staff at Brill, particularly Qin Higley, Judy Pereira, and Patrick Hunter, for their efforts to bring this project to completion. Last but not least, it has been a great pleasure to work with our contributors and we thank them for their unfailing patience with and prompt responses to our many queries and requests.

List of Contributors

Jennifer Altehenger

Dr. phil. in Modern Chinese Studies (University of Heidelberg, 2010) is Lecturer in Contemporary Chinese History at King's College London. She is interested in modern Chinese history, in particular the history of the People's Republic of China, publishing and propaganda production, popular legal knowledge, and the exchange of legal expertise among socialist countries during the Cold War and after. Recent publications include "A Socialist Satire? *Manhua* Magazine and Political Cartoon Production in the PRC, 1950–60," *Frontiers of History in China* (2013), and "Between State and Service Industry: Group and Collective Weddings in Communist Shanghai, 1949–56," *Twentieth-Century China* (forthcoming). She is currently completing a book manuscript that examines the dissemination of legal knowledge via propaganda in the PRC.

Daniel Asen

Ph.D. in History (Columbia University, 2012), is Assistant Professor of History at Rutgers University—Newark. His research interests include the intersection of law, science, and medicine in late imperial and Republican China, the cultural and social politics of expertise, and the history of death and the body. His publications include "The Only Options?: 'Experience' and 'Theory' in Debates over Forensic Knowledge and Expertise in Early Twentieth-Century China," in *Historical Epistemology and the Making of Modern Chinese Medicine*, ed. Howard Chiang (Manchester University Press, 2015), and "Vital Spots, Mortal Wounds, and Forensic Practice: Finding Cause of Death in Nineteenth-Century China," *East Asian Science, Technology and Society* (2009): 453–74.

Li Chen

J.D. (University of Illinois, 2002) and Ph.D. in History (Columbia University, 2009), is Assistant Professor of History at the University of Toronto and founding President of the International Society for Chinese Law and History. His research focuses on Chinese law and history, Sino-Western relations, empire and international law. His recent publications include "Law, Empire, and Historiography of Sino-Western Relations," *Law & History Review* (2009), "Universalism and Equal Sovereignty as Contested Myths of International Law," *Journal of the History of International Law* (2011), "Legal Specialists and Judicial Administration in Late Imperial China," *Late Imperial China* (2012),

"Power of Knowledge: The Role of Secret and Published Treatises of Private Legal Specialists in the Qing Juridical Field," *Zhejiang daxue xuebao* (2015), and *Chinese Law in the Imperial Eyes: Sovereignty, Justice, and Transcultural Politics, c. 1740s–1840s* (Columbia University Press, forthcoming 2015). He is completing *Invisible Power, Legal Specialists, and the Juridical Field in Late Imperial China, 1651–1911.*

Jianpeng Deng
Ph.D. in Legal History (Peking University, 2004), is Professor of Law at the Law School of the University of Nationalities (*Minzu daxue*) in Beijing, China. His research interests focus on law, custom, and litigation during the Qing dynasty, as well as Internet financial law in contemporary China. His recent publications include *Zhongguo fazhi shi* [Chinese Legal History] (Beijing daxue chubanshe, 2011), *Hulianwang jinrong falü yu fengxian kongzhi* (The Internet Finance Law and Risk Control) (Jixie chubanshe, 2014), *Caichan quanli de pinkun: Zhongguo chuantong minshifa yanjiu* (Deficiency in Property Rights: A Study of Traditional Chinese Civil Law) (Falü chubanshe, 2006), and "Cong choulou xianxiang dao fading shoufei: Qingdai songfei zhuanxing yanjiu (From Customary Fees to Legal Charges: On the Transformation of Qing Litigation Fees)," *Zhongguo zhengfa daxue xuebao* 18.4 (July 2010).

Bryna Goodman
Ph.D in History (Stanford University, 1990), is Professor of History and Director of Asian Studies at the University of Oregon. She is interested in modern Chinese urban culture, especially gender, colonialism, and new disciplinary formations. Her recent work examines early-20th-century Chinese print culture to map the interplay between everyday life and globally circulating institutions and categories of knowledge. She is the author of *Native Place, City, and Nation: Regional Networks and Identities in Shanghai, 1853–1937* (University of California Press, 1995), and co-editor of *Gender in Motion: Divisions of Labor and Cultural Change in Late Imperial and Modern China* (Rowman & Littlefield Publishers, 2005) and *Twentieth-century Colonialism and China: Localities, the Everyday and the World* (Routledge, 2012).

Weiting Guo
Ph.D. candidate in Asian Studies (University of British Columbia), is finishing up his doctoral dissertation at the University of British Columbia. His research focuses on late imperial and modern Chinese history, Taiwanese

history, law and society, violence, and local politics. His recent publications include "Living with Disputes: Zhang Gang Diary (1888–1942) and the Life of a Community Mediator in Late Qing and Republican China," *Journal of the Canadian Historical Association* (2013), and "In the Name of Justice: Summary Execution and the Politics of Rough Justice in Late-Qing China, 1864–1911," in *Global Lynching and Collective Violence*, ed. Michael J. Pfeifer (University of Illinois Press, forthcoming 2015).

Zhao Ma

Ph.D. in History (Johns Hopkins University, 2007), is Assistant Professor of Modern Chinese History and Culture at Washington University in St. Louis. His research interest and publications have concentrated on gender and family, law and punishment, and urban culture in modern China. He is the author of *Runaway Wives, Urban Crimes, and Survival Tactics in Wartime Beijing, 1937–1949* (Harvard University Asia Center, forthcoming 2015). It uses criminal case files to explore lower-class women's role in remaking wartime Beijing's social and moral order. His current work examines the rumor-mongering and political propaganda in Beijing during the Korean War period to study the transformation of urban informational space in Mao's China.

Janet Theiss

Ph.D. (University of California, Berkeley), is Associate Professor of Chinese History and Director of the Asia Center at the University of Utah. She is the author of *Disgraceful Matters: The Politics of Chastity in Eighteenth-Century China* (2004) and articles on various topics in Chinese legal, family and gender history, including "Love in a Confucian Climate: The Perils of Intimacy in Eighteenth-Century China." *Nan Nü: Men, Women and Gender in Early and Imperial China* (2009); and "Explaining the Shrew: Narratives of Spousal Violence and the Critique of Masculinity in 18th-Century Criminal Cases" in *Law and Writing in Late Imperial China*, ed. Robert Hegel and Katherine Carlitz (University of Washington Press, 2007).

Margaret B. Wan

Ph.D. (Harvard University), is Associate Professor of Chinese Literature at the University of Utah. She has published on Chinese fiction, popular culture, local literature, and cultural history. She is the author of *Green Peony and the Rise of the Chinese Martial Arts Novel* (SUNY Press, 2009), and coeditor of *The Interplay of the Oral and the Written in Chinese Popular Literature* (Nordic Inst. of Asian Studies, 2010) and *Yangzhou—A Place in Literature: The Local in Chinese Cultural History* (University of Hawaii Press, 2015). Her current project on drum ballads was awarded an American Council of Learned Societies Fellowship.

Yu Wang

Ph.D. Candidate in History (University of Toronto). His research interests focus on modern Chinese history, especially social and cultural history of early People's Republic of China. He is currently working on a doctoral dissertation that studies government regulation of sound in socialist broadcasting as part of the revolutionary propaganda and discipline and social transformation during the first few decades of the People's Republic of China.

Yanhong Wu

Ph.D. in History (Peking University, 1997) and Ph.D. in Sociology (Oklahoma State University, 2008), is Professor of History at Zhejiang University, China. Her research focuses on law and society in late imperial China, particularly legal institutions, legal practices, and legal culture from the fourteenth century to the seventeenth century. She is author of *Mingdai chongjun yanjiu* (Military Exile in the Ming dynasty) (Shehui kexue chubanshe, 2003), " 'Satisfying Both Sentiment and Law': Fairness-Centered Judicial Reasoning as Seen in the Casebooks of the Ming" (with Yonglin Jiang) in *Thinking with Cases*, ed. Charlotte Furth (University of Hawaii Press, 2007), and editor of *Mingdai zhidu yanjiu* (Studies of the Institutions of the Ming Dynasty) (Zhejiang daxue chubanshe, 2014). She is currently working on a book on legal experts, legal knowledge, and legal institutions in late imperial China.

Madeleine Zelin

Ph.D. in History (University of California at Berkeley, 1979), is Dean Lung Professor of Chinese Studies and Professor of History and East Asian Languages and Cultures at Columbia University. Her current research focuses on legal history and the role of law in the Chinese economy, including the evolution of shareholding and business organization in China, state handling of economic disputes, and the role of chambers of commerce as new sites for economic mediation. She has published extensively on Chinese legal and economic history, including *The Merchants of Zigong: Industrial Enterprise in Early Modern China* (Columbia University Press, 2005), a study of the indigenous roots of Chinese economic culture and business practice that was awarded the 2006 Allan Sharlin Memorial Prize of the Social Science History Association, the 2006 Fairbank Prize of the Association for Asian Studies and the 2007 Humanities Book Prize of the International Convention on Asian Studies.

Taisu Zhang
J.D. (Yale University, 2008) and Ph.D. in History (Yale University, 2014), is Associate Professor of Law at Duke University. His work covers comparative legal and economic history, property theory and contemporary Chinese law, and has been recently published in the *American Journal of Comparative Law*, the *Journal of Empirical Legal Studies*, and the *Columbia Journal of Asian Law*. His book manuscript, "Kinship, Property, and Agricultural Capitalism in Pre-Industrial China and England," is currently under review for publication.

Ting Zhang
Ph.D. in History (The Johns Hopkins University, 2014), is Assistant Professor of Chinese History at the University of Maryland, College Park. Her research focuses on the production and circulation of legal knowledge, and the role of legal information in the formation of early modern Chinese legal culture. Her publications include "Penitence Silver and the Politics of Punishment in the Qianlong Reign (1736–1795)," *Late Imperial China* (2010) and "The Code, Legal Secretaries, and Book Merchants: The Publication and Circulation of Legal Books in Qing Jiangnan," *Zhejiang daxue xuebao* (Jan. 2015).

Rethinking Chinese Law and History: An Introduction

Li Chen and Madeleine Zelin

This volume is the product of an ongoing collaboration among scholars from Asia, Europe, and North America to explore what might be called the life of the law in early modern China. We have chosen this term purposefully, in part for the attention it draws to the active role that law plays in everyday interactions, not simply as an instrument of governance but as a site of negotiation between people and the state, and as a part of the repertoire of ideas and devices used by people in their interactions with each other. We have also sought to avoid the essentializing and causal implications associated with terms such as "legal tradition" and "legal culture."[1] The period covered by the chapters in this volume extends from the sixteenth century through the Qing dynasty (1644–1911) and the turbulent Republican period (1912–49), to the early years of the People's Republic of China, as China is still known today. This was a period in which rulers and elites, the grounds of politics, the content of the law and the forms of its application, not to mention the territorial and demographic composition of the state itself, underwent multiple and dramatic transformations. "Culture" and "tradition" as conceived and reconceived are certainly part of the story of the law, but in China, as elsewhere, they must be viewed cautiously, with an eye to time, place, context, and a multiplicity of interpretive voices.

The contributors to this volume are particularly attentive to the perils of using "tradition" or "culture" as the overall framework for the study of law. Until the 1980s, scholarship on Chinese legal history focused largely on law as promulgated and administered by the state.[2] Western knowledge of Chinese ideas of the law depended largely on interpretations of Confucian social norms for a

1 The pitfalls associated with these concepts are discussed by Roger Cotterrell, "Comparative Law and Legal Culture," in *The Oxford Handbook of Comparative Law*, ed. Reinhard Zimmermann and Mathias Reimann (Oxford: Oxford University Press, 2006), 709–37.

2 See, e.g., Derk Bodde and Clarence Morris, *Law in Imperial China: Exemplified by 190 Ch'ing Dynasty Cases* (Cambridge: Harvard University Press, 1967); Marinus Meijer, *The Introduction of Modern Criminal Law in China* (Arlington: University Publications of America, 1950; repr., 1976); T'ung-tsu Ch'u, *Local Government in China under the Ch'ing* (Cambridge: Council on East Asian Studies, distributed by Harvard University Press, 1988); Sybille Van der Sprenkel, *Legal Institutions in Manchu China: A Sociological Analysis* (London: Athlone Press, 1962).

© KONINKLIJKE BRILL NV, LEIDEN, 2015 | DOI 10.1163/9789004288492_002

few centuries, and then on translations of the statutory parts of the Qing Code dating from the 1780s onward.[3] The code that formed the basis for formal justice appeared in close to its modern form in the seventh century, and although significantly revised through a process of accumulated amplification, reorganization, and revision, it was often misconstrued as a statement or symptom of the unchanging nature of the traditional Chinese legal system. As it was structured largely as an index of offenses and their appropriate punishments, from the modern Western perspective its overriding concerns were often viewed as administrative and penal. At the same time, legal codes throughout our period reflected a paradoxical commitment to both equality before the law and Confucian notions of the hierarchical nature of human relationships that often stymied outside observers.

This approach to Chinese legal history was transformed by the publication of *Essays on China's Legal Tradition* in 1980, which, with new access to Chinese archives beginning that year, was followed by a number of path-breaking studies based on extant legal cases and judicial archives at different levels.[4] In the United States, works by Jonathan Ocko, Philip Huang, Thomas Buoye, and Mark Allee on local or central adjudication, Madeleine Zelin on contract and business, Janet Theiss and Matthew Sommer on the gendered construction of law and social relations, and Melissa Macauley on litigation masters joined those of numerous Chinese and Japanese scholars determined to approach the history of Chinese law as revealed in court records, legal documents, political and private correspondence, and popular media and discourse.[5]

---

3 For a discussion of the Western discourse of Chinese law in the eighteenth and nineteenth centuries, see Li Chen, *Chinese Law in the Imperial Eyes: Sovereignty, Justice, and Transcultural Politics, c. 1740s–1840s* (New York: Columbia University Press, forthcoming 2015).

4 See Jerome A. Cohen, R. Randle Edwards, and Fu-mei Chang Chen, *Essays on China's Legal Tradition* (Princeton: Princeton University Press, 1980).

5 Philip C.C. Huang, *Civil Justice in China: Representation and Practice in the Qing* (Stanford: Stanford University Press, 1996); Mark A. Allee, *Law and Local Society in Late Imperial China: Northern Taiwan in the Nineteenth Century* (Stanford: Stanford University Press, 1994); Thomas M. Buoye, *Manslaughter, Markets, and Moral Economy: Violent Disputes over Property Rights in Eighteenth Eentury China* (New York: Cambridge University Press, 2000); Matthew H. Sommer, *Sex, Law, and Society in Late Imperial China* (Stanford: Stanford University Press, 2000); Madeleine Zelin, *The Merchants of Zigong: Industrial Entrepreneurship in Early Modern China* (New York: Columbia University Press, 2005). The Henry Luce Foundation was particularly important in this regard, supporting the collection of Qing law court documents and the convening of workshops at both UCLA and Columbia University, culminating in two volumes that serve as models for this collection: Kathryn Bernhardt and Philip C.C. Huang, *Civil Law in Qing and Republican China* (Stanford: Stanford University Press, 1994); Madeleine

The essays included here represent what may be thought of as the third wave in the historical study of Chinese law and society, alongside a series of recent publications informed by new sources or perspectives.[6] With one exception, the twelve chapters are based on papers selected from among twenty-six presentations at the International Workshop on Chinese Legal History, Culture, and Modernity held at Columbia University on May 4–6, 2012. As we shall note below, each moves in important new directions, employing methods anchored in economics, history of science, and cultural and gender studies, as well as the tools of case-based legal analysis. Nevertheless, they are linked by a commitment to the importance of empirically based research and innovative thinking, particularly in areas of inquiry in which the grounds of understanding are rapidly shifting. These are studies of Chinese law in practice, and as such they take us one step closer to a "thick description" of the worlds of the law in China. At the same time, they point to a number of common concerns that, approached from their unique vantage points or sources, contribute to ongoing discussions within the field of legal history as a whole. Among these are the grounds of the law and the interaction between state power/interests, cultural/religious identifiers, custom, and individual, class, and community interests. Religion

---

Zelin, Jonathan K. Ocko, and Robert Gardella, eds., *Contract and Property in Early Modern China* (Stanford: Stanford University Press, 2004).

6 We cannot list all the publications, but for some examples, see collections of essays in Chiu Pengsheng [Qiu Pengsheng] 邱澎生 and Chen Xiyuan 陈熙远, *Ming Qing falü yunzhuo zhong de quanli yu wenhua* 明清法律运作中的权力与文化 [Power and Culture in the Operation of Ming and Qing Law] (Taibei: Zhongyang yanjiuyuan, Shengjing chuban gongsi, 2009); Huang Zongzhi 黄宗智 (Philip C.C. Huang) and You Chenjun 尤陈俊, eds., *Cong susong dang'an chufa: Zhongguo de falü, shehui yu wenhua* 从诉讼档案出发：中国的法律、社会与文化 [Starting from the Archives: Chinese Law, Society, and Culture] (Beijing: Falü chubanshe, 2009); Robert E. Hegel and Katherine Carlitz, eds., *Writing and Law in Late Imperial China: Crime, Conflict, and Judgment* (Seattle: University of Washington Press, 2007). For monographs, see, e.g., Wu Peilin 吴佩林, *Qingdai xianyu minshi jiufen yu falü zhixu kaocha* 清代县域民事纠纷与法律秩序考察 [Study of County-Level Civil Disputes and Legal Order in the Qing Dynasty] (Beijing: Zhonghua shuju, 2013); Zhang Xiaobei 张小蓓, *Mianning Qingdai sifa dang'an yanjiu* 冕宁清代司法档案研究 [Study of the Qing Legal Archives in Mianning] (Beijing: Zhongguo zhengfa daxue chubanshe, 2010); Li Zan 里赞, *Wan Qing zhouxian susong zhong de shenduan wenti: Cezhong Sichuan Nanbu xian de shijian* 晚清州县诉讼的审断问题：侧重四川南部县的实践 [Adjudication in Late Qing County Courts: Focusing on Practice in Nanbu County of Sichuan] (Beijing: Falü chubanshe, 2010); Gong Rufu 龚如富, *Ming Qing songxue yanjiu* 明清讼学研究 [Study of the Profession of Litigation Specialists in the Ming and Qing] (Shanghai: Shangwu yinshuguan, 2008); Linxia Liang, *Delivering Justice in Qing China: Civil Trials in the Magistrate's Court* (Oxford: Oxford University Press, 2008).

or morality plays an important part in several chapters, as do contracts and other forms of private ordering as both supplements and challenges to formal law. Given the dramatic changes that took place during the period under study, it is not surprising that the impact of new political, social, and economic formations, including pressures exerted by Western ideals of law and science, emerge as important concerns in a number of chapters.

Most noticeable is the issue of legal knowledge in almost all of the studies in this volume, as an epistemological field whose modes of production, transmission, and contestation shape what constitutes law and justice and how the state is legitimized or imagined. While officials and private specialists were instrumental in developing late imperial law and judicial administration, authors of novels, drum ballads, or sensational journalistic reports of legal cases in Qing and Republican China dramatized popular ideas of justice as both theatrical entertainment and social critiques. Early-twentieth-century legal reformers and later socialist cadres also avidly promoted legal knowledge and consciousness to mold different kinds of modern subjects or citizens. Indeed, an important lesson of these studies and of the larger workshop was that a discourse of law pervaded Chinese society far more deeply and extensively than has previously been acknowledged. How this discourse evolved and continues to shape contemporary China's drive for a rule of law is clearly fertile ground for scholars going forward.

Jianpeng Deng addresses a debate that grew out of nineteenth-century critiques of Chinese law and was one of the first issues to be addressed by Chinese legal reformers in the early twentieth century—whether or not there existed a distinction between civil and criminal law in imperial China. Deng's intervention reflects a larger debate that continues within the PRC about the nature of China's legal culture and legal practice, a debate that has important implications for legal scholarship despite the enormous differences between the formal law of the PRC and that of the Qing dynasty. A particularly contentious part of that debate is over whether magistrates, as judges of the first instance, were bound to the law in making their decisions. Here, the distinction between serious "criminal" cases, which unquestionably required precise application of statutory punishment, and "civil" cases was key. Deng examines how Qing officials and legal specialists themselves considered this issue. Instead of focusing on the criminal/civil dichotomy informed by modern Western jurisprudence, he provides evidence that Qing local officials often used the terms *anjian* and *cisong* to distinguish different kinds of litigation, based not just on the severity of the offense/penalty but also on the nature of the substantive legal matters at issue. He then explores the institutional, juridical, and socio-economic reasons for the local officials' treatment of such different types of legal cases. Among other things, Deng argues that this *anjian-cisong* distinction could determine what legal procedures should be applied, or even whether the judges would strictly adhere to the Qing Code in a particular case. While the larger debate is far from being settled, Deng's study provides important data for further discussion. For scholars looking for the roots of modern legal reform in indigenous practice, Deng also raises some provocative issues, including the increasing inadequacy of the Qing Code to handle disputes anchored in rapidly commercializing urban spaces. While Deng suggests that litigants themselves were pushing the state to dissolve the distinction between serious and trivial matters, or between *anjian* and *cisong* cases, several contributors to this volume provide evidence of the multiple localities of legal knowledge that competed for authority in cases involving conflicting economic interests.

Taisu Zhang and Weiting Guo take radically different routes to their conclusion that in handling disputes over landed property, the Chinese state both took seriously the formal process of adjudication and incorporated community values of equity and religion in issuing its judgments. Zhang's is one of the first studies to apply the tools of law and economics scholarship to an evaluation of Chinese property disputes. And contrary to many more qualitatively based historical studies, he concludes that local Chinese dispute resolution favored the poor over wealthy litigants who may have held liens on their land. Zhang's argument hinges on the claim that kinship hierarchies strengthened the social status of small holders, who were thereby able to negotiate victories in key areas of property law, particularly in the handling of the *dian*, a Chinese practice that allowed redemption of land commended to a creditor in return for a loan. Zhang joins the growing consensus that Chinese institutions like *dian* and permanent tenancy were not products of a precommercial moral economy but rather grew out of a lively and relatively unencumbered market for land. Zhang tests his claim by mobilizing a large body of contracts and case files, many newly available to researchers. He also uses older sources, such as the interviews conducted with peasants in North China by the Japanese North Manchurian Railway authority and lineage registries and rules, to examine how rural communal property was governed and how local leaders were selected.

Guo employs the tools of the historical anthropologist to examine both the legal and religious ideals that governed land dedicated to burial of the dead. Focusing on the power of both geomancy and popular religious practices regarding the bodies of one's ancestors, Guo paints a complex picture of state adjudication of the competing moral and economic claims of litigants. Situating his study in Taiwan, a frontier area in the mid-Qing, he also reminds us how local contexts influenced judicial practice. As Taiwan's economy expanded from the late eighteenth century onward, land was increasingly commoditized and conflicts between those who occupied vacant land to inter their dead and those who sought to develop this for agriculture became more frequent. At the same time, the so-called geomantic benefits of gravesites were such that seemingly simple property disputes were always imbricated with complex social and economic meanings. Guo's evidence also points to the importance of contracts and steles as markers, both figurative and literal, of power and space. Pointing to the difficulties encountered in enforcement of judgments, Guo provides evidence of the importance of these two kinds of documents in establishing rights vis-à-vis the state, the community, and even the gods.

Janet Theiss and Bryna Goodman use thick descriptions of particular cases to shift our attention to the ways in which gender and status can influence judicial outcomes. While the question of whether the state is itself subject to the law is a frequent topic of discussion among legal historians, Theiss examines an aspect of the legal system in China that is given less attention: the subversive influence of powerful elites. Throughout her chapter we see the tension between officials seeking to uphold the rule of law, officials caught in a web of connections that provide both temptations and opportunities to enrich themselves at the expense of the law, and a state that applies sanctions against officials whose actions corrupt the law and enable elites. As in her earlier work, Theiss also demonstrates the value of legal records for social history. The many clandestine affairs, among high and low, that she documents also point to a degree of subversion of gender roles ignored in standard accounts of Qing society. Here we find a descendant of the literate and worldly women of Dorothy Ko's *Teachers of the Inner Chambers* using the legal system to defend her reputation and her claim to family wealth. At the same time, we are reminded that affective relationships do not keep people from going to court, especially if the case involves power asymmetries within the lineage itself. Nevertheless, as governor Lu Zhuo's memorial to the Board or Ministry of Rites reminds us, moral arguments still had a powerful hold on the imagination of that class of Chinese men charged with governance and judicial action. The "civilizing" role of the state helps explain many of the paradoxes noted by our authors, as moral imperatives confronted black-letter law and economic efficiency.

Goodman brings us to the "semi-colonial" world of early-twentieth-century Shanghai, in which "a maze of institutions and jurisdictions" formed the background to the tragic suicide of Xi Shangzhen and the trial and imprisonment of her employer, Tang Jiezhi. Goodman shows that the legal hybridity in which Tang's case was embedded was not just a matter of extraterritoriality, manifesting itself in mixed and consular courts, but also one of new collaborations between chambers of commerce, modern courts, and newly or partially promulgated modern codes that operated side by side with revised imperial codes well into the twentieth century. Eugenia Lean has demonstrated the ways in which the values of an earlier age could be mobilized to challenge and mold a modern Chinese legal culture.[7] In the case against Tang, the cultural associations attached to suicide and expectations regarding generational deference and responsibility were key to arguments in a case that sought to punish him for both driving his young employee to suicide and defrauding her of stock. In his favor were equally traditional native-place and associational networks that, though ultimately unsuccessful, pleaded a case that appealed to modern tropes of judicial independence and human rights.

Gender plays a critical role in the cases examined by Zhao Ma as well. Ma explores the reconceptualization of the family, family authority, and legal treatment of women's sexual autonomy through the lens of elopement and abduction cases in the 1940s. During this period, when sources of political authority were being hotly contested, social institutions that anchored society were particularly difficult to abandon. Ma highlights the contested values of individual autonomy and social stability at one of its most fragile sites. In the reformed law of the late Republican period, the freedom of young women to make sexual choices was upheld at the same time that families drew on traditional tropes to deflect social stigma away from daughters who took advantage of the opportunities provided by the collapse of the spatial and legal divide between the world and the woman's quarters in urban China. In addition to demonstrating the complexity of legal transformation, Ma's study provides a valuable window into the life of young urbanites and illustrates the usefulness of case testimonies for social history. It also points to the obstacles to female exercise of their subjectivity under conditions in which the outcome of cases often hinged not on a difference in the applicable law but on normative positions taken by the participants in a case. Moreover, as evidence of yet another continuity between the late Republic and the early People's Republic, Ma shows that besides familial supervision, police surveillance and residential registration became convenient ways for a state that was committed to both gender equality and the importance of the family as the pillar of social stability to regulate the rapidly changing social relations.

Whereas these chapters focus on the operation and effects of the law and judicial administration in late imperial and Republican China, the other contributors look at how legal knowledge was generated, commoditized, deployed, or changed over time. Yanhong Wu's essay traces the production of legal knowledge in the last century of the Ming dynasty (c. 1530s–1630s). By

7 Eugenia Lean, *Public Passions: The Trial of Shi Jianqiao and the Rise of Popular Sympathy in Republican China* (Berkeley: University of California Press, 2007).

examining thirty-six extant private commentaries on the Ming Code and their authors/editors, publishers, sponsors, and readers, she sketches out a hitherto little understood community of jurists and literati who shaped the development of the law and jurisprudence in Ming China. A number of official-jurists often collaborated to compile, critique, and revise commentaries on the code. Contrary to the once-dominant perception that popular knowledge of the law was strongly discouraged, Wu's research shows that these commentaries were designed not just to better prepare officials for administration but also to make the code more accessible to the general public. Most of the compilers and sponsors under study were governmental officials, and members of the central-level judicial agencies in particular played a leading role. Besides publishing or financing commentaries, these judicial officials also reviewed or recommended others' private treatises on the Ming Code, thus serving as both advocates and gatekeepers for the production of legal knowledge. For Wu, such concerted and conscientious efforts evidenced the emergence of a "community of legal experts," including the judicial officials and those who shared their interest in law and legal publications.

This kind of strong interest in publishing commentaries on the imperial law code, sometimes with updated legislative revisions and judicial precedents, continued into the Qing dynasty after 1644, but the imperial publishing houses and the official-jurists appear to have given way to other private legal experts and commercial publishers in this enterprise. In Ting Zhang's study of commentaries during the Qing period, we find that commercial publishers had largely replaced the inefficient imperial agencies in reprinting or updating the Qing Code by the late eighteenth century. More sensitive to profit and market demands, the commercial editions of the Qing Code often differed from the official ones by including more recent contents, useful commentaries, and other materials to appeal to potential readers. It had become a popular marketing cliché by the mid-eighteenth century to claim that these commercial editions included the newest statutory revisions and would be updated constantly in response to legislative or judicial changes.[8] Aside from reprinting the entire Qing Code and making it more widely available, these commercial editions often included the most recent substatutes, administrative regulations, or leading cases. Some of their innovations in form and substance, Zhang's study shows us, came to set the standards for other publishers and affected how the Qing Code was represented, read, or even applied in practice. Despite the Qing Court's brief attempt to regulate private legal publications in the mid-

8 E.g., see the announcements on the front pages of various editions of Sun Lun 孙纶, comp., *Dingli Cheng'an hejuan* 定例成案合镌 [A Combined Engraving of Regulations and Leading Cases] (1707, 1713, 1721, 1740s).

eighteenth century, commercial printing of the code and its commentaries soon revived and remained the major source of popular knowledge of the legal system for the remainder of the Qing period.

These Qing commercial editions were aimed at not just imperial bureaucrats and private legal specialists (including outlawed litigation masters) but all literate people who could afford to buy them. Zhang maintains that it was the private authors, publishers, and book industry, instead of the imperial state, that took the lead in providing the public with the most updated and helpful information about the Qing Code. Through meticulous research of more than 120 editions of the Qing Code, Zhang finds that at least from the 1790s onward, the extant commercial editions were mostly produced by private legal specialists (or what Li Chen has called "private legal advisors") rather than the judicial officials and local governments that published most of the Ming Code commentaries studied by Yanhong Wu.

Few historians of Chinese law have studied the print culture or sociocultural history behind the production and circulation of the imperial law codes and their commentaries. Likewise, we know relatively little about the jurists or legal specialists who produced or published them.[9] Therefore, together with his recent article on their emergence in the Ming-Qing period, Li Chen's analysis of private legal advisors (*muyou*) joins these recent studies to further illuminate the dynamics and implications of legal professionalization and knowledge production during this period. On the one hand, the Qing imperial authorities soon came to appreciate the nearly indispensable expertise of private legal advisors in local governance and judicial administration. The Yongzheng Emperor and his successors tried different means of providing incentives for legal advisors to serve the imperial government diligently and competently. On the other hand, the Qing Court expressed serious concerns about the growing influence of these legal specialists on judicial matters. The attempts in the mid-eighteenth century to regulate the recruitment, terms of employment, and geographical and social movement of these private legal experts were largely futile, however, as local officials had become so dependent upon these trained experts for their career success. Chen argues that understanding the tensions between official recognition of private legal advisors' crucial service and imperial anxiety about their excessive influence or possible corruption is essential for understanding the way Qing law and justice were administered.

Moreover, Chen suggests that underlying the almost contemporaneous governmental measures to ban litigation specialists and publications and to criminalize certain activities of legal advisors was the same concern about

9 For a few exceptions, see the relevant journal articles cited by authors in this volume.

the challenge that privatized and commercialized legal expertise posed to the imperial monopoly over the interpretation and administration of the law and justice. As the last stage of judicial review in major criminal cases, the Autumn Assizes thus vividly demonstrated these tensions and imperial ambivalence, with the desire for legal expertise and justice on the one hand and the desire for maximum control over the source of imperial legitimacy on the other. In response, Qing legal advisors emphasized their own professional ethics (or the "Way of Muyou") and the practical value of their expertise and services to the state, society, and the people. They also tried to win social recognition of their expertise and contributions by publishing influential adjudication handbooks, collections of leading cases, and legal commentaries, often with admiring prefaces by provincial officials. This is partly why so many editions of the Qing Code in Ting Zhang's sample were produced by private legal advisors.

More research is needed to fully explain this, but the three chapters just mentioned appear to show a trend of intensifying commodification and privatization of legal knowledge. Commercial editions and private commentaries on the imperial codes came to dominate the book market by 1800; litigation masters and legal advisors were perceived as an increasingly serious threat to imperial authority, thus provoking unprecedentedly strong legislative reactions in the mid-eighteenth century. In contrast with their crackdown on litigation masters, however, the Qing Court could do little to curtail the influence of private legal advisors, testifying to the limits of imperial power in judicial practice.

If the imperial authorities, legal specialists, and commercial publishers all shaped public knowledge of the law, then fictional literature enjoyed its own influence on popular understanding of the judicial system.[10] The court-case stories in drum ballad (*guci*) that circulated in North China in the late Qing and Republican periods, as Margaret Wan tells us, exemplifies the gap between official portrayals and popular imaginations of the legal system of the time. A modern reader might expect to see the state law and justice prevail in general in these popular stories, but the messages often turn out to be much more subtle and ambivalent. It is true that these very popular drum-ballad texts feature famous and incorruptible officials such as Judge Bao (Zheng) or Judge Liu (Yong) who bring powerful or crafty felons to justice. But the heroic images are frequently based on equally revealing details about official corruption, injustice, social inequity, and constitutional defects of the state or the legal system. The ballads also dramatize the disjuncture between the ideological propaganda and the commonsensical understanding of the law, morality,

10 For this, see also the three essays by James André, Daniel Youd, and Katherine Carlitz, in Hegel and Carlitz, *Writing and Law in Late imperial China*, 189–260.

power, and justice. Like jurists in real life, the model judges in the ballads also struggle with the tensions between human sentiments and formal justice, and between the law and morality. In this sense, they echo the findings of many chapters in this volume.

In contrast with earlier ballads of this kind, the stories that Wan examines places greater emphasis on realism and on the role of law in resolving grievances, indicating "contested" or multiple visions of law and justice within the same literary genre or anticipated audiences. Although copies of the imperial law codes or legal treatises for specialists were important for understanding judicial administration, Wan's study shows that the court-case fiction in the ballads, as artistic registers of popular sentiments, could also shape public opinion, or even judicial practice when its visions of ideal justice came to condition the readers' attitude and approach to the legal system. Alongside other recent studies, this chapter gives us glimpses of different articulations of law and justice from what one finds in the official judicial archives or non-fictional legal publications.

The popularity of these court-case ballads continued well into the Republican period, since the yearning for social justice and exemplary officials naturally did not vanish with the collapse of the Qing dynasty. In fact, the Republican judiciary even inherited personnel from the late Qing, although the legal system had been restructured since the start of the New Policy reform movement in 1902. Together with the Qing legal advisors, who were turned into local judges or bureaucrats after 1911, a number of forensic examiners (*wuzuo*) survived the changes in political regimes to play an active part in the "modernization" of Republican China's law and criminal justice.

Daniel Asen highlights the redefined roles of Chinese coroners in this period. The shortage of forensic examiners trained in Western legal medicine and anatomy made it necessary for the Republican judiciary to rely upon many traditionally trained Chinese coroners, but the way the latter's expertise was treated changed over time as "modern" legal professionals played an increasingly dominant role in administering justice. One can argue that earlier stages of "professionalization" (more broadly defined) of jurists, legal advisors, or litigation specialists were already seen in late imperial China, but what distinguished the professionalization in the twentieth century was an epistemological shift that often privileged foreign ideas and practices over indigenous ones. Besides other trappings of modern professions, new conceptions of professional expertise and qualification also took hold, giving greater authority to judges, prosecutors, and police with the new educational background. Nevertheless, utilizing the skills and expertise that were often passed down from one generation to another as a hereditary profession, coroners were still valued in the modern transformation of China's law and justice. The coroners in Republican Beijing, as Asen's study shows, illustrate how such an indigenous system of specialized knowledge was incorporated or reconfigured amid the changed terrains of epistemology and legal modernization. Although these forensic examiners were still essential functionaries for Republican criminal justice, they remained subordinate to other judicial officials and were bound now by modern judicial procedures and legal concepts. This placed them in a "productive" but "precarious" relationship with the latter at a time when the scientific and evidentiary authority of their still-needed expertise was being cast into serious doubt.

If the Qing and Republican authorities knew all too well the importance of capitalizing on law or other specialized knowledge to shore up their power and legitimacy, leaders of the newly founded People's Republic of China were even more acutely aware of what was at stake. Jennifer Altehenger's study demonstrates how the PRC government deployed mass campaigns of propaganda to improve popular knowledge of and obedience to the *Marriage Law* in the early 1950s. These mass campaigns were not as uniform or totalizing as might be assumed, however. In fact, the propaganda cadres often struggled to undo the damage caused by some of the campaign materials. People did not always follow the official line, and it was not easy to communicate or control the desired messages about the new law and the socialist political order. In Altehenger's analysis, we see how materials for popular legal education were designed and monitored by government officials, publishers, and individual authors. The linguistic simplification and wide promulgation of the law had always been crucial for its efficacy in earlier periods, but this new socialist state was far more aggressive and ambitious in trying to educate and reform the citizenry. Illustrated booklets, primers, short stories, songbooks, comic cartoons, poems, and operas all became part of the arsenal of the mass campaigners. The principal message was to represent the new *Marriage Law* as essential for harmonious families, gender equality, and free marriage, leading to a happy and productive socialist society. For such purposes, the new state and society were contrasted with the old, now recast as feudal and reactionary. At the same time, the propaganda officials could adapt the language of Confucian classics (otherwise dismissed as feudal) to promote the new *Marriage Law*. Altehenger draws our attention to an inherent contradiction of this type of socialist mass campaign: the people were mobilized to better understand their rights and duties, but they were told to do so only within the limits dictated by the socialist party-state. Her investigation of the dynamics of the popularization of the *Marriage Law* in 1950–53 illuminates the various challenges facing a government that struggles to maintain control of the masses it has mobilized and "awakened."

Most of the chapters that follow each are part of a larger project, so we have no doubt that our contributors will further develop and elaborate their analyses in the near future. While this volume may not be able to fully answer all the interesting questions raised herein due to the space limitation, it is our hope that our contributors' engagement with these questions and their fruitful dialogue with one another will continue the conversations about the underlying issues and help carry forward the recent efforts among scholars of China to rethink various aspects of the nature, history, transformation, and legacy of late imperial Chinese law and legal culture. With the founding of the International Society for Chinese Law and History in January 2014, we also expect this volume to introduce a series of such publication projects based on truly sustained international collaboration in order to better explore the intersections of Chinese law and history from a variety of perspectives.

Bibliography

Allee, Mark A. *Law and Local Society in Late Imperial China: Northern Taiwan in the Nineteenth Century*. Stanford: Stanford University Press, 1994.

Bernhardt, Kathryn, and Philip C. Huang. *Civil Law in Qing and Republican China*. Stanford: Stanford University Press, 1994.

Bodde, Derk, and Clarence Morris. *Law in Imperial China: Exemplified by 190 Ch'ing Dynasty Cases*. Cambridge: Harvard University Press, 1967.

Buoye, Thomas M. *Manslaughter, Markets, and Moral Economy: Violent Disputes over Property Rights in Eighteenth Century China*. New York: Cambridge University Press, 2000.

Ch'u, T'ung-tsu (Qu Tongzu). *Local Government in China under the Ch'ing*. Cambridge Council on East Asian Studies, distributed by Harvard University Press, 1988 [1961].

Chen, Li. *Chinese Law in the Imperial Eyes: Sovereignty, Justice, and Transcultural Politics, c. 1740s–1840s*. New York: Columbia University Press, 2015.

Chiu Pengsheng [Qiu Pengsheng] 邱澎生, and Chen Xiyuan 陈熙远, eds. *Ming Qing falü yunzhuo zhong de quanli yu wenhua* 明清法律运作中的权力与文化 [Power and Culture in the Operation of Ming and Qing Law]. Taibei: Zhongyang yanjiuyuan, Shengjing chuban gongsi, 2009.

Cohen, Jerome Alan, R. Randle Edwards, and Fu-mei Chang Chen, eds. *Essays on China's Legal Tradition*. Princeton: Princeton University Press, 1980.

Cotterrell, Roger. "Comparative Law and Legal Culture." In *The Oxford Handbook of Comparative Law*, edited by Reinhard Zimmermann and Mathias Reimann, 709–37. Oxford: Oxford University Press, 2006.

Gong Rufu 龚如富. *Ming Qing songxue yanjiu* 明清讼学研究 [Study of the Profession of Litigation Specialists in the Ming and Qing]. Shanghai: Shangwu yinshuguan, 2008.

Hegel, Robert E., and Katherine Carlitz, eds. *Writing and Law in Late Imperial China: Crime, Conflict, and Judgment*. Seattle: University of Washington Press, 2007.

Huang, Philip C.C. *Civil Justice in China: Representation and Practice in the Qing*. Stanford: Stanford University Press, 1996.

Huang Zongzhi 黄宗智 (Philip C.C. Huang), and You Chenjun 尤陈俊, eds. *Cong susong dang'an chufa: Zhongguo de falü, shehui yu wenhua* 从诉讼档案出发: 中国的法律、社会与文化 [Starting from the Archives: Chinese Law, Society, and Culture]. Beijing: Falü chubanshe, 2009.

Lean, Eugenia. *Public Passions: The Trial of Shi Jianqiao and the Rise of Popular Sympathy in Republican China*. Berkeley: University of California Press, 2007.

Li Zan 里赞. *Wan Qing zhouxian susong zhong de shenduan wenti: Cezhong Sichuan Nanbu xian de shijian* 晚清州县诉讼的审断问题: 侧重四川南部县的实践 [Adjudication in Late Qing County Courts: Focusing on Practice in Nanbu County of Sichuan]. Beijing: Falü chubanshe, 2010.

Liang, Linxia. *Delivering Justice in Qing China: Civil Trials in the Magistrate's Court*. Oxford: Oxford University Press, 2008.

Meijer, Marinus. *The Introduction of Modern Criminal Law in China*. Arlington: University Publications of America, 1976 [1950].

Sommer, Matthew H. *Sex, Law, and Society in Late Imperial China*. Stanford: Stanford University Press, 2000.

Sun Lun 孙纶, comp. *Dingli cheng'an hejuan* 定例成案合镌 [A Combined Engraving of Regulations and Leading Cases]. 1707, 1713, 1721, 1740s.

Van der Sprenkel, Sybille. *Legal Institutions in Manchu China: A Sociological Analysis*. London: Athlone Press, 1962.

Wu Peilin 吴佩林. *Qingdai xianyu minshi jiufen yu falü zhixu kaocha* 清代县域民事纠纷与法律秩序考察 [Study of County-Level Civil Disputes and Legal Order in the Qing Dynasty]. Beijing: Zhonghua shuju, 2013.

Zelin, Madeleine. *The Merchants of Zigong: Industrial Entrepreneurship in Early Modern China*. New York: Columbia University Press, 2005.

Zelin, Madeleine, Jonathan K. Ocko, and Robert Gardella. *Contract and Property in Early Modern China*. Stanford: Stanford University Press, 2004.

Zhang Xiaobei. *Mianning Qingdai sifa dang'an yanjiu* 冕宁清代司法档案研究 [Study of the Qing Legal Archives in Mianning]. Beijing: Zhongguo zhengfa daxue chubanshe, 2010.

PART 1

Meaning and Practice of Law

CHAPTER 1

Classifications of Litigation and Implications for Qing Judicial Practice

*Jianpeng Deng**

Translated by Li Chen and Yu Wang

Over the past few decades, historians of Chinese law have intensely debated the nature of the legal system in imperial China, often focusing on whether it made a distinction between civil and criminal law. Some historians have characterized it as a system that "had all laws in one code" but "distinguished civil from criminal law."[1] Related to this is the ongoing debate on the nature of Qing judicial administration and dispute resolution.[2] American scholar Mark A. Allee held that Qing courts treated all civil cases as "trivial matters" (*xishi*) and followed the same type of judicial procedure when adjudicating "civil" and "criminal" cases.[3] This view has since influenced French scholar Jérôme Bourgon.[4] However, Philip Huang has argued that county magistrates'

* The author wishes to thank Chen Li, Wang Yaxin, Li Honghai, Chen Xinyu, and Yang Songtao for their valuable advice, and the translators and editors. Responsibility for the article is the author's.

1 See Yang Yifan, "Dui Zhonghua faxi de zairenshi—jianlun 'zhufa heti, minxing bufen' shuo buneng chengli 对中华法系的再认识——兼论'诸法合体、民刑不分'说不能成立 [Rethinking the Chinese Legal Tradition, and the Unfounded Theory of 'No Separation between Civil and Criminal Laws and All Laws in One Code']" in *Pipan yu chongjian: Zhongguo fazhishi yanjiu fanbo* 批判与重建: 中国法律史研究反拨 [Critique and Reconstruct: Study of Chinese Legal History], ed. Ni Zhengmao 倪正茂 (Beijing: Falü chubanshe, 2002), 145–99.

2 Important studies on this topic include Philip C.C. Huang, *Civil Justice in China: Representation and Practice in the Qing* (Stanford: Stanford University Press, 1996); Philip C.C. Huang 黄宗智 and You Chenjun 尤陈俊, eds., *Cong susong dang'an chufa: Zhongguo de falü, shehui yu wenhua* 从诉讼档案出发: 中国的法律、社会与文化 [*Starting with the Judicial Archives: Chinese Law, Society, and Culture*] (Beijing: Falü chubanshe, 2009); Matthew H. Sommer, *Sex, Law, and Society in Late Imperial China* (Stanford: Stanford University Press, 2000).

3 Mark A. Allee, *Law and Local Society in Late Imperial China: Northern Taiwan in the Nineteenth Century* (Stanford: Stanford University Press, 1994), 4.

4 Jérôme Bourgon, "Rights, Freedoms, and Customs in the Making of Chinese Civil Law, 1900–1936," in *Realms of Freedom in Modern China*, ed. William C. Kirby (Stanford: Stanford University Press, 2004), 91.

© KONINKLIJKE BRILL NV, LEIDEN, 2015 | DOI 10.1163/9789004288492_003

handbooks evidenced a "distinct separation" between civil and criminal litigation that was absent "in theory" but present in practice.[5]

More recently, Zhang Xiaoye has suggested that as far as the Qing state and society were concerned, a distinction between *cisong* and *anjian* was recognized. *Cisong* refers to lawsuits over household, marriage, land, and some minor criminal matters. It was differentiated from *anjian* by the less severe penalties imposed on the litigants at fault. This distinction differed qualitatively from the modern "civil/criminal distinction" in the sense that the former operated not as a dichotomy but as a reflection of the Chinese juridical tradition of "arranging crimes by [different] punishments" (*yixing tongzui*). There was no strict boundary between *cisong* and *anjian* cases, and local officials had significant discretion over where to draw the line.[6]

For Li Zan, another Chinese legal historian, Qing litigation was divided into *zhongqing* (serious matters) and *xigu* (trivial matters), and this separation was based not on any written rules but on the magistrates' evaluation of the magnitude of the matters at issue. This then gave the magistrates a lot of leeway in deciding whether to treat the litigation as a trivial or a serious matter, depending on the final penalty rather than the nature of the legal case itself.[7] Li Zan also thought that the Qing legal system used these two rather ambiguous concepts, *zhongqing* and *xigu*, to classify legal cases and arrange the corresponding judicial proceedings. For him, the Qing distinction between *zhongqing* and *xigu* was not the same as that between criminal and civil cases in modern Western legal parlance, because *xigu* also included cases of personal injury and theft, which would be considered "criminal" in the modern sense.[8]

Japanese scholars have proposed another way of classification based on *zhouxian zili* (magistrate's self-managed cases) and *mingdao zhong'an* (serious cases involving homicide and robbery). *Zhouxian zili* refers to cases that

---

5 Huang, *Civil Justice in China*, 218–20.

6 Zhang Xiaoye 张小也, "Cong 'zili' dao 'xianlü': dui qingdai 'minfa' yu 'minshi susong' de kaocha 从"自理"到"宪律": 对清代"民法"与"民事诉讼"的考察 [From 'Self-Managed' Cases to State Law: On Civil Law and Civil Litigation in the Qing]," *Xueshu yuekan* 学术月刊 [Academic Monthly] 38, no. 8 (Aug. 2006): 139–47.

7 Li Zan 里赞, "Xingmin zhifen yu zhongqing xigu: qingdai fa yanjiu zhong de fa ji anjian fenlei wenti 刑民之分与重情细故: 清代法研究中的法及案件分类问题 [Distinction between Criminal and Civil Litigation and between Serious and Trivial Cases: Law and Litigation Classification in Qing Legal Study]," *Xi'nan minzu daxue xuebao* 西南民族大学学报 [Journal of the Southwest University of Nationalities] 208, no. 12 (Dec. 2008): 194–97.

8 Li Zan, "Zhongguo falüshi yanjiu de fangfa, cailiao he xijie 中国法律史研究的方法、材料和细节 [Methods, Materials, and Details in the Study of Chinese Legal History]," *Jindaifa pinglun* 近代法评论 [Modern Law Review] 2 (Dec. 2009): 184–85.

required no judicial review by superior officials unless the litigants appealed the county magistrate's decision. Most of these cases dealt with what would be called civil disputes and minor criminal matters in Western legal parlance. By contrast, *mingdao zhong'an* refers to cases that required automatic review of the county magistrate's decisions by superior officials, whether or not the litigants decided to appeal. Accordingly, cases of *mingdao zhong'an* were decided according to the formal written law, whereas cases of *zhouxian zili* were adjudicated based on the circumstances of the case and human sentiments and reason.[9] In addition, these Japanese scholars maintained that different kinds of legal cases, ranging from disputes over land boundary, debts, inheritance, and breach of marital agreements to cases of affrays, injury, and homicide, were all brought to the county government as the court of first instance before they were reviewed by higher courts if necessary.[10]

These interpretations often differ from or even contradict one another. Some of them are unduly influenced by modern Western legal categories and thus do not reflect how imperial Chinese jurists understood the Chinese legal system. It is true that the Qing legal system did not formally incorporate distinctions between "civil" and "criminal" law and their respective procedural law. Nevertheless, the Qing government developed its own method of differentiating types of litigation, one that suited the overall structure of its legal system and judicial practice.[11] Cases thus classified were handled according to different procedures of adjudication and judicial review, and the classification might even affect whether or not the judges should strictly apply the law. More careful perusal of Qing legal texts raises a series of questions regarding the

9 Hiroaki Terada 寺田浩明, "Riben de Qingdai sifa zhidu yanjiu yu dui fa de lijie 日本的清代司法制度研究与对'法'的理解 [Japanese Study of the Qing Judicial System and Understanding of the 'Law']," in *Ming Qing shiqi de minshe shenpan yu minjian qiyue* 明清时期的民事审判与民间契约 [Civil Adjudication and Contracts in the Ming-Qing Period], ed. Wang Yaxin 王亚新 and Liang Zhiping 梁治平 (Beijing: Falü chubanshe, 1998), 112.

10 Ibid., 115.

11 At the county level, Qing litigants brought an overwhelmingly large number of lawsuits to the court and caused a lot of judicial backlog. For relevant statistics about the lawsuits at the county level, see Deng Jianpeng邓建鹏, *Caichan quanli de pinkun: Zhongguo chuantong minshifa yanjiu* 财产权利的贫困：中国传统民事法研究 [Deficiency in Property Rights: A Study of Traditional Chinese Civil Law] (Beijing: Falü chubanshe, 2006), 107–8. Also see Fuma Susumu 夫马进, "Ming Qing shidai de songshi yu susong zhidu 明清时代的讼师与诉讼制度 [Litigation Masters and the Judicial System in the Ming-Qing Period]," in *Ming Qing shiqi de minshi shenpan yu minjian qiyue*, ed. Wang Yaxin and Liang Zhiping, 392–94.

abovementioned debates: Was there really no significant difference between the trial procedure for civil and criminal cases in Qing courts? Is it true that no strict boundary existed between *cisong* and *anjian*? Is it true that the distinction between *zhongqing* (serious matters) and *xigu* (trivial matters) existed only in the final penalties but not in the nature of the cases? Were *zili* (self-managed) cases and *mingdao zhong'an* (serious cases involving homicide and robbery) brought to the county magistrates with no regard for their different natures? To what extent did Qing magistrate handbooks evidence a distinct separation between civil and criminal litigation?

Some of these questions remain underanalyzed, and examining them in the context of the actual operation of Qing legal discourse and judicial practice may illuminate other important issues related to Chinese legal history. For instance, it could shed light on the debate between Shiga Shūzō and Philip Huang about whether Qing officials adjudicated according to the law, or on the debate among Zhang Weiren, He Weifang, and Gao Hongjun about whether judicial decisions were predictable in late imperial China.[12] The debate over whether Qing officials adjudicated according to the law or sentiments and reason can be reductive and misleading if we do not consider how different types of legal cases were actually categorized and treated during the Qing period. By studying the Qing Code, administrative handbooks, and judicial archives, this chapter will first try to clarify the concepts, institutional structure, and methods of Qing litigation classification. It then analyzes the government's approaches to different types of litigation and the litigants' counterstrategies. Finally, it discusses what types of cases must be decided according to the law and why. Instead of continuing to debate whether late imperial China had an indigenous tradition of civil-law jurisprudence or civil/criminal distinction, it might be more fruitful to analyze how Qing jurists utilized and rationalized their own ways of differentiating legal cases and what that tells us about the Qing judicial system. This may lead to some different and potentially more helpful perspectives on the ongoing debates over late imperial Chinese law.

The Basic Framework of Litigation Classification

Preliminary attempts to organize legal cases into different categories had already existed before the Qing dynasty. Administrative handbooks published

---

12 For a summary of these debates, please see Deng Jianpeng 邓建鹏, "Qingdai zhouxian songan de caipan fangshi yanjiu 清代州县讼案的裁判方式研究 [A Study of the Adjudication of Qing County-Level Litigation]," *Jiangsu shehui kexue* 江苏社会科学 [Jiangsu Social Science] 232, no. 3 (May 2007): 97–104.

in the late Ming advised officials to separate "major cases from minor cases" (*daxiao shi*), which would be subject to *different* procedures, ways of adjudication, and schedules. Ming administrator Jiang Tingbi of the Jiajing reign (1522–66) pointed out that when dealing with different kinds of cases, local officials "should promptly conclude or dismiss minor cases (*xiaoshi*) and carefully examine major cases (*dashi*) without taking litigants into custody in all cases."[13] While "major cases" involving homicide or robbery were sent to the relevant department (*fang*) of the county yamen (i.e., government office) to summon the parties concerned, "minor cases" that involved household issues, marriage, or affrays should be concluded promptly.[14] Jiang also suggested that legal complaints not be forwarded to the clerks or subofficials of the county yamen because the latter might attempt to extort money from the litigants. Instead, minor cases should be forwarded to the local residents who served as hundred captains (*lizhang*) or household heads (*huzhang*) for resolution; the local people understood the circumstances and would not dare to extort money.[15] In Jiang's words, "*cisong* should be sent to the hundred captains to summon the concerned parties and report the results [to the government]. Only complaints about major cases (*dashi*) should be accepted," and the parties would then be requested by the local officials to appear before the court. The judgment would be rendered only after the relevant evidence had been obtained. "If it involved serious matters (*zhongqing*) such as homicide, robbery, or a faked seal, etc., the case should first be reported to the superior authorities."[16] This view resonated with that of Wu Zun (*jinshi* or metropolitan degree, 1547), censor of the Henan circuit in the late Ming dynasty. According to Wu, "if the court accepted the plaint in a *cisong* case, the court should ask the relevant hundred captain rather than the yamen runners to get [the litigants and witnesses]."[17] For major cases involving homicide or robbery, the suspects might be dangerous and should be apprehended by the yamen runners. Wu also held: "Except for those involving homicide, robbery, rape and fraud, let the litigants do it if they want to settle a dispute over issues of household, marriage, and land outside the court." In contrast with homicide and robbery cases, which must be reviewed

---

13 Jiang Tingbi 蒋廷璧, *Pushan Jianggong zhengxun* 璞山蒋公政训 [Administrative Advice of Magistrate Jiang], in *Guanzhenshu jicheng* 官箴书集成 [Compendium of Administrative Handbooks], ed. Guanzhenshu jicheng bianzuan weiyuanhui (Hefei: Huangshan shushe, 1997), 2: 3.

14 Ibid.

15 Ibid.

16 Ibid., 13.

17 Wu Zun 吴遵, *Chushi lu* 初仕录 [Records for Novice Officials] (1629), in *Guanzhenshu jicheng*, 2: 52.

by superior officials after the preliminary adjudication, local officials had the power to allow the litigants to privately settle "minor cases" such as household or marriage disputes.[18]

Thus, one may conclude that the idea and practice of separating out different kinds of lawsuits and then treating them accordingly in judicial administration had taken shape by the mid-sixteenth century and continued into the Qing. During the process, the term *cisong* (or *xigu* or *xishi*) came to refer to lawsuits over household, marriage, and other kinds of (what we nowadays would call) civil cases, whereas the term *anjian* (or *zhongqing* or *dashi*) was used to refer to more serious criminal cases, including homicide, robbery, and so on. It is in this sense that I will use these two terms to discuss how different kinds of litigation were classified in the Qing. Accordingly, Qing legal cases can be roughly divided into *cisong* and *anjian*, although their usages in this regard were not universally agreed upon among Qing jurists and administrators.

The statute on "Bypassing the Proper Court" (*yuesu*) in the Qing Code stipulated: "Every *cisong* brought by a military person or a civilian must start from the lowest government office before moving to a higher one [according to the judicial procedure]. If someone bypasses the proper authorities and brings a lawsuit directly to a higher office, the complainant will receive 50 strokes of the light bamboo." The interlinear commentary, which provided a legally binding clarification of the preceding statutory language, then stated: "One is permitted to bring the plaint to a higher official only if the lower official with jurisdiction has refused to accept it or has handled it improperly."[19] Here the term *cisong* was used as a generic term to refer to all types of litigation. This was close to the usage in the *Placards for Instructing the People* (*Jiaomin bangwen*) of the early Ming, which stated: "Many people in places like Zhejiang and Jiangxi love to bring *cisong*, and even if only minor matters are at stake, they refuse to drop it but would rather travel to the imperial capital to complain."[20] Nevertheless, the Qing Code also provided: "For any *anjian* brought to the capital by subjects from other provinces, if the county official has judged unfairly and if his superiors including the provincial governors have then refused to

18 Ibid.

19 Tian Tao 田涛 and Zheng Qin 郑秦, eds., *Da Qing lüli* 大清律例 [The Great Qing Code] (Beijing: Falü Chubanshe, 1998), 473.

20 Liu Hainian 刘海年 and Yang Yifan 杨一凡, eds., *Zhongguo falü dianji jicheng* 中国珍稀法律典籍集成 [Compendium of Rare Chinese Law Books], *yibian* 乙编 [Series 2] (Beijing: Kexue chubanshe, 1994), 1: 639. For similar examples, see Tian and Zheg, *Da Qing lüli*, 490–93; Bao Shichen 包世臣, *Qimin sishu* 齐民四术 [Four Ways of Governing the People] (Beijing: Zhonghua shuju, 2001 (1846)), 252–53.

accept the appeal or judged [the case] incorrectly, or if the case has not been reviewed by the provincial governors but indeed involves serious matters, the Ministry of Justice (*Xingbu*) and the Censorate (*Duchayuan*) should verify the circumstances and memorialize the throne for a decree to handle it." The term *anjian* here obviously referred to serious criminal cases such as homicide and robbery because the next passage of the statute continued: "If the complaint [brought to the authorities in the imperial capital] is about a *xishi* ("minor") dispute over household, marriage, and land, it must be dismissed and the complainant must file the complaint with the local court with proper jurisdiction and be punished for having bypassed it."[21] Different judicial procedures were thus applied to *xishi* (or *cisong*) and *anjian* here: the latter could be appealed to the Ministry of Justice and the Censorate in the imperial capital and be adjudicated by them with the emperor's approval, but the former had to be decided first by the local officials, and those who bypassed the local courts would be punished.

Moreover, different types of litigation also involved different procedures and penalties. One Qing commentator described these differences quite accurately: "In other provinces [outside the imperial capital], they are known as *anjian* if the proposed penalty [in a case] is more severe than taking away the offender's civil-examination degree or than penal servitude or beating with the heavy bamboo, or if the proposed penalty and case record must be reviewed by the Ministry of Justice, or if the case is delegated by a superior office and its judgment has to be reported back to the latter." By contrast, "those self-managed cases and all disputes over issues of household, marriage, debts and affrays that may incur punishment of beating with the light bamboo or wearing a cangue, are called *cisong*." In other words, *anjian* referred to cases that were liable for punishment more severe than beating with the heavy bamboo or penal servitude and, procedurally, had to be reported to the Ministry of Justice or a superior government that had assigned the case to the lower-level office. *Cisong* referred to less serious offences and "civil" disputes that involved punishment lighter than wearing a cangue or beating with the bamboo.[22]

Although people might use different terms to refer to these two types of litigation, their respective scopes were quite clear. In numerous Qing official documents, *cisong* was understood to mean disputes over land, household, marriage, and the like. In the fifth year of the Yongzheng reign (1727), Sichuan

---

21 Based on a substatute proposed by the Censorate in 1769. See Wu Tan 吴坛, *Da Qing lüli tongkao jiaozhu* 大清律例通考校注 [The Great Qing Code with Comprehensive Notes and Annotation] (Beijing: Zhongguo zhengfa daxue chubanshe, 1992), 873.

22 Bao, *Qimin sishu*, 251–52.

Governor Xiande memorialized: "Seven or eight out of ten *cisong* in Sichuan concern land and one cannot adjudicate them without measuring the land."[23] Wang Huizu, a famous private legal advisor (*muyou*) in the Qianlong period (1736–95) and once a county magistrate in Hunan, also observed: "Not even half of the *cisong* really need be adjudicated. The litigants launched lawsuits on the spur of moment over quarrels between neighbors or trivial conflicts among family members."[24] These remarks suggest that the abovementioned distinction between *cisong* and *anjian* was already well recognized among some Qing local administrators by then.

Moreover, *anjian* (*zhongqing*) or serious cases concerning homicide and robbery could be brought to the court at any time, whereas plaints about *cisong* or minor disputes could be submitted only on certain designated days. In 1817, the Zhejiang provincial judge announced a rule: "Except for homicide and robbery which can be reported any time, all the other *cisong* cases can be brought to the court only on the designated days."[25] Otherwise, just as the Danshui sub-prefect in Taibei declared in 1883, plaints that were not submitted on the designated days would be rejected.[26] The Qing Code did not standardize the days for receiving plaints every month, but local officials frequently did that. Different jurisdictions therefore often had different days for receiving plaints. The *Imperially Approved Rules for County Magistrates*, distributed by the Yongzheng Emperor to all county magistrates, maintained that "county officials should not limit the receipt of plaints only to the third, sixth, and ninth day [of every ten days in each month]."[27] *The Provincial Regulation of Fujian*, however, threatened to punish those who "did not observe the designated days for submitting their plaints."[28]

Cisong and *anjian* were also handled by different departments (*fang*) of the local yamen. Most Qing county yamen, modeled after the six ministries in the central government, had six departments, in charge of personnel, revenue, rites, military, public works, and law/punishment. Different county

23 *Qingshi gao* 清史稿 [A Draft History of the Qing], 294: 10340.

24 Wang Huizu 汪辉祖, "Zuozhi yaoyan 佐治药言 [Medicinal Words for Assisting Governance]," in Wang Huizu, *Wang Longzhuang xiansheng yishu* 汪龙庄先生遗书 [Works Bequeathed by Wang Huizu] (Shenjiantang, 1871), in *Guanzhenshu jicheng*, 5: 317.

25 *Zhizhe chenggui* (1837), *juan* 8, in *Guanzhenshu jicheng*, 6: 656.

26 The *Dan-xin Archives*, No. 22609-32, microfilms at the Columbia University East Asian Library.

27 Tian Wenjing 田文镜, *Qinding xunchi zhouxian guitiao* 钦定训饬州县规条 [Imperially Approved Instructions for County Magistrates] (Hunan Hehuachi shuju, 1875), 13.

28 *Fujian shengli* 福建省例 [Provincial Regulations of Fujian] (Taiwan: Datong shuju gongsi, 1997), 971.

yamen might differ somewhat in the setup of the departments. Philip Huang found that in late Qing Xinzhu county, Taiwan, "cases concerning debts, land, marriage, etc. were sent to the *qiangu* advisor while cases about theft, robbery, affrays and gambling were sent to the *xingming* advisor" in the county yamen; the division [of labor] corresponded with that between the departments of revenue and punishment.[29] In Ba county of the Qing period, "the department of rites was responsible for disputes over the ancestral hall and temple, household, debt, marriage, and medicinal herbs. The department of punishment was responsible for cases of homicide, robbery, rape, prostitution, banditry, eloping, violence, and personal injury. The department of revenue was responsible for matters concerning land and house sales, grain, tax, mortgage and leasing, and wine levies."[30] Hence, it seems clear that during the Qing period, it was the department of revenue (or sometimes the department of rites as well) that was in charge of *cisong*, while the department of punishment handled *anjian*. Of course, yamen runners of the six departments sometimes overlapped in their case assignments, and that could cause competition among them for the case assignments and thus the litigation fees.[31]

Influenced by the distinction between different types of litigation, *muyou*, as the local officials' "private legal advisors," had division of labor among themselves. There were many types of *muyou* but the most important ones were criminal (*xingming*) and civil or fiscal (*qiangu*) *muyou*. The former focused on cases related to crimes, social order, and violation of "proper human relationships" (*gangchang*); the latter focused on civil disputes.[32] Their duties overlapped in some cases, however. According to Wang Youhuai, a famous legal specialist during the Qianlong reign and compiler of *Chongkan buzhu xiyuanlu jizheng*, if the cause of action concerned land, house, debt, sale of assets, taxation, or contract, the case should be handled by the *qiangu* advisor. If the

29 Huang, *Civil Justice in China*, 198–222.

30 *Qingdai Baxian dang'an huibian* (Qianlong chao) 清代巴县档案汇编(乾隆朝) [Collection of Qing Records from the Ba County Archives (the Qianlong Reign)], comp. Sichuan dang'anguan (Beijing: Dang'an chubanshe, 1992), 2–3.

31 For detailed analysis, see Deng Jianpeng 邓建鹏, "Cong lougui xianxiang dao fading shoufei: Qingdai songfei zhuanxing yanjiu 从陋规现象到法定收费：清代讼费转型研究 [From Customary Fees to Legal Charges: On the Transformation of Qing Litigation Fees]," *Zhongguo zhengfa daxue xuebao* 中国政法大学学报 [Journal of the Chinese University of Politics and Law] 18, no. 4 (July 2010): 5–23.

32 See Gao Huanyue 高浣月, *Qingdai xingming muyou yanjiu* 清代刑名幕友研究 [A Study of Qing *Xingming* Advisors] (Beijing: Zhongguo zhengfa daxue chubanshe, 2000), 36–40; Li Chen, "Legal Specialists and Judicial Administration in Late Imperial China, 1651–1911," *Late Imperial China* 33, no. 1 (June 2012): 3–4.

cause of action had to do with an affray, adultery, fraud, a fight over a graveyard, marriage, or violation of proper human relationships, the case should be handled by the *xingming* advisor.[33] As a result, a number of popular administrative handbooks, such as *Xingmu yaolüe* and *Zhaojie shuo*, instructed *xingming* advisors on how to deal with serious criminal cases such as robbery, homicide, and affray but said very little about civil lawsuits, or *cisong*.[34] This was also true of the many collections of cases decided by the Ministry of Justice that were published in the mid and late Qing period, including *Li'an quanji, Bo'an huibian*, and *Xing'an huilan*.[35] As proper handling of such serious (criminal) cases was considered crucial to the evaluation and promotion of local officials, such books were quite popular, whereas handbooks on the adjudication of less serious (civil) disputes were relatively few.

Bureaucratic and Popular Responses to Different Types of Litigation

Qu Tongzu observed that besides the maintenance of social order, the most important duties of Qing county magistrates were tax collection and judicial

33 See Wang Youhuai 王又槐, "Ban'an yaolüe 办案要略 [Essential Advice for Handling Cases]," in *Guanzhenshu jicheng*, 4: 770. [Translators'note: Wang Youhuai's handbook was actually copied from Bai Ruzhen's *xingming yide*. See Li Chen, "Zhishi de liliang: Qingdai muyou miben he gongkai chuban de lüxue zhuzuo dui qingdai sifa changyu de yingxiang 知识的力量：清代幕友秘本和公开出版的律学著作对清代司法场域的影响 [Power of Knowledge: The Role of Secret and Published Treatises of Private Legal Specialists in the Qing Juridical Field]," *Zhejiang daxue xuebao* 浙江大学学报 [Journal of Zhejiang University] 45, no. 1 (Jan. 2015)]

34 "Xingmu yaolüe 刑幕要略 [Essentials for *Xingming* Advisors]," in *Rumu xuzhi wuzhong*, 533–630; "*Zhaojie shuo* 招解说 [On Obtaining and Forwarding Confessions]," in *Ming Qing gongdu miben wuzhong* 明清公牍秘本五种 [Five Secret Administrative Handbooks from the Ming and Qing], ed. Guo Chengwei 郭成伟 and Tian Tao 田涛 (Beijing: Zhongguo zhengfa daxue chubanshe, 1999), 551–644; Bai Yuanfeng 白元峰, *Qintang bidu* 琴堂必读 [Required Readings for the Court Room] (Yunxiangtang cangban, 1840); Wan Weihan 万维翰, "Muxue juyao 幕学举要 [Key Points for Private Advisors]," in *Rumu xuzhi wuzhong*, 11–105; Wang Youhuai, "Ban'an yaolüe."

35 See, e.g., Zhiqiang Wang, "Case Precedent in Qing China: Rethinking Traditional Case Law," in *Columbia Journal of Asian Law* 19, no.1 (Spring-Fall 2005): 327–32. Also see Quan Shichao 全士潮, Zhang Daoyuan 张道源 et al., eds., *Bo'an huibian* 驳案汇编 [A Collection of Reversed Cases] (Beijing: Falü chubanshe, 2009 [reprint]); Zhu Qingqi 祝庆麒 et al., eds., *Xingan huilan quanbian* 刑案汇览全编 [A Complete Collection of Criminal Cases] (Beijing: Falü chubanshe, 2007 [reprint]).

administration. Judicial administration was tied closely to social order and was a major factor in evaluating the performance of local officials. The fact that how they handled *cisong* and *anjian* were weighed differently in their evaluation affected county magistrates' approaches to, and their allocation of time and efforts between, those two types of litigation. Zhang Wuwei, a Qing county magistrate in Jiangxi during the Jiaqing (1796–1820) period, wrote from personal experience: "Cases of homicide and robbery must be handled with great care and confidentiality and are often tried in the inner hall or side room" instead of the front hall of the yamen. Except for the staff members assigned to the case, even runners of the same yamen should not be allowed to stand by during the hearing "because neither they nor the public were supposed to hear the results of the case immediately." This was in contrast with the way in which a *cisong* (or minor dispute) was handled, for which even the exact time of a scheduled court hearing would be specified in a public advance notice.[36]

Bao Shichen (1775–1855), a famous Qing scholar and once a county magistrate in Jiangxi, succinctly summarized how many of his contemporaries probably viewed these two types of legal cases:

> Judicial officials in other provinces [than Beijing] are aided by *muyou*. The latter are mostly devoted to protecting the host officials' performance evaluation (*baoquan juting kaocheng*) and therefore focus their attention on *anjian* (serious cases) while being careless about *cisong* since they are self-managed matters of the office.... As far as I know, although [the former kind of cases] affect people's conviction and punishment, there are only a few of them in a county each year and the damages will be limited even if they are not handled properly. With regard to *cisong*, however, the court in a busy and populous county may receive more than one hundred plaints on a single day.
>
> Additionally, there are those who bring their lawsuits to the officials by stopping their sedan on the road or by hitting the drum in front of the yamen gate. As a result, *cisong* outnumber *anjian* by a hundred times and if they are hastily concluded or left unresolved for too long, they can affect every household. The officials who process *cisong* lawsuits promptly are loved by the people and those who are good at resolving *anjian* (or serious cases) are favored by their superiors. All county magistrates want to win the heart of their superiors; there are many who may be considered

36 Zhang Wuwei 张五纬, *Weinengxin lu* 未能信录 [A Record of the Unbelievable] (1807p), *juan* 1, in *Lidai panli pandu* 历代判例判牍 [Cases from Various Dynasties], ed. Yang Yifan 杨一凡 and Xu Lizhi 徐立志 (Beijing: Zhongguo shehui kexue chubanshe, 2005), 9: 504.

> capable officials by their superiors but are hated by the people. That is because the officials consider *cisong* irrelevant to their performance evaluation and disregard the hardships of the people, or because the officials choose to oppress the people at will after they have won their superiors' trust.... In recent years, provincial governors have all realized that hearing *cisong* promptly should be the top priority for purposes of caring for the people and that leaving these lawsuits unresolved is a main cause of people's hardships. So they have issued numerous orders to subordinate officials to clear up the judicial docket... but local administrators have treated such decrees as empty words and those officials commissioned [by the provincial governors] for that task also failed to do any better than sit idly in the prefectural yamen.[37]

What Bao Shichen described was quite typical in his time. *Anjian* had to go through a series of trials and reviews to reach the provincial governor, governor general, or even the emperor. In this process, local officials' decisions were monitored by their superiors, and the resulting performance evaluation would affect their career prospects. As local officials' private advisors, *muyou* were more likely to dedicate their efforts to dealing with these major cases. By contrast, *cisong* were managed by the local officials and freed from the mandatory reviewing process. Even though the county officials might be asked periodically to report how they had handled these less serious lawsuits, they had various ways of concealing the number of the unresolved lawsuits. For example, Fan Zengxiang (1846–1931), then Shaanxi provincial judge, criticized his subordinates as follows: "Most of the monthly reports [of *cisong*] listed two or three lawsuits at most. I have worked in the lower courts. Do you think I have no idea how many cases a county yamen would receive every month?... Some of the incompetent, cunning magistrates... have not only underreported but also reported no case at all."[38] Since local officials' evaluation and career success were determined more by how they handled *anjian* than by how they resolved *cisong*, it is not surprising that they might choose to neglect the latter and that the officials valued by their superiors could be disliked by the people.

The different attitudes of local officials towards *cisong* and *anjian*, especially their tendency to take the former less seriously, led litigants to adopt counterstrategies. It had already been pointed out in the Ming period: "Trivial matters are not actionable in the court. People who are obsessed with their own grievances would exaggerate the significance of the matter or bring the

37 Bao, *Qimin sishu*, 252.

38 Fan, *Fanshan zhengshu, juan* 12, in *Guanzhenshu jicheng*, 10: 259.

complaint to the superior yamen. People often try to make the case appear more serious than it is in order to get the government to hear it, so [officials should] be careful to detect this."[39] In the centralized Qing bureaucracy, the evaluation of local officials was primarily determined by criteria relating to their duties in support of the dynastic rule. The Qing Code provided different punishments for officials who mishandled different types of legal cases. According to the statute on "Failure to Take Action on Accusations" in the Qing Code, officials who refuse to receive an accusation of rebellion or high treason would receive the punishment of 100 strokes by the heavy bamboo and 3 years of penal servitude; not receiving accusations of petty treason (*e'ni*) would be punished with 100 strokes of the heavy bamboo; not receiving accusations of homicide or robbery would be punished with 80 strokes of the heavy bamboo; not receiving cases of affray, marriage, land and household should have the punishment of the offenders reduced by two degrees and up to 80 strokes of the heavy bamboo.[40] In comparison with *cisong*, those *anjian* involving homicide, robbery, rebellion, disobedience, and so on seriously threatened the imperial order and so how well local officials handled them significantly affected their performance evaluation. In addition, county magistrates were not allowed to delegate their staff members to adjudicate litigation. Whereas officials would forfeit their salaries for one year if they asked the local community heads (*xiangbao* and *dibao*) to conclude *cisong* disputes, they would suffer the more serious penalty of demotion by three grades if they asked them to investigate and report on crucial circumstances of homicide, robbery, or other serious cases.[41] Under the same statute, a substatute enacted in 1725 did state that "local officials should be impeached by their superiors if their intentional delay in processing self-managed *cisong* cases caused litigants to wait long and lose time and jobs or made women or the innocent suffer or even sell their wives and children."[42] However, these legal commands could not prevent local

39 Jiang, *Pushan Jianggong zhengxun*, 12.

40 Tian and Zheng, *Da Qing lüli*, 478. The offense of *e'ni* 恶逆 meant beating or murdering one's (or one's husband's) grandparent, parent, uncle, or aunt.

41 Yao Yuxian 姚雨芗 and Hu Yangshan 胡仰山, eds., *Da Qing lüli huitong xinzuan* 大清律例会通新纂 [New Comprehensive Compilation of the Great Qing Code] (Taibei: Wenhai chubanshe, 1987), 2945; Deng, "Qingdai Zhouxian song'an de caipan fangshi yanjiu"; You Chenjun 尤陈俊, "Qingdai jianyuexing sifa tizhi xia de 'jian song' wenti: Cong caizheng zhiyue de jiaodu qieru 清代简约型司法体制下的"健讼"问题—从财政制约的角度切入 [The Issue of Litigiousness in the Condensed Qing Judicial System: From the Perspective of Fiscal Constraints]," *Fashang yanjiu* 法商研究 [Studies in Law and Business] 148, no. 2 (March 2012): 154–60.

42 Tian and Zheng, *Da Qing lüli*, 479.

officials from overlooking *cisong* disputes; relatively few officials were actually punished for failing to conclude these disputes properly or promptly. As noted earlier, a litigant had to overcome more obstacles to get a court to accept a *cisong* accusation than an *anjian* one, including the different page limits for plaints in these two types of cases.

Under such circumstances, nonviolent disputes between private individuals were more likely to be overlooked by the imperial legislators and judicial authorities. In order to protect their own interests, litigants frequently exaggerated the nature of the dispute and might even distort a civil dispute to make it appear like a criminal case to attract the judge's attention.[43] At the same time, their plaints employed such [sensational] phrases as "crying for investigation," "begging for investigation," "*kowtow* for a hearing," and "please pity me and punish [the accused]" to appeal to the officials' sympathy and have their complaint accepted.[44] This practice existed throughout the Ming and Qing periods. The fact that many "secret handbooks for litigation masters" (*songshi miben*) were fond of teaching litigants to use flamboyant language to draft their plaints had a lot to do with this legal environment.[45] Unlike the handbooks for private advisors, those for litigation masters not only provided detailed advice on how to write a charge and how to litigate about homicide and robbery but also included equally detailed instructions on *cisong*. For example, besides discussing homicide cases, *Xiaocao zhijunshu* analyzed how to litigate in disputes over marriage, affrays, debts, real estate, succession, and graveyard.[46] The same is

---

43 For more about this, see Deng Jianpeng 邓建鹏, "Qingdai minshi qisu de fangshi 清代民事起诉的方式 [Ways of Launching Civil Litigation in the Qing]," in *Zhongguo wenhua yu fazhi* 中国文化与法治 [Chinese Culture and the Rule of Law], ed. Zhongguo falüshi xuehui 中国法律史学会 [Chinese Legal History Society] (Beijing: Shehui kexue wenxian chubanshe, 2007), 292–310.

44 For examples of plaints using such language, see Tian Tao 田涛, Xu Chuanxi 许传玺, and Wang Hongzhi 王宏治, eds., *Huangyan susong dangan ji diaocha baogao* 黄岩诉讼档案及调查报告 [The Judicial Archives of Huangyan and a Field Report] (Beijing: Falü chubanshe, 2004), 41; Wang Zhaowu 王昭武, *Wancheng suzhuang* 万承诉状 [Plaints from Wancheng] (Nanning: Guangxi renmin chubanshe, 2008), 3.

45 See Deng Jianpeng 邓建鹏, "*Songshi miben yu qingdai suzhuang de fengge* 讼师秘本与清代诉状的风格 [Secret Handbooks for Litigation Masters and Format of Qing Plaints]," *Zhejiang shehui kexue* 浙江社会科学 [Zhejiang Social Sciences]122, no. 4 (July 2005): 71–75.

46 See Wolongzi 卧龙子, *Xiaocao zhijunshu* 萧曹致君术 [The Art of Xiao He and Cao Can to Assist the Ruler]. undated.

true of another influential handbook for litigation masters, *Toudan han*.[47] All these handbooks more or less agreed that litigants should exaggerate to some extent in describing their cause of action so as to attract the judge's attention. This shared tendency among the litigation masters and litigants, as reflected in the judicial archives, was a reluctant but coordinated response to the state's passive treatment of *cisong*.

Some scholars outside China have recently questioned Max Weber's representation of traditional Chinese law and argued that there were far more serious limitations to Chinese officials' arbitrariness in adjudication than Weber ever acknowledged. Such limitations were not derived from "a sacred tradition" but from codified laws and restrictions on the conduct of judicial officials. In fact, more legal expertise was also required and manifested in imperial China's judicial administration than Weber realized. Chinese litigants were not just passive victims of a totalitarian regime.[48] This revisionist understanding was based on the formal state law, including the Qing Code, which had clear provisions restricting officials' arbitrariness in judicial administration.[49] Indeed, some scholars have argued that by the Qing period, the dynastic law was highly rationalized and sophisticated. This does not mean that it was unusual to find officials adjudicating arbitrarily, however. For example, Zhang Jixin, a prefect and then lieutenant governor who served in Shanxi, Shaanxi, Fujian, Sichuan, and Guizhou provinces during the Daoguang and Xianfeng reigns (1820–61), claimed that some county magistrates left all *cisong* disputes unprocessed, that his predecessors in Shanxi never held trials and therefore had cases piled up like a mountain, and that witnesses in *cisong* were jailed in Sichuan, suffering from the application of judicial torture at will.[50] At the same time, other Qing scholar-officials criticized those tendencies. For instance, Zhang Wuwei noted that officials who "generally attached importance to homicide and robbery cases and slighted *cisong*" failed to realize that the former happened only occasionally while the latter were "frequent occurrences among the people."[51] Fang Dashi echoed this: "Litigation over household, marriage, land, debts,

47 See Buxiang zi 补相子, *Xiangjian Buxiangzi yuanben xinjuan toudanhan* 湘间补相子原本新镌透胆寒 [Original Edition of Newly Printed *Toudanhan* (or *Scary Strategies*) by Buxiangzi of Hunan], undated.

48 See Robert M. Marsh, "Weber's Misunderstanding of Traditional Chinese Law," *American Journal of Sociology* 106, no. 2 (Sept. 2000): 298.

49 Tian and Zheng, *Da Qing lüli*, 579–602.

50 Zhang Jixin 张集馨, *Daoxian huanhai jianwenlu* 道咸宦海见闻录 [Things Seen and Heard as an Official in the Daoguang and Xianfeng Eras] (Beijing: Zhonghua shuju, 1981), 45, 95–97, 101, 104, 112.

51 Zhang Wuwei, *Weinengxin lu*, 504.

theft, and so on might be deemed trivial matters (*xigu*) by the government but were not trivial to the people whose interests were immediately affected thereby." Conscientious officials could not focus only on the few major cases (i.e. *zhongqing anjian*) while ignoring the many so-called minor disputes in a county.[52]

Litigation Classification and the Grounds for Adjudication

How *cisong* and *anjian* were adjudicated could also differ significantly in judicial practice. According to the Qing Code, when reviewing *anjian*, provincial governors must carefully examine the records to make sure that the punishment matched the offence and then report the decision to Beijing. Officials would be impeached if they distorted the law or made a serious mistake in adjudication, such as sentencing a capital offender to military exile or giving a death sentence to an offender punishable by military exile. Officials would be excused if the sentence was just a bit lighter than the due punishment, if the cited law was not perfectly appropriate, or if only a mistake or negligence was involved, as long as the officials had not acted for illicit purposes and the punishment for the wrongfully convicted person was below military exile.[53] Theoretically, once a case came under judicial review, the initial judge and subsequent reviewers were also under scrutiny by their superiors up to the emperor himself. Therefore, county magistrates as well as provincial governors had to follow the law when deciding *anjian* to avoid legal liabilities.

Over the past twenty years or so, legal historians such as Shiga Shūzō, Philip Huang, Zhang Weiren, and He Weifang have debated whether legal cases in traditional China (especially in the Qing period) were decided according to the law. That question might be better addressed by examining how Qing jurists felt about the application of the law. Fang Dashi (1821–96), Zhili provincial judge and then Shanxi lieutenant governor in the Guangxu reign (1875–1908), observed that not all self-managed cases of *cisong* had to be decided strictly according to the Qing Code. The magistrate might decide the case in light of the circumstances, reason, and local customs, although he should know what statute or substatute was applicable to the case and make sure that the judgment was not inconsistent with the applicable law. Otherwise, the magistrate was unable to explain his decision to his superiors if the case was appealed and

52 Fang Dashi, *Pingping yan* 平平言 [Ordinary Words] (Zizhou guanxie, 1892), *juan* 3, in *Guanzhenshu jicheng*, 7: 675.

53 Tian and Zheng, *Da Qing lüli*, 596.

sent back.[54] Of course, reference to specific provisions of the Qing Code was impossible when self-managed minor disputes concerned civil and commercial matters that were not covered by existing statutes during the late imperial period. Views similar to Fang's were quite common throughout the Ming and Qing dynasties. For example, a late Ming litigation handbook, *Erbi kenqing*, suggested this solution: "Assuming that it does not involve a junior family member accusing a senior relative in violation of the legal prohibition (*ganming fanyi*), the plaint for a dispute over family property will be good enough if it articulates the argument clearly and coherently and there is no need to cite specific legal provisions."[55] When dealing with *cisong*, local officials generally focused not so much on clarifying and protecting the two parties' rights and interests as trying to settle the disputes in such a way as to be acceptable to both parties. As a result, the formal state law might be referred to but not necessarily treated as binding. As an official honored by the Kangxi (1662–1722) Court as the best minister from the Confucian School of Principle (*lixue*), Lu Longqi and his approach to *cisong* litigation might represent the mainstream practice among the officials of his time. He wrote:

> When the litigants are summoned, [I] try to persuade them like this: "You two sides are relatives, acquaintances or neighbors and you have been close to each other. Now, you have brought the lawsuit about a trivial dispute over household, marriage, land, or debt just because you got mad for the moment and cannot let it go. But what you do not know is that once the lawsuit starts and before any decision can be made, you have to pay the yamen clerks for the paperwork … and it costs your time and interrupts your work since you have to wait in the county seat. Once the case is adjudicated, there will be a winner and a loser, which turns local allies into enemies and has exhausted all your limited wealth …" [I] then show them the statutory provisions and say: "As in this case, the accused should receive strokes by the bamboo according to the Code. But that statutory penalty will not be applied to those who are reasonable. X should bow down to Y and admit fault … If you both agree, you can submit an agreement to settle this case." More often than not … [the two sides] would restore their relationship like before.[56]

54 See Fang Dashi, *Pingping yan, juan* 2, in *Guanzhenshu jicheng*, 7: 653.

55 Juefei Shanren 觉非山人, "Erbi kenqing 珥笔肯綮 [Essentials for Writing Plaints]," annotated by Qiu Pengsheng 邱澎生, *Mingshi yanjiu* 明史研究 [Ming Studies], no. 13 (Dec. 2009): 244.

56 Wu Zhichang 吴炽昌, *Xu kechuang xianhua* 续客窗闲话 [Continued Casual Words at a Guest Room], in Zhou Hongxing 周红兴, *Zhongguo lidai fazhi zuopin xuandu*

The rationale underlying Lu's passage worked like this: Socially, since the litigants were relatives or friends, they should tolerate each other in disputes over household, marriage, land, and other minor issues. Economically, it cost both parties a lot of money and time and antagonized them once the lawsuit was started. Legally speaking, the party at fault would be punished with the bamboo but could be exempted from that if the two sides agreed to settle the case before trial. Therefore, by allowing the litigants to compare the costs and benefits of pressing or settling the lawsuit, the magistrate got the disputes resolved [without strictly applying the state law]. In a Qing collection of official documents [left by legal advisor Wu Hong], *Zhishang jinglun*, thirteen out of twenty-eight civil lawsuits mentioned that the litigants who should have been punished more severely according to the Code were pardoned due to their age, gender, or poverty. In these cases, it was stated that the accused would be punished harshly if they violated the law again, or that the litigants would be punished for the earlier offense as well if they refused to follow the ruling.[57] The primary function of the written law in such cases was to guide and even coerce the litigants to settle their disputes rather than to serve as the authority for final judgments.

The practice of dealing flexibly with *cisong* had a lot to do with how the role of a county magistrate was envisioned in late imperial China. He was known as the "father-mother official" and was expected to cherish the people. As Magistrate Dai Zhaojia of Tiantai, Zhejiang, put it in 1721, "the job of a county magistrate makes him the official closest to the people and responsible for everything that could cause benefit and happiness or harm and suffering to the county."[58] The duties of county magistrates covered all aspects of local administration and they administered justice but were not legal professionals. As noted above, the priorities of county magistrates were to hear lawsuits and maintain social order. In cases like *cisong* that need not be reviewed by their superiors, the magistrates were primarily interested in resolving conflicts and restoring order, so strict application of the state law might not help serve their purposes. In fact, adherence to the Qing Code in resolving these disputes was likely to escalate the hostilities between the litigants, cause financial difficulties, and turn *cisong* as "minor matters" into causes of deteriorating

---

中国历代法制作品选读 [Selected Legal Writings from Different Dynasties] (Beijing: Wenhua yishu chubanshe, 1988), 263.

57 See Wu Hong 吴宏, "Zhishang jinglun 纸上经纶 [Statesmanship on Paper]," *juan* 4, in *Ming Qing gongdu miben wuzhong*, 197–225.

58 Dai Zhaojia 戴兆佳, "Zixu 自序 [Preface]" (1721), in Dai Zhaojia, *Tiantai zhilüe* 天台治略 [A Brief Account of Governing Tiantai], in *Guanzhenshu jicheng*, 4: 76.

relationships between the disputants or of the breakdown of social order. That would be contrary to the goals of the officials as local administrators. As far as *cisong* were concerned, therefore, to rely on certain [adaptable] principles [based on both the law and local circumstances] to resolve these disputes rather than enforcing the codified law in a formalistic fashion was the preferred choice for pragmatically oriented county magistrates.

As evidenced in many collections of legal cases and local gazetteers, county magistrates might cite the Qing Code when deciding legal disputes over adoption, succession, or marriage since these cases had implications for "proper human relationships" (*lunchang gangji*) and were governed by specific provisions in the Qing Code. In most other circumstances, however, they often chose not to do so in their decisions, even though they might know the relevant laws or had even shown them to the litigants.[59] If the lawsuits, such as in property disputes, were unrelated to proper human relationships, local officials were likely to decide them based on common sense, circumstances, and the spirit of equity while rarely citing specific legal provisions. Fan Zengxiang was particularly good at resolving legal disputes by choosing or adapting laws in light of the circumstances of the case at hand. In his view, lawsuits were all different from one another and could not be governed by the same law with no adaptation. He stated on various occasions that adjudication should not be limited by old laws or precedents: "Rules or commands issued by superior officials to the local governments should be implemented according to the different circumstances of the locales and it is unreasonable to bind the living by the dead [i.e., fixed] rules."[60] This illustrated Qing officials' pragmatism in adjudicating *cisong* or minor disputes, in sharp contrast with the Legalists' ideas of

---

59 See Mio Kishimoto 岸本美绪, "Qike maifou?: Ming Qing shidai de maiqi, dianqi xisu 妻可卖否?—明清时代的卖妻、典妻习俗 [Could a Wife Be Sold?: Wife-selling and Wife-pawning in Ming-Qing China]," trans. Li Jihua 李季桦, in *Qiyue wenshu yu shehui shenghuo* 契约文书与社会生活 [Contracts and Social Life], ed. Chen Qiukun 陈秋坤 and Hong Liyuan 洪丽元 (Taibei: Zhongyang yanjiuyuan Taiwanshi yanjiusuo choubeichu, 2001), 225–64; Matthew H. Sommer, "Qingdai xianya de maiqi anjian shenpan 清代县衙的卖妻案件审判 [Adjudication of Wife-Selling Cases in Qing County Courts]," trans. Lin Wenkai 林文凯, in *Ming Qing falü yunzuo zhong de quanli yu wenhua* 明清法律运作中的权力与文化 [Power and Culture in Ming-Qing Legal Practice], ed. Chiu Pengsheng 邱澎生 and Chen Xiyuan 陈熙远 (Taibei: Zhongyang yanjiuyuan lianjing chuban gongsi, 2009), 345–96; Wang Zhiqiang 王志强, *Falü duoyuan shijiao xia de Qingdai guojiafa* 法律多元视角下的清代国家法 [Law of the Qing State in Multiple Perspectives] (Beijing: Beijing daxue chubanshe, 2003), 124–48.

60 Fan, *Fanshan zengshu, juan* 9, in *Guanzhenshu jicheng*, 10: 186.

strict obedience to the law and rule by law that prevailed in the Warring States (c. 475–221 BCE) period.

Nonetheless, county officials and their superiors differed notably in their approaches to the same kinds of cases. For example, in a case in the Kangxi period, Xu Shanhuang of Tiantai county, Zhejiang, accused Xu Shande of marrying a widowed sister-in-law. The circuit intendant ordered Magistrate Dai Zhaojia to send the litigants and witnesses to his yamen for trial, but Dai repeatedly refused to comply. Dai argued that the litigants were related to one another and that the case implicated a lot of people, including a person in his eighties and a pregnant woman, and that all these people had suffered and would suffer more if they had to travel so far to the circuit intendant's yamen in the cold winter. Based on his investigation, Magistrate Dai found the accusation groundless; besides, the two sides were willing to settle the dispute.[61] According to the Qing Code, anyone who married the wife of his deceased older brother was punishable by strangulation. If the accusation was true, Xu Shande, the accused, would be strangled. If it was not true, as Dai argued, the accuser would be punished with 100 strokes and exile to 3,000 *li* (Chinese miles) away, plus three years of penal servitude.[62] This case would be considered a major criminal case (or *anjian*) at the time. But Magistrate Dai acted differently from his superior, who wanted to handle it according to the Qing Code. Dai hoped to settle the dispute locally and save many people from the trouble and cost involved in the transfer. He claimed that as a local official interested in pacifying the people, he "always tried to settle conflicts and keep people in peace." This kind of thinking was closely related to his job as an administrator responsible for local order, and was very different from that of the superior officials (especially members of the Ministry of Justice).[63]

That local officials, influenced by pragmatism and the challenges of local governance, did not always enforce the codified law strictly when trying to resolve local disputes is something that has persisted in Chinese judicial practice at the lower level to this day. For example, according to the surveys of Su Li in the late twentieth century, a top priority of Chinese judges in the lowest courts was still to solve disputes instead of enforcing the existing law and regulations. Practically oriented, the judges weighed all the legal remedies available under the local constraints and circumstances and chose what they thought would best serve the interests of the litigants and be acceptable to the

61 Dai Zhaojia, "Zixu 自序 [Preface]," in Dai, *Tiantai zhilue*.

62 Tian and Zheng, *Da Qing lüli*, 209–10, 481.

63 See Wang Zhiqiang, *Falü duoyuan shijiao xia de qingdai guojiafa*, 139–44.

latter and the local community.[64] Like Qing county officials, local judges of the People's Republic of China, attached to the local communities, are influenced by local economic development, social stability, and litigants' sentiments, whereas their counterparts in higher courts tend to be more willing to decide such cases according to the law. As Wang Huizu put it in the nineteenth century, *muyou* could acquire legal knowledge by studying the law code, but to be really good at applying the law, one had to humbly consult [local people] about the customs and adapt the law to the local practice and circumstances [in adjudication].[65]

Most *cisong* were concluded at the county level. In regions that had developed commerce or powerful lineages, *cisong* with a lot at stake might be brought to the prefectural or provincial courts, or even to the imperial capital. For example, Qiu Pengsheng [i.e., Chiu Pengsheng] has suggested that commercial disputes (including those over shipping) in a commercially developed city like Chongqing were more likely to go beyond the county level to be handled by prefectural or higher officials as major cases. It would be a mistake to assume that cases of debts necessarily belonged to the county magistrates' self-managed cases in such economically developed places. It is also problematic to treat the judicial practice in a city like Chongqing (where commercial litigation frequently took place) the same as that of other counties.[66] On the one hand, this suggests that the distinction between *cisong* and *anjian* in Qing or traditional Chinese legal practice mainly applied to rural areas with relatively simple disputes. This distinction does not take into account the changes of time and location and the need to adapt to commercial development. On the other hand, *cisong* cases with greater consequences (such as commercial disputes and graveyard disputes) could be appealed to higher courts or even to the imperial capital.[67] Furthermore, we can also infer that litigants in the Ming and Qing periods (especially after the mid-Qing) were trying hard to break the imperial dichotomization between *cisong* and *anjian* even though their efforts received only limited recognition from the government, and only in special

64 Su Li 苏力, *Songfa xiaxiang: Zhongguo jiceng sifa zhidu yanjiu* 送法下乡：中国基层法律制度研究 [Delivering Law to the Countryside: A Study of the Chinese Legal System at the Local Level] (Beijing: Zhongguo zhengfa daxue, 2000), 181, 186, 189.

65 Wang Huizu, "Zuozhi yaoyan," in *Guanzhenshu jicheng*, 5: 323.

66 See Qiu Pengsheng 邱澎生, "Guofa yu banggui: Qingdai qianqi Chongqing cheng de chuanyun jiufen jiejue jizhi 国法与帮规：清代前期重庆城的船运纠纷解决机制 [State Law and Guild Rules: The Mechanisms for Resolving Shipping Disputes in Chongqing]," in *Ming Qing falü yunzuo zhong de quanli yu wenhua*, ed. Chiu and Chen, 329.

67 Zhang Xiaoye, "Cong 'zili' dao 'xianlü.' "

cases rather than "trivial" (*xishi*) disputes. Such classifications of litigation did not change until the late Qing legal reform.

As professional judicial officers, members of the Ministry of Justice in Beijing were removed from local society. Their adjudication was less influenced by administrative concerns with local social order or by local customs and economy as well as the litigants' sentiments. As illustrated by the *Xing'an huilan*, a Qing collection of major cases, these judges, under the direct scrutiny of the throne, generally followed the laws and procedures of the Qing Code or used circulars or leading cases when no law was clearly applicable to the case at hand.[68] Using the *Xing'an huilan* as his main source, legal historian Wang Zhiqiang has argued that officials in the Ministry of Justice cited and clarified the codified law, exercised discretion within the framework of the codified law, tried hard to rationalize their decisions, and emphasized the value of procedures as well as the formal logic and coherence of their legal reasoning.[69] In other words, the state law was the primary source of authority for their judicial administration. Institutionally, they became and should be the guardians of the legal system. Working under the emperor's watch, these relatively more professionalized judicial officials, unlike the county magistrates, had greater incentives or pressures to resort to the law code to decide legal cases.

In contrast with *cisong*, *anjian* involved issues of status, morality, homicide, or robbery, and the state law was more important as the basis of judicial decisions in such cases. Under the Qing Code, judicial officials needed to cite specific laws in judicial decisions. Improper judgment would make them liable to penalties. When dealing with *anjian*, local officials generally followed the law in order to avoid legal liability. Thus, even the author of *Erbi kenqing*, discussed above, chose to mention specific statutory laws when discussing cases of succession. As such cases affected proper human relationships, which were a fundamental concern of Chinese society and the state law then, both the government and litigants had to act according to the written law—even more so with cases of homicide and robbery. This was very different from other kinds of lawsuits over family property, as noted by the author of *Erbi kenqing* as well as Zhong Tizhi, a county magistrate in Jiangxi during the Guangxu period.[70]

In the Qing Code, the statute on "Officials Guilty of Misjudgment" focused on those misjudged cases involving penal servitude or more severe punishment.

68 Tian and Zheng, *Da Qing lüli*, 127.

69 Wang Zhiqiang, *Falü duoyuan shijiao xia de qingdai guojiafa*, 92.

70 Juefei Shanren, "Erbi kenqing," 259. See Zhong Tizhi 钟体志, "Liyan 例言 [Introductory Words]," in Zhong Tizhi, *Chaisang yonglu* 柴桑佣录 [Records of Office Held in Jiujiang] (Zaoxuetang cangban, 1890).

Therefore, even though the Qing Code did not spell it out, the statutory penalties for misapplying the law in adjudication were mostly aimed at serious criminal cases. By comparison, the Qing Code was very evasive as to whether the judges should cite provisions of the Code when deciding *cisong* that involved the lesser punishment of beating with the bamboo. As noted earlier, county magistrates had considerable discretion in adjudicating these cases and did not find it always necessary to cite the written law as the basis of their decisions. According to Wang Zhiqiang, the fact that the Ministry of Justice had trained judges, that some local officials had relatively solid legal knowledge, and that most local officials were advised by legal specialists also meant that judgments at different levels of the Qing judiciary were based not only on pragmatic considerations but also on legal reasoning based on the established written law. Given what has been discussed above, however, it is important for an accurate understanding of Qing judicial administration not to treat the judicial practices of the judges in the Ministry of Justice and of the county magistrates as though they were the same. In his study of the Sino-British legal dispute over the *Lady Hughes* homicide case during the Qianlong era, Li Chen showed that Guangdong officials initially tried to deport the British suspect to England in order to pacify the foreigners and settle the controversy, but that the Qianlong Emperor insisted on enforcing Chinese law and punishment against the British offender so that [the foreigners] would take Chinese law seriously.[71] Although this is a case study of Sino-British legal disputes, it does corroborate the analysis here that Qing local officials, operating under the pressure to maintain social order, tended to focus more on dispute resolution than on enforcement of the law, in contrast with their superiors, especially members of the Ministry of Justice or the emperor. Hu Xiangyu also suggested that when dealing with cases that occurred in the jurisdiction of Beijing, the Ministry of Justice clearly distinguished civil from criminal cases (even in minor matters) and adjudicated the latter strictly according to the Qing Code while allowing the litigants in the former to resolve their disputes privately or through communal mediation. These different tendencies in judicial administration on the part of local judges and those in the Ministry of Justice parallel the differences between judges of district courts and of appellate courts in Anglo-America today: the former are more concerned about dispute resolution whereas the latter are more committed to law enforcement.

---

71 Li Chen, "Law, Empire, and Historiography of Modern Sino-Western Relations: A Case Study of the Lady Hughes Controversy in 1784," *Law & History Review* 27, no. 1 (2009): 1–53. A translation by Deng Jianpeng and Song Sini of the article has been published in the *Peking University Law Review* 12, no. 2 (Sept. 2011): 437–81, esp. 460–67.

To sum up, if we are to truly understand the role of law in deciding cases in imperial China, it is important to take into account the differences in conception and treatment in judicial practice between *cisong* and *anjian*. After all, law was [and is] not the only way to solve various kinds of disputes. Influenced by the transplanted concepts of Western law, the late Qing government finally pushed forward the idea as well as the practice of classifying litigation along the Western model. In 1907, the *Provisional Organic Law for the Courts of Different Levels* (*Geji shenpanting shiban zhangcheng*) for the first time statutorily defined the difference between criminal and civil cases. Legal cases were divided into criminal and civil ones. Criminal cases were to determine whether a crime had been committed, whereas civil cases were to determine right and wrong.[72] This distinction ended the practice of conceptualizing and treating legal cases differently as either *cisong* or *anjian*. However, to understand late imperial Chinese judicial practice better, it is crucial to study what took place before 1907 without being straitjacketed by the modern civil/criminal dichotomy.

Glossary

anjian	案件	*qiangu*	钱谷
baoquan juting kaocheng	保全居停考成	*songshi miben*	讼师秘本
e'ni	恶逆	*xigu*	细故
cisong	词讼	*xishi*	细事
ganming fanyi	干名犯义	*xingming*	刑名
gangchang	纲常	*yixing tongzui*	以刑统罪
hushou	户首	*zhongqing*	重情
jinshi	进士	*zhongqing anjian*	重情案件
lizhang	里长	*zhouxian zili*	州县自理
lunchang gangji	伦常纲纪	*zili*	自理
mingdao zhong'an	命盗重案		

72 "Geji shenpanting shiban zhangcheng 各级审判厅试办章程 [Provisional Organic Law for the Courts of Different Levels], in *Da Qing fagui daquan* 大清法规大全 [Complete Collection of Qing Laws and Regulations] (Taibei: Kaozheng chubanshe, 1972), 1857.

Bibliography

Allee, Mark A. *Law and Local Society in Late Imperial China: Northern Taiwan in the Nineteenth Century*. Stanford: Stanford University Press, 1994.

Bai Yuanfeng 白元峰 (i.e., Bai Ruzhen 白如珍). *Qintang bidu* 琴堂必读 [Required Readings for the Court Room]. Yunxiangtang cangban, 1841.

Bao Shichen 包世臣. *Qimin sishu* 齐民四术 [Four Ways of Governing the People]. Beijing: Zhonghua shuju, 2001 (1846).

Bourgon, Jérôme. "Rights, Freedoms, and Customs in the Making of Chinese Civil Law, 1900–1936." In *Realms of Freedom in Modern China*, edited by William C. Kirby, 84–112. Stanford: Stanford University Press, 2004.

Buxiang zi 补相子. *Xiangjian Buxiangzi yuanben xinjuan toudanhan* 湘间补相子原本新镌透胆寒 [Original Edition of Newly Printed *Toudanhan* (or *Scary Strategies*) by Buxiangzi of Hunan]. Undated.

Chen, Li. "Law, Empire, and Historiography of Modern Sino-Western Relations: A Case Study of the Lady Hughes Controversy in 1784." *Law & History Review* 27, no. 1 (2009): 1–53. A translation by Deng Jianpeng and Song Sini of the article has been published in the *Peking University Law Review* 12, no. 2 (Sept. 2011): 437–81.

———. "Legal Specialists and Judicial Administration in Late Imperial China, 1651–1911." *Late Imperial China* 33, no. 1 (June 2012): 1–54.

———. "Zhishi de liliang: Qingdai muyou miben he gongkai chuban de lüxue zhuzuo dui qingdai sifa changyu de yingxiang 知识的力量：清代幕友秘本和公开出版的律学著作对清代司法场域的影响 [Power of Knowledge: The Role of Secret and Published Treatises of Private Legal Specialists in the Qing Juridical Field]." *Zhejiang daxue xuebao* 浙江大学学报 [Journal of Zhejiang University] 45, no. 1 (Jan. 2015).

Dai Zhaojia 戴兆佳. *Tiantai zhilüe* 天台治略 [A Brief Account of Governing Tiantai]. In *Guanzhenshu jicheng*, vol. 4.

Deng Jianpeng 邓建鹏. *Caichan quanli de pinkun: Zhongguo chuantong minshifa yanjiu* 财产权利的贫困: 中国传统民事法研究 [Deficiency in Property Rights: A Study of Traditional Chinese Civil Law]. Beijing: Falü chubanshe, 2006.

———. "Cong lougui xianxiang dao fading shoufei: Qingdai songfei zhuanxing yanjiu 从陋规现象到法定收费: 清代讼费转型研究 [From Customary Fees to Legal Charges: On the Transformation of Qing Litigation Fees]." *Zhongguo zhengfa daxue xuebao* 中国政法大学学报 [Journal of the Chinese University of Politics and Law] 18, no. 4 (July 2010): 5–23.

———. "Qingdai minshi qisu de fangshi 清代民事起诉的方式 [Ways of Launching Civil Litigation in the Qing]." In *Zhongguo wenhua yu fazhi* 中国文化与法治 [Chinese Culture and the Rule of Law], edited by Zhongguo falüshi xuehui

中国法律史学会 [Chinese Legal History Society], 292–310. Beijing: Shehui kexue wenxian chubanshe, 2007.

———. "Qingdai zhouxian songan de caipan fangshi yanjiu 清代州县讼案的裁判方式研究 [A Study of the Adjudication of Qing County-Level Litigation]." *Jiangsu shehui kexue* 江苏社会科学 [Jiangsu Social Science] 232, no. 3 (May 2007): 97–104.

———. "*Songshi miben yu qingdai suzhuang de fengge* 讼师秘本与清代诉状的风格 [Secret Handbooks for Litigation Masters and Format of Qing Plaints]." *Zhejiang shehui kexue* 浙江社会科学 [Zhejiang Social Sciences]122, no. 4 (July 2005): 71–75.

Fan Zengxiang. *Fanshan zhengshu*. In *Guanzhenshu jicheng*, vol. 10.

Fang Dashi. *Pingping yan* 平平言 [Ordinary Words]. Zizhou guanxie, 1892. Reprinted in *Guanzhenshu jicheng*, vol. 7.

Fujian shengli 福建省例 [Provincial Regulations of Fujian]. Taiwan: Datong shuju gongsi, 1997.

Fuma Susumu 夫马进. "Ming Qing shidai de songshi yu susong zhidu 明清时代的讼师与诉讼制度 [Litigation Masters and the Judicial System in the Ming-Qing Period]." In *Ming Qing shiqi de minshi shenpan yu minjian qiyu*, edited by Wang Yaxin 王亚新 and Liang Zhiping 梁治平, 389–430. Beijing: Falü chubanshe, 1998.

Gao Huanyue 高浣月. *Qingdai xingming muyou yanjiu* 清代刑名幕友研究 [A Study of Qing *Xingming* Advisors]. Beijing: Zhongguo zhengfa daxue chubanshe, 2000.

Geji shenpanting shiban zhangcheng 各级审判厅试办章程 [Provisional Organic Law for the Courts of Different Levels]. In *Da Qing fagui daquan* 大清法规大全 [Complete Collection of Qing Laws and Regulations]. Taibei: Kaozheng chubanshe, 1972.

Guanzhenshu jicheng 官箴书集成 [Compendium of Administrative Handbooks]. Edited by Guanzhenshu jicheng bianzuan weiyuanhui. 10 vols. Hefei: Hefei Huangshan shushe, 1997.

Huang, Philip C.C. *Civil Justice in China: Representation and Practice in the Qing*. Stanford: Stanford University Press, 1996.

Huang, Philip C.C. 黄宗智, and You Chenjun 尤陈俊, eds. *Cong susong dangan chufa: Zhongguo de falü, shehui yu wenhua* 从诉讼档案出发:中国的法律、社会与文化 [*Starting from the Judicial Archives: Chinese Law, Society and Culture*]. Beijing: Falü chubanshe, 2009.

Jiang Tingbi 蒋廷璧. *Pushan Jianggong zhengxun* 璞山蒋公政训 [Administrative Advice of Magistrate Jiang]. In *Guanzhenshu jicheng* 官箴书集成 [Compendium of Official Handbooks], edited by Guanzhenshu jicheng bianzuan weiyuanhui, 2: 1–16. Hefei: Huangshan shushe, 1997.

Juefei Shanren 觉非山人. "Erbi kenqing 珥笔肯綮 [Essentials for Writing Plaints]," annotated by Qiu Pengsheng 邱澎生. *Mingshi yanjiu* 明史研究 [Ming Studies], no. 13 (Dec. 2009): 233–90.

Kishimoto Mio 岸本美绪. "Qike maifou?: Ming Qing shidai de maiqi, dianqi xisu 妻可卖否?—明清时代的卖妻、典妻习俗 [Could a Wife Be Sold?: Wife-selling and Wife-pawning in Ming-Qing China]," trans. Li Jihua 李季桦. In *Qiyue wenshu yu shehui shenghuo* 契约文书与社会生活 [Contracts and Social Life], edited by Chen Qiukun 陈秋坤 and Hong Liyuan 洪丽元, 225–64. Taibei: Zhongyang yanjiuyuan Taiwanshi yanjiusuo choubeichu, 2001.

Li Zan 里赞. "Xingmin zhifen yu zhongqing xigu: qingdai fa yanjiu zhong de fa ji anjian fenlei wenti 刑民之分与重情细故: 清代法研究中的法及案件分类问题 [Distinction between Criminal and Civil Litigation and between Major and Minor Cases: Law and Litigation Classification in Qing Legal Study]." *Xinan minzu daxue xuebao* 西南民族大学学报 [Journal of the Southwest University of Nationalities] 208, no. 12 (Dec. 2008): 194–97.

———. "Zhongguo falüshi yanjiu de fangfa, cailiao he xijie 中国法律史研究的方法、材料和细节 [Methods, Materials, and Details in the Study of Chinese Legal History]." *Jindaifa pinglun* 近代法评论 [Modern Law Review], no. 2 (Dec. 2009): 181–208.

Liu Hainian 刘海年, and Yang Yifan 杨一凡, eds. *Zhongguo zhenxi falü dianji jicheng* 中国珍稀法律典籍集成 [Compendium of Rare Chinese Law Books], *yibian* 乙编 [Series 2], vol. 1. Beijing: Kexue chubanshe, 1994.

Marsh, Robert M. "Weber's Misunderstanding of Traditional Chinese Law." *American Journal of Sociology* 106, no. 2 (Sept. 2000): 281–302.

Qingdai Baxian dang'an huibian (Qianlong chao) 清代巴县档案汇编 (乾隆朝) [Collection of Qing Records from the Ba County Archives (the Qianlong Reign)], comp. Sichuan dang'anguan. Beijing: Dang'an chubanshe, 1992.

Qiu Pengsheng 邱澎生 [i.e., Chiu Pengsheng]. "Guofa yu banggui: Qingdai qianqi Chongqing cheng de chuanyun jiufen jiejue jizhi 国法与帮规: 清代前期重庆城的船运纠纷解决机制 [State Law and Guild Rules: The Mechanisms for Resolving Shipping Disputes in Chongqing]." In *Ming Qing falü yunzuo zhong de quanli yu wenhua*, edited by Chiu Pengsheng and Chen Xiyuan, 275–344.

Quan Shichao 全士潮, Zhang Daoyuan 张道源 et al., eds. *Bo'an huibian* 驳案汇编 [A Collection of Reversed Cases]. Beijing: Falü chubanshe, 2009 (reprint).

Sommer, Matthew H. "Qingdai xianya de maiqi anjian shenpan 清代县衙的卖妻案件审判 [Adjudication of Wife-Selling Cases in Qing County Courts]," trans. Lin Wenkai 林文凯. In *Ming Qing falü yunzuo zhong de quanli yu wenhua* 明清法律运作中的权力与文化 [Power and Culture in Ming-Qing Legal Practice], edited by Chiu Pengsheng 邱澎生 and Chen Xiyuan 陈熙远, 345–96. Taibei: Zhongyang yanjiuyuan lianjing chuban gongsi, 2009.

———. *Sex, Law, and Society in Late Imperial China*. Stanford: Stanford University Press, 2000.

Su Li 苏力. *Songfa xiaxiang: Zhongguo jiceng sifa zhidu yanjiu* 送法下乡：中国基层法律制度研究 [Delivering Law to the Countryside: A Study of the Chinese Legal System at the Local Level]. Beijing: Zhongguo zhengfa daxue, 2000.

Terada Hiroaki 寺田浩明. "Riben de Qingdai sifa zhidu yanjiu yu dui fa de lijie 日本的清代司法制度研究与对'法'的理解 [Japanese Study of the Qing Judicial System and Understanding of the 'Law']." In *Ming Qing shiqi de minshe shenpan yu minjian qiyue*, edited by Wang Yaxin and Liang Zhiping, 112–38.

———. "Quanli yu yuanyi: qingdai tingsong he minzhong de minshifa zhixu 权利与冤抑：清代听讼和民众的民事法秩序 [Rights and Injustice: Civil Justice and Civil-Law Order of the Qing-Dynasty People]," trans. Wang Yaxin 王亚新. In *Ming Qing shiqi de minshi shenpan yu minjian qiyue*, edited by Wang Yaxin and Liang Zhiping, 191–265.

Tian Tao 田涛, and Zheng Qin 郑秦, eds. *Da Qing lüli* 大清律例 [Statutes and Substatutes of the Great Qing, or the Great Qing Code]. Beijing: Falü chubanshe, 1998 (1740).

Tian Tao 田涛, Xu Chuanxi 许传玺, and Wang Hongzhi 王宏治, eds. *Huangyan susong dangan ji diaocha baogao* 黄岩诉讼档案及调查报告 [The Judicial Archives of Huangyan and a Field Report]. Beijing: Falü chubanshe, 2004.

Tian Wenjing 田文镜. *Qinding xunchi zhouxian guitiao* 钦定训饬州县规条 [Imperially Approved Instructions for County Magistrates]. Hunan Hehuachi shuju, 1875.

Wan Weihan 万维翰. "Muxue juyao 幕学举要 [Key Points for Private Advisors]." In *Rumu xuzhi wuzhong*, edited by Zhang Tingxiang, 11–105.

Wang Huizu 汪辉祖. "Zuozhi yaoyan 佐治药言 [Medicinal Words for Assisting Governance]." In Wang Huizu, *Wang Longzhuang xiansheng yishu* 汪龙庄先生遗书 [Works Bequeathed by Wang Huizu] (Shenjiantang, 1871). Reprinted in *Guanzhenshu jicheng*, vol. 5.

Wang Yaxin 王亚新, and Liang Zhiping 梁治平, eds. *Ming Qing shiqi de minshi shenpan yu minjian qiyue* 明清时期的民事审判与契约 [Civil Justice and Civil Contract in the Ming-Qing Period]. Beijing: Falü chubanshe, 1998.

Wang Youhuai 王又槐. "Ban'an yaolüe 办案要略 [Essential Advice for Handling Cases]." Reprinted in *Guanzhenshu jicheng*, vol. 4.

Wang Zhaowu 王昭武. *Wancheng suzhuang* 万承诉状 [Plaints from Wancheng]. Nanning: Guangxi renmin chubanshe, 2008.

Wang, Zhiqiang. "Case Precedent in Qing China: Rethinking Traditional Case Law." *Columbia Journal of Asian Law* 19, no. 1 (Spring-Fall 2005): 327–32.

———. *Falü duoyuan shijiao xia de Qingdai guojiafa* 法律多元视角下的清代国家法 [Law of the Qing State in Multiple Perspectives]. Beijing: Beijing daxue chubanshe, 2003.

Wolongzi 卧龙子. *Xiaocao zhijunshu* 萧曹致君术 [The Art of Xiao He and Cao Can to Assist the Ruler]. Undated.

Wu Hong 吴宏. "Zhishang jinglun 纸上经纶 [Statesmanship on Paper]." In *Ming Qing gongdu miben wuzhong*, 197–225.

Wu Tan 吴坛. *Da Qing lüli tongkao jiaozhu* 大清律例通考校注 [The Great Qing Code with Comprehensive Notes and Annotation]. Beijing: Zhongguo zhengfa daxue chubanshe, 1992.

Wu Zhichang 吴炽昌. *Xu kechuang xianhua* 续客窗闲话 [Continued Casual Words at a Guest Room]. In *Zhongguo lidai fazhi zuopin xuandu* 中国历代法制作品选读 [Selected Legal Writings from Different Dynasties], edited by Zhou Hongxing 周红兴, 263–65. Beijing: Wenhua yishu chubanshe, 1988. Wu Zun 吴遵. *Chushi lu* 初仕录 [Records for Novice Officials]. 1629 (1554p). In *Guanzhenshu jicheng*, 2: 35–56.

"Xingmu yaolüe 刑幕要略 [Essentials for *Xingming* Advisors]." In *Rumu xuzhi wuzhong*, edited by Zhang Tingxiang, 533–630.

Yang Yifan. "Dui Zhonghua faxi de zairenshi—jianlun 'zhufa heti, minxing bufen' shuo buneng chengli 对中华法系的再认识——兼论'诸法合体、民刑不分'说不能成立 [Rethinking the Chinese Legal Tradition, and the Unfounded Theory of 'No Separation between Civil and Criminal Laws and All Laws in One Code.']" In *Pipan yu chongjian: Zhongguo fazhishi yanjiu fanbo* 批判与重建: 中国法律史研究反拨 [Critique and Reconstruct: Study of Chinese Legal History], edited by Ni Zhengmao 倪正茂, 145–99. Beijing: Falü chubanshe, 2002.

Yao Yuxian 姚雨芗, and Hu Yangshan 胡仰山, eds. *Da Qing lüli huitong xinzuan* 大清律例会通新纂 [New Comprehensive Compilation of the Great Qing Code]. Taibei: Wenhai chubanshe, 1987.

You Chenjun 尤陈俊. "Qingdai jianyuexing sifa tizhi xia de 'jian song' wenti: Cong caizheng zhiyue de jiaodu qieru 清代简约型司法体制下的"健讼"问题——从财政制约的角度切入 [The Issue of Litigiousness in the Condensed Qing Judicial System: From the Perspective of Fiscal Constraints]." *Fashang yanjiu* 法商研究 [Studies in Law and Business] 148, no. 2 (March 2012): 154–60.

Zhang Jixin 张集馨. *Daoxian huanhai jianwenlu* 道咸宦海见闻录 [Things Seen and Heard as an Official in the Daoguang and Xianfeng Eras]. Beijing: Zhonghua shuju, 1981.

Zhang Tingxiang 张廷骧, ed. *Rumu xuzhi wuzhong* 入幕须知五种 [Five Essential Works for Entering the Muyou Profession]. Taibei: Wenhai chubanshe, 1968 [1892].

Zhang Xiaoye 张小也. "Cong 'zili' dao 'xianlü': dui qingdai 'minfa' yu 'minshi susong' de kaocha 从"自理"到"宪律": 对清代"民法"与"民事诉讼"的考察 [From 'Self-Managed' Cases to State Law: On Civil Law and Civil Litigation in the Qing]." *Xueshu yuekan* 学术月刊 [Academic Monthly] 38, no. 8 (Aug. 2006): 139–47.

Zhang Wuwei 张五纬. *Weinengxin lu* 未能信录 [A Record of the Unbelievable] (1807p). In *Lidai panli pandu* 历代判例判牍 [Legal Precedents and Cases from

Different Dynasties], edited by Yang Yifan 杨一凡 and Xu Lizhi 徐立志, vol. 9. Beijing: Zhongguo shehui kexue chubanshe, 2005.

Zhaojie shuo 招解说 [On Obtaining and Forwarding Confessions]. In *Ming Qing gongdu miben wuzhong* 明清公牍秘本五种 [Five Secret Administrative Handbooks from the Ming and Qing], edited by Guo Chengwei 郭成伟 and Tian Tao 田涛, 551–644. Beijing: Zhongguo zhengfa daxue chubanshe, 1999.

Zhong Tizhi 钟体志. *Chaisang yonglu* 柴桑傭录 [Records of Office Held in Jiujiang]. Zaoxuetang cangban, 1890.

Zhu Qingqi 祝庆麒 et al., eds. *Xingan huilan quanbian* 刑案汇览全编 [A Complete Collection of Criminal Cases]. Beijing: Falü chubanshe, 2007 (reprint).

CHAPTER 2

Kinship Hierarchies and Property Institutions in Late Qing and Republican China

*Taisu Zhang**

Introduction

One of the most striking things about Qing and Republican property institutions is that they were surprisingly protective—in some instances, overprotective—of the economic interests of poorer landholders. An especially compelling example is the redemption of collateralized property, a vital concern for lower-income households that relied on land-pawning instruments, typically the "dian" sale ("conditional sale"), for monetary liquidity.[1] Despite vigorous opposition by the wealthiest segments of society, customary law in most of China granted "dian" sellers—in other words, "land pawnors"—an essentially unlimited right of redemption, viable for decades after the initial sale.[2]

Preexisting studies tend to portray these norms as symptoms of a "precommercial" society: Philip Huang and others argue, for example, that the peculiarly strong protection of land redemption rights in Chinese property customs stem from certain cultural, even semi-religious, characteristics that directly encouraged such protection: Chinese rural communities adhered, they claim, to "precommerical" moral ideals of "permanence in landholding," partially due to the lack of market integration, labor mobility, and economic specialization.[3]

The problem, however, is that Qing and Republican China was far from "precommercial." Recent scholarship demonstrates that Chinese households,

* A longer version of this chapter, titled "Social Hierarchies and the Formation of Customary Property Law in Pre-Industrial China and England," appears in the *American Journal of Comparative Law* 62 (2014), at 171.

1 Philip C.C. Huang, *Code, Custom, and Legal Practice in China: The Qing and the Republic Compared* (Palo Alto: Stanford University Press, 2001), 71–98.

2 Taisu Zhang, "Property Rights in Land, Agricultural Capitalism, and the Relative Decline of Pre-Industrial China," *San Diego International Law Journal* 13 (2011): 156–74.

3 Huang, *Code*, 74; Melissa Macauley, *Social Power and Legal Culture: Litigation Masters in Late Imperial China* (Stanford: Stanford University Press, 1998), 234.

© KONINKLIJKE BRILL NV, LEIDEN, 2015 | DOI 10.1163/9789004288492_004

wealthy and poor alike, were, to an extent quite comparable with Western European households, economically rational and ruthlessly self-interested.[4] In addition, the economy was significantly market-based, while land ownership was increasingly commoditized and impersonal.[5] There is, in fact, no real evidence that people agreed on "precommercial" ideals of "permanence in landholding." Quite the opposite, this chapter presents considerable evidence that property norms, particularly "dian" redemption norms, were generally the product of fiercely self-interested negotiation: Higher-income households tended to resist generous "dian" redemption norms, whereas smallholders were almost uniformly in favor. But why, under those circumstances, were the actual institutional outcomes often more favorable to smallholders?

Utilizing several newly available court archives and contract collections from the late Qing and Republican eras, along with some more traditional sources such as Japanese rural surveys of North China, this chapter argues that some of the answer probably lies in the way rural Chinese society allocated social status, rank, and authority: The status and rank of many rural individuals in Qing and Republican China depended significantly on their generational seniority within their respective patrilineal descent groups. Both formal and customary law often recognized the sociopolitical dominance of senior relatives over junior ones, as did a plethora of private writings and lineage registries.

What scholars have largely failed to realize is that, despite creating systematic inequalities at the individual level, these kinship hierarchies also tended to confer large status benefits on lower-income households: Because status was so closely tied to age and generational seniority, the system allowed for significant status mobility within many individual lifetimes. Such people automatically gained status as they aged, theoretically independent of personal wealth. In practice, of course, wealth remained a valuable social asset, but even so, the

4 Lynda S. Bell, "Farming, Sericulture, and Peasant Rationality in Wuxi County in the Early Twentieth Century," in *Chinese History in Economic Perspective*, ed. Thomas G. Rawski & Lillian M. Li (Berkeley: University of California Press, 1992), 226–29, 232–39.

5 See, e.g., Kenneth Pomeranz, *The Great Divergence: China, Europe, and the Making of the Modern World Economy* (Princeton: Princeton University Press, 2000), 86–87. On the commoditization of land, see Thomas Buoye, *Manslaughter, Markets and Moral Economy: Violent Disputes over Property Rights in Eighteenth Century China* (New York: Cambridge University Press, 2000), 94; and Weiting Guo, "Social Practice and Judicial Politics in 'Grave Destruction' Cases in Qing Taiwan, 1683–1895," Chapter 3 in this volume (arguing that state officials would often sanction the desecration of graves in the interest of reclamation).

data below indicates that, at least in quite a few rural communities in North China and the Lower Yangtze, lower-income seniors could frequently obtain status and authority quite disproportionate to their wealth. Wealth still mattered, but it was not the only thing that mattered.

Higher status naturally led to stronger bargaining positions in the negotiation of property norms. Throughout Qing and Republican China, property norms were more often shaped by local custom rather than formal law. In other words, they were generally negotiated within local communities. The outcomes of such negotiation therefore tended to reflect the power balance between different interest groups in these communities: Because kinship hierarchies often strengthened the cumulative social status of smallholders, they were more likely to negotiate "victories" in key areas of property law.

To some extent, this is a classic political economy model of norm creation: people generally prefer property norms that advance their economic interests, and those with larger amounts of sociopolitical capital are more capable of obtaining their desired property norms. Some historians may be somewhat uncomfortable with the assumption that individuals are basically rational actors, at least when it comes to property norm negotiation, but this chapter does not ask them to *assume* that. Rather, to the extent it relies on individual self-interest and economic rationality, it seeks to demonstrate these behavioral patterns through archival sources, particularly through court documents and surveys that reveal the norm preferences of rich and poor landholders.

Readers will notice that the state has very little role to play in this thesis, and will perhaps wonder whether that is an oversight. It is not. The strong consensus of scholars who have studied property transaction norms in rural Qing and Republican China is that customary law was significantly more important in controlling property transactions than state legislation or regulation. Formal laws were, as discussed below, weakly enforced and very often ignored. Therefore, this thesis is explicitly a theory of communal self-regulation via customs and social norms. I would welcome, of course, any systematic evidence of strong and effective state intervention in these processes, but so far do not know of any.

Also, this thesis is by no means a comprehensive theory of social status in local Chinese communities. Its predominant goal is simply to argue for the existence of a reasonably powerful status axis that is both logically and practically distinct from conferring status by wealth, not to argue that it is the only axis that mattered, or even the axis that mattered the most. As many previous works suggest, there are very likely other status axis that are distinct from both kinship seniority *and* wealth. For example, the negotiation of popular religious beliefs clearly had significant import on the relative standing of individuals in rural communities.[6] To the extent that such processes led to status allocation on grounds other than wealth, they potentially reinforce, rather than damage, the claims advanced here. I do not expressly incorporate them into my analysis because, both in preexisting studies and in the case studies conducted here, it has been very difficult to systematically evaluate the impact of religious beliefs on status hierarchies, vis-à-vis the impact of more measurable factors like wealth or age. Nonetheless, it is clearly something that deserves future research, and may eventually lead to significant expansion of the model presented above.

Some basic qualifications: Given the size and regional diversity of China, a national-level analysis is prohibitively difficult to execute. Instead, this chapter focuses on two of China's comparatively developed coastline macroregions, the Lower Yangtze and North China, and indeed on a handful of villages and counties in each macroregion. A full discussion of representativeness is extremely difficult to pull off within a book chapter, so the claim here is simply that these case studies demonstrate that the effects I describe *could exist*. Temporally, the chapter's primary sources generally fall within 1865–1940, a period of relative social stability in most rural localities, despite turmoil on the national political stage. When possible, attempts are made to link socioeconomic patterns from that period to earlier developments in Qing history.

A final word about the use of "egalitarian" in this chapter: Although the term "egalitarian" may be used to describe any kind of equality-promoting behavior or policy,[7] within this article's context, it specifically describes institutions and actions that promote the political and economic interests of lower-income households. It is also used in a purely descriptive sense, without ideological connotations attached.

"Dian" Sales in Qing and Republican China

The Qing and Republican "dian" sale was, essentially, a collateralized loan: Like modern mortgages, it allowed landholders to secure large loans against real property. But while mortgages tend to conjure up images of back-breaking interest rates and the ever-looming threat of default and seizure, the "dian"

6 See, e.g., Rebecca Nedostup, *Superstitious Regimes: Religion and the Politics of Chinese Modernity* (Cambridge: Harvard East Asian Monographs, 2010); Prasenjit Duara, *Culture, Power and the State: Rural North China, 1900–1942* (Stanford: Stanford University Press, 1988).

7 "Egalitarianism," Stanford Encyclopedia of Philosophy, last accessed March 7, 2013, http://plato.stanford.edu/entries/egalitarianism/.

sale was a strikingly low-stress affair for the borrower—that is, for the "dian" seller: He conveyed land to the "buyer" for 60 to 80 percent of the property's full market value, but retained the right to redeem *at zero interest*.[8] The "dian" buyer's interest in lending money under such an arrangement was not monetary interest, but whatever profit the land could yield before the seller redeemed. He was, therefore, often protected by contractually-established "guaranteed usage periods" ("xian") of one or more years, during which the seller could not redeem. In addition, he could obtain full ownership of the land if the "dian" seller agreed to convert the transaction into a permanent sale ("mai"), upon which the seller would receive "additional payments" ("zhaotie") that made up the difference between the original transaction price and the land's present market value.

Most significantly, local "dian" customs generally allowed "dian" sellers to retain redemption rights *ad infinitum*—essentially, they would never terminate. Similar customs were commonplace throughout China's core regions, particularly North China and the Lower Yangtze.[9] Many explicitly forbid the original contract from setting any redemption deadline. Others allowed redemption rights to be exercised "any time after the guaranteed-usage period's expiration." These rules were not for show: Under their influence, very few "dian" contracts attempted to establish redemption deadlines, and many "dian" sales were apparently redeemed at some point.[10] Local legal archives contain, moreover, numerous cases where a "dian" seller or his descendants attempted to redeem after astonishingly long periods—sometimes a century.

This was an institutional arrangement rife with social tension. During the decades that often passed between "dian" sale and redemption request, families might move, or usage rights might be transferred to a third party. The swelling volume of related disputes brought before local courts eventually pushed the central government into action: It made several attempts to limit the redemption window of "dian" sales, ordering first in the *Qing Code* that all contracts must explicitly indicate whether they were permanent sales or "dian" sales,[11] and then, in the 1758 *Board of Finance Regulations*, that regular "dian" sales must be redeemed within ten years or be converted to a permanent sale, with at most a one-year extension.[12]

---

8 Zhang, "Property Rights," 156–57.

9 Ibid., 161–63.

10 Ibid., 161, 192–93.

11 *Da Qing lüli* 大清律例 [The Great Qing Code] [cited hereinafter as DQLL] (1905), § 95–107.

12 *Qingdai gebuyuan zeli: Qinding hubu zeli (Qianlongchao)* 清代各部院则例：清代户部则例 (乾隆朝) [Regulations of Qing Boards and Ministries: Imperial Board of Finance

Enforcement of these legal rules, however, was extremely weak. A survey of local case archives from the later Qing suggests that the great majority of redemption deadline cases—where the "dian" buyer refused to allow redemption because too much time had passed since the original contract—were eventually settled via external mediation, often at the court's behest.[13] Due to their lack of coercive authority, local magistrates were hesitant to formally adjudicate cases where central laws and regulations conflicted with local custom. This is unsurprising, as historians have long emphasized the serious weakness of the Qing state in local governance, especially in the regulation of commercial activity.[14]

By the Republican era, the government had basically admitted that Qing rules against excessive redemption were unenforceable: early Republican-era governments extended the national deadline for land redemption to sixty years, a clear concession to local custom.[15] After 1929, the newly-victorious Nationalist government attempted to impose a thirty year deadline nationwide,[16] but surveys of Northern Chinese peasants conducted a decade later suggest that their efforts were ineffectual: Most peasants had no knowledge of it, and most who did believed that no one followed it.[17]

For "dian" sellers, these customary norms offered tremendous advantages with very limited downside. The most obvious evidence of this is that, in the variety of disputes examined below, "dian" sellers universally argued in favor of these norms, whereas "dian" buyers were almost always opposed. This is unsurprising: Land was, to most rural residents in these early modern times, the single most valuable kind of property, not only because of its high market value but also because it was the foundation of most economic production. As various Qing and Republican era sources repeatedly claim, landowners generally sold land *only* when financial conditions made it absolutely necessary, and therefore usually preferred redeemable "dian" sales to permanent ones.[18]

Regulations (Qianlong Era)], vol. 1, ed. Fuchi shuyuan 蝠池书院 (Kowloon: Fuchi shuyuan, 2004) 83, 148–49.

13 Zhang, "Property Rights," 168–74.

14 Ch'u Tung-tsu, *Local Government in China under the Ch'ing* (Cambridge: Harvard University Press, 1962), 168–92.

15 *Faling jilan* 法令辑览 [Edited Collection of Laws and Regulations], ed., Sifa Bu 司法部 [Ministry of Justice] (Beijing: Sifa bu chubanshe, 1917), 6: 179–80.

16 *Zhonghua minguo minfadian* 中华民国民法典 [Civil Code of the Republic of China] (1929), arts. 912, 924.

17 *See* discussion at *infra*, pp. 59–60.

18 Huang, *Code*, 73; Madeleine Zelin, "The Rights of Tenants in Mid-Qing Sichuan: A Study of Land-Related Lawsuits in the Baxian Archives," *Journal of Asian Studies* 45 (1986): 515.

Under these conditions, an institutional framework that effectively eliminated the danger of default and seizure was highly attractive to cash-strapped landowners.

The only potential downside for "dian" sellers was that the inability to impose redemption deadlines could result in lower "dian" prices, which were, in fact, only 60 to 80 percent of the land's full value. Because, however, most "dian" sales were made under considerable financial stress, a lower "dian" value, so long as it covered immediate needs, was a far smaller concern than obtaining extended redemption rights. Moreover, there *were* ways to negotiate higher "dian" prices: the seller could simply grant a longer guaranteed-usage period ("xian"), which gave buyers greater security and larger returns.

On the other hand, customary law did "dian" buyers few favors. The constant danger of redemption after the guaranteed-usage period's expiration seriously decreased the land's value to buyers by discouraging both long-term investments to improve the land and use of the land as a reliable source of capital or collateral. The tremendous attractiveness of "dian" customs to potential land sellers also drained the supply of permanent land sales, further exacerbating the difficulty of secure land accumulation. Despite all this, the demand for "dian" sales remained high during times of relative peace, driven by a combination of population growth, commercialization, and nascent industrialization.

Generally speaking, "dian" sellers were much poorer compared to "dian" buyers: In one fairly typical North China village, for example, around 85% of "dian" sellers during the later 1930s possessed less land than the village average, and nearly 40% possessed less than a third of that average. In contrast, less than 3% belonged to the top 25% of landowners.[19] Additional circumstantial evidence can be found in contract collections from late Qing and Republican era Zhejiang Province: They commonly show one household conditionally buying multiple parcels from a wide assortment of sellers, which certainly suggests that a few relatively wealthy households were aggressively acquiring land from numerous poorer ones.[20]

The institutional protection of "dian" sellers was, therefore, also the protection of poor against rich. Indeed, as the author has argued elsewhere, the

---

19 *Chugoku noson kanko chosa* 中國农村惯行調査 [Investigation of Rural Chinese Customs] [hereinafter cited as *Mantetsu Surveys*] vol. 3, ed. Committee for the Publication of the Rural Customs and Practices of China (Tokyo: Iwanami shoten press, 1958), 5.

20 *Qingdai Ningbo qiyue wenshu jijiao* 清代宁波契约文书辑校 [Qing Contracts from Ningbo] [*hereinafter Ningbo qiyue*], ed. Wang Wanying 王万盈 (Ningbo: Tianjian guiji chubanshe, 2008); *Shicang qiyue* 石仓契约 [Shicang Contracts] vol. 3, ed. Cao Shuji 曹树基 (Hangzhou: Zhejiang daxue chubanshe, 2010).

institutional contrast between "dian" and mortgage significantly explains why landholding remained unusually equitable throughout China's pre-Communist history: "Landlords" and "large farmers" owned only 40 to 50 percent of arable land throughout the later Qing and Republic, and managed less than 15 percent.[21] To put this in a comparative perspective, conventional estimates of landownership by the English royalty, nobility and gentry—who comprised perhaps 5 to 6 percent of the English population—range from 65 to 75 percent of total land in 1690, 85 in 1790, and 90 by 1873.[22]

What explains the willingness of Chinese customary law to protect the economic interests of smallholders, but at significant cost to wealthier segments of rural society? Were wealthier Chinese households simply more generous to their less advantage neighbors—a form of "moral economy" that encouraged sharing of material resources? Or can we explain all this through a more rationalist perspective?

Models and Theories

Among legal historians, the traditional explanation for the customary protection of "dian" redemption rights in pre-industrial China has been exceedingly straightforward: They derived directly, as discussed above, from the moral embracement of "permanence in landholding" ideals in a "precommercial" society, where the economic value of land was much higher than in modern economies.

The evidence presented in support of these arguments, however, is thin—generally no more than vague moralizing by literati on the importance of land. The higher economic value of land in preindustrial societies, on the other hand, pushed in opposite directions: Apart from encouraging landowners to retain their properties, it also encouraged them to aggressively acquire new property. The stubbornly high demand for land sales, both permanent and "dian," from around 1870 to the 1930s certainly suggests that the latter dynamic was consistently at work in times of relative peace, despite the prevalence of highly burdensome "dian" customs. The attractiveness of landownership alone is, therefore, an inadequate explanation for the existence of those customs.

Moreover, the characterization of early modern Chinese society as "precommercial" has been severely challenged in recent scholarship: Studies of grain

21 Zhang, "Property Rights," 156–74.

22 J.V. Beckett, "The Pattern of Landownership in England and Wales, 1660–1880," *Economic History Review* 37 (1984): 1–22.

price fluctuations within and across macroregions show that large portions of the rural economy had become market-integrated.[23] This directly contradicts older assumptions about the dominance of subsistence agriculture.

Unsurprisingly, commercialization went hand-in-hand with individual economic rationality: most households were both calculating and resourceful. They invested in land when profitable, employed excess labor in non-agricultural production, reacted swiftly to fluctuations in land or commodity prices, and, as demonstrated below, tirelessly promoted economic institutions and norms that favored their own interests. Even within lineages, households often clashed over property, debt, and the rules that governed them. It is unclear how such a commercialized society could have sustained moral ideals of "permanence in landholding."

In fact, it probably did not. The evidence presented below strongly suggests that, very often, such "ideals" were embraced only by those who could economically benefit from them, and that "dian" and permanent tenancy customs were the result of intense and prolonged negotiation between highly self-interested parties, rather than simple moral derivatives of "precommercial" ideals. Bargained equilibriums could emerge where moral uniformity did not. The question, then, is why self-interested bargaining created a land collateralization regime in which the economic interests of smallholders were significantly privileged over wealthier landholders.

This chapter argues that the explanation lies in how Chinese societies allocated social status and rank: Because poorer households cumulatively possessed considerable social status in China—disproportionately large compared to their economic clout—they were often able to obtain favorable property norms. If and when richer households conceded certain property norms to poorer ones, it was not because they shared in some vaguely-defined "precommercial" ideal, but because the social cost of a prolonged standoff with high-status smallholders was too high.

The cumulative status of poorer Chinese households benefitted, as suggested above, from the "Confucian" emphasis on generational hierarchies: Virtually all levels of Qing law and society recognized systematic inequalities between different family members.[24] Parents naturally occupied a higher sociolegal position than their offspring, as did uncles over nephews, and elder brothers or

---

23 On the Lower Yangtze, see Li Bozhong, *Agricultural Development in Jiangnan, 1620–1850* (New York: St. Martin's Press, 1998). On North China, see Lillian M. Li, *Fighting Famine in North China* (Stanford: Stanford University Press, 2007), 196–220.

24 *Zhongguo fazhi tongshi* 中国法制通史 [History of Law in China], vol. 8, ed. Zhang Jinfan 张晋藩 (Beijing: Falü chubanshe, 1999), 208, 256–57, 508.

cousins over younger ones. Even disobedience or rudeness to a senior relative could constitute a punishable offense, if not by law then by lineage self-regulation or local custom. Unsurprisingly, major socioeconomic decisions were generally made by the household patriarch in consultation with other senior male members of his kinship group.

Kinship hierarchies retained much of their vitality even after the Qing's collapse. Republican legal codes narrowed the range of privileges afforded to senior relatives, but did not eliminate them altogether.[25] For example, killing or assaulting a senior relative continued to be punished more severely than usual homicide or assault. More importantly, the great majority of local communities continued to recognize and enforce traditional kinship hierarchies throughout the Republican era.[26]

However counterintuitively, these kinship hierarchies should theoretically have *promoted*, rather than damaged, status mobility, simply because everyone aged, which automatically boosted their status and rank both within and beyond their kinship network. This latter point requires some elaboration: Most kinship networks were of considerable size—several dozen households in North China, and considerably more than that in the Lower Yangtze—and, therefore, carried enough collective clout that high rank within the kinship network generally translated also into relatively high status beyond its borders.

Because kinship hierarchies were theoretically disconnected from wealth—a wealthy nephew owed the same sociolegal obligations to a penniless uncle as a penniless nephew to a wealthy one—they should have empowered large numbers of low-income but high-seniority individuals against their wealthier kin. In crude terms, even the wealthiest individuals probably had poorer relatives who were of similar or higher generational seniority. Correspondingly, these kinship hierarchies should have substantially boosted the cumulative social bargaining power of smallholders vis-à-vis landlords and other land-accumulators, helping them win substantial concessions over property norms.

---

25 Liu Guoqiang 刘国强, "Qingmo minguo shiqi xingfadian jianshe zhong qinshu lunli guanxi de chuancheng yu biange 清末民国时期刑法典建设中亲属伦理关系的传承与变革 [Continuity and Change in the Treatment of Kinship Ties in Late Qing and Republican Criminal Codes]," *Daode yu wenming* 道德与文明 [Morality and Civilization] 4 (2012): 67–72.

26 Feng Erkang 冯尔康, *18 shiji yilai Zhongguo jiazu de xiandai zhuanxiang* 18 世纪以来中国家族的现代转向 [The Modern Turn of Chinese Lineages Since the 18th Century] (Shanghai: Shanghai renmin chubanshe, 2011), 214–313.

Empirics

The remainder of this chapter provides empirical support for the above model, broken down into three sub-arguments: First, "dian" redemption customs were very often the source of widespread social tension and negotiation. In these cases, they were far more likely the equilibrium outcome of self-interested negotiation than the institutional manifestation of "precommercial" morality. Second, the prevalence of kinship hierarchies often allowed lower-income households to occupy, with some consistency, positions of considerable socio-political authority and dignity. Third, when this happened, kinship hierarchies and corresponding status distribution patterns tended to play a significant role in shaping the content and enforceability of "dian" redemption norms.

Section One: Conflict and Negotiation

The clearest indication that "dian" redemption customs were never fully internalized by Qing society is the sheer volume of litigation that they caused in many localities. This is best illustrated by statistics drawn from available local case archives. Within North China and the Lower Yangtze, there are two of these, one at Baodi County, Hebei Province, the other at Longquan County, Zhejiang Province. Only the latter is well preserved enough to project a reasonably solid statistical overview. It holds 18434 cases from 1910 to 1949, including 10614 civil suits and 7820 criminal cases.[27] Accounting for the loss of case files over time, the average number of civil cases per year probably ranged from 400 to 600—in a county of roughly 20,000 households. Within the 10614 civil suits, 430 stemmed from a dispute concerning "dian" sales, of which 386 focused on whether the "dian" seller should be allowed to redeem. Assuming a representative sample—there is little reason not to, as there is basically no evidence that the archives were ever consciously tampered with or even seriously damaged—this suggests that 4 to 5 percent of civil disputes were "dian" related, with around 85 percent of those related directly to redemption disputes. "Dian" redemption disputes were, therefore, one of the most significant sources of civil litigation. Of course, it seems unlikely that more than a fraction of contractual disputes ended up in court, which suggests that there may have been a hundred or more of these disputes in the county each year.

27 *Longquan Dang'an hebian mulu* 龙泉档案合编目录 [Index of Collected Archives from Longquan] (Dec. 5, 2011) (unpublished index, on file with the Zhejiang University History Department).

A more difficult question is how many "dian" redemption cases involved claims by the "dian" buyer that too much time had passed since the original contract for redemption to be allowable. Because access to the full case archive remains limited, this article relies on a randomly selected sample of sample of 80 "dian" cases, of which 65 were related specifically to "dian" redemption.[28] 26 of these featured express claims that the "dian" seller's redemption rights had expired after a certain period of time. This was the single most common rationale relied upon by "dian" buyers to reject redemption efforts.

Although precise projection is dangerous, these numbers do at least demonstrate that "dian" redemption deadlines, or the lack thereof, were in fact a frequently contested issue. Of the 26 "dian" expiration cases, 16 involved contracts that had been made more than 30 years prior to the redemption attempt, the oldest of which was made 72 years prior. In at least 5 of these 16, the "dian" buyer expressly cited a 1917 provincial regulation that banned redemption of "dian" contracts after 30 years.[29] "Dian" sellers avoided, naturally, any mention of this regulation. It should surprise no one that the parties' normative preferences dovetailed perfectly with their perceived economic interests: "Dian" sellers preferred the customary norms of unlimited redemption, whereas "dian" buyers petitioned the court to override those norms.

The substantive composition of "dian" disputes brought before Qing county courts elsewhere did not seem to differ significantly from the Republican-era patterns observed in Longquan. A large spate of such disputes can be found in three private case collections from the Lower Yangtze, covering the years 1875–1908.[30] Combined, they yield 1063 local civil disputes, including 96 "dian"-related cases, 59 of which involved a dispute over redemption.[31] 34 of the 59 focused specifically on whether redemption rights could expire. These ratios are similar to what we found in Baodi, Baxian, Danxin, or Longquan, clearly

28 Appendix A, Part I.

29 Longquan sifa dang'an 龙泉司法档案 [Longquan Legal Archives] [hereinafter cited as Longquan], No. M003-03-00038 (1919), M003-01-00586 (1921), M003-01-02147 (1920), M003-01-02160 (1925), M003-01-15483 (1932).

30 Ni Wangzhong 倪望重, "Zhuji yumin jiyao 诸暨谕民纪要 [Educating the People of Zhuji, Selected Records]," in *Lidai panli pandu* [Cases from Various Dynasties], ed. Yang Yifan 杨一凡 and Xu Lizhi 徐立志 (Beijing: Zhongguo shehui kexue chubanshe, 2005), 10: 301–497; Sun Dinglie 孙鼎烈, "Sixizhai jueshi 四西斋决事 [Decisions from Xisizhai]," in *Lidai panli pandu*, 10: 499–650; Zhao Youban 赵幼班, "Liren pandu huiji 历任判牍汇记 [Collections of Decisions from Past Appointments]," in *Lidai panli pandu*, 12: 109.

31 "Data Appendices," Appendix A, Part II.

indicating that "dian" redemption deadlines were a significant source of social tension throughout the late Qing and Republic.

Widespread social tension over "dian" redemption deadlines also surfaces in a variety of Republican-era social surveys. The most detailed of these are Japanese surveys of rural North China conducted around 1940, otherwise known as the "Mantetsu surveys."[32] Focusing primarily on six villages in Hebei and Shandong, they contain several hundred interviews with villagers on local governance, customary law, and other aspects of social organization. Naturally, general trends observed across the entire survey are more reliable than specific information drawn from individual interviewees.

One particularly striking trend is the extent to which interviewees from different economic backgrounds quarreled over property norms. In the two most extensively surveyed villages, Sibeichai and Shajing, researchers asked over twenty villagers about what they thought were the customs that governed "dian" transactions.[33] In Sibeichai, all interviewees agreed that "dian" redemption had no deadline,[34] but at least one local landlord complained that it was an "archaic" custom.[35] On several other issues, the landlords clashed openly with poorer village leaders over what the customs really were: One former village chief of middling wealth argued that "dian" sales could be redeemed even before the "guaranteed usage period" had expired, and even if the "dian" seller owed additional debt to the "dian" buyer.[36] Several others concurred.[37] Landlords and wealthier farmers disagreed: "Dian" buyers could deny redemption if the "dian" seller owed any outstanding debt, or if the guaranteed usage period had yet to expire.[38]

In Shajing, social discord existed not only over these comparatively minor issues, but also over whether "dian" redemption rights truly were interminable. Most interviewees stated that local custom allowed redemption regardless of time passage since the initial contract,[39] but one person, unsurprisingly one of the largest landowners in the village, declared that the true governing

32 *Mantetsu Surveys*, vols. 1–5.

33 Shajing is covered in *Mantetsu Surveys*, vols. 1 & 2. Sibeichai is covered in *Mantetsu Surveys*, vol. 3.

34 *Mantetsu Surveys*, 3: 166, 172, 176, 246, 273.

35 Ibid., 174.

36 Ibid., 170–71, 273, 275.

37 Ibid., 245, 263.

38 Ibid., 165–67, 173–174, 247–48.

39 *Mantetsu Surveys*, 2: 174, 187, 269.

principle was the thirty-year redemption deadline enacted by the 1929 Republican Civil Code.[40] According to a poorer interviewee, however, the rule was generally unenforceable in practice.[41]

Three other villages, Lengshuigou, Houxiazhai, and Wudian, resembled Sibeichai more than Shajing, in that all interviewees affirmed the basic principle of interminable redemption rights, but argued vigorously over more technical rules—for example, whether guaranteed usage periods were enforceable.[42] At Houjiaying, however, one interviewee—not coincidentally a relatively well-to-do "dian" buyer—declared that "although the traditional rule was that redemption could take place at any time, now it must be done within thirty years."[43] Other interviewees who were "dian" sellers disagreed in strong terms.[44]

The picture that emerges from this array of sources, both cases and interviews, is one of tension and dispute over customary norms, but not of social chaos in which no operative norm existed. Despite the large array of cases that involved the "dian" buyer arguing that redemption rights expired after either ten or thirty years, an equally eye-catching trend is that, when the great majority of these cases were resolved out-of-court, these same people almost always agreed to terms quite favorable to the "dian" seller, at least in cases that report the settlement terms. Most often, after further negotiation between senior relatives from both sides, they would simply allow the "dian" seller to redeem.[45] In the other cases, they retained possession of the land, but only after giving the seller an additional payment, and often without receiving any promise that redemption was henceforth prohibited.[46] The resigned complaints of the frustrated Sibeichai landlord reinforce this impression. Even in Shajing and Houjiaying, the few interviewees who proposed overriding traditional custom with legal regulations nonetheless recognized that those customs did provide for unlimited "dian" redemption.[47]

There is, therefore, strong historical evidence that a considerable number of—quite possibly most—local communities regulated "dian" transactions via

40 Ibid., 169.

41 Ibid., 269.

42 For Lengshuigou, see *Mantetsu Surveys*, 4: 205–06, 214, 222–24, 257. For Houxiazhai, see *Mantetsu Surveys*, 4: 482–85, 508–11. For Wudian, see *Mantetsu Surveys*, 5: 531, 562–63, 578, 583–84.

43 *Mantetsu Surveys*, 5: 286.

44 Ibid., at 266.

45 Longquan, No. M003-01-00642 (1919), M003-01-00787 (1947), M003-01-01166 (1920), M003-01-11063 (1922), M003-01-15821 (1943).

46 See, e.g., Longquan, No. M003-01-01283 (1923), M003-01-05358 (1948).

47 *Mantetsu Surveys*, 2: 174; *Mantetsu Surveys*, 5: 286.

customary law, but also that these customs were the source of much social contention. In all likelihood, they were created via negotiation between self-interested and, insofar as their preferred norms correlated to their perceived economic self-interest, basically rational parties. Strikingly, the wealthiest segments of rural communities frequently felt powerless against their poorer neighbors, and had to tolerate property norms that substantially damaged their socioeconomic interests.

Section Two: Patterns of Status Distribution

This section measures the relative effects of kinship and wealth on status distribution. It turns first to the Mantetsu surveys, which yield detailed demographic and landholding data for all surveyed villages. The interviews identify 126 political elites across seven villages, current and former, who can be matched with landownership and kinship information.[48] These included village chiefs and their deputies, major lineage chiefs, and "jiazhang" ("ten-household chiefs") or equivalent.

It turns out that lower-income households were quite proportionately represented among the village political elite. 63 of the 128–49 percent—owned less land than the village median. Nor were all 63 concentrated in "lower-tier" positions—"jiazhang" (head of a village subdivision) rather than village chief, for example. Of the 32 people identified to have been village chief during the past decade, 14 owned less land per-capita than the village average. Of the 35 largest landowners from the seven villages, only 9 had wielded any formal political authority in recent years. This was, of course, still a considerably higher ratio than among lower-income households, but nonetheless low enough to suggest that landed wealth was a weak determinant of sociopolitical authority.

On the other hand, the correlation between sociopolitical authority and generational seniority was extremely strong. At least 108 of the 128 individuals belonged to the most senior generation of what villagers identified as a "major kinship group." Only 9 people clearly belonged to a younger generation, whereas the generational standing of the other 11 are unclear. This suggests that at least 80–85 percent—but more probably well over 90 percent—of village political elites belonged to the senior generation of a major kinship group.

The above analysis assumes that political leadership positions were generally objects of social desire, and therefore fairly accurate proxies for high status and authority. But was this true? Based also on the Mantetsu surveys, Prasenjit

48 See Appendix B.

Duara has argued that the richest North China households actually avoided assuming direct political authority, considering it burdensome and risky.[49] The sole piece of evidence for these claims is an interview with Du Fengshan, a Lengshuigou village chief who had served for over two decades despite owning almost no land. Du notes that the village had undergone a political reorganization after 1935, in which 14 lüzhang (a jiazhang equivalent) replaced the 8 shoushi ("chief administrators") who had previously handled basic administration. He then lists from memory the names and landholdings of all 22 men. There was, as Duara points out, no overlap between the two administrations. Moreover, Du reports notably higher landholding figures for the 8 shoushi than for the 14 lüzhang. Duara argues, therefore, that the village economic elite, as represented by the 8 shoushi, had consciously withdrawn from political leadership positions.

However, Du's recollection is extraordinarily unreliable: no other interviewee ever mentions the 8 shoushi he lists, and only one of them can be found on the village land registry.[50] Moreover, that one person actually owned only 2 mu, not the 20 mu that Du reported.[51] Du's list of the 14 lüzhang was likewise inaccurate. He misstates the names of 4 people, and provides wildly inaccurate landholding numbers for another 5.[52] Whether Du was consciously misleading the Japanese researchers is unclear—his advanced age may have impaired his memory. Moreover, although there was no overlap between the 14 lüzhang and the 8 shoushi that immediately preceded them, one lüzhang had, in fact, been part of an earlier class of shoushi.[53] The two classes of shoushi also shared only one common member, suggesting that the large volume of personnel turnover was traditionally normal. There is simply no reliable evidence that Lengshuigou economic elites "withdrew" from village politics. Quite the opposite, some had considerable political aspirations, even in 1940: According to one interviewee, the village's largest landowner could not obtain his desired sociopolitical status "because he [was] only in his twenties."[54]

The conclusions drawn here stand in distinct opposition to two previous studies of the Mantetsu surveys: Duara's, of course, but also Philip Huang's important study of the North China economy. Both suggest that, quoting

49 Prasenjit Duara, *Culture, Power and the State: Rural North China, 1900–1942* (Stanford: Stanford University Press, 1988), 169–73.

50 *Mantetsu Surveys*, 4: 1–29, 386–89.

51 This would be Li Fenggui. See Ibid., 387.

52 Compare Ibid., 25 with Ibid., 386–89.

53 Ibid., 25.

54 Ibid., 8.

Huang, "lineage leaders and village 'councilmen' were generally also the village rich."[55] They rely, however, on highly incomplete surveys of village elite: Huang relies on a sample of 18 people;[56] while Duara provides only incomplete lists from Shajing, Houjiaying, and Lengshuigou.[57] More comprehensive coverage demonstrates, however, that lower-income households were hardly underrepresented among the political elite.

Certain regions of North China were, of course, more economically stratified than others. Joseph Esherick and Kenneth Pomeranz have noted, for example, that resident landlordism was more prevalent in the southwestern edge of Shandong Province than in other regions of North China, with large landlords owning perhaps a third or more of all arable land.[58] Whether this meant that they dominated local social and political authority, however, is ambiguous. The main sociopolitical function they controlled were organizing and funding local militias—something *only* the rich could provide.[59] Otherwise, there is no clear evidence that the ranks of local political elite were forcibly monopolized by higher-income households.

Social organization in the Lower Yangtze was different in several aspects, but nonetheless similar in that it revolved around large kinship networks. Compared to North China kinship groups, these lineages were better organized and more populous.[60] Whereas the average North China village might possess several kinship groups, each consisting of a few dozen households, Lower Yangtze villages were very often dominated by one large lineage, operating under published regulations and detailed conduct codes. Political authority

55 Philip C.C. Huang, *The Peasant Economy and Social Change in North China* (Stanford: Stanford University Press, 1985), 238.

56 Ibid., 238–39.

57 Duara, *Culture*, 162, 166, 171.

58 Joseph Esherick, *Origins of the Boxer Uprising* (Berkeley: University of California Press, 1988), 1–37; Kenneth Pomeranz, *The Making of a Hinterland: State, Society, and Economy in Inland North China, 1853–1937* (Berkeley: University of California Press, 1993), 101–04.

59 Esherick, *Origins of the Boxer Uprising*, 23.

60 See, however, Kathryn Bernhardt's characterization of Lower Yangtze lineages as "based in urban centers" and loosely organized in rural areas. Kathryn Bernhardt, *Rents, Taxes, and Peasant Resistance: The Lower Yangzi Region, 1840–1950* (Stanford: Stanford University Press, 1992), 19–21. More recent scholarship suggests that Bernhardt significantly underestimates the social importance of rural lineage groups. See Zhang Jinjun 张金俊, "Qingdai Jiangnan zongzu zai xiangcun shehui kongzhi zhong de zuoyong 清代江南宗族在乡村社会控制中的作用 [The Rural Social Control Function of Lineages in the Qing Lower Yangtze]," *Anhui Normal University Academic Journal* 34 (2006): 353–57.

and status in geographical communities were therefore inseparable from authority and status within lineages.

We focus here on the considerable number of lineage registries that were produced throughout the Qing and early Republic. Apart from recording the family tree, they also contained significant information on the use and maintenance of common property, rules of personal conduct, and rules on the selection of lineage heads and councilors. The collection of twelve registries analyzed here all hail from the Ningbo, Shicang and Longquan regions of Zhejiang Province, each correlating to a large lineage that dominated at least one village between 1870 and 1930.[61]

These lineages shared two basic organizational characteristics. First, *none* of the registries positively identify personal wealth with higher internal status and authority. At least three, in fact, expressly condemned as immoral the allocation of status based on material affluence. The natural order of families was, they stated, one that gave senior members precedence over junior ones, and any corruption of this principle by materialistic concerns was intolerable.[62] Second, of the seven lineages that published selection criteria for leadership positions, all seven highlight the importance of generational seniority.[63] The Jiang lineage of Ningbo, for example, divided its members into five subgroups, each of which sent the eldest member of the highest generation to the lineage council.[64] This five-person council arbitrated all internal disputes, represented the lineage in external negotiations, managed common property, coordinated

61 Eight of these are held at the Shanghai Library: *Nanjin Jiangshi minfang faxiang pu* 南津蒋氏闵房发祥谱 [Registry of the Min Branch of the Ningbo Jiang Lineage] (1890); *Jiangshi zhipu* 江氏支谱 [Branch Registry of the Jiang Lineage] (1934); *Siming Zhushi zhipu* 四明朱氏支谱 [Branch Registry of the Zhu Lineage of Siming] (1936); *Xudetang Yinjia pu* 徐德堂尹家谱 [Registry of the Yin Lineage of Xudetang] (1906); *Yongshang Tushi zongpu* 甬上屠氏宗譜 [Registry of the Tu Lineage of Yongshang] (1919); *Bianshi zongpu* 边氏宗谱 [Registry of the Bian Lineage] (1874); *Yaonan Dingshan Fangshi zongpu* 姚南丁山方氏宗谱 [Registry of the Fang Lineage from Dingshan, in Yaonan] (1921); *Dushi zongpu* 杜氏宗譜 [Registry of the Du Lineage] (1948). Three, from Longquan County, are held at the Zhejiang University History Department: *Nanyang Yeshi zongpu* 南阳叶氏宗谱 [Registry of the Ye Lineage of Nanyang] (1998); *Xushi zongpu* 徐氏宗谱 [Registry of the Xu Lineage] (1937); *Guanchuan Maoshi zongpu* 关川毛氏宗谱 [Registry of the Mao Lineage of Guanchuan] (late Qing, year unknown). One, from Shicang village, is held at the Shanghai Jiaotong University History Department: *Queshi zongpu* 阙氏宗谱 [Registry of the Que Lineage] (1896).

62 *Jiangshi zhipu; Dushi zongpu; Queshi zongpu.*

63 *Jiangshi zhipu; Siming Zhushi zhipu; Yongshang Tushi zongpu; Bianshi zongpu; Yaonan Dingshan Fangshi zongpu; Dushi zongpu; Queshi zongpu.*

64 *Jiangshi zhipu.*

labor and resource sharing, and enforced lineage regulations. In this latter task, the council could often count on the county government's backing, to the point where "bringing offenders to the county court" was listed as the punishment of last resort.[65]

Among members of the same generation, one lineage in our sample chose to rank individuals not by age, but by lineal proximity to a descent line of first-born males extending back to the founding ancestor: his eldest son, the eldest son's eldest son, and so on.[66] This line of eldest sons ("zongzi") enjoyed higher status than other members of their generation, regardless of age. All other members were ranked by their lineal proximity to him: his brothers would, for example, have social precedence over his cousins, usually through more prominent roles in ancestor worship rituals and easier access to lineage leadership positions. For the purposes of this article, these systems are not fundamentally different from straightforward ranking by seniority, in that they rank lineage members according to criteria that have little discernible correlation to wealth, especially after a few generations. Previous scholarship on Lower Yangtze lineages suggest, in any case, that straightforward ranking by generation and age gradually replaced "zongzi" systems during the Ming and Qing.[67]

Section Three: Kinship Hierarchies and Property Norms

The previous two sections have demonstrated that "dian" customs were often the product of self-interested negotiation in parts of North China and the Lower Yangtze, and that local status distribution probably correlated far better with "Confucian" kinship hierarchies in these localities than with wealth distribution. It remains to show that the relatively egalitarian distribution of status and rank facilitated by these kinship hierarchies affected norm negotiation and enforcement in ways that favored seller-friendly "dian" customs.

This is relatively straightforward for the North China locations, where the Mantetsu surveys provide numerous insights on the roles of village political elites in norm negotiation. First and foremost, village leaders of middling or lower wealth were often quite aggressive in protecting these customs against attempted erosion by landlords. The clearest example of this is when Zhang Leqing, former village chief of Sibeichai and middling landowner, engaged in a prolonged battle with local landlord Lin Fengxi over the proper procedure

65 Ibid.

66 *Nanjin Jiangshi Minfang faxiang pu.*

67 Feng, *18 shiji*, 95–96, 111–13, 248–56.

for "dian" redemption.[68] Zhang argued, internally and to county investigators, that his redemption of a "dian" sale from Lin was only dependent upon repayment of the initial "dian" price. He had later accrued additional debt to Lin, but that was unrelated and immaterial. Lin countered that, because he had allowed Zhang to remain on the "dian"-sold property as a rent-paying tenant, and because the additional debt was actually several years of unpaid rent, it was too closely tied to the initial "dian" transaction for Zhang to redeem without full repayment of all outstanding rent. This was, to Lin, what local custom "should" have been.

Several local landlords voiced their support for Lin, but other lower-income village elites sided with Zhang. By the time of the interview, the dispute was still ongoing, but Zhang was confident that his view would prevail. Lin, meanwhile, seemed resigned that he would be unable to recuperate the outstanding rent before Zhang redeemed, complaining that he could not fight the "stubborn" villagers who stuck to their "backwards customs."[69]

Although most disputes over "dian" customs in the surveyed villages were relatively narrow and technical, similar to the Zhang Leqing-Lin Fengxi dispute, they could sometimes trigger broader debates among village leaders about the expiration of "dian" redemption rights. As discussed above, a few wealthy interviewees suggested superseding traditional customs with national regulations that banned redemption after thirty years. Naturally, lower-income interviewees rejected this out-of-hand.

Many of these lower-income individuals were, in fact, members of the village political elite. For example, Li Liangfu, a Lengshuigou village official of middling wealth, seemed to know of the thirty-year legal deadline, but rejected outright any notion that it should be enforceable in his village. Similar statements were made by Zhao Shaoting, village councilor of Shajing, Hou Dingyi, former village chief of Houjiaying, and Hou Ruihe, also a member of Houjiaying's village administration.[70] Zhang and Hou Ruihe were both below-average landholders, whereas Hou Dingyi was slightly above-average in terms of overall household landholding, but probably below average on a per-capita basis due to the unusually large size of his household.[71] In the three other surveyed villages, the thirty-year redemption deadline was never openly discussed, but researchers nonetheless encountered middling or low-income village leaders who expressed preferences for "dian" customs that would allow

68 *Mantetsu Surveys*, 3: 170–71, 273–75.

69 Ibid., 174.

70 *See* notes 41 and 44 of this chapter.

71 Appendix B.

"dian" sellers to, for example, redeem even before the guaranteed-usage period had expired, or reject any right-of-first-purchase claim made by "dian" buyers.[72]

Another notable observation is that the only two villages, Shajing and Houjiaying,[73] where some interviewees expressly argued—if unsuccessfully—that "dian" redemption rights should expire beyond a certain deadline also happened to be the only two villages where large landlords appeared to enjoy some noticeable political advantage[74]: In Shajing, 5 of the top 8 village leaders ("huishou"), including the only identifiable village chief, owned significantly more land per-capita than the village average. In Houjiaying, 8 of 10 identifiable current and former village chiefs were above average landholders, including 5 people who owned at least three times the average amount. Additionally, 3 of 5 identifiable vice village chiefs were above-average landholders. In no other surveyed village do above-average landholders account for more than half of identifiable village chiefs, vice-village chiefs, or "huishou"/"baozhang"-level officials. While this may be pure coincidence—that possibility is hard to rule out in a sample of only seven villages—one reasonable interpretation is that the customary right of unlimited "dian" redemption was more secure in villages where large landholders were politically weaker.

All this suggests, ultimately, that vigorous support from lower-income political elites was quite instrumental in sustaining and enforcing seller-friendly "dian" norms. Their support could take effect in a variety of ways: village officials usually played crucial roles in mediating and settling "dian" and permanent sale related disputes, and therefore had numerous opportunities in everyday economic life to encourage and perhaps enforce adherence to their preferred institutional norms. The Zhang Leqing-Lin Fengxi dispute also highlights the somewhat higher-level forums, including formal litigation and village-wide "policy" debates, in which advocacy and support by sympathetic political elites could be particularly effective at reinforcing customary property institutions.

The Lower Yangtze locations pose greater empirical challenges. There are few sources there, if any, that directly document the positions of village or lineage elites in "dian"-related disputes—certainly nothing comparable to the Mantetsu surveys. Fortunately, there is much circumstantial evidence to be found, from both the county case archives discussed above and several major collections of land contracts from the same periods.

Whether in North China or the Lower Yangtze, few potential "dian" buyers and sellers negotiated contracts themselves. Rather, one side would typically

---

72 See notes 39–44 of this chapter.

73 See discussion at *supra*, pp. 59–60.

74 Appendix B.

ask a middleman to contact the other side, gather both sides' preferences, propose a reasonable compromise, measure the land, and, finally, draw up the deed. If any disputes flared up after the contract signing, the middleman would likewise supervise initial mediation and renegotiation attempts.[75] Given these expansive duties, he needed to command enough trust and respect within the community to effectively broker deals and settle disputes.

The argument here is that the great majority of Lower Yangtze middlemen were relatively senior members of either the "dian" seller's or the "dian" buyer's kinship group. These were usually identical, as most people preferred to do business with relatives. In any case, the near-omnipresence of senior kinsmen in "dian" sales strongly suggests that kinship groups were heavily involved with the negotiation and enforcement of proper behavior in these transactions.

These claims rely on data culled from two recently discovered contract collections in Zhejiang. The first is a set of 415 late-Qing land contracts from the Ningbo region, of which 412 were "dian" sales contracts, redemption contracts, or conversions from "dian" to permanent conveyance.[76] All 415 identify not only the names of middlemen, but also their kinship affinity, if any, with either contracting party—usually the seller. 403 contracts employed at least one elder relative as middleman. Moreover, of the 389 transactions made between members of the same lineage, 385 employed *only* fellow lineage members as middlemen. The most sought-after middlemen were generally senior members of one's lineage,[77] brokering contracts for nephews or junior cousins. There is no indication that personal wealth enhanced one's perceived fitness to be middleman—many, even the most popular, were themselves indebted "dian" sellers.[78]

The second contract collection is a batch of 140 land sales from Shicang Village, Songyang County, spanning the years 1865 to 1915.[79] 108 of these, or 77 percent, were "dian" transactions. The social composition of middlemen in these contracts was almost identical to the Ningbo collection: 130 of the 140 land sales, and 103 of 108 "dian" transactions, involved at least one middleman who was an elder relative of one contracting party, and the great majority

75 Huang, *Peasant* Economy, 52–58; Huaiyin Li, *Village Governance in North China, 1875–1936* (Stanford: Stanford University Press, 2005), 54–55.

76 *Ningbo qiyue*. The three exceptions are at nn. 81, 167, 169.

77 Examples include Mao Rongkun, Mao Renli, Mao Youpei and Mao Shengen. Ibid., 8, 23, 27, 98.

78 Ibid., 82, 87.

79 *Shicang qiyue*.

involved at least three. Here, too, certain senior members of the locally dominant lineage were in high demand.[80]

These empirical patterns highlight the influence that senior lineage members exerted on land transactions and their underlying social norms. Most importantly, middlemen were also mediators and arbitrators of first-resort in case of dispute, and therefore exercised considerable authority over the contracting parties. Employing senior relatives as middlemen further strengthened such authority and gave them a legitimate opportunity to advocate and enforce their understanding of local property norms. From there, it is but a small step to suggest that, because these senior relatives were often themselves low-income "dian" sellers, their wide-ranging influence over transactions weakened the ability of higher-income households to obtain their preferred normative and contractual outcomes.

One would also expect that this weakening effect was particularly strong in intra-lineage "dian" sales, as the influence of middlemen should have been significantly stronger when they were related to *both* parties. On the other hand, middlemen who were unrelated to either side possessed comparatively less authority, as the reputational costs of ignoring or contradicting them were significantly lower. This increased the potential for extended conflict and ruthless bargaining tactics in inter-lineage transactions. For example, inter-lineage sales accounted for a strong majority of "dian" disputes in the Lower Yangtze county cases discussed in Section One,[81] even though they probably accounted for only a small fraction of all "dian" sales. Therefore, if kinship hierarchies affected the negotiation and enforcement of "dian" customs in favor of lower-income households, their effect should have been greater in cases where buyer and seller belonged to the same lineage.

This is precisely what we find in these county-level cases.[82] In one 1896 case from Zhuji County, a relatively junior member of the local Zhou lineage attempted to ban a cousin-in-law from redeeming land her husband had conveyed to him five years ago.[83] The point of contention was whether the conveyance was a "dian" sale—here termed a "ya" transaction—or a permanent one. After consulting with other community members, the magistrate decided that the debate was immaterial: "[A]t the time of the transaction, the parties clearly should have understood that, because they were relatives, not only was a "dian"

80 Examples include Que Hansheng and Que Hanliu. Ibid., 8, 9.

81 Appendix A, Part II.

82 *Lidai panli pandu*, 10: 403–04, 443, 449, 484; 12: 303, 397.

83 *Lidai panli pandu*, 10: 443.

sale certainly redeemable, but there was also no reason why a permanent sale would not be."[84] Similar decisions appear in at least three other cases.[85]

The magistrate cites no clear authority for this extraordinary claim, but unless we assume incredible ignorance of central laws and regulations, he was probably aware that it violated every formal legal authority possible. Moreover, it seems implausible that he believed that this was some universal moral commandment—the steps he took to reach the conclusion, including meeting with community members, indicate that he was persuaded of its applicability under certain circumstances, not that he came in with a-priori moral faith in it. This strongly suggests that the claim derived from his understanding of local customary practices.

He was not alone in this observation. It also appears in three cases decided by another Lower Yangtze magistrate from the same era, who commented that, because "dian" buyers were expected to show greater leniency for low-income kinsmen, permanent sales between kinsmen were redeemable.[86] The vast majority of "dian" sellers would probably have appreciated this extra concession, especially if, as argued above, the selling of property was usually a last resort in times of extraordinary financial need. All this suggests, as argued above, that middlemen were often sympathetic towards the economic interests of lower-income relatives, and could act upon that sympathy more strongly in cases where the transacting parties were kinsmen.

Conclusion

The strongly egalitarian flavor of certain Chinese property institutions can be, at least in the cases I have studied here, paradoxically explained by the prevalence and influence of kinship hierarchies in rural communities. By creating a separate axis of status distribution that had little correlation with one's relative wealth, kinship hierarchies significantly boosted the cumulative status and bargaining power of lower-income households, and therefore their ability to establish favorable property institutions over the express opposition of wealthier landholders. Individual inequalities enhanced, in the broader scheme of things, balance and equality between rich and poor.

How do these conclusions relate to the main themes of this volume? In many ways, the account given here of how "dian" redemption norms were shaped by local interests and power balances is distinctly "modern," despite

84 Ibid.

85 Ibid., 403–04, 449, 484.

86 *Lidai panli pandu*, 12: 303, 397 (see the two cases).

the norms' highly questionable economic efficiency. They were generally negotiated based on rational calculations of economic self-interest, rather than cultural perceptions of morality. Of course, the power balances behind those negotiations *were* deeply influenced by cultural factors, but, at the very least, people tended to think of explicitly economic issues—property, contract, land use—in largely economic terms.

But what do we mean by "modern" in the first place? Preexisting studies of "dian" sales characterize "ideals of permanence in landholding" as "precommercial" or premodern, thus implying that a modern property regime should be unhampered by cultural undertones, but, ultimately, how much "culture" can modernity accommodate? If immediate perceptions of land use and property must be "deculturalized" to be modern, then what about understandings of kinship and social status? Does "modernity" leave no room for *any* moral internalization of status distribution norms?

The answer to the latter question, at least to most Chinese historians, would probably be "no." We now tend to think of Republican China as fluidly embracing "modernity"—if not already very "modern"—or at least not fundamentally averse to it. The various papers in this volume all speak to that basic point. It would be rather uncomfortable, therefore, to characterize kinship hierarchies as fundamentally "premodern," when they remained a central organizing principle of Chinese society throughout the Republican era. In fact, one could argue that they remain quite alive and well in China even today, not to mention in many other East and Southeast Asian countries. Of course, if one believes that substantive individualism and thorough materialism are indispensable components of a "modern" society, then perhaps one would happily label—*à la* Jürgen Habermas—all "Asiatic" societies as "not yet fully modern,"[87] but few historians, I suspect, would be quite so bold.

If so, then there is really nothing "premodern" at all about "dian" institutions, whether in the way they were immediately thought of and negotiated, or in the cultural structures that shaped underlying social power balances. That conclusion actually makes a good deal of sense when we place these largely stable property institutions back into the overarching historical context of late 19th and early 20th Century China, a time of rapid social and economic change at all levels of human life. If we think of "modernity" as a destabilizing force that dramatically altered the landscape of Chinese society, then perhaps the reason why it seemed to spare these oddly-shaped property norms was that they were very modern to begin with.

87 Jürgen Habermas, *The Postnational Constellation: Political Essays*, trans. Max Pensky (Cambridge: Massachusetts Institute of Technology Press, 2001), 124.

Appendix A List of "Dian"-Related Cases

Cases related to "dian" redemption are marked in bold type.

Cases involving claims by the "dian" buyer that the seller's redemption rights had expired are marked with @.

Part 1: Longquan Legal Archives, Zhejiang University

(Sorted by Archive Document Number)

Cases involving "dian" transactions of more than 30 years are marked with *

M003-01-00034 (1947) @
M003-01-00038 (1919) @*
M003-01-00044 (1948)
M003-01-00078 (1946) @
M003-01-00116 (1918)
M003-01-00126 (1928) @
M003-01-00191 (1931)
M003-01-00199 (1940)
M003-01-00277 (1941)
M003-01-00536 (1942)
M003-01-00549 (1926) @*
M003-01-00586 (1921) @*
M003-01-00642 (1919) @*
M003-01-00769 (1940)
M003-01-00787 (1947) @
M003-01-00821 (1926) @
M003-01-00847 (1920)
M003-01-00851 (1944)
M003-01-00872 (1927)
M003-01-00879 (1924) @*
M003-01-00915 (1941)
M003-01-00938 (1943)
M003-01-00956 (1942)
M003-01-01095 (1946)
M003-01-01119 (1919) @*
M003-01-01166 (1920) @
M003-01-01193 (1931)
M003-01-01229 (1926)
M003-01-01283 (1923) @*
M003-01-01412 (1944) @
M003-01-01480 (1933)
M003-01-01698 (1926) @*
M003-01-01778 (1945)
M003-01-01791 (1915)
M003-01-01923 (1937)
M003-01-01941 (1918)
M003-01-02104 (1923)
M003-01-02147 (1920) @*
M003-01-02160 (1925) @*
M003-01-02262 (1927) *
M003-01-02269 (1944)
M003-01-02484 (1927)
M003-01-02537 (1947)
M003-01-02543 (1912) @*
M003-01-02564 (1918)
M003-01-02553 (1926)
M003-01-02633 (1944)
M003-01-02715 (1942)
M003-01-02756 (1931) @*
M003-01-02781 (1921) @*
M003-01-02790 (1943) @*
M003-01-02792 (1930)
M003-01-03064 (1920)
M003-01-03427 (1946)
M003-01-03478 (1918)
M003-01-03653 (1948)
M003-01-04662 (1941)
M003-01-04738 (1924)
M003-01-04960 (1947)
M003-01-05358 (1948) @*

M003-01-06049 (1949)
M003-01-06251 (1931)
M003-01-06436 (1927)
M003-01-06546 (1922)
M003-01-06719 (1944)
M003-01-07697 (1935)
M003-01-10732 (1932)
M003-01-11063 (1922) @*
M003-01-11205 (1921)
M003-01-12468 (1944)
M003-01-14125 (1942)
M003-01-14275 (1944)
M003-01-14334 (1945)
M003-01-14772 (1941) @
M003-01-15067 (1932)
M003-01-15080 (1945)
M003-01-15483 (1932) @*
M003-01-15821 (1943) @
M003-01-16217 (1930)
M003-01-16292 (1931)

Part II: Cases from Lidai panli pandu

Ni Wangzhong, *Zhuji yumin jiyao*

This collection does not provide citation information other than page numbers (each corresponding to a single case in *Lidai panli pandu*, vol. 10). For example, "473" refers to the (only) case that is entirely on page 473, while "473–74" refers to the (only) case that spans pages 473 and 474. No case exceeds two pages.

Disputes between relatives are marked out with *.

313 @*
315 *
320–21 *
324 *
331 @*
332
336 *
344 @*
346 @*
348–49 @*
359 @*
375 *
377
380 *
386 *
393
403–04 @
410 @*
424 *
426
443 @*
446–47 *
449 @*
473 *
473–74 *
476–77 @
484 @*
487 @
490–91 @

Sun Dinglie, *Xisizhai jueshi*

Citation system is identical to the one above.

Disputes between relatives are marked out with *.

510
511–12
514
524
546
565–66 @
571 @*
581 *
585
592–93
602 @*
644
647

Zhao Youban, *Liren pandu huiji*

This collection does not provide citation information other than page numbers (in *Lidai panli pandu*, vol. 12). For example, "398" refers to the only case entirely on page 398, 398–99 refers to the (only) case spanning pages 398 and 399, whereas "398(1)" refers to the first case on a page with more than one case.

Disputes between relatives are marked out with *.

114(2) *
115–16
123(1)
128–29 @
132–33
136–37 *
138(2) *
142–43 @*
143 *
146–47
152
156 @
165–66 @
166–67
169(1)
172
178(1) *
212
215
216(1) @
222(2) *
224(1) *
239(1) *
245–46 @
250(2)
258(2) @
260–61
261(1)
271(1)
278(1) @*
303–04 @*
309
312 @
315(2)
320–21 @
321 @
328(2)
331(1) @
334(2) *
338(2)
342(2)
345(2) *347–48
348(2)
363(2) *
365–66
376–77 @
380–81 *
388(2) @
393–94
397(1) @*
397(2) @*
400(1)
402–03

Appendix B List of Political Elites from Seven North China Villages

Sources

1 *Chugoku noson kanko chosa* [Investigation of Rural Chinese Customs], 89–145, app. 2 (Committee for the Publication of the Rural Customs and Practices of China ed., Iwanami Shoten Press 1958)
2 *Chugoku noson kanko chosa*, apps. 2, 3
3 *Chugoku noson kanko chosa*, 27–51, app. 3
4 *Chugoku noson kanko chosa*, 1–29, 353–83, 385–89, 397–417, 555–63
5 *Chugoku noson kanko chosa*, 1–55, 63, 179–82, 406–31

Name	Landholding (number of mu/ household size (if available))	Belonging to the senior generation of a major lineage as identified by villagers)? (Y/N)	Position (current or former)
Sibeichai (median landholding per person: 2 mu)			
Zhang Leqing	48/10	Y	Village Chief
Hao Guodong	2/6	N	Id.
Hao Qingjun	"very average"	Y	Id.
Hao Yiwei	200+/?	Y	Id.
Hao Luozhuo	4/2	Y	Lüzhang (闾长)
Hao Baizi	28/14	Y	Id.
Hao Luozhen	3/7	Y	Id.
Zhao Luohan	23/5	Y	Id.
Liu Luoliu	25/10	Y	Id.
Zhao Luoxu	11/4	Y	Jiazhang (甲长)
Liu Yuande	10/5	Y	Id.
Zhao Luofeng	6/8	Y	Id.
Liu Luocun (Wuzi)	24/7	Y	Id.
Xu Laosi	7.5/5	Y	Id.
Hao Luojing (Luoping)	4/8	Y	Id.
Hao Luoxi (Luoji)	13/4	Y	Id.
Hao Luogeng	20/13	Y	Id.
Hao Luoxiang	8/8	Y	Id.
Shajing (median landholding per person: 2.5 mu)			
Yang Yuan	40/5	Y	Village Chief
Li Ruyuan	76/7	Y	Huishou (会首)
Zhang Rui	110/18	N	Id.
Du Xiang	11.5/10	Y	Id.
Zhao Tingkui	14/10	Y	Id.
Yang Ze	35/5	Y	Id.
Yang Run	11/5	Y	Id.
Zhang Yongren	46/13	Y	Id.
Li Xiufang	50/9	?	Xinminhui Officer
Yang Yongcai	18/8	Y	Councilor/Head of Kinship Group
Du Chun	4/5	Y	Id.
Zhang Wentong	110/18	Y	Id.

TABLE (*cont.*)

Name	Landholding (number of mu/ household size (if available))	Belonging to the senior generation of a major lineage as identified by villagers)? (Y/N)	Position (current or former)
Yang Zheng	40/5	Y	Id.
Zhao Shaoting	16/8	Y	Councilor/Village Chief Candidate
Lujiazhuang (median landholding per household: 10 mu)			
Xing Guanghua	10	Y	Village Chief
Chen Jirong	1.6	Y	Lüzhang
Xing Dawen	7	Y	Id.
Chen Dianxiang	13	Y	Id.
Yang Fenglin	8	Y	Id.
Yang Jinglin	8	Y	Jiazhang
Chen Jifu	14	Y	Id.
Xing Mingyun	10	N	Id.
Sun Riwen	3.3	Y	Id.
Chen Qingzhang	4.2	?	Id.
Yang Jinghe	2.7	Y	Id.
Lengshuigou zhuang (median landholding per household: ~13 mu)			
Du Fengshang	3	Y	Village Chief
Ren Fushen	27	Y	Jiazhang
Li Liangfu	17.8	Y	Id.
Ren Fuyu	27	Y	Baozhang (保长)
Zhang Zengjun	27	?	Id.
Li Yongxiang	16	Y	Id.
Li Fengkun	17	Y	Id.
Li Xiangling	80 (?)	Y	Shoushi (Id. as Lüzhang)
Ren Dexuan	50 (?)	Y	Id.
Li Wenhan	50 (?)	Y	Id.
Li Fenggui	2	Y	Id.
Yang Hanqing	80 (?)	Y	Id.
Yang Lide	30 (?)	Y	Id.

TABLE (*cont.*)

Name	Landholding (number of mu/ household size (if available))	Belonging to the senior generation of a major lineage as identified by villagers)? (Y/N)	Position (current or former)
Wang Weishan	40 (?)	Y	Id.
Li Fengjie	70 (?)	Y	Id.
Cheng Zhensheng	6	Y	Lüzhang
Yang Liquan	10	Y	Id.
Li Changhai	3	Y	Id.
Li Xingchang	17	?	Id.
Li Defu	20	Y	Id.
Li Zonglun	13	Y	Id.
Liu Xi'en	13	Y	Id.
Li Yongmao	14.5	Y	Id.
Ren Fuzeng	40	Y	Id.
Ren Furun	1	Y	Difang (地方)
Son of Yang Qingyun	3	N	Head of local militia
Houxiazhai (Median landholding per person: 3.6 mu)			
Ma Fengxiang	43/10	Y	Difang
Wu Yuheng	30/?	Y	Baozhang (same as village chief in this village)
Ma Wannian	7/4	Y	Id.
Wang Qinglong	30/?	?	Id.
Wu Yulin	36/11	Y	Id.
Wang Baotan	50 /?	?	Id.
Li Pu	30/?	?	Id.
Li Shengtang	22/7	Y	Jiazhang
Wei Jinsheng	28/7	?	Id.
Wang Baojun	35/11	Y	Head of Kinship Group
Wang Lianzhi	6/2	Y	Id.
Wang Junling	24/5	Y	Id.

TABLE (*cont.*)

Name	Landholding (number of mu/ household size (if available))	Belonging to the senior generation of a major lineage as identified by villagers)? (Y/N)	Position (current or former)
Ma Zhongting	30/14	Y	Id.
Wu Xiangzhong	27/8	Y	Id.
Wu Zhide	33/6	Y	Id.
Wang Qingyun	7/2	Y	Id.
Ma Xinggang	17/4	Y	Id.
Wang Zhende	10/2	Y	Id.
Wei Jizhou	11/4	Y	Id.
Houjiaying (median landholding per household: 25 mu)			
Hou Junliang	10	Y	Head of largest kinship group
Hou Dingyi	50, but supports household twice as large as average (p. 203, 96)	Y	Village Chief
Hou Quanwu	80	Y	Id.
Hou Yintang	70+	Y	Id.
Hou Rongkuan	25	Y	Id.
Liu Zixin	100+	Y	Id.
Hou Dasheng	40	Y	Id.
Hou Xianyang	150	Y	Id.
Hou Changzan	35	Y	Id.
Hou Baotian	25	Y	Id.
Hou Yuanguang	98	Y	Id.
Hou Yonghe	35, but supports household three times as large as average (p. 96)	Y	Vice Village Chief

TABLE (*cont.*)

Name	Landholding (number of mu/ household size (if available))	Belonging to the senior generation of a major lineage as identified by villagers)? (Y/N)	Position (current or former)
Hou Xichen	30	Y	Id.
Kong Ziming	20	Y	Id.
Hou Tingwu	35	Y	Id.
Xiao Huisheng	25 (p. 55)	Y	Id.
Hou Zhende	10	?	Jiazhang
Liu Wanchen	10	?	Id.
Hou Ruiwen	Less than 10	?	Id.
Hou Yuanzhao	Possibly landless	Y	Id.
Ye Runting	"Below average"	Y	Id.
Hou Ruihe	13 (p. 32)	N	Xiangding (a lower-level village official on the level of Jiazhang)
Wudian (median landholding per household: ~15 mu)			
Zhang Qilun	20	Y	Village Chief
Zhao Xianzhang	10–15	Y	Id.
Zhao Kai	10	Y	Id.
Pei Zhenyu	30	Y	Id.
Guo Ru	5–6	Y	Id.
Father of Jia Zhenheng	3–4	Y	Id.
Guo Kuan	70	Y	Id.
Yang Wenhai	3–4	Y	Id.
Zhang Wenzhong	3–4	Y	Id.
Pei Shun	No. 1 landowner	Y	Vice Village Chief
Zhang Wenhui	Landless	Y	Id.
Li Yongyu	30	Y	Id.
Guo Zhongsheng	70	N	Jiazhang
Li Rong	31	N	Id.

TABLE (*cont.*)

Name	Landholding (number of mu/ household size (if available))	Belonging to the senior generation of a major lineage as identified by villagers)? (Y/N)	Position (current or former)
Zhao Xiang	10	N	Id.
Hui Zhen	20	N	Id.
Yu Duo	30	Y	Id.

Lengshuigouzhuang landholding data marked out with (?) are highly unreliable

Individuals on the above list who were top-5 landowners in their respective villages:
Sibeichai: Hao Luozhen, Zhao Luofeng
Shajing: Zhang Rui
Lujiazhuang: none
Lengshuigouzhuang: Li Xiangling, Yang Hanqing
Houjiaying: Hou Xianyang, Liu Zixin
Wudian: Guo Kuan, Pei Shun.

Bibliography

Beckett, J.V. "The Pattern of Landownership in England and Wales, 1660–1880." *Economic History Review* 37 (1984): 1–22.

Bell, Lynda S. "Farming, Sericulture, and Peasant Rationality in Wuxi County in the Early Twentieth Century." In *Chinese History in Economic Perspective*, edited by Thomas G. Rawski and Lillian M. Li, 207–42. Berkeley: University of California Press, 1992.

Bernhardt, Kathryn. *Rents, Taxes, and Peasant Resistance: The Lower Yangzi Region, 1840–1950*. Stanford: Stanford University Press, 1992.

Bianshi zongpu 边氏宗谱 [Registry of the Bian Lineage]. Ningbo, 1874 (available at the Shanghai Public Library).

Buoye, Thomas. *Manslaughter, Markets and Moral Economy: Violent Disputes over Property Rights in Eighteenth Century China*. New York: Cambridge University Press, 2000.

Chugoku noson kanko chosa 中國农村惯行調查 [Investigation of Rural Chinese Customs] [cited as *Mantetsu Surveys*]. Edited by the Committee for the Publication of the Rural Customs and Practices of China 中国农村惯性調查会. Tokyo: Iwanami shoten 岩波書店, 1958.

Ch'u, Tung-tsu. *Local Government in China under the Ch'ing*. Cambridge: Harvard University Press, 1962.

Da Qing lüli 大清律例 [The Great Qing Code, or Statutes and Substatutes of the Great Qing]. 1905.

"Data Appendices for 'Social Hierarchies and the Formation of Customary Property Law in Pre-Industrial China and England.'" Last modified March 26, 2013. http://ssrn.com/abstract=2239843.

Duara, Prasenjit. *Culture, Power and the State: Rural North China, 1900–1942*. Stanford: Stanford University Press, 1988.

Dushi zongpu 杜氏宗譜 [Registry of the Du Lineage]. Ningbo, 1948 (available at the Shanghai Public Library).

Esherick, Joseph. *Origins of the Boxer Uprising*. Berkeley: Univ. of California Press, 1988.

Faling jilan 法令辑览 [Edited Collection of Laws and Regulations], vol. 6. Edited by Sifabu 司法部 [Ministry of Justice]. Beijing: Sifabu chubanshe, 1917.

Feng Erkang 冯尔康. *18 shiji yilai Zhongguo jiazu de xiandai zhuanxiang* 18 世纪以来中国家族的现代转向 [The Modern Turn of Chinese Lineages Since the 18th Century]. Shanghai: Shanghai renmin chubanshe, 2011.

Guanchuan Maoshi zupu 关川毛氏宗谱 [Registry of the Mao Lineage of Guanchuan]. Late Qing (available at Zhejiang University).

Guo, Weiting. "Social Practice and Judicial Politics in 'Grave Destruction' Cases in Qing Taiwan, 1683–1895." Chapter 3 in this volume.

Habermas, Jürgen. *The Postnational Constellation: Political Essays*. Translated by Max Pensky. Cambridge, Massachusetts Institute of Technology Press, 2001.

Huang, Philip C.C. *Code, Custom, and Legal Practice in China: The Qing and the Republic Compared*. Stanford: Stanford University Press, 2001.

———. *The Peasant Economy and Social Change in North China*. Stanford: Stanford University Press, 1985.

Jiangshi zhipu 江氏支谱 [Branch Registry of the Jiang Lineage]. Ningbo, 1934 (availableat the Shanghai Public Library).

Li, Bozhong. *Agricultural Development in Jiangnan, 1620–1850*. New York: St. Martin's Press, 1998.

Lidai panli pandu 历代判例判牍 [Cases from Various Dynasties]. Edited by Yang Yifan 杨一凡 et al. Beijing: Zhongguo shehui kexue chubanshe, 2005.

Li, Huaiyin. *Village Governance in North China, 1875–1936*. Palo Alto: Stanford University Press, 2005.

Liu Guoqiang 刘国强. "Qingmo Minguo shiqi xingfadian jianshe zhong qinshu lunli guanxi de chuancheng yu biange 清末民国时期刑法典建设中亲属伦理关系的传承与变革 [Continuity and Change in the Treatment of Kinship Ties in Late Qing and Republican Criminal Codes]." *Daode yu wenming* 道德与文明 [Morality and Civilization] 4 (2012): 67–72.

Longquan dang'an hebian mulu 龙泉档案合编目录 [Index of Collected Archives from Longquan]. Dec. 5, 2011. Unpublished index, on file with the Zhejiang University History Department.

Longquan sifa dang'an 龙泉司法档案 [Longquan Legal Archives], available at Zhejiang University.

Macauley, Melissa. *Social Power and Legal Culture: Litigation Masters in Late Imperial China*. Stanford: Stanford University Press, 1998.

Nedostup, Rebecca. *Superstitious Regimes: Religion and the Politics of Chinese Modernity*. Cambridge: Harvard East Asian Monographs, 2010.

Pomeranz, Kenneth. *The Great Divergence: China, Europe, and the Making of the Modern World Economy*. Princeton: Princeton University Press, 2000.

———. *The Making of a Hinterland: State, Society, and Economy in Inland North China, 1853–1937*. Berkeley: University of California Press, 1993.

Qingdai gebuyuan zeli: Qinding Hubu zeli (Qianlongchao) 清代各部院则例：清代户部则例（乾隆朝） [Regulations of Qing Boards and Ministries: Imperial Board of Finance Regulations (Qianlong Era)], Vol. 1. Edited by Fuchi shuyuan 蝠池书院. Kowloon: Fuchi shuyuan chubanshe, 2004.

Qingdai Ningbo qiyue wenshu jijiao 清代宁波契约文书辑校 [Qing Contracts from Ningbo] [cited as *Ningbo qiyue*]. Edited by Wang Wanying 王万盈. Ningbo: Tianjian guji chubanshe, 2008.

Queshi zongpu 阙氏宗谱 [Registry of the Que Lineage]. Songyang, 1896 (available at Shanghai Jiaotong University).

Shicang qiyue 石仓契约 [Shicang Contracts]. Edited by Cao Shuji 曹树基. Hangzhou: Zhejiang daxue chubanshe, 2010.

Siming Zhushi zhipu 四明朱氏支谱 [Branch Registry of the Zhu Lineage of Siming]. 1936 (available at the Shanghai Public Library).

Stanford Encyclopedia of Philosophy. "Egalitarianism." Last accessed March 7, 2013. http://plato.stanford.edu/entries/egalitarianism/.

Xudetang Yinjia pu 徐德堂尹家谱 [Registry of the Yin Lineage of Xudetang]. 1906 (available at the Shanghai Public Library).

Xushi zongpu 徐氏宗谱 [Registry of the Xu Lineage]. Longquan, 1937 (available at Zhejiang University).

Yaonan Dingshan Fangshi zongpu 姚南丁山方氏宗谱 [Registry of the Fang Lineage from Dingshan, in Yaonan]. 1921 (available at the Shanghai Public Library).

Yongshang Tushi zongpu 甬上屠氏宗譜 [Registry of the Tu Lineage of Yongshang]. 1919.

Zelin, Madeleine. "The Rights of Tenants in Mid-Qing Sichuan: A Study of Land-Related Lawsuits in the Baxian Archives." *Journal of Asian Studies* 45 (1986): 499–526.

Zhang Jinjun 张金俊. "Qingdai Jiangnan zongzu zai xiangcun shehui kongzhi zhong de zuoyong 清代江南宗族在乡村社会控制中的作用 [The Rural Social Control Function of Lineages in the Qing Lower Yangtze]." *Anhui Normal University Academic Journal* 34 (2006): 353–57.

Zhang, Taisu. "Property Rights in Land, Agricultural Capitalism, and the Relative Decline of Pre-Industrial China." *San Diego International Law Journal* 13 (2011): 129–200.

Zhongguo fazhi tongshi 中国法制通史 [History of Law in China], Vol. 8. Edited by Zhang Jinfan 张晋藩. Beijing: Falü chubanshe, 1999.

Zhonghua minguo minfadian 中华民国民法典 [Civil Code of the Republic of China]. 1929.

CHAPTER 3

Social Practice and Judicial Politics in "Grave Destruction" Cases in Qing Taiwan, 1683–1895

*Weiting Guo**

In recent years, a growing number of scholars have remarked on the importance of religious belief and practice in Chinese legal culture. We now have important studies of the dynamic interrelation and "distorting mimesis" between human legal practice and divine justice in various dimensions.[1] Scholars of Chinese religion have also explored how popular beliefs and practices were manipulated, regulated, standardized,[2] or "superscribed"[3] by the state and its agents. However, this scholarship has tended to focus on the relationship

---

* I want to thank Professor Madeleine Zelin for her generous support and insightful suggestions to my article. I also appreciate Jonathan Ocko, Pengsheng Chiu, Yanhong Wu, and Taisu Zhang for their valuable advice.

1 Among others, Paul Katz's *Divine Justice: Religion and the Development of Chinese Legal Culture* (New York: Routledge, 2009) represents the most comprehensive work on the interplay between Chinese law and religion. For other studies that also explore the mutual influences between human and divine justice, see, e.g., Valerie Hansen, *Negotiating Daily Life in Traditional China: How Ordinary People Used Contracts, 600–1400* (New Haven: Yale University Press, 1995); Timothy Brook, Jérôme Bourgon, and Gregory Blue, *Death by a Thousand Cuts* (Cambridge: Harvard University Press, 2008); Chen Dengwu 陈登武, *Cong renjianshi dao youmingjie: Tangdai de fazhi, shehui, yu guojia* 从人间世到幽冥界：唐代的法制、社会、与国家 [From Human World to Underworld: Law, Society, and the State in Tang Dynasty] (Taibei: Wunan, 2006); Chen Dengwu, *Diyu, falü, renjian zhixu: zhonggu zhongguo de zongjiao, shehui, yu guojia* 地狱、法律、人间秩序：中古中国的宗教、社会、与国家 [Hell, Law, and the Order of Human World: Chinese Religion, Society, and State during the Middle Age] (Taibei: Wunan, 2009).

2 See especially James Watson, "Standardizing the Gods: The Promotion of T'ien Hou ('Empress of Heaven') along the South China Coast, 960–1960," in *Popular Culture in Late Imperial China*, ed. David Johnson, Andrew J. Nathan, and Evelyn S. Rawski (Berkeley: University of California Press, 1985), 292–324.

3 Prasenjit Duara coined the term 'superscription' to describe how the state utilized the framework of popular symbolisms while adding new meanings to these symbolisms. Prasenjit Duara, *Culture, Power, and the State Culture, Power, and the State Rural North China, 1900–1942* (Stanford: Stanford University Press, 1988); Prasenjit Duara, "Superscribing Symbols: The Myth of Guandi, Chinese God of War," *Journal of Asian Studies* 47, no. 4 (1988): 778–95.

© KONINKLIJKE BRILL NV, LEIDEN, 2015 | DOI 10.1163/9789004288492_005

between the divine and mundane worlds, orthodoxy and heterodoxy, and formal and informal institutions. We have yet to explore the way in which popular beliefs were negotiated in adjudication, and the ways in which the violation of popular beliefs could be both overlooked and sanctioned in social and judicial practice. The goal of this chapter is to rethink the way we approach the interaction between religion and law by examining certain aspects of the process of negotiation in cases involving the religiously and culturally charged issue of grave desecration.[4]

Records preserved in the Danxin Archive (*Danxin dang'an*) and various other local sources from Qing-ruled Taiwan provide rich documentation for a study of "grave-destruction" (*huifen*) or "uncovering graves" (*fazhong*) cases. The tomb is one of the most consecrated and vulnerable sites. In China its sanctity was derived primarily from the cult of the ancestor, which influenced the way in which the deceased were imagined, and from ideas of *fengshui* or geomancy, which accorded transformative significance to the siting tomb itself. Because of its association with both geomancy and the corpse, disruption of the tomb could entangle kin and offenders in intense social conflicts. Maurice Freedman and subsequent anthropologists commented on the importance of geomantic disputes and the competition over geomantic sites, often referred to in Chinese as "stealing other's geomantic sites" (*qiang fengshui*).[5] Melissa Macauley drew attention to the practice of "body-snatching" of corpses as a unique feature of Chinese legal practice that frequently resulted in legal

4 Actually, disputes involved grave destruction were not uncommon in late imperial China. Many local gazetteers and legal handbooks provide vivid account of grave disputes particularly since late Ming period. Some grave disputes even triggered power struggles among local actors, officials, and the state. Timothy Brook discussed a Nanchang grave case that disturbed the imperial court and a wide range of higher officials. See Timothy Brook, *The Chinese State in Ming Society* (London: Routledge Curzon, 2005), 1–13.

5 Maurice Freedman, "Geomancy," in *Proceedings of the Royal Anthropological Institute of Great Britain and Ireland for 1968* (London: Royal Anthropological Institute of Great Britain and Ireland, 1969), 5–15; Maurice Freedman, "Chinese Geomancy: Some Observations in Hong Kong," in *The Study of Chinese Society: Essays by Maurice Freedman* (Stanford: Stanford University Press, 1979), 189–221. For the exploration of normalization and indigenization of geomantic order in local society through a historical anthropological approach, see Chen Jinguo 陈进国, *Xinyang, yishi, yu xiangtu shehui: fengshui de lishi renleixue tansuo* 信仰、仪式与乡土社会：风水的历史人类学探索 [Belief, Ritual, and Rural Society: The Anthropology of Fengshui in Fujian, China] (Beijing: Zhongguo shehui kexue chubanshe, 2005). For other comprehensive studies on Chinese geomancy, see Stephan Feuchtwang, *An Anthropological Analysis of Chinese Geomancy* (Vietnam: Vithagna, 1974); Ole Bruun, *Fengshui in China: Geomantic Divination between State Orthodoxy and Popular Religion* (Copenhagen: NIAS Press, 2003).

disputes.[6] The practice of tomb robbery further contributed to the vulnerability of graves.[7] The custom of "killing the drought demons" (*da hanba*) also had devastating effects on graves as it was widely believed that the corpses would attract moisture and eventually cause the drought.[8] As a result, grave destruction, whatever its motive, became an important source of litigation in Chinese courts.[9]

Previous studies have examined the cultural, material, and social context behind the destruction of graves, but have largely ignored desecration as a matter for adjudication and disputation. Most studies view this phenomenon merely as a "social problem," emerging out of disputes over geomancy or corpses, or as a byproduct of land disputes or lineage conflicts.[10] This

6 Melissa Macauley, *Social Power and Legal Culture: Litigation Masters in Late Imperial China* (Stanford: Stanford University Press, 1998), 195–227.

7 For the history of Chinese tomb robbery, see Wang Zijin 王子今, *Zhongguo daomu shi* 中国盗墓史 [A History of Chinese Tomb Robbery] (Beijing: Jiuzhou chubanshe, 2007).

8 For the culture of "killing the drought demons," see, for instance, Jeffrey Snyder-Reinke, *Dry Spells: State Rainmaking and Local Governance in Late Imperial China* (Cambridge: Harvard University Press, 2009), 108–10; Zhang Chuanyong 张传勇, "Hanba wei nue: Ming-Qing beifang diqu de 'da hanba' xisu' 旱魃为虐:明清北方地区的'打旱魃'习俗 [The Drought Demon Brings Disaster: The Custom of 'Killing the Drought Demon' in North China during the Ming-Qing Period]," *Zhongguo shehui jingji shi yanjiu* 中国社会经济史研究 [The Journal of Chinese Social and Economic History] 4 (2009): 51–60.

9 Another increasing threat to the graves is the government-sponsored campaign of removing graves (*pingfen yundong* or *qingshan baihua zhili*). Started first in the 1950s, this campaign has been represented by the authorities as one designed to promote agriculture and reuse land efficiently. In 2012, the Henan Province's grave removal project outraged local people and triggered a series of protest. Some netizens defied the government by creating a parody song called "Grave-flattening Style" (*pingfen style*). For the Henan incident, see Thomas Mullaney's report, at http://tsmullaney.com/?p=412. There are a number of news reports regarding the removal of grave across the nation. For a recent report on Wenzhou's *pingfen* campaign, see http://wz.people.com.cn/n/2014/0712/c139014-21646952.html.

10 See, e.g., Hong Jianrong 洪健荣, "Dang 'fengshui' chengwei 'huoshui': qingdai taiwan shehui de fengshui jiufen" 当'风水'成为'祸水'：清代台湾社会的风水纠纷 [When 'Wind and Water' Became 'Harmful Water': Fengshui Disputes in Qing-ruled Taiwan]," *Tainan wenhua* 台南文化 [Tainan Culture] 61 (2007): 27–54, and 62 (2008): 1–46; Zeng Guodong 曾国栋, "Cong shijinbei tantao qingdai taiwan de shehui xianxiang 从示禁碑探讨清代台湾的社会现象 [Qing-ruled Taiwan's Social Phenomenon: An Analysis of Banning Tablets]," *Shilian zazhi* 史联杂志 [Correspondence of Taiwan History and Relics] 35 (1999): 59–92; Han Xiutao 韩秀桃, *Ming Qing huizhou de minjian jiufen ji qi jiejue* 明清徽州的民间纠纷及其解决 [Local Dispute Resolution in Ming-Qing Huizhou] (Hefei: Anhui daxue chubanshe, 2004), 264–300; Zhang Xiaoye 张小也, *Guan, min, yu*

interpretation certainly conforms to imperial perceptions of social disorder, and also conforms to the literati's critique of the immorality of offenders in grave desecration cases. However, as this study argues, the records of court cases and other local historical sources reveal that grave violation was to some extent "sanctioned" in both social and judicial practice. The sanctioned violation of grave integrity left graves unprotected despite the highly charged emotional and religious associations with which they were endowed.

In the Qing legal system, the Qing Code imposed severe punishments for the offenses of exposing a coffin or a corpse.[11] Records of cases that underwent central government review, including those collected in the *Conspectus of Penal Cases* (*Xing'an huilan*), suggest that offenders who violated graves, even without engaging in homicide or robbery, were often sentenced to military servitude, exile, or branding.[12] However, when such cases were handled only by local officials, the officials often issued prohibitions without further investigation, handed down a lesser punishment, or sent the case for mediation before trial.[13] Evidence from Taiwan includes many cases in which communal

---

fa: Ming Qing guojia yu jiceng shehui 官、民、与法：明清国家与基层社会 [Official, Ordinary People, and Law: Ming-Qing State and Local Society] (Beijing: Zhonghua shuju, 2007); Lin Wenkai 林文凯, "Tudi qiyue zhixu yu difang zhili: shijiu shiji taiwan danxin diqu tudi kaiken yu tudi susong de lishi zhidu fenxi 土地契约秩序与地方治理：十九世纪台湾淡新地区土地开垦与诉讼的历史制度分析 [Local Governance and the Social Order of Land Contract: A Historical Institutionalist Analysis for Land Reclamation and Land Litigation in Danxin Region of the Nineteenth Century Taiwan]," Ph.D. diss., National Taiwan University, 2006.

11 In the Great Qing Code, the Article of "Uncovering Graves" dealt with grave-related offenses. Shen Zhiqi 沈之奇, *Da Qing lü jizhu* 大清律辑注 [The Great Qing Code with Collected Commentaries] (Beijing: Falü chubanshe, 2000), 623–34.

12 Zhu Qingqi 祝庆祺 et al., *Xing'an huilan sanbian* 刑案汇览三编 [Conspectus of Penal Cases] (Beijing: Beijing guji chubanshe, 2000), 220, 241, 726–63, 1043, 1232, 1513–14, 1681, 1776, 1789, 2047; vol. 4: 117–18, 186–98.

13 In late imperial law there was a statutory distinction between "trivial matters" (*xishi*) and "felony cases" (*zhong'an*). When an offense required a severe sentence it had to be sent to the magistrate's superior for review. However, as Thomas Buoye has demonstrated, it was possible for a magistrate to frame a case in such a way that the sentence did rise to the level of a mandatory review. By such means, magistrates might conceal case that the law would otherwise deem to be a felony case including cases of grave desecration. For the study on how local officials used rhetorical techniques to deal with the gap between central government policies and local reality, see Thomas Buoye, "Shiba shiji shandong de shahai qinren anjian: pinqiong, juewang, yu song'an shenli zhong de zhengzhi caozuo 18 世纪山东的杀害亲人案件：贫穷、绝望与讼案审理中的政治操作 [Killing the Family in Eighteenth-Century Shandong: Poverty, Despair

cemeteries (or "charitable cemeteries"; *yizhong* or *guanshan zhongdi*)—the public cemeteries built specifically for the poor, the homeless, fallen soldiers, or unidentified dead—were maliciously destroyed but the courts announced only prohibition to deter perpetrators.[14] In cases where land cultivators were involved, officials even favored compromise, allowing encroaching cultivators to pay compensation and continue to farm in the shadow of the graves. Local elites denounced offenders as "mountain demons" (*shan'gui*),[15] but they were often forced to accept the inevitability of violations and allow potential perpetrators to farm adjacent lands as "grave-managing tenant farmers" (*mudian, muding, dianding, xunding*, or *guanshi*), to safeguard their ancestor's graves.[16] Many locals vandalized each other's graves during family feuds or land competition, and in order to steal the benefits of efficacious geomantic sites. The prevailing custom of "bone collection re-burial" (*jian'gu*), in which the deceased was initially interred without a tombstone and subsequently reburied within six to ten years, frequently attracted offenders who would steal the gravesite

---

and Judicial Politics]," trans. by Weiting Guo, in *MingQing falü yunzuo zhong de quanli yu wenhua* 明清法律运作中的权力与文化 [Power and Culture in the Practice of Ming-Qing Law], ed. Chiu Pengsheng 邱澎生 and Chen Xiyuan 陈熙远 (Taibei: Lianjing, 2009), 255–74.

14 For recent studies on communal cemeteries, see Kawakatsu Mamoru 川胜守, "Min Shin irai, Kōnan shichin no kyōdō bochi. Gizuka: Shanghai fuki shichin shi no gizuka wo chūshin toshite 明清以来、江南市镇の共同墓地・义冢:上海附近市镇志の义冢を中心として [Communal Cemeteries in Jiangnan Cities and Towns: A Study of Shanghai and Its Surrounding Area]," *Kyūshū Daigaku Tōyōshi ronshū* 九州大学东洋史论集 [The Oriental Studies (of Kyushu University)] 24 (1996): 75–107; Feng Xianliang 冯贤亮, "Fenying yizhong: Ming Qing Jiangnan de minzhong shenghuo yu huanjing baohu 坟茔义冢：明清江南的民众生活与环境保护 [Graves and Communal Cemeteries: Everyday Life and Environmental Protection in Ming-Qing Jiangnan]," *Zhongguo shehui lishi pinglun* 中国社会历史评论 [Chinese Social History Review] 7 (2006): 161–84.

15 Taiwan yinhang jingji yanjiushi 台湾银行经济研究室 et al., *Taiwan nanbu beiwen jicheng* 台湾南部碑文集成 [Collection of Inscriptions from South Taiwan] (Taibei: Taiwan yinhang jingji yanjiushi, 1966), 69–70, 437–39; Taiwan yinhang jingji yanjiushi et al., *Taiwan zhongbu beiwen jicheng* 台湾中部碑文集成 [Collection of Inscriptions from Central Taiwan] (Taibei: Taiwan yinhang jingji yanjiushi, 1962), 86–88.

16 Inō Kanori 伊能嘉矩, Taiwan sheng wenxian weiyuanhui 台湾省文献委员会 trans., *Taiwan bunkashi* 台湾文化誌 [A History of Taiwanese Culture] (Taizhong: Taiwan sheng wenxian weiyuanhui, 1985–1991), *zhong juan*, 200; Taiwan yinhang jingji yanjiushi et al., *Fujian shengli* 福建省例 [Provincial Regulations of Fujian] (Taibei: Taiwan yinhang jingji yanjiushi, 1964), 447–48, 884–86; Gao Gongqian 高拱乾, *Taiwan fu zhi* 台湾府志 [Taiwan Prefecture Gazetteer] (Taibei: Taiwan yinhang jingji yanjiushi, 1960), juan 10, 249–50.

and discard the skeleton in order to bury their own relatives.[17] In cases where grave disputes involved land reclamation, officials appeared to give at least equal consideration to both the interests of land development and the need to protect the integrity of ancestral graves.[18]

The tension between ancestor worship and the sanctity of graves in normative practice and the apparent willingness of officials to endorse their violation raises important questions about the relationship between norms and legal practice in Chinese legal culture. It is not uncommon to find a gap between norms and practice, but the evidence that the violation of graves, sites so deeply embedded in local religious practice and social identity, was to a considerable extent sanctioned by both local actors and officials reveals an unexpected disparity between ideal and practice that requires further explanation. Through the exploration of grave destruction cases in Qing-ruled Taiwan, we can see the impact of social and economic changes from eighteenth to the nineteenth century on the treatment of sites whose economic and social meaning came into competition with new economic and social priorities. We can also see how grave integrity was negotiated during the course of social and economic change in both social and judicial practice. Actually, since the seventeenth and eighteenth centuries, the flood of migrants and the expansion of land reclamation have threatened the integrity of graves in Taiwan. The vast undeveloped lands (*kuangdi*) and vacant space (*kongdi*) in Taiwan attracted costal Chinese settlers, who were allowed to acquire these lands by applying for a cultivation license (*kenzhao*) and developing the lands.[19] Most of these undeveloped lands were home to communal cemeteries, however. Out of sympathy for the poor,

17 For the practice of bone collection re-burial in Taiwan, see Chen Ruilong 陈瑞隆, *Taiwan sangzang lisu yuanyou* 台湾丧葬礼俗源由 [The Origins of Death Rituals in Taiwan] (Tainan: Shifeng, 1997), 246–248; Li Xiu'e 李秀娥, *Taiwan chuantong shengming liyi* 台湾传统生命礼仪 [The Traditional Life Rituals of Taiwan] (Taizhong: Chenxing, 2003), 169–72. For the comparison of bone cleaning ritual between different regions in Asia, see Cai Wengao 蔡文高, *Senkotsu kaisō no hikaku minzoku gakuteki kenkyū* 洗骨改葬の比较民俗学的研究 [A Comparative Ethnographical Study of Bone-cleaning Reburial] (Tokyo: Iwata Shoin, 2004).

18 For the correlation between "geomantic approach" and the "utilitarian approach" in the practice of geomancy in premodern Taiwan, see Timothy Tsu, "Geomancy and the Environment in Premodern Taiwan," *Asian Folklore Studies* 56 (1997): 65–77.

19 Huang Fusan 黄富三 and Weng Jiayin 翁佳音, "Qingdai Taiwan hanren kenhu jieceng chulun" 清代台湾汉人垦户阶层初论 [A Preliminary Study on Han Chinese Land Developers in Qing-ruled Taiwan], in Zhongyang yanjiuyuan jindaishi yanjiusuo 中央研究院近代史研究所 ed., *Jindai Zhongguo quyushi yantaohui lunwenji shangce* 近代中国区域史研讨会上册 [Proceedings of the Conference on the Regional Histories

the Qing government allowed everyone to bury their deceased relatives in these places without charge. The relatively low value of the undeveloped lands and their distances from other cultivators' villages appeared to protect the graves from transgression by cultivators. The rugged terrain and the Qing government's settler/aborigine segregation also deterred cultivators from entering mountain regions. Nevertheless, the growing population and increasing pressure over land and resources encouraged land developers to trespass on communal lands and aboriginals' territories. During the nineteenth century, when the problem of land scarcity worsened, cemeteries in both plains and mountains fell prey to aggressive desecration. The competition over land also triggered battles in which a considerable number of homeless single migrants fought and died for land developers. At times, land developers donated funds and land to set up communal cemeteries, particularly for deceased single migrants and the soldiers killed in the feuds.[20] They were not averse, however, to encroaching on other developers' graves during cultivation, and even vandalized those graves during battles. Faced with the emerging grave violations, local governments attempted to protect communal cemeteries through a series of prohibitions and adjudication. In late seventeenth century, local officials proclaimed a standard that allowed anyone to bury his relatives in a vacant space that was located either on communal land or on land where the cultivator was licensed.[21] In some judicial cases, local officials even set up the land in question as a communal cemetery, as the magistrate found it difficult to determine ownership.[22] Such efforts had little effect on the trend of grave destruction, however. Officials usually announced warnings, but in practice they rarely took full measures to combat grave violation. As the following analysis demonstrates, local officials would never actively intervene in grave disputes unless a verdict was demanded or a crisis was imminent.

In addition to communal cemeteries, grave desecration also occurred in small cemeteries or private farmers' lands, even though these places were considered safer than communal lands as they were not accessible to everyone. Such violations differed from those in communal cemeteries. Most of the

---

of Modern China; Volume: Shang] (Taibei: Zhongyang yanjiuyuan jindaishi yanjiusuo, 1984), 249–70.

20 See, e.g., Taiwan yinhang, *Xinzhu xian caifang ce* 新竹县采访册 [Xinzhu County Local History and Information Book] (Taibei: Taiwan yinhang jingji yanjiushi, 1962), 134–35.

21 Gao Gongqian, *Taiwan fu zhi*, juan 10, 249–50.

22 He Peifu et al., *Taiwan diqu xiancun beijie tuzhi: Zhanghua xian pian* 台湾地区现存碑碣图志：彰化县篇 [Illustrations of Taiwan Old Inscriptions: Zhanghua County] (Taibei: Guoli zhongyang tushuguan, 1997), 117–18.

graves on private land belonged to those who owned the land (*yehu*) or worked as tenant farmers (*dianhu*). Since landowners usually resided or cultivated in other regions, they were not able to take care of their relatives' graves. Most tenant farmers also subleased the land to other farmers, so their residences were sometimes far from their relatives' graves. As a result, these landowners or tenant farmers often hired grave managers to guard the graves by leasing land to the latter. It was not unknown, however, for these managers to swindle the living kin of the deceased and participate in grave-damaging activities.[23] Unable to watch the graves themselves, the living kin had no choice but to continue to lease the land to grave managers. No matter whether the living kin looked after the graves by themselves or hired somebody else to do it, grave violations frequently took place due to disputes over swindling or management fees and the disputes over communal cemeteries or graves of relatives of tenant farmers tended to be particularly troublesome.[24]

All in all, although grave looting had a long history in China, it became particularly important as a social and legal issue as population growth and commercialization of land put increasing pressure on agricultural resources. In Taiwan this was largely a nineteenth-century problem, although elsewhere we see encroachment on cemeteries taking on its own local characteristics.[25] Whereas earlier graves were often situated in the middle of farmers' fields, by the turn of the century the need to preserve prime paddy land caused farmers to site their graves on lands that were unclaimed or unregistered, lands that still functioned as commons, where animals grazed or villagers foraged for wood and kindling. The ambiguity of ownership further exacerbated conflict, as one kinship group might establish gravesites in territory where another

23 Inō Kanori, *Taiwan bunkashi*, zhong juan, 200–202; Gao Gongqian, *Taiwan fu zhi, juan* 10, 249–250. In addition, the *Conspectus of Penal Cases* also contained several cases of punishing grave managers for their grave-damaging behavior. See Zhu, *Xing'an huilan sanbian*, 241; vol 4: 118, 186.

24 This is why on many occasions when the officials demanded the offenders pay for damages, they also required the victims to pay a cultivation and management fee. See Qiu Xiutang 邱秀堂, *Taiwan beibu beiwen jicheng* 台湾北部碑文集成 [Collection of Inscriptions from North Taiwan] (Taibei: Taibei shi wenxian weiyuanhui, 1986), 99.

25 Please refer to Madeleine Zelin, "Eastern Sichuan Coalmines in the Late Qing," in *Empire, Nation and Beyond: Chinese History in Late Imperial and Modern Times, A Festschrift in honor of Frederic Wakeman, Jr.*, ed. Joseph Esherick, Yeh Wen-hsin, and Madeline Zelin (Berkeley: Institute of East Asian Studies, University of California Berkeley, Center for Chinese Studies, 2006), 105–22, for destruction of graves in competition between owners of coal seams and owners of cemeteries.

had begun cultivation. As competition over land intensified, so did associated disputes.

Grave disputes were not simply a matter of resource scarcity, however. As a symbol of family prosperity, a hub of cosmic forces, and an exemplifier of human-environment relations,[26] the grave was a social and political as well as economic target. Political leaders and ordinary people destroyed these geomantic sites as a means of bringing supernatural disasters or "killing airs" (*shaqi*) upon their enemies.[27] During subethnic feuding and in battles between China and foreign countries,[28] soldiers and ordinary people used grave destruction as a tool for revenge. On many occasions grave-managing farmers ruined graves in order to extort gifts or higher wages.[29] The threat of grave desecration to the health and wealth of the family was such that parties to legal suits were known to carry out such acts to press for a settlement. There are even records of the construction of fraudulent tombs (*kongyin* or *xudui*), which were then damaged in order to levy accusations of grave destruction—a litigation tactic in Taiwan lawsuits.[30]

To the Chinese people, the sanctity of the grave and its significance in disputation are equally important. The grave became not only a tool for revenge

26 In the Republican and post-1949 eras, with the rise of the modern idea of sanitation, the pressure of increased population, and the increasing urban planning projects led by government or entrepreneurs, the grave also became one of the objects to be removed or relocated.

27 Among others, Chiang Kai-shek's attempt to destroy Mao Zedong's ancestral tomb is one of the most famous cases in modern Chinese history.

28 During the Sino-French War, for instance, Chinese soldiers in Jilong usually sneaked to French troop's area and vandalized French soldier's tombs. See Taiwan yinhang jingji yanjiushi et al., *Shubao fabing qin tai jishi canji* 述报法兵侵台纪事残辑 [Remnants on French Invasion to Taiwan during the Sino-French War] (Taibei: Taiwan yinhang jingji yanjiushi, 1968), 294–95.

29 Inō, Taiwan sheng wenxian weiyuanhui trans., *Taiwan bunkashi*, zhong juan, 200; Taiwan yinhang, *Fujian shengli*, 447–48; Gao, *Taiwan fu zhi*, *juan* 10: 249–50; Taiwan yinhang jingji yanjiushi et al., *Xinzhu xian caifang ce*, 208–10. Such phenomenon also happened in other regions of Fujian Province, see Su Liming 苏黎明, *Quanzhou jiazu wenhua* 泉州家族文化 [The Family Culture of Quanzhou] (Beijing: Zhongguo yanshi chubanshe, 2000), 177.

30 He Peifu 何培夫 et al., *Taiwan diqu xiancun beijie tuzhi: Taizhong xianshi Hualian xian pian* 台湾地区现存碑碣图志：台中县市.花莲县篇 [Illustrations of Taiwan Old Inscriptions: Taizhong County, Taizhong City, and Hualian County] (Taibei: Guoli zhongyang tushuguan, 1997), 110; He Peifu et al., *Taiwan diqu xiancun beijie tuzhi: Jiayi xianshi pian* 台湾地区现存碑碣图志：嘉义县市篇 [Illustrations of Taiwan Old Inscriptions: Jiayi County and Jiayi City] (Taibei: Guoli zhongyang tushuguan, 1994), 48.

but also a tool for protest and disputation. The potential harm of uncovering a grave could be used as a threat to individuals and families as well as a justification for pre-emptive and retaliatory action. As a result, both victims and perpetrators aimed to use grave destruction in their actions and arguments. The flexible use of grave violation in disputation demonstrates that the violation of such sanctified sites had become a useful legal tool that played a regular role in dispute resolution strategies, both within and beyond the courtroom. The sanctity of the grave imbued it with vulnerability, but in local society its vulnerability also gave it a peculiar power in structuring dispute resolution.

Nevertheless, popular culture alone could not endow the grave with such power. Equally important was the response of local magistrates to grave disputes. When local elites approached county magistrates in the hope that local government could capture and punish offenders, local officials usually issued banning tablets (*shijinbei*) to deter perpetrators without investigating the violation further. Such measures not only warned perpetrators but also avoided wasting time and resources in protracted investigation. Even in cases where the suspects were most likely those who cultivated nearby land, local officials preferred to issue a warning rather than proceed to formal adjudication. Since the officials employed a judicial economy approach, the investigation would never proceed if the disputants failed to complain further or attend the hearing. In some cases, local officials even required petitioners to pay the costs of establishing a banning tablet.[31] When cases contained geomantic disputes, officials rarely made a judgment and thus left the disputants to seek other resolution options. Even in the adjudication of cases that involved land cultivation, compensation was frequently adopted in actual dispute resolution, and victims may have preferred to accept these solutions rather than to punish the offenders. In most instances, grave destruction cases were not definitively resolved and similar offenses continued to occur. Under such circumstances, graveowners were forced to either rely on an official's prohibition or community pact or depend on nearby cultivators to safeguard their ancestors' graves, which in turn resulted in more disputes. To sum up, grave violation became relatively sanctioned in Chinese society because of officials' judicial economy approach, growing land reclamation, and the widspread disputation over grave integrity.

In the following sections, I will first describe the general development of grave protection and grave destruction in Qing-ruled Taiwan. I will then analyze three types of grave destruction: grave destruction in land reclamation,

31 He Peifu et al., *Taiwan diqu xiancun beijie tuzhi: Zhanghua xian pian*, 117–18; Chen Jinchuan 陈进传, *Qingdai gamalan gubei zhi yanjiu* 清代噶玛兰古碑之研究 [A Study on the Old Inscriptions in Qing Dynasty Kavalan] (Lugang: Zuoyang chubanshe, 1989), 148.

grave destruction and geomancy disputes, and grave disputes that involve fraud, swindle, and false accusation. These three specific phenomena will then be used to explain the manipulation and negotiation of the integrity of the grave. The chapter will conclude with a summary of the findings and a discussion of how they advance our understanding of the significance of grave destruction in Chinese legal culture.

Overview of Laws and Cases

Chinese law has long included articles prescribing serious punishment for the desecration of graves and protecting the graves of imperial and noble ancestors from tomb raiders. State law has also protected the tombs of ordinary people, demonstrating a general concern for the integrity of the corpse and the gravesite. During the Warring States period (475–221 BCE), political regimes enacted strict punishments for tomb raiders.[32] The Qin (221–206 BCE) and Han (206 BCE–220 CE) Empires continued to sentence offenders to death.[33] From the Tang Dynasty (618–906) onward, detailed provisions dealing with for grave uncovering were developed.[34] During the Qing Dynasty (1644–1912), the *Great Qing Code* made distinctions among several types of grave violations, with varying degrees of punishment. The violations listed in the article on "Uncovering Graves" in the chapter on "General Public Disorder and Theft" (*zeidao*) were primarily divided into four groups: (1) grave uncovering by ordinary persons, (2) grave uncovering by relatives, (3) discarding or destroying corpses, and (4) other grave-related offenses.[35]

The section on grave uncovering by ordinary persons states that "everyone who digs up another's burial mound or grave and causes the exterior or interior [of the coffin] to appear will receive 100 strokes of the heavy bamboo and be exiled to 3000 *li*. If one has opened the exterior and interior coffins and the

32 Lü Buwei 吕不韦, *Lüshi chunqiu* 吕氏春秋 [Spring and Autumn of Master Lü] (Shanghai: Shanghai guji, 2002), mengdong ji di shi, jiesang, 525–526.

33 He Ning 何宁, *Huainanzi jishi* 淮南子集释 [Commentaries on Huainanzi] (Beijing: Zhonghua shuju, 1998), zhongce: 976–77; Gao Heng 高恒, *Qin-Han jiandu zhong fazhi wenshu jikao* 秦汉简牍中法制文书辑考 [A Study on the Legal Documents in the Bamboo and Wooden Slips of Qin and Han Dynasties] (Beijing: Sheke wenxian chubanshe, 2008), 201–202.

34 See, e.g., the *Commentary of the Laws of Tang* (唐律疏议), the *Great Ming Code*, and the *Great Qing Code*.

35 Shen, *Da Qing lü jizhu*, 628.

corpse appears, the individual will be strangled with delay (*jiao jianhou*).[36] If one uncovers the grave but does not come to the exterior or interior coffin, then this person will receive 100 strokes of the heavy bamboo and penal servitude for three years ... If the offender opens the interior and exterior coffins and the corpse appears, punishment will be strangulation." In addition, the section on violation by relatives stated that "if an inferior and younger relative ... opens the exterior and interior coffins and causes the corpse to appear, he will be beheaded (with delay) [*zhan jianhou*]."[37] From these two sections, we can see that under Qing law, the appearance of the actual corpse required more severe punishment than simple grave uncovering. In addition, in keeping with the overall generational hierarchy embedded in the Code, grave destruction by inferior relatives with the exposure of a coffin and/or its corpse received severe punishment, whereas the same behavior by senior relatives received only the relatively light punishment of judicial beating. At the same time, the Qing substatutes made a distinction in the case of grave destruction for the purpose of acquiring good geomancy. The sentence for "desiring other's great geomantic sites and thus uncovering and robbing their graves" was strangulation with delay;[38] for "bone collection reburial" it was beheading with delay.[39]

Most intriguing, however, is the way in which Qing law handled damage to a gravesite for the purpose of agricultural development. "Leveling the grave mound of another person for building a field or garden" without exposure of the coffin or corpse merited only the minor punishment of judicial beating. However, if such behavior did result in uncovering of the coffin/corpse, the offender(s) would receive the death penalty.[40] The lesser punishment for "leveling the grave mound of another person for building a field or garden" suggested that the authorities weighed the relative interests of gravesite integrity and the need to maximize cultivated acreage, as long as the coffin and corpse were not disturbed. But the offenses of tomb robbery, corpse stealing, and despoliation of corpses were apparently not to be tolerated under any conditions.

---

36 "With delay" refers to the requirement that most death sentences be reviewed at the central government level prior to execution.

37 Shen, *Da Qing lü jizhu*, 624; William Jones trans., *The Great Qing Code* (Oxford: Clarendon Press, 1994), 260–63.

38 Xue Yunsheng 薛允升, Huang Jingjia 黄静嘉, ed., *Duli cunyi chongkanben* 读例存疑重刊本 [Questions about the Laws of Qing Dynasty: A Reprint and Annotated Version] (Taibei: Chengwen, 1970), 741.

39 Xue, *Duli cunyi chongkanben*, 742.

40 Xue, *Duli cunyi chongkanben*, 740; Shen, *Da Qing lü jizhu*, 624; Jones, *The Great Qing Code*, 262.

Qing law prescribed extreme punishment for grave desecration, but did local magistrates handle such cases according to the letter of the law? Under the centralized judicial system of the Qing empire, "felony cases" (*zhong'an*)—cases with sentences of exile, penal servitude, or the death penalty—could not be sentenced at the county level. Magistrates served as the entry point for consideration of such cases, undertaking the initial investigation and trial and submitting a suggested sentence along with all documentation and the offender to their immediate superiors. Death penalty cases were to be reviewed at the central government level, and, except in extreme cases, the approval of the emperor was required before all executions were carried out. As recent studies suggest, however, the problems of judicial backlog and limited budgets eroded the multi-tiered judicial review system. As early as the mid-eighteenth century, local governments extended the use of expedient measures to finalize certain types of felony cases without completing the entire procedure. Summary execution (*jiudi zhengfa*) was one of the most noted procedures that were used to avoid the protracted reporting and review process.[41] Other procedures, as Suzuki Hidemitsu has argued, included "quick case closure" (*xiangjie*), "execution by heavy bamboo stroke" (*zhangbi*), "heavy stroke with cangue" (*jiazhang*), and "confinement in chains" (*suodun*).[42] Matthew Sommer argues that much local adjudication was characterized by informality and flexibility, without

41 See Suzuki Hidemitsu 铃木秀光, "Shinmatsu shūchi seihō kō 清末就地正法考 [Summary Execution during the Late Qing Period]," *Tōyō Bunka Kenkyūjo kiyō* 东洋文化研究所纪要 [The Memoirs of the Institute of Oriental Culture] 145 (2004): 1–56; Zhang Shiming 张世明, "Qingmo jiudi zhengfa zhidu yanjiu 清末就地正法制度研究 [The Institution of Summary Execution during the Late Qing Period]," *Zhengfa luncong* 政法论丛 [Journal of Political Science and Law] 1 (2012): 46–57, 2 (2012): 59–70; Li Guilian 李贵连, "Wanqing 'jiudi zhengfa' kao 晚清'就地正法'考 ['Summary Execution' during the Late Qing Period]," *Fashang yanjiu* 法商研究 [Studies in Law and Business] 1 (1994): 81–87. In addition, my forthcoming dissertation will explore the dynamics of summary execution from late Qing through Republican era.

42 Suzuki Hidemitsu, "Zhangbi kao: qingdai zhongqi sixing anjian chuli de yixiang kaocha 杖毙考：清代中期死刑案件处理的一项考察 [Execution by Heavy Bamboo Stroke: A Study on Mid-Qing Capital Punishment Procedure]," in *Shijie xuezhe lun zhongguo chuantong falü wenhua, 1644–1911* 世界学者论中国传统法律文化, 1644–1911 [Recent International Scholarship on Traditional Chinese Law], ed. Zhang Shiming 张世明, Thomas Buoye, and Na Heya 娜鹤雅 (Beijing: Falü chubanshe, 2010), 209–34; Suzuki Hidemitsu, "Cong Danxin dang'an kan qingchao houqi xingshi shenpan zhidu de yiban 从淡新档案看清朝后期刑事审判制度的一斑 [A Preliminary Study on the Practice of Late-Qing Criminal Justice: From the Case of Danxin Archive]," conference paper, Academic Conference for Danxin Archive, National Taiwan University, Taibei, July 15, 2008.

cases being sent up through the bureaucracy for review.[43] Thomas Buoye also notes that lingering imprisonment in county or prefecture jails had become a de facto punishment for convicts who awaited final sentencing.[44] Although grave destruction was widely perceived as a behavior that "incurred the greatest indignation of men and gods," the interests protected by the punishments in the code—namely, the moral principles concerning the dead and ancestors and the property interest of the burial site and mortuary objects—were less urgent than the interests of life and public security. This was apparently the cause of local officials' policy towards grave disputes, as county magistrates usually sought informal approaches that could efficiently resolve disputes.[45]

Lest we think that the state did not take seriously the violation of moral principles and popular beliefs that its laws intended to protect, we should note that when a case did reach the Board of Punishments for review, offenders were indeed punished in accordance with the code and precedents. Nevertheless, the limited evidence available from magistrates' decisions in Taiwan suggests that the majority of such cases never reached the level of central review, and we can never know how many such cases did not even reach the magistrate's court. A sufficient number did, however, to enable us to consider what magistrates thought they could accomplish by exercising judicial discretion in handling these highly charged crimes.

For this study, I was able to obtain 102 texts referencing grave destruction or grave protection arrangements in Qing-ruled Taiwan. Of these, 50 out of 102 texts involved actual grave destruction; in 48, destruction of graves had not yet taken place. Four texts mentioned grave disputes in which the facts of the offense remained unconfirmed. Texts containing prohibitions due to detected offences included 22 cases in which officials failed to capture the suspects and only found the remains of ruined tombs; 11 of these prohibitions were at the request of local elites, while 3 were at the request of ordinary people. Thus, even when officials and local people failed to find the offenders, banning tablets were used as a deterrent to help protect the tombs.

---

43 Matthew H. Sommer, *Sex, Law, and Society in Late Imperial China* (Stanford: Stanford University Press), 2000.

44 Thomas Buoye, "Death or Detainment: The Dilemma of Eighteenth-century Chinese Criminal Justice," paper presented at the International Workshop on Chinese Legal History, Culture and Modernity at Columbia University on May 4–6, 2012.

45 C.K. Yang also suggests that the punishments against "heterodox" religious activities were not usually enforced during normal times. See Ch'ing K'un Yang, *Religion in Chinese Society: A Study of Contemporary Functions and Some of Their Historical Factors* (Berkeley: University of California Press, 1961), 181.

Actual Destruction (50)	
No official response	11
With official response	39
No offender captured but prohibition issued	22
Mediation ordered	4
Light punishment, compensation ordered, or other arrangements	13
No Destruction (48)	
Interfering with Others' Burial	2
Extorting Money from Worshippers	5
Land Reclamation	8
False Accusation	9
Mere Alert or Prohibition	16
Contract or Community Pact	5
Geomancy Dispute Only	3
Facts Unconfirmed (4)	

* *Sources*: *Danxin Archive* (stored in National Taiwan University Library); Taiwan yinhang jingji yanjiushi et al., *Taiwan wenxian congkan* (Taipei: Taiwan yinhang jingji yanjiushi, 1959–1972); He Peifu et al., *Taiwan diqu xiancun beijie tuzhi* (Taipei: Guoli zhongyang tushuguan, 1992–1999); Qiu Xiutang, *Taiwan beibu beiwen jicheng* (Taipei: Taipei shi wenxian weiyuanhui, 1986); Wang Shiqing, *Taiwan gongsi cang guwenshu* (stored in Fu Sinian Library, Academia Sinica, 1977); Sōsaku Ishizaka, *Kita Taiwan no kohi* (Taipei: Taiwan Nichinichi Shinpōsha, 1923); Taiwan sheng wenxian weiyuanhui trans., *Taiwan guanxi jishi* (Taizhong: Taiwan sheng wenxian weiyuanhui, 1991); Rinji Taiwan Kyūkan Chōsakai, *Rinji taiwan kyūkan chōsakai dai ichi bu chōsa dai san kai hōkokusho: furoku sankōsho* (Taipei: Rinji Taiwan Kyūkan Chōsakai, 1909)

FIGURE 3.1 *Textual references to grave dispute or grave protection arrangement*

Of the 11 cases that received no response from government, 4 cases were known to officials while 7 others were known only to gentry or ordinary people. Five of these 7 cases resulted in prohibitions proclaimed by local people. This suggests that local people had attempted to establish a means of grave protection without recourse to the state, perhaps because they did not consider the state to be effective in dealing with such issues. In addition, there were 17 cases in which officials responded with further arrangements; 4 of these cases were sent for mediation while the other 13 were resolved with lighter punishments or payment of compensation. Putting together these 17 cases and the 33 others, one sees that officials adopted flexible ways of coping with different situations. Banning tablets were used when magistrates found it necessary to deter perpetrators without further investigation. Lighter punishments and compensation were employed while officials intended to avoid the use of severe punishments. The government's efforts were undertaken within the larger framework of judicial economy. When the violations involved land disputes, as we shall analyze in later sections, magistrates would simply announce prohibition without further investigation, or even seek a compromise between land reclamation and grave integrity.

In the 48 texts where no grave destruction could be established, three types of cases (totaling 15 cases in all) had a high potential for future grave uncovering: interfering with others' burial, extorting money from kin of the deceased, and land reclamation. These types of behavior were typically carried out by what local people referred to as "mountain demons," persons who made a practice of preying on kin and who would not desist until the families of the deceased satisfied their demands. A high percentage of cases where no destruction had taken place were the result of false accusation. Here the tables were turned, and families of the deceased used accusations of grave violation as a tool in disputation. In other cases where no destruction had taken place, the fear or threat of grave violation was used as a tool of extortion against families of the deceased.

While most of these cases were accepted for consideration by the magistrate in his capacity as county judge, few were dealt with as stipulated by the Qing Code. Instead, the approach employed by the official was one of judicial economy. Eleven of the actual destruction cases handled by officials in which a culprit could be identified were dealt with by means of a light penalty or compensation, while the remaining four were sent for mediation. Although our sample is small, it suggests that compensation and mediation were commonly used in actual dispute resolution. Even victims may have preferred to accept such solutions rather than destroy the lives of offenders who might have been neighbors and acquaintances.[46] On the other hand, in twenty-two out of fifty cases of actual destruction, the perpetrators were not found, despite initial investigation by local elites before they reported to the officials. The high percentage of such cases demonstrates that capturing "mountain demons" was difficult in practice. Since the majority of graves were located on abandoned lands (*huangdi*) or unclaimed lands, offenders could easily commit a crime without being detected. It was not practical or always possible to deploy a security guard for every cemetery. Thus both officials and elites resorted to tablets warning offenders against desecration. Ultimately people could rely only on grave-managing tenant farmers or nearby cultivators, who, as stated earlier, might themselves be a source of disputes. In the end, although the law promised government protection of graves, officials lacked sufficient resources to honor this commitment. Instead, they usually resorted to banning tablets or

46 See, e.g., *Danxin Archive*, No. 35209.

a compromise between grave integrity and land cultivation and rarely adopted severe measures against grave violation. In essence, it was the paradox between grave protection and the relatively sanctioned violations that made the grave a vulnerable object in Chinese society.

The Negotiation over "Unclaimed Lands"

One reason why graves became such vulnerable sites was the growing pressure on arable land during the Qing period. It was during periods of active land reclamation that a large number of grave violations occurred. During the Qing Dynasty, Taiwan became home to a large number of Han Chinese migrants, primarily from southeast coastal China. Settlers with varied cultural and sub-ethnic backgrounds competed for cultivated land in various regions across the island. Violators destroyed graves for land cultivation,[47] herding,[48] and lumbering.[49] Only graves located on the land of a developer's own descendants were secure. Even these lands could provide only inadequate protection to the peace of the dead when they were transferred to others in Taiwan's increasingly active land market.

The situation was worse in the case of graves on "unclaimed lands" and in communal cemeteries. While wealthy households could afford to bury their dead in their own fields or in locations specially purchased for their geomantic properties, the poor had no access to these more secure gravesites.[50] Out of sympathy for the poor and respect towards the dead, the local government often allowed people to bury their deceased family members in public cemeteries. Local elites also established communal cemeteries in order to bury the poor, vagrants, or anonymous fighters who were killed in battle.[51] To distinguish these cemeteries from private land, they were usually located on undeveloped land, in herding areas (*mupu* or *niupu*), vacant space, or other unclaimed territory. It was the "communal" and "unclaimed" status of these lands that quickly

47 Taiwan yinhang, *Xinzhu xian caifang ce*, 136.

48 Taiwan yinhang, *Taiwan zhongbu beiwen jicheng*, 83–84.

49 Qiu, *Taiwan beibu beiwen jicheng*, 99.

50 Taiwan yinhang, *Xinzhu xian caifang ce*, 208–10.

51 Gao, *Taiwan fu zhi*, 249–50; Taiwan yinhang, *Taiwan zhongbu beiwen jicheng*, 30–31; Taiwan sheng wenxian weiyuanhui trans., *Taiwan guanxi jishi* 台湾惯习记事 [Taiwan Folk Custom] (Taizhong: Taiwan sheng wenxian weiyuanhui, 1991), di wu juan, 268; Jiang Yuanshu 蒋元枢, *Chongxiu Tai jun ge jianzhu tushuo* 重修台郡各建筑图说 [Illustrations of Restoring Buildings in Taiwan] (Taibei: Taiwan yinhang jingji yanjiushi, 1970), 69; Qiu, *Taiwan beibu beiwen jicheng*, 2.

attracted invasion by settlers. Many cultivators expanded their cultivation to these lands and herded their cattle around the cemeteries without regard to their impact on graves. Farmers or woodmen came to the cemeteries, removed the bush, herded their cattle, removed or disturbed the earth, and even trampled the graves. Some of them sold the tombstones and even opened the coffins, removed the skeletons, and put the burial site itself on sale.[52] On other occasions, graves may have been uncovered as a result of heavy rains, but it was the peasants' digging in the soil that allowed the coffins and corpses to appear.[53] Officials clearly knew of these offenses. Since the seventeenth century, local governments had repeatedly warned cultivators not to encroach upon any communal land (*guanshan* or *guandi*) or private land (*maiye*). Some officials even publicly criticized government clerks for their failure to fulfill their task of safeguarding the cemeteries.[54] In practice, however, local officials either failed to catch suspects or tolerated locals who simply continued herding and cultivating. To them, land reclamation enhanced local prosperity and increased tax revenues. As long as there were no violent conflicts, land reclamation and herding could be viewed by officials as an acceptable intrusion.

In fact, since local governments lacked sufficient resources to protect these unclaimed properties, they, like private employers of grave-managing tenant farmers, usually had to rely on local large cultivators to help secure the graves on these lands. In an 1851 case, the cultivators of Jinguangfu, one of the largest local-defense land development organizations (*ken'ai*),[55] vandalized the graves in a communal cemetery on Xiang Mountain and removed the skeletons from the tombs. The developer asked the families to pay a fee if they wished to have their relatives' skeletons returned. Some of the descendants paid the fee and repossessed the skeletons, while others could not afford to retrieve their ancestors' bones. The case was brought to Danshui Subprefecture, where Associate Prefect Zhang Qixuan criticized the cultivators' actions. However, he also ruled that people who wished to build a tomb had to pay a reasonable fee to nearby

52 Taiwan yinhang, *Taiwan nanbu beiwen jicheng*, 437–39.

53 Taiwan yinhang, *Taiwan zhongbu beiwen jicheng*, 83–84, 86–88.

54 Taiwan yinhang, *Taiwan nanbu beiwen jicheng*, 437–39; Taiwan yinhang, *Taiwan zhongbu beiwen jicheng*, 86–88.

55 For more information about Jinguangfu, see Wu Xueming 吴学明, *Jinguangfu ken'ai yanjiu* 金广福垦隘研究 [A Study on Jinguangfu] (Xinzhu: Xinzhu xian wenhuaju, 2000); Shi Tianfu 施添福, *Qingdai Taiwan de diyu shehui: Zhuqian diqu de lishi dilixue yanjiu* 清代台湾的地域社会：竹堑地区的历史地理学研究 [The Local Society of Taiwan during the Qing Dynasty: Studies in the Historical Geography of Zhuqian] (Xinzhu: Xinzhu xian wenhuaju, 2001).

cultivators.[56] Not every land developer enjoyed such privileges as Jinguangfu did. Its power and connections with local government were instrumental in causing officials to ignore its violation. Yet while Zhang's ruling appeared to have favored the cultivator and neglected the interests of the victims, in the end it satisfied the needs of both sides. On the surface, the ruling legalized and reaffirmed the de facto privilege of the large land cultivators concerning cultivation on land devoted to communal cemeteries. In reality, the developer's fee not only helped sustain cultivation but also allowed the developer to protect the graves from other perpetrators, thus aiding the victims in the future. This was certainly true of Jinguangfu, as it not only developed land but also served as a legitimate local self-defense organization. Only a few years before this incident, Jinguangfu, along with other community leaders and local organizations, had jointly sponsored the establishment of a communal cemetery in the same area.[57] On other occasions, cultivators who uncovered graves in communal cemeteries also made donations to set up such cemeteries.[58] Zhang's ruling reflected this paradoxical structure of grave management and also demonstrated the difficulty of protecting graves and the inevitability of compromise between grave protection and land cultivation.

The Making of "Killing Airs"

Destruction of graves in a quest for geomantic benefits proved to be a particularly vexing offense. Theft of geomantic benefits was marked by a profound belief in the efficacy of certain physical attributes of the landscape as a location for graves. In desecrating graves, however, offenders manifested a perplexing disregard for the equally strongly held popular belief that such acts would attract retribution from the gods. Geomancy dictates location within a precise arrangement of the natural landscape and other physical features, to evoke harmony with the universe, instill an aura of goodwill, and bring blessings upon the deceased and his descendants. It was the smooth flow of energy between heaven, earth, and man that strengthened the vital energy of the family. In order to acquire good geomancy, however, many people uncovered the graves of others and "stole" the blessings attached to the geomantic site. The Provincial Governor of Fujian commented in 1767 that some offenders had already incurred heavenly demerits by destroying others' graves, while

56 Taiwan yinhang, *Xinzhu xian caifang ce*, 208–10.

57 Ibid., 212–14.

58 Ibid., 134–35.

they could not be sure that they would receive a blessing from geomancy.[59] Selective belief in the power of natural and divine energies accounts in part for this paradoxical behavior. The practice of destroying other people's geomancy out of jealousy or revenge was perhaps an even stronger motivation for grave desecration.[60] The belief that uncovering a grave would bring misfortune or "killing airs" upon the victim's family was a powerful tool in the arsenal of vengeful adversaries. During feuds between indigenous peoples and Chinese[61] or between Han subethnic groups, grave uncovering was a common occurrence. Soldiers humiliated and weakened their enemies by damaging their graves and exposing their skeletons. This being the case, how did beliefs about graves and death impact judicial practice and dispute resolution strategy? How did local officials respond to this form of violation?

The most common forms of grave destruction in geomantic disputes were "stealing and burying" (*daozang*) and "occupying and burying" (*zhanzang*). In the former, the skeleton of a family's deceased ancestor was replaced with the corpse of the offender's relative. In the latter, the original corpse was not moved but a new grave was located adjacent to or on top of that of the original beneficiary of a coveted burial site. This action, it was believed, could bring negative effects from the burial site (*zangshang*) or negative effects from occupying and burying (*zhanzang shashang*) on the original occupant of the grave.[62]

---

59 *Fujian shengli*, 884–86. For the correlation between the principles of heaven (*tianli*) and retribution, see Ye Chunrong 叶春荣, "Fengshui yu baoying: yige Taiwan nongcun de lizi 风水与报应：一个台湾农村的例子 [Geomancy and Retribution: A Case of a Taiwanese Village]," *Zhongyang yanjiuyuan minzuxue yanjiusuo jikan* 中央研究院民族学研究所集刊 88 (1999): 233–57.

60 Taiwan yinhang, *Fujian shengli*, 884–86; Lin Baoxuan 林保萱, *Xihe linshi liuwu zupu* 西河林氏六屋族谱 [Genealogy of Lin Family in Xihe] (Taizhong: Taiwan sheng wenxian weiyuanhui, 1982), 21.

61 One of the most notorious incidents happened in 1815, when a Chinese settler Guo Bainian collaborated with his neighboring land developers to kill indigenous people, encroach upon their land, and ruin their ancestor's graves. The Taiwan Prefecture suppressed Guo and returned the lands to the aborigines. Nevertheless, due to the fear of potential uprising by Han settlers, Guo was only sentenced to heavy stroke with cangue, while his followers did not receive any punishment. See Lian Heng 连横, *Taiwan tongshi* 台湾通史 [General History of Taiwan], Taiwan wenxian congkan No. 128 (Taibei: Taiwan yinhang jingji yanjiushi, 1962), *juan* 15: 431–32; Yao Ying 姚莹, *Dongcha jilue* 东槎纪略 [A Brief Account of the Voyage to the East], Taiwan wenxian congkan No. 007 (Taibei: Taiwan yinhang jingji yanjiushi, 1957), *juan* 1: 34–40.

62 He Peifu et al., *Taiwan diqu xiancun beijie tuzhi: Tainan shi pian* 台湾地区现存碑碣图志：台南市篇 [Illustrations of Taiwan Old Inscriptions: Tainan City] (Taibei: Guoli zhongyang tushuguan, 1992), 69–70; *Danxin Archive*, No. 35202.

In some instances, people believed that the former violation could even bring "killing harm" (*shahai*) or "killing force that results in death" (*shabiming*). Most of these offenses were committed in order to partake of the good geomancy. Partaking of the good geomancy did not require permanent usurpation. Indeed, offenders indicated that they acted under the cover of night in the hope that they would enjoy the good luck the site promised for a time before being discovered.[63] This kind of desecration was more common in cases where the grave awaited bone collection reburial, as the original tomb was usually not yet marked by a tombstone.[64] Many people believed that an adversely located grave could interfere with the decay of the corpse. An undecayed corpse (*yinshi*) could bring misfortune to the descendants of the deceased. Thus, evidence of an undecayed corpse would lead to a search for a more auspicious place to inter the dead. Usually, the bone-cleansing ritual during the reburial prevented any inauspicious effects. However, if the descendants did not feel comfortable with the current site and envied another's geomancy,[65] they could look for a new one or secretly steal another's site. It was this complex of beliefs that led some offenders to steal the burial sites of others in order to conduct the bone collection ritual themselves, using the site as a place to rebury their relatives.[66]

Both reburial and stealing other's geomancy were statutory felony crimes.[67] While the *Conspectus of Penal Cases* also contained several cases of reburial offenders being punished, in practice evidence from Taiwan suggests that here too local officials expressed their criticism yet in adjudication they rarely punished the offense.[68] On some occasions, officials warned that the offenders should respect ghost and god and stated that the heavens would punish offenders who violated moral principles by desecrating graves.[69] However, in most of the prohibition or banning tablets that were erected in response to desecration where the offender had not yet been identified, officials merely mentioned that once the offenders were caught, they would be severely punished under state laws. For the offense of stealing other's geomancy, the

63 *Danxin Archive*, No. 35203, 35206.

64 Inō Kanori, *Taiwan bunkashi*, 200–01; Taiwan yinhang, *Fujian shengli*, 435–37, 447–48.

65 Taiwan yinhang jingji yanjiushi et al., *Penghu ting zhi* 澎湖厅志 [Penghu Subprefecture Gazetteer] (Taibei: Taiwan yinhang jingji yanjiushi, 1963), 18; Taiwan yinhang jingji yanjiushi et al., *Taiwan guanxi wenxian jiling* 台湾关系文献集零 [Some Documents about the History of Taiwan] (Taibei: Taiwan yinhang jingji yanjiushi, 1972), 206.

66 Taiwan yinhang jingji yanjiushi et al., *Xinzhu xian zhidu kao* 新竹县制度考 [The Institutions of Xinzhu County] (Taibei: Taiwan yinhang jingji yanjiushi, 1961), 121–22.

67 Xue, *Duli cunyi chongkanben*, 742.

68 Zhu, *Xing'an huilan sanbian*, 4: 232.

69 Taiwan yinhang, *Fujian shengli*, 884–86; Taiwan yinhang, *Xinzhu xian caifang ce*, 139–40.

official also frequently sent the case for mediation. In 1852, a Xinzhu villager, Liu Manfu, claimed that the tomb of his father, located on land purchased by his brother, was destroyed by another villager, Zeng Bu. The magistrate investigated the case and quickly confirmed that Zeng had indeed destroyed the senior Liu's grave. Instead of reporting the case to his superior officials, he sent it to the *baojia* head (*baozheng*), overseer (*zongli*), and local constable (*dibao*) for mediation.[70] In an 1878 case, the victim accused the perpetrator of destroying a grave of the vicitm's relative. The magistrate found that the defendant had vandalized this same grave on several occasions, and that the motive was to acquire the good geomancy of the land. Similar to the 1852 case, this one was eventually sent to local mediators.[71] On some occasions, officials even sent cases for mediation before an investigation.[72] In cases of lighter offenses without coffin damage or corpse exposure, officials would order the offender to pay compensation.[73] If locals filed a petition regarding serious offences without reference to specific suspects, officials would draft a prohibition with harsh terms to be posted as a banning tablet at the scene of the crime. Such a tablet could deter an offender as it indicated that both the official and the locals were aware of the crime and would pay more attention to any suspects in the vicinity. The tablet also offered local elites a certain degree of legitimacy in capturing suspects and delivering them to the authorities.[74]

In fact, however, most mediations and banning tablets did not prevent perpetrators from committing offences. To a county magistrate, the best strategy in dealing with a petition was to allow the disputant to decide how far to take the judicial process. This approach helped clear the magistrate's docket more quickly but also served to deflect responsibility for handling the offense away from the magistrate himself. In the case of a not-so-serious felony crime, the judicial process would not move to the next stage unless the petitioner continued to file petitions, attended the investigation, joined in confronting the accused, made a deposition, or signed the willing guarantee bond (*ganjiezhuang*) declaring the truth of his statement. Many disputants would abandon the

70 *Danxin Archive*, No. 35201.

71 Ibid., No. 22505.

72 Ibid., No. 35210.

73 Ibid., No. 22507.

74 He Peifu et al., *Taiwan diqu xiancun beijie tuzhi: Pingdong xian taidong xian pian* 台湾地区现存碑碣图志：屏东县.台东县篇 [Illustrations of Taiwan Old Inscriptions: Pingdong County and Taidong County] (Taibei: Guoli zhongyang tushuguan, 1995), 167; He Peifu et al., *Taiwan diqu xiancun beijie tuzhi: Taibei xian pian* 台湾地区现存碑碣图志：台北县篇 [Illustrations of Taiwan Old Inscriptions: Taipei County] (Taibei: Guoli zhongyang tushuguan, 1999), 66.

petition procedure after several attempts, and resort instead to other options for resolution or strike a compromise with the other party. If a petitioner suffered a huge loss in a grave case or his grievance remained after mediation, he could file another petition with the magistrate. In many grave disputes in the *Danxin Archive*, the investigation halted halfway as both sides ceased to file petitions. The magistrate usually ordered the runners and local heads to investigate the violation, but even after the clerks confirmed the violation and reported it to the official, the case would not proceed further if the disputants failed to attend the hearing.[75] In some instances, the runners did not even conduct an investigation. The magistrate usually warned that he would punish the runners if they "conducted their task perfunctorily," but this was itself a formality. As long as there were no follow-up petitions, the magistrate was happy to turn to other, more pressing judicial and administrative affairs. Under such circumstances, adjudication and prohibition had only limited effects in preventing grave violation.

On the other hand, as many studies have demonstrated, the Chinese populace during the late imperial period did not hesitate to participate in litigation. Philip Huang, Melissa Macauley, Terada Hiroaki, and Fuma Susumu have explored different dimensions of the culture of "litigiousness" (*jiansong*) and "redressing an injustice" (*shenyuan*).[76] Recourse to litigation and the use of false accusation (*hunkong*) was common in grave disputes in Qing-ruled Taiwan, as it was in other forms of "civil" disputation in late imperial China. Even in a lawsuit that ended without a ruling or investigation, disputants typically filed at least two to three petitions, and in some situations the number of rounds of petitioning could be as high as ten or more. Officials at times hesitated to issue a ruling as it was difficult to discern which claim was true. There is strong evidence that litigation masters in Taiwan, as elsewhere, were adept

75 *Danxin Archive*, No. 22505, 35202, 35211.

76 Philip C.C. Huang, *Civil Justice in China: Representation and Practice in the Qing* (Stanford: Stanford University Press, 1996); Macauley, *Social Power and Legal Culture*; Terada Hiroaki 寺田浩明, "Quanli yu yuanyi: qingdai tingsong he minzhong de minshifa zhixu 权利与冤抑：清代听讼和民众的民事法秩序 [Rights and Injustice: Civil Justice and Civil-Law Order of the Qing-Dynasty People]," trans. by Wang Yaxin 王亚新, in *Ming Qing shiqi de minshi shenpan yu minjian qiyue* 明清时期的民事审判与契约 [Civil Justice and Civil Contract in the Ming-Qing Period], ed. Wang Yaxin 王亚新 and Liang Zhiping 梁治平 (Beijing: Falü chubanshe, 1998), 191–265; Fuma Susumu 夫马进, "Ming Qing shidai de songshi yu susong zhidu 明清时代的讼师与诉讼制度 [Litigation Master and Litigation System of Ming and Qing China]," trans. by Fan Yu 范愉 and Wang Yaxin, in *Ming Qing shiqi de minshi shenpan yu minjian qiyue*, ed. Wang Yaxin and Liang Zhiping, 389–430.

at showing disputants how to use the claim of grave destruction to make the rivals liable for severe punishment.[77] Because officials were overworked and often rejected suits based on private economic conflicts, so-called minor matters, litigants were told that a false accusation could be used to catch the official's attention. Even if the false accusation was ultimately dropped, it could be a useful first step in getting a hearing in a land or debt dispute.

Of course, litigation masters were not the only ones who understood the rules of the game. Numerous cases reveal the care taken by magistrates to determine whether claims were fabricated. In an 1882 case, the plaintiff argued that the accused broke open his relative's grave, removed the coffin, and sold the *fengshui* spot in which it was located to others. The accused presented a land deed to the magistrate as proof that the land belonged to the accused's family and that the plaintiff had never owned any graves on the land. After this, he continued to file several petitions with the magistrate in the hope that the plaintiff would be charged with the crime of false accusation. The plaintiff, however, never made an argument in his defense and the magistrate did not hand down a judgment.[78] In another case in 1876, the magistrate confirmed that the plaintiff's claim was untrue. He then sentenced the plaintiff to beating with a light bamboo in accordance with the law of false accusation.[79]

Officials usually maintained a skeptical attitude towards all petitions, and on some occasions this may have led to the victim's being wronged by an official. In an 1886 case, the plaintiff accused his cousin of destroying his father's grave. He claimed that the cousin removed his father's remains and put the body of the cousin's brother into the *fengshui* spot. The magistrate strongly doubted the truth of the plaintiff's claim. He reached his conclusion without investigation, stating that such an offense could not possibly have transpired within a family, and suggested that the plaintiff resort to family mediation instead of trial. The magistrate then ordered a clerk to investigate the case, but the case was quickly terminated as records show there were no more documents presented or reported to the magistrate.[80] From these few cases, it seems clear that whatever the magistrate's predisposition in a case, the procedure he should follow was to remain open-minded, send a clerk to investigate, and then decide whether the case should proceed to trial or mediation.

77 Taiwan yinhang, *Fujian shengli*, 963–64, 989.

78 *Danxin Archive*, No. 35208.

79 Ibid., No. 35213.

80 Ibid., No. 35210.

The Combat against "Mountain Demons"

The frequent appearance of grave violation in written texts and legal documents demonstrates how widespread this practice must have been in Taiwan. This study uncovered 102 texts dealing with grave destruction and the prevention of grave disputes during the Qing dynasty. Because some of the texts contain more than one violation, the real number of incidents of this kind must have been far greater than those documented here. The terms that were chosen to label the offenders, such as "mountain demons," imply that the offenders were viewed like wandering ghosts—drifting around, looking for graves and worshippers, and disturbing them. Officials and locals encountered such a high volume of grave violations, so how did they deal with the problem? Figure 3.2 shows the final resolution of the three types of grave violation in Qing-ruled Taiwan.

First, more cases ended in prohibition announcements than in trial. This indicates that the prohibition procedure for the magistrate entailed actively resolving disputes more than it did the adjudication process. Out of 102 cases, 41 ended in prohibition announcements and 33 were resolved at trial. In land-related issues, 25 cases were settled by banning announcements, while only 10 cases were resolved at trial. Moreover, actual destruction was involved in 13 cases that ended in prohibition but in only 7 that ended in trial. This suggests that officials would rather issue a prohibition to settle cases where there was actual destruction than commence the trial procedure. The high percentage of prohibition announcements demonstrates that the approach employed by officials was one of judicial economy. Under such a framework, a case would not proceed further if the disputants ceased to argue or failed to attend the hearing.

Even during the trial process, different issues would result in different official reactions. In geomancy-related cases, magistrates hesitated to render a judgment. Ten out of thirty-two such cases were resolved at trial. Of these ten cases, seven had no outcome. In one case, the violator was required to render compensation, in a second it was decided that the grave had not been destroyed, and in a third case the offender was simply ordered to cease his offense. By comparison, in land disputes magistrates actively offered rulings and even reached some creative judgments during the trial procedure. In ten cases involving land-related issues that were resolved at trial, four required recovery, three required the offender to stop the offense, one resulted in compromise, one resulted in termination of the offender's cultivation license, and one set up a new communal cemetery. This would appear to indicate that officials intended to protect the graves or remedy the loss. Nevertheless, in all ten cases, officials provided only limited remedies to the victims and usually allowed perpetrators to continue cultivation. Out of the four recovery

Final Resolution	Land related issues				Geomancy related issues				Extortion, Disturbance, False Accusation				Others			
	Trial	Mediation	Official* Prohibition	Others	Trial	Mediation	Official* Prohibition	Others	Trial	Mediation	Official* Prohibition	Others	Trial	Mediation	Official Prohibition	Others
1680–1800	3	1	1:0	1			3:1	1	2		2:1		1			2
1800–1810											1:1					1
1810–1820	1		0:5								0:1		1			
1820–1830	1		0:1								0:1					1
1830–1840	1		0:2					3								
1840–1850				1				1			0:1					
1850–1860	1		1:2		1	1		2		1						2
1860–1870		1	1:1	1	2		0:1		1							
1870–1880	3		0:2	1	2	1			6							
1880–1890			1:5	1	4	2	0:2	2	2							
1890–1895			2:1		1	1	0:1									
Total	10	2	6:19	5	10	5	3:5	9	11	1	3:5		2			6

* *Sources*: see Figure 3.1.
** The ratio under the "Official Prohibition" refers to cases in which officials issued a prohibition on their own: cases in which officials issued a prohibition at the request of local people.

FIGURE 3.2 *Final resolution of cases*

cases, three involved trees surrounding cemeteries. In one of the three cases, the magistrate required the woodman to replant the trees adjacent to the gravesites, but he still allowed the woodman to cut trees in the surrounding area.[81] In the other two cases, the violation occurred in almost the same region where officials had commanded cultivators to remove the trees from the graves. Unlike the first case, where surrounding trees helped prevent trespassing on the cemeteries, the trees in the other two cases were located on the graves and were thus deemed to be harmful to the graves. However, after the official's ruling, as local elites argued, violations continued to occur and the magistrate's solution did not appear to deter the perpetrators at all.[82] Among the three cases where the offenders were required to stop offending, two cases occurred in the same region where officials had repeatedly warned different groups of perpetrators not to interfere with the cemeteries but the warnings never worked.[83] The third case involved the violation by Jinguangfu, which, as mentioned earlier, was permitted by local government to cultivate the lands and collect a cultivation fee from the graveowners. Apparently, magistrates tolerated the possibility of potential harm without further hindrance even after they offered remedies for the desecrated graves in the adjudication of land-related issues. Prior to the trial procedure for land disputes, magistrates even intended to settle disputes with mere prohibition, which, as we have seen, can hardly fulfill the task of safeguarding the cemeteries.

The officials' strategy of distinguishing land-related issues from geomantic disputes became more obvious when grave desecration cases increased during the latter half of the nineteenth century. After roughly 1850, as Figure 3.2 suggests, both cases resolved at trial and those resolved by prohibition increased sharply. Faced with this situation, local magistrates devoted more attention to land-related disputes while decreasing the use of prohibition in geomantic disputes unless it was actively requested by the locals. In land-related disputes before 1850, the ratio of cases where the official announced the prohibition without a request from local people to cases where there was such a request was 1:8; after 1850, it became 5:11. In the case of geomantic disputes, the ratio changed from 3:1 to 0:4. This confirms our earlier conclusion that magistrates

81 Rinji Taiwan Kyūkan Chōsakai 临时台湾习惯调查会, *Rinji Taiwan kyūkan chōsakai dai ichi bu chōsa dai san kai hōkokusho: furoku sankōsho* 临时台湾习惯调查会第一部调查第三回报告书台湾私法附录参考书 [Provisional Committee of Investigating Taiwanese Custom] (Taibei: Rinji Taiwan Kyūkan Chōsakai, 1909), 2: 321–323.

82 Taiwan yinhang, *Xinzhu xian caifang ce*, 136–38.

83 Ibid., 214.

were usually wary of geomantic disputes. The fact that the use of prohibition by officials increased after 1850 but the rate of proceeding to trial in land-related grave disputes did not also suggests that officials preferred to issue banning tablets when there was an increase in grave violations. Moreover, the change of ratio indicates an intriguing division of labor in which officials came to be more in charge of land-related grave disputes while society was more in charge of geomantic disputes. The category of "others," which consists of contracts and prohibitions made by locals without an official's involvement, also indicates such a division of labor. Of the forty-two cases of land-use-related issues, only five cases belong to this category. Of the thirty-two cases of geomantic disputes, nine cases belong to the category of "others." Whether or not this was intentional, as the problem of grave violation grew worse and magistrates merely provided prohibition, local society had no option but to increasingly employ its own mechanism of resolving disputes.

Besides prohibition announcements, local governments also adopted legislative measures to combat grave violation. Local regulations may have responded more flexibly than dynastic law to actual conflict situations, as evidenced by such a regulation that codified the practical standards for dealing with grave disputes in the nineteenth century. Nevertheless, like the use of *Great Qing Code* in actual adjudication, local officials usually had their own strategies for employing codified rules. In the "Regulations for Eight Review Divisions of Danshui Subprefecture" (*Danshui Ting bafang ban'an zhangcheng*, 1870), the local government of Danshui Subprefecture stipulated how grave disputes were to be dealt with in accordance with the administrative structure of local government. Article 5 of the regulations states that all litigation over "cemetery hill disputes" (*kongzheng fenshan*) shall be forwarded to the Division of Rites (*lifang*) in the local magistrate's yamen for further review. Article 7 requires that all the cases of "uncovering graves and robbing coffins" (*fazhong jieguan*), "destroying tombs and damaging corpses" (*huifen miehai*), and "devastating burial sites" (*qiangshang fenxue*) be forwarded to the yamen Division of Punishment (*xingfang*).[84] The distinction between "rites" (*li*) and "punishment" (*xing*) embodied in these separated offices, found in all magistrate's offices, resembled the distinction between ethical relations and the hierarchical structure of laws that had long been established in Chinese legal culture. Like the *Great Qing Code*, the regulation called for severe punishments for the offense of uncovering coffin and skeletons, but light punishment for other grave violations, particularly those involved in land-use disputes.

84 *Danxin Archive*, No. 11202.

As we have seen, however, in practice magistrates would further sanction those geomantic violations no matter what categories they belonged to. In the adjudication of land-use disputes where actual grave destruction took place, magistrates rarely punished offenders in accordance with statutory laws. On the other hand, even though the regulations had tolerated the use of non-severe measures in "cemetery hill disputes," as a written official document it would never abandon the severe punishments that had long been regarded as a legitimate deterrent tool. This is the Janus face of the magistrates' approach to a not-so-serious felony crime. While in theory local government was wobbling between informality and authority, in practice it adopted a flexible approach and sought the most efficient way to settle grave disputes. As a result, there was a sharp contrast between the worsening violations and the repeated warnings of local governments in nineteenth-century Taiwan. To a great extent, it was the officials' judicial economy approach that contributed to the vulnerability of the grave in Chinese society.

Local society also developed informal means of coping with grave disputes. One of the most popular was to initiate community pacts and conduct dramatic performances (*faxi*) to deal with grave disputes and to deflect the negative supernatural effects that would otherwise be visited upon the community. Community pacts required villagers not to damage cemeteries in the community. Failure to comply resulted in punishment, and the offender was required to underwrite a dramatic performance in honor of the deities to eliminate the harmful influences caused by the damage to geomancy or "injuries" to the dragon vein (*longmai*). On some occasions, violators also had to pay compensation to a local deity.[85] As local governments failed to effectively resolve geomantic disputes and remained suspicious of geomantic competition and even tolerated such practices, local people had no choice but to establish their own means of dealing with geomantic violations. It is also intriguing that during the nineteenth century such privately organized approaches increased sharply. Out of five cases of dramatic performance as punishment found in this study, four dated to the latter half of the nineteenth century.[86] The increased

85 He, *Taiwan diqu xiancun beijie tuzhi: Xinzhu xianshi pian*, 45.

86 He, *Taiwan diqu xiancun beijie tuzhi: Pingdong xian taidong xian pian*, 167; He Peifu et al., *Taiwan diqu xiancun beijie tuzhi: Taibei shi taoyuan xian pian* 台湾地区现存碑碣图志：台北市.桃园县篇 [Illustrations of Taiwan Old Inscriptions: Taipei City and Taoyuan County] (Taibei: Guoli zhongyang tushuguan, 1999), 109; He Peifu et al., *Taiwan diqu xiancun beijie tuzhi: Xinzhu xianshi pian* 台湾地区现存碑碣图志：新竹县市篇 [Illustrations of Taiwan Old Inscriptions: Taipei City and Taoyuan County] (Taibei: Guoli zhongyang tushuguan, 1998), 45; He, *Taiwan diqu xiancun beijie tuzhi: Taibei xian pian*, 66;

use of such community punishments indicates not only the prevailing land cultivation disputes and the remaking of the community dispute resolution mechanism but also a search for harmony between nature and humans and between the divine and mundane worlds that by no means disappeared in the last years of imperial rule. Although locals still followed official judicial procedures, they also resorted to such privately and religiously based resolution. This combination of official and unofficial dispute resolution resembles what Paul Katz terms the "judicial continuum," which he defines as "a holistic range of options for achieving legitimization and dispute resolution, including mediation ... formal legal procedure ... and performing rituals."[87] The increased use of such an approach during the nineteenth century also demonstrates how locals responded to officials' judicial economy approach by adjusting their strategies for the use of private and religious resolutions.

In addition to dramatic performance rituals, many local elites engaged in the development of a community agreement without rituals in the latter half of the nineteenth century. In some banning tablets established by local elites, the donors of the tablets stated that local heads had the authority to take necessary measures to stop future offenders.[88] In an 1867 community agreement, local elites made a detailed list of disallowed behaviors and the corresponding arrangements. The agreement stipulated that anyone who herded his cattle among the graves would have his cattle confiscated. Anyone who caught the transgressor would be rewarded with 600 copper *wen* for each head of cattle. Anyone who captured someone uncovering coffins and removing skeletons would be rewarded with twenty-four silver yuan. The public would determine which punishment the offender would be sentenced to. If the offender refused the punishment, he would be sent to the local official for further adjudication. During the Tomb Sweeping Festival (Qingming), only around ten beggars were allowed to beg in each tomb, and each beggar was allowed to beg for only one piece of rice cake. No one was allowed to extort or rob the worshippers.[89] Apparently, locals had recognized that grave violation was inevitable and that local governments could not provide effective protection. The fines imposed for both serious and light violations were more effective than official adjudication

---

Sōsaku Ishizaka 石坂庄作, *Kita Taiwan no kohi* 北台湾の古碑 [Ancient Inscriptions in North Taiwan] (Taibei: Taiwan Nichinichi Shinpōsha, 1923), 75.

87 Katz, *Divine Justice*, 7, 47–60; Paul Katz, "Swearing down the Law—A Debate," available at the website of The China Beat: http://www.thechinabeat.org/?p=3653.

88 Chen Jinchuan, *Qingdai gamalan gubei zhi yanjiu*), 148.

89 He, *Taiwan diqu xiancun beijie tuzhi: Taibei xian pian*, 66.

or punishment. The agreement even institutionalized begging around the tombs, which was usually conducted by an abundance of "mountain demons."

Finally, contracts usually served as an important means of preventing grave disputes. Many land deeds required tenants or buyers not to ruin the existing graves on the land. On many occasions, the contracts stated that the parties wished to protect geomancy and prevent "killing airs" and besought heaven and the cosmic forces to punish the offenders through supernatural means.[90] Parties to the contract were required to follow the agreement not to harm the geomancy of a site and cause misfortune. Since the location of a grave was included in a land contract, the contract gave the owner of the grave proof if litigation was triggered. The contractually stated threat of curses reminds us of the degree to which individuals believed in the retribution of the gods and heavenly punishment. To sum up, in order to protect graves, people appeared to have relied on the use of compensation and religious rituals as a more efficient means of dispute resolution than official litigation. The growing use of these methods in the nineteenth century demonstrates that as local governments failed to provide sufficient protection for the graves, community pacts and religious rituals gained more importance as dispute resolution mechanisms.

Conclusion

As a sanctified object containing both tangible and intangible interests, the grave had been long entangled in various social conflicts. Land reclamation, geomantic competition, revenge, and deliberate disturbance to cemeteries and worshippers all challenged the integrity of the grave in late imperial Taiwan. Victims resorted to trial, mediation, and community pacts in order to achieve resolution. However, as this chapter demonstrates, local officials adopted different strategies for handling grave disputes depending on their social context. In the adjudication of cases that involved land cultivation, officials usually resorted to a compromise between grave integrity and land reclamation. On the other hand, when the cases involved geomantic disputes, officials rarely made a judgment and thus left the disputants to seek other resolution options. On most occasions, grave destruction cases were not thoroughly resolved and similar offenses continued to take place. Moreover, protection of nearby graves was often made the responsibility of those who moved to cultivate lands

90 *Danxin Archive*, No. 35207; Rinji Taiwan Kyūkan Chōsakai, *Rinji Taiwan kyūkan chōsakai dai ichi bu chōsa dai san kai hōkokusho: furoku sankōsho*, 3: 17–18; He, *Taiwan diqu xiancun beijie tuzhi: Taibei shi taoyuan xian pian*, 343–44.

abutting graves and cemeteries. The frequency of grave violation was closely related to prevailing beliefs in geomancy, the growing importance of land reclamation from the eighteenth century onward, and the paradoxical system of grave management. It was also due to the attitude of officials who chose not to employ limited judicial resources to cope with grave violation. All of these created a paradoxical phenomenon: while officials and locals upheld the sanctity of grave, they also sanctioned various kinds of violations against grave integrity in both the social and judicial realms. As a result, as an illicit yet relatively sanctioned practice, grave destruction was a product not only of social practice but also of official adjudication strategy.

Furthermore, if such an illicit practice has been constantly negotiated and even perceived as one of the inevitable aspects of land reclamation and the grave management system, how should one understand its role in Chinese legal culture? Even as the state consistently enacted strict laws against grave desecration, officials usually adopted a flexible approach to distinguish between "legal" and "illicit" and between "punishable" and "unpunishable." In the process of drawing the boundaries between these categories, the sanctioning of an "illicit" practice also served as an important resource for the formulation of a magistrate's policies towards land reclamation and geomantic disputes. The prevailing grave desecration was not separated from the manipulation of grave order and the surrounding interests. In this sense, the adjudication of grave destruction cases in late imperial China constituted a special arena for negotiation of local governance, judicial politics, and the integrity of popular beliefs.

Glossary

baojia	保甲	*fazhong jieguan*	发冢劫棺
baozheng	保正	*fengshui*	风水
da hanba	打旱魃	*ganjiezhuang*	甘结状
Danshui	淡水	*guandi*	官地
Danshui Ting bafang ban'an zhangcheng	淡水厅八房办案章程	*guanshan*	官山
		guanshan zhongdi	官山冢地
Danxin dang'an	淡新档案	*guanshi*	管事
daozang	盗葬	Guo Bainian	郭百年
dianding	佃丁	*huangdi*	荒地
dianhu	租户	*huifen*	毁坟
dibao	地保	*huifen miehai*	毁坟灭骸
faxi	罚戏	*hunkong*	混控
fazhong	发冢	*jian'gu*	捡骨

jiansong	健讼
jiazhang	枷杖
jiao jianhou	绞监候
Jinguangfu	金广福
jiudi zhengfa	就地正法
ken'ai	垦隘
kenzhao	垦照
kongdi	空地
kongyin	空窨
kongzheng fenshan	控争坟山
kuangdi	旷地
li	礼
lifang	礼房
Liu Manfu	刘满福
longmai	龙脉
maiye	买业
mudian	墓佃
muding	墓丁
mupu	牧埔
niupu	牛埔
pingfen	平坟
pingfen yundong	平坟运动
qingshan baihua zhili	青山白化治理
qiang fengshui	抢风水
qiangshang fenxue	戕伤坟穴
Qingming	清明
shabiming	煞毙命
shahai	煞害
shan'gui	山鬼
shaqi	煞气
shenyuan	伸冤
shijinbei	示禁碑
suodun	锁礅
wen	文
xiangjie	详结
xing	刑
Xing'an huilan	刑案汇览
xingfang	刑房
Xinzhu	新竹
xishi	细事
xudui	虚堆
xunding	巡丁
yehu	业户
yinshi	荫尸
yizhong	义冢
zangshang	葬伤
zeidao	贼盗
Zeng Bu	曾不
zhan jiaohou	斩监候
zhangbi	杖毙
Zhang Qixuan	张启煊
zhanzang	占葬
zhanzang shashang	占葬杀伤
zhong'an	重案
zongli	总理

Bibliography

Brook, Timothy. *The Chinese State in Ming Society*. London: Routledge Curzon, 2005.

Brook, Timothy, Jérôme Bourgon, and Gregory Blue. *Death by a Thousand Cuts*. Cambridge: Harvard University Press, 2008.

Bruun, Ole. *Fengshui in China: Geomantic Divination Between State Orthodoxy and Popular Religion*. Copenhagen: NIAS Press, 2003.

Buoye, Thomas. "Shiba shiji shandong de shahai qinren anjian: pinqiong, juewang, yu song'an shenli zhong de zhengzhi caozuo 18 世纪山东的杀害亲人

案件：贫穷、绝望与讼案审理中的政治操作 [Killing the Family in Eighteenth-Century Shandong: Poverty, Despair and Judicial Politics]," trans. by Weiting Guo. In *Ming Qing falü yunzuo zhong de quanli yu wenhua* 明清法律运作中的权力与文化 [Power and Culture in the Practice of Ming-Qing Law], edited by Chiu Pengsheng 邱澎生 and Chen Xiyuan 陈熙远, 255–74. Taibei: Lianjing, 2009.

———. "Death or Detainment: The Dilemma of Eighteenth-century Chinese Criminal Justice," conference paper presented at the International Workshop on Chinese Legal History, Culture, and Modernity at Columbia University, New York, May 4–6, 2012.

Cai Wengao 蔡文高. *Senkotsu kaisō no hikaku minzoku gakuteki kenkyū* 洗骨改葬の比较民俗学的研究 [A Comparative Ethnographical Study of Bone-cleaning Reburial]. Tokyo: Iwata Shoin, 2004.

Chen Dengwu 陈登武. *Cong renjianshi dao youmingjie: tangdai de fazhi, shehui, yuguojia* 从人间世到幽冥界: 唐代的法制、社会、与国家 [From Human World to Underworld: Law, Society, and the State in Tang Dynasty]. Taibei: Wunan.

———. *Diyu, falü, renjian zhixu: zhonggu zhongguo de zongjiao, shehui, yu guojia* 地狱,法律,人间秩序：中古中国的宗教、社会、与国家 [Hell, Law, and the Order of Human World: Chinese Religion, Society, and State during the Middle Age]. Taibei: Wunan, 2009.

Chen Jinchuan 陈进传. 1989. *Qingdai gamalan gubei zhi yanjiu* 清代噶玛兰古碑之研究 [A Study on the Old Inscriptions in Qing Dynasty Kavalan]. Lugang: Zuoyang chubanshe, 1989.

Chen Jinguo 陈进国. *Xinyang, yishi, yu xiangtu shehui: fengshui de lishi renleixue tansuo* 信仰、仪式与乡土社会：风水的历史人类学探索 [Belief, Ritual, and Rural Society: The Anthropology of Fengshui in Fujian, China]. Beijing: Zhongguo shehui kexue chubanshe, 2005.

Chen Ruilong 陈瑞隆. *Taiwan sangzang lisu yuanyou* 台湾丧葬礼俗源由 [The Origins of Death Rituals in Taiwan]. Tainan: Shifeng, 1997.

Duara, Prasenjit. *Culture, Power, and the State Culture, Power, and the State Rural North China, 1900–1942*. Stanford: Stanford University Press, 1988.

———. "Superscribing Symbols: The Myth of Guandi, Chinese God of War," *Journal of Asian Studies* 47, no. 4 (1988): 778–795.

Feng Xianliang 冯贤亮. "Fenying yizhong: Ming Qing Jiangnan de minzhong shenghuo yu huanjing baohu 坟茔义冢：明清江南的民众生活与环境保护 [Graves and Communal Cemeteries: Everyday Life and Environmental Protection in Ming-Qing Jiangnan]." *Zhongguo shehui lishi pinglun* 中国社会历史评论 [Chinese Social History Review] 7 (2006): 161–84.

Feuchtwang, Stephan. *An Anthropological Analysis of Chinese Geomancy*. Vietnam: Vithagna, 1974.

Freedman, Maurice. "Geomancy." In *Proceedings of the Royal Anthropological Institute of Great Britain and Ireland for 1968*, 5–15. London: Royal Anthropological Institute of Great Britain and Ireland, 1969.

———. "Chinese Geomancy: Some Observations in Hong Kong." In *The Study of Chinese Society: Essays by Maurice Freedman*, 189–21. Stanford: Stanford University Press, 1979.

Fuma Susumu 夫马进. "Ming Qing shidai de songshi yu susong zhidu 明清时代的讼师与诉讼制度 [Litigation Master and Litigation System of Ming and Qing China]," trans. by Fan Yu 范愉 and Wang Yaxin. In *Ming Qing shiqi de minshi shenpan yu minjian qiyue* 明清时期的民事审判与契约 [Civil Justice and Civil Contract in the Ming-Qing Period], edited by Shiga Shūzō 滋贺秀三 et al., 389–430. Beijing: Falü chubanshe, 1998.

Gao Gongqian 高拱乾. *Taiwan fu zhi* 台湾府志 [Taiwan Prefecture Gazetteer]. Taibei: Taiwan yinhang jingji yanjiushi, 1960.

Gao Heng 高恒. *Qin-han jiandu zhong fazhi wenshu jikao* 秦汉简牍中法制文书辑考 [A Study on the Legal Documents in the Bamboo and Wooden Slips of Qin and Han Dynasties]. Beijing: Sheke wenxian chubanshe, 2008.

Han Xiutao 韩秀桃. *Ming Qing huizhou de minjian jiufen ji qi jiejue* 明清徽州的民间纠纷及其解决 [Local Dispute Resolution in Ming-Qing Huizhou]. Hefei: Anhui daxue chubanshe, 2004.

Hansen, Valerie. *Negotiating Daily Life in Traditional China: How Ordinary People Used Contracts, 600–1400*. New Haven: Yale University Press, 1995.

He Ning 何宁. *Huainanzi jishi* 淮南子集释 [Commentaries on Huainanzi]. Beijing: Zhonghua shuju, 1998.

He Peifu 何培夫 et al. *Taiwan diqu xiancun beijie tuzhi: tainan xian pian* 台湾地区现存碑碣图志：台南县篇 [Illustrations of Taiwan Old Inscriptions: Tainan County]. Taibei: Guoli zhongyang tushuguan, 1992.

———. *Taiwan diqu xiancun beijie tuzhi: Tainan shi pian* 台湾地区现存碑碣图志：台南市篇 [Illustrations of Taiwan Old Inscriptions: Tainan City]. Taibei: Guoli zhongyang tushuguan, 1992.

———. *Taiwan diqu xiancun beijie tuzhi: Jiayi xianshi pian* 台湾地区现存碑碣图志：嘉义县市篇 [Illustrations of Taiwan Old Inscriptions: Jiayi County and Jiayi City]. Taibei: Guoli zhongyang tushuguan, 1994.

———. *Taiwan diqu xiancun beijie tuzhi: Pingdong xian taidong xian pian* 台湾地区现存碑碣图志：屏东县.台东县篇 [Illustrations of Taiwan Old Inscriptions: Pingdong County and Taidong County]. Taibei: Guoli zhongyang tushuguan, 1995.

———. *Taiwan diqu xiancun beijie tuzhi: Taizhong xianshi hualian xian pian* 台湾地区现存碑碣图志：台中县市.花莲县篇 [Illustrations of Taiwan Old Inscriptions: Taizhong County, Taizhong City, and Hualian County]. Taibei: Guoli zhongyang tushuguan, 1997.

———. *Taiwan diqu xiancun beijie tuzhi: zhanghua xian pian* 台湾地区现存碑碣图志：彰化县篇 [Illustrations of Taiwan Old Inscriptions: Zhanghua County]. Taibei: Guoli zhongyang tushuguan, 1997.

———. *Taiwan diqu xiancun beijie tuzhi: Xinzhu xianshi pian* 台湾地区现存碑碣图志：新竹县市篇 [Illustrations of Taiwan Old Inscriptions: Taipei City and Taoyuan County]. Taibei: Guoli zhongyang tushuguan, 1998.

———. *Taiwan diqu xiancun beijie tuzhi: Taibei shi taoyuan xian pian* 台湾地区现存碑碣图志：台北市.桃园县篇 [Illustrations of Taiwan Old Inscriptions: Taipei City and Taoyuan County]. Taibei: Guoli zhongyang tushuguan, 1999.

———. *Taiwan diqu xiancun beijie tuzhi: Taibei xian pian* 台湾地区现存碑碣图志：台北县篇 [Illustrations of Taiwan Old Inscriptions: Taipei County]. Taibei: Guoli zhongyang tushuguan, 1999.

Hong Jianrong 洪健荣. "Dang 'fengshui' chengwei 'huoshui': qingdai Taiwan shehui de fengshui jiufen 当'风水'成为'祸水'：清代台湾社会的风水纠纷 [When 'Wind and Water' Became 'Harmful Water': Fengshui Disputes in Qing-ruled Taiwan]." *Tainan wenhua* 台南文化 [Tainan Culture] 61 (2007): 27–54, 62 (2008): 1–46.

Huang Fusan 黄富三, and Weng Jiayin 翁佳音. "Qingdai Taiwan hanren kenhu jieceng chulun 清代台湾汉人垦户阶层初论 [A Preliminary Study on Han Chinese Land Developers in Qing-ruled Taiwan]." In *Jindai Zhongguo quyushi yantaohui lunwenji shangce* 近代中国区域史研讨会上册 [Proceedings of the Conference on the Regional Histories of Modern China; Volume: Shang], edited by Zhongyang yanjiuyuan jindaishi yanjiusuo 中央研究院近代史研究所, 249–70. Taibei: Zhongyang yanjiuyuan jindaishi yanjiusuo, 1984.

Huang, Philip C.C. *Civil Justice in China: Representation and Practice in the Qing*. Stanford: Stanford University Press, 1996.

Inō Kanori 伊能嘉矩. Taiwan sheng wenxian weiyuanhui 台湾省文献委员会, trans. *Taiwan bunkashi* 台湾文化志 [A History of Taiwanese Culture]. Taizhong: Taiwan sheng wenxian weiyuanhui, 1985–1991.

Jiang Yuanshu 蒋元枢. *Chongxiu Tai jun ge jianzhu tushuo* 重修台郡各建筑图说 [Illustrations of Restoring Buildings in Taiwan]. Taibei: Taiwan yinhang jingji yanjiushi, 1970.

Jones, William, trans. *The Great Qing Code*. Oxford: Clarendon Press, 1994.

Katz, Paul. *Divine Justice: Religion And The Development Of Chinese Legal Culture*. New York: Routledge, 2009.

Kawakatsu Mamoru 川胜守. "Min Shin irai, Kōnan shichin no kyōdō bochi. Gizuka: Shanghai fuki shichin shi no gizuka wo chūshin toshite 明清以来、江南市鎮の共同墓地・义冢: 上海付近市镇志の义冢を中心として [Communal Cemeteries in Jiangnan Cities and Towns: A Study of Shanghai and Its Surrounding Area]." *Kyūshū Daigaku Tōyōshi ronshū* 九州大学东洋史论集 [The Oriental Studies (of Kyushu University)] 24 (1996): 75–107.

Li Guilian 李贵连. “Wanqing ‘jiudi zhengfa’ kao 晚清‘就地正法’考 [“ ‘Summary Execution’ during the Late Qing Period].” *Fashang yanjiu* 法商研究 [Studies in Law and Business] 1 (1994): 81–87.

Li Xiue 李秀娥. *Taiwan chuantong shengming liyi* 台湾传统生命礼仪 [The Traditional Life Rituals of Taiwan]. Taizhong: Chenxing, 2003.

Lian Heng 连横. *Taiwan tongshi* 台湾通史 [General History of Taiwan], Taiwan wenxian congkan No. 128. Taibei: Taiwan yinhang jingji yanjiushi, 1962.

Lin Baoxuan 林保萱. *Xihe linshi liuwu zupu* 西河林氏六屋族谱 [Genealogy of Lin Family in Xihe]. Taizhong: Taiwan sheng wenxian weiyuanhui, 1982.

Lin Wenkai 林文凯. “Tudi qiyue zhixu yu difang zhili: shijiu shiji Taiwan danxin diqu tudi kaiken yu tudi susong de lishi zhidu fenxi 土地契约秩序与地方治理：十九世纪台湾淡新地区土地开垦与诉讼的历史制度分析 [Local Governance and the Social Order of Land Contract: A Historical Institutionalist Analysis for Land Reclamation and Land Litigation in Danxin Region of the Nineteenth Century Taiwan].” Ph.D. diss., National Taiwan University, 2006.

Lü Buwei 吕不韦. *Lüshi chunqiu* 吕氏春秋 [Spring and Autumn of Master Lü]. Shanghai: Shanghai guji, 2002.

Macauley, Melissa. *Social Power and Legal Culture: Litigation Masters in Late Imperial China*. Stanford: Stanford University Press, 1998.

Qiu Xiutang 邱秀堂. *Taiwan beibu beiwen jicheng* 台湾北部碑文集成 [Collection of Inscriptions from North Taiwan]. Taibei: Taibei shi wenxian weiyuanhui, 1986.

Rinji Taiwan Kyūkan Chōsakai 临时台湾习惯调查会. *Rinji Taiwan kyūkan chōsakai dai ichi bu chōsa dai san kai hōkokusho: furoku sankōsho* 临时台湾习惯调查会第一部调查第三回报告书台湾私法附录参考书 [Provisional Committee of Investigating Taiwanese Custom]. Taibei: Rinji Taiwan Kyūkan Chōsakai, 1909.

Shen Zhiqi 沈之奇. *lü jizhu* 大清律辑注 [The Great Qing Code with Collected Commentarires]. Beijing: Falü chubanshe, 2000.

Shi Tianfu 施添福. *Qingdai Taiwan de diyu shehui: Zhuqian diqu de lishi dilixue yanjiu* 清代台湾的地域社会：竹堑地区的历史地理学研究 [The Local Society of Taiwan during the Qing Dynasty: Studies in the Historical Geography of Zhuqian]. Xinzhu: Xinzhu xian wenhuaju, 2001.

Snyder-Reinke, Jeffrey. *Dry Spells: State Rainmaking and Local Governance in Late Imperial China*. Cambridge: Harvard University Press, 2009.

Sommer, Matthew. *Sex, Law, and Society in Late Imperial China*. Stanford: Stanford University Press, 2000.

Sōsaku Ishizaka 石坂庄作. *Kita Taiwan no kohi* 北台湾の古碑 [Ancient Inscriptions in North Taiwan]. Taibei: Taiwan Nichinichi Shinpōsha, 1923.

Su Liming 苏黎明. *Quanzhou jiazu wenhua* 泉州家族文化 [The Family Culture of Quanzhou]. Beijing: Zhongguo yanshi chubanshe, 2000.

Suzuki Hidemitsu 铃木秀光. "Shinmatsu shūchi seihō kō 清末就地正法考 [Summary Execution during the Late Qing Period]." *Tōyō Bunka Kenkyūjo kiyō* 东洋文化研究所纪要 [The Memoirs of the Institute of Oriental Culture] 145 (2004): 1–56.

———. "Cong danxin dang'an kan qingchao houqi xingshi shenpan zhidu de yiban 从淡新档案看清朝后期刑事审判制度的一斑 [A Preliminary Study on the Practice of Late-Qing Criminal Justice: From the Case of Danxin Archive]." Conference paper, Academic Conference for Danxin Archive, National Taiwan University, Taibei, July 15, 2008.

———. "Zhangbi kao: qingdai zhongqi sixing anjian chuli de yixiang kaocha 杖毙考：清代中期死刑案件处理的一项考察 [Execution by Heavy Bamboo Stroke: A Study on Mid-Qing Capital Punishment Procedure]." In *Shijie xuezhe lun zhongguo chuantong falü wenhua, 1644–1911* 世界学者论中国传统法律文化, 1644–1911 [Recent International Scholarship on Traditional Chinese Law], edited by Zhang Shiming, Thomas Buoye, and Na Heya 娜鹤雅, 209–34. Beijing: Falü chubanshe, 2010.

Taiwan sheng wenxian weiyuanhui, trans. *Taiwan guanxi jishi* 台湾惯习记事 [Taiwan Folk Custom]. Taizhong: Taiwan sheng wenxian weiyuanhui, 1991.

Taiwan yinhang jingji yanjiushi 台湾银行经济研究室 et al. *Xinzhu xian zhidu kao* 新竹县制度考 [The Institutions of Xinzhu County]. Taibei: Taiwan yinhang jingji yanjiushi, 1961.

———. *Xinzhu xian caifang ce* 新竹县采访册 [Xinzhu County Local History and Information Book]. Taibei: Taiwan yinhang jingji yanjiushi, 1962.

———. *Taiwan zhongbu beiwen jicheng* 台湾中部碑文集成 [Collection of Inscriptions from Central Taiwan]. Taibei: Taiwan yinhang jingji yanjiushi, 1962.

——— *Penghu ting zhi* 澎湖厅志 [Penghu Subprefecture Gazetteer]. Taibei: Taiwan yinhang jingji yanjiushi, 1963.

———. *Fujian shengli* 福建省例 [Provincial Regulations of Fujian]. Taibei: Taiwan yinhang jingji yanjiushi, 1964.

———. *Taiwan nanbu beiwen jicheng* 台湾南部碑文集成 [Collection of Inscriptions from South Taiwan]. Taibei: Taiwan yinhang jingji yanjiushi, 1966.

———. *Shubao fabing qin tai jishi canji* 述报法兵侵台纪事残辑 [Remnants on French Invasion to Taiwan during the Sino-French War]. Taibei: Taiwan yinhang jingji yanjiushi, 1968.

———. *Taiwan guanxi wenxian jiling* 台湾关系文献集零 [Some Documents about the History of Taiwan]. Taibei: Taiwan yinhang jingji yanjiushi, 1972.

Terada Hiroaki 寺田浩明. "Quanli yu yuanyi: qingdai tingsong he minzhong de minshifa zhixu 权利与冤抑：清代听讼和民众的民事法秩序 [Rights and Injustice: Civil Justice and Civil-Law Order of the Qing Dynasty People]," trans. by Wang Yaxin 王亚新. In *Ming Qing shiqi de minshi shenpan yu minjian qiyue*

明清时期的民事审判与契约 [Civil Justice and Civil Contract in the Ming-Qing Period], edited by Wang Yaxin 王亚新 and Liang Zhiping 梁治平, 191–265. Beijing: Falü chubanshe, 1998.

Tsu, Timothy. "Geomancy and the Environment in Premodern Taiwan." *Asian Folklore Studies* 56 (1997): 65–77.

Wang Shiqing 王世庆 ed. *Taiwan gongsi cang guwenshu* 台湾公私藏古文书, stored in Academia Sinica, Fu Sinian Library, 1977.

Wang Zijin 王子今. *Zhongguo daomu shi* 中国盗墓史 [A History of Chinese Tomb Robbery]. Beijing: Jiuzhou chubanshe, 2007.

Watson, James. "Standardizing the Gods: The Promotion of T'ien Hou ('Empress of Heaven') along the South China Coast, 960–1960." In *Popular Culture in Late Imperial China*, edited by David Johnson, Andrew J. Nathan, and Evelyn S. Rawski, 292–324. Berkeley: University of California Press, 1985.

Wu Xueming 吴学明. *Jinguangfu ken'ai yanjiu* 金广福垦隘研究 [A Study on Jinguangfu]. Xinzhu: Xinzhu xian wenhuaju, 2000.

Xue Yunsheng 薛允升. *Duli cunyi chongkanben* 读例存疑重刊本 [Questions about the Laws of Qing Dynasty: A Reprint and Annotated Version]. Edited by Huang, Jingjia 黄静嘉. Taibei: Chengwen, 1970.

Yang, Ch'ing K'un. K. *Religion in Chinese Society: A Study of Contemporary Functions and Some of Their Historical Factors*. Berkeley: University of California Press, 1961.

Yao Ying 姚莹. *Dongcha jilue* 东槎纪略 [A Brief Account of the Voyage to the East], Taiwan wenxian congkan No. 007. Taibei: Taiwan yinhang jingji yanjiushi, 1957.

Ye Chunrong 叶春荣. "Fengshui yu baoying: yige Taiwan nongcun de lizi 风水与报应：一个台湾农村的例子 [Geomancy and Retribution: A Case of a Taiwanese Village]." *Zhongyang yanjiuyuan minzuxue yanjiusuo jikan* 中央研究院民族学研究所集刊 88 (1999): 233–57.

Zelin, Madeleine. "Eastern Sichuan Coalmines in the Late Qing." In *Empire, Nation and Beyond: Chinese History in Late Imperial and Modern Times, A Festschrift in honor of Frederic Wakeman, Jr.*, edited by Joseph Esherick, Yeh Wen-hsin, and Madeleine Zelin, 105–22. Berkeley: Institute of East Asian Studies, University of California Berkeley, Center for Chinese Studies. 2006.

Zeng Guodong 曾国栋. "Cong shijinbei tantao qingdai taiwan de shehui xianxiang 从示禁碑探讨清代台湾的社会现象 [Qing-ruled Taiwan's Social Phenomenon: An Analysis of Banning Tablets]." *Shilian zazhi* 史联杂志 [Correspondence of Taiwan History and Relics] 35 (1999): 59–92.

Zhang Chuanyong 张传勇. "Hanba wei nue: Ming-Qing beifang diqu de 'da hanba' xisu 旱魃为虐: 明清北方地区的'打旱魃习俗' [The Drought Demon Brings Disaster: The Custom of 'Killing the Drought Demon' in North China during the Ming-Qing Period]." *Zhongguo shehui jingji shi yanjiu* 中国社会经济史研究 [The Journal of Chinese Social and Economic History] 4 (2009): 51–60.

Zhang Shiming 张世明. "Qingmo jiudi zhengfa zhidu yanjiu 清末就地正法制度研究 [The Institution of Summary Execution during the Late Qing Period]." *Zhengfa luncong* 政法论丛 [Journal of Political Science and Law] 1 (2012): 46–57, 2 (2012): 59–70.

Zhang Xiaoye 张小也. *Guan, min, yu fa: Ming Qing guojia yu jiceng shehui* 官、民、与法：明清国家与基层社会 [Official, Ordinary People, and Law: Ming-Qing State and Local Society]. Beijing: Zhonghua shuju, 2007.

Zhu Qingqi 祝庆祺 et al. *Xing'an huilan sanbian* 刑案汇览三编 [Conspectus of Penal Cases]. Beijing: Beijing guji chubanshe, 2000.

CHAPTER 4

Elite Engagement with the Judicial System in the Qing and Its Implications for Legal Practice and Legal Principle

Janet Theiss

Historians of Chinese law are much concerned these days with questions about the extent to which the Qing judicial system functioned according to the "rule of law," informed by ideas of justice, impartiality, and legal professionalism. Most research done on the Qing judicial system has been based on the vast extant case record of crimes and disputes involving commoners and, occasionally, lower level gentry. My current research into the legal entanglements of two elite Zhejiang families linked by marriage, the Wangs, an extremely wealthy merchant family, and the Feis, a long-respected family of officials, suggests that the Qing judicial system functioned very differently for the wealthy and well-connected than it did for commoners. Patterns of elite engagement with the judicial system had significant implications for judicial principle and practice that challenged the legitimacy and integrity of the judicial system. While historians commonly assume that the wealthy and powerful had the resources and *guanxi* either to avoid airing their conflicts in the courts or to prejudice judicial outcomes in their favor, little attention has been paid to the mechanisms of such evasion and manipulation and their effects. The legal system was a critical arena, for the interaction of local elites and officialdom, and its workings demonstrate the mutual dependence between the two that made legal process essentially a negotiation of power. Degree status, professional connections to officialdom from their own service in the bureaucracy, wealth, and business ties to local officials influenced both family decisions on how and when to take disputes to court and the response of local magistrates, prefects, and governors to their lawsuits.

Literati families were, of course, uniquely dependent on the state for their status, careers and reputation. Linked to officialdom through personal, political, professional and business networks, elite families encountered the judicial system not as fathers and mothers of the people, as the locus of state authority or justice, but as a set of relationships to be worked and manipulated. Local officials dealt with elites as allies, enemies, competitors, and sometimes creditors, within the complex web of local politics. In effect, magistrates,

© KONINKLIJKE BRILL NV, LEIDEN, 2015 | DOI 10.1163/9789004288492_006

prefects, and governors unavoidably had conflicts of interest and tangled connections with the elites whose cases entered their purview.

The Wang and Fei cases came into public focus (and into the historical record) in 1741, when the Governor of Zhejiang Province, Lu Zhuo, was impeached for taking advantage of his post for personal gain and accepting bribes from subordinates. The charges focused on several instances of officials bribing him with one or two thousand taels of silver to support their promotions and two intertwined cases in which the governor accepted bribes from women in the Fei and Wang families to prejudice the outcome of lawsuits resulting from internal family conflicts.

The Wang Family Inheritance Case

The first case involved the family of Wang Wenbo, a well-known poet and art collector from Tongxiang County, Zhejiang whose grandfather, a wealthy salt merchant, had migrated from Xiuning County, Anhui in the early Qing. Wenbo and his two older brothers, Wang Sen (1653–1726) and Wang Wengui, known in Tongxiang as "the three brothers of the Wang Clan," were all highly accomplished poets, who were friends of prominent scholars like Huang Zongxi (1610–1695). After Wenbo's death, a dispute broke out between his eldest son, Wang Zhaojing and his second son's widow, Wang Sun Shi, who, having no sons of her own, had adopted one of Zhaojing's sons as an heir. Wang Sun Shi was anxious to divide the property between the heirs quickly and sent her adopted son in 1738 (QL 3) to file a petition in the Jiaxing prefectural court requesting division. It is not clear exactly why she wanted the intervention of the court in this matter, but one might surmise from the later unfolding of the case and subsequent behavior of Wang Zhaojing, that he was, in fact, trying to give her adoptive heir less than his fair share. As soon as her plaint was filed, Wang Zhaojing and his eldest son Wang Kentang, fled to Suzhou to avoid appearing in court and the case was suspended with the prefect ordering that the lineage mediate the dispute on its own. The inability and/or unwillingness of county magistrates to exercise their authority in civil disputes within large lineages is a common theme in this and the Fei family case as it is in the case record in general.[1] But given the fact that the status and wealth of the Wang and Fei families far exceeded that of the magistrates and given their

1 See, e.g., Maura Dykstra's paper presented at the International Workshop on Chinese Legal History, Culture and Modernity at Columbia University on May 4, 2012, organized by Madeline Zelin and Li Chen.

subsequent ability to bypass the county and prefecture and take their cases to the provincial level, their initial filing of plaints at the local level seems to be a procedural convenience without any expectation of resolution at this stage or any fear of being caught. There is no indication that the Jiaxing prefect made any attempt to contact his counterparts in Suzhou for assistance in apprehending Zhaojing and Kentang. Families like the Wangs may well have assumed that local officials already overloaded with underfunded mandates would not have the means or motivation to track them down for court proceedings that were likely to be complicated.

In any case, according to Governor-General Depei, who was in charge of the investigation of the corruption charges against Governor Lu Zhuo, when Lu took office in 1739 he was sympathetic to Wang Sun Shi's position.[2] That same year, Governor Lu transferred in a new prefect to Jiaxing, Yang Jingzhen. With the arrival of the new governor and new prefect, Wang Sun Shi spearheaded a complex strategy of bribery to get a hearing for her case and a favorable judgment. As wealthy merchant families, both Wang Sun Shi's natal family and the Wangs were well connected within the merchant community and within official circles. Wang Sun Shi took full advantage of these connections. She enlisted the help of her brother Sun Shimian, Wang Shideng, a Hangzhou copper merchant who had once served as a clerk in the Provincial Treasurer's office, and two other copper merchants, Qian Zhoushu and Fan Sinian. Provincial and local officials were especially beholden to copper merchants, who imported the copper used by mints in Zhejiang and Jiangsu to make coins and who made loans to officials for administrative and personal use.[3] It is a commonplace of Qing history that low salaries and inadequate funding for local administration made officials at the county, prefectural and provincial level chronically dependent on merchant payment of customary fees and philanthropic contributions to deal with crises.[4] The responsibility of officials in Zhejiang and Jiangsu for procurement of copper for provincial mints exacerbated official dependence on such merchants, especially in the period between 1736–1744 when revisions to the copper importation regulations stipulated that these two provinces were responsible for convincing merchants who imported

2 *Lufu zouzhe* 录副奏折 [Copies of Memorials at the Grand Council], Memorial of Depei, QL 6/6/23.

3 Helen Dunstan, "Safely Supping with the Devil: The Qing State and Its Merchant Suppliers of Copper," *Late Imperial China* 13, no. 2 (December 1992): 42–81 and Hans Ulrich Vogel, "China's Central Monetary Policy, 1644–1800," *Late Imperial China* 8, no. 2 (Dec. 1987): 1–52.

4 Madeleine Zelin, *The Magistrate's Tael: Rationalizing Fiscal Reform in Eighteenth-Century Ch'ing China* (Berkeley: University of California Press, 1984), 46–71.

the copper to sell them sufficient quantities at fixed official rates that were often below market price. Copper deficits were a common problem for such officials.[5] In his previous posting in Quzhou, Prefect Yang had become friends with Wang Shideng because Wang arranged for Yang to borrow copper from a relative who imported it from Japan in order to make up a deficit from another merchant.

Sun Shimian and Wang Shideng approached Lu Zhuo's brother Lu Bian, who as the Commissioner of the Zhejiang West Road Market (*Zhejiang xilu changdashi*) was well connected with merchant and official circles, to offer him a bribe to use his influence with Lu Zhuo.[6] They paid Lu Bian 3,000 taels of silver and had him give Lu Zhuo 10,000 taels. After Lu Zhuo accepted the plaint, they sent him another 20,000 taels with the request that Lu Zhuo allow the division of the property rather than letting the lineage mediate the matter itself. This silver was transmitted by Zhang Zihui, the head of the Provincial Office of Military Affairs (*fu zhongjun*) who handed it over to a senior official (*tangguan*) surnamed Yao. At the same time, Wang Sun Shi had Wang Shideng and the two other copper merchants negotiate with Prefect Yang Jingzhen, offering him 30,000 taels of silver and asking him to give Lu Zhuo 50,000. Wang Sun Shi sent her brother Sun Shimian to deliver the money to Prefect Yang at his home in Yangzhou.

The result of this staggering quantity of bribe money was that Prefect Yang re-opened the case, arrested Wang Zhaojing, and incarcerated him in the prefectural prison on the grounds that since he had earlier escaped to the city of Suzhou to avoid the case and his son was still in hiding, he was a flight risk. In Depei's interpretation, Yang Jingzhen "saw how the wind was blowing and prejudicially protected Sun Shi while flagrantly humiliating Wang Zhaojing" (*yangcheng fengzhi piantan* Sun Shi *jiang* Wang Zhaojing *hengjiao zheru*).[7] In other words, he took the cue from Lu Zhuo to settle the case as Wang Sun Shi wished.

---

5 See Dunstan, "Safely Supping with the Devil," and Vogel, "China's Central Monetary Policy."

6 The appointment of brothers in the same province would appear to violate rules of avoidance for officials, however, according to a precedent established by the Yongzheng emperor in 1724, these rules did not apply to special appointees like governors, especially if the relative in the subordinate position had been appointed first. See R. Kent Guy, *Qing Governors and Their Provinces: The Evolution of Territorial Administration in China, 1644–1796* (Seattle: University of Washington Press, 2010), 174, and personal communication. Of course this case illustrates precisely the dangers of allowing relatives to serve in the same jurisdiction.

7 *Lufu zouzhe*, Memorial of Depei, QL6/6/23.

In the 7th month of 1739, Wang Kentang from his hideout (seemingly one of his houses) in Suzhou initiated his own series of bribes to the prefect and the governor through various negotiators. First, he asked a senior family relative from Huzhou, the 83-year-old Wang Shao to intercede with Prefect Yang on behalf of Wang Zhaojing. According to Wang Shao's testimony in the impeachment proceedings against Prefect Yang, he got involved because he was elderly, suggesting perhaps that he would be immune from criticism or perhaps that his lobbying would carry more weight than that of another family member.[8] He went to Wang Shideng's house in Hangzhou to ask him to intercede with Prefect Yang to request that he give him a little face (*shuoqing quanxie timian*) and tell him that they were willing to give him a gift in gratitude (*songta xieyi*). Wang Shideng refused to help. Wang Kentang then consulted with Zhang Baotian, a 72-year-old relative of Wang Zhaojing's who was also his grandson's tutor, and one of his retainers, Yu Shengfan who was also an acquaintance of Wang Shideng. Zhang and Yu visited Kentang in his hideout and reported that since Prefect Yang displayed "such a stern tone and severe countenance, he could not be without enmity" (*ruci yansheng lise bu'neng wuyuan*) towards Wang Zhaojing. When Zhang then visited Zhaojing in prison, Zhaojing said "I have committed no crime in this property dispute. It's not worth using silver" (*wo wei jiacai de shi bing bu fanfa, fanbuzhao yong yinzi*).

Zhaojing changed his strategy when Prefect Yang brought him into court and told him he was "a rich man without benevolence who is cheating a widow" (*weifu buren qiling guafu*). Prefect Yang claimed he merely wanted Zhaojing to know shame, but Zhaojing and his supporters interpreted this as abusive humiliation. In the meantime, too, Zhaojing fell ill in prison. So Zhang Baotian and Yu Shengfan again sought out Wang Shideng, who was at the dock where he was meeting his boat with an incoming shipment of copper. They asked him to plead with Prefect Yang for a reexamination of the case to "give him some face" and offered him 18,000 taels of silver. This time Wang Shideng went to Prefect Yang with the offer of the bribe, but Yang refused, emphasizing his view that Zhaojing was a wealthy man without benevolence trying to cheat a widow. Yu, Zhang and Wang Kentang himself went again to Wang Shideng's boat to beg him to try again. At first he refused, but they offered to increase the bribe to 28,000 and Wang took this offer to Prefect Yang. This time, the prefect

8 All of the details of the bribery negotiation process are from the routine memorial on Prefect Yang's impeachment for accepting the bribes. See *Like tiben: jiucan chufen lei* 吏科提本:纠参处分类 [Routine Memorials to the Ministry of Personnel: Impeachment and Discipline], Memorial of Lu Zhuo, QL6/6/17.

finally agreed to accept the silver but told Wang that it had to be delivered to his house in Yangzhou. He also told him, "Do not tell people outside that I wanted silver. Just say that I did you a favor so as to avoid any criticism outside" (*ni zai waibian buyaoshuo wo yao yinzi, zhishi shuo wo songqing yu ni de yimian waimian zhaoyao*). This intriguing comment suggests that the prefect thought popular opinion would condone the *guanxi* logic of prejudicing a verdict as a personal favor but not the purchase of a favorable verdict with a bribe.

The next day, Yang released Wang Zhaojing from prison and Yu went to Suzhou to get the silver. The Wang family accountant delivered 20 packets of silver to Yu Shengfan's boat. Wang Shideng picked it up, kept his portion of 4,000 taels and took the rest to Prefect Yang. The prefect used some of it pay off a debt and some to cover his expenses for an official trip to Beijing, but when he returned to Jiaxing, he told Wang Shideng that he regretted taking the bribe and asked Wang to return the remainder of the silver to Wang Zhaojing's family. He was impeached before he could do this. Yang Jingzhen insists in his confession that he incarcerated Wang Zhaojing because he was a flight risk, not because he wanted to extort money from him. While admitting that taking the bribe was wrong, he also stressed his reluctance to take the money and claimed that when he judged the case he "made an impartial verdict and was not at all crooked" (*xiangjie jiacai de an doushi pinggong duangei bingwu wangqu*). Of course, this assertion that he acted in accordance with established judicial norms is belied by his comment to Wang Shideng about doing favors. Still, this defense does indicate that judicial norms mattered in assessments of official integrity and competence. In fact, the outcome after all the bribery, was Zhaojing's release from prison and the official authorization of division of property between Wang Wenbo's two grandsons. This ruling in effect overturned the previous prefect's decision to let the Wang family mediate the dispute itself but was in accordance with inheritance law.

Whatever his motivations, Prefect Yang was very concerned about angering public opinion. According to Governor-General Depei, this case was revealed because "popular criticism was boiling over" so much that Depei began an investigation. To cover his tracks in the matter, Governor Lu Zhuo then quickly launched his own investigation and impeached Prefect Yang for accepting bribes from Wang Zhaojing. His indictment of Prefect Yang made no mention of Madame Wang's own bribery. Indeed, he affirmed the prefect's claim that he judged her case fairly, dividing the property equally in half in accordance with the law and that far from persecuting Wang Zhaojing, he simply accused him of "being a wealthy man without benevolence who tried to cheat and humiliate a widow" and wanted to make him "know shame." Lu's own acceptance of bribes in the Wang case was not revealed until his indictment in 1741 after he had also accepted bribes in the intrafamilial lawsuit of the Fei family.[9]

Between them, Wang Sun Shi and Wang Zhaojing paid a total of 30,000 taels of silver to Prefect Yang, 50,000 to Governor Lu Zhuo, and over 50,000 to the various go-betweens, negotiators, yamen clerks, and runners who facilitated the transactions. The payments were all made in installments over a period of less than a month, to obtain particular goals: some to procure a hearing for Wang Sun Shi's petition, some later to ensure her desired outcome of property division, some to get Wang Zhaojing out of prison, and final payments to express gratitude for the outcome. I would argue, however, that the twisting of judicial procedure in this case cannot be explained simply through a rubric of corruption. Studies of the endemic corruption in eighteenth-century China have demonstrated that it was a complex phenomenon caused by a variety of factors including the chronic underfunding of the bureaucracy, low official salaries and the expansion of the commercial money economy which promoted both a culture of extravagance and a fee-for-service mentality in which anything could be bought and everything had to be paid for.[10] Susumu Fuma has argued that given the variety and variability of fees and payments for litigation, there was no clear distinction between bribery and payment for services rendered.[11] Nancy Park has also emphasized the blurriness of definitions of corruption within the law, official circles and popular opinion caused

9 Lu Zhuo's complicity in the Wang family bribery scheme of course calls into question the accuracy of his accounts of Prefect Yang's actions in his routine memorial indicting him. It is always impossible to assess fully the authenticity of information in such case files. But here because of the correspondence between the account of the bribery in Lu Zhuo's memorial on the prefect and Depei's memorial on Lu Zhuo's corruption, I think the basic narrative of the individuals involved, the process for transmitting bribes, and the language used by participants to explain them is probably fairly accurate.

10 See for example, Guo Chengkang 郭成康 and Zheng Baofeng 郑宝凤, "Qianlong nianjian qintan wenti yanjiu 乾隆年间侵贪问题研究 [Research on the Problem of Corruption in the Qianlong Era]," *Qingshi yanjiu ji* 清史研究集 [Collection of Qing Studies] 8 (Beijng: Zhongguo renmin daxue chubanshe, 1997); Nancy Park, "Corruption in Eighteenth-Century China," *The Journal of Asian Studies* 56, no. 4 (Nov. 1997): 967–1005; and Bradley Reed, *Talons and Teeth: County Clerks and Runners in the Qing Dynasty* (Stanford: Stanford University Press, 2000). See also Nancy Park's paper presented at the International Workshop on Chinese Legal History, Culture and Modernity at Columbia University in May 2012.

11 Susumu Fuma, "Litigation Masters and the Litigation System of Ming and Qing China," *International Journal of Asian Studies* 4, no. 1 (2007): 79–111.

in large part by a gift-giving culture that legitimated the exchange of goods and favors to build and maintain social and political relationships. Wang Sun Shi's intermediaries use the language of "giving a gift out of gratitude" to describe the bribe and Prefect Yang comments in his defense that he wanted his acceptance of the money to be presented as essentially a gift in gratitude for a favor. These statements attest to the blurriness of the boundaries between gifts, fees for service, and bribes that may have been intentional and certainly worked in the interests of those on the giving and receiving ends of such transactions.

The Wang case shows that transmission of bribes by elite families to resolve their lawsuits required the use of social, business and political networks that linked elite families to state officials. The process of negotiating bribes mobilized these networks to support and actively lobby for particular legal outcomes. Bribery was thus integral to the process of mediating such cases in a way that did not offend local merchant and literati elites who could make trouble for a governor, let alone a magistrate or prefect. Yet the motivations of the many people who accepted bribes varied and the money did not simply purchase a single outcome. The officials adjudicating a case like this were influenced by moral and political agendas in addition to money and, indeed, the bribes did not just present an opportunity for personal gain, but for the maintenance of good working relationships with local elites.

It is noteworthy that neither Wang Sun Shi nor Wang Zhaojing seems to have feared the consequences of airing their disgraceful family squabbles in court (in contrast with members of the Fei family who cared deeply about this, as we will see later) or about their bribery becoming public news. Zhaojing's behavior suggests that he thought his wealth and vast connections across several cities put him out of reach of the law, while Wang Sun Shi saw the court as providing external leverage that was much needed in such a powerful family. For both, the yamen, to which they were connected through a dense network of diverse ties, was merely an extension of their social and business circles, not a source of authority. By incarcerating Wang Zhaojing, Prefect Yang tried to assert the superior authority of the state, but that authority, already shown to be quite tenuous by Zhaojing's effective escape to Suzhou earlier, dissipated completely with the lobbying and transmission of bribes by Wang Shideng, a merchant to whom he was beholden.

Given the power and wealth of the Wang family this case carried many dangers for Prefect Yang and Governor Lu. Wang Zhaojing and Wang Kentang's ability to abscond to a well-known hideout in Suzhou to avoid capture for trial proceedings demonstrates their ability to evade official control and the strength of their political alliances. The enormous size of these bribes, of course, illustrates the Qianlong era culture of extravagance and greed that was one of the underlying causes of corruption.[12] Angering either party in this family fight would have made their official duties much more difficult. The offering of such huge bribes also emphasized to Yang Jingzhen and Lu Zhuo the power of the merchant community and the depth of their dependence on it. In accepting the bribes, which Yang, at least, seems to have been reluctant to do, these officials were seemingly motivated by the need for money and the desire to maintain good relations with the merchant community, as well as the temptations of wealth. Indeed, the career of Wang Shideng as copper merchant and clerk in the Provincial Treasury office demonstrates the permeability of the boundaries between officials and merchants. At various points, Prefect Yang invokes each of the elements of Qing judicial principle, *qing* in the reference to doing favors, *li* in the reference to protecting chaste widows, and *fa* in the reference to ruling by principles of impartiality. But in the end he bows to political pressure, which was made more palatable with a bribe.

The Fei Family Adultery Case

If the Wang case exemplifies how merchant ties to officials could distort legal process and principle, the Fei case demonstrates the judicial implications of ties between scholar-official families and local officials. The case had its beginnings in 1733 (YZ 11), when, three years after the death of his father who had just been appointed Governor of Hunan Province, Fei Yuyou, left his home in Huzhou to become an expectant official in Beijing.[13] He left behind his wife, Fei Li Shi, who had been managing the large Fei family compound for several years and two sons, two daughters, and a daughter-in-law, ranging in age from 16 to 22 *sui*. Their eldest son, Fei Shupian was married to Wang Sun Shi's daughter. In 1737 (Qianlong 2) Fei Yuyou arranged to hire a tutor for his two sons back home in Huzhou. The tutor, a *shengyuan* named Xu Yantan who was a maternal cousin of his two charges, Fei Shupian and Fei Shunan, moved into their quarters to take up his duties. At some point within the first year of his service in the Fei household, Xu Yantan and Fei Li Shi began to have an affair. In the

12 Guo Chengkang and Zheng Baofeng emphasize this point in "Qianlong nianjian qintan wenti yanjiu."

13 The following discussion of the case is all based on a single very large case file from the Number One Historical Archive in Beijing: *Xingke tiben: hunyin jianqing lei* 刑科题本: 婚姻奸情类 [Routine Memorials to the Ministry of Justice: Marriage and Adultery], QL5/7/8.

fourth month of 1739 (QL 4) their relationship was exposed when Fei Li Shi's maid, Guanhua, revealed love letters she had carried back and forth to a senior family servant, Wang Wancheng, with whom she was herself having an affair. Wang then copied the letters and showed them to the Fei family head, Yuyou's elder brother Fei Qianliu, a former Circuit Intendant who came home to head the household after being impeached for mishandling a homicide case. What transpired next was the subject of much controversy.

According to Fei Li Shi's version of events, one night in the fourth month of 1739, after she and her family had retired for the night, Fei Qianliu led a posse of some ten people, including his brother, Fei Luxiang, his nephew, Fei Zifu, Fei Li Shi's own brother, Li Zhoule (who was not informed of what Qianliu intended to do), and several servants, including senior family retainer, Wang Wancheng, to Fei Li Shi's house. They barged into the study where Tutor Xu was sleeping with his students, ordered him to get up and accused him of having illicit sex with Fei Li Shi, waving a stack of love letters as proof. Tutor Xu protested his innocence saying that the handwriting was not his. But Qianliu told him that the servant Wang Wancheng had discovered the letters and recopied them to show them to his master. Qianliu drew a sword to threaten Tutor Xu into writing a letter of apology for his misdeeds and resignation. Fei Li Shi's brother came to her quarters to tell her what was happening and she ran out and tried to reason with her brother-in-law, who, in her words, "humiliated and cursed me saying that I was a woman who had committed one of the seven offenses justifying divorce."[14] She stated that she then ran back to her room outraged, wanting to kill herself, but was dissuaded by her brother.

The next day, she claimed, she tried to see her mother-in-law, Fei Jinwu's widow, Fei Fan Shi, the matriarch of the family, but Qianliu had people block the way to prevent her from entering the gate. Left with no options, she went home with her brother to seek the help of her father, Li Zilan. The next day, the 15th, one of Qianliu's servants delivered a writ of divorce to her family's house forbidding her from returning to her husband's house. Qianliu also had her four children along with her furniture and belongings moved to his own house and pressured her eldest son, Fei Shupian, to sign a deed selling her house to another member of the lineage for 600 taels of silver. Shupian received 100 taels while Qianliu took 400 and another 100 was to be paid later.

According to Depei's interpretation of the case in his investigation of Lu Zhuo, "[Fei Li Shi's] indecent behavior became known and [Fei Li Shi's eldest son] Shupian often wept to his uncle Qianliu imploring him to do something

14 In addition to adultery, the seven offenses included childlessness, unfiliality to parents-in-law, quarrelsomeness, stealing, jealousy, and malignant disease.

about it. Qianliu felt this matter concerned the family's reputation and so on the one hand, sent a letter to [his brother in] the capital and on the other, requested orders from his mother to order Li Shi to return home temporarily to her family and had Xu Yantan dismissed. He led his brothers … to audit Yuyou's household wealth and property and then handed a list over to Shupian and his brother to keep. The money from the sale of the house was handed over to Shupian to await Yuyou's return."

In the seventh month of the fourth year of the reign of the Qianlong Emperor (1739), Fei Li Shi filed a plaint in the county court against the family head Fei Qianliu, his younger brother, Fei Zifu, and the nephew, Fei Luxiang. She accused them of slandering her chastity with a false accusation of adultery, divorcing her without her husband's consent, and confiscating her property. According to her plaint, Fei Qianliu conspired with a resentful senior family servant, one Wang Wancheng, to forge 16 love letters attributed to her and Xu Yantan to slander them. She accused Fei Qianliu of "conspiring with the wayward servant, Wang Wancheng, and others to baselessly and falsely accuse [me] of having illicit sex with the private tutor, Government Student (*shengyuan*) Xu Yantan. Together with Fei Luxiang, Fei Zifu, and others, [Fei Qianliu] then [issued a writ of] divorce and forced me to return [to my family]. [He] sold my rooms and confiscated my property."

As in the Wang case, the magistrate declared that this was an internal family matter (an extremely messy one at that) and declined to intervene. So in the ninth month, Fei Li Shi took her suit directly to the Governor, Lu Zhuo, with a series of bribes. She did so without the assent of her husband, who read about the lawsuit in the Peking Gazette and was deeply distraught at the damage it would do to the family's reputation and his own career. She consulted with a pettifogger who advised her that Wang Sun Shi (of the case above) had bribed the governor's staff in her own inheritance case and was thus "familiar with the narrow paths around the Governor."[15] So Fei Li Shi relied on Wang Sun Shi's connections to make contact with the staff of Governor Lu's yamen, using her own natal relatives, including her brother and two others, to represent her in negotiations. According to Depei's investigation, Wang Sun Shi, worried about a female relative's adultery damaging the family reputation, "naturally wanted to overturn the case and cleanse her reputation, so she represented her in squandering money." Lu Zhuo had a secretary surnamed Mei, who was a Yangzhou man and Wang Sun Shi's mother's family was from Yangzhou and knew him.

15 The description of the bribery process is from Depei's memorial, cited above, reporting on his investigation of the charges against Lu Zhuo. *Lufu zouzhe*, Memorial of Depei, QL6/6/23.

So she directed Fei Li Shi's relatives Zhao Baoshan and Zhang Guoqian to enlist Mei's help to conspire with the governor's inner secretary Chen Peicai to look after the case when it crossed Governor Lu Zhuo's desk. They first gave Mei 160 taels of silver. Then after the plaint was made, they also gave Chen Peicai 300 taels. Fei Li Shi was afraid that if the case were tried in her hometown of Huzhou, "popular opinion in Huzhou would be outraged and difficult to quell." So she requested that it be moved to the Hangzhou Provincial Court, sending Peicai another 120 taels to facilitate the move. The money was actually handed over to Chen Peicai at his residence in Hangzhou by Zhao Baoshan, Zhang Guoqian and Fei Li Shi's older brother Li Gongfu.

Fei Li Shi's bribes facilitated access to the ear of the Governor and many manipulations of judicial procedure. The conclusion presented in the original case file finds Fei Li Shi to be a chaste woman who was the victim of a slander perpetrated entirely by Wang Wancheng who resented his mistress for firing him after discovering him having sex with another servant, and resented Tutor Xu for meddling in family business and suggesting that Wang was embezzling rents from the family's land. The magistrate, under Lu Zhuo's instructions, rejected Fei Li Shi's accusation that Qianliu masterminded the slander and instead supported his own claim that he had merely been too gullible in believing Wang's story. Yet the magistrate does condemn Qianliu's failure to investigate the slander before jeopardizing the life and reputation of a chaste woman. This was a verdict that amounted to a kind of compromise, salvaging some face for both Fei Li Shi and Fei Qianliu as head of the family by having the servant take the fall for the whole incident.

The testimonies recorded in the Board of Punishments' routine memorial on the case are full of anomalies and unanswered questions, suggesting manipulation of witnesses and twisting of facts to produce the awkward compromise Lu Zhuo wanted. The assessment of the servant Wang's guilt turned ultimately on an evaluation of his literacy level in comparison with that of Fei Li Shi. The interrogation of Wang is one of the more awkward sections of the case file, marked by abrupt changes in story, failure to reproduce the characters in the courtroom with full accuracy, and obvious manipulation of the evidence of his writing ability. The nature of Fei Li Shi's literacy remains suspiciously vague in the case record. Her son Shupian claims she knows only a few characters for household accounts, but cannot write coherent sentences. Yet letters sent from her husband in Beijing to her son indicate that he should give them to her to "read" (*yuekan*). Despite this mixed evidence on the literacy of both Fei Li Shi and Servant Wang Wancheng, the presiding magistrate finally accepted the story of the forgery, giving Fei Li Shi the benefit of the doubt. Wang is convicted of slandering his mistress and sentenced to exile. The case was then sent up to the Board of Punishments where Board officials found this verdict to be too lenient and recommended a death sentence. But not too long after this recommendation, the fate of the case became tangled up with Lu Zhuo's impeachment proceedings.

The judicial trajectory of the Fei case cannot be explained solely by the bribe which did not get Fei Li Shi precisely what she wanted. The verdict issued in the wake of the bribes reflected Lu Zhuo's complex and conflicted relationship with the Fei family. Boasting several generations of high office-holders and imperial emoluments, the Fei lineage was one of the most prominent in Huzhou. The chief target of the lawsuit, Fei Qianliu, was the heir of an impressive line of officials and scholars stretching back to the Song Dynasty (960–1279). His grandfather, Fei Zhida, had passed the Zhejiang Provincial examination with the number one rank in 1672 and gone on to pass the highest level Palace Examinations and serve as a Hanlin Compiler and Metropolitan Examiner before retiring early to live as a Buddhist monk. The family's prestige continued under the leadership of Zhida's son, Qianliu's father, Fei Jinwu, who died in 1730 at the peak of his career, having just been appointed Governor of Hunan Province. Jinwu became a protegé of Tian Wenjing (1662–1732), one of the most powerful men in the empire and one of the Yongzheng Emperor's (1723–36) most trusted provincial officials, when he served in succession as Administrative Commissioner of Henan (1725–28) and Shandong Provinces while Tian was the Governor of Henan and then Governor-General of Henan and Shandong. His close political association with Tian was confirmed in 1727 when Tian was accused of corruption and injustice as an administrator. Jinwu was one of his six highest level subordinates in Henan who, apparently under orders from the Yongzheng Emperor himself, co-authored a letter to Tian requesting compilation of administrative documents from his tenure as Governor to showcase his virtue and accomplishments as examples for other governors to follow, a gesture intended to shore up Tian's reputation in response to the political assault launched against him.[16]

At the time of the lawsuit, Jinwu's three living sons (several others appear to have died young) had achieved only modest career success. Fei Yuyou, Fei

---

16 The collection (*Fu Yu xuanhua lu*) was widely circulated among officials in the Qing. Tian Wenjing 田文镜, *Fu Yu xuanhua lu* 抚豫宣化录 [Records on Propagating Civilization as Henan Governor] (Zhengzhou, Henan: Zhongzhou guji chubanshe, 1995 [1727]); Arthur W. Hummel, *Eminent Chinese of the Ch'ing Period* (Washington: The Library of Congress, 1943. Reprint, Taibei: SMC Publishing, 1996), 720; and Pierre-Etienne Will, *Official Handbooks and Anthologies of Imperial China: A Descriptive and Critical Biography* (Brill, forthcoming), 328–29.

Li Shi's husband, was an expectant official in Beijing and Fei Zifu had a *juren* degree. Fei Qianliu had advanced the farthest with his official postings, but his career, especially in comparison with that of his father, was striking for its mediocrity. It started with a purchased Tribute Student degree (acquired in 1718, KX 57) and then a purchased position as acting magistrate of Yongshou County in Shaanxi Province (in 1720, KX 59). He served as magistrate of several counties in the province and was finally promoted to a secretarial position in the Yunnan Section of the Board of Revenue in 1724 (YZ 2) after he made a donation for disaster relief as magistrate of Fengxian County. From 1726 (YZ 4) he served concurrently in the Office on Irrigation. In 1728 (YZ 6), Zhang Tingyu recommended him for promotion to Vice Director of the Fujian Section of the Board of Revenue and only a few months later recommended him for Prefect of Chenzhou in Hunan Province. He served as Prefect of several prefectures in Hunan and Henan before being promoted to Circuit Intendant of Nanru District in Henan in 1732 (YZ 10). He had just been appointed Salt Distribution Commissioner of Changlu, Zhili, when, in 1734 (YZ 12), he was dismissed from official service for his failure to investigate a death under torture that took place during a homicide investigation in a county court under his jurisdiction as Prefect of Runing Fu.

It is very clear that Fei Qianliu was a mediocre official, at best, who owed his career entirely to his father's excellent reputation. The Yongzheng Emperor noted in a marginal comment on a palace memorial recommending him for promotion to Chenzhou Prefect, "Of middling talents. Employed because he is recommended by [Zhang Tingyu) and is Fei Jinwu's son. Yet he is honest and knows his place."[17] By 1734, serious problems had emerged with Qianliu. In the wake of his appointment as Changlu Salt Distribution Commissioner, Henan Governor Wang Shijun memorialized in secret to Yongzheng to register his growing concern over Qianliu's behavior and performance:

> As for Nanru Circuit Intendant Fei Qianliu, he appears on the outside to be sincere and conscientious. When your minister came into office last year, I visited Xinyang Zhou in this Circuit Intendant's jurisdiction. When I first saw this person, I had the impression that he had a bit of talent. He spoke persuasively. Hence, when your minister memorialized in the winter on the situation with sitting officials, I reported that he was diligent and conscientious. Recently, I further investigated him and found, unexpectedly, that in fact his disposition is stubborn and recalcitrant.

17 *Qingdai guanyuan luli* 清代官员履历 [Resume of Officials of the Qing Dynasty] (Shanghai: Huadong shifan daxue chubanshe, 1997), 1: 94.

> I heard that when he arrived to investigate the areas under his jurisdiction, he was always dissatisfied with the accommodations and threw his weight around with the result that those serving under him were forced to inquire after him daily. Moreover, he did not get along at all with the two prefects in the Nanru Circuit and imposed his own personal opinions about what was right and wrong for the prefectures and counties. None of those under him respected his authority. Your minister admonished him repeatedly, but did not see any sign of reform. Whenever I deputed someone [to investigate him], he tried to avoid him and when his misdeeds were brought up, he invented excuses to retire and ignore official business. For example, in the case of land reclamation,[18] all of his subordinates diligently carried out orders, but this Circuit Intendant then argued against them and hindered them. Some of his subordinates tried to be conciliatory, but he reproved them. He completely uses his own likes and dislikes as the arbiter of right and wrong and pays no attention to public opinion.[19]

Wang says he was hesitant to report this earlier because he had no concrete proof of any malfeasance, but now that Fei Qianliu was being promoted, he felt it important to inform the Emperor of his misgivings. In his rescript, Yongzheng notes that since all of his superiors had always praised his performance and because he was Fei Jinwu's son, it would not be good to censure him. However, he expressed concern about the seriousness of Qianliu's behavior and suggests keeping close watch on him in his new position. Merely two weeks later, the torture case came to the Emperor's attention and he recommended that

18 Reclamation of marginal land for cultivation to enhance rural livelihoods and increase tax revenue was a hallmark policy of the Yongzheng emperor's reform program championed by Tian Wenjing and his protégés like Wang Shijun. The *kaiken* policy, as it was called, had many critics who cited widespread mismanagement, abuse, and corruption in its implementation. One of Qianlong's first actions upon succeeding to the throne in 1735 was to end the program. Wang Shijun memorialized to defend it in the name of the Yongzheng Emperor prompting Qianlong to order his execution for sedition. That Fei Qianliu was implicated in resisting *kaiken* (albeit for reasons that are not clear) indicates the complexity of the political rivalries and maneuvering that lay behind impeachments of officials.

19 *Yongzheng chao hanwen zhupi zouzhe huibian* 雍正朝汉文朱批奏摺汇编 [Collection of Vermillion-Rescripted Chinese-Language Palace Memorials of the Yongzheng Reign] (Nanjing: Jiangsu guji chubanshe, 1989), 26: 739, Memorial of Wang Shijun, YZ12/7/25.

Qianliu be demoted and impeached along with several other officials implicated in the case of failure to investigate a death under torture.[20]

Lu Zhuo was a complicated character himself, and in many ways the opposite of Fei Qianliu. Three biographies of him, written decades later after his death in 1767 by Chen Hongmou, Yuan Mei, and Lu Xinheng, all praise him for his great virtue, competence, and benevolence in his years as an official. A Han bannerman from Fengtian, he was the son of Lu Chenglun who had attained the post of Vice Minister of the Court of Judicial Review (*Dalisi*). His family's hereditary rank entitled him to office via the *yin* privilege, but he also demonstrated talent from early on: Yuan Mei describes him as "outstanding from birth, a very great talent expected to attain great accomplishments."[21] Between 1728 and 1734, he advanced very rapidly from county magistrate to prefect of Dongchang Fu in Shandong to Nanru Circuit Intendant in Henan to Henan Judicial Commissioner, then Administrative Commissioner, and finally Governor of Fujian. He, like Fei Jinwu, who was Shandong Administrative Commissioner and then Acting Governor during Lu Zhuo's years as Prefect of Dongchang, was a favored protégé of Tian Wenjing. According to Yuan Mei and Lu Xinheng, Lu impressed him in particular by clearing a huge backlog of cases and emptying the hugely overcrowded prison. Yuan states, "Tian cherished him and when [Tian] died [in 1732], he was left without support," a comment that may allude to the political motivations behind the governor's impeachment. Lu Zhuo seems also to have felt some allegiance to Fei Jinwu, who as his superior early on in his career may have played an important role in his advancement. It is striking in this regard that only days before Fei Li Shi's first bribe to the governor's staff on the 11th day of the 9th month of QL 4, Lu Zhuo submitted a memorial endorsing the request of several Wucheng County literati, to have Fei Jinwu admitted to the provincial Shrine for Local Worthies, a request that was granted by the emperor in an edict dated to the 13th day of the tenth month.[22]

Lu Zhuo was also quite familiar with Fei Qianliu. Although Governor-General Depei had no direct proof that Lu Zhuo himself accepted money in

20 *Yongzheng chao qijuzhu* 雍正朝起居注 [Diaries of the Yongzheng Emperor] (Beijing: Zhonghua shuju, 1993), 5: 3943–44.

21 Qian Yiji 钱仪吉, comp., *Beizhuanji* 碑传集 [Collection of Stele Biographies] (Reprint Shanghai: Zhonghua shuju, 1993), *juan* 71: 2050.

22 *Shishu* 史書, QL4/9/11, *like tiben* by Lu Zhuo. On the same day, Lu Zhuo memorialized with a parallel request for Li Wei, another favorite of the Yongzheng Emperor, to be admitted to the Shrine for Famous Officials for his service as Governor and then Governor-General of Zhejiang from 1727–29.

this case, he argued that the governor was predisposed to dislike Fei Qianliu because the two "had longstanding mutual resentments from their time serving together as officials in Henan." The torture case that ended Qianliu's official career had initially been discovered by Lu Zhuo who had just been promoted to Henan Judicial Commissioner from Nanru Circuit Intendant, the post to which Qianliu had just been appointed. A few months later, at the beginning of 1734 (YZ 12), Lu Zhuo became Henan Administrative Commissioner, the post he held at the time of Fei Qianliu's impeachment and dismissal. Lu's biographers all note his commitment to and success at reversing unjust verdicts and clearing up judicial backlogs. Chen Hongmou writes that in his posts in Henan, he "excelled at questioning criminals and never resorted to using torture for interrogations. He reversed unjust verdicts in over thirty cases."[23] Fei Qianliu was thus implicated in a judicial and moral matter, the use of torture, about which Lu felt deeply. Given his reputation for upholding justice and the integrity of the judicial system, Governor Lu's impeachment for violating the integrity of judicial process is poignantly ironic.

The accusations of corruption against Lu Zhuo were raised in 1741 (QL 6) by Left Censor-in-Chief Liu Wulong, who, in a palace memorial, accused Lu Zhuo of taking advantage of his post for personal gain and accepting bribes from subordinates. Governor-General Depei concludes that Lu Zhuo's corruption in this instance happened because he was both "narrow-mindedly obsessed with his resentment and coveted bribes." This led him to bypass the county and prefectural channels to take the case on himself, and ultimately to "attribute responsibility for forging the eleven love letters that were obviously written in [Tutor] Xu Yantan's hand to a household servant named Wang Wancheng who only knew a few characters." The Governor-General exclaims, "This was extremely unbelievable…, public sentiment was furious with the confounding of right and wrong and there were people writing jokes about it everywhere. If Lu Zhuo did not receive a bribe, then why did he turn truth and falsehood upside down like this?"

According to Feng Erkang's interpretation of the case, the Qianlong Emperor was very reticent to believe the charges and delayed investigation for some months because he respected Lu Zhuo as a highly capable and upright official.[24] Based on Yuan Mei's comment about the significance of losing Tian Wenjing and the timing of Governor Lu's public honoring of Li Wei and Fei Jinwu, his impeachment may have been part of ongoing fallout from the decline of Tian Wenjing's reputation after the death of the Yongzheng Emperor.

---

23 *Beizhuanji, juan* 71: 2048.

24 Feng Erkang 冯尔康, *Qingchao tongshi* 清朝通史 [A General Qing History] (Beijing: Zijincheng chubanshe, 2003), 1: 495–500.

Lu Zhuo's biographers offer quite a different interpretation of his actions in this case. Chen Hongmou and Yuan Mei both became protegés of Depei during his tenure as Liang-Jiang Governor-General in 1742–3 immediately after he oversaw Lu Zhuo's impeachment as Governor-General of Zhejiang and Fujian. One thus assumes that they had inside knowledge of the case. Intriguingly, they describe Lu's impeachment as the result of his unfortunate, yet innocent entanglement with the Fei case, not even mentioning the other cases involving far greater amounts of money and thus greater levels of culpability. Although all three biographers are convinced that Fei Li Shi had committed adultery, they insist that Lu did not know this and took up the Fei case out of genuine concern for the reputation of a chaste woman. Lu Xinheng writes, "There was a younger brother's wife [whose secret indiscretion] was exposed. [Lu Zhuo] cherished virtuous reputation and mistakenly sought to redress a miscarriage of justice that was a ruse" (*you jie diqi zhe, gong lianxi mingjie, yi weixing wufang pingfan zhi*).[25]

These retrospective accounts, highlighting Lu Zhuo's integrity and commitment to justice, indicate that we should take seriously his own interpretation of the significance of the Fei case that he presented to the Board of Rites in his memorial requesting removal of the degree titles of three of the male heads of the Fei family so that they could stand trial. Describing the Fei men as "evil bullies," he argued that it was imperative for the imperial state to defend the reputation and social standing of this woman against the patriarchs of her husband's family because such "disgrace of a woman of pure virtue" by men, who were not only her close relatives but part of the degree-holding elite, threatened the moral civilization of the empire. Deeply disturbed by the moral implications of this affair, the Governor framed the complicated details of the case in vociferous condemnation of the moral turpitude of the implicated literati men:

> I write in the interest of flushing out corruption and promoting purity so as to rectify human relationships and defend moral civilization. I believe that the women's inner quarters are the source of cultural restoration and moral transformation. If they suffer humiliation without redress, then how can honor and chastity be protected? The common people look up to officials. If they dare to disdain proper human relationships and corrupt laws then indeed they can hardly masquerade as gentlemen of the cloth and hat. Truly they do nothing for the cause of eliminating base customs, promoting loyalty, civilizing customs, and transforming the minds of the common people through their instruction and example.

25 *Beizhuanji, juan* 71: 2050.

Here Lu Zhuo articulates both the passionate commitment to defense of female chastity and the activist vision of the state's civilizing role in society that were hallmarks of Qing policy and politics in the Yongzheng and early Qianlong years. Lu Zhuo was not motivated by greed in the Fei case given that the amount of money involved here, 580 taels in total, was tiny and insignificant. As in the Wang case, the bribes, transmitted via friends, relatives, and political allies opened a channel of communication on a case that local officials did not want to hear, though once Lu Zhuo was apprised of it, he needed no background information on the Fei family. Like Prefect Yang Jingzhen, Lu Zhuo justified his actions in this case as a defense of female chastity, which is consistent with his reputation for virtue and fairness. But moral transformation (*jiaohua*) was clearly not his only motivation. His preferred verdict in the case was shaped both by his documented contempt for Fei Qianliu and his great respect for Fei Jinwu.

All three of Lu Zhuo's biographers also emphasize his popularity with the people of Zhejiang who took to the streets to protest his arrest. Chen Hongmou writes, "Mistakenly implicated in Fei Li Shi's case, he was arrested and taken to Beijing. The people of Zhejiang escorted him with tears falling, but could not stop [his arrest] and it became a major case." In his eulogy for Lu Zhuo, Yuan Mei recounts his surprise when he heard of his impeachment and describes the virulent popular reaction to it:

> The people of Zhejiang clamored in opposition and went on strike, demanding that [the governor] be shown leniency. They climbed up to Wu Mountain Temple supplied with food provisions. The multitudes were like a wall moving forward. In the places they passed by, women shouted out that an injustice had been done. Tens of thousands of people entered the gate of the Governor-General's yamen and beat on the drum to call for [Lu Zhuo to be] maintained.

There were other interpretations of the nature of these demonstrations. Governor-General Depei's months-long investigation of the case created quite a circus with hundreds of witnesses held for questioning and housed in local homes. The Qianlong Emperor excoriated Depei for his handling of the investigation and blamed his bungling and inefficiency for arousing public ire and instigating the riots.[26] According to Yuan Mei's understanding of events, the Qianlong Emperor "knew that [Lu Zhuo] was without blame, but did not

26 Nancy Park discusses these events in Nancy Park, "Corruption and Its Recompense: Bribes, Bureaucracy, and the Law in Late Imperial China," Ph.D. diss., Harvard University, 1993.

want to prolong the wicked behavior of the mobs (literally, blackheads), so [he was sentenced to] military exile. For a moment, court and people feared [Lu Zhuo's] ability to win over the people."

Throughout these cases there is frequent mention of public opinion. Given the local prominence of these families, the disgraceful nature of these disputes, and the huge network of people involved in the bribery, it is hardly surprising that such cases would fuel the tabloid-type gossip of the day. But beyond prurient curiosity, the public, as described by Lu Zhuo, Prefect Yang, Depei, and Qianlong was concerned about the fairness of these judicial proceedings. Prefect Yang assumed that his acceptance of bribes would anger the public. When she requested transfer of her case to Hangzhou, Fei Li Shi assumed that the local public in Huzhou, which had already heard rumors of her adultery, would oppose a verdict clearing her name. And masses of people opposed the impeachment proceedings against Lu Zhuo, perhaps because of his popularity as governor and perhaps also because of the perception that the judicial proceedings against him were mishandled and harmed numerous people associated with his case. The legitimacy of judicial proceedings, however vaguely understood, was clearly important to the public as were perceptions of corruption in the system.[27]

Conclusion

Examination of the Wang, Fei and Lu Zhuo cases allows us to identify a number of distinctive aspects of the engagement of degree-holding and merchant elites with the judicial system. The array of connections between these elites and the magistrates, prefects, and governors who presided over legal process in their districts made it impossible for officials to be impartial or even to follow the dictates of the law if they wanted to. Not only were they peers—socially, economically, politically, or in all three ways—they were bound in relationships of mutual dependence and social obligation forged through business interactions or overlapping service in the bureaucracy. Sometimes they knew each other quite well and had emotional attachments or animosities. Ironically, the lack of distance between adjudicating officials and elites did not necessarily work in elite favor. Embarrassing entanglements with the judicial system often

27 The role of public opinion in judicial proceedings and what it tells us about popular perceptions of the law and of justice is a theme addressed in several of the papers in this volume or presented at the International Workshop on Chinese Legal History, Culture and Modernity at Columbia University in May 2012, including those by Margaret Wan for the Qing, and for the Republican period, by Bryna Goodman, Daniel Asen and Xiaoping Cong.

had more severe consequences for elite families than for commoners. Bribery was an integral component of elite engagement with the judicial system, yet it was often ruinously expensive and officials were perpetually vulnerable to impeachment, a judicial proceeding that routinely destroyed the lives and careers of bureaucratic elites. The Wang and Fei families were devastated by the outcomes of their cases. Both seem to disappear from the historical record and we know from an epitaph for Fei Li Shi's son, Fei Shupian, that he and his wife, Wang Liang, the daughter of Wang Sun Shi, ended their days in poverty and obscurity, completely estranged from both of their families. Lu Zhuo was convicted, had all his property confiscated by the state and was sent into military exile. Qianlong rehabilitated him shortly before his death in 1767, far too late to salvage what had been a brilliantly promising career. In some ways, elites had more to lose in judicial proceedings than commoners since the state that granted them their degrees and status could readily take them away. The Fei and Wang family use of legal system for leverage in their familial disputes indicates that they saw it as vital and useful despite the dangers. But what they wanted out of the system was not a fair legal judgment but an arena for their own social negotiations. They assumed that through their money, *guanxi* with officials, and even local and national reputation, they could dominate that arena by making the adjudicating official their ally. Official response to these cases might well be characterized as a kind of improvisation in which they tempered the standard Qing legal principles of *qing, li, and fa* with personal sympathy or animosity, debts of various kinds to various parties, political utility, and desire for monetary gain. Even the impeachment proceedings against Lu Zhuo and his own prosecution of Yang Jingzhen were driven by politics as much as by legal imperative. One might say that the judicial system for elites was all about politics and that politics was personal. In the person of Lu Zhuo, we see how an official who cared deeply about the integrity of the legal system as it applied to commoners threw judicial integrity to the winds when faced with these plaints by elite families and was in turn subject to impeachment proceedings that were tainted by politics.

Qing rulers and the imperial officials who shaped the expansion of the Qing Code and thus the reach of the judicial system into society in the eighteenth century understood the law to be one of the most important tools for the moral transformation of society (*jiaohua*), that is for the enhancement of a paternalistic state's control over society and exercise of its role as chief arbiter of moral norms.[28] The *jiaohua* paradigm for state-society relations presumed

28 Janet Theiss, *Disgraceful Matters: The Politics of Chastity in Eighteenth-Century China* (Berkeley: University of California Press, 2005); Matthew H. Sommer, *Sex, Law and Society in Late Imperial China* (Stanford: Stanford University Press, 2002).

the superior authority of the state over all imperial subjects who in principle were equally subject to the state's control and civilizing force. Lu Zhuo and Yang Jingzhen both invoke the *jiaohua* function of the law when they reference the upholding of chastity in the Wang and Fei cases, noting explicitly that elites were supposed to conform to the same moral norms as people of lower social status, to set an example for them but also to ensure the state's ideological monopoly. The glimpses of public concern with the proceedings in the Wang, Fei and Lu Zhuo cases suggests that whichever parties they sympathized with, urban residents in fact agreed with key elements of the *jiaohua* paradigm, namely that the state ought to be the arbiter of justice and that legal norms should apply to everyone, regardless of status, including adjudicating officials. Yet the ability of members of the Wang and Fei families to evade and manipulate the legal process, the inability of officials to enforce the law and proper judicial procedure in their cases, and official use of legal mechanisms for political purposes, indicates that the judicial system for elites did not function to uphold the state's authority, let alone impartiality or judicial principles like justice, but instead was an arena for negotiation and political struggle.

Glossary

Changlu	长芦
Chenzhou Fu	郴州
Chen Peicai	陈佩采
Depei	德沛
fa	法
Fei Li Shi	费李氏
Fei Qianliu	费谦流
Fan Sinian	笵司年
Fei Shunan	费树楠
Fei Shupian	费树楩
Fei Yuyou	费豫游
Fengxian	凤县
fu zhongjun	抚中軍
Guanhua	官花
Huang Zongxi	黄宗羲
Huzhou	湖州
jiaohua	教化
Jiaxing	嘉兴
li	理
Li Gongfu	李工扶
Liu Wulong	刘吴龙
Lu Bian	卢变
Lu Zhuo	卢焯
kaiken	开垦
Mei	梅
Nanru	南汝
ni zai waibian buyaoshuo wo yao yinzi, zhishi shuo wo songqing yu ni de yimian waimian zhaoyao	你在外边不要说我要银子只是说我送情与你的以免外面招摇
Qian Zhoushu	钱舟书
qing	情
Quzhou	衢州
ruci yansheng lise bu'neng wuyuan	如此严声厉色不能无怨
Runing	汝宁
Shengyuan	生员
Shupian	树楩

shuoqing quanxie timian	说情全些体面	Xiuning	休宁
songta xieyi	送他谢仪	Xu Yantan	徐延菼
Sun Shimian	孙士勉	Yang Jingzhen	杨景震
tangguan	堂官	*yangcheng fengzhi piantan* Sun Shi *jiang* Wang Zhaojing *hengjiao zheru*	仰承风旨偏袒孙士将汪兆鲸横加折辱
Tongxiang	桐乡	Yao	姚
Wang Kentang	汪肯堂	Yongshou	永寿
Wang Sen	汪森	*you jie diqi zhe, gong lianxi mingjie, yi weixing wufang pingfan zhi*	有讦弟妻者，公矜惜名节，以微行误访平反之
Wang Shao	汪燿	yuekan	阅看
Wang Shideng	汪士登	Yu Shengfan	俞圣凡
Wang Shijun	王士俊	Zhang Baotian	张保天
Wang Sun Shi	汪孙氏	Zhang Guoqian	张果千
Wang Wancheng	汪万程,	Zhang Tingyu	张廷玉
Wang Wenbo	汪文柏	Zhang Zihui	张自譓
Wang Wengui	汪文桂	Zhao Baoshan	赵宝山
Wang Zhaojing	汪兆鲸	Zhejiang xilu changdashi	浙江西路场大使
weifu buren qiling guafu	为富不仁欺凌寡妇		
wo wei jiacai de shi bing bu fanfa, fanbuzhao yong yinzi	我为家财的事并不犯法犯不着用银子		
xiangjie jiacai de an doushi pinggong duangei bingwu wangqu	详解家财的案都是凭公断给并无枉屈		

Bibliography

Dunstan, Helen. “Safely Supping with the Devil: The Qing State and Its Merchant Suppliers of Copper.” *Late Imperial China* 13, no. 2 (December 1992): 42–81.

Feng Erkang 冯尔康. *Qingchao tongshi* 清朝通史 [A General Qing History]. Beijing: Zijincheng chubanshe, 2003.

Fuma, Susumu. “Litigation Masters and the Litigation System of Ming and Qing China.” *International Journal of Asian Studies* 4, no. 1 (2007): 79–111.

Guo Chengkang 郭成康, and Zheng Baofeng 郑宝风. “Qianlong nianjian qintan wenti yanjiu 乾隆年间侵贪问题研究 [Research on the Problem of Corruption in the Qianlong Era].” *Qingshi yanjiu ji* 清史研究集 [Collection of Qing Studies] 8. Beijng: Zhongguo renmin daxue chubanshe, 1997.

Guy, R. Kent. *Qing Governors and Their Provinces: The Evolution of Territorial Administration in China, 1644–1796*. Seattle: University of Washington Press, 2010.

Hummel, Arthur W. *Eminent Chinese of the Ch'ing Period*. Washington: The Library of Congress, 1943. Reprint, Taibei: SMC Publishing, 1996.

Like tiben: jiucan chufen lei 吏科提本:纠参处分类 [Routine Memorials to the Ministry of Personnel: Impeachment and Discipline], Number 1 Historical Archives, Beijing.

Lufu zouzhe 录副奏折 [Copies of Memorials at the Grand Council], Number 1 Historical Archives, Beijing.

Park, Nancy. "Corruption in Eighteenth-Century China." *The Journal of Asian Studies* 56, no. 4 (Nov. 1997): 967–1005.

———. "Corruption and Its Recompense: Bribes, Bureaucracy, and the Law in Late Imperial China." Ph.D. diss., Harvard University, 1993.

Qian Yiji 钱仪吉, Comp. *Beizhuanji* 碑传集 [Collection of Stele Biographies. Reprint Shanghai: Zhonghua shuju, 1993.

Qingdai guanyuan luli 清代官员履历 [Resume of Officials of the Qing Dynasty]. Shanghai: Huadong shifan daxue chubanshe, 1997.

Reed, Bradley. *Talons and Teeth: County Clerks and Runners in the Qing Dynasty*. Stanford: Stanford University Press, 2000.

Sommer, Matthew. *Sex, Law and Society in Late Imperial China*. Stanford: Stanford University Press, 2002.

Theiss, Janet. *Disgraceful Matters: The Politics of Chastity in Eighteenth-Century China*. Berkeley: University of California Press, 2005.

Tian Wenjing 田文镜. *Fu Yu xuanhua lu* 抚豫宣化录 [Records on Propagating Civilization as Henan Governor]. Zhengzhou, Henan: Zhongzhou guji chubanshe, 1995 [1727].

Vogel, Hans Ulrich. "China's Central Monetary Policy, 1644–1800." *Late Imperial China* 8, no. 2 (Dec. 1987): 1–52.

Will, Pierre-Etienne, ed. *Official Handbooks and Anthologies of Imperial China: A Descriptive and Critical Biography*. Brill, forthcoming.

Xingke tiben: hunyin jianqing lei 刑科题本: 婚姻奸情类 [Routine Memorials to the Ministry of Justice: Marriage and Adultery], Number 1 Historical Archives, Beijing.

Yongzheng chao hanwen zhupi zouzhe huibian 雍正朝汉文朱批奏摺汇编 [Collection of Vermillion-Rescripted Chinese-Language Palace Memorials of the Yongzheng Reign]. Nanjing: Jiangsu guji chubanshe, 1989.

Yongzheng chao qijuzhu 雍正朝起居注 [Diaries of the Yongzheng Emperor]. Beijing, Zhonghua shuju, 1993.

Zelin, Madeleine. *The Magistrate's Tael: Rationalizing Fiscal Reform in Eighteenth-Century Ch'ing China*. Berkeley: University of California Press, 1984.

CHAPTER 5

"Law is One Thing, and Virtue is Another": Vernacular Readings of Law and Legal Process in 1920s Shanghai

*Bryna Goodman**

The new Chinese republic, established in 1912, repositioned people as citizens in a polity governed by law. But the new state could not achieve full judicial sovereignty. How did people negotiate political and cultural identity in legal practice? And how did ideas of citizenship and Chinese judicial sovereignty influence public discussion of the law? This chapter uses trial transcripts, reportage, and commentary from a controversial case in the early 1920s to map ideas of law in the early Chinese republic, a time of draft provisional codes, new-style courts (civil and criminal), and ideas of judicial independence.

A Multitude of Laws and Institutions

Chinese understandings of law in this era were framed by a semicolonial array of legal institutions with contested and overlapping jurisdictions. This unsettled legal framework shaped the political and intellectual context for the 1922 case that is discussed here, and for the contemporary legal reform and judicial sovereignty movements that infused the rhetoric of its legal proceedings and commentary.

The partial, but multiple presence of foreign authorities across China's landscape, and the imposition of varying degrees of extraterritoriality in different spaces created a panoply of judicial arrangements that required practicing lawyers, Chinese and foreign, to gain expertise in multiple legal systems. The legal patchwork of early twentieth-century Shanghai included areas of Chinese jurisdiction, an Anglo-American dominated International Settlement, and a French Concession. Chinese courts adjudicated in Chinese areas. Hybrid "mixed courts" in the International Settlement and the French Concession

* I am grateful to Teemu Ruskola, Sophie Volpp, and the volume editors for their insightful suggestions.

© KONINKLIJKE BRILL NV, LEIDEN, 2015 | DOI 10.1163/9789004288492_007

brought together elements of extraterritorial privilege and Chinese sovereignty in joint hearings by a foreign assessor and a Chinese judge. There were, in addition, consular courts and extraterritorial courts for foreign nationals, like the U.S. Court for China. Foreign courts on Chinese soil, the stigmata of impaired sovereignty, disadvantaged Chinese in globally asymmetrical relations of power, but also created accidental spaces and opportunities that could be manipulated in practice by Chinese groups or individuals.[1]

Under these circumstances, judicial reform in China was predominantly Western-modeled and linked, from its inception, to Chinese efforts to regain legal sovereignty. The legal reforms of the late Qing New Policies era (1901–11) followed several decades of translation of Western and Japanese law. Following Western notions of humanitarianism, reforms emphasized incarceration over corporal punishment, judicial independence, drafting of a civil code, and creation of independent courts.[2] The creation of a republic and the touted transformation of the Chinese people from subjects to citizens brought a new emphasis on the rule of law, human rights, people's rights, and the protection of property. Although differences of opinion persisted in regard to the preservation of elements of Chinese law and notions of justice (and the selection of Chinese and Western features to be combined in the new judicial system), the New Policies reforms were generally enshrined in the new draft legal codes. Judicial independence, if elusive, was salient as a deeply felt imperative of the new republic. In the spatially differentiated political landscape, new-style courts and judicial personnel concentrated in major cities where they

1 Bryna Goodman and David S.G. Goodman, "Introduction: Colonialism and China," in Goodman and Goodman, eds., *Twentieth-Century Colonialism and China: Localities, the Everyday, and the World* (New York: Routledge, 2012). From the 1860s, Chinese residence in the foreign settlements complicated principles of extraterritoriality, necessitating mixed tribunals. Thomas B. Stephens, *Order and Discipline in China: The Shanghai Mixed Court 1911–27* (Seattle: University of Washington Press, 1992), Teemu Ruskola, "Colonialism Without Colonies: On the Extraterritorial Jurisprudence of the U.S. Court for China," *Law and Contemporary Problems* 17 (2008): 217; Charles Sumner Lobinger, ed., *Extraterritorial Cases, U.S. Court for China* (Manila: Bureau of Printing, 1920), vol. 1. Chinese businesses acquired extraterritorial protection by taking foreign partners and registering businesses with foreign consulates. See also Teemu Ruskola, *Legal Orientalism: China, the United States, and Modern Law* (Cambridge: Harvard University Press, 2013).

2 Chinese magistrates formerly adjudicated without civil/criminal distinctions. By 1912, 345 civil courts were established nationwide (Beijing Supreme Court, provincial high courts, county courts of first instance, urban district courts; with procuratorial courts at each level for criminal cases). Xiaoqun Xu, *Trial of Modernity: Judicial Reform in Early Twentieth-Century China* (Stanford: Stanford University Press, 2008), 29–31, 43.

were visible to foreign authorities. Inland courts were largely unchanged, with the result that two modes of judicial administration coexisted for much of the Republican era, depending on location.[3] Further complicating the mix were military courts that followed exceptional military law. These latter institutions have passed largely under the radar of Chinese legal history research, though they complete the institutional context for the case in question.

May Fourth nationalism heightened the impetus for judicial reform and abolition of extraterritorial jurisdiction, particularly in the aftermath of the 1921–22 Washington Conference, at which the Chinese delegation lobbied for recognition of China's full sovereignty. The U.S., Belgium, Great Britain, France, Italy, Japan, the Netherlands, and Portugal responded that they would reconsider extraterritorial rights when the Chinese government fulfilled "its expressed desire to reform its judicial system [to] bring it into accord with that of Western nations."[4] China's frustrations at the conference were publicized in the expansive May Fourth press. Public associations enunciated the slogans "judicial reform," "sovereignty," and "Mixed Court rendition." The Shanghai Lawyers' Association advocated the unconditional rendition of the Mixed Court at a national judicial conference in September 1922, the same month as the suicide of the female secretary, Xi Shangzhen, which precipitated the case that is examined here, the trial and imprisonment of her employer, Tang Jiezhi.[5] Before his trial, the U.S.-educated Tang was managing director of a major Shanghai newspaper and a leader of the Shanghai Federation of Street Unions, a grass-roots organization that agitated for social, economic, and national rights.[6] This organization and others would mobilize a judicial reform movement to protest Tang's conviction.

Vernacular Understandings of Law and Judicial Procedure

Public discussion of the Xi-Tang case sheds light on urban expectations regarding legal practice in the early Republican era. The trial commentary, not surprisingly, reveals continuity with late imperial legal understandings as well as the strong imprint of ideas of republican governance. Public contro-

3 Goodman and Goodman, "Introduction."

4 Commission on Extraterritoriality, ed., *Provisional Code of the Republic of China* (Peking: Commission on Extraterritoriality, 1923), preface.

5 "Judicial Reform Discussed by Meeting Here," *China Press*, September 29, 1922.

6 Another federation leader, lawyer Chen Zemin 陈则民, authored "Fei jiancha zhidu zhi yundong 废检察制度之运动 [Procuratorial-System Abolition Movement]," (Shanghai, 1922), pamphlet.

versy surrounding the case also suggests tension between the goal of judicial independence and the national imperative of judicial sovereignty. The linking of judicial reform to the abolition of extraterritoriality subjected the former to the disciplinary constraints of Chinese nationalism.

Contestations over Chinese legal modernity, judicial reform, and judicial sovereignty infused public discussion of law and legal process. The actions of Chinese litigants and judicial personnel were judged in the context of new political sensibilities. New courts were compared to old imperial courts. Old courts were tainted, in the May Fourth-era press, by despotism, corruption and the violation of human rights. Western-style judicial reform was valued as modern, but also questioned as foreign, inappropriate for the character of Chinese society, and empty of virtue. If the new courts were found deficient in terms of the rule of law and the protection of human rights, on nationalist grounds they were to be defended. The Mixed Courts, in contrast, however they performed in terms of the rule of law, encroached on Chinese sovereignty. Chinese litigants who hired foreign lawyers or tried to avoid Chinese jurisdiction risked branding as hypocrites and traitors. Critics of Chinese judicial administration were targeted as national traitors who imperiled China's chances of attaining legal sovereignty at a time when foreigners were evaluating the Chinese judicial system.

In practice, residents could only negotiate the maze of institutions and legal jurisdictions with the help of Chinese and foreign lawyers. It was difficult to find one's bearings in the new system, let alone navigate the thicket of political significations that accompanied judicial gestures. New categories of law, transitional legal codes and new courts added to the confusion of frameworks and jurisdictions. Yao Gonghe observed in 1917 that "eight or nine of ten average citizens" could not distinguish between a civil or criminal complaint. The ability to differentiate was critical to determining venues and filing legal paperwork.[7]

The republic also ushered in a new emphasis on legal literacy. The Commercial Press published popular guidebooks that were premised on the growing assumption that citizens needed basic legal knowledge. As one such book argued:

> All litigants, whether civil or criminal, need basic legal knowledge to avoid the torturous pain of engaging the law without preparation. Today the complexity of laws and decrees is extreme. Legal scholars continue to lack knowledge. How much more so the common people!... This book

7 Yao Gonghe 姚公鹤, *Shanghai xianhua* 上海闲话 [Idle Talk about Shanghai] (Shanghai: Shanghai gujichubanshe reprint, 1989), 46. The forms were not easily distinguishable even for legal scribes. Xu, *Trial*, 71.

> specifies [costs, timing, and procedures for appeals] ... For criminal cases [it covers] reporting, accusation, confession, surrender, appeal, and all basic items.... The low price of this brief guide for citizens and merchants enables wide circulation.[8]

Such guidebooks introduced readers to law and legal institutions in theory. Brevity and national orientation ruled out examination of the extraterritorial complications of judicial procedure. The practical and formal focus elided the question of how readers made sense of law and justice, Chinese and Western, or how they deployed their social networks in interaction with legal institutions. To see how political, social and cultural elements—extraterritoriality, social relations, notions of virtue—affected popular reception of the new laws and the dramas of crime and justice that appeared in the daily newspapers it is useful to examine the unfolding of a case.

A Suicide, and the Trial of Tang Jiezhi

Xi Shangzhen was twenty-four *sui* and unmarried at the time of her suicide on September 8, 1922, at the Shanghai *Journal of Commerce* (*Shangbao*).[9] Although her nuclear family was poor, their Dongting Dongshan Xi lineage was prominent in Shanghai financial and journalistic circles. According to newspaper accounts, when Xi was absent from an employee dinner, Wang Jipu, an older staff member dropped by her desk to check on her. Something in her manner worried him and he left to alert her family. Xi closed the door, climbed onto a chair, slipped a cord from an electric teakettle through a metal ring in the window frame, arranged it around her neck, and stepped into the air. When Wang returned with Xi's sister-in-law, less than an hour later, they found Xi dangling from the window frame. Office employees lifted her body,

8 Hu Xia 胡暇 and Huang Yan 黄岩, eds., *Susong changshi* 诉讼常识 [Basic Knowledge about Lawsuits], (Shanghai: Shangwu yinshuguan, 1922), preface; see also *Susong xuzhi* 诉讼须知 [Necessary Knowledge about Lawsuits] (Shanghai: Shangwu yinshuguan, 1917). A 1923 guide is cited in Herbert Huey, "Law and Social Attitudes in 1920s Shanghai," *Hong Kong Law Journal* 14, no. 3 (1984): 306–22.

9 On gender issues in the case, see Bryna Goodman, "The New Woman Commits Suicide: Press, Cultural Memory, and the New Republic," *Journal of Asian Studies* (JAS) 64, no. 1 (Feb. 2005): 67–101.

removed the cord, and gently laid her down. A doctor summoned to the scene pronounced Xi dead at approximately 8:00 p.m.[10]

Xi's desk was in Tang's office. Tang appears in a list of Shanghai's most newsworthy individuals, published by the tabloid newspaper, *Crystal* (*Jingbao*).[11] He had led a recent tax strike against the governing Shanghai Municipal Council of the International Settlement in which he rallied Chinese commercial leaders under the slogan, "no taxation without representation." His politically bold newspaper advocated the mobilization of what he called the Chinese middle class (*zhongliu jieji*)—an imprecise term in Chinese society that reflected the influence of Tang's U.S. education. Although his Chinese-language newspaper was staffed almost entirely by Chinese, Tang's Western partner, the Russian-American journalist George Sokolsky, telephoned the International Settlement police to report the suicide.[12]

Because the *Journal* was located in the International Settlement, the inquest that followed was at the Mixed Court, where a Chinese magistrate and a British assessor jointly presided. Police detectives, a coroner, and witnesses corroborated the judges' verdict of suicide. This did not resolve the legal questions that surrounded Xi's death, however, because Republican law retained provisions of late imperial code that held individuals responsible for driving others to suicide.[13]

At the inquest Xi's family accused Tang of wrongdoing, though their arguments were not legally focused, logical, or consistent.[14] Xi's widowed mother, née Fang, testified that Tang had caused Xi to commit suicide because he had failed to return a large sum of money. Xi's married elder sister described the

---

10 This narrative is based on reports in *Xinwenbao* (XWB) (September 10, 1922); *Shenbao* (September 10, 1922), *Minguo ribao* (MGRB) (September 11, 1922); *China Press* (CP) (September 9, 1922; September 10, 1922) and *North China Daily News* (NCDN) (September 12, 1922; September 16, 1922).

11 "Shanghai zuijin yibai mingren biao 上海最近一百名人表 [Most Recent List of 100 Shanghai Celebrities]," *Jingbao* (JB), March 30, 1922.

12 Shanghai Municipal Council, *Daily Police Reports*, September 9, 1922 (Shanghai Archives 1-1-1135); PRO FO 228/3291 (Intelligence Report September 1921). A Chinese version of Sokolsky's name (not his official Chinese name) appears unexplained in XWB, September 10, 1922.

13 Provisional code chapters 23 and 26, "Offences against Morality," and "Homicide and Causing Injury," contain punishments for individuals who caused others' suicides. Commission on Extraterritoriality, ed., *Provisional Code of the Republic of China*.

14 The narrative that follows is assembled from reportage and court transcripts in *Shenbao*, MGRB, XSB, SSXB (September–December 1922); Cui Weiru, ed., *Xi Shangzhen* (2 volumes), (Shanghai: Funü zhiye yanjiu she, 1922).

financial crux of the case in confused terms that articulated both a debt and a purchase of stock:

> [After telling Xi about the profitability of stock] Mr. Tang, borrowed five thousand *yuan*, but he didn't give her any stock. When my sister asked for the money, Tang said the stock was pawned, but that things would work out. These were empty words, and my sister [began attempting suicide. On her second attempt] she didn't return home. Cherishing hope, we waited until dawn, when the newspaper sent her home in a horse-carriage, saying that she had had a fever. Unexpectedly, Sister refused to come out of the carriage and said she wanted to die in the Journal of Commerce office ... Sister also said [she swallowed] tranquilizers because Mr. Tang had not returned the money. He had said, "your money is with me, why worry?" [After Sister took tranquilizers] Mr. Tang wrote an IOU ... [This] was clearly an empty show, leading Sister to commit suicide.[15]

In contrasting testimony, Tang denied borrowing Xi's money. He stated that she gave him the money to invest on her behalf in the recent stock market boom.[16] In spring 1921, in the heady atmosphere of a bull market, Tang had launched the China Commercial Trust Company. People in his office clamored to purchase stock from him, Xi among them. Unfortunately the market fell and Xi's money was lost, a common, if nonetheless devastating experience. He had given her some stock certificates when they became available; others he had held for her in his safe. Tang vigorously denied suggestions made by Xi's family that he had pressured her to become his concubine.[17] It was not the task of the inquest to reconcile the discrepant accounts. The presiding officials nonetheless indicated that if Xi's family wished to pursue the financial losses, they could lodge a *civil* complaint against Tang.[18]

As reportage of the case unfolded, drawing readers as surely as the serialized fiction that drove newspaper sales,[19] the press became a vehicle for contending enunciations of law and morality. Responding to the shadow of

15 XWB, September 10, 1922.

16 Bryna Goodman, "Things Unheard of East or West: Colonial Contamination and Cultural Purity in Early Chinese Stock Exchanges," in Goodman and Goodman, *Twentieth*, 57–77.

17 *Shenbao*, September 10, 1922; MGRB, September 11, 1922.

18 CP and XWB, September 10, 1922.

19 Alexander Des Forges, "Building Shanghai, One Page at a Time: The Aesthetics of Installment Fiction at the Turn of the Century" *Journal of Asian Studies* 62, no. 3 (August 2003): 781–810; Eileen Chow, *Spectacular Novelties: "News" Culture, Zhang Henshui, and Practices of Spectatorship in Republican China*, Ph.D. dissertation, Stanford University, 2000.

legal vulnerability cast by the inquest, as well as to rumors about his relations with Xi, Tang published a front page announcement to clarify his economic entanglement with Xi:

> In regard to Miss Xi Shangzhen's suicide, I make a declaration for society and for my friends. The deceased bought shares ... through me with money she had borrowed. I believed it was her money. She wanted to buy more shares but I refused because I felt she was engaging in excessive speculation. [After the collapse] she begged me for help with her creditors. Twice she attempted suicide. Motivated by a benevolent desire to ameliorate her distress, I gave her a promissory note on August 19 that stated I would pay a first installment of 1500 *yuan* within twelve months, a second installment of 1500 *yuan* within twenty-four months, and a final payment of 2000 *yuan* within thirty-six months. [This note] is still in the hands of Xi's family. Apart from this I undertook no responsibility....[20]

Tang's statement was quickly challenged. On September 13, the Dongting Dongshan native-place association published a letter of accusation against Tang, addressed "to all circles of Shanghai society," based on its own investigation of the case. The association pressed the Shanghai procuratorial court (*jiancha ting*) to initiate proceedings. The legal status of Tang's crime, and whether it was civil or criminal, was obscured by the moral economy of grievances and retribution that informed the association's rhetoric:

> ... Shangzhen naively gave him 500 *yuan* to buy stock.... Instead of handing over the shares, Tang urged her to become his concubine ... Thus Shangzhen not only lost her money, but she was so insulted and angry that she didn't want to live.... [It was family money], and when she couldn't recover it she resolved to die. She told her sister, "I will leave a detailed note of grievance." ... Tang has now printed a notice admitting that Xi Shangzhen entrusted him to buy her stock. [But the] stock never reached Xi's hands.... How is it he doesn't mention turning over the stock? How is it that she ... attempted suicide three times at the office?[21]

---

20 "Tang Jiezhi jinyao shengming 汤节之紧要声明 [Important Declaration of Tang Jiezhi]," *Shenbao*, September 11, 1922; XWB, September 11, 1922; *North China Herald* (NCH), September 16, 1922.

21 "Dongting dongshan tongxiang dai wei suyuan 洞庭东山代为诉冤 [Dongting Association Redresses Grievances]," *Shenbao*, September 13, 1922. Also published in XWB and MGRB.

The thrust of this statement, if translated into a legal argument, was that Tang 1) bore responsibility for Xi's suicide and 2) fraudulently induced her to purchase stock that he did not intend to deliver.

Tang responded swiftly, bringing libel suits against two high-circulation papers that published this statement, *Xinwenbao*, and *China Press*.[22] Because they were registered under U.S. ownership, the lawsuits were brought in the U.S. Court for China.

Other groups published statements to stir public opinion in favor of Xi and against Tang.[23] Their statements highlight contemporary concern for reputation, communal responsibility, and public demonstration of vital social connections (or community ostracism). Commentators evoked an economy of right and wrong that was independent of legal process:

> The Xi-Tang case is a major social incident.... Women's circles and several public associations have spoken. [But] Tang [is] director, manager, board member and supervisor [of various organizations] and we haven't heard a word from them.... They should investigate.... [If Tang's] behavior corresponds to newspaper reports, they should protect their reputation and quickly expel this mad horse from their organizations. If investigation [reveals that Tang] has been slandered, they should intervene to protect his and their own reputation.[24]

The reading public was quickly caught up in the contradictory accounts. Commentators placed themselves in the character of the Sherlock Holmesian detectives popular in serialized fiction, tracing clues and formulating hypotheses. Also captivating was the spectacle of conflict between the prominent Xi lineage, backed by Jiangsu native-place associations, and Tang, who served on the boards of the Chamber of Commerce, Commercial Federation, Federation of Commercial Street Unions, and his native-place association, the Guang-Zhao *gongsuo*.

By mid-October, notice of the affair began to slip from reportage into the literary supplement pages, transforming what had been news into literary memory. But just as the drama might have melted into didactic remembrance,

---

22 MGRB September 24, 1922; CP, November 14, 1922. "Chinese Files Libel Suits," *Weekly Review of the Far East* (WRFE), September 23, 1922.

23 Between September 15 and September 18, 1922, East City Women's School, three Jiangsu native-place associations, a women's professional association, and an office workers' association published notices in MGRB, *Shenbao* and XWB.

24 MGRB, September 17, 1922.

the plot deepened with the thrilling cloak-and-dagger spectacle of Tang's kidnapping and arrest by Chinese police, in the middle of the night.

Tang's residence on Alabaster Road, like his business, was located in the International Settlement. By the rules of extraterritoriality, this meant that the exercise of a Chinese court warrant for his arrest at his home or workplace constituted an illegal trespass on Settlement jurisdiction. The Chinese police argued, however, that Gongyi Li alleyway, where Tang garaged his car, marked the boundary between the Settlement and the Chinese city. On the night of the arrest, as many as ten deputies of the Chinese court staked out this lane. Members of the Dongting association, disguised as peddlers, served as lookouts. When Tang stepped from his car at two o'clock in the morning the police pounced, seized him and his chauffeur-bodyguard, and placed them in a Chinese jail.[25]

Tang's arrest transformed what the inquest judged to be a possible civil suit, and what most Chinese residents had seen as an injustice and moral failure, into a criminal case, a surprise to the principals and most observers. *Weekly Review of the Far East* suggested that Tang's unusual arrest resulted from a political sleight-of-hand, and directly compared it to the recent arrest on dubious charges of the Finance Minister, Lo Wengan.[26] Chinese newspapers focused instead on sensation and morality.

Tang stood accused of two crimes: 1) compelling Xi's suicide, a charge that was dropped, and 2) defrauding Xi of stock, for which he would be convicted. At a preliminary hearing at the Chinese court, Tang was refused bail. Confusion reigned over the question of bail and the criminal character of the case. To maintain pressure on the court to refuse bail, the Dongting association organized a public "indignation meeting" that gathered over two hundred people.[27] Tang's associates, in contrast, notified the head of the Consular Body, Italian Consul-General De Rossi, that Tang had been arrested in the International Settlement.[28]

---

25 MGRB, September 13, 14, and 19, 1922; "Dr. Tong Kidnapped," NCDN, November 14, 1922; "Dr. F.C. Tong Arrested by Chinese Police," *China Press*, November 14, 1922; *Dongting dongshan lü Hu tongxianghui sanshi zhounian jinian tekan* 洞庭东山旅沪同乡会三十周年纪念特刊 [30-year Commemoration of Shanghai Dongting Association] (Shanghai: 1944), 79.

26 WRFE, v. 23, December 2, 1922.

27 CP, November 14, 1922; *Shenbao*, November 14, 1922.

28 MGRB, November 15, 16, 19, 20, 1922; "Jianting qisu Xi Shangzhen an yuan wen 检厅起诉席上珍案原文 [Prosecution Document in Xi Shangzhen Case]," *Shenbao*, November 27, 1922.

In practice, the exercise of extraterritorial jurisdiction was imprecise. The Consular Body upheld Tang's account of the arrest, but was unable, or unwilling, to secure Tang's release.[29] The Chinese authorities that had gone to such lengths to arrest Tang were disinclined to give him up. Without possession of the accused, extraterritoriality could not prevail without considerable effort. Such effort—for a nationalist activist who had led a tax protest against the municipal council of the foreign settlement—may not have seemed worthwhile. Tang's trial for fraud took place in the Chinese district court on December 2 and 8, 1922.

The publication of transcripts in Shanghai dailies indicates enormous public interest in the case and concern to showcase Chinese judicial proceedings. In the context of the movement for recovery of China's legal sovereignty and a concurrent national meeting on Chinese judicial process, the proceedings were infused with emphasis on the independence of the Chinese judiciary. The irony of Tang's appeal for help from the foreign consuls was not lost on his audience.

Justice was swift, and, for Tang, disastrous, despite his eminent legal team.[30] Transcripts suggest that the prosecution's presentation of the case followed closely the narrative of events published earlier by the Dongting association. Although the indictment found insufficient evidence for the charge of compelling suicide, the prosecution and the Xi family continued throughout the trial to assert Tang's responsibility for Xi's death. The crux of the criminal case for fraud, however, was claim that Tang induced (*quanyou*) Xi to purchase stock that was not delivered. According to the indictment, this second charge "could not be considered empty" because of the compelling testimony of Xi's mother.[31]

Issues raised by the defense complicated the prosecution's evident plan to swiftly demonstrate guilt. Witnesses recalled how the journal employees had vied to purchase stock. Tang provided financial documents and explained the financial practices that developed during the exchange fever. He substantiated his disputed claim that he had given Xi stock certificates, showing that she had used stock as collateral for a bank loan and to qualify for purchases on another exchange. Tang stuck to his position that his promissory note reflected only altruism. When Xi confided her financial troubles she had suggested that he write the note to fend off her creditors. Asked why he had not given her

29 WRFE, December 2, 1922.

30 Qin Liankui 秦联奎, Li Shirui 李时蕊, and Xu Huilin 徐惠霖. The Chinese court disallowed a foreign lawyer. SSXB, December 3, 1922; CP, December 9, 1922.

31 "Jianting qisu Xi Shangzhen yuanwen 检厅起诉席上珍原文 [Procuratorial Indictment in Xi Shangzhen Case]," *Shenbao*, November 27, 1922.

money, Tang answered that he, too, had lost money in the crash and lacked cash. Tang stated that Xi gave him various certificates as collateral for his note. He could produce them in court. The defense argued that criminal prosecution was inappropriate and ignored commercial practice and market behavior. If Xi wanted stock certificates at the time of her suicide attempts, Tang could have easily provided them. By that time they were worth considerably less than his promissory note. He had certificates for over a thousand shares of stock of his own.[32]

The court adjourned to evaluate the new evidence. Records of the second hearing suggest that, despite an appearance of procedural attentiveness, Tang's evidence was dismissed. Witness statements that corroborated Tang's delivery of stock certificates to Xi were struck from the record as "confusingly irrelevant."[33] Witnesses who might have explained crucial details of financial practice fielded instead extraneous questions. One key witness, the guarantor for the pawning of Xi's stock, was not called. Tang's exculpatory documentary evidence was declared counterfeit and tossed aside without expert examination. The judge went to extraordinary lengths to discount financial transaction records that bore Xi's chop. In an apparently rehearsed move, he showed these to Xi's mother and asked if the seal was Xi's. She testified that the documents must have been counterfeited, producing from her sleeve what she identified as Xi's exclusive chop. Tang's lawyer asked how Xi's mother knew to bring the chop to court. The judge explained that it was discovered the day before, when he personally visited Xi's house to investigate.[34]

After this hearing, sympathetic newspapers published a defense argument that Tang had been framed. The charge that Tang had induced Xi to buy stock was risible in the context of the stock-purchasing frenzy. A journal employee attested to Xi's "unusual lust" (*qingre yichang*) for stock. Tang's lawyer summarized evidence that had been ignored by the court, arguing that the documents showed lawful contractual commercial relationships, and also indicated Xi's possession of stock. The court had accepted instead the uncorroborated statements of Xi's family. Even if Tang had violated a commercial agreement, legally this would constitute at most a breach of contract. But the court had pursued an unwarranted criminal prosecution: "Those bringing suit bear responsibility

---

32 "Xi Shangzhen an zuo ri bianlun zongjie 席上珍案昨日辩论总结 [Yesterday's Summation in Xi Case]," MGRB, December 9.

33 CP, December 9, 1922.

34 MGRB, December 9, 1922, "Magistrate Tu Turns Detective in Tong Trial, Rules Out Evidence: Drama Enacted in Crowded Courtroom as Mother of Suicide Denounces Accused," CP, December 9, 1922.

for demonstrating that their accusations are not groundless. What evidence do they have that the accused didn't turn over the stock or that Xi demanded it? ... Only when they produce positive evidence are their accusations worth considering."[35]

More than twenty public associations with connections to Tang condemned court bias and denounced the judge. The Guang-Zhao *gongsuo* organized a meeting of Guangdong associations, the Ningbo native-place association and the Federation of Commercial Street Unions. Speakers denounced the judge's ignorance about exchanges and stock ownership rules, and his rejection of conclusive evidence. Tang's lawyer Li Shirui reviewed judicial irregularities in the arrest and trial and presented a proposal for judicial reform.[36] Rhetorically linking human-rights and national sovereignty, Tang's supporters argued that the judge's actions injured Chinese sovereignty and exemplified corruption and national weakness:

> Tang is a prestigious director of the [Chamber of Commerce]. If he is subjected to such abuses, how will ordinary merchants be treated by these butchers? In this moment of concern for judicial sovereignty, with the Shanghai court under the scrutiny of [foreign] countries, [these] judges dare to trample on human rights.... Their unrestrained recklessness [makes] China a global laughing-stock.[37]

Representatives of twenty-four public associations (native-place, street, and trade associations, worker unions, a self-government society, a workers' mutual aid society) gathered on December 10 to protest bias and advocate judicial reform to protect human rights. The assembly sent telegrams to the Ministry of Justice in Beijing and to civil and military courts in Jiangsu, calling for dismissal of the offending judges, "to save the spirit of the judicial process [and] protect our international status."[38]

---

35 "Tang Jiezhi bianhu liyou 汤节之辩护理由 [Tang's Defense]," *Shenbao*, December 10, 1922 (also published in ZHXB and MGRB); Zhou Dongbai 周东白, *Quanguo lüshi ming'an huilan* 全国律师名案汇览 [Famous Cases of the Nation's Lawyers] (Shanghai: Shijie shuju, 1923), 8: 6–7.

36 "Liang gongtuan dui Tang an fayan 两公团对汤案发言 [Two Groups Speak in Tang Case]," MGRB, December 10, 1922; "Ge tuanti dui Tang an zhi ji'ang 各团体对汤案之激昂 [Indignation of Groups in Tang Case]," MGRB, December 11, 1922.

37 MGRB, December 11, 1922.

38 Ibid.

On December 11, a similar group met with the chief judge. Following this energetic but useless protest, the participants formalized a judicial reform movement, denouncing China's court as part of an "authoritarian government to which Chinese have been subjected from ancient times." It was "unsuitable for modern life, in this time of contesting foreign control over Chinese courts." The movement advocated abolition of the procuratorial system, establishment of a jury system, creation of a commercial court, supervision of lower courts by higher courts, and compensation for improper arrest and detention.[39]

Protests escalated after December 18, when Tang was pronounced guilty of fraud and sentenced to three years in prison. Tang's sympathizers denounced the judges for "trampling the human rights of the majority," and "inflicting hardship on the body of the people."[40] They articulated an alternate scenario behind the Xi family suit: In her naiveté, Xi was tempted by the exchange boom and urged her family to invest. Her investment failures were compounded by the recrimination of her family members. The bitter situation caused her suicide. The family (which relied on Xi's salary, in the absence of able-bodied male earners) then held Tang responsible for her death and their financial losses. This motivated their false charge that Tang fraudulently induced Xi to purchase stock that he didn't deliver.[41]

In a last-ditch effort to influence the course of justice, the protesting groups fired off telegrams to Ningbo, Suzhou and Shanghai officials, the Beijing government, and to Sun Yatsen, who was in temporary residence in Shanghai. These telegrams, published in the Shanghai papers, reprised a history of abuses and likened Shanghai judicial cruelty to the barbarity of warlords.[42] Although it is not clear what, if anything, other recipients made of such appeals, the out-of-power Sun used the occasion to position himself against the arbitrary exercise of power: "This case is extremely significant [and] affects all citizens. [I] will try to prevent legal officials from depriving people of human rights …"[43]

Tang futilely appealed his case from prison. He was instead transferred to a military jail for involvement in illegal arms trading, a charge for which he never stood trial. Tang would not emerge from the military jail until 1928, three years after the expiration of his sentence.[44]

---

39 MGRB, December 12, 1922.

40 MGRB, December 24, 1922.

41 ZHXB, December 10, 1922; SSXB, December 24, 1922.

42 ZHXB, December 26, 1922; MGRB, December 26, 1922.

43 MGRB, December 31, 1922.

44 "Tang Jiezhi shangsu an shenli ji 汤节之上诉案审理记 [Tang's Appeal Hearing]," *Shenbao*, January 7, 1923; "Tang an zhao yuanpan 汤案照原判 [Tang Case Follows

On the face of the evidence, the outcome of the case is surprising, although public opinion, stirred by Xi's suicide, stood against Tang. The persistent intervention of Tang's critics suggests that they may not have been confident of the outcome. Tang's supporters, in contrast, clearly felt that the evidence would vindicate him. They only belatedly organized meetings and protests after the second trial, when crucial evidence was dismissed.[45] It is unlikely that the individuals and organizations concerned would have gone to such lengths to defend Tang (given the social scandal that surrounded the case) had they not felt a credible argument could be made for his innocence. The judgment of the legal scholar Zhou Dongbai, who analyzed the case in 1923, reinforces this impression. Zhou applauded the "brilliance" of the defense summary of Li Shirui and questioned the legal reasoning behind the verdict.[46]

The court verdict is only surprising, however, if one dismisses both public distraction with issues tangential to the law, and the practical power relations that governed the administration of justice in the early republican era. Bringing the practical authority of the local military over the Chinese court into the picture—though the issue was never mentioned in the court proceedings—is essential to understanding both the disposition of the case and why the Chinese police went to such lengths, at the outset, to ensure that Tang would come under the jurisdiction of the Chinese district court. He Fenglin, the local military commander, does not appear explicitly in the public discussion of the case, but Tang's defenders certainly understood that the judges were his pawns. In the several years before Xi's suicide, Tang had repeatedly clashed with He in his campaigns for Chinese rights. He had also publicly embarrassed He on the pages of his newspaper. One can only imagine He's delight when Tang was delivered into his hands by means of a scandal that destroyed his social reputation.[47] From this perspective, Tang's sentencing may have been a foregone conclusion for the judges, which obviated their serious review of the evidence of the case. This "backstory" to the trial proceedings nonetheless did not deliver them of the need to maintain their public deference to proper legal procedure, nor did it protect them from criticism on these grounds. Proper legal procedure was not, however, the primary concern in the public discussion that enveloped the case.

Original Verdict]," MGRB February 24, 1923; Xi Shangzhen an zhi zuoxun 席上珍案之昨讯 [Yesterday's News on Xi Case]," *Shenbao*, August 23, 1923; "Xi Shangzhen an chong tiqi 席上珍案重提起 [Xi Case Raised Again]," MGRB, August 10, 1928.

45 ZHXB, December 11, 1922.

46 Zhou, *Quanguo*, 8: 1.

47 PRO FO 228/3291 (Shanghai Intelligence Report, September 1921).

Vernacular Understandings of Law and Justice

Because the episode invoked judicial reform and judicial sovereignty, involved a well-known figure in a social scandal that touched on suicide, gender, and the new exchanges, not to mention a cloaked political subtext, it was particularly productive of public controversy. The commentary that is preserved in print permits a sketch of vernacular understandings of justice, law, and legal procedure in early Republican Shanghai.

Morality, Grievance, and Retribution

Relatively little Chinese comment, with the exception of Tang's defense, focused on legal issues. Most discussion, in the statements of associations, essays, reader letters, and poetry, focused on morality, grievance, redress, and even ghostly retribution, language evoked by the cultural associations of suicide.[48] Numerous commentators invoked Tang's paternalistic responsibility: "[As employer] Tang bears moral responsibility for protecting Miss Xi. [She] belongs to the junior generation. Therefore Tang is responsible to guide and protect [her].... If he thought it would be profitable for her to buy stock, he should have helped her to profit and avoid failure."[49] The logic of a revenge suicide was explicit in the court's reasoning, and taken as evidence that Tang could not have delivered the stock (even in the face of contrary documentary evidence).

Public Opinion, Investigation, and Collective Social Agency

The language of grievance/retribution was joined in print discussion to ideas of public opinion (*yulun, gonglun*), infusing the new public of newspapers with older notions of community responsibility and behavior. Commentators did not view investigation of the facts as the exclusive preserve of judicial professionals. Instead, public investigation—by associations, journalists, and newspaper readers—was necessary, preferable, and was linked to the desirable dissemination of public information and negative exposure of wrongdoers. Public justice, executed by newspapers, not the law, was the solution: "Only public opinion circles can punish him in terms of his reputation."[50]

48 Goodman, "New," 91–94.

49 ZHXB, September 18, 1922, editorial.

50 XSB Sept 17, 1922, special supplement.

By the same token, the social production of justice, which interacted only unevenly with the formal administration of justice, was a collective, not an individual or impersonal affair. Social groups that weighed in on the case conducted and publicized their own investigations and pressured court officials. The Dongting association covered Xi family legal costs and assisted with Tang's arrest. Various women's groups and three Jiangsu associations all agitated on Xi's behalf.[51] The efforts of native-place and women's associations on Xi's behalf were seen as natural and unexceptional. Since Tang was a public figure, the involvement of organizations he represented had a different valence. Their involvement in the case did not arouse surprise. Nonetheless, at the time of construction of a public realm that was defined by impersonal bonds of citizenship, the involvement of associations that claimed to represent sectors of citizens risked the accusation of masking private connections as public opinion.[52]

Disregard for Law, Legal Professionals, and Legal Procedure

In vernacular discussion, from the moment of Xi's suicide, morality trumped law: "It is a problem of human integrity. The legal issues are secondary."[53] The strict provisions of law served to exasperate: "As for him angering [Xi] unto death…how can this remain beyond the law?"[54] Some insisted that morality must be key to the law. As women's rights activist, Zhou Fengxia, argued, "Law protects people's rights, and justice is in people's hearts. Since law proceeds from justice.… If you have justice, you have law." But law was not her primary concern: "His behavior is absolutely not upright." If Tang had been a good employer, "he should have taken care of things for her."[55] Like others, Zhou combined moral emphasis with disregard, misunderstanding, or refusal to accept the impersonal logic of market mechanisms.

Legal maneuvering and recourse to lawyers generated suspicion. Tang was criticized for consulting a lawyer after the inquest: "He printed his

51 MGRB, September 15, September 16, September 17, 1922; SB, September 15, and 16, 1922; XWB, September 18, 1922. *Dongting dongshan lü Hu tongxianghui di shi'er ci baogao shu* 洞庭东山旅沪第十二报告书 (Shanghai: 1924), 29.

52 Bryna Goodman, "What is in a Network? Local, Personal, and Public Loyalties in the Context of Changing Conceptions of State and Social Welfare," in *At the Crossroads of Empires*, ed. Nara Dillon and Jean Oi (Stanford: Stanford University Press, 2007), 155–78.

53 "Xiao Shenbao" (Special Xi-Tang issue), XSB, September 17, 1922.

54 *Shenbao*, September 16, 1922.

55 SSXB December 26, 1922.

announcement in each newspaper, in consultation with the lawyer Fei-xin-dun [Fessenden]. This intimidates people with legal authority, so they don't dare speak. However, law is one thing and virtue is another."[56] Legal action by Xi's family was met with surprise: "It is said that Xi's family members are innocent and timid people. But [Tang's arrest] seems rather sharp and goes beyond normal expectations."[57] Tang was similarly denounced for his libel suit. He was advised instead to bend to social criticism, heed public opinion, and compensate Xi's family: "Where justice exists, you can't lightly pass over it. The newspapers are the organ of public opinion.... The greater the uproar, the more useless it is to resist."[58]

Distrust of law and legal proceedings was ubiquitous. Even a legal casebook of the period begins with a strikingly negative characterization of law: "If we look at the history of law it is evident that law is the personal tool of the strong and the victorious. Thus the majority of sociologists disdain the law as a tool of the powerful and attack it." Although gestures of ritual humility are characteristic in such prefaces, nonetheless the editors justification for the publication of a casebook appears remarkably apologetic, reasoning that in China's current situation, "even the most intelligent and most strongly opposed to the law would still not go so far as to argue that law may be abandoned altogether. [Therefore] study of law retains some value."[59]

Suspicion of law and the administration of justice was nonetheless not uniform. Some writers alluded to law as an "empty form." Others expressed distaste for Western legal culture as a model for China. One article that was reprinted in several venues criticized both the corruptions of Chinese culture and the lack of virtue in Western society, finding law impotent in both cases:

> Chinese society is infinitely evil. To rely on law to correct these evils is useless. This is because the law is matter of form. If you break the form, you break the law. It is not the case that doing evil counts as breaking the law. Therefore, despite its meticulous laws, the West is still incessantly evil.[60]

---

56 XSB, September 17, 1922. Another article on this date noted, "Tang's statement already bears the name of a lawyer's office. Everyone should pay attention."

57 ZHXB, November 15, 1922

58 SSXB September 28, 1922, "Qingguang" supplement.

59 Zhou, *Quanguo*, preface.

60 Cha Mengci 查孟词, "Nüzi jiaoyu de quexian 女子教育的缺陷 Limitations of Female Education]," ZHXB, reprinted in MGRB, September 16, 1922.

Tang's defenders, in contrast, showed regard for legal principles in the abstract, but problematized the Chinese judges who implemented the law.

Inattention to Evidence

Tang's lawyers emphasized the compelling weight of witness testimony and financial documents. Most public commentary followed the prosecution in ignoring key pieces of evidence, especially financial evidence. Tang's lawyer, Qin Liankui, complained of court inattention to evidence and public distraction from the substance of the law:

> Social opinion has focused on this case, but [it] is actually focused on Xi's suicide ... Public opinion is not focused on the idea that Tang defrauded Xi of money. In regard to the suicide, investigation revealed no legal doubt [that Tang was innocent of causing her death]. It is not permissible for this reason to simply level another accusation against Tang [for fraud].[61]

Commentators acknowledged that the evidence supported Tang, but directed attention elsewhere:

> Tang's advantage is that there is no evidence against him, only evidence on his behalf.... Nonetheless, his advantage in terms of the law is a disadvantage in the face of social opinion.... I advise Mr. Tang to seriously consider his social position. He should help her family. He should rectify the situation to pacify people's minds.[62]

Disregard for evidence in this case appears strange in the context of Qing legal tradition.[63] The judge's dismissal of evidence (and creative production of new evidence) may certainly have reflected political expedience. Nonetheless, for the court and the public, the unfamiliarity of financial documents and the seeming unnaturalness of the logic of finance capitalism may have facilitated its dismissal. As the judge narrated the events, he questioned the logic of market speculation as well as the possibility of female agency: "[How could] a weak woman think that investing in trust company stock would be so profitable that

61 SSXB, December 9, 1922.

62 ZHXB, September 18, 1922.

63 Li Chen, "Legal Specialists and Judicial Administration in Late Imperial China, 1651–1911," *Late Imperial China* 33, no. 1 (June 2012): 27–31.

she would purchase so much stock? Why, with no guarantee of profit, should you have accepted her 5000 *yuan* to invest?"[64] One might imagine, from the judge's question, that Shanghai had not just witnessed a wave of popular investment that bridged class and gender.[65]

Conclusion

The vernacular understandings of law and legal practice in the Xi-Tang case, not surprisingly, reveal areas of broad continuity with the late Qing era, together with Republican language of citizenship, nationalism, human rights, judicial reform, and judicial independence. The continuing sway of notions of communal and cosmic justice in the Republican era is perhaps not surprising, thought it was also problematized. Tang's lawyer, Li Shirui characterized such reasoning as outmoded: "The court's arbitrary decision that Xi's suicide was revenge required [substantial] denial of evidence. Following this logic, whenever someone dies outside their house, they are seeking revenge against the site of death. Can such logic exist in this world?"[66] His challenge appears to have made as little impression on the public as on the court.

The Xi-Tang case also exhibits strategic use of the judicial process by socially disadvantaged social actors, through the mechanism of false accusations. The Xi family logic resembles the late imperial false accusation cases examined by Quinn Javers.[67] The social expectation was that Tang, as Xi's employer, should compensate the family for losses from Xi's failed investment and her death, whether or not he was legally responsible. Concern for justice on behalf of their aggrieved family member as well as compensation from her employer were fundamental to the Xi women's actions.

Despite this continuity in vernacular expectations, the trial outcome also suggests a rupture between social expectations and the administration of justice. For the late Qing, Javers describes a dynamic state/society reciprocity that enabled weak parties to draw the power of the state at times into their local disputes. Javers reasons that the redistributive logic behind this socially-recognized strategy underlay judicial decisions to overlook the strict provisions

64 "Tang Jiezhi shangsu an shenliji 汤节之上訴案审理纪 [Tang Jiezhi's Appeal]," *Shenbao*, January 7, 1923.

65 Bryna Goodman, "Things Unheard" (2012).

66 Zhou Dongbai, p. 19 (appeal document, January 6, 1923).

67 Quinn Doyle Javers, *Conflict, Community, and Crime in Fin-de-siecle Sichuan*, Ph.D. dissertation, Stanford University (2012), chapter 4.

of the law and facilitate compensation of the weaker party. Court attentiveness to collective understandings of justice, rather than the letter of the law, contributed to the legitimacy of the administration of justice. In the Xi-Tang case, the guilty verdict certainly gratified Xi family enmity and moral sentiment against Tang. However, it would be inappropriate to conclude that the court was motivated by notions of moral economy. In fact the court showed little concern for compensating the family. The arms trading charge lodged against Tang shifted emphasis away from Xi's grievance. More than a year after Tang was moved to military prison, the Xi women were still petitioning the court for compensation. [68] Political exigency, rather than concern for the weak, provides a better explanation of court disregard for the evidence.

A similar logic may apply to expectations for community intervention. The involvement of public associations and institutions testifies to community agency in the judicial process. Understandings of community in the new republic included but also exceeded the legally engaged elites that Janet Theiss has examined for the late Qing,[69] and encompassed both older networks and new-style associations, bringing into one arena the paternalism of the Dongting Dongshan Xi lineage and newer notions of public representation, expressed through the mediated public opinion of Republican-era newspapers. Insofar as community intervention bore the mantle of popular opinion, public response to the case suggests a robust early Republican-era climate of what Ben Liebman, in the context of contemporary China, terms legal populism, the notion that the populace has a right to weigh in on court decisions.[70] It is perhaps in character with contemporary understandings of legal process in China that a recent PRC study of the Xi-Tang case reasoned that the court's decision was motivated by concern to appease social sympathy for Xi.[71]

Although the verdict aligned with community sentiment, it would nonetheless be unwise to uncritically emphasize the power of public opinion. The broad expression of public feeling in this instance offered a useful cloak for an inappropriate but politically expedient application of the criminal code to

68 "Xi Fang Shi qing dui Tang Jiezhi zhi caichan 席方氏情对汤节之财产 [Madam Xi's Request in Regard to the Property of Tang Jiezhi]," *Shangbao*, April 8, 1924.

69 Janet Theiss, "Elite Engagement with the Judicial System in the Qing and its Implications for Legal Practice and Legal Principle," in this volume.

70 Benjamin Liebman, "A Return to Populist Legality? Historical Legacies and Legal Reform," in *Mao's Invisible Hand: The Political Foundations of Adaptive Governance in China*, ed. Sebastian Heilmann and Elizabeth Perry (Cambridge: Harvard University Asia Center, 2011), 165–200.

71 Lu Zhiqi 卢志奇, "Xi Shangzhen zisha de yanjiu 席上珍自杀的研究 [Research on Xi Shangzhen's Suicide]," M.A. thesis, Zhongshan University Law School (2012), 24.

ensnare Tang. The political backstory and the close interaction of court personnel with the Dongting association and the Xi family suggest the difficulty of disentangling community initiative and official manipulation in what appear to be spontaneous expressions of popular opinion in the legal process.[72]

The vernacular expectations expressed in the print discussion of the case and the protest movement that followed nonetheless reveal a strand of legal populism that predates the communist revolutionary tradition invoked by Liebman. This populism drew on republican notions of popular sovereignty and citizenship, the hegemonic principles of legitimacy after 1912, despite widespread recognition that the new republic had failed to produce a credible state.

The predicament of extraterritoriality exacerbated tensions in vernacular discussion between the imagined rights born of popular sovereignty and the duties and discipline of nationalism. The idea of popular sovereignty undergirded the militant assertions of citizen rights that were visible in protests of the Tang verdict. But citizen rights claims were vulnerable to the prerogatives of the nation and nationalism made it awkward to criticize Chinese judicial practice. Failure to critique foreign courts could disarm criticism of Chinese courts. After the inception of the reform movement that protested court bias, a reporter interviewed the protestors. He asked, "Did you mistrust the court and administration of justice prior to this case, or did this mistrust begin with this case? They responded, "We have always mistrusted the courts."[73] The protestors had nothing to say when asked whether a similar protest would have followed a judgment in the Mixed Court. By printing this detail, the reporter interrogated the protestors' loyalty.

Similarly, the language of judicial independence, which Xu Xiaoqun identifies as an ideal of the early republic,[74] was unsettled and available for conflicting interpretation. A court administrator, who was interviewed by the same journalist, used the ideal of judicial independence to cast aspersions on the integrity of the judicial reform movement. In his rendering, judicial independence necessitated the protection of the court against pressure from individuals or the popular masses: "This [protest] by these groups [oppresses] the court to please a private individual. It is bad for the masses to interfere with the administration of justice." He suggested that the reputation of the court

72 See also Bryna Goodman, "Review of Eugenia Lean, *Public Passions: The Trial of Shi Jianqiao and the Rise of Popular Sympathy in Republican China*," *Journal of Asian Studies* 67, no. 3 (August 2008): 1063–65.

73 ZHXB, December 12, 1922.

74 Xu Xiaoqun, "The Fate of Judicial Independence in Republican China, 1912–1937," *China Quarterly* 149 (March 1997): 9.

remained intact, but worried nonetheless that the protestors incurred "the derision of foreigners." His musings were tone-deaf in terms of contemporary anti-Japanese sentiment: "Recently the Japanese Consul General spoke to me about [a case in which] more than twenty outsiders interfered, something he found especially regrettable."[75]

Similar concern to protect Chinese legal process from popular interference appeared in the press. A *Shishi xinbao* editorial highlighted the neologism, "legal rights movement," and argued for a rectification of names. Those protesting the verdict had created a "false legal sovereignty movement" or a "destroy legal sovereignty movement," because the organizers' activities "destroyed the spirit of judicial independence," making the abolition of extraterritoriality more difficult: "The abolition of consular jurisdiction requires two things: 1) wholesome judicial institutions, fully developed law, and upright officials; 2) citizens who know and respect the law." The writer suggested that it was only because protest leaders lived in the International Settlement that "they could indignantly attack the court." The author was critical of Chinese judicial personnel ("we frankly admit that we have no faith in them"). Nonetheless, he argued, "citizens should respect the law," and reforms must have limits: "If you want to reform the judicial system, citizens must first gain legal knowledge.... If their acts destroy the judiciary, it is useless to sing out 'legal rights movement.' "[76]

Another editorial pleaded for judicial lenience for the defendant, noting that there was no evidence of criminal behavior. The writer argued, nonetheless, that society must uphold the sanctity of the court. At a consequential moment for the return of Chinese sovereignty, criticism of Chinese courts was unfortunate, especially if the criticism came from people who lived within the International Settlement.[77]

These views of national loyalties, citizen duty, and restraint on public criticism of Chinese courts provoked a discredited but eloquent rebuttal in Tang's own newspaper:

> [Some people] make the criticism that "this [protest] intrudes on the independence of the law" ... [But protest] is exactly what citizens *should* do. If they insist that this infringes on judicial independence and citizen rights, how may we speak of legal literacy?

---

75 ZHXB, December 12, 1922. Quoting the Japanese Consul made sense in terms of solicitude for the Japan-connected He Fenglin.

76 SSXB, December 12, 1922.

77 ZHXB, December 11, 1922.

> "Judicial independence" refers to independence from the legislative and administrative branches of government. It is not that [the court] should be independent of citizens, who suffer grievances, insult, and murder, without being able to register their objections. Such critics' solicitousness for the judges resembles the subservience of slaves.... They forget they are fundamental republican citizens of the national body. [They] say that the [protests of the public organizations harms our legal sovereignty, reveals our judicial underside, and that this is what citizens should not do. From this we see that they cheat themselves in order to cheat others.[78]

This exchange illuminates the predicament of vernacular understandings of democracy and legal process in the early Republican era. The extraordinary multiplicity of legal institutions on Chinese soil, old and new, Chinese and foreign, worked to denaturalize all of them, making them appear more like arbitrary constructs than embodiments of rooted law.[79] In late Qing vernacular understandings of law, as analyzed by Margaret Wan, vernacular criticism was directed, not at the law itself, but at the gap between legal ideals and practice.[80] Once sovereignty was no longer self-evident, nothing was ineluctable. In a fractured political landscape, older, morally-inflected notions of justice provided a familiar language to navigate the social disruptions of new urban arrangements and the modern confusions of sexually integrated workplaces, stock exchanges, and market speculation.

Chinese courts were tokens of national aspiration, but difficult to criticize, and troubled in practice, bent to the contingencies of local military governance. In the absence of a state that was perceived to be legitimate, the principle of popular sovereignty nonetheless assumed unusual rhetorical independence from notions of state constraint. This form of "de-institutionalized democracy" (or "deconstructed political form," as Yves Chevrier has described it)[81] coexisted in tension with a powerful nationalism that was similarly fueled by the dream of an unrealized state. The consequences for Chinese judicial process and understanding of the rule of law, compounded by the institutional disruptions of first decades of the People's Republic, continue to resonate today.

78 December 14, 1922.

79 In the new Republic, the law itself was unsettled.

80 Margaret Wan, "Justice and Corruption: Legal Ideals in Qing Ballads," in this volume.

81 Yves Chevrier, "Elusive Democracy," in *China, Democracy, and Law: A Historical and Contemporary Approach*, ed. Mireille Delmas-Marty and Pierre-Etienne Will (Leiden: Brill, 2012), 459–77.

Glossary

Dongting Dongshan	洞庭东山	*Shishi xinbao*	时事新报
gonglun	公论	Tang Jiezhi	汤节之
Guang-Zhao *gongsuo*	公所	*Xinwenbao*	新闻报
jiancha ting	检察厅	Xi Shangzhen	席上珍
Jingbao	晶报	Yao Gonghe	姚公鹤
Li Shirui	李时蕊	*yulun*	舆论
Qin Liankui	秦联奎	*zhongliu jieji*	中流阶级
qingre yichang	情热异常	Zhou Dongbai	周东白
quanyou	劝诱	Zhou Fengxia	周凤暇
Shangbao	商报		

Bibliography

Newspapers

China Press (CP)
Jingbao 晶报 (JB)
Minguo ribao 民国日报 (MGRB)
North China Daily News (NCDN)
North China Herald (NCH)
Shangbao 商报
Shenbao 申报
Shishi xinbao 时事新报 (SSXB)
Weekly Review of the Far East (WRFE)
Xinwenbao 新闻报 (XWB)
Xin Shenbao 新申报 (XSB)

Cha Mengci 查孟词. "Nüzi jiaoyu de quexian 女子教育的缺陷 [Limitations of Female Education]." ZHXB, reprinted in MGRB, September 16, 1922.

Chen Zemin 陈则民. "Fei jiancha zhidu zhi yundong 废检察制度之运动 [Procuratorial-System Abolition Movement]." Shanghai, 1922 (pamphlet).

Chen, Li. "Legal Specialists and Judicial Administration in Late Imperial China, 1651–1911." *Late Imperial China* 33, no. 1 (June 2012): 1–54.

Chevrier, Yves. "Elusive Democracy." In *China, Democracy, and Law: A Historical and Contemporary Approach*, edited by Mireille Delmas-Marty and Pierre-Etienne Will, 459–77. Leiden: Brill, 2012.

"Chinese Files Libel Suits." *Weekly Review of the Far East* (WRFE), September 23, 1922.

Chow, Eileen. *Spectacular Novelties: "News" Culture, Zhang Henshui, and Practices of Spectatorship in Republican China*. Ph.D. dissertation, Stanford University, 2000.

Commission on Extraterritoriality, ed. *Provisional Code of the Republic of China*. Peking: Commission on Extraterritoriality, 1923.

Cui Weiru 崔蔚茹, ed. *Xi Shangzhen* 席上珍 (2 volumes). Shanghai: Funü zhiye yanjiu she, 1922.

Des Forges, Alexander. "Building Shanghai, One Page at a Time: The Aesthetics of Installment Fiction at the Turn of the Century." *Journal of Asian Studies* 62, no. 3 (August 2003): 781–810.

Dongting dongshan lüHu tongxianghui di shi'er ci baogao shu 洞庭东山旅沪第十二报告书 [Twelfth Report of the Dongting Association]. Shanghai, 1924.

Dongting dongshan lüHu tongxianghui sanshi zhou jinian tekan 洞庭东山旅沪同乡会三十周年纪念特刊 [30-Year Commemoration of Shanghai Dongting Association]. Shanghai: 1944.

"Dongting dongshan tongxiang dai wei suyuan 洞庭东山代为诉冤 [Dongting Association Redresses Grievances]." *Shenbao*, September 13, 1922.

"Dr. F.C. Tong Arrested by Chinese Police." CP, November 14, 1922.

"Dr. Tong Kidnapped," NCDN, November 14, 1922.

"Ge tuanti dui Tang an zhi ji'ang 各团体对汤案之激昂 [Indignation of Groups in Tang Case]." MGRB, December 11, 1922.

Goodman, Bryna. "New Woman Commits Suicide: Press, Cultural Memory, and the New Republic." *Journal of Asian Studies* 64, no. 1 (February 2005): 67–101.

———. "Review of Eugenia Lean, *Public Passions: The Trial of Shi Jianqiao and the Rise of Popular Sympathy in Republican China*." *Journal of Asian Studies* 67, no. 3 (August 2008): 1063–65.

———. "Things Unheard of East or West: Colonial Contamination and Cultural Purity in Early Chinese Stock Exchanges." In *Twentieth-Century Colonialism and China: Localities, the Everyday, and the World*, edited by Goodman and Goodman (New York: Routledge, 2012), 57–77.

———. "What is in a Network? Local, Personal, and Public Loyalties in the Context of Changing Conceptions of State and Social Welfare." In *At the Crossroads of Empires*, edited by Nara Dillon and Jean Oi (Stanford: Stanford University Press, 2007), 155–78.

Goodman, Bryna, and David S.G. Goodman. "Introduction: Colonialism and China." In *Twentieth-Century Colonialism and China: Localities, the Everyday, and the World*, edited by Goodman and Goodman (New York: Routledge, 2012), 1–22.

Great Britain. PRO FO 228/3291 Shanghai Intelligence Report, September 1921.

Hu Xia 胡暇, and HuangYan 黄岩, eds. *Susong changshi* 诉讼常识 [Basic Knowledge about Lawsuits]. Shanghai: Shangwu yinshuguan, 1922.

Huey, Herbert. "Law and Social Attitudes in 1920s Shanghai." *Hong Kong Law Journal* 14, no. 3 (1984): 306–22.

Javers, Quinn Doyle. *Conflict, Community, and Crime in Fin-de-siecle Sichuan*. Ph.D. dissertation, Stanford University, 2012, chapter 4.

"Jianting qisu Xi Shangzhen yuanwen 检厅起诉席上珍原文 [Procuratorial Indictment in Xi Shangzhen Case]." *Shenbao*, November 27, 1922.

"Judicial Reform Discussed by Meeting Here." *China Press*, September 29, 1922.

"Liang gongtuan dui Tang an fayan 两公团对汤案发言 [Two Groups Speak in Tang Case]." MGRB, December 10, 1922

Liebman, Benjamin. "A Return to Populist Legality? Historical Legacies and Legal Reform." In *Mao's Invisible Hand: The Political Foundations of Adaptive Governance in China*, edited by Sebastian Heilmann and Elizabeth Perry (Cambridge: Harvard University Asia Center, 2011), 165–200.

Lu Zhiqi 卢志奇. "Xi Shangzhen zisha de yanjiu 席上珍自杀的研究 [Research on Xi Shangzhen's Suicide]." M.A. thesis, Zhongshan University Law School, 2012.

"Magistrate Tu Turns Detective in Tong Trial, Rules Out Evidence: Drama Enacted in Crowded Courtroom as Mother of Suicide Denounces Accused." CP, December 9, 1922.

Ruskola, Teemu. "Colonialism Without Colonies: On the Extraterritorial Jurisprudence of the U.S. Court for China." *Law and Contemporary Problems* 17 (2008): 217

———. *Legal Orientalism: China, the United States, and Modern Law*. Cambridge: Harvard University Press, 2013.

Shanghai Municipal Archives 1-1-1135. Shanghai Municipal Council, *Daily Police Reports*, September 9, 1922.

"Shanghai zuijin yibai mingren biao 上海最近一百名人表 [Most Recent List of 100 Shanghai Celebrities]." *Jingbao* (JB), March 30, 1922.

Stephens, Thomas B. *Order and Discipline in China: The Shanghai Mixed Court 1911–27*. Seattle: University of Washington Press, 1992.

Susong xuzhi 诉讼须知 [Necessary Knowledge about Lawsuits]. Shanghai: Shangwu yinshuguan, 1917.

"Tang an zhao yuanpan 汤案照原判 [Tang Case Follows Original Verdict]." MGRB February 24, 1923.

"Tang Jiezhi bianhu liyou 汤节之辩护理由 [Tang's Defense]." *Shenbao*, December 10, 1922.

"Tang Jiezhi jinyao shengming 汤节之紧要声明 [Important Declaration of Tang Jiezhi]." *Shenbao*, September 11, 1922. Also printed in XWB, September 11, 1922; NCH, September 16, 1922.

"Tang Jiezhi shangsu an shenli ji 汤节之上诉案审理记 [Tang's Appeal Hearing]." *Shenbao*, January 7, 1923.

Theiss, Janet. "Elite Engagement with the Judicial System in the Qing and its Implications for Legal Practice and Legal Principle." In this volume.

Wan, Margaret. "Justice and Corruption: Legal Ideals in Qing Ballads." In this volume.

"Xi Fang Shi qing dui Tang Jiezhi zhi caichan 席方氏情对汤节之财产 [Madam Xi's Request in Regard to the Property of Tang Jiezhi]." *Shangbao*, April 8, 1924.

"Xi Shangzhen an chong tiqi 席上珍案重提起 [Xi Case Raised Again]." MGRB, August 10, 1928.

Xi Shangzhen an zhi zuoxun 席上珍案之昨讯 [Yesterday's News on Xi Case]." *Shenbao*, August 23, 1923.

"Xi Shangzhen an zuo ri bianlun zongjie 席上珍案昨日辩论总结 [Yesterday's Summation in Xi Case]." MGRB, December 9.

"Xiao Shenbao" (Special Xi-Tang issue). XSB, September 17, 1922.

Xu, Xiaoqun. "Fate of Judicial Independence in Republican China, 1912–1937." *China Quarterly* 149 (March 1997): 1–28.

———. *Trial of Modernity: Judicial Reform in Early Twentieth-Century China*. Stanford: Stanford University Press, 2008.

Yao Gonghe 姚公鹤. *Shanghai xianhua* 上海闲话 [Idle Talk about Shanghai]. Shanghai: Shanghai gujichubanshe reprint, 1989.

Zhou Dongbai 周东白. *Quanguo lüshi ming'an huilan* 全国律师名案汇览 [Compilation of Famous Cases of the Nation's Lawyers]. Shanghai: Shijie shuju, 1923.

CHAPTER 6

Wayward Daughters: Sex, Family, and Law in Early Twentieth-Century Beijing

*Zhao Ma**

On July 23, 1946, Li Haiquan rushed to police station and reported to officers that his daughter Li Shuying was abducted by her boyfriend Li Duxiao. Haiquan was manager of an iron works and lived with his wife and seventeen-year-old daughter in the Inner-3 District in Beijing. In his neighborhood, there lived Duxiao, a twenty-two-year-old shop assistant of a pharmacy store. Shuying became acquainted with Duxiao because she often went to his home to use his telephone, and over time the casual encounter grew into an intimate relationship. Haiquan did not intervene, but secretly arranged his daughter's engagement to a man surnamed Jiao. Once he told Shuying of the engagement plan, Shuying declined, and she even attempted to commit suicide by taking arsenic after learning that Jiao's mother had a difficult personality. On July 19, Shuying ran away from home. She took money from the family to finance her elopement and also persuaded Duxiao to run off with her. Three days after she fled, Haiquan ran into his neighbor who told him that Shuying had taken his rickshaw to the railway station on the day of her disappearance. The neighbor recalled that Shuying said she was going to Nankou in Beijing's northern suburb. Haiquan alerted police immediately and together they took the train to Nankou and arrested the absconding couple at a hostel near the train station.[1]

The case of Shuying and Duxiao shows that the law enforcement and criminal justice in Republican Beijing played an active role in handling cases involving absconding unmarried women. Police officers investigated abduction allegations. They patrolled train stations, long-distance bus terminals,

* For giving me generous and insightful comments, I want to thank Susan Brownell, Bob Hegel, Madeleine Zelin, Li Chen, Steve Miles, Tobie Meyer-Fong, Harold Tanner, Linda Nicolson, and participants of the Colloquium Series of Women, Gender, and Sexuality Stuides Program at Washington University in St. Louis in fall 2012. I thank my research assistant, Clarissa Polk, who came to my aid with tireless support on writing and editing.

1 Beijing Municipal Archives (cited hereinafter as BMA), No. J65-13-3974, Li Duxiao, 1946. All citations from the Beijing Municipal Archives in this article follow their cataloging conventions. The citation numbers refer to category (*quanzong*), catalogue (*mulu*), and volume (*juan*).

© KONINKLIJKE BRILL NV, LEIDEN, 2015 | DOI 10.1163/9789004288492_008

and city gates in search of suspicious elements, especially people who were traveling without proper documentation. They also conducted periodic raids of wayside inns to arrest couples who failed to prove their relationship. Men and women arrested on a charge of abduction typically were detained in the police station where a preliminary interrogation could be held. After gathering testimony and physical evidence, the Police Department filed a concise investigation report and transferred the case to the procuracy at the Beijing District Court. Procurators held preliminary hearings to determine if there was sufficient evidence to hold the accused men and women for trial in criminal court. As the prosecution moved forward, as happened in Shuying and Duxiao's case, the judge presided over trials, summoned witnesses, cross-examined testimonies and evidence, heard lawyer's statements, and then issued the sentence. In cases where the defendant decided to appeal, the Hebei Provincial High Court would review case files and issue the final sentence.[2] Legal proceedings document every step as the case was moved through the Republican system of law enforcement and criminal justice, and are now preserved in the Beijing Municipal Archives. They allow us to examine the pattern of unmarried women's sexuality and the meaning of the sexual encounters to unmarried women themselves, their male partners, their families, and judicial officials who conducted criminal investigations. It is through this kind of family crisis—escalating tensions between daughters and parents, and through official's adjudicative and legislative responses, that this article seeks to examine some of the core twentieth-century conceptions of women, family, and the power dynamic inside the family.

During court hearings, most parents, including Shuying's father Haiquan, insisted on their daughters' innocence and blamed their male friends for the affair. Haiquan described Shuying as "young and naïve" (*nianyou tianzhen*) and "ignorant of worldly affairs" (*buzhi shili*), while her boyfriend, Duxiao, was accused of instigating Shuying's wild behavior. Haiquan wrote in his complaint: "Without Duxiao's instigation, Shuying would never have agreed to her engagement; moreover, she would not have attempted to commit suicide if Duxiao had not given her poison." Such rationale explained why most parents refused to describe their runaway daughters' action as elopement (which implied a degree of women's consent) but, instead, called it an act of abduction perpetrated by men. The depiction of runaway daughters as victims of male seduction and exploitation echoed the late imperial conception of women's sexuality. According to Philip Huang, the Qing codes perceived man as "the active agent" in sexual crimes such as seduction and rape, whereas woman

2 BMA, No. J65-3-287, "Susong xuzhi 诉讼须知 [Guidelines of Litigation]," December 21, 1935.

maintained agency by either consenting or resisting man's advance.[3] "Women have fickle temperaments," Huang Liuhong, a seventeenth-century magistrate warned, and "they will be unable to control themselves" when facing men's propositions.[4]

Judicial officials, however, were cautious about the kind of testimonies that regarded women as sexually passive. They saw runaway daughters responsible for more than consenting to male advance. As the case of Shuying demonstrates, they often took matters in their own hands in terms of initiating social relationship and sexual encounter. It was not uncommon that the runaway daughters testified in their boyfriends' defense during court hearings. They claimed they "were deeply in love with" (*liangqing xianghao*) their boyfriends and they absconded not because of male predation but because of parental opposition to their relationship. As women became increasingly socially and sexually assertive, the laws adopted new principles to recognize woman as "an independent agent" capable of, among other things, initiating and maintaining sexual liaisons with men. The case of Shuying and Duxiao, along with others prosecuted at the Beijing District Court, allows us to study how such a new conception of women's sexual agency and the new criminal laws were applied in actual adjudication process and radically changed the way laws scrutinized women's social and sexual behaviors.

While recognizing women's sexual urges and autonomy, judicial officials did not necessarily endorse unmarried women's actions to run away from home with their male friends. They clearly understood that women eloping signified a family crisis—a daughter's open challenge to parental authority. They were also aware of the entrenched social disapproval of elopement as unruly and immoral behavior. Furthermore, judicial officials knew that, if the elopement was the product of a sexual liaison that resulted in out-of-wedlock pregnancy, it not only caused significant damage to a women's sexual respectability and the family's social standing, but also threatened the family's financial well-being (especially in the lower echelon of society). These practical concerns and pervasive social stigma attached to elopement drove parents to seek judicial intervention to punish the wayward daughter and her male friend for their unapproved relationship and behavior.

3 Philip C.C. Huang, *Code, Custom, and Legal Practice in China: The Qing and the Republic Compared* (Stanford: Stanford University Press, 2002).

4 Janet Theiss, *Disgraceful Matters: The Politics of Chastity in Eighteenth-Century China* (Berkeley: University of California Press, 2004), 184. See also Matthew H. Sommer, *Sex, Law, and Society in Late Imperial China* (Stanford: Stanford University Press, 1999).

In this regard, Republican lawmakers and judicial officials, though operating within a legal context that claimed radically different political and cultural foundations, found themselves embarking on the same mission as their imperial counterparts did centuries earlier: a mission to define women's sexuality and defend the integrity of the family in the face of drastic and often disruptive changes. Imperial lawmakers in the eighteenth century, as Matthew Sommer has suggested, engaged in a concerted campaign to make the humble peasant household "the foundation of late imperial order."[5] They enlisted women's moral consciousness and sexual purity to defend a patriarchal family order. Such ideologically and legislatively fortified families allowed the Qing state to contain the increasing physical mobility that released people from traditional familial and communal control, while also allowing it to counter the grave and growing threat posed by underclass "rogue males"—men displaced by the commercialized economy and forced to stray from normative family relations. The social and legal reform since the late Qing sought to dislodge the family from its underlying traditional values such as female chastity, gender segregation, and parental authority. Yet, the reform efforts changed neither the essential meanings of the family as the basic unit of economic production, nor did it change the family as an anchor of social order in a society torn apart by political crisis and socioeconomic changes. The case of Shuying and Duxiao, together with other cases heard before the Beijing District Court, enables us to explore how Republican judicial officials responded to women's growing assertion of social and sexual autonomy on the one hand, and parents' tangible concerns about their authority and the integrity of the family on the other hand, within the framework of the new Republican criminal law.

The Qing Practice

Historians have shown that lawsuits involving runaway women, both married and unmarried, constituted a significant portion of late imperial Chinese officials' regular judicial docket.[6] In the Qing Code, "to run away from one's husband or father," Paola Paderni argues, "was a crime, because it challenged the

5 Sommer, *Sex, Law, and Society*, 310.

6 Paola Paderni, "I Thought I Would Have Some Happy Days: Women Eloping in Eighteenth-Century China," *Late Imperial China* 16, no. 1 (1995): 1–32; Jonathan Spence, *Death of Woman Wang* (New York: Penguin, 1998); Wang Yuesheng 王跃生, *Qingdai zhongqi hunyin chongtu touxi* 清代中期婚姻冲突透析 [Marital Disputes in the Mid-Qing Period] (Beijing: Shehui kexue chubanshe, 2003).

family, the institution on which the state based its power."[7] The family envisioned by the Qing state was a patriarchal unit. Those who helped her elope violated one of the patriarchal household's property rights—the right to control a woman's body. As Philip Huang has argued, Qing laws "even implicitly equated those women with things taken by theft or robbery" by placing abduction and seduction under the statutory section of *zeidao*—"theft and robbery."[8] Because promotion and protection of family order became a top priority on the government's political and social agendas, elopement was deemed a serious offense. The Qing laws prescribed various penalties, ranging from strangulation to flogging, in order to punish men who seduced women away from their families and women who submitted to such seduction. With these rather draconian laws, Qing officials reaffirmed their social mission and sent a stern warning to anyone who dared to undermine the normative family order.

Officials considered a number of factors when determining penalties. At the outset, the Qing laws upheld the principle of "status performance," a term coined by Matthew Sommer, which made social status the central arbiter of sexual morality and criminal liability. People were divided into two opposing categories, *liang* (honorable persons or free commoners) vs. *jian* (mean or debased persons), and each was "held to different standards of sexual and familial morality."[9] Commoners were to follow Confucian ritual norms to support the hierarchy in terms of gender roles and family obligations, while the debased group was seen as incapable—unnecessary, even—to live up to the standard of sexual morality. Therefore, the seduction law strove to defend the status boundary by protecting women's body and the integrity of common families. As far as the law was concerned, the worst-case scenario was to have a debased male lure away a daughter of a commoner's household; such act not only threatened the generational notion of patriarchy but also transgressed the status boundaries.

However, Sommer points out that many statutes in the *Great Qing Code* "embodied timeless moral ideals" but ceased to function in everyday adjudication. It is the substatutes that "gave the principles to be applied in practice."[10] In the eighteenth century, Qing laws went through "a fundamental shift in the organizing principle for the regulation of sexuality," from "status performance" to "gender performance, in which a uniform standard of sexual morality and criminal liability was extended across old status boundaries and all

7 Paderni, "I Thought I Would Have Some Happy Days," 2.

8 Huang, *Code, Custom, and Legal Practice in China*, 158–9.

9 Sommer, *Sex, Law, and Society*, 2.

10 Ibid., 26.

people were expected to conform to gender roles strictly defined in terms of marriage."[11] In place of social status, a victim's consent now assumed the paramount importance when assigning legal liabilities. The statute set the age of consent at ten; if a woman was ten years old or younger, then "although she agree[d], it is the same as the law of kidnapping and enticing" and she "[was] not to be punished."[12] The substatute added to the code book in the eighteenth century increased the penalty by one degree: "All persons who are guilty of enticing children by means of tricks or drugs will be punished by strangulation immediately." A woman above the age of ten "[would] not be punished" but instead "reunited with her family" if she was a victim of abduction; in contrast, if a woman gave her consent, her punishment would be one degree less than that of her seducer.[13] To determine whether consent was given, a woman's conduct before the crime and her reactions to the crime often came under strict scrutiny. One statutory explanation summarized that: to convict a man of abduction, the abducted person must "neither have previous knowledge of the plot prior to the abduction" (*shiwei buzhi*), "nor give up to the abduction when it was committed" (*houwei buyuan*).[14] The seduction law did not specify what behaviors and circumstances would prove or disqualify a woman's innocence, but the rape law in the Qing Code offers some clues.

Seduction and rape, though two distinct types of crime, posed a similar threat to imperial morals and social order. They both represented a blunt attack on family by licentious males from the outside; and if a woman failed to uphold the moral code of conduct, both crimes also signified the internal collapse of family. Historians including Vivien Ng, Matthew Sommer, and Janet Theiss have demonstrated that late imperial judges in rape cases closely examined the alleged victim's conduct prior to the crime.[15] More important than the record of chaste behavior is that women were asked to present evidence of active resistance throughout the crime. If a woman gave up her resistance at any moment, "the case was not considered rape, but one of 'illicit intercourse by

11 Ibid., 5.

12 Article 275.3, *The Great Qing Code*, William C. Jones, trans. (New York: Oxford University Press, 1994), 258.

13 Article 275.1, *The Great Qing Code*, 258.

14 *Da Qing lüli zengxiu tongzuan jicheng* 大清律例增修通纂集成 [Enlarged and Revised Collectanea of the *Great Qing Code*, 1899], Vol. 25, "Theft and Robbery: Abducting and Selling People," 24.

15 Sommer, *Sex, Law, and Society*, 68. Also see Vivien Ng, "Ideology and Sexuality: Rape Laws in Qing China," *Journal of Asian Studies* 46, no. 1 (1987): 57–70; Theiss, *Disgraceful Matters*, 170.

mutual consent,' in which case the woman would be subject to punishment."[16] Janet Theiss also reminds us that imperial officials expected woman not only to resist physical assault but also to fend off any unwanted propositions (e.g. flirtation, verbal insult, and unwitting impropriety) that could compromise one's moral integrity and credentials of being a victim of sexual crimes.[17] Following the same rationale, the seduction law also put women in a perilous position: It treated women as accomplices, *not* victims, if they failed to present an impeccable record of chaste behaviors or if they showed any sign of submitting to the attackers; a woman's penalty would be one degree less than her attacker's.[18] In sum, sexual promiscuity destroyed female virtue and family honor. When they failed to live up to the state's moral expectations, women would be punished along with the male offenders.

This kind of patriarchal family order and ideal of female chastity came under attack in the era of twentieth-century social and cultural reforms. Susan Glosser has argued that reformers, particularly of the May Fourth generation, "accused the traditional patriarchal family of sacrificing China's youth on the altar of filial obligation, teaching them dependency, slavishness, and insularity, and robbing them of their creative energy."[19] The reform started as a cultural and social movement to create a world in which women could enter public spaces, pursue education and professional careers, and participate in politics more freely. It also inspired and drove legal reform, whereby political and social leaders expected laws to safeguard women's rights and to remold family structure and gender relations. In 1910, the late Qing regime revised its criminal code and drafted its first civil code. In the following two decades, Republican lawmakers drafted five criminal codes and four civil codes.[20] The legal reform movement, in particular its final product—the 1935 Criminal Code, promised to redefine female sexuality and the pattern of domestic authority.

16 Such evidence, according to Vivien Ng, must include: "(1) witnesses, either eyewitnesses or people who had heard the victim's cry for help; (2) bruises and lacerations on her body; and (3) torn clothing." Ng, "Ideology and Sexuality," 58.

17 Theiss, *Disgraceful Matters*, 11–2.

18 Article 275.1, *The Great Qing Code*, 258.

19 Susan Glosser, *Chinese Visions of Family and State, 1915–1953* (Berkeley: University of California Press, 2003), 3.

20 Xie Zhenmin 谢振民, *Zhonghua minguo lifa shi* 中华民国立法史 [Legislative History of the Republic of China] (Beijing: Zhongguo zhengfa daxue chubanshe, 1999).

Elopement in Republican Laws

The judges at the Beijing District Court in the 1940s all held college degrees from national universities, private colleges, and even foreign institutions.[21] Contemporary surveys indicate that college students at the time overwhelmingly supported new ideals such as "freedom of marriage" (*ziyou jiehun*), "freedom of love" (*ziyou lian'ai*), "open social contact" (*shejiao gongkai*), "coeducation" (*nannü tongxue*), and "conjugal family structure" (*xiao jiating zhi*).[22] As legal professionals, they also witnessed several fundamental changes to the *Criminal Code*. Simply put, the new law considered woman "an independent agent," capable of having sexual liaisons with men.[23] Moreover, a woman did not have to prove her chastity in order to be considered a legitimate victim of sexual crimes. This article will now examine criminal cases heard before the Beijing District Court to explore how judges applied the reformist ideals and laws in actual adjudication.

Credentials of the Victim

When a seventeen-year-old Li Huanchen could not get along with her stepmother in 1942, she decided to run away from her home in Beijing and go back to her hometown in Hebei Province. Huanchen told the plan to her friend, Shao Shuqin, who convinced her to stay in Beijing for just one more day so that they could spend some more time together. On February 24, they walked to the Business Encouraging Bazaar (Quanyechang) to watch a film and left there around five o'clock. Shuqin ran into a man named Zhang Wenlu, a friend of her sister's. At eight o'clock in the evening, Shuqin went home while Huanchen and Wenlu walked back to the bazaar. Around eleven o'clock, Wenlu spotted his friend, Liu Wenxuan, a twenty-year-old shop assistant. The three people chatted for a while and eventually Wenlu left. Before he departed, Wenlu

---

21 BMA, No. J65-3-161, "Beiping difang fayuan 1943 nian disan jidu banshi renyuan xueli 北平地方法院1943年第三季度办事人员学历 [Educational Credentials of Judicial Officials at the Beijing District Court during the Third Quarter of 1943]," 1943.

22 For social surveys of students' views of marriage and family, see Chen Heqin 陈鹤琴, "Shehui wenti: xuesheng hunyin wenti zhi yanjiu 社会问题：学生婚姻问题之研究 [Social Problems: Study of the Problems of Student's Marriage]," *Dongfang zazhi* 东方杂志 [Oriental Miscellany] 18, no. 4 (Feb. 25, 1921), 18, no. 5 (March 10, 1921), and 18, no. 6 (March 25, 1921). Reprinted in *Minguo shiqi shehui diaocha congbian: hunyin jiating juan* 民国时期社会调查丛编：婚姻家庭卷 [Republican Social Surveys: Marriage and Family], ed. Li Wenhai et al. (Fuzhou: Fujian jiaoyu chubanshe, 2004), 1–33.

23 Huang, *Code, Custom, and Legal Practice in China*, 182.

whispered to Wenxuan that Huanchen was a street prostitute. It is not clear what happened afterwards. According to Huanchen, she checked into an inn with Wenxuan. When the innkeeper asked about her relationship with Wenxuan, Huanchen claimed that she was his wife. They stayed in the same hotel room. Huanchen alleged that Wenxuan raped her that night. In contrast, Wenxuan considered everything that happened consensual. After the first sexual episode, he saw Huanchen bleeding and realized that she was not a prostitute. But Huanchen did not resist Wenxuan's further advances and had sex with him twice again that night. Huanchen woke up and found Wenxuan gone. Consumed by anger, shame, and despair, Huanchen attempted to commit suicide. The hotel servant, twenty-six-year-old Li De, came to her rescue. After listening to her story, he offered to take her to his hometown. They traveled a few miles and checked in at the Quanshun Inn. Before they could travel any further, however, they were stopped by policemen. The police found Li De and Huanchen sharing a hotel room. Without proper documentation to support a spousal relationship, the two were arrested. One month later, the prosecutor at the Beijing District Court filed an indictment charging Li De with abduction and Wenxuan, the man who had sex with Huanchen the night before she was intercepted by police, with rape. However, they did not file a charge against Huanchen.[24]

Huanchen's experience and the court's investigation showcase the radical change from the imperial laws to the Republican codes with regard to the roles and rules of women in public. Imperial gender norms held that once women left their domestic sphere and made contact with male strangers, they would be tempted into improper behavior and licentious activities, which would upset the moral order based on the spatial division between domestic and public spaces.[25] Recent studies have pointed out that such spatial seclusion reflected more of "a rhetorical distinction" than "actual practices;" the *nei/wai* dichotomy was not fixed but flexible, permeable, and relative in everyday life.[26]

24 BMA, No. J65-6-2177, Liu Wenxuan, (1942).

25 Weikun Cheng, "In Search of Leisure: Women's Festivities in Late Imperial Beijing," *The Chinese Historical Review* 14, no. 1 (Spring 2007): 1–28.

26 Historians since the 1990s have become increasingly familiar with the study of the gendered division of space (both as social ideal and everyday experience) in late imperial China. For an overview of important scholarly works, please see Bryna Goodman and Wendy Larson, "Axes of Gender: Divisions of Labor and Spatial Separation," in *Gender in Motion: Divisions of Labor and Cultural Change in Late Imperial and Modern China*, ed. Bryna Goodman and Wendy Larson (Lanham, MD: Rowman & Littlefield Publishers, 2005), 1–25.

Nevertheless, gendered seclusion remained normative in late imperial China and therefore cultivated hostility towards women's public visibility. On the one hand, Qing laws profiled victims of sexual crimes as those who "remained unambiguously within the domestic sphere proper to them," as Matthew Sommer puts it. Therefore, "[t]hey could not be blamed for provoking rape through some questionable activity of their own."[27] On the other hand, Janet Theiss argues that "coping with perpetual compromises of idealized gender norms in their living and work situations," Qing laws required women to maintain "the inner-outer distinction by cultivating a 'sense of shame' that guided them in 'avoiding suspicion' of impropriety in their inevitable interactions with men."[28]

Nevertheless, early twentieth-century reforms rejected this gendered division of space, as both an ideal and a practice. In Beijing of the early 1940s, there were two cinemas, an acrobatic ground, seven Peking Opera houses, two billiards, a dancing hall, a café, 131 restaurants, four teahouses, thirty-six bars, and two temple fairs in the Outer-2 District where Huanchen lived.[29] Many of these businesses admitted women; and as the population of female consumers grew, some businesses even tailored their products and services to the needs of female customers.[30] The growing level of women's public visibility constituted, in Paul Bailey's terms, "one of the most striking social and cultural changes of the period."[31] Government officials and intellectuals were concerned about "bad behaviors," which included women attending licentious shows; but they still encouraged women to enter the public realm as political activists,

27 Sommer, *Sex, Law, and Society*, 103.

28 Theiss, *Disgraceful Matters*, 11–2.

29 In addition to these entertainment facilities, there were 128 brothels in the district. BMA, No. J2-7-337, "Beijing tebieshi dianyingyuan diaochabiao 北京特別市电影院调查表 [Survey of Cinemas in Beijing]," March 1943; J2-7-337, "Beijing tebie shi qiushe, chashe, jiugang, fanguan, zajichang diaochabiao 北京特别市球社、茶社、酒缸、饭馆、杂技场调查表 [Survey of Billiards, Teahouses, Bars, Restaurants, and Acrobatic Grounds in Beijing]," December 1943; J183-2-23990, "Benshi ge wuchang mingcheng biao 本市各舞场名称表 [List of Dance Halls in Beijing]," 1942; J2-7-414, "Beijing tebie shi fanguan diaocha biao 北京特别市饭馆调查表 [Survey of Restaurants in Beijing]," June 1943.

30 Leo Ou-fan Lee, "The Urban Milieu of Shanghai Cinema, 1930–40: Some Explorations of Film Audience, Film Culture, and Narrative Conventions," in *Cinema and Urban Culture in Shanghai, 1922–1943*, ed. Yingjin Zhang, 74–98 (Stanford: Stanford University Press, 1999), 74–98.

31 Paul Bailey, " 'Women Behaving Badly': Crime, Transgressive Behaviour and Gender in Early Twentieth Century China," *Nan Nü* 8, no. 1 (April 2006): 194.

productive laborers, and consumers. In the court, judges encountered numerous cases in which women engaged in "bad behaviors" in public spaces. But women's conduct before, during, and after the crime was only relevant in differentiating coercive action from consensual relations. Judges did not use these behaviors to disqualify women as sexual crime victims.

Relevance of Woman's Sexual Past

In March 1943, Li Ben filed a lawsuit at the Beijing District Court accusing thirty-five-year-old Wang Yiqian of abducting and attempting to rape his daughter. Li Ben was a tanner and owned a courtyard house in Beijing. In 1942, his family lived in the east wing and he rented the rest of the house out to three families. Among his tenants was the family of Wang Yiqian, a truck driver. He was married and lived in the north wing with his wife. In February 1942, his wife went back to Manchuria and Yiqian was left alone in Beijing. To cook meals, he often borrowed Li Ben's stove, and as a result he became acquainted with Li Ben's daughter, the twenty-year-old Li Lezi. When the relationship between Lezi and Yiqian got serious, Li Ben banned Lezi from seeing Yiqian and moved his home to another place. Lezi attempted to run away from Beijing with Liqian but failed. After this incident, Li Ben became very watchful of his daughter. One day he learned from a neighbor that a night soil carrier brought Lezi a message from Yiqian. In the message, Yiquan told Lezi that he would be waiting for her in the morning at a nearby teahouse. Li Ben suspected Yiqian was plotting to run off with his daughter, so he called the police to arrest him.

Over the course of the investigation, all the people involved in this case were summoned to court and questioned about Lezi's liaison with Yiqian, and they each provided graphic accounts of Lezi's sexual behavior. Li Ben did not hide his daughter's sexual delinquency from the court. In his words, "My daughter did not 'behave dutifully and exercise proper self-control' (*anfen shouji*) which 'had earned her a not-so-good reputation' (*mingyu bu haoting*)." This statement displayed his frustration of Lezi's behavior, referring not only to her relationship with Yiqian, but also her sexual liaisons with other men in the neighborhood. The defendant, Yiqian, had a similar testimony: "She is pregnant, but I am not the father. I know she has other friends." Lezi's account further suggests that she approached Yiqian not simply for a romantic encounter; she was probably expecting him to help her out of another disgraceful love affair. According to her, in February 1942, she had sexual encounters with another neighbor several times and became pregnant. Six months later, Lezi realized her growing body would soon expose her disgraceful behavior to family members and neighbors. She further testified that she had intercourse with Yiqian before the alleged abduction took place. She often went to his place when her father was out. According to Lezi, "[Yiqian] never forced me [to have sex with him]" and "we both did so willingly."

Under imperial law, Lezi's sexual liaisons with her neighbor and Yiqian prior to the crime would have disqualified her as a victim of either rape or abduction. However, Lezi's sexual past became irrelevant during prosecution under the new criminal code. The 1935 Criminal Code indirectly touched upon the issue of a woman's sexual record and employed the term "a woman from a respectable family" (*liangjia funü*) in one statute. By definition, "a woman of respectable character," would be "determined by whether or not she is currently engaged in prostitution (*xiyu yinhang*)."[32] In another sentencing hearing in 1936, the judge stressed: "If a woman has been engaged in prostitution and remains practicing, when she goes to the home of the petitioner to provide sexual services, [her conduct] is merely 'moving to a different place to offer service (*qiandi yingye*). Had the petitioner connived and sheltered [her activities], [the petitioner's conduct] is as a matter of fact different from sheltering a woman belonging to a respectable family for the purpose of having illicit intercourse with any person."[33] Therefore, in Lezi's case, because there was no evidence showing that she was engaged in prostitution, Lezi was a legitimate victim of abduction or rape, despite her record of delinquent sexual behavior.

Qing laws put women's chastity "on the frontlines to defend the familial order."[34] Women who misbehaved, along with the men who put them in those compromising positions, were subjected to intense moral scrutiny and stern corporal punishment. Nevertheless, in the 1940s' Beijing District Court, a woman's sexual past, if not directly related to the crime, was no longer an issue in the prosecution.

Re-Defining Female Agency

In Auguest 1942, Gao Yongquan, thirty years old, stood trial in the Beijing District Court, facing charges of abducting and raping Zhang Xiuhua. The relationship between Yongquan and Xiuhua started about two years before, in early 1941. Yongquan was married and had a sister who lived in a courtyard compound where Xiuhua and her family resided. Due to his frequent visits to his sister's home, Yongquan became acquainted with Xiuhua. Over time, their

---

32 1932: 718, in Fu Bingchang 傅秉常 and Zhou Dingyu 周定宇, eds. *Zhonghua minguo liufa liyou panjie huibian* 中华民国六法理由判解汇编 [Compendium of the Six Laws of the Republic of China, with Rationales, Judgments, and Explanations] (Taibei: Xinlu Shudian, 1964).

33 1936: 5406, from Fu and Zhou, *Zhonghua minguo liufa liyou panjie huibian*.

34 Sommer, *Sex, Law, and Society*, 14.

casual encounters developed into a close relationship, and they secretly had sex one night. The sexual liaison continued for a few months and Xiuhua became pregnant. In panic, she brought this terrible news to Yongquan and asked for help. It is not clear who first proposed the idea of elopement; but according to the police report, they met in April 1942, and ran away to a hostel outside the city gate. They spent a night together and had sex three times. They were discovered by the police the next morning. While in custody, Yongquan was tied up but Xiuhua was not. When they were finally left alone, Yongquan managed to untie himself with Xiuhua's help and sneaked out of the cell. No one noticed him as he walked out of the front gate of the police station and fled. Xiuhua was transferred to the district civil office, which notified her family to take her home. Although their first elopement had failed, Yongquan never gave up hope of reuniting with Xiuhua and attempted to get in touch with her through letters. However, Xiuhua's family intercepted the letters and then had the police arrest Yongquan outside his workplace.[35]

While facing two serious charges at court, Yongquan hoped that Xiuhua would confirm before the judge that their relationship was consensual. To Yongquan's disappointment, Xiuhua testified that he ordered her to go out of the city with him. When the judge asked Xiuhua if she had resisted Yongquan's advance during the night in the inn, she answered, "I cried. But under his threat and intimidation, I dared not resist." The judge asked a similar question during the second court hearing, and Xiuhua said she did not resist because Yongquan threatened to choke her if she cried. Xiuhua and her brother reiterated the late imperial tropes that blamed male lust for women's moral downfall. However, the judges focused less on the emotional charges. After having cross-examined Yongquan and heard the testimonies of other witnesses, the judge found at least three critical pieces of evidence that negated the plaintiff's charges of rape and abduction. First, the judge asked what had caused Xiuhua to leave home in the first place (before she ran into Yongquan on the street). Xiuhua said she had left home to find her mother who had gone to her relative's place earlier in the morning, but the judge determined that this did not amount to an urgent situation that would require Xiuhua to rush to her aunt's home. Second, the judge found that the route of Xiuhua's travel with the defendant Yongquan suggested that Xiuhua consented to their elopement. The court sentence read:

> The Wangfujing Avenue (home of Xiuhua's aunt) is to the southwest of Dongsi pailou. But on the day when [Xiuhua] walked together with Gao Yongquan and reached Dongsi Pailou, [she] allowed the pedi-cab to head

35 BMA, No. J65-6-4586, Gao Yongquan, 1942.

> east toward Chaoyang Gate, which is in the opposite direction [from her aunt's home]. After getting out of the pedi-cab, she again walked with Gao Yongquan out of the Chaoyang Gate.... Despite the long distance they had covered and the fact that it was already after sunset, she walked with him anyway. This clearly speaks to Zhang Xiuhua's willingness to stay with [Yongquan].

Lastly, the judge noticed that the language in Yongquan's letters to Xiuhua was "exceedingly sentimental" (*yuyi chanmian*) which, in the judge's opinion, definitely revealed a relationship far deeper than a fleeting encounter as the plaintiff had claimed. In the end, the court confirmed Xiuhua's active part in their sexual relationship, despite her denial.

In adjudicating such cases, both Qing magistrates and Republican judges carefully examined evidence for the plausibility of vague and oftentimes conflicting testimonies. Notwithstanding the similar legal reasoning, their views of young women's agency in their sexual relationships differed markedly. To explain women's perilous situation under Qing laws, Philip Huang argues that a woman was given "a measure of choice" but "limited to what we might term a 'passive agency': she could resist or she could submit."[36] "The law protected their 'right' to say no," Huang stresses, "but it also made them criminally liable when they did not."[37] In sharp contrast, the Nationalist *Criminal Code* of Republican China recognized a woman as an independent agent capable of making autonomous decisions on sexual matters.

In this regard, Chinese lawmakers joined a global discourse that had been seeking to re-define female sexuality and punish sexual delinquency since the late nineteenth century. Scholars of juvenile delinquency have demonstrated that the sweeping social and cultural changes as a result of industrialization, urbanization, and migration fueled a global anxiety regarding the sexuality of young single women. The public concerns about sexual dangers and temptations in cities mounted, leading to spirited discussion and debate on how to redefine female sexuality and a heightened campaign to police sexual misconduct.[38] In the United States, for instance, Mary Odem finds that the moral reformers, police officers, and state officials in the Progressive era

36 Huang, *Code, Custom, and Legal Practice in China*, 166.

37 Ibid., 175.

38 See Mary Odem, *Delinquent Daughters: Protecting and Policing Adolescent Female Sexuality in the United States, 1885–1920* (Chapel Hill: The University of North Carolina Press, 1995); Anne Meis Knupfer, *Reform and Resistance: Gender, Delinquency, and America's First Juvenile Court* (New York: Routledge, 2001); Joan Sangster, *Regulating Girls and Women:*

(1890s–1920s) rejected "the Victorian belief in inherent female purity and passionlessness" and began to acknowledge women's sexual urges and autonomy.[39] In Taisho Japan (1912–1926), policy makers also expressed great concerns about such women's sexual agency. As David Ambaras points out, "fears that young women were not simply victims of delinquent male predations but increasingly self-directed agents in the pursuit of illicit pleasure spurred authorities to intensify their crackdowns on alleged disruptions of public morality."[40] In China, Paul Bailey finds that public media in Beijing and elsewhere "began to pay increasing attention to perceived transgressive behavior amongst women (young and old)." More importantly, while seeking to contain sexual crimes and uphold moral standards, the media stopped portraying women "principally as the helpless victims of crime or passive casualties of fate."[41] Republican lawmakers now acknowledged women's social agency and sexual urges.

De-Criminalizing Runaway Daughters

In May 1947, Feng Fuzhen reported to a local police station that his sixteen-year-old daughter, Feng Guilan, was missing. He suspected that a Gao Jifu, thirty-one years old, might know where she was. While processing Fuzhen's report, the police officers learned that officers in the household registration unit had captured a man and a woman the day before. The persons under custody happened to be Fuzhen's runaway daughter Guilan and her boyfriend. The police arrested them because they could not provide valid registration cards. A week later, Jifu stood trial at the Beijing District Court on an abduction charge.[42]

In court, Jifu insisted that Guilan ran away from home on her own accord. According to Jifu, Guilan just showed up at at his home. Guilan testified in defense of Jifu. She said: "I cannot remember how many times [we had] sex together but now I am two months pregnant. Last night my father, Feng Fuzhen, told me that he was planning my engagement to another man [whom I have never met]. I rejected these plans and went to Gao Jifu for help. I was unwilling to return home and live without [him]." Guilan apparently stood firm with Jifu throughout the trial. When judge asked her whether Jifu used any trick to

---

Sexuality, Family, and the Law in Ontario, 1920–1960 (Oxford: Oxford University Press, 2001).

39 Odem, *Delinquent Daughters*, 17.

40 David Ambaras, *Bad Youth: Juvenile Delinquency and the Politics of Everyday Life in Modern Japan* (Berkeley: University of California Press, 2006), 5.

41 Bailey, " 'Women Behaving Badly,' " 159.

42 BMA, No. J65-13-3010, Gao Jifu, 1947.

entice her, she denied that; and when the judge asked whether she was willing to be with Jifu, she answered affirmatively.

These statements convinced the judicial officials that Guilan played an equal, if not a leading, role in her relationship with Jifu. Guilan's testimonies would have been unthinkable in a Qing magistrate's court. In her study of eloping women in eighteenth-century China, Paola Paderni finds that runaway women exhibited a degree of internal struggle. They "displayed the desire and the determination to pursue the happiness that life had denied them" by escaping from a repressive family or a depressing marriage. But facing criminal punishment under imperial law in a court, women called upon "the traditional view of women as dependent and subject to men's influence to hide the extent to which they have consciously chosen to risk the law's sanctions to pursue their desires."[43]

To be clear, many runaway daughters in twentieth-century Beijing repeated the imperial stereotypes of "women-as-victims" and "women-without-agency" to maintain their innocence. Some might have believed in such tropes; others were likely to use them to please their parents or to get themselves out of embarrassing situations as quickly as possible. Yet, the court and laws adopted new measures that allowed women like Guilan to acknowledge their active role in sexual liaison without facing legal sanctions. The *Criminal Code* renounced the Qing state's position that criminalized any attempt to run away from one's family. A woman was viewed as a free and independent individual. In terms of sexual relations, an unmarried woman or widow was not liable for punishment if she willingly had sex with a man. Moreover, as Philip Huang argues, "a mature woman who voluntarily agreed to be sold to someone as a wife, concubine, or prostitute was generally not liable to punishment."[44] Republican lawmakers once stated, "Only rape and adultery are considered as being illicit sex." The law did not "carry any statute punishing conduct like 'pre-martial sex between unmarried adults' (*sitong yehe*)." Even though sex between unmarried adults "was contrary to Chinese moral teachings and thereby the law should make consensual seduction of either an unmarried virgin or a widow a criminal offense," the lawmakers decided that such actions "should be deterred by family education, school education, and media criticism, not by criminal punishment."[45] Put differently, a woman's consent to a sexual relationship might mean a moral stain but would not make her liable for criminal

43 Paderni, "I Thought I Would Have Some Happy Days," 26.

44 Huang, *Code, Custom, and Legal Practice in China*, 182.

45 Fu and Zhou, *Zhonghua minguo liufa liyou panjie huibian*, 638.

punishment. In Guilan's case, despite her sexual affairs with Jifu and her elopement, she did not face any criminal charge.

On July 26, 1947, Guilan's father decided to withdraw his complaint. The court document did not explain what motivated him to do that. It is likely that he found it hard to sustain his complaint when all evidence suggested that his daughter Guilan initiated and willingly had the sexual relationship with Jifu and later eloped. The court thereby dropped the charge against Jifu and set him free immediately. Defendants in other cases cited above were not as lucky as Jifu. For example, Gao Yongquan, who wrote passionate love letters to his girlfriend, was convicted of seducing an unmarried woman and removing her from the control of her family guardian. He appealed the verdict to the Hebei Provincial High Court but his appeal was denied. He was ultimately sentenced to a two-year prison term. His girlfriend, Zhang Xiuhua, was not in court when he was sentenced as she had been married to a man surnamed You a month earlier. After the judge announced the verdict and prison sentence, Yongquan was unable to contain his frustration and lashed out: "Zhang Xiuhua ordered me to take her away, and she said she would rather commit suicide than returning home if I didn't help her! It is not my fault!" The court actually had an answer for Yongquan and other defendants in similar situations. These men, the court reasoned, had committed "Offences against the Family"; they had not violated a woman's will but had instead damaged the integrity of her family.

Defending the Family

The new criminal laws purported to support women's social and economic independence, recognize their sexual desires, and protect their sexual choices. By renouncing the chastity cult and decriminalizing elopement, it removed many legal sanctions and much of the moral pressure on women who were brought to court for promiscuous activity. While doing that, however, the lawmakers realized that they faced a grave challenge in that both female agency and sexuality could threaten the institution of family. The above-cited cases of eloping women show that consensual sexual relationships shocked their parents and upset domestic order. Women's actions became more than individual choices and expressions of autonomy, but affected constructions of family and social order. Therefore, controlling hetero-social contacts and sexual relationship outside of legitimate marriage remained an essential task in twentieth-century social and legislative campaigns. The criminal cases at the Beijing District Court shed light on Republican lawmakers' solution to defending the family. As the next part of this article will argue, the seduction law decriminalized the act of women elopement but punished men with whom they eloped. More importantly, by raising the age of consent to sixteen and the age of mandatory parental protection to twenty, Republican laws limited women's right to freely enter into sexual relationship and thus retained the authority of parents, who in most cases still found their daughters' assertion of social and sexual autonomy objectionable.

Moral Codes in Beijing's Neighborhood

The social and cultural reforms in China in the late nineteenth century called for the reshaping of intimacy—hetero-social contacts, courtship, sexual relations, and marriage. Sociologists who conducted surveys during the 1920s and the 1930s on Chinese college campuses, the epicenter of the reform movements, found that new ideals of gender roles and family relations became both propagandist catchphrases and principles to be applied in everyday practice. However, when sociologists walked through Beijing's myriad courtyard neighborhoods in the 1940s and surveyed society beyond intellectual and student circles, they found that reformist ideals were anything but accepted as new social norms. In one survey, Zhou Enci, a sociology major at Yenching University, examined customs of nuptials in Beijing in the 1940s and found that chastity still held a considerable force in defining female virtue. Families placed a high value on maintaining their daughters' pre-marital virginity. Promiscuous conduct would bring shame not only upon a daughter but also upon her entire family. Local custom required the bridegroom's family to display the nuptial blood-spotted bed sheet as proof of consummation of marriage and the bride's virginity.[46] Moreover, a daughter's sexuality played a vital role in establishing both her marriage prospects and the family's moral respectability. It was still prevalent at the time in Beijing for parents to arrange a child's marriage, despite the reformers' attack on such customary authority of parents. Court case files show that many runaway daughters were already engaged when pursuing their unapproved romantic encounters. An engagement in the 1940s still followed the imperial ritual practice, which normally involved the exchange of a "birthday card" (*xiaotie*), drawing up a "preliminary agreement" (*xiaoding*), informing relatives and close family friends of the upcoming marriage, and the fiancé's family delivering several pieces of jewelry to the fiancée's family. After these steps, local custom required the bride's family to limit her contact with males (including male relatives and her fiancé) and even take into

46 Zhou Enci 周恩慈, "Beiping hunyin lisu 北平婚姻礼俗 [Wedding Customs in Beijing]," Senior Thesis, Department of Sociology, Yanching University, 1940.

consideration her menstrual cycle when determining the wedding date.[47] When a betrothed daughter ran away from home, she put her own moral standing and her family's reputation at risk. Furthermore, for many lower-class families, the elopement, or even worse, an out-of-wedlock pregnancy, threatened the family's economic stability. Parents were concerned about either the loss of daughter's productive labor or covering the cost incurred by pregnancy.

Since stakes were high, parents worked hard to monitor their daughters' behavior and they had a range of methods to do so. They teamed up with the relatives and friends to monitor the interactions between their daughters and the latter's friends. Their watchful neighbors were also helpful in detecting suspicious conduct when parents were not around, and the neighbors' gossip provided information on secret relations. In one case, Yang Wang Shi noticed that her eighteen-year-old Yang Zhanying's relationship with her boyfriend, Zhang Kexian, was spinning out of control. Without her mother's permission, Zhanying often met the boyfriend at parks or went out to watch movies until late at night. Yang Wang Shi decided to separate the two by sending Zhanying to stay with a relative. However, a few days later, Yang Wang Shi was surprised to learn that Zhanying had run off, and she had to ask her relatives and friends to search for Zhanying.[48]

When domestic and neighborhood methods of supervision failed, parents went to the police and the law court for assistance. In Zhanying's case, although the family was able to locate her, she ran away again within a few short hours. Her mother's instincts told her that Zhanying must have gone to Kexian's place; there, she found her daughter standing by Kexian's side. Enraged, she wrestled with Kexian before the police arrived to arrest him. To make their case, parents often invoked traditional moral norms such as filial piety and chastity to defend their daughter's innocence. They also reiterated the late imperial tropes that blamed male lust for women's moral downfall. In Yang Wang Shi's case, she went to the Beijing District Court and filed a lawsuit, accusing Kexian of seducing, abducting, and raping her daughter. She denounced Kexian as someone who "always used tricks to seduce young girls in the neighborhood and had many victims." His "licentious character" (*yindang chengxing*) and "bandit-like behavior" (*tufei zhi xingwei*) threatened her household stability and was "harmful to the society." While condemning Kexian as a licentious and deceptive person, Yang Wang Shi praised her daughter's purity, morality, and filial piety. She claimed that her family "emphasized 'moral teachings' (*lijiao*) and

47 Zhou, "Beiping hunyin lisu," 28–41.

48 BMA, No. J65-13-804, Zhang Kexian, 1945.

'strict child discipline' (*guanjiao shenyan*), which was well known to the neighbors." Raised in such a traditional family, Zhanying was an obedient and filial girl. To further testify to Zhanying's moral uprightness, Yang Wang Shi provided an example: "When Kexian flirted with my daughter by riding his bicycle into her on purpose, she felt she was offended. Only after her friend Guo Shuzhen's mediation, my daughter let him go." To explain how Zhanying ended up being sexually involved with Kexian, Yang Wang Shi stressed that her daughter "lost her senses for a moment" (*yishi hutu*) and yielded to Kexian's deception and threats. In her words, "with the strict moral discipline she received at home, [Zhanying] never would have followed the plan through without encouragement." Yang Wang Shi requested the judge to punish Kexian severely in order to "stop the degenerate practice" (*yi wan tuifeng*) of rape.

The cases from the Beijing District Court in the 1940s and the case files from magisterial adjudications in late imperial China show a striking degree of similarity in the parents' testimonies. Qing officials and family elders denied that women were autonomous agents who were capable of starting sexual liaisons on their own; and a record of chastity precluded women's liability in illicit sexual liaisons and enhanced a daughter's reputation and the family's honor. Parents in the 1940s' Beijing upheld the same rationale of sexual morality and litigation strategies by portraying their runaway daughters as naïve and innocent victims of male seduction and exploitation. It provided the parents with a plausible narrative of seduction and abduction and, as the parents hoped, would wash away their daughter's shame in sexual crimes as well as the loss of respect suffered by her family.

Profiling Villains

The majority of the male offenders charged with seduction in the Beijing District Court during the 1940s were in their twenties and were unmarried while some had wives and even children. They were not "rootless" at all, as they had homes, jobs, steady incomes, and were often acquaintances and neighbors of the victims' families. Many had good knowledge of urban entertainment facilities and frequented parks, cinemas, and dance halls. These places of public entertainment played an important role in many of cases under study.

In one case, Zhao Wenlian, a twenty-eight-year-old rickshaw puller, was arrested for rape in January 1948. The alleged victim was his neighbor, a sixteen-year-old Liu Shuying. They had been dating since summer 1947. In one of their excursions to the Beihai Park, they found an isolated place and had sex for the first time. In December 1947, Shuying learned that her parents had found out about the affair and she was scared and fled with Weilian to Fengtai, a southern suburb in Beijing, where they lived together for a month. Shuying's family did not report her missing to the police but secretly kept their eyes on Wenlian's family. Their patience finally paid off and they intercepted Shuying at Wenlian's home a few weeks later.[49]

Criminal cases show that parks appealed to young people for a number of reasons. Built on the grounds of former imperial palaces and gardens, parks in twentieth-century Beijing presented scenic landscapes. Moreover, many runaway daughters and their boyfriends chose to stroll around the park at the time when large crowds left, taking advantage of the darkness and tranquility to be intimate and have sex. Lastly, the admission charge to parks seemed to be fairly insignificant to many local residents in 1940s Beijing. Besides strolling in parks, frequenting commercial and entertainment facilities became a new urban pastime. For example, seventeen-year-old Liu Shuying worked in a Japanese household and in her spare time she often went to the Business Encouraging Bazaar in Qianmen and further south to the Tianqiao district. The former was a giant five-floor concrete building decorated with carved marble. The Xinluotian Amusement Park where Shuying often visited occupied the top floor and its daily programs featured movie shows, storytelling, and folklore performances. The Tianqiao district that Shuying regularly visited was, in Madeleine Yue Dong's words, "a one-square-mile space of bustling chaos," clustered with retailers of all kinds, restaurants and tea houses, folklore performances, and brothels, all catering to the city's low-end customers.[50] At Tianqiao, Shuying met a seventeen-year-old dealer of used clothing, Li Baoli. In November 1946, they watched films at the Sunlight Cinema till evening. Not returning home for fear of being scorned by her parents, Shuying followed Baoli to his brother's home. There, they shared a bed and had sex. Afterward, their romantic encounter took a radical turn. At dawn, several police officers showed up at the door during a routine patrol to verify household registration. They found Shuying and Baoli suspicious and arrested them. After a brief questioning, the officers notified Shuying's parents but kept Baoli under custody. Shuying's parents later filed a lawsuit accusing Baoli of raping and abducting Shuying.[51]

Movies were introduced to Beijing at the turn of the twentieth century and the first cinema was opened there in 1913. By 1942, an incomplete municipal survey indicated that the number of cinemas in two inner city districts (Inner-1

49 BMA, No. J65-26-2115, Zhao Wenlian, 1947.

50 Madeleine Yue Dong, "Juggling Bits: Tianqiao as Republican Beijing's Recycling Center," *Modern China* 25, no. 3 (July 1999): 305.

51 BMA, No. J65-11-1598, Li Baoli, 1946.

and Inner-2) grew to eleven. With a capacity of 7,748 seats, the average daily attendance was approximately 7,820.[52] Legal documents suggest that not all moviegoers in the 1940s came from better-off families. Women from the lower echelon of society were among the moviegoers, especially when their male companions covered the cost of admission.[53]

The rapid development of cheap amusement created new spaces for young people to pursue romantic relationships and sexual encounters. Kathy Peiss demonstrates that the emergent of cheap forms of urban amusement in early twentieth-century New York embodied the rise of a youth-oriented culture of "individualism, ideology of consumption, and affirmation of dating and courtship outside parental control."[54] It would be hasty to argue that urban amusements in Beijing had a similarly profound impact on social relationships, but criminal case files do suggest that recreational facilities helped young women and men assert social and sexual autonomy that challenged both conventional moral code and parental authority.

The Age of Protection

Lawmakers, as well as political leaders, promised that new laws would grant women unprecedented freedom and protect their social autonomy and sexual choices. While upholding these liberal ideals, they also made it clear that they were committed to protecting the institution of family. To achieve both objectives, the Nationalist lawmakers introduced two new categories of crime: "Offences against Personal Liberty" (*fanghai ziyou zui*) to protect the individual's free will and "Offences against the Family" (*fanghai jiating zui*) which made the protection of family integrity its overriding objective. Lawmakers claimed that new laws allowed them to defend family without sacrificing individual free will, but, as the last section of this article will demonstrate, parents found that they gained more power vis-à-vis their daughters. How could this be? The age of consent stipulated by the new criminal code holds the key.

The age of consent was raised from ten under the Qing laws to sixteen under the new law. To seduce a woman under sixteen years of age, with her consent, would be tried as abduction. If convicted, the defendant faced a

52 BMA, No. J2-7-339, "Beijing tebieshi dianyingyuan diaochabiao: neiyiqu he neierqu 北京特別市电影院调查表: 内一区和内二区 [Survey of Cinemas in Beijing: Inner-1 District and Inner-2 District]," 1942.

53 The exact percentage of women ticket-buyers remains unclear, since recreational facilities never kept records on their customers.

54 Kathy Peiss, *Cheap Amusements: Working Women and Leisure in Turn-of-Century New York* (Philadelphia: Temple University Press, 1986), 6.

minimum prison term of one year and a maximum of seven years. If the defendant committed this crime "for lucrative purpose" and had illicit sex with the victim the penalty would be three to ten years of imprisonment. Whoever seduced woman between sixteen and twenty years of age, with her consent, faced a prison term of not more than three years. In practice, a defendant who seduced an unmarried woman above fourteen but below sixteen was normally sentenced to one year of imprisonment. If the victim was between sixteen and twenty, the prison term varied from three months to one year.[55] In summary, under the 1935 Criminal Code, seducing a married woman or an unmarried woman under twenty years of age was a punishable offense. The accused men in such cases could be acquitted *only* if their girlfriend was unmarried and older than twenty.

The age of protection for unmarried woman was *unusually* high when compared to other statutes in both civil and criminal codes of Republican China. For example, the most important age mark for women in the civil code was fifteen and sixteen. Women under fifteen should not be engaged, and those under sixteen were not permitted to get married.[56] In the criminal code, fourteen and sixteen were significant thresholds. Laws saw women under fourteen as minors lacking the capacity for conducting autonomous actions. Crimes against them would attract maximum penalty. Women between fourteen and sixteen were viewed by the law as neither minors nor adults. The law seems to hold that crimes against them were not as serious as crimes against minors, but definitely more serious than those against adults.

Lawmakers did not explain why they chose *not* to follow these common thresholds but set the age of protection at twenty in punishing seduction. If we take into consideration contemporary social surveys on marriage customs, we will find clues to explain this particular legislation. Many surveys found

---

55 Once convicted, the defendant might be given a lighter sentence, depending on a number of grounds. Judges calculated the sentence by the perceived harm that the crime had caused the woman and her family. An elopement was deemed less harmful, and subsequently received lighter sentence, than a relationship involving sexual contact or resulting in pregnancy. Also, judges tended to give young offenders lighter sentences on the grounds that a short prison term would teach them a lesson while allowing them to quickly rejoin society as a useful member. Finally, judges considered seduction a minor offense and were willing to shorten the period of incarceration in order to move "petty criminals" out of the cash-strapped and overcrowded prison system as quickly as possible.

56 Article. 973, Chapter 2: Marriage, Title 1: Betrothal; Article. 980, Chapter 2: Marriage, Title 2: Conclusion of Marriage, in *The Civil Code of the Republic of China*, Book IV: Family, 5 and 8, translated by Hsia Ching-lin, James Chow, and Yukon Chang (Shanghai: Kelly & Walsh, Limited, 1930).

that the average age for women to marry was categorically below twenty in most rural communities then, and slightly over that in metropolitan areas. In other words, most women would marry by the time they turned twenty.[57] A higher age threshold would allow the law to greatly reduce the possibility of un-punishable elopement. This meant that when elopement was brought to a court, the woman and man involved were more likely to be prosecuted, and punished not for violating a woman's right to exercise free will but for destabilizing her family.

This new law reflected legislative and judicial efforts to address the social concern about sexual delinquency and the fragility of the institution of family. It proclaimed to safeguard family integrity without sacrificing women's freedom. Republican lawmakers denounced their imperial predecessors' attempt to contain the breakdown of moral and social order by promoting female chastity and reinforcing the patriarchal household. They claimed that the reconfigured family institution was built on women's social autonomy, productive labor, and sexual abstinence. However, cases from the Beijing District Court in the 1940s disclosed some ironic effects of the ambitious liberal legal reform. The chastity cult was eliminated under the new laws, but patriarchal power remained. Although parents lost some of their customary authority (such as forcing their daughters into an arranged marriage), they could still block their daughters from the latter's free choice. Therefore, the legislative efforts did not fundamentally change the male-centered household authority and kinship hierarchy that the Nationalist lawmakers and political leaders claimed to reject.

Conclusion

In a book to chronicle key reform measures and legislative milestones during the previous two decades or so starting from the late Qing, Xie Zhenmin, a Nationalist lawmaker and legal scholar, remarked in 1937: "As the human race evolves, so do crimes. Unless we scrutinize [the existing laws] and pass new ones, we will not be able to demonstrate our judicial prudence and legal insights."[58] Xie's statement highlighted the Republican legal modernization

---

57 For social surveys of age at marriage in the 1920s and 30s, see Li Wenhai 李文海, Huang Xingtao 黄兴涛, and Xia Mingfang 夏明方, eds. *Minguo shiqi shehui diaocha congbian* 民国时期社会调查丛编 [Collection of Republican-era Social Surveys] (Fuzhou: Fujian jiaoyu chubanshe, 2004).

58 Xie, *Zhonghua minguo lifa shi*, 903.

as a consistent and determined attempt to break away from China's imperial legal tradition. The imperial legal philosophy and institution became a natural point of departure, from which the twentieth-century legal reform charted its course and measured its successes and setbacks. The reform was celebrated as a collective effort by lawmakers and political and social leaders to adopt liberal ideals such as gender equality and conjugal family, to import the continental European model of law, to promote new legal education and professions, and to institutionalize new concept and practice of punishment. Legal reform culminated in the early 1930s under the Nationalist government with the enactment of the *Civil Code* in 1930–31 and the *Criminal Code* in 1935.

One of the most significant discontinuities from the Qing to the Republic is the law that regulated gender relations and family structure. Under the Nationalist government, from the draft criminal code of 1928 to the promulgated code of 1935, lawmakers made changes in sixteen areas, half of which concerned statutes on sexual crimes and domestic relations. They abolished the rape law, divorce law, marriage law, and inheritance law of the Qing Code and overturned a significant number of Qing precedents. For example, the *Civil Code*, as Kathryn Bernhardt points out, "allowed easy 'no fault' mutual consent divorce" in order to "provide women with the means to liberate themselves from oppressive marriages."[59] Philip Huang argues that the new Criminal Code began to recognize women as independent agents, socially and sexually, capable of making autonomous decisions.[60] It is understandable why lawmakers like Xie Zhenmin were so eager to repudiate the imperial laws regarding gender and sexuality. Women's liberation and family reform were two driving forces behind the social reforms and political revolutions in modern China. Many social and political leaders genuinely believed that it was on the ruins of the imperial past that China could recover its lost greatness. The vision of reformed womanhood and family even overrode political differences and ideological rivalries between the Nationalists and the Communists. For all their legislative efforts, Chinese judicial officials and lawmakers claimed that they actively participated in the social and cultural reform movements of the early twentieth century and attempted to use liberal legislation to spearhead changes in gender and family relations.

---

59 Kathryn Bernhardt, "Women and the Law: Divorce in the Republican Period," in *Civil Law in Qing and Republican China*, ed. Kathryn Bernhardt and Philip C.C. Huang (Stanford: Stanford University Press, 1994), 188.

60 Huang, *Code, Custom, and Legal Practice in China*, 181.

Mindful of these profound changes, however, this article has drawn attention to the continuities. So far as this article is concerned, the Nationalist lawmakers and judicial officials inherited a social mission to protect the integrity of the family. More importantly, the privileged position of men as the head of household, along with their authority over family affairs, was also retained. In the Qing code, unmarried women were subjected to patriarchal surveillance and discipline. Such generational hierarchy was preserved in Republican laws through the invention of a new category of crime, "Offenses against the Family," despite the lawmakers' promise to support women's social autonomy and protect their sexual choices. Cases from the Beijing District Court of the 1940s reveal that parents used the new seduction law as an effective means to restrain daughters whose choices went against the family's moral code. The legal reform that appeared so beneficial to women on the surface still managed to entrap them in a family system that subordinated their individual interests to those of their parents. This Nationalist seduction law was abolished in 1949 in the wake of the communist victory. However, the tension it sought to address, between women's assertion of social and sexual freedom and family control, continued well into the second half of the twentieth century. It continued to drive future generations of lawmakers, in both revolutionary and post-socialist China, to reconfigure the relationship between women and their families in legislation.

Glossary

anfen shouji	安分守己	*Quanyechang*	劝业场
buzhi shili	不知事理	*shejiao gongkai*	社交公开
fanghai jiating zui	妨害家庭罪	*shiwei buzhi*	始为不知
fanghai ziyou zui	妨害自由罪	*sitong yehe*	私通野合
guanjiao shenyan	管教甚严	*tufei zhi xingwei*	土匪之行径
houwei buyuan	后为不愿	*xiyu yinhang*	习于淫行
jian	贱	*xiaoding*	小定
liang	良	*xiao jiating zhi*	小家庭制
liangjia funü	良家妇女	*xiaotie*	小帖
liangqing xianghao	两情相好	*yishi hutu*	一时糊涂
lijiao	礼教	*yi wan tuifeng*	以挽颓风
mingyu bu haoting	名誉不好听	*yindang chengxing*	淫荡成性
nannü tongxue	男女同学	*yuyi chanmian*	语义缠绵
nianyou tianzhen	年幼天真	*ziyou jiehun*	自由结婚
qiandi yingye	迁地营业	*ziyou lian'ai*	自由恋爱

Bibliography

Ambaras, David. *Bad Youth: Juvenile Delinquency and the Politics of Everyday Life in Modern Japan*. Berkeley: University of California Press, 2006.

Bailey, Paul. "'Women Behaving Badly': Crime, Transgressive Behaviour and Gender in Early Twentieth Century China." *Nan Nü* 8, no. 1 (April 2006): 157–97.

Bernhardt, Kathryn. "Women and the Law: Divorce in the Republican Period." In *Civil Law in Qing and Republican China*, edited by Kathryn Bernhardt and Philip Huang, 187–214. Stanford: Stanford University Press, 1994.

Chen Heqin 陈鹤琴. "Shehui wenti: xuesheng hunyin wenti zhi yanjiu 社会问题: 学生婚姻问题之研究 [Social Problems: Study of the Problems of Student's Marriage]." *Dongfang zazhi* 东方杂志 [Oriental Miscellany] 18, no. 4 (Feb. 25, 1921); 18, no. 5 (March 10, 1921); 18, no. 6 (March 25, 1921). Reprinted in *Minguo shiqi shehui diaocha congbian: hunyin jiating juan* 民国时期社会调查丛编：婚姻家庭卷 [Republican Social Surveys: Marriage and Family], edited by Li Wenhai et al. (Fuzhou: Fujian jiaoyu chubanshe, 2004), 1–33.

Cheng, Weikun. "In Search of Leisure: Women's Festivities in Late Imperial Beijing." *The Chinese Historical Review* 14, no. 1 (Spring 2007): 1–28.

The Civil Code of the Republic of China, translated by Hsia Ching-lin, James Chow, and Yukon Chang. Shanghai: Kelly & Walsh, Limited, 1930.

Da Qing lüli zengxiu tongzuan jicheng 大清律例增修通纂集成 [Enlarged and Revised Collectanea of the *Great Qing Code*], 1899.

Dong, Madeleine Yue. "Juggling Bits: Tianqiao as Republican Beijing's Recycling Center." *Modern China* 25, no. 3 (July 1999): 303–42.

Fu Bingchang 傅秉常, and Zhou Dingyu 周定宇, eds. *Zhonghuaminguo liufa liyou panjie huibian* 中华民国六法理由判解汇编 [Compendium of the Six Laws of the Republic of China, with Rationales, Judgments, and Explanations]. Taibei: Xinlu Shudian, 1964.

The Great Qing Code. Translated by William C. Jones. New York: Oxford University Press, 1994.

Glosser, Susan. *Chinese Visions of Family and State, 1915–1953*. Berkeley: University of California Press, 2003.

Goodman, Bryna, and Wendy Larson. "Axes of Gender: Divisions of Labor and Spatial Separation." In *Gender in Motion: Divisions of Labor and Cultural Change in Late Imperial and Modern China*, edited by Bryna Goodman and Wendy Larson, 1–25. Lanham, MD: Rowman & Littlefield Publishers, 2005.

Huang, Philip C.C. *Code, Custom, and Legal Practice in China: The Qing and the Republic Compared*. Stanford: Stanford University Press, 2002.

Knupfer, Anne Meis. *Reform and Resistance: Gender, Delinquency, and America's First Juvenile Court*. New York: Routledge, 2001.

Lee, Leo Ou-fan. "The Urban Milieu of Shanghai Cinema, 1930–40: Some Explorations of Film Audience, Film Culture, and Narrative Conventions." In *Cinema and Urban Culture in Shanghai, 1922–1943*, edited by Yingjin Zhang, 74–98. Stanford: Stanford University Press, 1999.

Li Wenhai 李文海, Huang Xingtao 黄兴涛, and Xia Mingfang 夏明方, eds. *Minguo shiqi shehui diaocha congbian* 民国时期社会调查丛编 [Collection of Republican-era Social Surveys]. Fuzhou: Fujian jiaoyu chubanshe, 2004.

Ng, Vivien. "Ideology and Sexuality: Rape Laws in Qing China." *Journal of Asian Studies* 46, no. 1 (1987): 57–70.

Odem, Mary. *Delinquent Daughters: Protecting and Policing Adolescent Female Sexuality in the United States, 1885–1920*. Chapel Hill: The University of North Carolina Press, 1995.

Paderni, Paola. "I Thought I Would Have Some Happy Days: Women Eloping in Eighteenth-Century China." *Late Imperial China* 16, no. 1 (1995): 1–32.

Peiss, Kathy. *Cheap Amusements: Working Women and Leisure in Turn-of-Century New York*. Philadelphia: Temple University Press, 1986.

Sangster, Joan. *Regulating Girls and Women: Sexuality, Family, and the Law in Ontario, 1920–1960*. Oxford: Oxford University Press, 2001.

Sommer, Matthew. *Sex, Law, and Society in Late Imperial China*. Stanford: Stanford University Press, 1999.

Spence, Jonathan. *Death of Woman Wang*. New York: Penguin, 1998.

Theiss, Janet. *Disgraceful Matters: The Politics of Chastity in Eighteenth-Century China*. Berkeley: University of California Press, 2004.

Wang Yuesheng 王跃生. *Qingdai zhongqi hunyin chongtu touxi* 清代中期婚姻冲突透析 [Marital Dispute in the Mid-Qing Period]. Beijing: Shehui kexue chubanshe, 2003.

Xie Zhenmin 谢振民. *Zhonghua minguo lifa shi* 中华民国立法史 [Legislative History of the Republic of China]. Beijing: Zhongguo zhengfa daxue chubanshe, 1999.

Zhou Enci 周恩慈. "Beiping hunyin lisu 北平婚姻礼俗 [Wedding Customs in Beijing]." Senior Thesis, Department of Sociology, Yanching University, 1940.

PART 2

Production and Application of Legal Knowledge

CHAPTER 7

The Community of Legal Experts in Sixteenth- and Seventeenth-Century China

Yanhong Wu

Introduction

Professions and professionalism are a modern product. They constitute an essential part of civil society and play an important role in structuring power and generating culture. In China, the legal profession centered on the lawyer system was officially formed in 1912. Over the past century, it has matured and its growth has accompanied China's steps towards modernity. Although the contemporary Chinese legal profession has by and large been patterned after the Western model, it is instructive to consider what the legal domain looked like prior to the twentieth century and examine how its function both resembled and differed from that of its modern counterpart.

This chapter focuses on legal practitioners and legal professionalism in the last hundred years of the Ming dynasty (1368–1644), a period that is considered part of China's "early modern era."[1] The conventional wisdom is that, as

1 In their discussion of visual materials and printing culture, both Craig Clunas and Kai-wing Chow use the term "early modern China" to refer to the 16th and 17th century Chinese society. See Craig Clunas, *Pictures and Visuality in Early Modern China* (London: Reaktion Books Ltd, 1997), 9; and Kai-wing Chow, *Printing, Culture, and Power in Early Modern China* (Stanford: Stanford University Press, 2004), 1. In mainland China, the thesis that "Capitalist sprouts" could be identified in the mid- and late Ming dynasty was shared among various historians in the 1950s. See works such as Department of Chinese History of Renming University 中国人民大学中国历史教研室, ed., *Zhongguo zibenzhuyi wenti taolunji* 中国资本主义问题讨论集 [Collected articles on Chinese Capitalism] (Beijing: Sanlian shudian, 1957). Contemporary historians such as Niu Jianqiang 牛建强, Wan Ming 万明, Zhang Xianqing 张显清, and Zhao Yifeng 赵轶峰 focus on the social change witnessed in the 16th- and 17th-century China and believe that it involved profound social transformation. See Niu Jianqiang, *Mingdai zhonghouqi shehui bianqian yanjiu* 明代中后期社会变迁研究 [Studies on the Social Change of the Mid-and Late Ming Society) (Taibei: Wenjin chubanshe, 1997); Wan Ming, ed., *Wanming shehui bianqian: Wenti yu yanjiu* 晚明社会变迁：问题与研究 [The Social Change in Late-Ming Society: Issues and Studies] (Beijing: Shangwu yinshuguan, 2005); Zhang Xianqing 张显清, ed., *Mingdai houqi shehui zhuanxing yanjiu* 明代后期社会

© KONINKLIJKE BRILL NV, LEIDEN, 2015 | DOI 10.1163/9789004288492_009

John Langlois put it, "legal professionalism [in the Ming dynasty] was relatively undeveloped."[2] As a matter of fact, very little is known about the legal profession during this period. Many important questions remain unanswered: Who practiced law? How was legal knowledge produced, disseminated, and obtained? How did the legal experts interact with each other? The answers to these questions will not only enrich our understanding of the development of legal practice and of the unique societal nature of the early modern period in China but also facilitate a more rigorous assessment of the origins and transformation of modern legal professionalism in general.

This chapter aims to understand legal experts in the sixteenth- and seventeenth-century Ming dynasty. To identify these legal experts, the chapter relies on the commentaries on the *Great Ming Code* and regulations (*li*), the major legal sources of the dynasty. Unlike the Tang dynasty, the Ming government never issued a uniform official commentary of the *Great Ming Code*.[3] In the sixteenth and the seventeenth centuries, after the Code had been completed and kept unchanged for over one hundred years, it became difficult to comprehend. In addition, starting from the Hongzhi reign (1488–1505), regulations became a form of legal source. The existence of a large number of regulations placed additional burdens on officials in terms of grasping the legal rules and applying them properly to daily legal affairs. To alleviate such burdens, private commentaries began to be composed to help officials understand the Code and the regulations.

The earliest extant commentary on the *Great Ming Code* from the Ming dynasty was *Lüjie bianyi* (Code with Commentaries and Explication of Questions),[4] which includes a preface dated the nineteenth year of the Hongwu reign (1386). Such commentaries were scarce before the sixteenth century, however. Out of the thirty-six commentaries examined in this study, only two were produced before 1500; the rest were published in the sixteenth and seventeenth centuries. Indeed, the significant increase in the production and dissemination of commentaries on the *Great Ming Code* in sixteenth- and

转型研究 [A Study on the Social Transformation in Late Ming Society] (Beijing: Zhongguo shehui kexue chubanshe, 2008); Zhao Yifeng 赵轶峰, *Mingdai de bianqian* 明代的变迁 [Social Change of the Ming Dynasty] (Beijing: Sanlian chubanshe, 2008).

2 John Langlois, "Ming Law," in *The Cambridge History of China*, vol. 8, eds., Denis Twitchett and Frederick W. Mote (Cambridge: Cambridge University Press, 1998), 172–220, at 207.

3 Wu Yanhong 吴艳红, "Guojia zhengce yu Mingdai de lüzhu shijian 国家政策与明代的律注实践 [State Policy and the Practice of Interpreting the Code in the Ming Dynasty]," *Shixue yuekan* 史学月刊 [Journal of Historical Science], no. 1 (2013): 52–62, at 52.

4 He Guang 何广, *Lüjie bianyi* 律解辩疑 [Code with Commentaries and Explication of Questions] (1386p).

seventeenth-century China was an unprecedented social phenomenon. The state's legal rules were commented upon and interpreted by individuals who were interested in and capable of compiling such works. Contradictory interpretations of certain legal provisions existed side by side and were circulated widely. The Ming government appears to have adopted a detached policy towards the production of such commentaries. Although legal officials suggested the compilation of a uniform official commentary on the Code and the regulations, it appears that such proposals were never taken seriously by the Ming government.[5]

Drawing on those commentaries of the *Great Ming Code*, together with legal archives, published writings of legal officials, local gazetteers, and so on, this chapter explores the legal domain during the last century of the Ming dynasty. Through a study of the authors, compilers, sponsors, and publishers of such commentaries, it aims to outline the community of legal experts in sixteenth- and seventeenth-century China, to determine who the members were, how they worked, and what the community was like.

The Community of Legal Experts: Authors, Compilers, and Sponsors

Producing commentaries in the sixteenth and the seventeenth centuries seemed to be a project involving wide collaboration among authors, compilers, and sponsors. *Da Ming lü jishuo* (Collected Explications of the Great Ming Code) (cited as *DMLJS* hereafter) is a commentary on the *Great Ming Code* published in the twentieth year of the Wanli reign (1592).[6] The unique feature of this commentary is that it contains detailed information regarding how it was produced and circulated, which many other commentaries do not have.

The original author of the commentary was Feng Zi.[7] Feng Zi was a native of Tongxiang, now part of Zhejiang province. Feng received his *jinshi* degree in the second year of the Longqing reign (1568)[8] and took various positions related to law in the Wanli period (1573–1620). In 1583, Feng, now a director in the Ministry of Justice, received a work evaluation of "having fine legal

5 Wu Yanhong, "Guojia zhengce yu Mingdai de lüzhu shijian," 54.

6 Feng Zi 冯孜 and Liu Dawen 刘大文, *Da Ming Lü jishuo* 大明律集说 [The Collected Explications of the *Great Ming Code*] (1592p). Cited as *DMLJS* hereafter.

7 Feng Zi and Liu Dawen, *DMLJS, juan* 1: 1.

8 Gao Ju, "Preface," 6a, in Feng Zi and Liu Dawen, *DMLJS*.

knowledge" from the ministry.[9] Seven months later, he was promoted to Vice Surveillance Commissioner of Henan.[10] According to Wang Zhiyou, who assumed the same post about ten years later, Feng Zi served in the Ministry of Justice for nine years. It was during this period that he authored the commentary *DMLJS*.[11] Besides *DMLJS*, Feng also compiled a book titled *Mingxing Lu* (A Book to Illuminate Legal Affairs) in 1590 when he was Surveillance Commissioner of Guizhou.[12] Feng Zi was clearly a legal expert.

After *DMLJS* was completed, it was not published immediately but circulated in the form of handwritten copies. When Liu Dawen entered his office after receiving his *jinshi* degree in 1586, he encountered a copy of Feng's commentary. Liu mentioned that at that time, he was serving in the Court of the Judicial Review. Although he felt very lucky to see this book, the book was in bad shape and some parts were missing. Liu did manage to purchase a good copy later, however.

Like Feng Zi, Liu Dawen was a legal expert and was interested in the *Great Ming Code* and its commentaries. He appreciated Feng's work as he recognized that Feng had closely studied the *Great Ming Code*. According to Liu, Feng collected all the existing annotations and commentaries on the Code, compared and contrasted them, and then "integrated them and created the unbiased commentaries of his own."[13] It seems, however, that Liu also added much of his own work to this commentary. He noted that he had edited the book and added new regulations under the original structure of the book.[14] According to Zhao Shouzu, whenever Liu had some spare time during his tenure in the Court of Judicial Review, he would read and work on Feng's book, together with *Dulü suoyan* and *Du Lü Guanjian*, two popular commentaries on the *Great Ming Code* at the time.[15] Before 1592, however, the main audience of the revised version of *DMLJS* was Liu Dawen himself, who said that all through the years he had kept the book to cope with his "simplicity and ignorance."[16]

In the summer of 1591, Liu Dawen was serving as a case reviewer at the Court of Judicial Review and was dispatched to Nanzhili, the southern metropolitan

9 *Ming Shenzong shilu* 明神宗实录 [Veritable Record of Ming Shenzong] (Taibei: Zhongyanyuan shiyusuo, 1962), *juan* 133: 2473.

10 *Ming Shenzong shilu*, *juan* 141: 2634.

11 Wang Zhiyou, "Preface," 3a, in Feng Zi and Liu Dawen, *DMLJS*.

12 *Guizhou tongzhi* 贵州通志 [A General Gazetteer of Guizhou], *juan* 24: 81a.

13 Liu Dawen, "Preface," 2b, in Feng Zi and Liu Dawen, *DMLJS*.

14 Ibid., 3a.

15 Zhao Shouzu, "Preface," 3a, in Feng Zi and Liu Dawen, *DMLJS*.

16 Liu Dawen, "Preface," 3a, in Feng Zi and Liu Dawen, *DMLJS*.

area, to direct the "Grand Review."[17] He was stationed in Anqing and worked with both local officials and those who were sent to the area by the central government, including Zhao Shouzu, Prefect of Anqing; Wang Deguang, Prefectural Judge of Anqing; Wang Zhiyou, Vice Surveillance Commissioner of Henan (who was appointed as the commander of granaries of the state farms and the restorer of the military defense at Yinzhou area by imperial order); and Gao Ju and Wang Ming, Regional Inspectors of Zhili. They were all legal experts and had common interests in legal issues.

Prefect Zhao Shouzu had served as a director in the Ministry of Justice before he took the position in Anqing. He recalled his days in the Ministry of Justice and how he worried about the situation where various contradictory interpretations of the Code were circulated and legal clerks easily took advantage of this situation to manipulate legal cases.[18] Wang Deguang admitted that as the prefectural judge of Anqing he tried hard to follow the legal rules but every day he feared that he would fail in his duty. He showed great passion for DMLJS, as he believed that commentaries like it would provide the basic guidelines for legal practice, and that officials like him would benefit tremendously from such works.[19]

Wang Ming also observed that he gave a lot of thought to legal issues. He concurred with Liu Dawen that the text of the law was so concise and the meaning so subtle that it was very difficult for new officials, who had just laid down the Confucian classics, to understand the law. Therefore, he really appreciated the value of works such as DMLJS.[20] Wang Zhiyou shared similar sentiments. He identified three merits (*sanshan*) in compiling and publishing commentaries on the Code such as DMLJS. First, it would benefit officials like him. With this book at hand, previous confusion about the law would be dispelled and the Code would be understood much better. Second, it would benefit clerks. The book would help the clueless ones avoid misusing the law, and warn the "cunning ones" against manipulating the law. And third, the

17 The grand review is a review process that was held every five years at the provincial level starting from the Chenghua reign (1465–1488). The main purpose of the review was to show the leniency and benevolence of emperors. In it, various suspects would be pardoned, some criminals would be exonerated, and some of the inmates would be released. See Wu Yanhong, "Mingdai de falü jiqi yunzuo 明代的法律及其运作 [The Legal System of the Ming Dynasty and its Operation]," in *Mingdai zhengzhi shi* 明代政治史 [A Political History of the Ming Dynasty], ed. Zhang Xianqing 张显清 and Lin Jinshu 林金树 (Guilin: Guangxi shifan daxue chubanshe, 2003), 710.

18 Zhao Shouzu, "Preface," 2b, in Feng Zi and Liu Dawen, DMLJS.

19 Wang Deguang, "Preface," 1b–2b, in Feng Zi and Liu Dawen, DMLJS.

20 Wang Ming, "Preface," 1a, 2b–3b, in Feng Zi and Liu Dawen, DMLJS.

commentary would benefit commoners, by making it much clearer to them what should be followed and what should be avoided.[21]

Of all of Liu Dawen's colleagues in Anqing, Gao Ju was a genuine co-worker. Gao Ju received his *jinshi* degree in 1580. In the same year that Liu was sent to Anqing, Gao was appointed regional inspector of Nanzhili and met Liu in the area. Both Gao and Liu were dispatched to the locale by the central judicial agencies to review cases. Gao was also a legal expert. Four years later, when he served as regional inspector of Henan, he participated in the compilation and publication of the commentary *Da Ming lü jijie fuli* (The Collected Commentaries of the *Great Ming Code* with Regulations) with Zhong Zhenji as the author.[22] In 1610, as grand coordinator of Zhejiang province, Gao sponsored the publication of a commentary with the same title.[23] When working with Liu, Gao described the difference between them. According to Gao Ju, Liu Dawen's goal in judicial review was to demonstrate the benevolence of the emperor, whereas he himself, as a regional inspector, was to "follow the law of the emperor."[24] But Gao appreciated the commentary that Liu shared with him. He commented that the annotations included in *DMLJS* were "fine and brilliant" and that both Feng and Liu had made a significant contribution to the existing legal knowledge.[25]

In 1592, thanks to the group's efforts, the commentary *DMLJS* was published at Anqing. On the cover page, Feng Zi was listed as the author, Liu Dawen as the compiler, Zhao Shouzu as the reviewer, and Wang Deguang as the proofreader. Liu Dawen, Wang Zhiyou, Wang Ming, Gao Ju, and Zhao Shouzu wrote prefaces, and Wang Deguang wrote the postface.

The *DMLJS* case shows how collaboration among legal experts facilitated production of the commentaries on the *Great Ming Code*. In the sixteenth and the seventeenth centuries, such collaboration was common although it took different forms. Some would focus on the authors more than on other participants. For example, although it is evident that the production of the commentary *Dulü suoyan* (Miscellaneous Notes on Reading the Code) was a joint effort, much less is known about the sponsor and the publishing process than about the author, Lei Menglin, the legal expert who closely studied the

21 Wang Zhiyou, "Preface," 3b–4a, in Feng Zi and Liu Dawen, *DMLJS*.

22 Zhong Zhenji 衷贞吉, *Da Ming lü jijie fuli* 大明律集解附例 [The Collected Commentaries of *the Great Ming Code* with Regulations) (1596), 16a.

23 Gao Ju 高举, *Da Ming lü jijie fuli* 大明律集解附例 [The Collected Commentaries of *the Great Ming Code* with Regulations] (Taibei: Xuesheng shuju, 1970).

24 Gao Ju, "Preface," 4a, in Feng Zi and Liu Dawen, *DMLJS*.

25 Ibid., 6a.

Great Ming Code and finished the commentary while serving in the Ministry of Justice in the mid-sixteenth century.[26] In many other cases, however, it was the compilers and sponsors instead of the authors who were highlighted. In 1585, Sun Xun, Regional Inspector of Jiangxi, ordered the local government to print a commentary titled *Da Ming lüli fushu* (The Great Ming Code and Regulations with Commentaries). In the preface, Sun clearly stated that he had purchased the commentary when he first entered officialdom. He believed that the interpretations of the law in this commentary were comprehensive and profound, and that the work also provided various original interpretations of the meanings and connotations of the *Great Ming Code*. Sun therefore wished to sponsor its publication. Unlike Liu Dawen, however, who gave credit to the author of the commentary, Sun did not include any information about the author of *Da Ming lüli fushu*.[27] Indeed, many authors of the commentaries remained anonymous.

The case of Ying Jia and his commentary *Da Ming lü shiyi* (The Commentary of the Great Ming Code) demonstrates another form of collaboration among Ming jurists. After receiving his *jinshi* degree in 1526, Ying Jia became an official in the Ministry of Justice. He worked on the *Great Ming Code* in his spare time, and finally completed a draft of *Da Ming lü shiyi*. According to Ying, he was then sent to Jiangnan for judicial review. Although he benefited from the commentary, he had little time to do further work on it. After he returned to the capital, some of his acquaintances approached him and requested copies of the work. As a result, Ying resumed the revision of the commentary and finally published it, hoping that its publication might benefit a wider audience.[28] In other words, the publication was encouraged by those who shared the same interests in legal knowledge in general and in the *Great Ming Code* in particular.

In his preface to *DMLJS*, Wang Zhiyou used the term "people like us" (*wobei*) to refer to his group that cared about law.[29] In the words of Zhao Shouzu, from now on, "if all of the people who share my calling (*fanwo tongzhi*) can use this book as the guideline and follow it, then the benevolence of the emperor will be carried even beyond the sea."[30] In 1632, in the preface to the commentary *Linmin baojing* (Precious Mirror for Governing the People), the author

---

26 Lei Menglin 雷梦麟, *Dulü suoyan* 读律琐言 [Miscellaneous Notes on Reading the Code], reprint ed., Huai Xiaofeng 怀效峰 and Li Jun 李俊 (Beijing: Falü chubanshe, 2000), 3.

27 Sun Xun 孙旬, "Preface," in Sun Xun, *Da Ming lüli fushu* 大明律例附疏 [The Great Ming Code and Regulations with Commentaries] (1585p), 1a–1b.

28 Ibid.

29 Wang Zhiyou, "Preface," 3b, in Feng Zi and Liu Dawen, *DMLJS*.

30 Zhao Shouzu, "Preface," 4b, in Feng Zi and Liu Dawen, *DMLJS*.

also hoped that those "who shared the same commitment" would not ignore the law just because it seemed easy. They should follow the law, from which, he hoped, both the state and the people would benefit.[31] Thus, collaboration among legal experts on the production and dissemination of commentaries on the *Great Ming Code* appears to reveal the existence of a community of legal experts. In the sixteenth and seventeenth centuries, a sense of "we" seems to have developed among its members.

Legal Experts and Legal Institutions

It is evident from a close look at the thirty-six commentaries on *the Great Ming Code* examined in this study that officials, especially judicial officials, occupied the central positions in the community. Indeed, of the thirty titles for which the names of either the authors, compilers, or sponsors were given, twenty-eight were produced by government officials while the other two contain little information about the producers.[32] It is known that the commentary *Da Ming lüli zhushi xiangxing bingjian* (Lucid Commentaries on the *Great Ming Code* and Regulations), was authored by a student of the Nanjing Imperial Academy. This might be the only author who could be clearly identified as coming from outside officialdom. And Dong Yu, who served as Minister of Justice in the Wanli reign, endorsed the publication of the commentary by providing a preface.[33]

With only handful of exceptions, most of the government officials were judicial officials when they participated in the production and dissemination of the commentaries. For the commentary *Santai Ming lü zhaopan zhengzong* (Standard Formats for Making Judgments According to the Code), Yu Yuan, a registrar of Kaipin Guard (Kaipin *wei*), was listed as the author.[34] Sun Cun, author of *Da Ming lü dufa*, was a prefect when he compiled this work.[35] When

31 See Qingbaili 清白吏, "Preface," in Su Maoxiang 苏茂相, *Linmin baojing* 临民宝镜 [Precious Mirror for Governing the People] (1632p), 6a.

32 Gong Ju 贡举, *Da Ming Longtou biandu pangxun lüfa quanshu* 大明龙头便读傍训律法全书 [An Encyclopedia of Ming Laws with Commentaries and Readings at the Top of the Pages] (undated Ming edition); Peng Yingbi 彭应弼, *Xingshu juhui* 刑书据会 [Essentials of the Code] (undated Ming edition).

33 Dong Yu 董裕, "Preface," 3, in Dong Yu, *Da Ming lüli zhushi xiangxing bingjian* 大明律例注释祥刑冰鉴 [Lucid Commentaries to the *Great Ming Code* and Regulations] (1599p).

34 Yu Yuan 余员, *Santai Ming lü zhaopan zhengzong* 三台明律招判正宗 [Standard Formats for Making Judgments According to the Code] (1606), *juan* 1: 1.

35 Sun Cun 孙存, *Fengshan ji* 丰山集 [Collected Works of Sun Cun] (1555p), *juan* 4: 3–6.

Wang Zongyuan worked on his commentary, he was the provincial administration commissioner of Sichuan.[36] Table 7.1 shows the dominant role that judicial officials played in the community of legal experts in sixteenth- and seventeenth-century China, especially officials from the three central-level judicial agencies: the Ministry of Justice, the Court of Judicial Review, and the Censorate.

TABLE 7.1 *Institutions of the producers of thirty-four commentaries published in the sixteenth and seventeenth centuries*

Ministry of Justice	9
Court of Judicial Review	3
Censorate (Regional Inspectors)	11 (9)
Surveillance Commission	1
Other Agencies	4
Unknown	6
Total	34

Although government agencies such as the Grand Secretariat and the Imperial Bodyguard might get involved in legal issues,[37] the three judicial agencies were mainly responsible for handling legal cases in the Ming central government. The Ministry of Justice was responsible for trying and reviewing all cases that occurred in the capital area (including supervising capital punishment) and for reviewing most severe cases from other provinces.[38] The main function of the Court of Judicial Review was to review cases that were tried or reviewed by the Ministry of Justice and the Censorate.[39] The Censorate was responsible for reviewing cases and clarifying cases of injustice as well as directing trials of

36 Pan En 潘恩, "Postface," 2b, in Wang Zongyuan 汪宗元, *Da Ming lüli* 大明律例 [The *Code* and Regulations of the Great Ming] (1554pf).

37 Na Silu 那思陆, *Mingdai zhongyang sifa shenpan zhidu* 明代中央司法审判制度 [The Central Legal Institutions in the Ming Dynasty] (Taibei: Zhengdian chuban wenhua youxian gongsi, 2002).

38 *Ming huidian* 明会典 [Collected Statutes of the Ming Dynasty] (Beijing: Zhonghua shuju 1989), *juan* 159: 819.

39 *Ming huidian, juan* 214: 1068; *Mingshi* 明史 [History of Ming] (Beijing: Zhonghua shuju, 1974), *juan* 73: 1781.

official offenders.[40] Within the Censorate, regional inspectors played significant roles in judicial matters. Corresponding to the thirteen provinces, a total of 110 censors in the Censorate were divided among thirteen circuits. Every year, censors would be dispatched to tour their designated regions, one censor to each of thirteen provinces, together with three censors to Nanzhili, Xuanda, Liaodong, and Gansu, respectively. They were known as regional inspectors.[41] In 1393, the *Government Statutes* were promulgated, which provided that when regional inspectors arrived in their designated areas, they should "first review the case records of the convicts."[42] Regional inspectors were required to go through every relevant document to decide whether the judicial proceedings were legal, the evidence convincing, the law applied appropriately, the sentencing suitable, and so on.[43]

In the Ming dynasty, legal knowledge was required for all the government officials. The *Great Ming Code* stated: "It is essential that officials and functionaries in all the government offices thoroughly read them and be able to explain clearly the meaning of the Code so that they can analyze and decide matters."[44] But it was the legal officials who were obligated to acquire enough legal knowledge to function in their positions. When Kong Gongxun was promoted to the post of vice-minister of the Court of Judicial Review at the beginning of the Chenghua reign (1465–87), he was very unhappy. He confessed to the emperor that he did not know enough about the law and would like to return to his previous position, junior supervisor of the Household Administration of the Heir Apparent.[45] The famed legal scholar Wang Kentang mentioned that his father, Wang Qiao, cited inappropriate legal provisions in judgments when he was vice director in the Ministry of Justice in the Jiajing reign, and was reprimanded by the minister for it. According to Wang Kentang, Wang Qiao regarded this incident as a humiliation and studied the Code very hard afterwards. He eventually became a legal expert and authored the commentary *Dulü sijian*.[46] Even more emphasis was placed on the possession of legal knowledge in the appointment process of the Censorate. According to the *Guidelines for*

40 *Mingshi, juan* 73: 1768.

41 Na Silu, *Mingdai zhongyang sifa shenpan zhidu*, 44–46.

42 *Zhusi zhizhang* 诸司职掌 [Government statutes], in *Huang Ming zhishu* 皇明制书 [Government Documents of the Great Ming], *juan* 5 (Beijing: Shumu wenxian chubanshe, 1998), vol. 46: 245.

43 *Ming huidian, juan* 210: 1048–1049.

44 Yonglin Jiang, *The Great Ming Code* (Seattle: University of Washington Press, 2005), 59.

45 *Ming xianzong shilu* 明宪宗实录 [Veritable Record of Ming Xianzong], *juan* 98: 1862.

46 Chiu Pengsheng [Qiu Pengsheng] 邱澎生, "Youzi yongshi huo fuzuo zisun 有资用世或福祚子孙—晚明有关法律知识的两种价值观 [To Help Statecraft or Promote the

the Censorate issued in 1439, all the selected censors should spend one year in the Censorate or a half-year in personally taking charge in judicial trials. When the term ended, their legal skills would be examined. Only those who received a positive evaluation could become censors and, when dispatched from the capital, regional inspectors.[47]

In the sixteenth and the seventeenth centuries, legal affairs appeared to be the major topic of discussion in interactions within certain judicial agencies. Wang Qiao clearly pointed out that officials in the Ministry of Justice discussed legal matters whenever there were doubtful questions.[48] Officials who worked hard on cultivating their legal knowledge would be highly appreciated and encouraged in the agencies. When Zheng Rubi, compiler of *Da Ming lüjie fuli* (The Commentary of the *Great Ming Code* with Regulations),[49] worked in the Ministry of Justice early in the Wanli reign, he was appraised by Minister Wang Zhigao for his legal expertise.[50] Xu Changzuo (1558–1609), author of *Da Ming lüli tianshi pangzhu* (Commentaries and Interlinear Notes on the *Great Ming Code* and Regulations),[51] was also commended by Minister Dong Yu for his study of law and adjudication when Xu was a secretary in the bureau of the Ministry of Justice.[52]

Furthermore, the three central-level judicial agencies were structured to collaborate on both judicial review and trials. According to Na Ssu-lu, judicial reviews by the three agencies were arranged along two parallel venues: for non-official legal cases, the Ministry of Justice served as the first reviewer and the Court of Judicial Review the second; for official cases, the Censorate would serve as the first reviewer while the Court of Judicial Review would serve

---

Happiness for Offsprings: Two Views on Legal Knowledge in the Late Ming]," *Tsinghua faxue* 清华法学 [Tsinghua Legal Studies], no. 3 (2006): 141–174, at 145.

47 *Xiangang* 宪纲 [Guidelines for the Censorate], in *juan* 10 of *Huangming zhishu*, 307; Wang Shu 王恕, *Wang Duanyi zouyi* 王端毅奏议 [Collected Memorials of Wang Shu], *juan* 8: 1–2, in *Wenyuange siku quanshu* (Taibei, Shangwu yinshuguan, 1986).

48 Wang Qiao 王樵, *Fanglu ji* 方麓集 [Collected Works of Wang Qiao], *juan* 6: 28, in *Wenyuange siku quanshu* (Taibei: Shangwu yinshuguan, 1986), *ce* 1285: 97–476.

49 Zheng Rubi 郑汝璧, *Da Ming lüjie fuli* 大明律解附例 [The Commentary of the *Great Ming Code* with Regulations] (1594).

50 *Chuzhou fu zhi* 处州府志 [The Local Gazetteer of Chuzhou] (Taibei: Chengwen chubanshe, 1974), *juan* 18: 631.

51 Xu Changzuo 徐昌祚, *Da Ming lüli tianshi pangzhu* 大明律例添释旁注 [Commentaries and Interlinear Notes on the *Great Ming Code* and Regulations] (Undated Ming edition).

52 Xu Fuzuo 徐復祚, *Jiaer siyu* 家儿私语 [Private Accounts of Family Issues], in Zhao Yichen 赵饴琛, *Bingzi congbian* 丙子丛编 [The Book Series Compiled in the Year of Bingzi) (1936), 2b.

as the second.[53] The co-trials by these agencies might take different forms. Some of the joint trials were under the order of emperors. In 1434, for example, twenty-four monk rebels were arrested and sent to the capital. The emperor ordered the three judicial agencies to conduct a joint trial.[54] Other joint trials by the three judicial trials were more regular, especially for serious cases and benevolent trials (*xuxing*).[55]

It is also interesting to note that while the Ministry of Justice and the Court of Judicial Review worked as the major judicial institutions, in the late Ming they were often viewed as having a very light workload. In the Jiajing reign (1522–66), officials from the Ministry of Justice frequently held literary gatherings.[56] Why officials there enjoyed such leisure time requires further study, but it was evident that this environment significantly enhanced the cultivation of legal expertise of certain judicial officials. Indeed, various officials attributed their acquisition of legal knowledge to the light workload in the Ministry of Justice. Ying Jia felt fortunate that there was not much to do in the Ministry of Justice, which made it possible for him to focus on studying the Code.[57] Wang Qiao also said that the Ministry of Justice was well known for "having little work to do." Directors spent only three *shichen* (*sanshi* or about six hours) every day taking care of official business and were able to spend the rest of the time reading.[58] Being a director of the Ministry of Justice in the Wanli period, Wang Qiao was able to read the *Great Ming Code* as closely as scholars studied the Confucian classics.[59] The situation might have been similar in the Court of Judicial Review. Liu Dawen mentioned that when he served as a judicial reviewer in the latter office, he spent a great deal of time working on the DMLJS.

It seems safe to argue that Ming judicial institutions, especially the three central-level agencies, acted as the main venues for nurturing and cultivating legal expertise. Thus, the operation of these institutions in the sixteenth and

53 Na Ssu-lu, *Mingdai zhongyang sifa shenpan zhidu*, 212.

54 *Ming Xuanzong shilu* 明宣宗实录 [Veritable Record of Ming Xuanzong], *juan* 108: 2436.

55 *Mingshi*, *juan* 94: 2306–2308; *Minghui dian*, *juan* 214: 1072.

56 Zhang Dejian 张德建, "Mingdai Jiajing jian xingbu de wenxue huodong 明代嘉靖间刑部的文学活动 [The Literary Activities in the Ministry of Justice in the Jiajing Reign of the Ming Dynasty]," *Zhongguo wenhua yanjiu* 中国文化研究 [Chinese Cultural Studies], no. 4 (winter 2011): 40–50.

57 Ying Jia 应槚, "Postface," in *Da Ming lü shiyi* 大明律释义 [The Commentary of the *Great Ming Code*], 227, in Xuxiu siku quanshu (Shanghai, Shanghai guji chubanshe, 2002).

58 Wang Qiao, *Fanglu ji*, *juan* 6: 28.

59 Ibid.

the seventeenth centuries significantly affected the composition of the community of legal experts.

The Structure of the Community

Judicial institutions also shaped the structure of the community of legal experts. To ensure that government officials were well equipped with legal knowledge, the *Great Ming Code* decreed: "At the end of every year, they [officials] shall be examined: in the capital, by the Investigation Bureau, and outside the capital, by investigating censors and officials of Provincial Surveillance Commissions within their jurisdictions."[60] In the sixteenth and the seventeenth centuries, these investigating censors, i.e. regional inspectors, played a significant role in ordering the community.

Touring their designated areas, regional inspectors often found various problems concerning legal affairs. Many of them attributed these problems to the lack of legal knowledge and legal expertise on the part of local officials. For example, Regional Inspector Chen Yuwen mentioned that the reason why local officials violated the laws was that "they do not understand the law."[61] Regional Inspector Sun Xun also pointed out that according to his inspection, some of the legal decisions made by the local legal officials were inappropriate, mainly because local officials did "not understand the law well."[62]

This presumption explains why regional inspectors frequently sponsored the publication of commentaries at the local level. Both Chen Yuwen and Sun Xun sponsored such publications in their designated regions and required local officials to use these commentaries. Chen Xing, regional inspector of Huguang in the early years of the Longqing reign (1567–72), compiled and sponsored the publication of the commentary *Da Ming lüli* (The Code and the Regulations of the Great Ming).[63] In the postscript, Chen not only described how he worked on this commentary but also mentioned that as a regional inspector, he felt that his responsibility was somehow fulfilled when he sponsored the publication of the commentary.[64]

60 Jiang Yonglin, *The Great Ming Code*, 59.

61 Chen Yuwen 陈遇文, "Preface," 3b–4a, in *Da Ming lü fujie* 大明律附解 [The *Great Ming Code* with Commentaries] (1592p).

62 Sun Xun, "Preface," 1a, in Sun Xun, *Da Ming lüli fushu*.

63 Chen Xing 陈省, *Da Ming lüli* 大明律例 [The Code and the Regulations of the Great Ming] (1567pf).

64 Chen Xing, "Postface," 2b, in *Da Ming lüli*.

In the publication process, therefore, regional inspectors served as the providers while local officials were regarded as the receivers and beneficiaries, although local officials also participated in the production process. While regional inspectors would often be the sponsors, most of the local officials would work as editors and proofreaders. In other words, local officials were followers rather than initiators, assistants rather than principals. At the local level, the surveillance commissions used to be regarded as the local counterpart of the Censorate at the central government.[65] In the early Ming, officials from the surveillance commissions were often considered the equals and colleagues of regional inspectors dispatched by the Censorate. In the later Ming period, however, regional inspectors gained more power in dealing with local affairs and surveillance commission officials, along with their local colleagues, gradually became their assistants.[66]

As a matter of fact, the community of legal experts did extend to the local areas. In 1532, Sun Cun, prefect of Jingzhou in Huguang province, presented his fine commentary *Da Ming lü dufa* to the Jiajing emperor. The work was said to have included the following parts: the Code, the imperial documents related to the Code, the imperially approved regulations, interpretations from earlier commentaries for each article of the Code cited from existing commentaries, the new regulations issued in the Zhengde reign, and the current cases in the Jiajing reign. Beginning in 1523, Sun Cun spent about seven years on this work during his tenure as the prefect of Ganzhou, Changsha, and Jingzhou. According to his friend Wen Zhengming, Sun was viewed as a legal expert by his contemporaries, and Sun himself was proud of this.[67]

It is interesting to note that Zhang Lu, regional inspector of Huguang, offered Sun Cun advice during Sun's work on the commentary. When the work was finished, it was also Zhang Lu who approved its publication and financed it through the redemption money collected by the local government.[68] Wang Zongyuan's case was similar. When he was promoted to the post of left provincial administration commissioner of Jiangxi, he wanted to publish his commentary, *Da Ming lüli*. He asked for and received permission for its publication

65 Wang Tianyou 王天有, *Mingdai guojia jigou yanjiu* 明代国家机构研究 [A Study on the Government Institutions of the Ming Dynasty] (Beijing: Beijing daxue chubanshe, 1992), 220.

66 Gao Chunping 高春平, "Lun Mingdai de tixing ancha shisi 论明代的提刑按察使司 [On Provincial Surveillance Commission in the Ming Dynasty]," *Jinyang xuekan* 晋阳学刊 [Scholarly Journal of Jinyang], no. 3 (1992): 92–97.

67 Wen Zhengming, "Preface," 3, in Sun Cun, *Fengshan Ji*.

68 Sun Cun, *Fengshan ji*, *juan* 4: 4.

from both Grand Coordinator Chen and Regional Inspector Wu of Jiangxi.[69] Thus, regional inspectors appeared to have worked as gatekeepers as well as builders for the community of legal experts.

It is worth pointing out, however, that the regional inspectors' control was limited to the commentaries published by local governments. As in the case of Sun Cun, publication of the commentaries was financed by local governments and the main audience consisted of officials within these touring inspectors' jurisdictions. In a sense, the regional inspectors' impact on the configuration of the community of legal experts had some limitations.

In the mid- and late-Ming, two other factors appeared to have affected the community of legal experts. One was the emphasis on legal expertise. Within the community of legal experts, members paid close attention to what had been produced previously and what was newly created. This kind of attention was accompanied by critical evaluation of the works. In the case of *DMLJS*, Liu Dawen closely studied the work together with the popular commentaries of his time, *Dulü suoyan* and *Dulü guanjian*, and provided a very positive review of *DMLJS*. Such evaluations then resulted in a work's being selected for improvement or further distribution. If a certain commentary was recognized as valuable by members of the community, joint efforts were more likely to be made to revise and compile the work and sponsor its publication. For already-published commentaries, positive reviews meant more appreciation and citations. Recognized as the model commentary, Zhang Kai's *Lütiao shuyi*, which was published in 1461, was widely cited in the commentaries of the sixteenth and the seventeenth centuries.[70] Ying Jia acknowledged that his commentary, *Da Ming lü shiyi*, was based on existing commentaries such as *shuyi* (*Lütiao shuyi*) and *zhiyin*, together with his own understanding.[71] *Dulü suoyan* was so popular that not only was it cited in various other commentaries but its annotations and interpretation were widely followed by legal officials.[72]

The *jijie* (collected commentaries) format became popular in this period.[73] It further indicated the community members' broad knowledge of the field,

69 Pan En, "Preface," 2b–3a, in Wang Zongyuan, *Da Ming lüli*.

70 Zhang Boyuan 张伯元, *Lüxue wenxian congkao* 律学文献丛考 [Studies on the Law Codes), in *Zhongguo fazhishi kaozheng xubian* 中国法制史考证续编 [The Sequel to *Studies on Chinese Legal History*], ed. Yang Yifan (Beijing: Sheke wenxian chubanshe, 2009), 187, 202–204.

71 Ying Jia, "Postface," in Ying Jia, *Da Ming lü shiyi*, 227.

72 Chen Xing, "Preface," 1b, in Chen Xing, *Da Ming lüli*.

73 Chiu Pengsheng, "You Mingdai lüli zhushixue fazhan kan shangye yu falü de hudong 由明代律例注释学发展看商业与法律的互动" [Understanding the Interaction between Commerce and Law from the Commentaries on the Code and Regulations], paper

their constant evaluation of new works, and the selection and inclusion of valuable commentaries. The *jijie* format required authors and compilers to make references to all the pre-existing commentaries on the Code, critically evaluate them, select the more reliable and worthy ones, and either include them directly or integrate them into their own commentaries. This *jijie* format was already in use as early as the *Da Ming lüjie fuli* (A Commentary on the Great Ming Code with Regulations), compiled in the Zhengde reign (1506–21).[74] It became more popular later. By the early seventeenth century, when Zhong Zhenji's and Gao Ju's commentaries were compiled, both were titled *Da Ming lü jijie fuli*.[75]

Such evaluation and selection emphasized the value of the commentaries and the legal expertise that the producers could provide to the community. Sun Cun's case is a good example of how the emphasis on legal expertise affected the making of the community. Not only was he a local official but he also offended the Jiajing emperor when he presented his work to the throne in 1532. The emperor blamed Sun for having worked on the dynastic code and publishing the commentary without authorization, and ordered this work to be destroyed.[76] In a sense, Sun's commentary was politically suppressed. However, Sun's work was still quite popular and widely cited and appreciated during the Ming dynasty right after the political incident. In 1533, Fan Yongluan published his commentary on the *Da Ming lü*, which not only copied a significant amount of information from Sun's work but also had Sun's book title, *Da Ming lü dufa*, in the central margin of the leaves of the book. Indeed, Fan Yongluan's work looks so similar to Sun Cun's that Shen Jiaben, a leading legal scholar in the late Qing, believed that it was the same book.[77] A number of commentaries that appeared later also cited extensively from Sun Cun's work, including Ying Jia's *Da Ming lü shiyi*, Lu Jian's *Dulü guanjian*, and Xu Changzuo's *Da Ming lüli tianshi pangzhu*.[78] It seems certain that although Sun Cun's work was politically denounced, both his biographer and his compatriots were proud

presented at the conference *Quanqiu hua xia Mingshi yanjiu zhi xin shiye* 全球化下明史研究之新视野 [New Perspectives on Ming Studies under the Globalization Context), Taibei, October 27–31, 2007.

74 Compiler Hu Qiong specifically mentioned that this work was "a collected commentary compiled by censor Hu Qiong." Hu Qiong 胡琼, *Da Ming lüjie fuli* 大明律解附例 [A Commentary of *the Great Ming Code* with Regulations] (1521pf), *juan* 1: 1.

75 Zhong Zhenji's *Da Ming lüjie fuli* was published in 1596, while the extant Gao Ju's work was published in 1610.

76 *Ming Shizong shilu* 明世宗实录 [Veritable record of Ming Shizong], *juan* 137: 3229.

77 Shen Jiaben 沈家本, *Shen Jiyi xianshen yishu* 沈寄簃先生遗书 [The Posthumous Works of Shen Jiaben] (Beijing: Zhongguo shudian, 1990), 978.

78 Zhang Boyuan, *Lüxue wenxian congkao*, 242–243, 292.

of this work and emphasized its legacy in both his biography and the local gazetteer.[79] It seems that in the mid- and late-Ming, legal expertise began to have some professional value apart from political influence. It became a significant factor in affecting the structure of the community of legal experts.

Another factor was the flourishing of commercial printing. Although we know little about how commercial printing shops produced the commentaries, we do know that commercial printing provided lesser-known authors with a venue for getting their works published and distributed. Out of the thirty-six commentaries under study here, about twelve were published through commercial printing enterprises. Most of the producers of these 12 commentaries fall into either the "Other agencies" or the "Unknown" category in Table 7.1. In reality, however, commercial printing may have played a greater role than these numbers indicate. For example, before Wang Kentang published his father's *Dulü sijian*, he mentioned that some commercial printers had already published the work.[80]

In other words, commercial printing opened another door for individuals to enter the community of legal experts, especially those who were from local areas and lower socio-economic backgrounds. Furthermore, although commercial printing was often criticized for poor quality, it significantly enhanced the circulation of legal knowledge, providing another resource for cultivating legal experts. Thus, during this period, while the hierarchical order of the community of legal experts was still being shaped by legal institutions or political power, commercial printing did affect the structure of the community.

Conclusions

This chapter has examined the community of legal experts in sixteenth- and seventeenth-century China. It has traced the community's formation and operation by studying the legal experts' participation in the production and dissemination of the commentaries on the *Great Ming Code*. Drawing on thirty-six commentaries, it has focused on the authors, compilers, revisers, sponsors, editors, and proofreaders of these commentaries as a community of legal experts. This community was by no means exclusive or all-inclusive. There were certainly commentaries that are not included in this study, and many Ming legal experts might not have worked on commentaries on the Code. Nevertheless,

79 Wu Yanhong 吴艳红, "Sun Cun an yu Mingdai zhonghouqi de falü ahishi 孙存案与明代中后期的法律知识 [The Case of Sun Cun and Legal Knowledge in Mid- and Late-Ming]," *Faguo hanxue* 法国汉学 [French Sinology] vol. 12 (2014), forthcoming.

80 Chiu Pengsheng, "Youzi yongshi huo fuzuo zisun," 155.

our study of this community of legal experts should improve our understanding of who they were and how they worked in Ming China.

Three distinctive features of this community of legal experts are worth mentioning. First, members of the community had a shared interest in law and legal affairs. In particular, they possessed expertise in interpreting the law. Within the community, members not only paid close attention to new works in the field but also constantly collected, studied, evaluated, and revised them. Indeed, shared legal knowledge served as a crucial tie binding members of the community. Through these ties, they got to know other members and interacted with them. In the mid- and late-Ming, it was not uncommon for members of the community to refer to each other as "all the people who share my calling" (*fanwo tongzhi*). A sense of common identity appeared to have developed within the community. We do not know much, however, about whether this community was recognized by outsiders. Unlike the leaders of literary communities, who were often well known,[81] leaders of the legal community were often little known to outsiders.

Second, the community was mainly composed of officials, especially those from the three central judicial agencies. The flourishing commercial printing industry during this period helped extend the community to non-legal officials, lower-ranking officials, and even experts outside of the bureaucracy, but it did not change the main features of the community. Being colleagues, many of the members were bound by their working relations. Judicial institutions also played a significant role in shaping the community. Indeed, the legal specialists mentioned above either developed their interests in legal affairs on their own or cultivated their legal expertise while holding a judicial office. They became legal experts through extensive working experience with trials and judicial reviews. In order to work effectively in these judicial institutions, they had to acquire extensive legal knowledge. In this sense, the Ming legal system was able to transform inexperienced Confucian scholar-officials into learned jurists by providing them with the opportunity and incentive to study law and judicial administration on the job. Modern scholars tend to compare legal experts in imperial China with their modern counterparts, namely, lawyers. In the existing literature, therefore, non-official legal experts, such as litigation masters, have received much attention.[82] By comparison, studies of legal

81 Liao Kebin 廖可斌, *Mingda wenxue fugu yundong yanjiu* 明代文学复古运动研究 [A Study of the Movement of Classicism in Ming Literature] (Shanghai: Shanghai guji chubanshe, 1994), 55.

82 For some of the works, see Melissa Ann Macauley, *Social Power and Legal Culture: Litigation Masters in Late Imperial China* (Stanford: Stanford University Press, 1998); Chiu Pengsheng, "Yifa weiming: Songshi yu muyou dui Mingdai falü de chongji 以法为名:

officials, or legal experts who worked within the official legal domain, appear to have been somehow overlooked.[83] The community of legal experts examined in this chapter demonstrates how legal professionalism was developed within the imperial legal system.

Third, legal institutions and political power provided the basic structure of the community of legal experts. Regional inspectors, in particular, acted as both the gatekeepers and patrons of the community. Not only did they approve the publication of commentaries authored by non-officials but they also seemed responsible for sponsoring quality commentaries for local legal officials. Other factors began to affect the composition of the community, however. Within the community, independent criteria were sometimes created to evaluate works in the field. Such criteria emphasized the legal expertise demonstrated by the works at issue, together with the arrangement, originality, and comprehensiveness of the knowledge, producers and writers from lower positions in the political strata might enjoy some popularity if their works were favorably reviewed by the legal experts within the community. The growth in commercial printing in Ming China was an unprecedented social phenomenon that, according to Kai-wing Chow, fostered various literary professionals and helped them gain power and challenge government authority, thus creating a kind of "literary public sphere."[84] In the community of legal experts, commercial printing appears to have been less powerful than in the literary world, but it did provide those who enjoyed less political power another avenue for gaining membership in the community.

讼师与幕友对明清法律秩序的冲击 [In the Name of Law: The Impact of Litigation Masters and Legal Advisors on the Legal Order]," *Zhongxi falü chuantong* 中西法律传统 [Sino-Western Legal Traditions] (2008): 222–277; Li Chen, "Legal Specialists and Judicial Administration in Late Imperial China, 1651–1911," *Late Imperial China* 33, no. 1 (June 2012): 1–54.

83 About the legal training and legal expertise of officials in the Qing dynasty, see, e.g., Xu Zhongming 徐忠明, and Du Jin 杜金, "Qingdai sifa guanyuan zhishi jiegou de kaocha 清代司法官员知识结构的考察 [A Study on the Knowledge of Judicial Officials in the Qing Dynasty]," *Huadong zhengfa xueyuan xuebao* [Journal of East China University of Politics and Law] 5 (2006): 69–90; Ibid., "Dulü shengya: Qingdai xingbu guanyuan de zhiye suyang 读律生涯: 清代刑部官员的职业素养 [A Life of Reading the Code: Professionalism of the Judicial Officials in the Qing]," *Fazhi yu shehui fazhan* 法制与社会发展 [Law and Social Development], no. 3 (2012): 36–67; Gong Rufu 龚汝富, "Ming Qing shiqi sifa guanli de falü jiaoyu 明清时期司法官吏的法律教育 [Legal Education of Judicial Officials in the Ming and Qing Dynasties]," *Jiangxi caijing daxue xuebao* 江西财经大学学报 [Journal of the Jiangxi University of Finance and Economics], no. 5 (2007): 54–57.

84 Kai-wing Chow, *Printing, Culture, and Power in Early Modern China*, 1–2.

Glossary

ancha si	按察司
ancha fushi	按察副使
Changsha	长沙
Chen Xing	陈省
Chen Yuwen	陈遇文
Dashen	大审
Dong Yu	董裕
Fanwo tongzhi	凡我同志
Fan Yongluan	范永銮
Feng Zi	冯孜
fengchi tidu nanzhili cangchang zhengchi yingzhou deng chu bingbei henan ancha fushi	奉敕提督南直隶屯种仓场整饬颖州等处兵备河南按察副使
Ganzhou	赣州
Gao Ju	高举
Grand Secretariat	内阁
Guozijian	国子监
Jijie	集解
Jingzhou	荆州
Jinyi wei	锦衣卫
Kaipingwei jingli	开平卫经历
Kong Gongxun	孔公恂
Lei Menglin	雷梦麟
li	例
Liu Dawen	刘大文
Nanzhili	南直隶
pingshi	评事
qinchai xunan zhili jianchayushi	钦差巡按直隶监察御史
sanshan	三善
sanshi	三时
Shen Jiaben	沈家本
Shujin	赎金
Sun Cun	孙存
Sun Xun	孙旬
Tongxiang	桐乡
Wang Deguang	王德光
Wang Kentang	王肯堂
Wang Ming	王明
Wang Qiao's	王樵
Wang Zhigao	王之诰
Wang Zhiyou	王之猷
Wang Zongyuan	汪宗元
Wobei	我辈
xuxing	恤刑
Xu Changzuo	徐昌祚
xunan zhili jianch yushi	巡按直隶监察御史
Ying Jia	应檟
Yu Yuan	余员
yuanwai lang	员外郎
Zhang Lu	张禄
zhanshifu shaozhanshi	詹事府少詹事
Zhao Shouzu	赵寿祖
Zheng Rubi	郑汝璧
Zhengming	文征明
Zhong Zhenji	衷贞吉

Bibliography

Chen Xing 陈省. *Da Ming lüli* 大明律例 [The Code and the Regulations of the Great Ming]. 1+30+1 *juan*, 1567pf.

Chen Yuwen 陈遇文. *Da Ming lü fujie* 大明律附解 [The *Great Ming Code* with Commentaries]. 8 *juan*. 1592p.

Chen, Li. "Legal Specialists and Judicial Administration in Late Imperial China, 1651–1911." *Late Imperial China* 33, no. 1 (June 2012): 1–54.

Chiu Pengsheng 邱澎生. "Yi fa wei ming: Songshi yu muyou dui Mingdai falü de chongji 以法为名：讼师与幕友对明清法律秩序的冲击 [In the Name of Law: The Impact of Litigation Masters and Legal Advisors on the Legal Order]." *Zhongxi falü chuantong* 中西法律传统 [Sino-Western Legal Traditions] 6(2008): 222–277.

———. "You Mingdai lüli zhushixue fazhan kan shangye yu falü de hudong 由明代律例注释学发展看商业与法律的互动 [Understanding the Interaction between Commerce and Law from the Commentaries on the Code and Regulations]." Paper presented at the Conference *Quanqiu hua xia Mingshi yanjiu zhi xin shiye* 全球化下明史研究之新视野 [New Perspectives on Ming Studies under the Globalization Context]. Taibei, October 27–31, 2007.

———. "Youzi yongshi huo fuzuo zisun—wan Ming youguan falü zhishi de liangzhong jiazhiguan 有资用世或福祚子孙—晚明有关法律知识的两种价值观 [To Help Statecraft or Promote the Happiness for Offsprings: Two Views on Legal Knowledge in the Late Ming]. *Tsinghua faxue* 清华法学 [Tsinghua Legal Studies] 3 (2006): 141–174.

Chow, Kai-wing. *Printing, Culture, and Power in Early Modern China*. Stanford: Stanford University Press, 2004.

Chuzhou fu zhi 处州府志 [The Local Gazetteer of Chuzhou]. Taibei: Chengwen chubanshe, 1974.

Clunas, Craig. *Pictures and Visuality in Early Modern China*. London: Reaktion Books Ltd, 1997.

Department of Chinese History, China Renming University 中国人民大学历史教研室, ed. *Zhongguo zibenzhuyi wenti taolunji* 中国资本主义问题讨论集 [Collected Essays on Chinese Capitalism] Beijing: Sanlian shudian, 1957.

Dong Yu 董裕. *Da Ming lüli zhushi xiangxing bingjian* 大明律例注释祥刑冰鉴 [Lucid Commentaries to the *Great Ming Code* and Regulations. 1+30 *juan*, 1599p.

Du Jin 杜金, and Xu Zhongming 徐忠明. "Dulü shengya: Qingdai xingbu guanyuan de zhiye suyang 读律生涯：清代刑部官员的职业素养 [A Life of Reading the Code: Professionalism of the Judicial Officials in the Qing]. *Fazhi yu shehui fazhan* 法制与社会发展 [Law and Social Development] no. 3 (2012): 36–67.

Feng Zi 冯孜, and Liu Dawen 刘大文. *Da Ming lü jishuo* 大明律集说 [The Collected Explications of the *Great Ming Code*]. 30 *juan*, 1592p.

Gao Chunping 高春平. "Lun Mingdai de tixing ancha shisi 论明代的提刑按察使司 [On Provincial Surveillance Commissioners in the Ming Dynasty]. *Jinyang xuekan* 晋阳学刊 [Scholarly Journal of Jinyang] 3 (1992): 92–97.

Gao Ju 高举. *Da Ming lü jijie fuli* 大明律集解附例 [The Collected Commentaries of *the Great Ming Code* with Regulations]. 1+30 *juan*. 1610. Taibei: Xuesheng shuju, 1970.

Gong Ju 贡举. *Da Ming Longtou biandu pangxun lüfa quanshu* 大明龙头便读傍训律法全书 [An Encyclopedia of Ming Laws with Commentaries and Readings at the Top of the Pages]. 1+11 *juan*. Undated Ming edition.

Gong Rufu 龚汝富. "Ming Qing shiqi sifa guanli de falü jiaoyu 明清时期司法官吏的法律教育 [Legal Education of Judical Officials in the Ming and Qing Dynasties]." *Jiangxi caijing daxue xuebao* 江西财经大学学报 [Journal of Jiangxi University of Finance and Economics] 5 (2007): 54–57.

Guizhou tongzhi 貴州通志 [A General Gazetteer of Guizhou]. Undated Ming edition.

He Guang 何广. *Lüjie bianyi* 律解辩疑 [Code with Commentaries and Explication of Questions]. 30 *juan*. 1386p.

Hu Qiong 胡琼. *Da Ming lüjie fuli* 大明律解附例 [A Commentary of *the Great Ming Code* with Regulations]. 1+30 *juan*. 1521pf.

Jiang, Yonglin. *The Great Ming Code*. Seattle: University of Washington Press, 2005.

Langlois, John. "Ming Law." In *The Cambridge History of China*, vol. 8, eds. Denis Twitchett and Frederick W. Mote, 172–220. Cambridge University Press, 1998.

Lei Menglin 雷梦麟. *Dulü suoyan* 读律琐言 [Miscellaneous Notes on Reading the Code]. 30+1 *juan*. 1563. Reprint ed., Huai Xiaofeng 怀效锋 and Li Jun 李俊. Beijing: Falü chubanshe, 2000.

Liao Kebin 廖可斌. *Mingda wenxue fugu yundong yanjiu* 明代文学复古运动研究 [A Study of the Movement of Classicism in Ming Literature]. Shanghai: Shanghai guji chubanshe, 1994.

Macauley, Melissa A. *Social Power and Legal Culture: Litigation Masters in Late Imperial China*. Stanford: Stanford University Press, 1998.

Ming huidian 明会典 [Collected Statutes of the Ming Dynasty]. Beijing: Zhonghua shuju 1989.

Ming shilu 明实录 [Veritable Record of the Ming]. Taibei: Zhongyanyuan shiyusuo, 1962.

Mingshi 明史 [History of Ming]. Beijing: Zhonghua shuju, 1974.

Na Silu 那思陆. *Mingdai zhongyang sifa shenpan zhidu* 明代中央司法审判制度 [The Central Legal Institutions in the Ming Dynasty]. Taibei: Zhengdian chuban wenhua youxian gongsi, 2002.

Niu Jianqiang 牛建强. *Mingdai zhonghouqi shehui bianqian yanjiu* 明代中后期社会变迁研究 [Studies on Social Change of the Mid-and Late Ming Society]. Taibei: Wenjin chubanshe, 1997.

Peng Yingbi 彭应弼. *Xingshu juhui* 刑书据会 [Essentials of the Code]. 3+12 *juan*. Undated Ming edition.

Shen Jiaben 沈家本. *Shen Jiyi xianshen yishu* 沈寄簃先生遗书 [The Posthumous Work of Shen Jiaben]. Beijing: Zhongguo shudian, 1990.

Su Maoxiang 苏茂相. *Linmin baojing* 临民宝镜 [Precious Mirror for Governing the People]. 3+10+3 *juan*. 1632p.

Sun Cun 孙存. *Fengshan ji* 丰山集 [Collected Works of Sun Cun]. 40 *juan*, 1555p.

Sun Xun 孙旬. *Da Ming lüli fushu* 大明律例附疏 [The Great Ming Code and Regulations with Commentaries]. 1585p.

Wan Ming 万明, ed. *Wanming shehui bianqian: Wenti yu yanjiu* 晚明社会变迁: 问题与研究 [The social change in late Ming society: Issues and studies]. Beijing: Shangwu yinshuguan, 2005.

Wang Qiao 王樵. *Fanglu ji* 方麓集 [Collected Works of Wang Qiao]. Wenyuange siku quanshu edition. Taibei: Shangwu yinshuguan, 1986, *ce* 1285, 97–476.

Wang Shu 王恕. *Wang Duanyi zouyi* 王端毅奏议 [Collected Memorials of Wang Shu]. Wenyuange siku quanshu edition. Taibei: Shangwu yinshuguan, 1986, *ce* 427, 453–704.

Wang Tianyou 王天有. *Mingdai guojia jigou yanjiu* 明代国家机构研究 [A Study on the Government Institutions of the Ming Dynasty]. Beijing: Beijing daxue chubanshe, 1992.

Wang Zongyuan 汪宗元. *Da Ming lüli* 大明律例 [The Code and Regulations of the Great Ming], 1554pf.

Wu Yanhong 吴艳红. "Mingdai de falü jiqi yunzuo 明代的法律及其运作 [The Legal System of the Ming Dynasty and Its Operation]." In *Mingdai zhengzhi shi* 明代政治史 [A Political History of the Ming Dynasty], edited by Zhang Xianqing 张显清, and Lin Jinshu 林金树, 661–745. Guilin: Guangxi shifan daxue chubanshe, 2003.

———. "Sun Cun an yu Mingdai zhonghouqi de falü zhishi 孙存案与明代中后期的法律知识 [The Case of Sun Cun and the Legal Knowledge in Mid- and Late- Ming]." *Faguo hanxue* 法国汉学 [French Sinology], 2014, forthcoming.

———. "Guojia zhengce yu Mingdai de lüzhu shijian 国家政策与明代的律注实践 [State Policy and the Practice of Interpreting the Code in the Ming Dynasty]." *Shixue yuekan* 史学月刊 [Journal of Historical Science] 1 (2013): 52–62.

Xiangang 宪纲 [Guidelines for the Censorate]. In *Huangming zhishu* 皇明制书 [Government Documents of the Great Ming], 302–317 (*ce* 46, *juan* 10). Beijing: Shumu wenxian chubanshe, 1998.

Xu Changzuo 徐昌祚. *Da Ming lüli tianshi pangzhu* 大明律例添释旁注 [Commentaries and Interlinear Notes on the *Great Ming Code* and Regulations]. 30 *juan*. Undated Ming edition.

Xu Fuzuo 徐復祚. "Jia'er siyu 家儿私语 [Private Accounts of Family Issues]." In Zhao Yichen 赵饴琛, *Bingzi congbian* 丙子丛编 [The Book Series Compiled in the Year of Bingzi]. Kunshan, 1936.

Xu Zhongming 徐忠明, and Du Jin 杜金. "Qingdai sifa guanyuan zhishi jiegou de kaocha 清代司法官员知识结构的考察 [A Study on the Knowledge Structure of Legal Officials in the Qing Dynasty]. *Huadong zhengfa xueyuan xuebao* 华东政法学院学报 [Journal of the East China University of Politics and Law] 5 (2006): 69–90.

Yu Yuan 余员. *Santai Ming lü zhaopan zhengzong* 三台明律招判正宗 [Standard Formats for Making Judgments According to the Code]. 13 *juan*. 1606.

Zhang Boyuan 张伯元. *Lüxue wenxian congkao* 律学文献丛考 [Studies on the Law Codes]. In *Zhongguo fazhishi kaozheng xubian* 中国法制史考证续编 [A Sequel to *Studies on Chinese Legal History*], edited by Yang Yifan. Beijing: Sheke wenxian chubanshe, 2009.

Zhang Dejian 张德建. "Mingdai Jiajing jian xingbu de wenxue huodong 明代嘉靖间刑部的文学活动 [Literary Activities in the Ministry of Justice in the Jiajing Reign of the Ming Dynasty]." *Zhongguo wenhua yanjiu* 中国文化研究 [Chinese Cultural Studies] (winter 2011): 40–50.

Zhang Xianqing 张显清, ed. *Mingdai houqi shehui zhuanxing yanjiu* 明代后期社会转型研究 [A Study on Social Transformation in the Late Ming Society]. Beijing: Zhongguo shehui kexue chubanshe, 2008.

Zhao Yifeng 赵轶峰. *Mingdai de bianqian* 明代的变迁 [Social Change of the Ming Dynasty]. Beijing: Sanlian chubanshe, 2008.

Zheng Rubi 郑汝璧. *Da Ming lüjie fuli* 大明律解附例 [The Commentary of the *Great Ming Code* with Attached Regulations]. 30 *juan*. 1594.

Zhong Zhenji 衷贞吉. *Da Ming lü jijie fuli* 大明律集解附例 [The Collected Commentaries of *the Great Ming Code* with Attached Regulations]. 1+30 *juan*. 1596.

Zhusi zhizhang 诸司职掌 [Government Statutes]. In *Huang Ming zhishu* 皇明制书 [Government Documents of the Great Ming], 59–259 (*ce* 46, *juan* 5). Beijing: Shumu wenxian chubanshe, 1998.

CHAPTER 8

Marketing Legal Information: Commercial Publications of the *Great Qing Code*, 1644–1911

Ting Zhang

As the most important book of the Qing legal world, the *Great Qing Code* (*Da Qing lü jijie fuli* or *Da Qing lüli*) was compiled, revised, and published many times in various editions by both official and commercial publishing houses. An increasingly competitive market for the Code, centered in Hangzhou, emerged in the mid-Qing period as commercial publishing houses gradually took the place of official publishing houses in printing the Code. Commercial editions were printed in large quantities and updated frequently, and they usually included additional legal information. The popular design of commercial editions was different from that of the imperially authorized (*qinding*) editions of the Code. Editors of commercial editions were usually "private legal advisors" (*muyou*). Target readers not only included officials and legal advisors but also extended to all educated men who could afford to buy a copy. I argue that over the course of the Qing period, the book market, rather than the state, became the major force in disseminating accurate and up-to-date legal information. The flourishing legal book market challenged the Qing state's authority in producing and organizing legal knowledge.

Insufficiency of the Imperial Editions

Qing lawmakers made great efforts to promulgate up-to-date laws for the bureaucracy and society.[1] Qing laws were frequently updated, and the Code was enlarged by the revision and periodical addition of a number of new substatutes (*li*). From the first imperially promulgated edition of the Code (the Shunzhi Code) to the last one (the Tongzhi Code), the number of substatutes increased from 449 to 1,892.[2] In the early Qianlong period, the Qing Court

1 See Qin Zheng and Guangyuan Zhou, "Pursuing Perfection: Formation of the Qing Code," *Modern China* 21, no. 3 (1995): 310.

2 The number is cited from Su Yigong 苏亦工, "Lüli guanxi kaobian 律例关系考辨 [Investigation and Analysis on the Relations between Statutes and Substatutes]," in *Zhongguo*

© KONINKLIJKE BRILL NV, LEIDEN, 2015 | DOI 10.1163/9789004288492_010

decided to establish a schedule for the regular revision of substatutes, which was carried out at approximately five-year intervals until 1852.[3] Active legislation requires an efficient dissemination system, otherwise law cannot be effectively implemented. This was especially true for the Qing, a vast empire that had numerous judicial officials working in the huge bureaucracy. However, despite the fact that the Qing central government enthusiastically updated the laws while strictly requiring all judicial officials to sentence criminal cases according to the law,[4] it did not engage as ardently in providing its bureaucracy and society with updated printed editions of the Code.

As far as I have found, only eight imperial editions were published in the Qing period (see Chart 8.1), which means that the publication of the imperial editions occurred much less frequently than revisions of the Code. For most revisions, therefore, updated substatutes were published and issued separately from the Code. For Qing judicial officials, the separation of new substatutes from the Code was an ongoing problem since it easily led to confusion and sometimes wrong citations. For example, in 1671, an official of the Ministry of Justice pointed out such problems in a memorial. In judicial practice, he said, some officials sentenced a case according to an old statute in the Code while others cited a new one from *Xingbu xianxing zeli* (Substatutes of the Ministry of Justice Currently in Operation)—a compilation of new substatutes issued by the Ministry separately from the Code. He warned that this situation could result in injustice and corruption in the judicial system.[5]

Even after the Qing Court set up the standard revision process for the Code in the early Qianlong period, which was designed to codify new substatutes and eliminate possible inconsistencies between pre-existing substatutes in the Code, the problem of separation still existed. After each scheduled revision, instead of publishing the revised Code, the Qing Court usually only printed and issued to judicial officials *Da Qing lü xuzuan tiaoli* ("Expanded Substatutes of the Great Qing Code," henceforth cited as the *Expanded Substatutes*), which

fazhishi kaozheng 中国法制史考证 [Research on Chinese Legal History] (Beijing: Zhongguo shehui kexue chubanshe, 2003), ed. Yang Yifan 杨一凡, Series 1, Vol. 7: 273.

3 *Qing shilu* 清实录 [Veritable Records of the Qing Dynasty] (Beijing: Zhonghua shuju, 1985), 12: 539–540 (*juan* 271).

4 See *Qinding Da Qing huidian shili* 钦定大清会典事例 [Collected Statutes of the Great Qing with Precedents and Substatutes] (Qing huidian guan, 1899), *juan* 852: 1a–2b.

5 Zhang Weichi 张惟赤, *Haiyan Zhangshi Sheyuan congke* 海盐张氏涉园丛刻 [Collected Printings of the Zhang Lineage in the She Garden of Haiyan], reprinted in *Congshu jicheng xubian* 丛书集成续编 [Collections of the Books, Supplemented Compilation] (Shanghai: Shanghai shudian chubanshe, 1994), Vol. 58, *juan* 3: 15b.

contained only new and revised substatutes.[6] The accumulation of new and revised substatutes and their separation from the Code made it even more difficult for officials to read and cite the Code—a multivolume book that was already challenging to handle. For example, Wang Ding (1768–1842), Minister of Justice in the Daoguang period, said: "The substatutes accumulated quickly…Nowadays the *Expanded Substatutes* issued by the Ministry has amounted to a large number of volumes. Because [the new substatutes] have not been sorted out, it is unavoidable for us to feel perplexed and confused."[7]

Besides the separation of new substatutes from the Code, Qing readers faced another problem: the printing and publishing process of the imperial editions of the Code was painfully slow. The Qing imperial publishing house in Beijing—the Wuyingdian Book Editing Department (*Wuyingdian xiushuchu*, henceforth cited as "the Wuyingdian")—printed most of the imperial editions of the Code. Although the Wuyingdian printed an enormous number of books in the Qing period and its books were famous for their high quality, it was not an efficient publishing operation.[8] The proofreading, printing, and publishing of a new edition of the Code usually took several years. For example, about three years after the promulgation of the 1740 Code, the Wuyingdian copy finally arrived on the Jiangsu provincial judge's desk.[9] The delay became much longer after the High Qing period, when the Wuyingdian's efficiency declined significantly because of budget cuts and poor management. In the Jiaqing and Daoguang periods, it could take the Wuyingdian ten or even twenty years to

---

6 According to my estimation, of the 23 standard Code revisions after 1740, the Qing Court published only 5 editions of the Code. In the other 18 revisions, it only published the *Expanded Substatutes*. The data is collected from various editions of the *Great Qing Code* and its *Expanded Substatutes*. Several indexes of Chinese law books are also considered, including Zhongguo zhengfa daxue tushuguan 中国政法大学图书馆, ed., *Zhongguo falü tushu zongmu* 中国法律图书总目 [Comprehensive Catalog of China's Law Books] (Beijing: Zhongguo zhengfa daxue chubanshe, 1991).

7 Yao Run 姚润, ed., Hu Zhang 胡璋 revised, *Da Qing lüli xing'an tongzuan jicheng* 大清律例刑案统纂集成 [Comprehensive Complete Compilation of the Great Qing Code with Leading Cases] (Hangzhou: Sanshantang, 1859), "Wang Ding's Preface," 1b.

8 See Xiao Li 肖力, "Qingdai Wuyingdian keshu chutan 清代武英殿刻书初探 [Research on the Wuyingdian's Book Printing in the Qing Period]," *Tushu yu Qingbao* 02 (1983): 56.

9 See Qingshi bianzuan weiyuanhui 清史编纂委员会, Zhupi zouzhe shujuku 硃批奏折数据库 [Database of Imperial Memorials with Red Rescripts], Archival No. 04-01-01-0101-045, 1743.

print a book with multiple volumes.[10] The Wuyingdian was therefore unable to provide updated editions of the Code in a timely fashion.

The imperial editions of the Code and the *Expanded Substatutes* were usually printed in small numbers and issued only to high-ranking officials.[11] The print run of the Shunzhi Code was so small that no official editions survive today. Only a very small number of officials received the Code from the court in the early Qing period, including a number of high officials in the central government, Manchu generals, governors general, governors, and provincial judges.[12] In the mid-Qing period, the Wuyingdian probably produced more copies of the Code, but it was still difficult for lower-ranking officials and common people to see imperial editions. The editors of the 1790 Code indicated that "the yamens inside and outside [the capital] with judicial responsibilities" (*neiwai wenxing yamen*) could receive the *Expanded Substatutes*. They listed high provincial officials and prefects as the recipients.[13] However, county magistrates, who had the most important responsibility for local judicial administration, were not included on the list. They might have had to buy commercial editions of the Code from the book market, as other non-official readers of the Code did.

The imperial editions of the Code symbolized imperial judicial authority. The front page of imperial editions was printed in vermillion ink with a unique decoration that no other editions were allowed to use: the title of the Code was printed in a square frame surrounded by flying dragons. When receiving an imperial edition of the Code, an official had to treat it with the same utmost reverence as pertained to other imperial gifts from the court. For example, Li Xueyu, Jiangsu provincial judge, recorded the ritual he performed when receiving the 1740 imperial edition of the Code: "Upon hearing that the imperial edition of the Code had arrived, we set up an incense table, kowtowed towards the direction of the imperial palace, and respectfully received the Code. Then we asked the governor to submit a memorial to the emperor

10 Weng Lianxi 翁连溪, *Qing neifu keshu dang'an shiliao huibian* 清内府刻书档案史料汇编 [Collection of the Archives and Historical Materials of the Qing Court's Book Printing] (Yangzhou: Guangling shushe, 2007), 484.

11 In theory, individual readers could buy the imperial editions of the Code and the *Expanded Substatutes* from the Wuyingdian. However, based on the Wuyingdian's archives, few copies were sold out through this channel. See Weng Lianxi, *Qing Neifu keshu dang'an shiliao huibian*, 689–721.

12 *Qing shilu*, 4: 505 (*juan* 38).

13 Yao Guan 姚观 et al., *Da Qing lüli quanzuan* 大清律例全纂 [Complete Compilation of the Great Qing Code] (Hangzhou: Mingxintang, 1796), 9b.

expressing our gratitude for this imperial grace (*tian'en*)."[14] Then the Code would probably be enshrined in the government's library. As an official working in the Ministry of Justice complained, the Code issued by the Court was difficult to access: "Nowadays each yamen only has one copy of the Code, which is locked up tightly and hidden in the inner chamber (*bisuo shencang*). There is no way for people to see it."[15] In other words, the Code issued by the Court was the emperor's gift and the government's property—a book to revere, not to consume. In fact, the imperial editions of the Code that I have seen usually show few, if any, traces that anyone actually read them: there are few marks, notes, or worn pages. If people actually read these editions, they must have done so with extreme care.

Evidence suggests that the Qing Court did not provide enough usable copies of the Code to the bureaucracy and society. Local governments in the Qing period were also much less enthusiastic than Ming local governments in terms of publishing the Code and statutory commentaries.[16] Thus far, I have found only three official editions published by local governments.[17] Why, then, did the Qing state not actively engage in publishing the Code? Although Qing officials provided few explicit explanations, the available evidence appears to indicate that considerations of cost and efficiency were the reason. The Wuyingdian, a bureaucratically run agency of the Imperial Court, was an expensive and inefficient publishing institution. When the Wuyingdian finished printing an edition of the Code—a huge book that was updated constantly—there was a good chance that it was already outdated. The Qing government therefore opted for a more efficient and economical way to circulate updated laws—it published the *Expanded Substatutes*, which contained only new and revised substatutes. The Code issued by the Court served more to symbolize the imperial judicial authority than to convey updated legal information. However, no judicial official could sentence cases by using only the *Expanded Substatutes*, and the separation between the Code and updated substatutes caused problems. Commercial editions, as we shall discuss, filled this void and largely solved the problems.

---

14 Zhupi zouzhe database, Archival No. 04-01-01-0101-045.

15 *Qing shilü*, 3: 699 (*juan* 88).

16 For Ming local governments' involvements in publishing law books, see Yanhong Wu's chapter herein.

17 These three editions are: *Da Qing lüli* (1768), published by the Office of Jiangsu Provincial Judge; *Da Qing lüli* (1778), published by Jiangning prefectural school; and *Da Qing lüli huiji bianlan* (1872), edited and published by the Hubei Adjudicating Bureau (*yanju*).

Evolution of Commercial Editions of the Code

Commercially compiled and printed editions of the Code far outnumber the imperial editions. I have found about 120 different commercial editions in several major libraries around the world (see Chart 8.1), and the actual number of commercial editions printed in the Qing period was probably far beyond that. Generally speaking, commercial editions of the Code in the Qing period had two features. First, their printing format, structure, and content gradually departed from those of the imperial editions. From the mid-Qing period, commercial publishers established their own well-accepted standard of printing the Code. Second, the commercial editions incorporated more and more extra information that the imperial Code did not include, such as private commentaries, administrative regulations, cross-indexes, and leading cases (*cheng'an*).

CHART 8.1 *Editions of the Code printed in the Qing period*[18]

Reign (date)	Number of imperial editions	Number of commercial editions
Shunzhi (1644–61)	1	5
Kangxi (1662–1722)	0	11
Yongzheng (1723–35)	1	0
Qianlong (1736–95)	3	11
Jiaqing (1796–1820)	1	17
Daoguang (1821–50)	1	17
Xianfeng (1851–61)	0	4
Tongzhi (1862–74)	1	14
Guangxu (1875–1908)	0	38
Xuantong (1909–11)	0	1
Date unknown	0	2
Total	8	**120**

18 The data of editions is collected from the Qing Wuyingdian's archives and extant imperial and commercial editions that I collected from several major libraries around the world, including the National Library of China, the Library of Congress, the Library of the Institute of Oriental Culture in University of Tokyo, the Harvard-Yenching Library, the Library of Waseda University, the Hathitrust Digital Library. I also refer to several indexes of Chinese law books, such as *Zhongguo fazhi tushu zongmu*. Some scholars suggested

So far I have found five commercial editions of the Code printed in the Shunzhi period. These early Qing editions did not include information about the editors or publishers, annotations or commentaries, updated substatutes, administrative regulations, or leading cases. Moreover, they resembled each other in terms of their structure and layout, although their printing styles indicate that they were obviously printed by different publishing houses.[19] It seems that they were following a common format, probably that of the imperial edition of the Code published in 1647.

Compared with commercial editions from the Shunzhi period, those from the Kangxi period were more diverse and reflected a livelier publishing milieu. Although five of the Kangxi commercial editions still adhered to the format and content of the imperial edition, six departed by adding private commentaries and updated substatutes into the Code. For example, *Da Qing lü jianshi hechao* adopted *Lüli jianshi* (Annotations and Explanations on the Statutes and Substatutes), a famous late Ming commentary published in 1612. Each page of *Da Qing lü jianshi hechao* was divided into two horizontal registers (*lan*): the original statutes and substatutes were printed in larger characters in the lower registers; commentaries were printed in smaller characters in the upper registers, usually in the order of the statutes and substatutes on the same page.[20] This arrangement made it convenient for readers to locate the statutes and related commentaries. Shen Zhiqi's influential *Da Qing lü jizhu*, published in 1715, also followed this two-register-per-page arrangement.[21] Not all of the commercial editions published in the Kangxi period used this format, however. For example, *Da Qing lü jianshi* used the traditional single-register format, in which commentaries were printed in small characters after each group of

---

that the 1670 edition of the Code is probably an official edition published by the Ministry of Justice (Zheng Qin 郑秦, "Da Qing lüli kaoxi 大清律例考析 [Research and analysis on the Great Qing Code]," in *Zhongguo fazhishi kaozheng*, Series 1, Vol. 7, 45). I saw the Code in the Library of Congress and found no conclusive evidence that this Code is indeed an official edition.

19 Most of these editions contain 30 chapters (*juan*), which are bound into 10 volumes (*ce*). Each page has 9 columns, and each column contains 20 characters. See *Da Qing lü jijie fuli* (1646 preface), and *Da Qing lü jijie fuli*, (1647 preface). See also Su Yigong 苏亦工, "Shunzhi lü kao 顺治律考 [Research on the Shunzhi Code]," in *Zhongguo fazhishi kaozheng*, Series 1, 7: 144–49.

20 Qian Zhiqing 钱之青 and Lu Fenglai 陆凤来, eds., *Da Qing lü jianshi hechao* 大清律笺释合抄 [A Combined Copy of the Great Qing Code with Annotations and Explanations] (Zundaotang, 1705).

21 See Shen Zhiqi 沈之奇, *Da Qing lü jizhu* 大清律辑注 [The Great Qing Code with Collected Commentaries] (1715).

statutes and substatutes.[22] *Da Qing lüli zhuzhu guanghui quanshu* combined upper-register commentaries and interlinear commentaries in one book.[23]

Commentaries appear to have been a selling point of these diverse Kangxi commercial editions. Commercial publishers added eye-catching words like *jianshi hechao* (combined compilation with annotations and explanations) and *zhuzhu guanghui* (extensive collection of vermillion commentaries) to the title of the Code. They also printed short phrases prominently on the front colophon pages, indicating that the books included commentaries. For example, the colophon page of *Da Qing lü zhuzhu guanghui quanshu* states in red ink to the left of the book's title: "Various annotations and explanations are completely included and printed in vermillion ink."[24] Similarly, the colophon page of *Da Qing lü jianshi* shows that this work was to update and expand Wang Kentang's *Lüli jianshi*, and the publisher apparently tried to capitalize on the appeal of Wang's commentary besides the statutes and substatutes.[25]

The Shunzhi and Kangxi governments did not regulate commercial publications of the Code. However, in the Yongzheng and early Qianlong periods, when the Qing state was at the zenith of its power and wealth, the Court attempted to regulate and control commercial publications of law books. In 1725, the Yongzheng Emperor banned commercial printing and sale of the administrative regulations of the Six Ministries (*Liubu zeli*).[26] In 1742, the Qianlong Emperor launched an empire-wide campaign to eliminate the printing and sale of "secret handbooks for litigation masters" (*songshi miben*) and other books that would "incite litigation" (*gousong*).[27] Although it was not the main target of this campaign, commercial publication of the Code suffered too. Tighter regulation and censorship, as well as the relative abundance of official editions, meant that fewer commercial editions of the Code were printed in the mid-Qing period. Thus far, I have found no commercial edition of the Code published in the Yongzheng reign, and only five commercial editions in the Qianlong period

22 Li Nan 李枏 and Cai Fangbing 蔡方炳, eds., *Da Qing lü jianshi* 大清律笺释 [The Great Qing Code with Annotations and Explanations] (1689).

23 Wanguzhai zhuren 万古斋主人, *Da Qing lüli zhuzhu guanghui quanshu* 大清律例朱注广汇全书 [Complete Book of the Great Qing Code with Extensive Collection of Vermillion Commentaries] (Tingsonglou, 1706).

24 *Da Qing lü zhuzhu guanghui quanshu*, the colophon page.

25 *Da Qing lü jianshi* (1689), the colophon page.

26 *Qing shilü*, 7: 513–14 (*juan* 34).

27 *Da Qing lü xuzuan tiaoli* 大清律续纂条例 [Expended Substatutes of the Great Qing Code] (Beijing: Wuyingdian, 1743), *juan* 1: 16a. See the relevant discussion in Li Chen's chapter in this volume, and Melissa Macaulay, *Social Power and Legal Culture: Litigation Masters in Late Imperial China* (Stanford: Stanford University Press, 1998).

before the revival of commercial editions of the Code in 1790s.[28] Only the best editions could survive this shrinking market, which contributed to the standardization of the structure and printing format of commercial editions. The two-register-per-page format (i.e., commentaries in the upper register and the statutes and substatutes in the lower register) began to dominate the mid-Qing market, as evidenced in all of the commercial editions from this period.

After the late Qianlong period, the policy on commercial legal publications was eased. This coincided with the decline of official publishing houses, and commercial editing, printing, and publishing of the Code began to rebound. The late Qianlong and early Jiaqing period (1790s–1810s) was an important transition period for commercial publishing of the Code. There were at least five major commercial editions that laid the foundation for all later editions published in this period, including Shen Shucheng's *Da Qing lüli huizuan* (1789), and Wang Youhuai's *Da Qing lüli huizuan* (1793), *Da Qing lüli quanzuan* (1796), *Da Qing lüli huizuan jicheng* (1799), and *Da Qing lüli tongzuan* (1805). All five editions were compiled by different groups of editors and printed in Hangzhou.

In spite of obvious competition among them, these commercial editions had many more similarities than differences. One the one hand, unlike earlier commercial editions, which were usually compiled by one or two scholars, all of the influential commercial editions of the Code from this period were collectively compiled and proofread. On the other hand, all five commercial editions have three registers per page for the main body of the contents, an updated version of the earlier popular two-register format. A cross-index was usually printed in the upper register.[29] Shen Shucheng's *Da Qing lüli huizuan* is the earliest edition that I have seen with a cross-index. Evidently readers appreciated this feature. Almost all of the commercial editions of the Code published after 1789 adopted a similar cross-index in their upper registers. In the middle register, editors compiled not only private and collective commentaries but also a large number of administrative regulations, leading cases, and other valid rules and regulations. The authorized Code text was kept in the bottom register with some interlinear private commentaries.

In 1805, two private legal advisors, Zhou Menglin and Hu Zhaokai, published a revised edition of the Code, named *Da Qing lüli tongzuan* (General

28 These five editions are *Da Qing lü jizhu*, originally compiled by Shen Zhiqi in 1715, but revised and republished by Hong Hongxu in 1745 and 1755; Wan Weihan's *Da Qing lüli jizhu*, published in 1769 and revised by Hu Qian and Wang Youhuai in 1784 and 1786.

29 The function of the cross index is to help readers locate similar statutes and substatutes. See Shen Shucheng 沈书成 et al., *Da Qing lüli huizuan* 大清律例汇纂 [Amalgamated Compilation of the Great Qing Code] (1792), "Fanli," 2b.

Compilation of the *Great Qing Code*). Zhou and Hu followed the popular three-register format of the period, but they carefully revised the middle register. They deleted the miscellaneous commentaries typically found in other popular editions and included only Shen Zhiqi's commentaries in *Da Qing lü jizhu*, which they praised as the most accurate interpretations.[30] They also updated and enlarged leading cases, administrative regulations, and other legal information in the middle registers. This edition seems to have been popular among readers, and in 1811 Hu and Zhou updated the book and republished it under a new name—*Da Qing lüli tongzuan jicheng* (Comprehensive Complete Compilation of the *Great Qing Code*, henceforth cited as "TZJC"). Hu and Zhou's TZJC won the support of several prominent judicial officials. For example, Qin Ying (1743–1821), Guangdong provincial judge, wrote a preface to the 1805 edition and called it "a guide for judicial administration" (*yanyu zhi zhinan*).[31] Chen Ruolin (1759–1832), a Guangdong provincial judge who later became Minister of Justice, also wrote a preface to the 1811 edition, praising it for making great contributions to justice and judicial administration.[32]

The rise of TZJC heralded the end of the competitive era of the Qianlong-Jiangqing transition, when several major commercial editions compiled by different groups of private advisors competed with one another. Soon after its publication, TZJC dominated the Code market. A number of prominent legal experts continued to update and enlarge it in the Jiaqing and Daoguang period, such as Yao Run, the private legal advisor of the Zhejiang provincial judge, and Hu Zhang, the private legal advisor of the Hangzhou prefect. Many high-ranking judicial officials continued to enthusiastically support the revisions and publications of TZJC. Each time it underwent a major revision, editors usually invited a leading judicial official to write a new preface for the book. For example, Yao Run, editor of the 1823, 1826, 1829, 1833, 1836, and 1838 editions, invited Yunnan Provincial Judge Wu Tingchen (1773–1844); Zhejiang Provincial Judge Qi Gong (1777–1844), who later became Minister of Justice; and Wang Ding (1768–1842), Assistant Grand Secretary (*Xieban daxueshi*), who was in charge of the Ministry of Justice at the time, to write for his revised editions of TZJC. In their preface, these officials usually confirmed and celebrated the authority, accuracy, and reliability of TZJC. For example, in his 1836 preface,

---

30 Hu Zhaokai 胡肇楷 et al., *Da Qing lüli chongding tongzuan jicheng* 大清律例重订统纂集成 [Revised Comprehensive Complete Compilation of the Great Qing Code] (1815), "Preface," 43a–b.

31 Ibid., 35a–b.

32 Ibid., 38a–39a.

Wang Ding commended the book's quality and encouraged "all readers of the Code in the realm" (*tianxia dulüzhe*) to read it:

> This book collects all of [the laws] with no omissions, and sorts them into categories, in order to make it easy for people to read and understand. It is precisely "the secret book for legal experts" (*fajia zhi miji*) ... When I received this book and read it, I found that everything in it is carefully selected and clearly categorized, and all of the details are listed. It is indeed "an excellent edition of the Code" (*lüli shanben*), which will contribute to our Sacred Dynasty's benevolent judicial administration. That is why I am willing to write this preface and introduce the book to all readers of the Code in the realm.[33]

Supported by these leading officials in the Qing judicial system, *TZJC*'s authority was unchallenged.

Commercial publishing of the Code flourished in the late Qing period. From the Jiaqing reign to the end of the Qing dynasty, at least ninety-one commercial editions of the Code were published (see Chart 8.1), far more than the imperial editions (only three) published in the same period. Almost all of these commercial editions closely followed *TZJC*'s content and format. Even provincial publishing bureaus (*guanshuju*) established by officials after the Taiping Rebellion discarded the design of the imperial editions of the Code and adopted *TZJC*'s content and format.[34] After 1805, therefore, the *TZJC* editions gradually replaced the imperial editions and other commercial editions of the Code, and dominated the printed world of the *Great Qing Code*.

Compared with the imperial editions, commercial editions of the Code were usually updated more frequently and contained much more legal information. Commercial editions always emphasized that they included the newest substatutes, and many even promised that they would follow the legislative progress and be updated accordingly. For example, the editors of *Da Qing lüli quanzuan* said that they kept updating the new substatutes in their book until the last day of the compilation, and they promised: "In the future if there are new substatutes in circulation, we will print them [into this book] as soon as we see them (*suijian suikan*); we expect that our book has no inconsistencies with any of the current laws."[35] Commercial publishers apparently believed

33 Ibid., 49a–b.

34 See Hubei yanju 湖北谳局, ed., *Da Qing lüli huiji bianlan* 大清律例汇集便览 [Comprehensive Compilation of Brief Guide to the Great Qing Code] (1872).

35 *Da Qing lüli quanzuan*, "Fanli," 4b.

that only editions containing new substatutes and other up-to-date legal information would attract readers. Most mid and late Qing commercial editions claimed on their front colophon page that their book was newly carved (*xinjuan*) according to the latest substatutes and leading cases issued by the Ministry of Justice. Many commercial editors indicated that the *Expanded Substatutes*, the *Peking Gazette* (*dibao*), and legal documents circulated inside the bureaucracy, such as memoranda (*shuotie*) and general circulars (*tongxing*), were their main source of updated legal information. Commercial editions of the Code usually included new substatutes before the imperial editions did,[36] and therefore largely solved the problem caused by the separation between new substatutes and the Code that bothered many Qing readers.

In commercial editions of the Code, the body of additional legal material missing in the imperial editions was expanded during the Qing period. As we have seen, in the Shunzhi period, all commercial editions loyally reprinted the texts of the imperial edition. In the Kangxi period, half of the commercial editions that I have found added private commentaries. In the Qianlong period and afterwards, most commercial editions included not only commentaries but also a cross-index, leading cases, and administrative regulations. Such additional material in late Qing editions accounted for a much larger portion than the original contents of the imperial editions. For example, in the Tongzhi Code (1870), the Article on Fornication (*fanjian*) had only one statute and fourteen substatutes. In a commercial edition published in 1873, the editors attached to the article at least eight paragraphs of commentaries, two administrative regulations, twenty-eight leading cases, and a cross-index.[37] By adding such additional legal information, commercial editors intended to help readers find the statute or substatute that best fitted the circumstances of a case. Commentaries and leading cases in commercial editions seldom directly contradicted original laws in the imperial editions of the Code; rather, in most cases, they defined various subtle circumstances of crimes and suggested suitable punishments that statutes and substatutes did not specify.

36 E.g., see Wan Weihan 万维翰 and Teng Jingshan 滕京山, eds., Hu Qian 胡钤 and Wang Youhuai 王又槐 revised, *Da Qing lüli jizhu* 大清律例集注 [The Great Qing Code with Collective Annotations] (Suzhou: Yunhuitang, 1784), "Fanli," 1a.

37 See Yao Run and Hu Zhang, eds., *Da Qing lüli huitong xinzuan* 大清律例会通新纂 [New Comprehensive Compilation of the Great Qing Code] (Beijing: Diqisuo guanfang, 1873), reprinted in *Jindai zhongguo shiliao congkan* 中国近代史料丛刊 [A Collection of Historical Sources of Modern China] (Taibei: Wenhai chubanshe, 1964), Series 3, 211: 3197–3224 (*juan* 31).

The Qing judicial system required judges to decide a case according to a statute or substatute that precisely fit the circumstances of the crime. The designers of the Code also tried to define each crime narrowly and provide exact punishments for each possible variation.[38] In judicial practice, however, the circumstances of real cases were infinite in variety and usually not precisely covered by any statute or substatute; it was thus a constant challenge for Qing judges to find the closest statute or substatute.[39] The commercial editions thus helped judges make their choice by providing interpretations and leading cases that more specifically defined the circumstances of crimes. Although the Qing regulations strictly banned local judges from citing private commentaries or leading cases in determining a sentence, commentaries and leading cases did influence their choice in many ways.[40] As a matter of fact, some scholars have found that leading cases played an increasingly important role in judicial practice as a "source of law" (*fayuan*) in the Qing period.[41] The popularity of commercial editions, which contained so many leading cases, might have contributed to this change in Qing judicial administration.

Editing and Marketing Commercial Editions of the Code

Most editors of the commercial editions under study were from the Jiangnan area, mainly Hangzhou and Shaoxing prefectures. This is not surprising because this area was famous for producing a large number of private legal advisors in the Qing period.[42] Private legal advisors were true legal experts. They not

38 See Derk Bodde and Clarence Morris, *Law in Imperial China: Exemplified by 190 Ch'ing Dynasty Cases* (Cambridge: Harvard University Press, 1967), 496.

39 Ibid., 175.

40 Wang Zhiqiang 王志强, "Qingdai cheng'an de xiaoli heqi yunyong zhong de lunzheng fangshi 清代成案的效力和其运用中的论证方式 [The Effect of Qing's Leading Cases and Their Logic in Practice]," *Faxue yanjiu* 3 (2003): 147. For detailed discussions on the functions of leading cases and commentaries in the Qing laws, see also Fu-mei Chang Chen, "Private Code Commentaries in the Development of Ch'ing Law, 1644–1911" (Ph.D. diss., Harvard University, 1970).

41 Wang Zhiqiang, "Qingdai cheng'an de xiaoli heqi yunyong zhong de lunzheng fangshi," 147; Su Yigong 苏亦工, *Ming Qing lüdian yu tiaoli* 明清律典与条例 [The Codes and Substatutes in the Ming and Qing] (Beijing: Zhongguo zhengfa daxue chubanshe, 1999), 40.

42 See James Cole, *Shaohsing: Competition and Cooperation in Nineteenth-Century China* (Tucson: University of Arizona Press, 1986); Li Chen, "Legal Specialists and Judicial Administration in Late Imperial China, 1651–1911," *Late Imperial China* 33, no. 1 (June 2012): 1–54.

only usually went through years of legal training but also accumulated experience in dealing with real cases.[43] Working in the Qing government although not officials themselves, they had access to all the up-to-date legal information distributed by the central government through administrative channels.

There were two distinct patterns in terms of the compilation and editing of commercial editions of the Code. One was individual endeavor. One or two editors did all compiling and editorial work, which usually took several years. Many early Qing commercial editions were individually compiled. The other pattern was collective endeavor, involving a larger group of editors working together. Most of the popular editions in the late Qianlong and early Jiaqing periods were compiled through this collective method. Groups of editors compiled and proofread more efficiently and cooperatively, and they usually finished their project within a year. For instance, Hu Zhaokai, Zhou Menglin, and eleven other editors took only seven months to finish *Da Qing lüli tongzuan*.[44] Editorial teams systematically collected useful information from various books, classified it according to the chapters and categories in the Code, and proofread it together. For example, a preface writer described how *Da Qing lüli quanzuan* was compiled:

> The editors broadly collected all [the books and documents] they could find, and compiled statutory annotations and commentaries, case precedents, administrative sanctions of the Ministry, and memorials. They sorted them into categories, selected [the useful ones], and made notes and tags on them. Then they examined and questioned each other's work as they proofread over and over again.[45]

Because of such joint efforts, collectively compiled editions usually had more comprehensive and updated information as well as fewer mistakes than the earlier individual works. Collective editing contributed to the development of commercial editions in the 1790s–1810s, when the textual contents of such editions expanded greatly—a lot of supplemental legal information, such as cross-indexes, leading cases, and administrative regulations, was incorporated. Accuracy, comprehensiveness, and up-to-date information were important reasons for the popularity of commercial editions during this period. In many

43 See Wejen Chang, "Legal Education in Ch'ing China," in Benjamin Elman and Alexander Woodside, eds., *Education and Society in Late Imperial China, 1600–1900* (Berkeley: University of California Press, 1994), 292–339.

44 Hu Zhaokai et al., *Da Qing lüli chongding tongzuan jicheng* (1813), "Preface," 43b.

45 *Da Qing lüli quanzuan*, "Preface," 24b–25a.

ways, collectively compiled commercial editions from the 1790s–1810s established the foundation and standard for all subsequent commercial editions.

Compared with the imperial editions, which were mainly supplied to various government offices, commercial editions of the Code had a broader readership. Many editors and preface writers emphasized the importance of the Code and encouraged people to purchase and own it. They claimed that not only should each official and private legal advisor who had to deal with legal cases have one such book, but scholars and students who aspired to become officials in the future should also own and read the Code. For example, a preface writer of *Da Qing lüli huizuan* pointed out:

> The *Great Qing Code* is issued by the emperors to all of the people of the realm. Not only should every official working in various yamens with judicial responsibilities have it, but also all of the students in schools and the gentry interested in the way of ruling should have it in order to prepare for being officials and governing people in the future.[46]

In another commercial edition, a preface writer also said that officials should not put aside the Code even for one day, and that every scholar and gentleman (*shijunzi*) should have a copy at hand in order to cultivate his morality (*xiushen*) and establish himself in life (*liming*).[47] Besides officials and scholars, private legal advisors were apparently major target readers. Referred to as "friends who share the same interests," "people who learn the laws" (*xi fajiayan zhe*), and "guests who handle the legal cases" (*bing'an zhike*), private legal advisors were frequently mentioned as potential readers in prefaces to these commercial editions.[48]

Although designed primarily for officials, scholars, and private legal advisors, commercial editions were available to anyone who could afford it and were sold freely in major book markets in the empire. Jiangsu was an important printing center and book market for the Code in the early Qing period. After the late Qianlong period, Hangzhou became the largest book market for the Code. Among the 120 commercial editions of the Code I have collected, 71 had information on the place where they were published or sold. Thirty-three of

46 *Da Qing lüli huizuan* (1792), "Qian Qi's Preface," 1b.

47 *Da Qing lü jizhu* (1746), "Jiang Chenxi's Preface," 1a.

48 See *Da Qing lüli jizhu* (1784), "Wan Fengjiang's Preface," 2b; *Da Qing lüli huizuan* (1792), "Qian Qi's Preface," 4a–b; Tao Jun 陶骏 and Tao Nianlin 陶念霖, eds., *Da Qing lüli zengxiu tongzuan jicheng* 大清律例增修统纂集成 [Expanded Comprehensive Complete Compilation of the Great Qing Code] (Hangzhou: Juwentang, 1907), 38b.

these 71 commercial editions were compiled and published in Hangzhou (see Chart 8.2), including almost all the important and influential commercial editions after the mid-Qianlong period, such as Shen Shucheng's *Da Qing lüli huizuan*, Yao Guan's *Da Qing lüli quanzuan*, Wang Youhai's *Da Qing lüli quanzuan jicheng*, and various editions of *TZJC*. Several bookstores and publishing houses in Hangzhou were active in printing and selling commercial editions of the Code, including the Mingxintang, Youyizhai, Wubentang, Sanshantang, Tongwentang, Qinglaitang, and Juwentang. Editions produced in Hangzhou were famous for their high quality in compilation and printing, and had a reputation as the best editions of the Code in the mid and late Qing. A Shanghai publisher of an 1891 commercial edition observed: "[These Hangzhou editions of the Code] have become a fashion within the Four Seas (*fengxing hainei*), and people view them ... as excellent editions (*shanben*)."[49]

Another center for commercial legal publishing was Beijing. Of the seventy editions of the Code under consideration here, sixteen were printed and sold in Beijing (see Chart 8.2). Most of these bookstores, like the Rongjintang, Shanchengtang, and Hongdaotang, were on the famous Liulichang Street, the largest book market in North China. Shanghai was also a printing center of the Code in the late Qing period. When western lithographic printing technology was introduced to China in the late nineteenth century, Shanghai quickly emerged as a major publishing center.[50] Publishing houses there printed at least nine editions (see Chart 8.2). Several famous Shanghai publishing houses, such as the Wenyuan shanfang and the Saoye shanfang, engaged in printing and selling the Code.

The market for commercial editions of the Code was competitive, especially in the late Qing period, when many bookstores in cities like Hangzhou and Beijing were selling similar editions at similar prices. Fierce competition was reflected in the editions' front colophon pages, in which publishers usually announced that their edition was newly updated, more comprehensive, and more precise than other editions. They also criticized other publishing houses for "pirating" their books,[51] and dismissed those "pirated editions" as being low in quality and full of mistakes. For example, on the front colophon page of the

49 *Da Qing lüli zengxiu tongzuan jicheng* (Shanghai: Zhenyi shuju, 1891), 1a.

50 See Christopher A. Reed, *Gutenberg in Shanghai: Chinese Print Capitalism, 1876–1937* (Vancouver: University of British Columbia Press, 2004).

51 The Qing laws did not specifically protect copyright. Unauthorized reprinting was not illegal, and publishers felt no guilt when they pirated others' publications. See William P. Alford, *To Steal a Book Is an Elegant Offense: Intellectual Property Law in Chinese Civilization* (Stanford: Stanford University Press, 1995), 9–29.

CHART 8.2 *Place of publication of commercial editions of the* Great Qing Code (*1644–1911*)

Place	Number of editions
Hangzhou	33
Beijing	16
Shanghai	9
Suzhou	7
Ningbo	1
Quzhou	1
Nanjing	2
Changzhou	1
Xiugu	1
Total	71

Lüsutang's *Da Qing lüli xinxiu tongzuan jicheng*, the publisher printed the following statement in red ink:

> Recently, there are unauthorized reprinted editions that are full of errors. Some bandits (*feitu*) even forged the stamp of our publishing house and pirated [our book] to pursue profit. [I] hope that those gentlemen who know well about the book can distinguish [our book from these fake ones].[52]

Many other publishers made similar statements in their books. Expressions such as "The woodblocks are stored in our [publishing] house" (*benya cangban*) and "Unauthorized reprinting will definitely be investigated" (*fanke bijiu*) frequently appeared at the beginning of commercial editions. Competition among publishing houses indicated that commercial editions of the Code were in great demand and were a profitable business.

Such editions were not cheap, but they were affordable for their target readers. In the early Qing period, the price was relatively low. *Da Qing lüli zhuzhu*

52 Yao Run et al., *Da Qing lüli tongzuan jicheng* 大清律例统纂集成 [Comprehensive Complete Compilation of the Great Qing Code] (Anchang: Lüsutang, 1826), the front colophon page.

guanghui quanshu (1706), a beautiful ten-volume book printed in black and red ink, cost only 2.2 taels.[53] The prices of these publications increased over time due to inflation as well as expansion of their contents, but they were still affordable. *Da Qing lüli chongding tongzuan jicheng*, printed in 1823 by the Wubentang bookstore in Hangzhou, for sold for 3.2 taels at the time.[54] In the late Qing period, the price of such commercial editions increased to around 6 taels. *Da Qing lüli xing'an huizuan jicheng* (1859) was sold by the Sanshantang bookstore in Hangzhou for 6.4 taels.[55] *Da Qing lüli zengxiu tongzuan jicheng*, a very popular edition in the late Qing period printed by the Juwentang bookstore in Hangzhou in 1878, 1890, 1891, 1892, 1896, 1898, and 1907, was also priced at 6.4 taels.[56] The Qinglaitang bookstore's edition of *Da Qing lüli zengxiu tongzuan jicheng*, published in 1894 in Hangzhou, was a little more expensive at 7 taels.[57] Editions printed and sold in Beijing cost about 6 taels.[58] Although it might have been difficult for ordinary people to afford them, these books cost only a small fraction of the annual incomes of the main target readers—officials and private advisors, who usually earned from several hundred to several thousand taels per year.[59]

Conclusion

Commercial publishing has flourished since the boom in the late Ming period. Although a large number of books in various genres were commercially published during that period, the rise of commercial editions of the dynastic law code can be viewed more as a Qing phenomenon than as a Ming one. Yanhong Wu's research on over thirty statutory commentaries sheds new light on the publishing history of the Ming Code. Many of these commentaries can be viewed as predecessors of commercial editions of the Qing Code. According to Wu's study, most authors, editors, and compilers were Ming officials, and the majority of them worked for the Ministry of Justice and other central-level

53 *Da Qing lüli zhuzhu guanghui quanshu* (1706), the front colophon page.

54 *Da Qing lüli chongding tongzuan jicheng* (1823), the front colophon page.

55 *Da Qing lüli xing'an tongzuan jicheng* (1859), the front colophon page.

56 *Da Qing lüli zengxiu tongzuan jicheng* (1878, 1891, 1898 and 1907), the front colophon page.

57 *Da Qing lüli zengxiu tongzuan jicheng* (Hangzhou: Yixizhai, 1894), the front colophon page.

58 *Da Qing lüli huiji bianlan* (1892), the front colophon page.

59 For the discussion on legal advisors' salaries, see Chen, "Legal Specialists and Judicial Administration in Late Imperial China": 18–21.

judicial offices, which provided them with the authority and privilege to write and compile the books. Wu has also pointed out that publishers of these books were usually local governments.[60] In her opinion, therefore, judicial officials in the Ming government by and large monopolized the production of commentaries and texts of the Ming Code.

This situation changed dramatically in the Qing period. Having explored both official and commercial editions of the Qing Code, I find that compared with the Ming period, non-official editors and commercial publishers played a far more important role than official publishers in producing commentaries and reproducing the text of the Qing Code. Editors, compilers, and proofreaders in the Qing period were overwhelmingly private legal advisors. They worked for Qing officials but were not a formal part of the Qing bureaucracy. They could access the latest legal information circulating through the bureaucracy because of their work, and they took advantage of their access to that information when compiling, editing, and updating the Code. As Li Chen points out, legal advisors had considerable power and influence in the judicial administration and the production of legal knowledge in the Qing.[61] Although officials still participated in publishing commercial editions of the Qing Code, usually by writing prefaces for the books, they no longer directly engaged in editing, compiling, and publishing tasks. Compared with their Ming predecessors, their importance had diminished in the publication of the Code. Moreover, during the Qing period, most editions of the Code were published by commercial publishing houses and sold by bookstores in Hangzhou, Beijing, Suzhou, and other urban centers, with the participation of only a few provincial or local governments. Therefore, from the Ming to the late Qing period, we see a trend of increasing commercialization and commodification of printing and publishing of the Code. Market forces gradually took the place of the government in disseminating up-to-date legal knowledge.

The proper functioning of the Qing judicial administration depended upon timely dissemination and circulation of up-to-date legal information and knowledge. The Qing official publishing houses did not provide enough updated editions of the Code to support the judicial system. Commercial publications, to a large extent, provided this information to people working in the Qing legal system, especially low-level officials of the bureaucracy and private legal advisors. Qing officials sponsored the compilation and publication of commercial editions of the Code by writing prefaces that elevated the

60 See Yanhong Wu's chapter in this volume.

61 See Chen, "Legal Specialists and Judicial Administration in Late Imperial China," and his chapter herein.

legitimacy and authority of these books among readers. It is fair to say that the Qing judicial system even had a symbiotic relationship with the commercial publishing industry, depending on each other for proper functioning and survival. However, commercial editors and publishers increasingly challenged the central government's authority in defining how the Code should be edited and printed. Commercial editions gradually departed from imperial editions in terms of their contents and printing styles. Although the original texts of the imperial editions were kept in the bottom register of each page, more and more extra materials were added in commercial editions. From the early Jiaqing period, *TZJC* editions began to dominate the market, and their editing and printing principles were widely accepted and adopted by various commercial and even official publishers. Finally, private legal advisors and commercial publishers, under the sponsorship of judicial officials, redefined the standard of Code printing and publishing. Together, they transformed the form and content of the most authoritative body of legal knowledge in the Qing period.

Glossary

benya cangban	本衙藏板	*Liubu zeli*	《六部则例》
bing'an zhike	秉案之客	Liulichang	琉璃厂
bisuo shencang	闭锁深藏	*Lüli jianshi*	《律例笺释》
ce	册	*lüli quanshu*	《律例全书》
Changzhou	常州	*lüli shanben*	律例善本
Chen Ruolin	陈若霖	Lüsutang	履素堂
cheng'an	成案	Mingxintang	铭心堂
fajia zhi miji	法家之秘笈	*muyou*	幕友
fanjian	犯奸	*neiwai wenxing yamen*	内外问刑衙门
fanke bijiu	翻刻必究	Qin Ying	秦瀛
feitu	匪徒	*qinding*	钦定
fengxing hainei	风行海内	Qinglaitang	清来堂
gousong	构讼	Quzhou	衢州
guanshuju	官书局	Rongjintang	荣锦堂
Hongdaotang	宏道堂	Sanshantang	三善堂
Jianshi hechao	《笺释合抄》	Saoye shanfang	扫叶山房
juan	卷	*shanben*	善本
Juwentang	聚文堂	Shanchengtang	善成堂
lan	栏	*shijunzi*	士君子
li	例	*shuotie*	说帖
Li Xueyu	李学裕	*songshi miben*	讼师秘本
liming	立命	*suijian suikan*	随见随刊

tian'en	天恩	Xieban daxueshi	协办大学士
tianxia dulüzhe	天下读律者	*Xingbu xianxing zeli*	刑部现行则例
Tongwentang	同文堂	*xinjuan*	新镌
tongxing	通行	*xinli jianjia jiubian nandu*	新例渐加旧编难读
Wang Ding	王鼎	*xiushen*	修身
Wenyuan shanfang	文渊山房	*yanju*	谳局
Wu Yuan'an	吴元安	*yanyu zhi zhinan*	谳狱之指南
Wubentang	务本堂	Youyizhai	友益斋
Wuyingdian xiushuchu	武英殿修书处	*zhuzhu guanghui*	朱注广汇
xi fajiayan zhe	习法家言者		

Bibliography

Alford, William P. *To Steal a Book Is an Elegant Offense: Intellectual Property Law in Chinese Civilization*. Stanford: Stanford University Press, 1995.

Bodde, Derk, and Clarence Morris, *Law in Imperial China: Exemplified by 190 Ch'ing Dynasty Cases*. Cambridge: Harvard University Press, 1967.

Chang, Wejen. "Legal Education in Ch'ing China." In *Education and Society in Late Imperial China*, 1600–1900, edited by Benjamin Elman and Alexander Woodside, 292–321. Berkeley: University of California Press, 1994.

Chen, Fu-mei Chang. "Private Code Commentaries in the Development of Ch'ing Law, 1644–1911." Ph. D. dissertation, Harvard University, 1970.

Chen, Li. "Legal Specialists and Judicial Administration in Late Imperial China, 1651–1911." *Late Imperial China* 33, no. 1 (June 2012): 1–54.

Cole, James H. *Shaohsing: Competition and Cooperation in Nineteenth-Century China*. Tucson: University of Arizona Press, 1986.

Da Qing lü jijie fuli 大清律集解附例 [Statutes of the Great Qing with Collected Commentaries and Appended Substatutes]. 1647, 1670, 1725.

Da Qing lü xuzuan tiaoli 大清律續纂條例 [Expended Substatutes of the Great Qing Code]. Beijing: Wuyingdian, 1743.

Da Qing lüli 大清律例 [Statutes and Substatutes of the Great Qing, or the Great Qing Code]. Beijing: Wuyingdian, 1740, 1768, 1790, 1825, 1870.

Da Qing lüli huiji bianlan 大清律例汇辑便览 [Comprehensive Compilation of Brief Guide for the Great Qing Code]. Edited by Hubei yanju 湖北谳局, 1872; reprinted by unidentified publishing house in 1892.

Hu Zhaokai 胡肇楷 et al., eds. *Da Qing lüli chongding tongzuan jicheng* 大清律例重订统纂集成 [Revised Comprehensive Complete Compilation of the

Great Qing Code]. 1813 and 1815. Revised by Yao Guan 姚观, Hangzhou: Wubentang, 1823.

Li Nan 李柟, and Cai Fangbing 蔡方炳, eds. *Da Qing lü jianshi* 大清律笺释 [The Great Qing Code with Annotations and Explanations]. 1689.

Qian Zhiqing 钱之青, and Lu Fenglai 陆凤来, eds. *Da Qing lü jianshi hechao* 大清律笺释合钞 [A Combined Copy of the Great Qing Code with Annotations and Explanations]. Zundaotang, 1705.

Qing shilu 清实录 [Veritable Records of the Qing Dynasty]. Beijing: Zhonghua shuju, 1985.

Qinding Da Qing huidian shili 钦定大清会典事例 [Collected Statues of the Great Qing with Precedents and Substatutes]. Qing huidian guan, 1899.

Reed, Christopher A. *Gutenberg in Shanghai: Chinese Print Capitalism, 1876–1937*. Vancouver: University of British Columbia Press, 2004.

Shen Shucheng 沈书成 et al., eds. *Da Qing lüli huizuan* 大清律例汇纂 [Amalgamated Compilation of the Great Qing Code]. 1792. Revised by Wang Youhuai 王又槐, 1793.

Shen Zhiqi 沈之奇. *Da Qing lü jizhu* 大清律辑注 [The Great Qing Code with Collected Commentaries]. 1715. Revised by Hong Hongxu 洪弘绪, 1746.

Su Yigong 苏亦工. *Ming Qing lüdian yu tiaoli* 明清律典与条例 [The Codes and Substatutes in the Ming and Qing]. Beijing: Zhongguo zhengfa daxue chubanshe, 1999.

Tao Jun 陶骏, and Tao Nianlin 陶念霖, eds. and rev. *Da Qing lüli zengxiu tongzuan jicheng* 大清律例增修统纂集成 [Expanded Comprehensive Complete Compilation of the Great Qing Code]. Hangzhou: Juwentang, printed in 1878, 1891, 1898, and 1907; Shanghai: Zhenyi shuju, 1891; Hangzhou: Yixizhai, 1894.

Wanguzhai zhuren 万古斋主人, ed. *Da Qing lüli zhuzhu guanghu quanshu* 大清律例朱注广汇全书 [Complete Book of the Great Qing Code with Extensive Collection of Vermillion Commentaries]. Tingsonglou, 1706.

Wang Zhiqiang 王志强. "Qingdai cheng'an de xiaoli heqi yunyong zhong de lunzheng fangshi 清代成案的效力和其运用中的论证方式 [The Effect of Qing's Leading Cases and Their Logic in Practice]." *Faxue yanjiu* 法学研究 [Legal Studies] 3 (2003): 146–60.

Wan Weihan 万维翰, and Teng Jingshan 滕京山, eds. *Da Qing lüli jizhu* 大清律例集注 [The Great Qing Code with Collective Annotations]. Suzhou: Yunhuitang, 1769. Revised by Hu Qian 胡钤, and Wang Youhuai 王又槐. Suzhou: Yunhuitang, 1784.

Weng Lianxi 翁连溪, ed. *Qing neifu keshu dang'an shiliao huibian* 清内府刻书档案史料汇编 [Collection of the Archives and Historical Materials of the Qing Court's Book Printing]. Yangzhou: Guangling shushe, 2007.

Xiao Li 肖力. "Qingdai Wuyingdian keshu chutan 清代武英殿刻书初探 [Research on the Wuyingdian's Book Printing in the Qing Period]." *Tushu yu qingbao* 图书与情报 [Library and Information] 2 (1983): 56–60.

Yang Yifan 杨一凡, ed. *Zhongguo fazhishi kaozheng (jiabian)* 中国法制史考证(甲编) [Research on the Chinese Legal History (Series 1)]. Beijing: Zhongguo shehui kexue chubanshe, 2003.

Yao Guan 姚观, and Hu Zhang 胡璋, eds. *Da Qing lüli huitong xinzuan* 大清律例会通新纂 [New Comprehensive Compilation of the Great Qing Code]. Beijing: Diqisuo guanfang, 1873, reprinted in *Jindai zhongguo shiliao congkan* 中国近代史料丛刊 [A Collection of Historical Sources of Modern China], Taibei: Wenhai chubanshe, 1964.

Yao Guan 姚观 et al., eds. *Da Qing lüli quanzuan* 大清律例全纂 [Complete Compilation of the Great Qing Code]. Hangzhou: Mingxintang, 1796.

Yao Run 姚润 et al., eds. *Da Qing lüli tongzuan jicheng* 大清律例统纂集成 [Comprehensive Complete Compilation of the Great Qing Code]. Anchang: Lüsutang, 1826.

Yao Run 姚润, ed. *Da Qing lüli xing'an tongzuan jicheng* 大清律例刑案统纂集成 [Comprehensive Complete Compilation of the Great Qing Code with Leading Cases]. Revised by Hu Zhang 胡璋. Hangzhou: Sanshantang, 1859.

Zhang Weichi 张惟赤. *Haiyan Zhangshi Sheyuan congke* 海盐张氏涉园丛刻 [Collected Printings of Zhang Lineage in the She Garden in Haiyan]. Reprinted in *Congshu jicheng xubian* 丛书集成续编 [Collections of the Books, Series 2], Vol. 58. Shanghai: Shanghai shudian chubanshe, 1994.

Zheng, Qin. "Pursuing Perfection: Formation of the Qing Code." *Modern China* 21, no. 3 (1995): 310–44. Translated by Guangyuan Zhou.

Zhongguo zhengfa daxue tushuguan 中国政法大学图书馆 [Library of Chinese University of Political Science and Law], ed. *Zhongguo falü tushu zongmu* 中国法律图书总目 [Comprehensive Catalog of China's Law Books]. Beijing: Zhongguo zhengfa daxue chubanshe, 1991.

CHAPTER 9

Regulating Private Legal Specialists and the Limits of Imperial Power in Qing China

Li Chen

Private legal advisors (*xingming* and *qiangu muyou*) were the backbone of judicial administration in Qing China (1644–1911). They handled legal and other administrative matters for local officials in most jurisdictions of the empire. They also published most of the leading legal treatises and commentaries on the Qing Code, exerting an enormous impact on the study of law and judicial practice and indirectly on legislation during the Qing period.[1] The Qing ruling house in Beijing became increasingly concerned about losing its presumptive monopoly over the interpretation of the law and administration of justice as a key source of its legitimacy or claim to the Mandate of Heaven. This chapter will show that the tensions between the Qing government's recognition of the indispensable service of these private legal specialists and its desire for maximum control over them and their legal knowledge profoundly shaped the Qing judicial system. I will examine the motives, strategies, and limited effects of the Qing government's efforts to regulate private legal advisors. In the process, my analysis will draw attention to the significant limitations, beyond a very small portion of cases, to the supposedly absolute power of the Qing

1 About Qing legal advisors, see, e.g., Li Chen, "Legal Specialists and Judicial Administration in Late Imperial China, 1651–1911," *Late Imperial China* 33, no. 1 (June 2012): 1–54; Gao Huanyue 高浣月, *Qingdai xingming muyou yanjiu* 清代刑名幕友研究 [Study of Qing Legal Advisors] (Beijing: Zhongguo zhengfa daxue chubanshe, 2000). For their influence on Qing legal publications, see, e.g., Li Chen, "Zhishi de liliang: Qingdai muyou miben yu gongkai chuban de lüxue zhuzuo dui qingdai sifa changyu de yingxiang 知识的力量：清代幕友秘本和公开出版的律学著作对清代司法场域的影响 [Power of Knowledge: The Role of Secret and Published Treatises of Private Legal Specialists in the Qing Juridical Field]," *Zhejiang daxue xuebao* 浙江大学学报 [Journal of Zhejiang University], forhcoming in 2015; Zhang Ting's chapter in this volume; Tanii Yoko 谷井阳子, "Qingdai zeli shengli kao 清代则例省例考 [Study of Qing Ministerial and Provincial Regulations]," in *Zhongguo fazhishi kaozheng (bingbian disijuan)* 中国法制史考证(丙编第四卷) [Evidentiary Study of Chinese Legal History, Series 3, Vol. 4], ed. Terada Hiroaki 寺田浩明 (Beijing: Zhongguo shehui kexue chubanshe, 2003), 120–214.

© KONINKLIJKE BRILL NV, LEIDEN, 2015 | DOI 10.1163/9789004288492_011

rulers in trying to control the operation of the legal system. The first part of the chapter will trace the various policies of the Qing government in response to the growing influence of private legal advisors on local judicial administration. The regulatory impulses of the early Qing rulers to control these legal specialists culminated in the issuance and then codification of a series of imperial edicts as ministerial regulations in the early 1770s, but these regulatory endeavors proved to have very little momentum and efficacy in the next century. To some extent, the resulting official discourse did serve to warn legal advisors against abusing their expertise or power when helping local officials, just as the contemporary official portrayal of "evil pettifoggers" (*esongshi*) was meant to deter private litigation specialists (*songshi*) from inciting "ignorant" people to frivolous litigation that would flood the judicial docket. But the Qing government could not dispense with the services of private legal advisors, in contrast with the litigation specialists who were viewed as counterproductive and thus outlawed. As a result, the Qing policies on legal advisors reflected a mix of expectations, anxieties, and frustrations regarding these Confucian-literati-turned-specialists. The second part of the chapter will briefly discuss the operation of the Autumn Assizes (*qiushen*) of capital cases to illustrate the tensions, limitations, and ambivalence of the Qing government in this regard. Although it was the emperor's prerogative to review and decide whether to sanction any death sentence, the original legal reports that formed the basis of the imperial review in the Autumn Assizes were drafted in most cases by legal advisors in the provincial and lower courts. The Qing rulers—the Yongzheng (r. 1723–35) and Qianlong (r. 1736–95) Emperors in particular—were repeatedly alarmed at the near-dominant influence of legal advisors on the judicial system, but they never figured out how to effectively solve this "problem." In this sense, the presumably unlimited power of the Qing rulers was significantly diluted or fragmented in practice when much of the actual operation of the government fell into the hands of legal and administrative specialists such as private advisors, who turned out to be more difficult to monitor or regulate than imperial bureaucrats.

Policies of the Qing Court: Ambivalence towards Private Legal Specialists

Co-opting and Regulating Legal Advisors in the Early Qing

In 1651, the Shunzhi Emperor (r. 1644–61) lamented that the less experienced (*bushi wenyi*) local officials relied upon private advisors (*mubin*) to draft all their official documents.[2] That was actually a serious understatement of the situation of Qing local governments. As I have discussed elsewhere, this practice had become widespread at least by 1600, as more and more local officials in the Ming dynasty (1368–1643) hired private administrative specialists to perform their duties, a strategy previously adopted by local yamen clerks since the late Yuan (1279–1368).[3] Such heavy dependence upon private advisors during the Qing was certainly not confined to just inexperienced officials. This is evidenced in the extant judicial records or testimonies left by early Qing legal advisors such as Pan Biaocan (1630s–?1680s), Sun Hong, Wu Hong, Sun Lun, and Li Gong (1659–1733).[4] The overwhelming workload and increasingly complex institutions of judicial administration made it almost inevitable that even competent veteran administrators would turn to trained specialists for help.

Shen Zhiqi, author of an influential commentary on the Qing Code that was first published in 1715, still found it not easy to accurately explain and apply the law after thirty years of practice as legal advisor to local officials at all levels.[5] In a secret memorial to the Yongzheng Emperor in 1730, Ma Weihan, Jianchang

2 *Qing shilu* 清实录 [Veritable Records of the Qing Dynasty] (Beijing: Zhonghua shuju, 1985), 3: 427 (*Shizu silu, juan* 54: 4, sz8/r2/9 or March 29, 1651); *Donghua lu* 东华录 [Records from the Donghua Gate], in *Xuxiu Siku quanshu* 续修四库全书 [Supplement to the *Full Library of the Four Treasures*], ed. Xuxiu Siku quanshu bianzhuan weiyuanhui (Shanghai: Shanghai guji chubanshe, 2002), 369: 315.

3 Chen, "Legal Specialists," 5–10.

4 For reliance of Fujian Governor General Fan Chengmo (1624–76) on his *xingming, qiangu, zhangfang* (accounting), and *zouzhe* (memorial) *muyou*, see Xu Xu 许旭, *Minzhong jilüe* 闽中纪略 [Brief Notes about Occurrences in Fujian], ed. Taiwan yinhang jingji yanjiushi (Taibei: Taiwan yinhang, 1968 [1675]), 22–23, also 2, 6–7, 15–19. Li Gong (1659–1733) worked as a legal advisor himself periodically around 1700, and mentioned various local officials hiring legal advisors. See Feng Chen 冯辰 et al., eds., *Li Shugu xiansheng nianpu* 李恕谷先生年谱 [A Chronological Biography of Mr. Li Gong] (1836 [1714p]), 1: 21b, 2: 1a, 4a, 3: 4a, 32b, 5: 3a, 41b. Also see Sun Hong 孙宏, *Weizheng diyibian* 为政第一编 [Manuals for Governance, Part I], 8 *juan* (Benfu cangban, 1702p); Sun Lun 孙纶, *Dingli cheng'an hejuan* 定例成案合镌 [A Collection of Regulations and Leading Cases], 30 *juan* (Wujiang: Lejingtang, 1721 [1707p]); Chen Wenguang 陈文光, *Bu Weixinbian* 补未信编 [Supplement to *An Unreliable Treatise*], 4 *juan* (Sanduozhai cangban, 1707p). For Pan Biaocan 潘杓灿, Wu Hong 吴宏, and Gu Ding 顾鼎, see Chen, "Legal Specialists, 9–10."

5 Shen Zhiqi's preface (1707), in Shen Zhiqi 沈之奇 and Hong Hongxu 洪弘绪, *Da Qing lü jizhu* 大清律辑注 [The Great Qing Code with Collected Commentaries], 30 *juan* (Hangzhou: Sanyutang, 1755 [1715]), 11a. See Fu-mei Chang Ch'en, "The Influence of Shen Chih-Ch'i's Chi-Chu Commentary upon Ch'ing Judicial Decisions," in *Essays on China's Legal Tradition*, ed. Jerome Alan Cohen, R. Randle Edwards, and Fu-mei Chang Ch'en (Princeton: Princeton University Press, 1980), 170–221. For recognition of the importance of legal advisors, also

Circuit Intendant in Sichuan, even attributed the problems with local governance in that province partly to the insufficient number of *muyou*, or private advisors, there.[6] Numerous other senior officials would readily echo Huguang Governor General Fuming, who told the emperor in 1727 that "the *xingming qiangu* matters of the two provinces [Hunan and Hubei] were so overwhelming that he must hire *mubin* to help out."[7]

It is little wonder, then, that the Qing Court also found it essential to retain the services of these private advisors. To afford their relatively high salaries was one of the reasons for reforming the empire's fiscal system in the eighteenth century by legalizing customary surcharges paid by taxpayers to provide the honesty-nurturing (*yanglian*) stipends for local officials.[8] In 1725, for instance, Jiangxi Lieutenant Governor Changdeshou set aside 1,500 taels of silver—amounting to one-quarter of the total *yanglian* budget for that provincial yamen—to pay for his *muyou*.[9] As the Yongzheng Emperor himself noted, compensation for private advisors was one of the few items on a local government's budget that "could by no means be saved" (*duan buke sheng*).[10]

Pursuant to Shunzhi's edict of 1651, the Ministry of Personnel (*libu*) was directed to test all future official candidates' ability to write official (including judicial) documents (*wenyi gaoshi*), while provincial governors were to check their subordinates' qualification and diligence in performing their duties.[11] This hardly reduced the growing need and importance of private legal advisors in local governments, however.[12] From the beginning of his reign, the

---

see Huang Liuhong 黄六鸿, *Fuhui quanshu* 福慧全书 [The Complete Book Concerning Happiness and Benevolence], ed. Guanzhenshu jicheng bianzuan weiyuanhui, *Guanzhenshu jicheng* 官箴书集成 [Compendium of Administrative Handbooks] (Hefei: Huangshan shushe, 1997 [1694p]), 3: 228–29.

6 *Shizong xianhuangdi zhupi yuzhi* 世宗宪皇帝朱批谕旨 [Emperor Yongzheng's Imperial Edicts with Rescripts], *juan* 132 (*xia*): 7, in *Siku quanshu* 四库全书 [The Full Library of Four Treasures], 1500 *ce* (Taibei: Shangwu yinshuguan, 1986), 422: 144 (YZ8/3/20).

7 *Shizong xianhuangdi zhupi yuzhi*, 25: 54 (YZ5/3/16), in *Siku quanshu*, 417: 524; see *Siku quanshu*, 418: 488 (YZ5/11/1), 418: 654 (YZ7/9/3). Also see sources cited below. For more about this fiscal reform, see Madeleine Zelin, *The Magistrate's Tael: Rationalizing Fiscal Reform in Eighteenth-Century Ch'ing China* (Berkeley: University of California Press, 1984).

8 See, e.g., *Shizong xianhuangdi zhupi yuzhi*, 41: 3a (YZ2/6/8), in *Siku quanshu*, 418: 236; also see *Siku quanshu*, 418: 205 (YZ5/2/1), 416: 658 (YZ6/1/29).

9 *Shizong xianhuangdi zhupi yuzhi*, 54: 3 (YZ3/4/3), in *Siku quanshu*, 418: 667; Chen, "Legal Specialists," 18–20.

10 *Shizong xianhuangdi zhupi yuzhi*, 25: 54, in *Siku quanshu*, 417: 524.

11 *Qing shilu*, 3: 427.

12 See, e.g., in *Qing shilu*, 3: 663 (SZ11/6), 6: 261 (KX24/3) (warning Fan Chengmo not to listen to his *mubin* blindly), 6: 575 (KX53/12) (governors fighting for *muyou*), 6: 865 (KX60/11).

Yongzheng Emperor stepped up efforts to rein in private advisors, who had spread across the empire by then. In early 1725, he approved a memorial prohibiting them from working in government offices within their home province, a ban similar to the long-standing rule of avoidance for all ranking officials or subofficials (*zuoza*). Unlike the latter rule, however, the penalty for breaking this new prohibition would fall on the hiring officials instead of the private advisors. Its harsh treatment of litigation specialists or masters (*songshi*) in the eighteenth century notwithstanding, the Qing rulers did not, and practically could not, outlaw private legal advisors as a profession or exclude them from government service. In an edict that was later codified as a ministerial regulation (*shili*), the Yongzheng Emperor explained in 1723: "The large volume of work at the provincial yamen makes it impossible for any governor to handle it single-handedly. They have to turn to private advisors for help. This [practice] has long existed." According to this new rule, provincial governors general and governors should hire only experienced and trustworthy private advisors, and file their names and resumes (*lüli*) with the Ministry of Personnel. After several years of flawless service, these advisors could be recommended for an official rank (*guanxian*) or an actual official appointment.[13]

In 1736, the newly enthroned Qianlong Emperor also realized the importance of this matter and further extended his father's policy to require officials below provincial governors to report to the latter the names and native places of their *muyou* in charge of *xingming* and *qiangu* matters—that is, their legal advisors. Local officials could recommend those advisors with proven "ability, virtue, talent, and wisdom" after six years of service. The governors would then examine their skills before forwarding the names of the truly outstanding advisors to the Ministry of Personnel for final review and award. The original recommenders or the provincial assessors would be penalized if the recommended advisors turned out to be poor in writing and reasoning (*wenli huangmiu*) and ignorant about the law (*bu'an lüli*). Those advisors who had previously been fired for misconduct, who were relatives of the host officials, or who

---

13 *Qing shilu*, 7: 114–15 (about the recommendation); *Qing huidian shili* 清会典事例 [The Collected Qing Regulations with Precedents] (Beijing: Zhonghua shuju, 1991), 1: 963 (1723) (*juan* 75: *libu* 59, "chushou") (based on Santai's memorial in 1724 [YZ2/10/2]). See the two rules quoted in Li Wei's memorial (YZ4/3/15) at Zhang Shucai 张书才, ed., *Yongzheng chao hanwen zhupi zouzhe huibian* 雍正朝汉文朱批奏摺汇编 [Collection of Vermillion-Rescripted Chinese-Language Palace Memorials of the Yongzheng Reign], 40 *ce* (Nanjing: Jiangsu guji chubanshe, 1989), 6: 931. For Santai's memorial, ibid., 31: 2.

managed less important matters such as accounting (*shusuan*) or registration (*neihao*) in the local yamen were ineligible for such recommendations.[14]

A few things are worth noting about these attempts to co-opt and regulate Qing legal advisors. First, the Qing emperors apparently believed that the time-honored mechanism of winning the loyalty of Chinese talents by granting them official honors or positions was still effective. Second, contrary to traditional historiography, these edicts at least *partially* demonstrated the Qing rulers' appreciation of the practical value of legal and administrative expertise in governing the empire. Third, the fact that *xingming* and *qiangu* advisors were privileged in this regard supports my suggestion that, because of their specialized training and importance, these two types of *muyou*, the legal advisors, should be distinguished from other types of *muyou* or yamen clerks as well as most other alternative careers pursued by late imperial Chinese literati.

This carrot-and-stick policy did not work out well. Shortly after the rule of avoidance for legal advisors was promulgated in 1725, Yongzheng received a steady stream of requests from provincial officials for exemption from the injunction. The example of Li Wei (1686–1738), one of Yongzheng's most trusted officials, is both typical and revealing. As Yunnan lieutenant governor (*buzhengshi*) in 1724, Li Wei hired Zeng Zhi as legal advisor. When he was promoted to the post of Zhejiang governor the next year, advisor Zeng also became a subofficial (*jingji*) in Yanzhou prefecture. Since the judicial and fiscal matters in Zhejiang "were mounting up on the desk and truly impossible to handle by one person," Li explained in a secret memorial to the emperor, he then hired Lu Jin, a native of Zhejiang and junior staff member (*ban'gao tiexie*) at the Ministry of Justice in Beijing. Lu knew the laws and leading cases well but knew nothing about local administration. Therefore, Governor Li also brought in Zhu Lunhan, a bureau chief (*langzhong*) in the Ministry of Justice, to help him temporarily. In the meantime, he searched anxiously for another private legal advisor in neighboring provinces but was unsuccessful. Finally, he learned from Lieutenant Governor Tong Jitu that Pan Zhaoxin, a *juren* who had previously advised Zhejiang and Fujian Governor General Manbao, was an outstanding advisor (*mucai pohao*). Because Pan was a native of Hangzhou in Zhejiang, Governor Li now had to ask the emperor to waive the prohibition of 1725 in this case. Conscious of the emperor's concerns about the excessive influence of private advisors, Li assured His Majesty that he had

14 *Qing huidian shili*, 1: 963, 2: 248 (*juan* 97: *libu* 81). In 1739, Qianlong also approved the suggestion that local officials not allow their advisors to go home frequently, that those advisors whose families lived in the same city not be hired, and that provincial officials and circuits not hire advisors from the same province.

hired Pan only to "handle miscellaneous cases to reduce the workload," not to usurp his full control over important matters. The emperor apparently saw through this familiar type of defense, but his reply also manifested his ambivalence on this issue: "Your wish has been granted. If the person has good character and handles the job well, why cling to the native-place restriction or care about others' opinion?"[15] Thus Yongzheng implicitly admitted the impracticability of strictly enforcing the restrictions on private legal advisors in light of their indispensable role in local governance.

This policy of rewarding the best private legal advisors appears to have had only limited effects in transforming local governance or judicial administration in the next century. Yongzheng observed in 1731 that only a few governors had bothered to recommend their advisors to the court. If neither the host officials nor their advisors were interested in that opportunity, reasoned the emperor, the court could not force them to avail of it.[16] The fairly high income and social status, and the relative freedom from the institutional constraints and bureaucratic hierarchy that bound local officials, made the career of legal advisor attractive enough for numerous Qing literati to pursue it

15 *Shizong xianhuangdi zhupi yuzhi*, 174(2): 12–13 (YZ4/3/15), in *Siku quanshu*, 423: 38; also available at *Qingdai gongzhongdang ji junjichu dangzhejian* 清代宫中档及军机处档折件 [Qing Palace Memorials and Grand Council's Memorials] (Archives in Taibei: Gugong bowuyuan) (cited as *QGJJD*), No. 402007591 (YZ4/3/15). Through Li Wei's recommendation, Zhu Lunhan later became Acting Ningbo Prefect and then Quzhou prefect in 1727 (*Siku quanshu*, 419: 21), and Li Wei later lent Lu Jin to Acting Zhejiang Governor Cai Shishan as legal advisor in 1729 (*Siku quanshu*, 419: 64 [YZ7/7/25]). For similar requests of waiver, see *QGJJD*, No. 402011264 (YZ3/3/3) (also at *Shizong xianhuangdi zhupi yuzhi*, 70: 13, in *Siku quanshu*, 419: 200) (Zhejiang Provincial Judge Gan Guokui), 402011351 (YZ5/11/1) (Suzhou Lieutenant Governor Zhang Tanlin), 402012949 (YZ13/6/2) (Minzhe Governor General Hao Yulin) (also at *Yongzhengchao hanwen zhupi zouzhe huibian*, 10: 900 and 28: 506, respectively).

16 *Shizong xianhuangdi zhupi yuzhi*, 132 (*xia*): 7–8, in *Siku quanshu*, 422: 144–45 (YZ8/3/20). In the same year, Wang Shijun (?–1756, *jinshi* 1722), then Guangdong lieutenant governor, recommended to the emperor his legal advisor, Tong Fan, from Guiji of Shaoxing, for official appointment. Tong had been with him for six years since Wang was magistrate of Xiangfu county, Henan (*Shizong xianhuangdi zhupi yuzhi*, 73 [*xia*]: 28–29 [YZ8/2/26], in *Siku quanshu*, 419: 282). Three years later, Tong became Xiangfu county magistrate and Wang Shijun, then Hedong governor, asked whether their prior relationship triggered the rule of avoidance for officials. See *Yongzhengchao hanwen zhupi zouzhe huibian*, 23: 933 (YZ11/2/6). For other instances of recommendation, see ibid., 23: 918 (YZ11/8/8) (by Hubei Governor Deling); *QGJJD*, No. 00543 (QL12/4/11) (Yunnan governor recommending his *mubin* Zhu Xiangcai).

and to remain in that profession for decades.[17] At the same time, Li Wei's example shows how much even experienced Qing officials came to depend on their private legal advisors.

Emergence of a Criminalizing Identity for Wayward Private Advisors

The lack of effective surveillance or leverage over legal advisors who de facto managed the daily operation of local governments posed a real threat to the Qing Court's control over the empire's governance. As judicial administration was considered essential to the ruling house's claim to legitimacy and authority, the Qing emperors jealously guarded against such private encroachment on their sovereign power. In numerous cases, however, adjudication during the Qing often became a battlefield between the central imperial authorities (including the emperor and the Ministry of Justice), private legal advisors on behalf of local judges, and litigation masters who coached individual litigants behind the scenes. This triangular dynamic of power relations in Qing juridical politics has not received enough attention from historians of Chinese law and society, who have often focused on the contestation between private litigants or between litigants and local officials.[18]

The Yongzheng and Qianlong Emperors repeatedly expressed displeasure over the fact that numerous provincial officials relied upon private advisors to draft even the "secret imperial memorials" or review capital cases in the Autumn Assizes, two of the presumably most important duties of the provincial officials.[19] Unable to dissuade the officials from ignoring its repeated admonitions, the Qing Court could only resort to a strategy of terror, occasionally meting out exemplary, harsh punishments in some high-profile cases involving egregious misconduct of local officials and their advisors. In one of the early instances, Yongzheng penalized Fujian Provincial Judge Qiao Xueyi

17 For more about this, see Chen, "Legal Specialists," 17–21.

18 For two exceptions where the authors discussed some aspects of these tensions, see Chiu Pengsheng, *Dang falü yushang jingji: Ming Qing zhongguo de shangye falü* 当法律遇上经济: 明清中国的商业法律 [When Law Meets Economy: Business and Law in Ming and Qing China) (Taibei: Wunan tushu chuban gongsi, 2005); Gong Rufu 龚如富, *Ming Qing songxue yanjiu* 明清讼学研究 [Study of the Profession of Litigation Specialists in the Ming and Qing] (Shanghai: Shangwu yinshuguan, 2008).

19 For the emperors censuring senior local officials for this, see, e.g., *QGJJD*, No. 402018220 (YZ11/2/6), 402022237 (YZ2/12/20), 403009113 (QL20/4/15). Fujian Governor Zhao Guolin 赵国麟 had to excuse himself by arguing that he had drafted the secret memorials but asked his *muyou*, Liu Guangyu 劉光煜 from Shanyin, to *copy* them because he was poor in eyesight and handwriting (*QGJJD*, No. 402009893; *Shizong xianhuangdi zhupi yuzhi*, 206: 13 [YZ8/9/6], in *Siku quanshu*, 424: 550).

and his legal advisor, a certain Pan, for reportedly mishandling several legal cases or being too lenient with serious offenders.[20]

What prompted the Imperial Court to institute more stringent measures was a notorious case that implicated a number of senior officials in Hubei province. In 1760, two brothers, Zhang Hongshun and Zhang Honggui, were initially convicted of robbery by Magistrate Zhao of Guizhou for breaking into a house, but they later recanted their confessions at the provincial court and were eventually acquitted. The robbery victim and the local constable (*dibao*) were sentenced to military exile and labor servitude, respectively, for false accusations, and the magistrate was sentenced to exile for abusive judicial torture and wrongful judgment. Two years later, the Zhang brothers committed another robbery, were again convicted, and also confessed to the earlier robbery. To avoid potential disciplinary sanctions for the earlier wrongful acquittals during his term as the Hubei provincial judge, Lieutenant Governor Shen Zuopeng pressured other provincial officials to report only the second robbery to the Ministry of Justice, without disclosing or correcting their earlier mistake. The ministry and the Qianlong Emperor eventually found this out. In the end, the Zhang brothers were executed, and so was Lieutenant Governor Shen. Governor General Aibida (?–1771) and former Governor Zhou Wan were sentenced to strangulation after the Autumn Assizes (later commuted to exile to Xinjiang) for covering up Shen's misconduct. The incumbent provincial judge, Gao Cheng, and two governors (Tang Pin and Song Bangsui) who succeeded Zhou Wan were dismissed for having failed to impeach their colleagues or superiors. For the same reason, several prefects who had been delegated by the guilty provincial officials to try the two robbery cases were also penalized.[21]

Given that the sentences of the wronged Guizhou magistrate and the victim of the first robbery had not yet been carried out, the fact that so many high-ranking officials were punished so harshly made this a very unusual case. This was mainly because the emperor believed this to be one of the most outrageous instances ever of so many provincial officials conspiring to cover up a wrongful judgment and deceive the Imperial Court. For the same reason, the emperor even brought the principal offenders and witnesses from Hubei and elsewhere to Beijing to interrogate them himself. Magistrate Zhao, now vindicated and restored, informed the emperor that a clique of Shaoxing *muyou* long in the Hubei government offices were also responsible for the miscarriage of

---

20 *Shizong xianhuangdi zhupi yuzhi*, 72: 4–5 (YZ6/8/4), in *Siku quanshu*, 415: 117.

21 *Qianlongchao shangyudang* 乾隆朝上谕档 [Imperial Edicts of the Qianlong Reign], comp. Zhongguo diyi lishi dang'anguan, 18 *ce* (Beijing: Dang'an chubanshe, 1991), 4: 189 (QL28/5/18)–202, 211–14, 236, 242–44, 312.

justice. Xu Zhangsi, legal advisor to then Provincial Judge Shen Zuopeng, had a brother, Xu Dengsan, advising Governor General Aibida, and their brother-in-law, Lu Peiyuan, was Governor Tang Pin's legal advisor. According to Zhao, all the legal decisions concerning the two robbery cases at the different provincial yamen were made by these few advisors. While admitting that the officials themselves were no less guilty, Qianlong argued: "This kind of bad *muyou* (*liemu*) dared to form secret networks with one another [and local officials] and thereby control [local governance]. They are truly a source of evil for the local [people]. Their guilt must be publicized and punished so that all *muyou* will heed the warning."[22] The three Xu brothers were later exiled to Xinjiang for having illicitly communicated with one another and for manipulating the law and official writings (*antong shengqi wuwen wangfa*).[23]

Until this incident, private legal advisors in general would only have been dismissed and sent home in a case like this. The Qianlong Emperor, however, demanded that Xu Zhangsi and his relatives be brought to Beijing for interrogation and strict punishment. It might well have been true that the three relatives were partly responsible for what went wrong in this case, but we should not take at face value the emperor's justification of the harsh penalties meted out to them as being intended only to enforce the law, prevent injustice, and protect the innocent from malfeasant administrators. The strong imperial reaction was the culmination of the Qing Court's concerns about the growing influence of private legal advisors on local governance on the one hand, and about bureaucratic entrenchment and collusion among local officials on the other. As Qianlong implied in late 1763, these developments threatened to seriously undermine the power and moral legitimacy of the Qing ruling house.[24] In a remarkable study of the widespread persecution of the so-called soul-stealers in the same decade, Philip Kuhn has also shown the Qing Court's enormous anxiety about these kinds of perceived political threats.[25] From the emperor's point of view, the legal advisors' judicial and administrative expertise and social networks made it much easier for local officials to defeat or even

---

22 *Qianlongchao shangyudang*, 4: 242–43 (QL28/7/7), 279 (QL28/8/12); QGJJD, No. 403015472; *Neige daku dang'an* 内阁大库档案 [Archives of the Grand Secretariat] (Archives in Taibei: Academia Sinica), No. 078533-001 (on punishments of the provincial officials) (QL28/7), 078518 (QL28/7/15). Also see QGJJD, No. 403014962, 403015128, 403015149, 403015581, 403015811.

23 *Neige daku dang'an*, No. 151457-001 (QL28/9, Xingbu's memorial).

24 *Qianlongchao shangyudang*, 4: 243–44.

25 Philip Kuhn, *Soulstealers: The Chinese Sorcery Scare of 1768* (Cambridge: Harvard University Press, 1990).

challenge the Qing Court's control and surveillance. The prompt and severe penalties in this case were designed to deliver a stern message to all the local administrators (as well as their legal advisors) that they could not prioritize personal interest over that of the throne.[26]

Over the short span of four months, the label for Xu Zhangsi and his ilk went from "bad advisors" (*liemu*) to "evil advisors" (*emu*) in the imperial edicts and memorials. This new criminalizing identity for wayward advisors soon took root in the Qing official discourse.[27] Melissa Macauley and Fuma Susumu have shown how the increased use of the professional services of litigation masters contributed to the *intensified* imperial hostility towards those private legal specialists in late imperial China. In consequence, a Ming statute of 1503 was retained in the Qing Code in 1646 and then in 1740, punishing those "who incited litigation, or who added or omitted facts in order to falsely accuse people" with the same penalties as for the false accusers. A substatute was added in 1756 to penalize repeat offenders or "habitual litigation hooligans" (*jiguan songgun*) under that statute.[28] In 1742, it was further legislated that all handbooks for instructing people on litigation, such as *Jingtian lei* (Advice for Thunderous [Victories]), *Xiang jiao* (To Fight), *Fajia xinshu* (A New Book for Legalists), or *Xingtai qinjing* (A Divine Mirror [for Legalists]), should be banned and destroyed just as pornographic literary works had been since 1738, with the offending publishers punishable by 100 strokes of the heavy bamboo and exile.[29]

It was more than sheer coincidence that the efforts of Yongzheng and Qianlong in the 1720s to 1760s to more aggressively prosecute and penalize legal advisors (often based on evidence of the host officials' misconduct) came almost at the same time as they sought to statutorily criminalize

26 *Qianlongchao shangyudang*, 4: 244.

27 Ibid., 4: 288–89 (QL28/9/9).

28 If the inciter or plaint writer was punishable by death hereunder, the punishment would be reduced by one grade under the Qing Code unless the writer was hired to draft the false accusation. See Xue Yunsheng 薛允升, *Duli cunyi* (*chongkan ben*) 读例存疑(重刊本) [Doubtful Points While Reading the Substatutes] (Taibei: Chengwen chubanshe, 1970), 4: 1019; *Qing huidian shili*, 2: 438 (*juan* 112). Melissa Macauley, *Social Power and Legal Culture: Litigation Masters in Late Imperial China* (Stanford: Stanford University Press, 1998), 18–46; Fuma Susumu, "Litigation Masters and the Litigation Systems of Ming and Qing China," *International Journal of Asian Studies* 27, no. 1 (2007 [1993]): 79–111.

29 The substatute was based on Sichuan Provincial Judge Li Rulan's memorial. See Xue Yunsheng, *Duli cunyi* (*chongkan ben*), 4: 1021. Penalties for officials negligent in enforcing this law were added in a ministerial regulation in 1765. See *Qing huidian shili*, 2: 438 (*juan* 112).

litigation masters. These measures, I suggest, indicated that the Qing rulers' anxiety about private use of legal knowledge to influence judicial administration had reached such a critical threshold that they felt compelled to take more drastic measures than before to cope with it. About the Qing criminalization of unauthorized proxy writers under the ambiguous label of "habitual litigation hooligans" in this period, Macaulay has observed that "the issue was no longer simply one of litigation abuse; it was the fact that a person outside of official auspices made a living out of assisting people in a lawsuit."[30] In comparison, the issue here was more about the fact that private advisors' legal expertise and administrative experience threatened to thwart any effective imperial control over them and, by extension, over local administration.

It is worth noting that such obvious distrust in private legal expertise existed side by side with official promotion of popular knowledge of the law. For instance, in 1737, Jiangxi Provincial Judge Huang Yuemu suggested to Qianlong that printed copies of statutes relevant to commoners should be widely distributed in all places. In contrast with the outlawed litigation handbooks, however, such dissemination of authorized legal knowledge was supposed to deter or save the otherwise ignorant people from breaking the law.[31] This kind of imperial ambivalence towards privatization of legal knowledge continued to influence Qing policies towards legal advisors.

Needless to say, legal advisors to local officials differed considerably from the long-despised litigation specialists in their legal and social status and in their relationship with the Qing authorities. Besides, the latter's activities made the job of legal advisors at once more valuable (to local officials) and more difficult. Naturally, Qing private advisors frequently echoed the official denunciation of these litigation specialists for instigating meritless lawsuits that overburdened the local administrators (and their advisors). Nevertheless, given their shared appreciation of legal knowledge, it is not hard to understand why some legal advisors, such as Wang Youfu, would suggest that a distinction be made between benign "litigation masters" (*songshi*),[32] who provided

30 Macauley, *Social Power*, 18–20. She highlighted a case in 1820, although the same tendency predated that. For another recent study of litigaiton masters and their practice, see Gong Rufu, *Ming Qing songxue yanjiu*.

31 *QGJJD*, No. 001540 (QL12/11/6). For a similar memorial by Shanxi Judicial Judge Li Chengye 李承邺, see *QGJJD*, No. 40303343 (QL42/11/28).

32 Wang Youfu 王有孚, *Yide outan* 一得偶谈 [Casual Talk on Small Points] (1804p), 1 (i.e., *chuji*): 39b–40a, in Wang Youfu, *Bu'aixuan dulü liuzhong* 不碍轩读律六种 [Six Works for Legal Studies from the Bu'ai Pagoda] (1807). See Philip C.C. Huang, *Civil Justice in China: Representation and Practice in the Qing* (Stanford: Stanford University Press, 1996), 165, 220–21.

much-needed legal advice to laypeople, and abusive "litigation hooligans" (*songgun*), who profited from swindling litigants and inciting frivolous litigation. Echoing Wang Youfu (c. 1750–post-1807), other famous Qing legal advisors, including Wang Huizu (1730–1807) and Zhang Tingxiang (1842–post-1915), likewise called for a parallel distinction to be made between "good advisors" (*liangmu*) who honored the Way of Muyou (*mudao*) and the relatively small number of "bad advisors" (*liemu*).[33] Out of practical necessity, as noted earlier, the Qing Court had to agree with them on the legitimacy of the latter distinction even though it might disagree on how and where to draw the line on a particular occasion.

Failure of the Qing Court to Control Private Legal Advisors

As in the case of litigation masters, who were frequently dubbed as habitual litigation hooligans in this period, an ill-defined, criminalizing identity was hence constructed for those disliked legal advisors in the official and popular discourses by the early 1760s. It presumably provided the juridical and moral authority for the Qing Court to prosecute certain private advisors by labeling them as habitually bad or evil advisors even though there was apparently little evidence of direct responsibility for their host officials' misconduct at issue. These discourses and judicial practice in turn exerted a great deal of influence on the public perception and the professional training, practice, and identity of these Qing private legal practitioners.[34]

The Qing Court did not face much backlash in outlawing litigation specialists, whose legal advice was deemed a major cause of false accusations, judicial backlog, and moral decay of society.[35] In contrast, it faced a far more daunting challenge in dealing with legal advisors. After all, even Yongzheng and Qianlong, two of the most aggressive emperors in this regard, acknowledged that their services were indispensable to local governance and judicial administration.[36] A more realistic goal was to contain the side effects of utilizing legal advisors' expertise by carefully circumscribing their social space and political influence.

The rules of avoidance and mandatory reporting, introduced in 1725 and revised in 1736, were designed for those purposes. In the next three decades, other restrictions were added, banning officials and their advisors from

33 Chen, "Legal Specialists," 24–37.

34 For a discussion of Qing legal advisors' responses to such pressure, see Chen, "Legal Specialists," 25–35.

35 Macauley, *Social Power*; Fuma, "Litigation Masters."

36 *Qing shilu*, 10:1068 (*Gaozong chunhuangdi shilu, juan* 144, QL6/6 or 1741).

pressuring a subordinate official to hire someone as an advisor (*lejian* or *yajian*). Private advisors were forbidden to freely socialize with other government employees or subordinate officials.[37] In response to the 1763 case of Shen Zuopeng and several similar instances, Qianlong approved censor Hu Qiaoyuan's proposal in 1772 that codified and further expanded the earlier rules as a set of formal regulations. Accordingly, all local officials were prohibited from hiring any *muyou* who was a native of that province, or any *muyou* who, though from another province, was residing or had a family living in that province and within 500 *li* of the hiring official's jurisdiction. All *muyou* had to be replaced after five years of service; provincial officials could not leave behind their *muyou* for their successors. Each year, provincial officials were to send the Ministry of Personnel background and residential information for all the *muyou* employed in the province. All officials had to prevent their *muyou* from leaving the yamen to socialize or engage in power brokering. As noted above, these restrictions applied only to *xingming* and *qiangu muyou*, or private legal advisors. Officials who disobeyed the regulations would be demoted two grades and their private advisors would be expelled.[38]

Although these regulations were short-lived, they did shed light on how and why the Qing Court desired to utilize and control such legal and administrative specialists. Designed purportedly to prevent bad advisors (*liemu*), the spatial and social restrictions were ultimately intended to keep private legal advisors as *useful but docile experts* subservient to the command of the throne and its designated officials (*yizi quce*).[39] Nevertheless, legal and administrative expertise had become such a highly valued commodity that it empowered private legal advisors and redefined the dynamic of their relationship with their host officials and the central imperial government.

37 *Qing huidian shili*, 2: 248–251 (*juan* 97) (1735–62).

38 The provincial officials were to send information about their new advisors to Beijing immediately, but submit such information about lower officials' advisors only at the end of each year. About these regulations, see *Qing shilu*, 20: 291–93 (*Gaozong chunhuangdi shilu, juan* 917, QL37/9/21 or Oct. 21, 1772) (imperial edict approving Hu's memorial after the Ministry's deliberation); *Qing huidian shili*, 1: 963 (*juan* 75); 2: 251 (*juan* 97). For useful memorials quoting them, see *Qianlongchao junjichu lufu zouzhe* 乾隆朝军机处录副奏折 [Copies of Memorials of the Qianlong Reign at the Grand Council] (Archives in Beijing: Zhongguo diyi lishi dang'anguan), No. 03-0135-052 (Shandong Governor Xu Ji 徐绩, QL38/12/26), 02-0141-061 (QL39/12/15); *QGJJD*, No. 018229 (QL37/9/25). Another immediate cause of these restrictions involved Yunnan Lieutenant Governor Qian Du and his *muyou* Ye Muguo (Shiyuan). See *QGJJD*, No. 016921 (QL37/5/4), 017596, 017598 (QL37/6/18), 017635, 017657.

39 *Qing shilu*, 20: 291–93 (*Gaozong chunhuangdi shilu, juan* 917, QL37/9/21).

Unsurprisingly, most local officials found it difficult to abandon their trusted advisors. They attempted to bypass the new restrictions while making strenuous efforts to convince the superior authorities of their independence from their advisors in handling all the major matters.[40] In 1773, for instance, the Zhejiang governor told officials in Hangzhou, Jiaxing, and Huzhou Prefectures to retain their current legal advisors, including natives of that province, until they had found qualified advisors from other provinces. Many naturally claimed that they had difficulty getting a replacement. This was how Magistrate Liu Yanti managed to keep Wang Huizu as his legal advisor despite the prohibitions. In fact, from 1761 through 1782, Wang Huizu worked successively for thirteen different officials in eleven different local yamen in Zhejiang, his home province.[41]

Four years had hardly elapsed when the Qing Court decided to abolish the regulations on annual reporting and residential and term limitations. As Qianlong explained in early 1776, the reporting requirement must have been a dead letter (*jüwen*) since none of the provincial reports had disclosed any instance of violation. In any event, he further admitted, officials should be able to neutralize the potential harm of private advisors by keeping them under close surveillance and confinement (*yanmi guanfang*), without which the residential and term limitations could do little good. What local officials now had to do was to prevent private advisors from socializing and forming cliques and to punish those "evil advisors" for misconduct.[42]

The emperor made this rather quick reversal and implicit admission of defeat apparently because the annual reports further proved that legal advisors were indispensable to local officials. As discussed in my earlier study, the surviving annual provincial reports from 1772–75 revealed that virtually all local administrators in the nineteen provinces, ranging from county magistrates to governors general, hired one or more private legal advisors, with an estimated

40 See, e.g., *QGJJD*, No. 019143 (QL37/12/12) (Memorial by Acting Zhejiang Governor Xiong Xuepeng 熊学鹏).

41 Wang Huizu 汪辉祖, "Bingta mengheng lu 病榻梦痕录 [Trace of Tears in the Dream of a Sickbed]," 1: 35b (1773), in *Wang Longzhuang xiansheng yishu* 汪龙庄先生遗书 [Works Bequeathed by Wang Huizu] (Shandong shuju, 1886). For his employment history, see Bao Yongjun 鲍永军, *Shaoxing shiye Wang Huizhu yanjiu* 绍兴师爷汪辉祖研究 [A Study of Shaoxing Private Advisor Wang Huizhu] (Beijing: Renmin chubanshe, 2006), 140. During that period, he also worked for a circuit intendant (Zhejiang ningshaotai) in 1771.

42 *Qing shilu*, 21: 382 (*Gaozong chunhuangdi shilu, juan* 1000, QL41/1/6 or Feb. 24, 1776); *Qing huidian shili*, 1: 964, 2: 252.

total of more than 3,000 trained specialists advising local officials across the country at the same time.[43]

During the next century, sporadic attempts were made to regain control over legal advisors, but little progress was achieved.[44] When it was suggested in 1817 that governors should resume briefing the Ministry of Personnel about private advisors in their jurisdictions, the Jiaqing Emperor (r. 1796–1820) rejected it as useless since local officials changed their advisors so often that the ministry had no way to keep track.[45] As an increasing number of degree-holders or official candidates chose to temp as private advisors to powerful provincial officials in order to get a recommendation for official appointment later, the Qing Court also abolished the rule regarding recommending and rewarding private advisors in 1824.[46] The century-long experiment ended silently in failure.

Legal advisors remained the de facto judicial administrators in most jurisdictions. In contrast with their official representation as profit-driven and corruption-prone, many legal advisors took pains to prove themselves to be professionally competent, morally principled, and socially responsible experts who were key to local governance and public interest. By publishing many of the most influential legal treatises and administrative handbooks, private advisors also established themselves as leading authorities in law and judicial administration, and in statecraft literature or "practical learning" (*shixue*). Their promotion of a discourse on the Way of Muyou countered the disparaging official discourse and carved out a respectable social and public space for these private legal practitioners.[47] Imperial censors continued to complain that some private advisors formed powerful and abusive cliques, manipulated local officials, or caused injustice, but many of the stories turned out to be false

43 Chen, "Legal Specialists," 23–24. I am revising a paper that analyzes the statistics in the reports in detail.

44 In 1801, it was further stipulated that private advisors were liable to the same punishment as their host officials if the former had "incited" (*zhushi*) the latter to commit misconduct. See *Qing huidian shili*, 2: 252 (*juan* 97).

45 *Qing shilu*, 32: 436 (*Renzong ruihuangdi shilu*, *juan* 336, JQ22/11/22 or Dec. 29, 1817) (Edict on Censor Tan Ruidong).

46 See *Qing huidian shili*, 1: 964 and 2: 252 (prohibiting hiring subordinate officials as advisors in 1801, reconfirmed in 1828, 1833, 1847). Those like Zeng Guofan and Li Hongzhang clearly ignored these prohibitions.

47 See, e.g., Chen, "Legal Specialists," 24–36; ibid., *Zhishi de liliang: Qingdai muyou miben he gonkai chuban de lüxue zhuzuo dui qingdai sifa changyu de yingxiang*. For analysis of a somewhat similarly dismissive attitude towards forensic experts as only petty technicians, see the chapter by Daniel Asen in this volume and his dissertation cited herein.

or exaggerated. As in the case of Xu Zhangsi in 1763, the investigations also generally confirmed one thing: legal advisors not only were essential to judicial administration but also had enormous clout with local officials at all levels.[48]

The Role of Legal Advisors in the Autumn Assizes

By way of illustration, this section will discuss the Autumn Assizes in order to provide a glimpse of the ambivalent attitudes of the Qing Court towards private legal advisors. It is worth emphasizing that this should by no means be seen as a systematic treatment of the Autumn Assizes. Rather, my purpose is only to contextualize the issues discussed above within the specific institutional setting of the Autumn Assizes to demonstrate how the tensions between the Qing government's desire for the services of legal experts on the one hand and its distrust of private legal specialists on the other came to affect the actual operation of Qing judicial administration.

Many other societies also gave their monarchs the power to grant royal pardons or amnesty, but late imperial China was one of the few that also required the monarchs to review and sanction all sentences of capital punishment.[49] The annual review of capital cases would be conducted by the provincial authorities and then by multiple central government agencies in the Autumn Assizes, and finally by the emperor himself. The so-called Grand Procedure of the Autumn Assizes (*qiuyan dadian*) enabled the ruling house to exercise both imperial benevolence and sovereign power by demonstrating to the offenders and the public at large that the emperor was divinely endowed with the mission and sagacity to decide on life and death and to dispense ultimate justice to all the imperial subjects. As a result, how the Autumn Assizes

48 See, e.g., *Daoguangchao junjichu lufu zouzhe* 道光朝军机处录副奏折 [Copies of Memorials of the Daoguang Reign at the Grand Council] (Archives in Beijing: Zhongguo diyi lishi dang'anguan), No. 3-65-4053-19 (DG16/12/10) (memorial by Jiangsu Governor Lin Zexu); *QGJJD*, No. 405000227 (DG3/6/13) (Censor Cheng Yica), 405004467 (DG21/11/6) (Shanxi Governor Yang Guozhen), 127778 (GX10/5/25) (Zhang Shusheng).

49 Even those cases of immediate execution (*zhengfa* or *jiudi zhengfa*) involving unusually brutal or dangerous crimes, which rose significantly in number after the 1850s, were technically subject to imperial review and sanction after the execution. For recent studies of European royal pardons, see, e.g., Natalie Z. Davis, *Fiction in the Archives: Pardon Tales and Their Tellers in Sixteenth-Century France* (Stanford: Stanford University Press, 1987); Carolyn Strange, ed., *Qualities of Mercy: Justice, Punishment, and Discretion* (Vancouver: University of British Columbia Press, 1996); Krista J. Kesselring, *Mercy and Authority in the Tudor State* (New York: Cambridge University Press, 2003).

were operated or perceived was of enormous importance to the ruling regime's continued legitimacy and authority.

From very early on, the Qing rulers adopted the discursive tradition of imperial Chinese jurisprudence to claim their benevolent rulership and the Mandate of Heaven in the newly conquered empire. For instance, the Kangxi Emperor (r. 1661–1722) issued numerous edicts, declaring that he paid extraordinary attention to capital cases and exhorting all officials to "be careful about punishment and compassionate to the people" (*shenxing aimin*). He explained in 1679: "Human lives are of vital importance (*renming youguan*); improper judgment [in such cases would endanger human lives and] disturb cosmological harmony (*yougan tianhe*)."[50] Subsequent emperors likewise emphasized on many occasions that they carefully reviewed each of the capital cases to determine whether the offenders should be executed or treated more leniently.[51]

Beginning from 1673, parallel to but several months before the Autumn Assizes in Beijing, senior officials in each provincial capital would also meet annually to review and divide capital cases into three different categories: cases for immediate execution (*qingzhen* or *qingshi*), cases for postponed execution (*huanjue*), and other cases for judicial mercy (*jinyi* or *kejin*).[52] Besides

50 *Shengzu renhuangdi shengxun* 圣祖仁皇帝圣训 [Sacred Instructions of the Kangxi Emperor], *juan* 28: 6 (KX12/11/1 or Dec. 8, 1673), 28: 7 (KX14/5/17), 28: 8 (KX18/4/4) (for the quotations), 28: 10(KX20/1/27), 28: 13 (KX23/1/20) (applying the same reasoning to judicial torture), 28: 15 (KX25/3/16), 28: 16 (KX25/6/7), 29: 9 (KX41/1/24 or Feb. 20, 1702) (royal pardons), all in *Siku quanshu*, 411: 477–89. My discussion here of the ideology of "cosmological harmony" or *tianhe* is different from the interpretation by many earlier Western Sinologists who tended to imply that the imperial Chinese legal system cared only about the "cosmic harmony," with little regard for justice or law. See a critique of that interpretation in Li Chen, "Law, Empire, and Historiography of Sino-Western Relations: A Case Study of the *Lady Hughes* Controversy in 1784," *Law & History Review* 27, no. 1 (Spring 2009): 46–49.

51 *Shengzu renhuangdi shilu*, 29: 7 (KX40/11/11 or Dec. 10, 1701) (Kangxi had "carefully read each of the cases in the Autumn Assizes" and censured the Ministry for printing wrong words in the case records), in *Siku quanshu*, 411: 488. See *Qianlong dang'an* 乾隆档案 [Archives of the Autumn Assizes in the Qianlong Period] (Undated MS); *Jiaqing dang'an* 嘉庆档案 [Archives of the Autumn Assizes in the Jiaqing Period] (Undated MS). Also see *Qing shilu*, 18: 445 (*Gaozong chunhuangdi shilu, juan* 769, QL31/9/26 or Oct. 29, 1766), 18: 746 (*Gaozong chunhuangdi shilu, juan* 796, QL32/10/2 or Nov. 10, 1767).

52 A fourth category of "staying to support a senior relative (*liuyang*)" was later created for the Autumn Assizes. For details on the procedure of the metropolitan Autumn Assizes, see Gangyi 刚毅, "Qiushen shiyi 秋审事宜 [Things about the Autumn Assizes]," in *Qiuyan jiyao* 秋谳辑要 [Essentials on the Autumn Assizes], ed. Gangyi 刚毅 (Jiangsu shuju, 1889), *juan shou*: 1a–4a. Also see Shen Jiaben 沈家本, "Qiuyan xuzhi 秋谳须知

the county magistrate (or, more accurately, his legal advisor) who made the initial judgment, the provincial judge's office and the Ministry of Justice were the two major agencies responsible for the Autumn Assizes in the provincial and national capitals, respectively. However, legal advisors affected the outcomes of these capital cases not only as the de facto adjudicators or reviewers at the local levels but also as the actual drafters of the legal reports that were relied upon in Beijing. As the Kangxi Emperor observed in 1686: "Once the legal report (*yuci*) [of the trial court] was submitted and then the memorial [of the provincial tribunals] was inked, it would be very hard to save the convict even though [the central government agencies and the emperor] had many rounds of careful reviews."[53] Such reliance on these *private* legal specialists raised various issues for the throne's claim to be the ultimate arbiter of justice.

As early as June 1735, the Yongzheng Emperor publicly lamented the dominance of legal advisors over this judicial process:

> It has long been reported that all the provinces concluded their joint session [of the Autumn Assizes] within one day, no matter how many cases were under review. The governors general or governors dictated everything with no regard for the provincial judges or circuit intendants, let alone the prefects or magistrates in attendance. The penal sentence was fixed within seconds, and one voice determined whether it was correct or not. But the truth is that even the governors general and governors might not really know (*weibi liaoran*) [what was going on] but only read the summaries (*lüejie*) prepared by their advisors (*muke*). What they did [in the joint session] was just for show.

Yongzheng exhorted local officials to treat the Autumn Assizes more seriously and to spend more time reviewing the capital cases.[54] Perhaps only a minority of the provinces conducted the Autumn Assizes as summarily and superficially as portrayed by the emperor, but he seems well justified in believing that it was legal advisors who conducted the substantial judicial review.

[Essential Things about the Autumn Assizes]," in Shen Jiaben, *Shen Jiaben weikan'gao qizhong* 沈家本未刊稿七种 [Seven Unpublished Works of Shen Jiaben], 1–242, esp. 149–54 (on changes over time).

53 *Shengzu renhuangdi shengxun, juan* 28: 15 (KX25/3/16 or Apr. 8, 1686), 29: 6 (KZ39/9/21 or Nov. 1, 1700) (also on relying on provincial officials to supervise their subordinates in these matters), in *Siku quanshu*, 411: 481 and 488, respectively.

54 *Qing shilu*, 8: 900-1 (YZ 13/r4/29 or June 19, 1735).

A few examples may suffice to show this. Legal advisor Xie Chengjun spent about six years in the 1840s compiling a treatise on how to conduct the Autumn Assizes because he was acutely aware that lives were at stake, based on his experience of reviewing dozens of capital cases each year as legal advisor to the Zhili provincial judges for twenty years. As with many other legal advisors, Xie's sense of responsibility testified to the centrality of his role in the provincial Autumn Assizes.[55] Remarkably, several of the provincial judges he advised were themselves "legal experts" (*jing xingming zhiyan*).[56] For instance, Dai Zongyuan (?–1833, *jinshi* 1813) worked for a few years in the Ministry of Justice before he became Zhili provincial judge in 1826–29 and then vice minister of justice. Hua Jie (1779–1859, *jinshi* in 1799) had been a bureau chief (*langzhong*) in charge of the Autumn Assizes in the Ministry of Justice for almost a decade (1811–19) before he was appointed a local official and then Zhili provincial judge (1829–31). Likewise, before his transfer to the post of Zhili provincial judge in 1831–33, Guang Congxie (*jinshi* 1809) had been a senior official in the Ministry of Justice and then Fujian provincial judge.[57] If they all found it necessary to rely on their advisors to handle the judicial work, the vast majority of local officials, without such extensive legal knowledge or experience, would feel far more compelled to do so.

Four decades later, Xie's treatise was updated by Xu Shenwang, a legal advisor from Hubei. Xu valued this treatise because it had guided him in handling the Autumn Assizes when working for Henan Provincial Judge Jiang Qixun (1837–1902) for some years around 1880. He further explained why he reprinted Xie's collection of rules and leading cases for the Autumn Assizes: "There was

---

55 See Xie's preface at Xie Chengjun 谢诚钧, *Qiushen bijiao shihuan tiaokuan* 秋审比较实缓条款 [*Rules for Confirming or Postponing Execution in the Autumn Assizes*] (Jiangsu shuju, 1878), 1: 1a. It was cited approvingly by Shen Jiaben 沈家本, *Qiushen tiaokuan fu'an* 秋审条款附案 [Rules for the Autumn Assizes with Comments] (Xiuding falüguan, 1906), 1: 2a. For similar concerns, see Wu Kun 吴坤, *Xingyou liangfang shize* 刑友良方十则 [Ten Good Suggestions for Legal Advisors], 3a–b.

56 See Xie's preface in Xie, *Qiushen shihuan bijiao tiaokuan*, 1b.

57 About Dai Zongyuan 戴宗沅, see *Qing guoshiguan zhuangao* 清国史馆传稿 [Draft Biographies of the Qing Historiography Institute] (Archives in Taibei: National Palace Museum), No. 701000998, and 701003972; about Hua Jie 花杰, see Qin Guojing 秦国经, Tang Yinian 唐益年, and Ye Yunxiu 叶云秀, eds., *Qingdai guanyuan lüli dang'an quanbian* 清代官员履历档案全编 [A Complete Collection of Qing Officials' Resumes] (Shanghai: Huadong shifan daxue chubanshe, 1997), 25: 174–75, 2: 652; about Guang Congxie 光聪谐, see *Qing guoshiguan zhuangao*, No. 701007314 (not specifying when he was *langzhong*); Qian Shifu 钱实甫, ed., *Qingdai zhiguan nianbiao* 清代职官年表 [Chronological Charts of Qing Officials] (Zhonghua shuju, 1980), 3: 2136–38.

only one *mubin* [i.e., advisor] in charge of the Autumn Assizes at the provincial judge's office. Limited by his own knowledge and experience, one person can hardly avoid mistakes when examining the myriad circumstances in all the cases unless he has precedential cases available for ready reference and comparison."[58] The message was again unmistakable: legal advisors were *the* key players in the reviewing process. In the same period and for similar reasons, Lin En'shou and Sun Wenyao, both veteran legal advisors to the Sichuan provincial judges, and Wu Wu'an, another legal advisor in that province, were also compiling a compendium of Autumn-Assizes regulations and cases.[59] Guangdong even enacted provincial regulations to set aside 300 taels of silver from the Autumn Assizes budget as extra stipends for the provincial judge's three legal advisors.[60]

In a letter in 1871 to his legal advisor Chen Jian, Zhili Governor General Li Hongzhang (1823–1901) shows us how the Autumn Assizes were handled in his office then. Having noted that he was busy with other matters in Tianjin, Li continued: "Any discrepancy in the Autumn Assizes might have serious consequences. It is a testimony to your care and ability that you have managed to affirm or reverse each of the cases ... I will be obliged if you continue to supervise [the subordinates] to ensure that all will be done properly and in

58 See Xu's preface in Xu Shenwang 许伸望, *Qiuyan zhi* 秋谳志 [*Records of the Autumn Assizes*] (Hui budushu zhai, 1880).

59 Lin was assisted by two persons and relied upon materials provided by Sichuan Provincial Judge Yingxiang 英祥. See Lin Enshou 林恩绶, Li Xian'gen 李仙根, and Wang Lantian 王蓝田, comps., *Qiushen shihuan bijiao cheng'an* 秋审实缓比较成案 [Leading Cases of the Autumn Assizes], 24 *juan* (Sichuan nieshu cangban, 1873). Sun Wenyao had been working for seventeen years at the Sichuan provincial judges' office. See prefaces by Sun Wenyao (1881) and Chonggang 崇纲 (1881), in Sun Wenyao 孙文耀 and Sun Guangxie 孙光燮, comps., *Qiushen shihuan bijiao cheng'an xubian* 秋审实缓比较成案续编 [A Sequel to *Leading Cases of the Autumn Assizes*]. It was collated (*jiaokan* 校勘) by Wu Wu'an 吴悟安, Lin Enshou 林恩绶, and Zhu Rong 朱溶, based on materials provided by Acting Sichuan Provincial Judge Chonggang. About Wu, see Zhou Xun 周询, *Shuhai congtan* 蜀海丛谈 [Miscellaneous Remarks about Sichuan] (Chengdu: Bashu chubanshe, 1986 [1948]), 171.

60 The three divisions (*gu*) were Guangzhou, Chaozhou, and Huizhou. See Huang Entong 黄恩彤, ed. *Yuedong shengli xinzuan* 粤东省例新纂 [New Compendium of Provincial Regulations of Guangdong], 8 *juan* (Guangdong: Fanshu cangban, 1846), 7: 33b. Sichuan also had three legal advisors to the provincial judges, responsible for the eastern, western, and adjudication division, respectively. There were also three advisors to the provincial treasurer. Zhou Xun, *Shuhai tongtan*, 170.

accordance with the law."[61] In other words, it was his legal advisor in Baoding (the seat of his office and that of the provincial judges) who handled the judicial review in his absence. During his combined tenure of twenty-three years in that post, Li relied heavily on another renowned legal advisor, Lou Chunfan (1850–1912), to handle his memorials and judicial work. Lou's judicial work even won praises from prominent jurists, including Ministers of Justice Ting Jie (?–1910) and Shen Jiaben (1840–1913).[62] These examples were corroborated by the published judgments of legal advisors like Zhou Shouchi and Meng Hushi on behalf of provincial officials in Anhui and Jiangxi, respectively, in the nineteenth century.[63]

It is little wonder, then, that the Qing rulers worried about the excessive influence of legal advisors on local judicial administration, especially regarding the Autumn Assizes. By the 1740s, one of the major complaints of the Qing emperors had been that the legal reports of capital cases tended to include stretched or fabricated mitigating circumstances for the offenders because the legal advisors who authored the reports were led by the "vulgar" idea of "saving the living rather than the dead" (*jiusheng bu jiusi*).[64] Thomas Buoye

61 See "Fu xingmu Chen Jian 复刑幕陈鉴 [Reply to Legal Advisor Chen Jian]," in Li Hongzhang 李鸿章, *Li Hongzhang quanji* 李鸿章全集 [A Complete Collection of Li Hongzhang's Work], ed. Dai Yi 戴逸 and Gu Yanlong 顾延龙 (Hefei: Anhui jiaoyu chubanshe, 2008), 30: 226 (TZ10/5/1). Chen Yunzhai was a legal advisor from Chengxian 塍县 of Shaoxing, and his grandson, Chen Chuqing, was an early Republican revolutionary who led an anti–Yuan Shikai revolution in 1913 in Shaoxing.

62 Lou was recruited by Li from the Rehe Circuit Intendant's office and remained to advise several Zhili governors general during the next thirty years. About him, see Shen Zuxian 沈祖宪 (Luo's old friend and Li's *muyou*), "Qingfeng ronglu dafu erpinxian baojian daoyuan loujun jiaosheng muzhiming 清封荣禄大夫二品衔保荐道员娄君椒生墓志铭 [Epitaph of Lou Jiaosheng]," at Shaoxing xian tushuguan 绍兴县图书馆.

63 Zhou Shouchi 周守赤, *Xinji Xing'an huibian* 新辑刑案汇编 [A New Compendium of Legal Cases], 16 *juan* (Shanghai: Tushu jicheng shuju, 1896); Meng Hushi 孟壶史, *Xing'an chengshi* 刑案成式 [Model Cases for Adjudication], 10 *juan* (Mochi shuwu, 1877). I study these records in detail in my larger project.

64 Gangyi, *Qiuyan jiyao, juan shou*: 15a–17a (1757), 47a–48a (1782), 77a (1806); Dong Jianzhong 董建中, ed., *Qianlong yupi* 乾隆御批 [Qianlong's Imperial Rescripts], 773 (1748), 775 (1764, blaming *mubin*). For general information about the Autumn Assizes, see Song Beiping 宋北平, *Qiushen tiaokuan jiqi yuyan yanjiu* 秋审条款及其语言研究 [Study of the Rules for the Autumn Assizes and Their Language] (Beijing: Falü chubanshe, 2011); Sun Jiahong 孙家红, *Qingdai de sixing jianhou* 清代的死刑监候 [Capital Punishment and Postponed Execution in the Qing] (Beijing: Shehui kexue chubanshe, 2007). For instance, seven Autumn Assizes cases from Jiangsu province (Zhuang Yougong as governor) were changed from postponed execution to execution by the nine central

has shown that Qing reports of homicide cases had become fairly standardized and uniform in their narrative style by this time, and that many homicide reports indeed reflected a desire to win sympathy for the offenders *at the time of sentencing* in the Autumn Assizes by including details of mitigating circumstances after the initial judgment had been made more strictly according to the law.[65] Consistent with the Chinese juridical tradition of urging compassion even when inflicting penalties, this practice might have significantly tempered the harsh side of Qing criminal justice, especially if those mitigating circumstances were not groundless. From the Qing rulers' viewpoint, however, what the local officials or their legal advisors did was highly problematic.

A few cases will illustrate this. On June 2, 1774, Anhui Governor Pei Zongxi reported that a Xu Youren in Suzhou district broke his father's hand in a scuffle when he *was drunk and frantically tried to stop his father's chase*, and that the father eventually died of the injury. Based on an imperial edict of 1761, Pei and his colleagues had the offender executed for parricide by slicing (*lingchi*) immediately after the provincial Autumn Assizes. The emperor agreed with the final sentence and ratified the immediate execution (*zhengfa*). However, some words in the legal report appeared to call for mitigation and reminded him of the popular tendency in such homicide reports. Where a man killed an older brother when trying to save their parent, the emperor reasoned, the former might deserve a reduction of the penalty in the Autumn Assizes because the older brother was punishable by death in the first place for attacking a parent. This was totally different from many other cases in which someone was killed by a younger brother in an affray but was represented in the legal report as the aggressor so as to permit a commuted sentence for the killer in the Autumn Assizes. For Qianlong, these farfetched excuses were provided by "wicked litigations masters and cunning yamen clerks" (*diao'e songshi huali*) for the "vulgar advisors" (*yongmu*) who were "influenced by the idea of collecting merits (or karma) for their afterlives" (*anji yingong*) by winning mercy for the capital offenders.[66] It is worth noting the emergence in the Qing imperial

---

government agencies (*jiuqin*). *Qianlongchao shangyudang*, 4: 313 (QL28/10/15). The Qing official perception that some jurists purposely bent on the lenient side (*yiwei congkuan*) even in cases with no doubt about the charged offence can be traced back at least to the Kangxi era (see *Shengzu renhuangdi shengxun, juan* 29: 9 (KX45/10/15 or Nov. 30, 1705), in *Siku quanshu*, 411: 489.

65 Thomas Buoye, "Suddenly Murderous Intent Arose: Bureaucratization and Benevolence in Eighteenth-Century Qing Homicide Reports," *Late Imperial China* 16, no. 2 (1995): 62–97, esp. 64–92.

66 For Qianlong's comments, see *Qing shilu*, 21: 983–84 (*Gaozong chunhuangdi shilu, juan* 958, QL39/5/6 or June 14, 1774). On Pei's memorial, Qianlong highlighted in vermillion

discourse of a trilogy or axis of evil, consisting of the habitual litigation hooligans, cunning clerks, and unethical legal advisors. What they had in common was their possession of specialized expertise or local experience, and their ability to manipulate local officials and the judicial system beyond the central government's effective scrutiny.

Just four months later, the emperor rebuked Jiangsu Governor Sazai for letting his legal advisor play the same trick of including similar mitigating language in the report of a parricide case in which a *drunken* Liu Bingruo killed his father in a scuffle with a knife.[67] Particularly worrisome to the Qing Court was the fact that even highly capable officials like Gansu Governor Bi Yuan or Jiangxi Governor Haicheng (who had worked for years at the Ministry of Justice) also fell prey to such an "absurd" practice of their "vulgar advisors."[68] Legal advisors, including Wan Weihan and Wang Huizu, strenuously denied this charge of distortion of the law or immoral judicial practice. Instead, they contended that they strove to follow their professional ethics or the Way of Muyou in enforcing the law and administering justice. In fact, Wang Youfu, a veteran legal advisor in the Qianlong-Jiaqing period, explicitly argued that to let a homicide offender escape the due penalty would win the judicial administrator not any divine blessing (*yinde*) but condemnation in the afterlife (*mingqian*), since the excessive leniency for the living (offender) at the expenses of the dead (victim) would leave the latter's wrongs unaddressed.[69]

Fortunately, we do have information about the legal advisors who presumably prepared or reviewed some of these legal reports criticized by Qianlong. Governor Pei reported in 1774 that the five senior provincial offices in Anhui hired ten legal advisors, including two for himself: Chen Zhanglun for *xingming* matters and Zhou Mengban for *qiangu* and *zhezou* (memorials). Anhui Provincial Judge Wang Xianxu was advised by Luo Yuanrui and Li Gui in legal

---

the following clauses: "因父无人服侍仍欲搬回 [Wanted to move back as nobody supported his father]," "情急回身 [turned around in desperation]," "酒醉昏迷 [drunk and unconscious]." See "Pei Zongxi zoubao shenli Suzhou min Xu Youren oushang fu Xu Jing zhisi an lingchi chusi lü zhengfa shi 裴宗锡奏报审理宿州民徐有仁殴伤父徐景至死按凌迟处死律正法事 [Report by Pei Zongxi about the Immediate Execution by Slicing of Xu Youren of Suzhou for Killing His Father by Injuries]," at *QGJJD*, No.403028785 (QL39/4/24 or June 2, 1774).

67 *Qing shilu*, 20: 1167–68 (*Gaozong chunhuangdi shilu, juan* 967, QL39/9). For the response of Sazai 萨载, see *QGJJD*, No.403030302 (QL39/10/16).

68 *Qing shilu*, 23: 163 (*Gaozong chunhuangdi shilu, juan* 1135, QL46/6/18 or Aug. 7, 1781, on Bi Yuan 毕沅); 20: 1220–21 (*Gaozong chunhuangdi shilu, juan* 969, QL39/10, on Haicheng 海成); 21: 214 (*Gaozong chunhuangdi shilu, juan* 990, QL40/9).

69 See Chen, "Legal Specialists," 30–31; Wang Youfu, *Yide outan* (*chuji*), 19b–20a.

matters. In the same year, Jiangsu Governor Sazai had two advisors: Yang Jingshui (for *xingming* matters) and Hu Lingyi. The Jiangsu provincial judge then had three legal advisors: Zhu Yiyuan, Wang Qisan, and Cai Jieshan. Among the eleven legal advisors for eight provincial officials in Jiangxi, Governor Haicheng had two, Wang Qian from Wanping county in Shuntian and Wu Yi from Guian county in Zhejiang, while the provincial judge's advisors consisted of Shen Zhaobang and Wang Jian, both from Shanyin county, Zhejiang.[70] Qianlong had access to such information in the annual reports, but he apparently resigned himself to the reality that he could exert little influence on those private legal specialists and do little other than castigate their host officials.

Aside from reiterating the lofty goal of doing justice to the victims, a perhaps equal, if not more important, consideration for the Qing rulers was to prevent the local officials (or, more accurately, their legal advisors) from undermining the throne as the supreme dispenser of justice in the empire. What mattered was not just whether justice or benevolence was served but also who got credit for doing so. If local judicial administrators could effectively determine whether a capital offender deserved to live or die, much of the authority and legitimacy of the imperial ruling house would be undermined. Even though the final outcome might be the same, it was the Ministry of Justice and then the emperor that should make the ultimate decision on the fate of those who had committed the most serious offences and thus challenged the fundamental law and order of the empire.[71] That was partly why the Qing emperors frequently emphasized that they attached the greatest importance and solemnity to the final review of the Autumn Assizes, when they would decide whether the name of each convicted capital offender should be checked (*goujue*) and thus the offender executed that year. As the emperors often had to review as many as 600 capital cases over six or seven days, they apparently could only glance through the short summaries prepared by the Ministry of Justice rather than the detailed legal reports (*zhaoce*) or the original trial records in most capital cases.[72] However superficial the imperial review might

70 *Qianlongchao junjichu lufu zouzhe*, No. 03-0141-055 (QL39/11/30, for advisors in Anhui), 03-0142-062 (QL39/12/04, on Sazai's advisors), and 03-0142-062 (QL39/12/04, for 17 advisors in the provincial offices of Jiangsu in 1774), 03-0142-007 (QL39/11/27, for advisors in Jiangxi).

71 See, e.g., the case of Huang Chaodai at *Qing shilu*, 18: 191–92 (*Gaozong chunhuangdi shilu, juan* 745, QL30/9/22 or Nov. 5, 1765).

72 For instance, for the Autumn Assizes convicts (excluding those for the *chaoshen* (Court Assizes) from the Beijing area), Qianlong reviewed 594 (and checked 529) convicts in 1765, reviewed 496 (and checked 486) in 1766, reviewed 542 (and checked 481) in 1767, and

appear to us, the fact that all capital sentences required the throne's (sometimes retrospective) sanction played a real and important juridical and political function at the time.

The Qing rulers wanted to have maximum control over the Autumn Assizes and retain their exclusive discretionary power to decide how and when judicial mercy should be granted. Throughout the Qing period, only an ad hoc body of imperial edicts, ministerial circulars, and precedential cases were circulated among a small circle of officials in Beijing and the provincial capitals to guide the Autumn Assizes. Legal advisors, including Wang Youfu, Xie Chengjun, and Xu Shenwang, tried to obtain and publish a copy of those internal guidelines to help themselves and other private legal professionals to better anticipate and prevent fault finding and reversal by the Ministry of Justice and the emperor.[73] Thus, the Autumn Assizes might be seen as the final stage of the negotiation between legal advisors and the central authorities in Beijing.

The Qing rulers claimed that their role was to perform their duty as the Son of Heaven to ensure that nothing but justice and fairness should guide their review of capital cases. What Qianlong stated in 1766 captured the desired message of many such imperial edicts throughout the Qing period:

> The Autumn Assizes were a solemn occasion for clarifying and enforcing the law. When reading the reports of conviction, I have always been extremely careful and striven for the best of impartial justice (*dazhong zhizheng*). If there remained any doubtful point about even just a commoner, I would thoroughly investigate it to ensure that no one was wrongfully punished or let free ... [When conducting the final review of the capital offenders] I am never influenced by any prejudgment.

---

reviewed 498 (and checked 424) convicts in 1768. This is culled from records for those years in *Qing Shilu*, 18: 165–1200 (*Gaozong chunhuangdi shilu, juan* 742–824, QL30/8–QL33/11).

73 See the relevant private publications cited earlier, and Wang Youfu 王有孚, "Qiushen zhizhang 秋审指掌 [A Guide to the Autumn Assizes] (1799p), in Wang Youfu, *Bu'aixuan dulü liuzhong* (1807). Cf. *Qiushen zongli* 秋审总例 [General Rules for the Autumn Assizes] (undated MS, covering 1735–79); *Qiushen zhenmi* 秋审枕秘 [Secret Tips for the Autumn Assizes], 5 *juan* (undated MS); Xue Yunsheng 薛允升(?), *Qiucao gaoshi* 秋曹稿式 [Models for Drafting Reports of the Autumn Assizes], 4 *juan* (1886p ms, and 1901p for another printed version); Lai Leshan 来乐山, *Qiushen suojianji* 秋审所见集 [*Works Seen about the Autumn Assizes*], 5 *juan*/*ce* (undated MS). Song Beiping 宋北平, ed., *Qiushen tiaokuan* 秋审条款 [Rules for the Autumn Assizes], in *Lidai zhenxi sifa wenxian* 历代珍稀司法文献 [Rare Judicial Materials from Various Dynasties], ed. Yang Yifan 杨一凡 and Guan Zhiguo 关志国 (Beijing: Shehui kexue wenxian chubanshe, 2012), vols. 13–15.

> Whether I settle on a heavier or lighter sentence is all determined by what the offenders themselves have done. Publicize this and let all the people understand it.[74]

It was essential for the emperor to convince his subjects that no matter what punishment he eventually meted out, he was guided by the spirit of pure impartiality and justice (*yibing dagong*), that even "His Majesty could not make the decision based on his own [sentiments]" (*zhen yi bude zizhu*), and that the offenders brought all the punishment upon themselves."[75] That claim to fully objective justice could not disguise the fact that the emperor alone had the final say in deciding whether the name of a convicted capital offender should be checked or left unchecked (repetition of the latter for a few years could lead to a commutation). He would not allow the local officials, let alone their private advisors, to usurp his role in performing that act of supreme sovereignty. Nonetheless, after the legal reports of the initial judgments and subsequent reviews were prepared or refined by legal advisors at different local levels of the judiciary, the Ministry of Justice and the emperor, relying on those reports, had to confirm them in the vast majority of the cases. They could only read between the lines of those reports to spot the most egregious inconsistencies or mistakes of law in a small number of cases in order to challenge the local decisions and claim their own expertise and authority.

Given the highly complex nature of the judicial system and their own overwhelming administrative duties, local officials in general did not have the time or expertise to challenge the authority or agendas of the Qing ruling house in judicial administration. The intervention of legal advisors as trained legal practitioners and de facto judicial administrators had the potential to undermine the power of the Qing Court when their judicial practice departed from the desired policy lines or undercut the image of the throne as the benevolent legitimate sovereign. This was the case even though the services of legal advisors also helped the Qing ruling house keep the local governments and the judicial system working. The (contested) belief that legal advisors or local officials distorted the law or facts for personal benefit (including the desire for either afterlife blessings or a benevolent reputation) simply fuelled the imperial distrust in them. Given their indispensable services in local governments, however, the Qing Court never developed effective methods of maximizing

---

74 *Qing shilu*, 18: 445 (*Gaozong chunhuangdi shilu, juan* 769, QL31/9/26 or Oct. 29, 1766), also included in Gangyi, *Qiuyan jiyao, juan shou*: 25b.

75 *Qing shilu*, 18: 746 (*Gaozong chunhuangdi shilu, juan* 796, QL32/10/2 or Nov. 10, 1767); also in Gangyi, *Qiuyan jiyao, juan shou*: 27b–28a.

their knowledge while minimizing their potential harm. The official Qing discourse and policies thus wavered uneasily between implicit recognition and deep distrust of these late imperial Chinese legal practitioners. The unsuccessful imperial regulatory attempts and the complaints about legal advisors' excessive influence or abuses of power throughout the eighteenth and nineteenth centuries testified to both their importance for Qing judicial administration and local governance and the possible limits of the Qing rulers' actual control over those domains.

Glossary

angao tiexie	案稿贴写
anji yingong	暗积阴功
antong shengqi wuwen wanfa	暗通声气舞文枉法
bu'an lüli	不谙律例
bushi wenyi	不识文义
buzhengshi	布政使
dazhong zhizheng	大中至正
dibao	地保
diao'e songshi huali	刁恶讼师猾吏
duan buke sheng	断不可省
emu	恶幕
esongshi	恶讼师
Fajia xinshu	《法家新书》
goujue	勾决
guanxian	官衔
huanjue	缓决
jiguan songgun	积惯讼棍
jingji	经纪
Jingtian lei	《惊天雷》
jing xingming zhiyan	精刑名之言
jinyi	矜疑
jiusheng bu jiusi	救生不救死
jüwen	具文
kejin	可矜
langzhong	郎中
lejian	勒荐
liangmu	良幕
liemu	劣幕
libu	吏部
lingchi	凌迟
lüejie	略节
lüli	律例
mingqian	冥谴
mubin	幕宾
mucai pohao	幕才颇好
mudao	幕道
muke	幕客
neihao	内号
qingzhen/qingshi	情真/情实
qiushen	秋审
qiuyan dadian	秋谳大典
renming youguan	人命攸关
shenxing aimin	慎刑爱民
shili	事例
shixue	实学
shusuan	书算
songshi	讼师
qiangu	钱谷
weibi liaoran	未必了然
wenyi gaoshi	文移告示
Xiang jiao	《相角》
xingming	刑名
Xingtai qinjing	《刑台秦镜》
yajian	压荐
yanglian	养廉

yanmi guanfang	严密关防	*zhaoce*	招册
yibing dagong	一秉大公	*zhengfa*	正法
yizi quce	以资驱策	*zhen yi bude zizhu*	朕亦不得自主
yongmu	庸幕	*zhushi*	主使
yougan tianhe	有干天和	*zuoza*	佐杂
yuci	狱词		

Bibliography

Bai Ruzhen. *Xingming yide* 刑名一得 [Things Learned from Legal Practice]. 2 *juan*. Kunming: Diannan nieshu cangban, 1784p.

Bao Yongjun 鲍永军. *Shaoxing shiye Wang Huizhu yanjiu* 绍兴师爷汪辉祖研究 [A Study of Shaoxing Private Advisor Wang Huizhu]. Beijing: Renmin chubanshe, 2006.

Buoye, Thomas. "Suddenly Murderous Intent Arose: Bureaucratization and Benevolence in Eighteenth-Century Qing Homicide Reports." *Late Imperial China* 16, no. 2 (1995): 62–97.

Ch'en, Fu-mei Chang. "The Influence of Shen Chih-ch'i's *Chi-chu* Commentary upon Ch'ing Judicial Decisions." In *Essays on China's Legal Tradition*, edited by Jerome Alan Cohen, R. Randle Edwards, and Fu-mei Chang Ch'en, 170–221. Princeton: Princeton University Press, 1980.

Chen, Li. "Legal Specialists and Judicial Administration in Late Imperial China, 1651–1911." *Late Imperial China* 33, no. 1 (2012): 1–54.

———. "Zhishi de liliang: Qingdai muyou miben he gongkai chuban de lüxue zhuzuo dui qingdai sifa changyu de yingxiang 知识的力量：清代幕友秘本和公开出版的律学著作对清代司法场域的影响 [Power of Knowledge: The Role of Secret and Published Treatises of Private Legal Specialists in the Qing Juridical Field]." *Zhejiang daxue xuebao* 浙江大学学报 [Journal of Zhejiang University] 45, no. 1 (Jan. 2015), forthcoming.

Chen Wenguang 陈文光. *Bu Weixinbian* 补未信编 [Supplement to *An Unreliable Treatise*]. 4 *juan*. Sanduozhai cangban, 1707p.

Chiu Pengsheng [i.e., Qiu Pengsheng] 邱澎生. *Dang falü yushang jingji: Ming Qing Zhongguo de shangye falü* 当法律遇上经济: 明清中国的商业法律 [When Law Meets Economy: Business and Law in Ming and Qing China]. Taibei: Wunan tushu chuban gongsi, 2005.

Daoguangchao junjichu lufu zouzhe 道光朝军机处录副奏折 [Copies of Memorials of the Daoguang Reign at the Grand Council]. See *Junjichu lufu zouzhe*.

Davis, Natalie Z. *Fiction in the Archives: Pardon Tales and Their Tellers in Sixteenth-Century France*. Stanford: Stanford University Press, 1987.

Dong Jianzhong 董建中, ed. *Qianlong yupi* 乾隆御批 [Qianlong's Imperial Rescripts]. Beijing: Zhongguo huaqiao chubanshe, 2001.

Donghua lu 东华录 [Records from the Donghua Gate]. In Xuxiu siku quanshu [Supplement to the Library of the Four Treasurers], edited by *Xuxiu Siku quanshu* bianzhuan weiyuanhui, Vol. 369. Shanghai: Shanghai guji chubanshe, 2002.

Feng Chen 冯辰 et al., eds. *Li Shugu xiansheng nianpu* 李恕谷先生年谱 [A Chronological Biography of Mr. Li Gong]. 1836 [1714p].

Fuma, Susumu. "Litigation Masters and the Litigation Systems of Ming and Qing China." *International Journal of Asian Studies* 27, no. 1 (2007 [1993]): 79–111.

Gangyi. *Qiuyan jiyao* 秋谳辑要 [Essentials on the Autumn Assizes]. 1 (*juan shou*) + 6 *juan*. Jiangshu shuju, 1889 (also reprinted in 1884, 1886).

Gao Huanyue 高浣月. *Qingdai xingming muyou yanjiu* 清代刑名幕友研究 [Study of Qing Legal Advisors]. Beijing: Zhongguo zhengfa daxue chubanshe, 2000.

Gatrell, Vic A.C. *The Hanging Tree: Execution and the English People 1770–1868*. Oxford: Oxford University Press, 1994.

Hong Hongxu 洪弘绪, ed. *Cheng'an zhiyi* 成案质疑 [On Doubtful Issues in Leading Cases]. 31 *juan*. Hangzhou: Sanyutang (Benya cangban), 1746.

Huang Entong 黄恩彤, ed. *Yuedong shengli xinzuan* 粤东省例新纂 [New Compendium of Provincial Regulations of Guangdong]. 8 *juan*. Guangdong: Fanshu cangban, 1846.

Huang Liuhong. "Fuhui quanshu 福慧全书 [The Complete Book Concerning Happiness and Benevolence]. 32 *juan*. 1694p. In *Guanzhenshu jicheng*, 3: 22–591.

Huang, Philip C.C. *Civil Justice in China: Representation and Practice in the Qing*. Stanford: Stanford University Press, 1996.

Jiaqing dang'an 嘉庆档案 [Archives of the Autumn Assizes in the Jiaqing Reign]. 10 *ce*. Undated MS (covering 1796–1812).

Junjichu lufu zouzhe 军机处录副奏折 [Copies of Memorials at the Grand Council]. Archives in Beijing: Zhongguo diyi lishi dang'anguan.

Kesselring, Krista J. *Mercy and Authority in the Tudor State*. New York: Cambridge University Press, 2003.

Kuhn, Philip A. *Soulstealers: The Chinese Sorcery Scare of 1768*. Cambridge: Harvard University Press, 1990.

Lai Leshan 来乐山, comp. *Qiushen suojianji* 秋审所见集 [*Works Seen about the Autumn Assizes*], 5 *juan*/*ce*. Undated MS.

Li Hongzhang 李鸿章. *Li Hongzhang quanji* 李鸿章全集 [Complete Collection of Writings of Li Hongzhang]. Edited by Dai Yi 戴逸 and Gu Yanlong 顾延龙. 39 vols. Hefei: Anhui jiaoyu chubanshe, 2008.

Lin Enshou 林恩绶, Li Xian'gen 李仙根, and Wang Lantian 王蓝田, comps. *Qiushen shihuan bijiao cheng'an* 秋审实缓比较成案 [Leading Cases of the Autumn

Assizes], 24 *juan*. Sichuan nieshu cangban, 1873. Partly based on materials provided by Yingxiang 英祥, who was often listed as the author/compiler of this title.

Macauley, Melissa. *Social Power and Legal Culture: Litigation Masters in Late Imperial China*. Stanford: Stanford University Press, 1998.

Meng Hushi 孟壶史. *Xing'an chengshi* 刑案成式 [Model Cases for Adjudication]. 10 *juan*. Mochi shuwu, 1877.

Neige daku dang'an 内阁大库档案 [Archives of the Grand Secretariat]. Archives in Taibei: Academia Sinica.

Pan Biaocan 潘杓灿. *Weixin bian* 未信编 [An Unreliable Treatise]. 6 *juan*. 1704 [1684].

Qin Guojing 秦国经, Tang Yinian 唐益年, and Ye Yunxiu 叶云秀, comps. *Qingdai guanyuan lüli dang'an quanbian* 清代官员履历档案全编 [A Complete Collection of Qing Officials' Resumes]. 30 *ce*. Shanghai: Huadong shifan daxue chubanshe, 1997.

Qian Shifu 钱实甫, ed. *Qingdai zhiguan nianbiao* 清代职官年表 [Chronological Charts of Qing Officials]. 4 *ce*. Zhonghua shuju, 1980.

Qianlong dang'an 乾隆档案 [Archives of the Autumn Assizes in the Qianlong Reign]. 12 *ce*. Undated MS (covering 1735–95).

Qianlongchao junjichu lufu zouzhe 乾隆朝军机处录副奏折 [Copies of Memorials of the Qianlong Reign at the Grand Council]. See *Junjichu lufu zouzhe*.

Qing guoshiguan zhuangao 清国史馆传稿 [Draft Biographies of the Qing Historiography Institute]. Archives in Taibei: National Palace Museum.

Qing huidian shili 清会典事例 [Collected Regulations of the Qing Dynasty]. 12 vols. Beijing: Zhonghua shuju, 1991.

Qing shilu 清实录 [Veritable Records of the Qing Dynasty]. Beijing: Zhonghua shuju, 1985.

Qingdai gongzhongdang ji junjichu dangzhejian 清代宫中档及军机处档折件 [Qing Palace Memorials and Grand Council's Memorials]. Archives in Taibei: Gugong bowuyuan. Cited as *QGJJD*.

Qiushen zhenmi 秋审枕秘 [Secret Tips on the Autumn Assizes]. 5 *juan*. Undated MS.

Qiushen zongli 秋审总例 [General Rules for the Autumn Assizes]. Undated MS (covering 1735–79).

Shen Jiaben 沈家本. *Shen Jiaben weikan'gao qizhong* 沈家本未刊稿七种 [Seven Unpublished Works of Shen Jiaben]. In *Zhongguo zhenxi falü dianji jicheng* (bingbian, disance) 中国珍稀法律典籍集成(丙编第三册) [Compendium of Rare Chinese Law Books], Series 3, Vol. 3, edited by Liu Hainian 刘海年 and Yang Yifan 杨一凡. Beijing: Kexue chubanshe, 1992.

———. *Qiushen tiaokuan fu'an* 秋审条款附案 [Rules for the Autumn Assizes with Comments]. 4 *juan*. Xiuding falüguan, 1906.

Shen Zhiqi 沈之奇, and Hongxu Hong 洪弘绪. *Da Qing lü jizhu* 大清律辑注 [The Great Qing Code with Collected Commentaries]. 30 *juan*. Wulin [Hangzhou]: Sanyutang, 1755 [1715].

Shen Zuxian 沈祖宪. "Qingfeng ronglu dafu erpinxian baojian daoyuan loujun jiaosheng muzhiming 清封荣禄大夫二品衔保荐道员娄君椒生墓志铭 [Epitaph of Lou Jiaosheng]." At the Shaoxing xian tushuguan 绍兴县图书馆.

Shengzu renhuangdi shengxun 圣祖仁皇帝圣训 [Sacred Instructions of the Kangxi Emperor]. See *Siku quanshu*.

Shizong xianhuangdi zhupi yuzhi 世宗宪皇帝朱批谕旨 [Emperor Yongzheng's Imperial Edicts with Rescripts]. See *Siku quanshu*.

Siku quanshu 四库全书 [The Complete Library of Four Treasures]. 1772–83. Taibei: Shangwu yinshuguan, 1986 (reprint). 1500 *ce*.

Song Beiping 宋北平, ed. *Qiushen tiaokuan* 秋审条款 [Rules for the Autumn Assizes]. In *Lidai zhenxi sifa wenxian* 历代珍稀司法文献 [Rare Judicial Materials from Various Dynasties], vols. 13–15, edited by Yang Yifan 杨一凡 and Guan Zhiguo 关志国. Beijing: Shehui kexue wenxian chubanshe, 2012.

———. *Qiushen tiaokuan jiqi yuyan yanjiu* 秋审条款及其语言研究 [Study of the Rules for the Autumn Assizes and Their Language]. Beijing: Falü chubanshe, 2011.

———. "Qiushen zhidu tiaokuan yanjiu 秋审制度条款研究 [Study of the Rules of the Autumn Assizes System." PhD dissertation, Zhongguo zhengfa daxue, 2004.

Strange, Carolyn, ed. *Qualities of Mercy: Justice, Punishment, and Discretion*. Vancouver: University of British Columbia Press, 1996.

Sun Hong 孙宏. *Weizheng diyibian* 为政第一编 [Manuals for Governance, Part 1], 8 *juan*. Benfu cangban, 1702p.

Sun Jiahong 孙家红. *Qingdai de sixing jianhou* 清代的死刑监候 [Capital Punishment and Postponed Execution in the Qing]. Beijing: Shehui kexue chubanshe, 2007.

Sun Lun 孙纶. *Dingli cheng'an hejuan* 定例成案合镌 [A Collection of Regulations and Leading Cases], 30 *juan*. Wujiang: Lejingtang cangban, 1721 [1707p].

Sun Wenyao 孙文耀, and Sun Guangxie 孙光燮, comps. *Qiushen shihuan bijiao cheng'an xubian* 秋审实缓比较成案续编 [A Sequel to *Leading Cases of the Autumn Assizes*]. 24 *juan*. Sichuan nieshu cangban, 1881. Collated (*jiaokan* 校勘) by Wu Wu'an 吴悟安, Lin Enshou 林恩绶, and Zhu Rong 朱溶, based on materials provided by Acting Sichuan Provincial Judge Chonggang.

Tanii Yoko 谷井阳子. "Qingdai zeli shengli kao 清代则例省例考 [Study of Qing Ministerial and Provincial Regulations]." In *Zhongguo fazhishi kaozheng* (*bingbian disijuan*) 中国法制史考证(丙编第四卷) [Evidentiary Study of Chinese Legal History, Series 3, Vol. 4], edited by Terada Hiroaki 寺田浩明, 120–214. Beijing: Zhongguo shehui kexue chubanshe, 2003.

Wang Huizu 汪辉祖. “Bingta mengheng lu 病榻梦痕录 [Trace of Tears in the Dream at a Sickbed].” 1796p. In *Wang Longzhuang xiansheng yishu* 汪龙庄先生遗书 [Works Bequeathed by Wang Huizu]. Shandong shuju, 1886.

Wang Youfu 王有孚. “Qiushen zhizhang 秋审指掌 [A Guide to the Autumn Assizes].” 1799p. In Wang Youfu 王有孚, *Bu'aixuan dulü liuzhong* 不碍轩读律六种 [Six Works for Legal Study from the Bu'ai Pagoda], 1807.

———. *Yide outan* 一得偶谈 [Casual Talk on Small Points]. 2 *ji* (*chuji* 初集+*erji* 二集). 1804p. Printed together with *Bu'aixuan dulü liuzhong*.

Wei Jirui 魏际瑞. *Sicitang gao* 四此堂稿 [Drafts from the Sici Hall]. 10 *juan*. 1863 [1675].

Wenyuange Siku quanshu 文渊阁四库全书 [The Complete Library of Four Treasures at the Wenyuan Pavilion]. See *Siku quanshu*.

Wu Kun 吴坤. *Xingyou liangfang shize* 刑友良方十则 [Ten Good Suggestions for Legal Advisors]. 1850p.

Xie Chengjun 谢诚钧. *Qiushen bijiao shihuan tiaokuan* 秋审比较实缓条款 [Rules for Confirming or Postponing Execution in the Autumn Assizes]. 2 *ce*. Jiangsu shuju, 1878.

Xu Shenwang 许伸望. *Qiuyan zhi* 秋谳志 [*Records of the Autumn Assizes*]. 4 *juan* + *shou juan*. Hui budushu zhai, 1880.

Xu Xu 许旭. *Minzhong jilüe* 闽中纪略 [Brief Notes about Occurrences in Fujian]. 1675p. Edited by Taiwan yinhang jingji yanjiushi. Taibei: Taiwan yinhang, 1968.

Xue Yunsheng 薛允升. *Duli cunyi* (*chongkan ben*) 读例存疑(重刊本) [Doubtful Points While Reading the Substatutes], annotated by Huang Jingjia 黄静嘉. Taibei: Chengwen chubanshe, 1970.

———. *Qiucao gaoshi* 秋曹稿式 [Models for Drafting Reports of the Autumn Assizes]. 4 *juan*. 1886p. MS (another printed version, 1901p).

Zelin, Madeleine. *The Magistrate's Tael: Rationalizing Fiscal Reform in Eighteenth-Century Ch'ing China*. Berkeley: University of California Press, 1984.

Zhang Guangyue 张光月. *Li'an quanji* 例案全集 [A Complete Collection of Legal Precedents]. 35 *juan*. Sijingtang, 1722p.

Zhang Shucai 张书才, ed. *Yongzheng chao hanwen zhupi zouzhe huibian* 雍正朝汉文朱批奏摺汇编 [Collection of Vermillion-Rescripted Chinese-Language Palace Memorials of the Yongzheng Reign]. 40 vols. Nanjing: Jiangsu guji chubanshe, 1989.

Zhou Shouchi 周守赤. *Xinji xing'an huibian* 新辑刑案汇编 [A New Compendium of Legal Cases]. 16 *juan*. Shanghai: Tushu jicheng ju, 1897.

Zhou Xun 周询. *Shuhai congtan* 蜀海丛谈 [Miscellaneous Remarks about Sichuan]. Chengdu: Bashu chubanshe, 1986 [1948].

CHAPTER 10

Court Case Ballads: Popular Ideals of Justice in Late Qing and Republican China

Margaret B. Wan

Drum ballad texts (*guci*) evoke one of the most popular of performance genres, the drum ballad, in north China in the late Qing and Republican period (1800–1937). These texts not only drew on oral literature but also served as vehicles for the dissemination of popular stories throughout north China. Many drum ballad texts recount stories of incorruptible judges who help the powerless gain justice. Drum ballads reached audiences ranging from the nobility to men and women of low social status. Study of this body of narratives opens up new perspectives on Chinese culture by examining the attitudes toward justice in these widely-read texts.

Precisely because they are a kind of popular literature, drum ballads provide an interesting complement to historians' usual sources for the study of Chinese legal culture. Studies of legal history have revealed much about non-elite practices in the Qing. By mining case records, scholars like Matthew Sommer and Thomas Buoye observed striking differences between prescription and practice among lower socio-economic groups.[1] Still, these case records were written by officials for officials, and thus reflect their interpretation. Drum ballads have received little scholarly attention but provide another perspective, because the ballads' ties to the oral tradition and easy-to-read rhymed format meant they could be read by less educated audiences.[2]

The legend of a wise judge inspired by the historical official Liu Yong (1719–1805) provides fertile ground to explore ideals of justice in popular culture. Drum ballads on Judge Liu[3] generated at least nineteen woodblock editions in

1 Thomas Buoye, *Manslaughter, Markets, and Moral Economy* (Cambridge: Cambridge University Press, 2000); Matthew Sommer, *Sex, Law and Society in Late Imperial China* (Stanford: Stanford University Press, 2000).

2 Margaret Wan, "Audiences and Reading Practices for Qing Dynasty Drum Ballad Texts," in *The Interplay of the Oral and the Written in Chinese Popular Literature*, Vibeke Børdahl and Margaret Wan (Copenhagen: Nordic Institute of Asian Studies Press, 2010), 41–60.

3 The legends of Liu Yong frequently refer to him as "Liu Gong." I am translating the informal title "Liu Gong" as Judge Liu because it evokes a longstanding tradition of "wise judge" stories, among which the legend of Judge Bao (Bao Gong) is the most famous. Historically, the

© KONINKLIJKE BRILL NV, LEIDEN, 2015 | DOI 10.1163/9789004288492_012

the mid- to late Qing, and twenty lithographic editions from 1908–1931. These court case stories are little studied, but were hugely popular in their day. They allow us to look at the 'same' story across a range of forms within North China.

Drum ballads on Judge Liu circulated in manuscript, woodblock, and eventually lithographic editions. While many of the texts are not dated, it is likely that the manuscript in the Chewangfu collection is the earliest, with internal evidence suggesting a date between 1797 and 1804.[4] Cases in the manuscript include murder, adultery, rape, property disputes, heterodox teachings, and rebellion. Most of the woodblock editions of drum ballads on Judge Liu are not dated, but internal evidence shows one text can be no earlier than Daoguang (1821), and another can be no earlier than Tongzhi (1862). Those that are dated are from 1881 and 1894. The corpus of woodblock and lithographic editions of the Judge Liu drum ballads consists almost entirely of a linked trilogy of case stories: *Bailing ji* (The Story of the White Silk Plaint), *Xuanfeng an* (The Case of the Whirlwind), and *Na Guotai* (Nabbing Guotai), also known as *Jinan fu* (The Prefecture of Jinan) or *Xia Jinan* (Going to Jinan).[5] *The Case of the Whirlwind*, which falls in the middle of the trilogy, is a case of murder and adultery. The other two stories center on a boy who takes his case to Beijing in a quest to avenge his father's death after a high-level official abuses power (*The Story of the White Silk Plaint*),[6] and Judge Liu's campaign to oust the abusive official

men these legends were based on were not "judges" but held more general administrative positions, such as prefect or magistrate. Still, the court case tradition of fiction and drama (*gongan*) emphasizes their role as judge.

4 This range of dates is suggested since the text refers to Liu Yong as being alive, and it refers to the Qianlong emperor as the former emperor (*taishang huangye*). See the preface to Yan Qi 燕琦, ed. *Liu Gong an: Chewangfu quben* 刘公案： 车王府曲本 [Cases of Judge Liu: The Songbook from the Chewangfu Collection] (Beijing: Renmin wenxue chubanshe, 1990): 1.

5 The drum ballad texts make extensive use of homophonic substitution, shorthand characters, and simplified characters. Where I suspect homophonic or orthographic substitution, I give the "correct" character in brackets.

6 In the ballad, the boy's father was a local elite, the richest man in Shandong and a Provincial Graduate (*juren*). However, wealth plays no role in the boy's quest, and he does not draw upon any particular networks of influence. Instead he goes alone to Beijing to have his case heard. Thus he seems to represent the ordinary man, and is even more vulnerable by virtue of being a child. While Nancy Park mentions that commoners could and did bring cases against officials, in the Qianlong era only three commoners brought charges against a Governor or Governor-General. Although two of those cases resulted in punishment of the official, in all three cases the commoner was punished. Nancy Park, "Corruption and Its Recompense: Bribes, Bureaucracy, and the Law in Late Imperial China," Ph.D. dissertation, Harvard University, 1993, 188–93. Capital appeals were frequent, but in reality a youth was not permitted to present a capital appeal. See Jonathan Ocko, "I'll Take It All the Way to

(*Nabbing Guotai*). They are loosely based on a case that sealed the reputation of the historical Liu Yong, when he was sent to investigate Guotai, the Governor of Shandong and a protégé of the notorious Heshen, in 1782 and "proved an incontestable case of corruption" against him.[7]

The Terminology of Justice

From the way the plots are constructed—a crime is exposed and the judge resolves it by punishing the wrongdoer—one could say that justice is a central concept in these court-case drum ballads. Intriguingly, there is no one term that clearly means "justice" in these stories.[8] Martial arts novels use the terms "justice" (*zhengyi*), but in the court case drum ballads the emphasis seems to be on the injustice (*yuan*). The solutions to injustice are varied: they involve Heavenly Principle (*tianli*), the King's Law (*wangfa*), retribution (*baoying*), truth (*zhen qingshi*), fairness (*gongdao*), and reason or common sense (*li*). The three major terms relating to Qing justice—*qing* (compassion or feeling), *li* (principle or reason), and *fa* (law)[9]—all appear in the ballads, but often lend themselves to different interpretations than in "orthodox" understandings of the law and morality.

Reason, Truth and Evidence

Overall the drum ballads present a fairly utilitarian morality. The most frequent critique in the drum ballads seems to be that acts are "unreasonable."[10] In the Chewangfu manuscript this critique is employed by plaintiffs bringing a case as well as by Judge Liu himself. Often it indicates a discrepancy in

---

Beijing: Capital Appeals in the Qing," *Journal of Asian Studies* 47, no. 2 (1988): 291–315. In the ballad Judge Liu brings the situation to the emperor's attention.

7 Arthur W. Hummel, *Eminent Chinese of the Ch'ing Period* (Taibei: Chengwen, 1972), 537. For more on the Guotai case and Heshen's influence, see David S. Nivison, "Ho-Shen and His Accusers: Ideology and Political Behavior in the Eighteenth Century," in *Confucianism in Action*, edited by David S. Nivison and Arthur F. Wright (Stanford: Stanford University Press, 1959), 209–43; and Nancy Park, "Corruption and Its Recompense," 278–85.

8 This line of inquiry was inspired by a question Robert Hegel posed at the Association of Asian Studies annual meeting in 2009.

9 For the terms *qing*, *li*, and *fa*, see Phillip Huang, *Civil Justice in China: Representation and Practice in the Qing* (Stanford: Stanford University Press, 1996), 12–13.

10 "Unreasonable" is *libutong*.

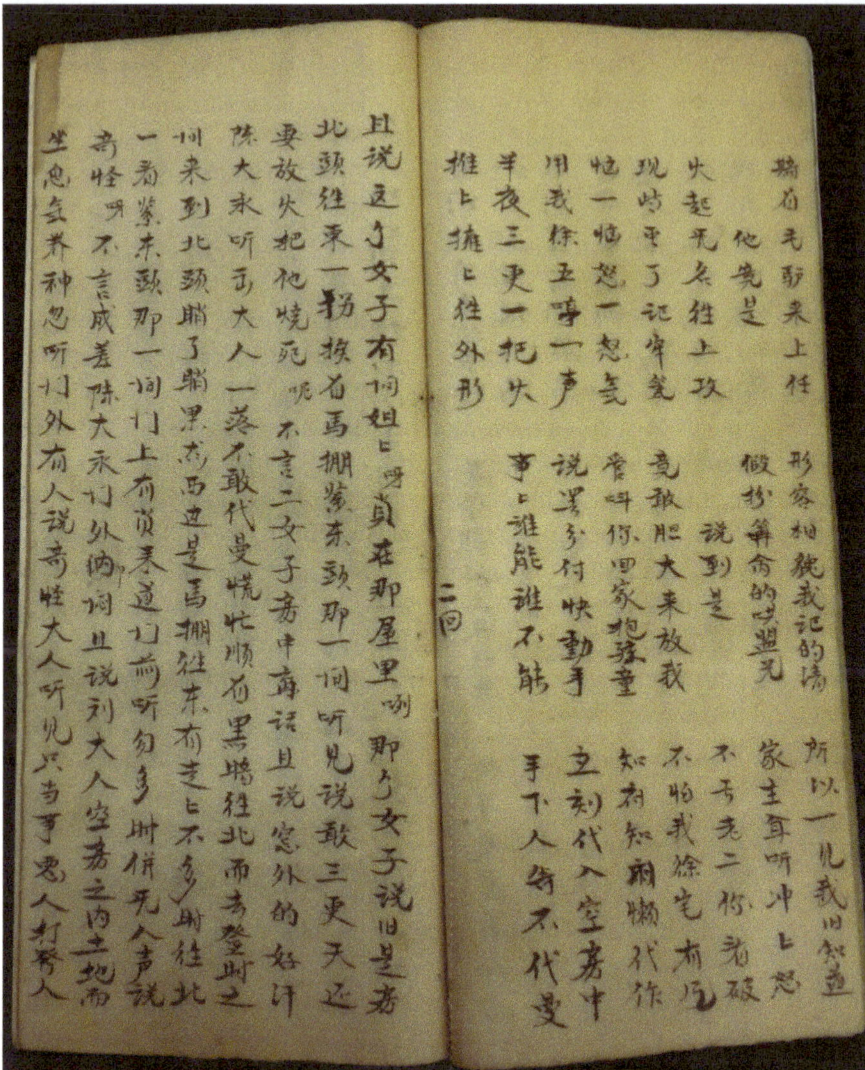

FIGURE 10.1 *The manuscript* Cases of Judge Liu *from the Chewangfu Collection (1797–1804?)*

FIGURE 10.2 *The woodblock print* Nabbing Guotai, *also known as* Going to Jinan (*Beijing: Jukui tang, 1862 or later*)

testimony that helps to expose the facts. In the woodblock ballad *Xuanfeng an*, reason also contrasts with emotion. During the escalation of tensions revolving around the as-yet-inconclusive examination of a corpse in a case of murder and adultery, both the accused and Judge Liu are seen as acting unreasonable. The bystanders note, "This is difficult for His Honor Old Liu. / The woman at the grave wouldn't recognize reason / at that, in court, he got angry."[11] Judge Liu's underling has to stop him from summarily executing the woman, saying, "If an official doesn't stick to reason, the people will become unmanageable and hard to deal with."[12] In some editions, Judge Liu's threat is part of a plan to expose the woman's lover, but in other editions it is presented at face value.

As in most Chinese court-case stories, the interest is not in "whodunit" but how the judge will prove the case and punish the culprits. Both the Chewangfu manuscript and the woodblock drum ballads on Judge Liu employ an omniscient narrator and dramatic irony—the reader knows more than Judge Liu does. In the drum ballads, the narrator makes it very clear to the reader who the culprit is through labels like "the criminal" or "the adulteress," but Judge Liu must find the evidence or get their confession in order to punish them. Even when the Judge knows or suspects something is morally wrong, he must be able to prove it. Legal judgment only extends as far as the evidence will support it. This sets up the basic tension driving the plot. As long as the judge cannot prove the crime, the law and morality are at odds. Once the evidence is obtained, the case can be solved, and law and morality harmonized.

The importance of evidence corresponds with the emphasis on "truth" in the ballads. In the woodblock *Xuanfeng an*, as soon as the Judge sees a whirlwind expose the adulteress, he says, "If I can get at the true situation through interrogation, I will certainly execute the woman."[13] Even exhuming the grave and

11 *Xuanfeng an* 旋风案 [The Case of the Whirlwind] (Tianjin, n.d.), 4.2: 7b.

12 "Doesn't stick to reason" is *bu lun li*. See *Xuanfeng an* [The Case of the Whirlwind] (Shandong, 1894), 2: 24a.

13 "The true situation" is *zhen qingshi*. *Xuanfeng an* (Tianjin), 2.1: 2b. The centrality of facts also figures prominently in the handbook *Xiyuan jilu* 洗冤集录 [*Washing Away of Wrongs*]: "Supposing an examination is held to get the facts, the clerks will sometimes accept bribes to alter the reports of the affair. If the officials and clerks suffer for their crimes, that is a minor matter. But, if the facts are altered, the judicial abuse may cost someone his life. Factual accuracy is supremely important." Brian E. McKnight, trans., *The Washing Away of Wrongs* (Ann Arbor: Center for Chinese Studies, University of Michigan, 1981), 72. For the same passage in the 1843 edition of *Xiyuan jilu*, see Herbert Giles, "The 'Hsi Yuan Lu' or 'Instructions to Coroners,'" *Proceedings of the Royal Society of Medicine* 27 (1924): 87.

FIGURE 10.3 *The whirlwind exposing the adulteress at the graveside, in the only illustration in a woodblock edition of* The Case of the Whirlwind (*Tianjin: Dehetang, n.d.*)

examining the corpse[14] fail to uncover any signs of wrongdoing, however, and Judge Liu becomes upset. His servant advises Judge Liu to go undercover:

> Once you go outside and visit [the dead husband Pu] Xian,
> if Pu Xian did die a wrongful death,
> the crowd will certainly talk wildly.
> Once Your Honor has found the truth (*zhen qingshi*)
> the people will say we're upright officials.[15]

This passage links the facts, public opinion, and the need to go to the scene of the crime to investigate.[16]

Going undercover is a recurring trope in the drum ballads. The assumption behind going undercover is that people in the community know what really happened. This makes sense in terms of Qing society. Robert Hegel notes: "As Buoye suggests, most major criminal cases involved people who knew one another: family members, neighbors, partners in small businesses. Thus, the details of most crimes were familiar to neighbors, who sometimes knew about dangerous situations long before violence resulted.... Consequently, the culprits' identity was seldom at issue."[17]

In the drum ballads, Judge Liu must find the evidence or get their confession in order to punish the criminals. In nearly every case, this means travelling to the scene of the crime to look for facts. Many of the central scenes are scenes of confrontation, with incriminating evidence or witnesses testifying

---

14 To the extent that it is described, the procedure followed in the both the Chewangfu manuscript *Liu Gong an* and the woodblock *Xuanfeng an* for the inquest is consonant with that prescribed by Qing law and the forensic handbook *The Washing Away of Wrongs*. See Daniel Asen, "Dead Bodies and Forensic Science: Cultures of Expertise in China, 1800–1949," Ph.D. dissertation, Columbia University, 2012, at 39–53; and McKnight, trans., *The Washing Away of Wrongs*, 76–94. Cf. Giles, "The 'Hsi Yuan Lu,'" 65, 67. See also Daniel Asen's paper in this volume.

15 *Xuanfeng an* (Tianjin, n.d.), 4.2: 7a.

16 A similar concern with public opinion is clear in Janet Theiss' paper in this volume, "Elite Engagement with the Legal System in the Qing." Officials worry what people will think, and the public in their accounts is concerned with the fairness of judicial proceedings. When the official gets the verdict wrong, public sentiment is angry.

17 Robert Hegel, "Introduction: Writing and Law" in *Writing and Law in Late Imperial China: Crime, Conflict, and Judgment*, ed. Robert Hegel and Katherine Carlitz (Seattle: University of Washington Press, 2007), 16. See Thomas Buoye, "Suddenly Murderous Intent Arose: Bureaucratization and Benevolence in Eighteenth-Century Homicide Reports," *Late Imperial China* 16, no. 2 (1995): 62–97.

against the accused in what can sometimes seem like a psychological game—what will finally convince them to confess? Asen's account of one Republican inquest shows a similar dynamic, in which public opinion was employed to make a killer confess, and the same may have been at work in "Ma Xiwu's adjudication method" as discussed by Cong Xiaoping.[18] The ballads' emphasis on on-site investigation and considering public opinion was still evident in how Ma Xiwu, a model judge in the early Communist era, handled cases, as Cong demonstrates.[19]

Law and Social Justice

In his study of law in rural North China, Philip Huang finds that the law (*guofa*) entered little into the actual resolution of many less serious cases, which generally were crimes of petty theft resolved through mediation.[20] In contrast, the vast majority of the stories in the drum ballads about Judge Liu are about major criminal cases, and in them the law (*wangfa*) seems to be the main weapon against abuses of power.

How is the law invoked in the drum ballads, and by whom? In the Chewangfu manuscript *Liu Gong an* (Cases of Judge Liu), the law is invoked with some frequency by characters ranging from local elites to the destitute, not to mention Judge Liu himself. Sometimes it is used in a self-serving manner. Thus a Provincial Graduate who murdered his brother says to Judge Liu, "Look in the Qing legal code, are graves to be exhumed lightly?"[21] Judge Liu eventually retorts, "You're relying on the fact that you're a Provincial Graduate… How

18 Asen, "Old Forensics in Practice," 30; Cong, "Ma Xiwu's Way of Judging," 33.

19 Ma Xiwu eschewed written plaints in favor of "a thorough on-site investigation." Cong notes the most important aspect of the investigation was collecting the views of the masses and examining community opinions regarding the case. See Cong Xiaoping, "Ma Xiwu's Way of Judging," presented at the International Workshop on Chinese Legal History, Culture and Modernity at Columbia University on May 4–6, 2012. In the case Bryna Goodman discusses in this volume, the evidence was on the defendant's side, but public opinion was against him, and he was found guilty.

20 Huang notes that most crimes in the villages were petty theft, and murder was unheard of. Thus "the criminal justice system figured relatively little in the lives of villages. Most village 'crimes' were dealt with informally by the community itself, without involving outside authorities. When peasants did come in contact with the formal legal system, it was more often with its civil rather than its criminal arm." Huang, *Civil Justice in China*, 46. The ballads use the term *wangfa* more frequently than *guofa*.

21 The term used here for Qing legal code is *Da Qing lü. Liu Gong an: Chewangfu quben*, 132.

can you not know a prince who breaks the law bears the same punishment as a commoner!"[22] When the Provincial Graduate tries to dismiss the plaint against him as slander motivated by greed, the impoverished plaintiff protests:

> Bright Heaven and Earth are governed by the king's laws (*wangfa*),
> I'd never dare to be stupid or wild.
> Don't listen to Wu Ren's empty trap
> relying on his clever tongue.[23]

Even the poor invoke the law when bringing a plaint.

Even though the law can be invoked by anyone, effectively knowing the law is often related to education. The drum ballad tells of a merchant, Zhao, who is a good man but becomes implicated in a murder case when someone plants a severed head in his yard. The narrator notes that Zhao could recognize characters but could not really read; he was a businessman, so how could he know the law?[24] Lack of education and consequent lack of knowledge of the law causes costly lapses in a person's judgment. Afraid of being involved in a lawsuit, Zhao goes along with his worker's plan to move and bury the head. When the case is solved, Zhao is punished because he buried the head instead of reporting it.

Yamen runners are portrayed as having greater understanding of the law, including the consequences of particular crimes. Thus, when the local official's son wants to marry Yamen Runner Duan's beautiful daughter, the yamen runner is disgusted. He says:

> Young Master, you really don't understand reason! Your father is an imperial officer of the third rank, how can Young Master fool around like this? Won't it make people laugh at you? My daughter is engaged, but even if she weren't, an official over a local area can't marry a girl from a commoner family. If you really don't understand the Great Qing law code, in the end your father's career will be wrecked by a bad son like you![25]

22 *Liu Gong an: Chewangfu quben*, 138. Officials actually were treated differently under the law.

23 *Liu Gong an: Chewangfu quben*, 131.

24 "The law" here is *lüli*. *Liu Gong an: Chewangfu quben*, 236–237. Zhao was afraid of what a lawsuit would cost. He said to his worker: "When the official asks me about this, how will it ever be straightened out? I'm just afraid that although I'm in the right the wrong circumstances will make the false true (*lizheng qingqu jia zuozhen*). If they torture me, I'll confess to something I didn't do and be a headless wronged ghost."

25 "Reason" here is *daoli*; "the Great Qing law code" is *Da Qing guo lü*. *Liu Gong an: Chewangfu quben*, 452.

Duan refuses the proposal, and the official's son has Duan framed and thrown in prison. Duan's friends are outraged; they raid the yamen, kill the official and his family, and break Duan out of jail. Duan, being a yamen runner, is fully aware of the consequences. He says: "Brothers, although you've rescued me, this is no small catastrophe! For a yamen runner to kill an official is a huge treason, the whole family should be executed and the ancestral graves leveled."[26] This incident is the beginning of a White Lotus rebellion in the Chewangfu manuscript *Cases of Judge Liu*.

So in the ballads the problem is that, even among officials, the law is not being followed. The law itself is good, but its implementation is a problem. The woodblock drum ballad *Nabbing Guotai* clearly recognizes the agency of officialdom in how the law is implemented. "All under Heaven is decided by the ruler,/ half is up to him and half up to his officials."[27] The well-connected and powerful Guotai has no respect for the law[28] and he even wrecks the law.[29] He is far from alone in this. At one point, *Nabbing Guotai* goes so far as to say, "The Great Qing Law Code was dead / because all the officials were greedy."[30]

This brings us to the other major issue raised by the drum ballads: social justice. The woodblock printed drum ballad *The Story of the White Silk Plaint* presents a moving picture of suffering under corruption. In this ballad Guotai, the Governor of Shandong, reports a good harvest despite three consecutive years of famine, and presses the people for taxes.

> For three years running Shandong had poor harvests
> Families great and small were impoverished.
> The price of wheat rose to eight and a half strings of cash,
> Sorghum was over six strings of cash.
> ....
> River weeds were put on scales to weigh [and sell].
> First-rate families sold donkeys and horses,
> second-rate families sold fields.
> Third-rate families had nothing to sell,
> they took their sons and daughters by the hand in the streets,

---

26 Ibid., 465.

27 "*Tianxia zong ze jun you zhu / ban you Tianzi ban you chen*," at *Xia Jinan* 下济南 [Going to Jinan] aka *Na Guotai* 拿国泰 [Nabbing Guotai] (Beijing: Jukuitang, n.d.), 2: 3b.

28 "*Lütiao wangfa quan bu zun*," at Ibid., 1: 5b.

29 "*Chengshang lütiao ta quan huai*," at Ibid., 3: 9b.

30 "*Da Qing fadu lüli si / jie yin guanyuan dou tancang*," at *Jinan fu* 济南府 [The Prefecture of Jinan] (Shandong, 1894), 3: 8a.

Leading by the hand they walked the street with their sons and daughters.
(Spoken:) Gentlemen, why did they take their children by the hand and go to the streets? Since Shandong had had three years of famine, there was a market for people in Jinan Prefecture.
(Sung:) They waited for those going south to buy a life.
A girl of seventeen or eighteen was only worth two strings of cash,
a newly married daughter-in-law only one string of cash.
No one wanted a forty year old;
one in her early thirties had to bring money with her.
If a twenty-something widow wanted to find a husband,
she had to give the rascal two pieces of flatbread.
Three years of famine in Shandong.
You see, isn't that a bitter situation?[31]

The difference between the elevated price of staple grains and the cheapness of human life drives home the desperation felt in famine-stricken Shandong.

Based on Guotai's report, the emperor allows regular taxes to be collected, and Guotai is ruthless in pressing the people to pay.

He promulgated the edict to the prefectural and county officials to begin collecting.
The big officials asked for it from the little officials,
the little officials collected from the common people.
The people
having eaten breakfast, don't know when their next meal will be;
where can they get grain or money to present?
But if they say they can't,
they'll be hauled into the city.
They'll be brought to Guotai's great hall.
Entering the hall, first they'll be beaten forty strokes.
Being beaten hard forty strokes doesn't count,
they still have to present grain and money.
If they present grain and money, nothing happens.
If they don't come up with the grain, Guotai has another five punishments.

31 "Rascal" is *guanggun*. See *Bailing ji* 白绫记 [The Story of the White Silk Plaint] (Beijing: Jukuitang, [1862 or later]), 11: 6b–7a.

> Spoken: What other five punishments does he have, eh? This is the Qing dynasty, in the Great Qing Code there's only the ankle press and the bamboo.[32]

The storyteller goes on to describe the strange tortures Guotai invents for the people, including making them stand barefoot on ice at night in the winter, three in one cangue, five on one rope. There were so many families who could not present grain that the cangues were all used up and they made makeshift ones out of roof beams. Thus part of the corrupt official's villainy is inventing his own tortures.

In these dire circumstances, the local elites are portrayed positively as they try to intervene on the people's behalf. Twelve local elites (ten *shengyuan*, one *xiucai*, and one *jinshi*) go successively to Jinan to remonstrate but are summarily executed by Guotai.[33] The people then appeal to a local Provincial Graduate (*juren*), Zuo Duheng, who is from the richest family in Shandong. He offers to pay the taxes from his county. Hearing this, Guotai says Zuo can pay taxes for the whole province and in addition demands a personal loan of 8,000,000 taels of silver.[34] Zuo refuses to loan him the money, saying if he had it he would use it for charity. Guotai then accuses Zuo of rebellion, and immediately has him dismembered and his head boiled in oil.

The problem in *Nabbing Guotai* is favoritism. In the ballad, Guotai is an imperial favorite and relative by marriage. His powerful connections give even Judge Liu pause about taking on the case:

> Master Liu called the Zen Master,
> "You don't know Guotai's background.
> His father is Circuit Intendant of Ganning, Shanxi;
> with one flag he can command the troops of 10 Prefectures.
> Guotai is the official in Jinan,
> like another palace outside the capital.
> His brother is called Guosheng,
> he's Vice Minister in the Ministry of Revenue.
> The emperor gave him a horse that can ride into the palace;

32 "The Great Qing Code" is *Da Qing lü*. See *Bailing ji* 白绫记 [The Story of the White Silk Plaint] (Nanyang fu: Jingyuan tang, 1881), 2: 1b.

33 In 1808–09 a powerful local official actually did execute a *jinshi* who was going to expose his corruption. See Joanna Waley-Cohen, "Politics and the Supernatural in Mid-Qing Legal Culture," *Modern China* 19, no. 3 (1993): 330–53.

34 *Bailing ji* (Nanyang, 1881), 3: 4a.

he can go in or out of the imperial halls at will.
His sister is now in the Western Palace.
She is the emperor's favorite darling.
Whenever she says anything to the emperor,
it's like setting a nail in iron.
The Military Commander of the Capital, He Shougui,
is Guotai's cousin.
Then there's another Censor
who is his elder cousin.
Guotai as an official has strong roots
If you want me to take this plaint, it will never happen."[35]

The portrayal of Judge Liu in *Nabbing Guotai* is not as fearless as he seems to be, at least publicly, in the Chewangfu manuscript ballad.[36] However, he is persuaded to take the case. To solve the case, Judge Liu overcomes Guotai by getting his confession in advance, thereby cutting the emperor and his subjectivity out of the process.[37] Social justice is the ideal throughout; all are in theory equally subject to the law. But this ideal is attainable only when the judge clearly sees the factors obstructing it—special relationships and favoritism—and take pains to see that evidence is gathered and justice is done. Thus Judge Liu interrogates Guotai in private, rather than at court in the presence of the emperor, because he recognizes that the emperor would probably intercede. The conclusion of the ballad calls Judge Liu "fair and without bias."[38]

In dealing with corruption among powerful officials, the woodblock ballad *Nabbing Guotai* places great emphasis on the law and its impartiality.

---

35 "Strong roots" is *genzi ying*. Ibid., 11: 4b–5a.

36 If Guotai is clearly abusing his power in the woodblock *Na Guotai*, a similar predicament occurs with some of the local officials or strongmen in the Chewangfu manuscript *Liu Gong an*. In the manuscript, however, Judge Liu shows public fearlessness. For example, one local despot, Zhou Tong, is described as absolutely lawless. Judge Liu is told that his underlings have influence at every court, and his predecessor lost his position because of him. Judge Liu says since I took the case, I'll take down that rascal if it means losing my post! *Liu Gong an: Chewangfu quben*, 284–285.

37 In the historical case, the Qianlong emperor may have tried to limit the investigation. In the end, he decided on a lighter sentence than his review board recommended, then allowed Guotai to commit suicide rather than be strangled. Nancy Park, "Corruption and its Recompense," 280, 282–284.

38 "*Gongping wu sixin.*" See *Jinan fu* (Shandong, 1894), 4: 22b.

Being an official, the law cannot be broken;
in all matters, reason comes first.
Great worthies and sages handed down the law;
it does not wrong people, nor is it partial.[39]

The most frequently invoked formulation states, "A prince who breaks the law gets the same punishment as a commoner."[40] Judge Liu is able to put this into practice, even under the most difficult circumstances. A summary verse on Guotai's case says:

Liu and He administered the law without partiality,
They punished corrupt officials and people who broke the law.
With loyal and righteous hearts they eliminated the evil and stupid.[41]

Thus Judge Liu embodies impartiality; he is praised for having "an iron face, utterly selfless and not yielding to *qing*."[42]

The Problem of *renqing*

This brings us to the problem of *renqing*. Literally "human feeling," the term *renqing* appears in the Han-dynasty *Book of Rites* (*Li ji*) as a term for familial affection. By the late Ming and early Qing it nearly always had positive connotations, with a meaning ranging from "empathy," "reciprocal obligation," "romantic attachment," "common sense," and "popular attitudes," to "public opinion."[43] In late imperial legal cases, the term *qing* from which *renqing* is derived could mean at least three different things: "truth" or the facts of the case; the motives

39 *Xia Jinan fu* 下济南府 (Beijing: Jukuitang, [1862 or later]), 2: 9b. Cf. "All you officials, big and small, need to understand the imperial law (*huangshang fadu*)," at *Jinan fu* (Shandong, 1894), 2: 3a.

40 "*Wangzi fan fa shumin tong zui*," at *Jinan fu* (Shandong, 1894), 2: 12b, 4: 16b.

41 *Xinke Jinan fu* 新刻济南府 (Shandong, 1894), 2: 12b.

42 "*Tiemian wusi bu shunqing*," at Ibid., 2: 7b.

43 William T. Rowe, *Saving the World: Chen Hongmou and Elite Consciousness in Eighteenth-Century China* (Stanford: Stanford University Press, 2001), 103. In contrast, in Song neo-Confucianism, *qing* or emotions lead people astray. Rowe notes that Chen Hongmou acknowledges the tendency for *renqing* in the realm of individual actions to become self-interest. Ibid., 107.

of the perpetrator; or the judge's capacity for judicial compassion.[44] In the third usage, Confucian legal theory understood *renqing* as "human compassion" exercised in the application of law, an ideal close to humaneness. Philip Huang argues that in actual mediation it meant something more like the "*renqing* ('human feeling') of human relations, in which the emphasis was on maintaining decent relationships among those living in close proximity to one another." [45] In this sense, it would mean considering and maintaining the web of mutual obligation that ties people together, a meaning close to *guanxi*. In the drum ballads, however, *renqing* is never mentioned in a positive light. Part of what sets Judge Liu apart from other officials—and makes him capable of solving these difficult cases—is his absolute refusal to consider *renqing*. Here *renqing* can mean the social network (including hierarchy), as well as out-and-out bribes.

In both the Chewangfu manuscript *Cases of Judge Liu* and the woodblock ballads, bribery is a given. In the Chewangfu manuscript, Judge Liu pretends to be open to a bribe in order to put the adulterer and adulteress off their guard. The narrator exposes this to the reader as a conscious plan, and the adulteress' reaction shows how well it works. Provincial Graduate Wu and his lover find completely believable Judge Liu's rhetoric about officials taking care of each other and his underling's suggestion to the adulteress to bribe the witness to change his testimony. Thus, although no bribes are actually given in this version of the story, the practice of bribery is so commonplace that Judge Liu can play on those expectations. The implication of Judge Liu playing this role, however, is that corruption is simply a part of how things are usually done. In *The Case of the Whirlwind*, most of the characters recognize that Judge Liu is immune to bribery, but that others in the system are not. An actual bribe to the coroner serves to suppress evidence of murder. Liu realizes the coroner was probably bribed when he looks at the body. The dead husband is ugly, short, and pockmarked, while the widow is as pretty as Pan Jinlian. Judge Liu concludes that if the man is ugly and the woman is pretty it must be a case of adultery. Here the allusion to Pan Jinlian, the notorious adulteress and murderer in *Shuihu zhuan* (Outlaws of the Marsh), shows how powerful "types" and familiar stories give the judge (and audience) a way to interpret the case. In the magistrate's handbook *Xiyuan jilu* (The Washing Away of Wrongs), a similar situation

44 Eugenia Lean, *Public Passions: The Trial of Shi Jianqiao and the Rise of Popular Sympathy in Republican China* (Berkeley: University of California Press, 2007), 111.

45 Huang, *Civil Justice in China*, 12–13.

is mentioned: in the case of an old husband and a young wife, one must suspect murder by his co-worker.[46]

Later in the same story, an old man's advice gives an interesting perspective on how the justice system is perceived to work. When Judge Liu orders the adulteress executed before he has found evidence of the crime, her lover Zhang Peiyuan gets ready to fight him. An old man stops him, saying: "I know how they work, he is just trying to scare the woman; I guarantee they will take her into custody tonight, then you can go and bribe them." This piece of advice suggests that judges regularly use scare tactics, and that bribes are generally expected and effective.[47]

Although bribes are recognized as common practice in the ballads, Judge Liu is the upright official who refuses to take part. Since official salaries were meager, any official without supplementary income could not hope to live in a manner fitting for his status.[48] Thus in the Chewangfu manuscript *Cases of Judge Liu*, Judge Liu is shown to be extremely parsimonious, eating only the simplest food and wearing tattered clothes. When Judge Liu arrives at his new post, the people gape at him and laugh at his faded hat and old clothes—"his whole get-up from head to toe / altogether wasn't worth two strings of copper

46 McKnight, *The Washing Away of Wrongs*, 63.

47 *Xuanfeng an* (Tianjin, n.d.), 4.2: 5b–6a. In another woodblock edition of *Xuanfeng an*, the old man's characterization of Judge Liu in the middle of his advice is fairly positive. He says, Judge Liu is no ordinary official passing by, he's a loyal and good official (*zhongliang daren*). He has thousands of military officials at his beck and call. Today you were going to hit him with a brick—that would be like throwing an egg at Taishan Mountain. *Xuanfeng an* 旋风案 [The Case of the Whirlwind] (Wannan, n.d.), 2.7b. Still, Judge Liu is thought susceptible to bribes. Neither version reveals the source of the old man's knowledge. It is tempting to think that he may have seen trials or inquests before.

48 "Even the most virtuous and frugal of local officials would have found it difficult to operate.... Although all *ts'un-liu* allocations included a category of official salaries, the amounts granted for this purpose were miniscule, comprising neither a living wage nor an administrative budget. Yet, as we have seen, along with runners' wages, these were almost the only funds legally available to civil officials for the purposes of local government." Madeline Zelin, *The Magistrate's Tael: Rationalizing Fiscal Reform in Eighteenth-Century Ch'ing China* (Berkeley: University of California Press, 1984), 37. Nancy Park notes, "According to one estimate by an 18th-century Chinese observer, the average yearly expenses for local officials ranged from 5,000 to 10,000 taels, several times more than the income they received from the central government." Thus officials made up the difference through informal funding sources, including gifts, fees, bribes and extortion. Park, "Corruption and Its Recompense," 40–41.

cash."[49] He refuses any welcoming gifts of food and has gruel and left-over buns for supper. Later, a yamen runner who works under Judge Liu comments:

> In my view
> even if he's poor he should think about money,
> change his clothes to show his power and prestige.
> When salt merchants present gifts he won't accept them.
> In deciding cases
> you'll never see Hunchback [Liu] go along with *renqing*.
> If you want to speak of
> what he eats, its even more of a joke.
> Listen to me tell you, brother.
> Since he's arrived
> no one's seen him touch meat.
> He seems to be vegetarian.
> His servant frequently comes out to buy dried veggies,
> and then there's
> soybeans and onions.
> I asked the servant what they were for.
> He said, 'It's
> to make tofu.
> His Honor likes to eat that.
> Each month he uses six strings of cash.
> The two of us, master and servant, spend 200 cash a day.
> How could we think of touching meat!
> It could never happen.
> We just wait
> for the Moon Festival on the fifteenth of the eighth month.
> His Honor resumes a normal diet
> and we eat a *jin* of onions apiece!'[50]

Judge Liu becomes an extreme illustration of what it would mean to be incorruptible. His frugality also makes him more 'ordinary' in that his lifestyle is closer to that of a commoner. He does not live up the expected status of an official in his dress, food, entourage (a single manservant), or even his dilapidated sedan-chair. Thus his extreme parsimony serves both as proof of his honesty

49 *Liu Gong an: Chewangfu quben*, 3.

50 *Liu Gong an: Chewangfu quben*, 26–27. Usually resuming a normal diet (*kaizhai*) would mean eating meat—the joke here is that even then, they still eat vegetarian dishes.

and as an antidote to the possibility of corruption. This aspect of his image is fully elaborated in the Chewangfu manuscript, but echoes of it persist in some of the woodblock ballads. For example, *The Story of the White Silk Plaint* describes Judge Liu's sedan-chair as patched, with only half a roof, and ropes tied around the carrying bars.[51]

Judge Liu's parsimony in the Chewangfu manuscript *Cases of Judge Liu* soon leads to a conflict with his superior, Governor-General Gao. Judge Liu is invited to his superior's birthday party, and brings a simple gift of food worth only two strings of cash. Governor-General Gao is incensed at the cheap gift, which he takes as an insult, and refuses to accept it.[52] Judge Liu thinks:

> The Governor-General really has gone too far bullying people.
> That gift of
> mine, in not accepting he is out of luck.
> If you think you'll get others' gifts, no way!
> Taking advantage of your superior position to bully your inferiors—
> is Hunchback [Liu] really a coward?
> If you're going to give gifts, it should be in private,
> it's not something we officials should do.
> It is often said that if someone brings a swan feather a thousand *li*,
> even if the gift is cheap the person's intentions are valuable.
> Even if it were just cold water that I had warmed,
> you should have accepted it for appearances' sake.
> ....
> Only those who are upright and selfless have nothing to fear.
> I am also
> happy to be pure and tend to the people's matters.
> If you make a single misstep,
> our debt cannot be settled![53]

Judge Liu gets even by standing in the doorway and turning away all the other well-wishers by telling them that Governor-General Gao is not accepting gifts.

Besides the poking fun inherent in the episode, it reflects the discussion of gifts among officials (and even as tribute to the emperor) current in the Qianlong era. Judge Liu defends his choice by saying gifts are just to express feelings, so what is given is not important. This is similar to the rhetoric the

51 *Bailing ji* (Nanyang, 1881), 8: 3a.

52 *Liu Gong an: Chewangfu quben*, 71–73.

53 *Liu Gong an: Chewangfu quben*, 74.

historical Qianlong emperor used regarding tribute from officials.[54] Moreover, bribery laws in the Qianlong period prohibited any gifts to officials except foodstuffs.[55] However, in practice, gifts were an important source of income for officials. As Madeline Zelin points out, "All officials and functionaries, from the lowest assistant magistrate to the governor-general, periodically sent gifts of customarily established sums of silver to their superiors.... These gifts could amount to a considerable sum, especially when the recipient was a high provincial official such as the governor or financial commissioner."[56]

Thus in 1724, the Liangguang Governor General confessed to receiving 47,110 taels in gifts from his subordinates.[57] While the laws regarding gifts to officials were rarely enforced in practice,[58] in this ballad Judge Liu's rigid adherence to the letter of the law sets him apart. Judge Liu proves "supermoral" in his ethical stance, in that he goes above and beyond the social expectations of morality.

The episode also shows the practical consequences of sticking to principle. Governor-General Gao is incensed over losing all the valuable birthday gifts, and gives Judge Liu an impossible case to solve: an unidentified head that was found in a public well. As Judge Liu mulls over the case, he thinks:

> Governor-General Gao hates and resents me,
> He must have said I
> should send that Liu to solve a case.
> If I can't solve it in five days,
> Governor-General Gao probably won't allow it.
> He'll say I
> am lacking in talent and wisdom, without learning,
> not fit to serve
> as Prefect in this office.
> Using public means for a private grudge, he'll certainly impeach me.
> I only fear
> because of this case Gao will memorialize the cinnabar palace.

---

54 Nancy Park shows that the Qianlong Emperor had no compunction about keeping valuable items, but sent down edicts starting in 1740 discouraging or prohibiting tribute from governors or governor-general beyond foodstuffs. Still, his private messages to particular governors berated them for "ordinary" gifts and complimented unusual or expensive ones. "Corruption and its Recompense," 51–53.

55 Ibid., 70.

56 Zelin, *The Magistrate's Tael*, 55.

57 Ibid.

58 Nancy Park, "Corruption in Eighteenth-Century China," *Journal of Asian Studies* 56, no. 4 (1997): 979.

> What I fear
> is that our sagely Emperor's dragon heart will anger
> and I, Liu,
> will lose my office and have to leave my post.
> If I, Liu, have to leave Jiangning Prefecture,
> that would suit Gao's plan.
> After that he could ask for all the money he wants
> without any fear
> that his name would live in infamy.[59]

Later, the same Governor-General Gao tries to block Judge Liu's investigation of his friend, Provincial Graduate Wu. Judge Liu "secretly berated the avaricious official. / 'You take advantage of your superior position to pressure your underlings. / How could I, Liu, go along with *renqing?* /At worst, I won't be Prefect of Jiangning.' "[60] Judge Liu decides he does not care if he loses his career over it, he will not do any favors. Under ordinary circumstances, someone in his position would have had difficulty pursuing the matter, since his sentence in a murder case would be subject to review by the very man trying to block his investigation. However, Judge Liu is able to get around the power structure and achieve justice precisely through his own network, in this case his personal connection with the emperor. After mentioning Judge Liu's decision to write the emperor directly, the narrator comments:

> Someone said, 'There's a problem with the tale. Judge Liu is only the Prefect of Jiangning, a fourth-rank official, how can he have the power to memorialize to the emperor?' Gentlemen, there's something you don't know. When Old Buddha Qianlong appointed Liu to Prefect of Jiangning, before he set out from the capital, he promised that Liu could memorialize. That's why he dared to memorialize about this.[61]

Thus, however problematic the drum ballads find *renqing* in the sense of social networks to be, these texts cannot imagine a system without it. On the other hand, in the Chewangfu manuscript, Judge Liu's honesty leads directly to his promotion. An imperial edict states:

---

59 *Liu Gong an: Chewangfu quben*, 82.

60 Ibid., 150. In another case someone says Liu will never decide a case based on *renqing*. Ibid., 26.

61 Ibid., 150–151.

We understand the worthy official Liu Yong
We have heard you
in Jiangning have been honest and upright,
regulating the country, pacifying the masses and caring for the people.
We hereby promote you to the Censorate.[62]

As Judge Liu leaves for the capital, countless commoners come see him off with wine and lambs.

The woodblock texts, especially *The Story of the White Silk Plaint*, also emphasize Liu's connections. When Judge Liu expresses qualms at taking on Guotai, the boy's advocate reminds Judge Liu of his own privilege as the Empress Dowager's godson.[63] This convinces Judge Liu to take the case, and also suggests to the audience that he is the one who can successfully take down Guotai. Similarly, Guotai's influence through his sister, the emperor's favorite concubine, makes the women's quarters part of the problem, but they are also part of the solution in the Empress Dowager's patronage of Judge Liu.

Before the boy seeking justice against Guotai finds Judge Liu, he runs across the self-important General Wu Neng. In this comic episode, the role of connections is both underscored and satirized. The boy insists on knowing the official's name, home, and position before presenting his plaint. The General replies:

"If you want to ask how big a position I hold at court,
I am the Defender of the Palace General Wu Neng."
When His Honor Wu said his name and office,
Liancheng picked up his bundle and was about to leave.
When Master Wu saw this he was incensed,
He quickly opened his tiger mouth and cried, "Child!
You blocked my sedan to bring a plaint,
asked my home and name,
asked how big a position I have.
I told it all to you clearly,
from top to bottom I explained it to you.
Why aren't you putting your injustice in my hands?"
When Liancheng heard this,

62 "Honest and upright" is *qing zheng*. The Censorate is *Duchayuan*. Ibid., 360.

63 *Bailing ji* (Nanyang, 1881), 11: 5a–12: 1b.

he said, "Master,
it's not that I won't put my case in your hands.
You said already that you're incompetent."

The name Wu Neng sounds like the word for incompetent (*wu you neng*). Once the pun on his name is cleared up, the General tries to allay the child's concerns about his ability to handle the case of injustice by parading his connections.

> Master Wu said, "Child, you needn't say it. The person you're accusing is someone with wealth and prospects. My position is General, Defender of the Palace. I've seen a lot of the Nine Chief Ministers, Four Grand Councilors, eight Grand Ministers, Five Military Commissions and Six Ministries, nobles and their descendants, Imperial In-laws and Imperial Clansmen, and Supervising Secretaries and Censors. Those provincial, prefectural, and county officials, degree holders, and gentry are just ordinary and incapable."[64]

Wu Neng brags about his network, but will not take on the powerful. Since the boy insists on finding out his position, it shows the boy's way of judging whether an official can help him. After Wu Neng refuses to take the case, the child says:

If as an official you don't act on the people's behalf,
you're receiving a salary from the emperor for nothing.
You may as well go home and retire early.[65]

To the boy, social justice should be everyone's duty.

The ballads' perception of the importance of networks and their implications is borne out by historical records. As Nancy Park notes, favoritism and nepotism were illegal in the Qing, but

> it was widely understood among officials that striving for unattainable levels of incorruptibility—which could not only lead to administrative ineffectiveness but could also alienate less scrupulous members of the bureaucracy—was not a guarantee for professional success. More important for an up-and-coming official was to keep his nose clean

64 *Bailing ji* (Nanyang, 1881), 8: 2a.

65 Ibid., 8: 3a.

> politically, which meant successfully fulfilling the requirements of office, currying favor with the right people, and not making enemies.[66]

This led to a widespread reluctance to expose the powerful and well-connected.[67]

How well connected were the historical Guotai and Liu Yong, and how much of this is poetic license? In history, Heshen was the emperor's favorite, and the investigation of Guotai was an indirect attack on Heshen's own power and corruption. In the ballad, however, Heshen is whitewashed; he helps to investigate the case, and thus is part of the solution rather than being part of the problem. The ballads thus emphasize Guotai's own connections to the palace, rather than his connection to Heshen.

The historical Liu Yong was the son of Grand Secretary Liu Tongxun, whom the Qianlong Emperor respected. Liu Yong was appointed prefect of Jiangning (Nanjing) in 1769 as a favor by the emperor to his father, and upon Liu Tongxun's death the Qianlong Emperor came to their house to pay his respects.[68] The emperor exchanged poetry with both father and son, which suggests a social connection between them. Liu Yong had a successful career, including posts as President of the Censorate and Grand Secretary, and in his sixties was given the privilege of riding a horse inside the Forbidden City.[69] So there is some basis for Liu Yong's purported connection with the emperor. The idea that Liu Yong was the Empress Dowager's godson is pure fiction.

Judge Liu Ballads in the Republican Era

The trilogy of Judge Liu cases from the woodblock drum ballads continued to be published and read in lithographic editions in the late Qing and Republican era. Indeed, given the larger print runs for lithographic editions, they may have been even more available in this period. What accounts for their continued appeal?

---

66 Nancy Park, "Corruption in Eighteenth-Century China": 999.

67 Ibid.

68 See the entries on Liu Tongxun and Liu Yong in Hucker, ed., *Eminent Chinese of the Ch'ing Period*, 534, 536.

69 Liu Xiangyu 刘祥雨, "Liu Yong nianpu 刘墉年谱 [The Chronicle of Liu Yong]," Master's Thesis, Lanzhou University, 2007.

FIGURE 10.4 *A lithographic edition of* Cases of Judge Liu *(Shanghai: Guangyi shuju, n.d.). In the Hanan collection of the Harvard-Yenching Library.*

Legal practice did not change overnight.[70] The Republican legal system was a mix of new and old, and this may have been even more true in the rural areas where institutional change was slower. Even in the cities, ideas were often slower to change than institutions.

Social justice against one's superiors had been a powerful ideal in court-case fiction going back to the Judge Bao *chantefables* of the early Ming;[71] it found renewed emphasis in these Qing court-case drum ballads. Could this be one reason why these court case narratives remained appealing in the Republican era, as social justice became an explicit concern of legal reform?

Prefaces to late-Qing- and Republican-era lithographic editions emphasize Judge Liu's fairness and incorruptibility. The preface to the 1908 Zhangfuju edition holds Judge Liu up as a model, "to exhort those in power."

> With great integrity he could not be forced, meeting with a prosperous enterprise he would stay clean and hide himself. Corrupt officials hearing his name lost heart, bribe-taking officials seeing his shadow were startled. He spoke straightforwardly, dared to remonstrate, and didn't avoid the powerful.[72]

The idea that narrative about good judges could serve as a model for real judges appeared frequently in Qing-dynasty prefaces to court-case fiction like *Longtu gongan* (Cases of Bao Longtu, 1776 preface) and *Shi Gong an* (Cases of Judge Shi, 1839 preface).[73] Those earlier prefaces also emphasize the good judge's straightforward and incorruptible nature. The preface to the drum ballad *Cases of Judge Liu*, however, is unusual in its emphasis on eliminating the corrupt.

Another preface, to a 1911 lithographic edition of the drum ballad *Cases of Judge Liu*, echoes the previous one in many respects, but adds some new keywords in praise of Judge Liu:

---

70 Xiaoqun Xu, *Trial of Modernity: Judicial Reform in Early Twentieth-Century China, 1901–1937* (Stanford: Stanford University Press, 2008), 13–20, 65, 73–74; Jennifer Neighbors, "The Long Arm of Qing Law? Qing Dynasty Homicide Rulings in Republican Courts," *Modern China* 35, no. 3 (2009): 3–37.

71 For a translation of these early ballads, see Wilt Idema, *Judge Bao and the Rule of Law: Eight Ballad-Stories from the Period 1250–1450* (Singapore: World Scientific, 2010).

72 *Xiuxiang Liu Gong an quanzhuan* 绣像刘公案全传 [The Illustrated Cases of Judge Liu] (Shanghai: Zhangfuju, 1908).

73 See the prefaces for *Longtu gongan* and *Shi Gong an* in Ding Xigen 丁锡根, *Zhongguo lidai xiaoshuo xu ba ji* 中国历代小说序跋集 [A Collection of Prefaces and Postfaces from Chinese Novels of Various Dynasties] (Beijing: Renmin, 1996), 3: 1601–1602, 1610–1611.

> Nothing among all the strange tales of past and present outdoes the book *Cases of Judge Liu* for loyalty and righteousness. It is set in the Qianlong period and records several true events. Judge Liu was from Zhucheng county in Shandong and was a loyal and straightforward official of the Qing. He wasn't afraid of big cases. Avaricious officials were afraid of him. He was straightforward in speech and dared to remonstrate, he wasn't afraid of power. Nabbing Guotai in Shandong, investigating the white horse on the road, he went undercover to investigate the truth of the matter. He entered the bandit's lair, not afraid of difficulties. He is first among the pure officials of past and present.... I hope those who investigate cases in the future learn from his example.[74]

This preface ties the character Judge Liu to the historical official, emphasizing his loyalty, righteousness, and courage in facing the powerful. His talent lies in investigating the truth of the matter. By calling him the "first among pure officials of past and present," this preface implicitly elevates Judge Liu above even Judge Bao and Judge Shi.

Of course, this is not to deny that the court-case stories and ballads also served as entertainment. An advertisement in another lithographic edition of *Cases of Judge Liu* for the *Xinji fenlei gujin qi'an huibian* (*Newly Compiled Categorized Strange Cases Old and New*) goes,

> This compilation searched broadly for especially strange cases, old and new. They have been categorized as robbery, scheming for wealth, adultery, disputes over property, secret killings, mistaken killings, revenge, marriage, new marriage, trickery, letters, illusion, ghosts and spirits, oddities, retribution, frame-ups, injustice, and difficult cases. There are twenty kinds of cases, all true; things seldom seen or heard, every incident startling, a must-read for everyone and the only 'marvelous book'.[75]

The pitch claims the cases are "true," but at the same time it primarily emphasizes their entertainment value. While it is referring to another book, by

74 "The truth of the matter" is *shi zhi xushi*. "Learn from his example" is *yi Liu Gong wei fa*. See *Xiuxiang shuochang Liu Gong an* 绣像说唱刘公案 [The Illustrated Telling-and-Singing Cases of Judge Liu] (Shanghai: Zhuji shuju, 1911).

75 Advertisement for *Xinji fenlei gujin qi'an huibian*, in *Zuben dazi Xiuxiang quantu Liu Gong an* 足本大字绣像全图刘公案 [The Original, Large-Print, Fully Illustrated Cases of Judge Liu] (Shanghai: Guangyi shuju, n.d.).

implication the audience of the drum ballad *Cases of Judge Liu* might be reading it in a similar fashion.

Conclusions

While the drum ballads ultimately uphold the effectiveness of the legal system, they also demonstrate its weaknesses in considerable detail. It takes an exemplary official like Judge Liu to make it work in the face of favoritism, bribery, and the manipulation of rhetoric. Suspense lies in how the judge will handle the case and the personal consequences to him if he does not handle it well. Thus much of the heart of the story is about interpersonal dynamics and social expectations. The law is the weapon the upright judge wields against those who abuse their power. He battles corruption and favoritism in part by acting supermoral and refusing to acknowledge *renqing*. However, in the end, he often has to rely on his own network to ensure that justice is done.

The ballads also serve as a reminder of the multiple sources of legal knowledge. In the ballads, characters gain legal knowledge through education, through experience as a yamen runner, or quite possibly by having seen inquests. Specialists like litigation masters rarely appear;[76] when they do, they are in the employ of the rich, and are satirized as twisting rhetoric to immoral ends. In the analysis of the ballads of Judge Liu we have seen that certain elements of legal culture run through literature and legend, administrative handbooks, and the practice of public inquests. For example, the suspicion raised by the death of an older man with a pretty wife plays out similarly in these ballads, the novel *Outlaws of the Marsh*, and the magistrate's handbook *The Washing Away of Wrongs*. Legal procedure is at the heart of *The Washing Away of Wrongs*, but is also portrayed with surprising accuracy in *Outlaws of the Marsh*[77] and the Judge Liu ballads. Thus these disparate texts seem to be in conversation with each other regarding the actual practice of law, perhaps informed by, or forming the basis for, a kind of legal "common sense."

The drum ballads on Judge Liu expose a gap between the code of law and how it was put into practice; this gap is also a recurring theme in the actual cases examined by Janet Theiss in this volume, as well as the research of Thomas Buoye and Nancy Park. In these ballads, law is good, but implementation is a

76 On litigation masters, see Melissa Macauley, *Social Power and Legal Culture: Litigation Masters in Late Imperial China* (Stanford: Stanford University Press, 1998).

77 Robert Hegel notes the accuracy of legal procedure in *Shuihu zhuan* in his "Introduction," 11–12.

problem. The theory of law in China encompasses both the code of law and the morality informing it. The tension between the law and morality seems to be an ongoing theme in Chinese legal culture. The Judge Liu ballads try to resolve that contradiction. Law is invoked in the drum ballads most often in cases where social justice is at stake. Judge Liu frequently cites the formulation that the law applies equally to princes in the drum ballads when he is taking on the powerful, but the idea of the law is also called upon by the underprivileged in their pursuit of justice. Judge Liu seeks to go by the code, regardless of who is being investigated, and tries to eradicate differences between elites and commoners regarding the judicial system. Structurally, much of the dramatic tension in the ballads comes when the Judge knows something is morally wrong, but is not able to prove it or prosecute legally. This tension is resolved when evidence is finally forthcoming. Once the evidence allows prosecution, the law and morality are reconciled; law upholds morality.

Whereas in theory *renqing* is supposed to be a positive element, in the popular discourse of the drum ballads *renqing* is almost always portrayed as negative, either explicitly as outright corruption or implicitly as a kind of favoritism perpetuated by social connections. Thus, when *renqing* is mentioned, it is in the context of the upright Judge Liu flatly refusing to be influenced by it. If *qing* or *renqing* was important to mediation in North China, as Philip Huang demonstrates,[78] its disadvantages are stressed in the Judge Liu ballads.

This negative view of *renqing* in practice is substantiated in Nancy Park's research on corruption and Janet Theiss' paper in this volume. Theiss suggests that Prefect Yang understood *qing* as favors, and *fa* as impartiality. Thus his understanding in practice would be commensurate with how these terms were used in the ballads. Networks of power were the reality: as Janet Theiss explains in this volume, "elite families encountered the judicial system not… as the locus of state authority or justice, but as a set of relationships to be worked, manipulated."[79] This reality is acknowledged in the drum ballads not only in Judge Liu's crusades against *renqing*, but ironically in his own reliance on such personal networks of power.

The degree to which the Judge Liu ballads emphasize the law is unusual even for the genre of court case fiction. Earlier ballads like the Judge Bao *chantefables*, which had developed by the early Ming, show a similar concern with abuses by the powerful, but never invoke the code of law. Instead, Judge Bao fights the powerful using the special privilege granted to him by Emperor in

78 Huang, *Civil Justice in China*, 12–13.

79 Theiss, "Elite Engagement with the Judicial System in the Qing."

the form of magical weapons.[80] The Judge Liu ballad manuscripts are also unusual in that they relate stories of fairly recent events, and insist on their own "realism." Thus even within one tradition of popular fiction, we find contested visions of justice and the role the law plays in it. The drum ballads critique the system of legal administration, but they also imagine how it might work and try to fix it; as David Wang notes of other court-case fiction, they present a "fantasy of cleansing" the existing order. The martial arts novel, in contrast, sees corruption as sufficient reason for the martial heroes to disregard the law and take morality into their own hands. Its vigilante justice is a "fantasy of overcoming" the system.[81] These two closely related genres debate what constitutes justice and how it should be achieved. Indeed, these discourses are placed in dialogue with each other in the court-case adventure novels and many of the martial arts novels that were widely popular in the late Qing and early Republic.[82]

Did the imagined justice of popular Chinese fiction or ballads influence public opinion? Bryna Goodman's paper shows that many of the same themes—injustice and its solution—are invoked in Republican newspapers. She sees a clear tension between morality and the law in the case she examines, as one activist in her study states in the newspapers: "If you have justice, you have law."[83] Goodman's research shows that the rhetoric of grievance common in popular fiction was still powerful in the discussion of an actual court case in newspapers in 1920s Shanghai.[84] This serves as a reminder that fiction not only represents experience artistically; the ideals fiction presents also shape people's understanding of real events, or the way they frame the issues in interpreting those events for others. Thus fiction can serve as a model for life, or a lens through which the perception of events is filtered.[85]

80 Wilt Idema, "Introduction," in *Judge Bao and the Rule of Law*, especially xxxi–xxxii. Cf. *Ming Chenghua shuochang cihua congkan* [Collection of Telling-and-Singing Ballads from the Ming Chenghua Reign Period] (Shanghai: Shanghai Museum, 1973).

81 David Der-wei Wang, *Fin de Siecle Splendor: Repressed Modernities of Late Qing Fiction, 1849–1911* (Stanford: Stanford University Press, 1997), 117–118.

82 For the dialogization of values in martial arts novels and their relationship to court-case adventure novels (*gongan xiayi xiaoshuo*), see Margaret Wan, *"Green Peony" and the Rise of the Chinese Martial Arts Novel* (Albany: State University of New York Press, 2009), 10–12, 57–59, 93–98.

83 Bryna Goodman, " 'Law Is One Thing, and Virtue Is Another': Vernacular Readings of Law and Legal Process in 1920s Shanghai," in this volume.

84 Ibid.

85 Margaret Wan, *"Green Peony" and the Rise of the Chinese Martial Arts Novel*, 11, 103, 144–45, 149–51. Cf. M.M. Bakhtin, *The Dialogic Imagination*, ed. Michael Holquist (Austin: University of Texas, 1981), 288–92, 413.

Glossary

Bao Gong	包公
Baoying	报应
bu lun li	不论理
Chengshang lütiao ta quan huai	呈上律條他全坏
Da Qing fadu lüli si / jie yin guanyuan dou tancang	大清法度律例死 皆因官员都贪藏
Da Qing guo lü	大清国律
Da Qing lü	大清律
daoli	道理
Duchayuan	都察院
fa	法
genzi ying	根子硬
gongan	公案
gongan xiayi xiaoshuo	公案侠义小说
gongdao	公道
Gongping wu sixin	公平无私心
Guci	鼓词
guanxi	关系
guanggun	光棍
guofa	国法
Guotai	国泰
Heshen	和珅
huangshang fadu	皇上法度
Jiangning	江宁
jinshi	进士
juren	举人
kaizhai	开斋
li	理
libutong	理不通
lizheng qingqu jia zuozhen	理正情屈假作真
Liu Gong	刘公
Liu Tongxun	刘统勋
Liu Yong	刘墉
Longtu gongan	龙图公案
lüli	律例
Lütiao wangfa quan bu zun	律條王法全不尊
qing	情
qing zheng	清正
renqing	人情
shengyuan	生员
Shi Gong an	施公案
shi zhi xushi	事之虚实
Shuihu zhuan	水浒传
taishang huangye	太上皇爷
tianli	天理
Tianxia zong ze jun you zhu / ban you Tianzi ban you chen	天下总则君有主 半由天子半由臣
Tiemian wusi bu shunqing	铁面无私不顺情
Wangfa	王法
Wangzi fan fa shumin tong zui	王子犯法 庶民同罪
Wu Neng	吳能
wu you neng	无有能
xiucai	秀才
Xiyuan jilu	洗冤集录
Xinji fenlei gujin qi'an huibian	新辑分类古 今奇案汇编
yi Liu Gong wei fa	以刘公为法
yuan	冤
zhen qingshi	真情事
zhengyi	正义
zhongliang daren	忠良大人

Bibliography

Asen, Daniel. "Dead Bodies and Forensic Science: Cultures of Expertise in China, 1800–1949." Ph.D. dissertation, Columbia University, 2012.

———. "Old Forensics in Practice: Investigating Suspicious Deaths and Administering Justice in Republican Beijing." In this volume.

Bailing ji 白绫记 [The Story of the White Silk Plaint]. Beijing: Jukuitang, [1862 or later].

Bailing ji 白绫记 [The Story of the White Silk Plaint]. Nanyang fu: Jingyuan tang, 1881.

Bakhtin, M.M. *The Dialogic Imagination*. Edited by Michael Holquist. Austin: University of Texas, 1981.

Buoye, Thomas. *Manslaughter, Markets, and Moral Economy*. New York: Cambridge University Press, 2000.

———. "Suddenly Murderous Intent Arose: Bureaucratization and Benevolence in Eighteenth-Century Homicide Reports." *Late Imperial China* 16, no. 2 (1995): 62–97.

Ding Xigen 丁锡根. *Zhongguo lidai xiaoshuo xu ba ji* 中国历代小说序跋集 [A Collection of Prefaces and Postfaces from Chinese Novels of Various Dynasties]. Beijing: Renmin, 1996.

Giles, Herbert. "The 'Hsi Yuan Lu' or 'Instructions to Coroners.'" *Proceedings of the Royal Society of Medicine* 27 (1924): 87.

Goodman, Bryna. "'Law Is One Thing, and Virtue Is Another': Vernacular Readings of Law and Legal Process in 1920s Shanghai." In this volume.

Hegel, Robert. "Introduction: Writing and Law." In Hegel and Katherine Carlitz, eds. *Writing and Law in Late Imperial China: Crime, Conflict, and Judgment*, 3–23. Seattle: University of Washington Press, 2007.

Huang, Phillip C.C. *Civil Justice in China: Representation and Practice in the Qing*. Stanford: Stanford University Press, 1996.

Hummel, Arthur W. *Eminent Chinese of the Ch'ing Period*. Taibei: Chengwen, 1972.

Idema, Wilt. *Judge Bao and the Rule of Law: Eight Ballad-Stories from the Period 1250–1450*. Singapore: World Scientific, 2010.

Jinan fu 济南府 [The Prefecture of Jinan]. Shandong, 1894.

Lean, Eugenia. *Public Passions: The Trial of Shi Jianqiao and the Rise of Popular Sympathy in Republican China*. Berkeley: University of California Press, 2007.

Liu Xiangyu 刘祥雨. "Liu Yong nianpu 刘墉年谱 [The Chronicle of Liu Yong]." Master's thesis, Lanzhou University, 2007.

Macauley, Melissa, *Social Power and Legal Culture: Litigation Masters in Late Imperial China*. Stanford: Stanford University Press, 1998.

McKnight, Brian E., trans. *The Washing Away of Wrongs*. Ann Arbor: Center for Chinese Studies, University of Michigan, 1981.

Ming Chenghua shuochang cihua congkan 明成化说唱词话丛刊 [Collection of Telling-and-Singing Ballads from the Ming Chenghua Reign Period]. Shanghai: Shanghai Museum, 1973.

Neighbors, Jennifer. "The Long Arm of Qing Law? Qing Dynasty Homicide Rulings in Republican Courts." *Modern China* 35, no. 3 (2009): 3–37.

Nivison, David S. "Ho-Shen and His Accusers: Ideology and Political Behavior in the Eighteenth Century." In *Confucianism in Action*, edited by David S. Nivison and Arthur F. Wright, 209–43. Stanford: Stanford University Press, 1959.

Ocko, Jonathan. "I'll Take It All the Way to Beijing: Capital Appeals in the Qing." *Journal of Asian Studies* 47, no. 2 (1988): 291–315.

Park, Nancy. "Corruption and Its Recompense: Bribes, Bureaucracy, and the Law in Late Imperial China." Ph.D. dissertation, Harvard University, 1993.

———. "Corruption in Eighteenth-Century China." *Journal of Asian Studies* 56, no. 4 (1997): 967–1005.

Rowe, William T. *Saving the World: Chen Hongmou and Elite Consciousness in Eighteenth-Century China*. Stanford: Stanford University Press, 2001.

Sommer, Matthew. *Sex, Law and Society in Late Imperial China*. Stanford: Stanford University Press, 2000.

Theiss, Janet. "Elite Engagement with the Judicial System in the Qing and its Implications for Legal Practice and Principle." In this volume.

Waley-Cohen, Joanna. "Politics and the Supernatural in Mid-Qing Legal Culture." *Modern China* 19, no. 3 (1993): 330–53.

Wan, Margaret. "Audiences and Reading Practices for Qing Dynasty Drum Ballad Texts." In *The Interplay of the Oral and the Written in Chinese Popular Literature*, edited by Vibeke Børdahl and Margaret Wan, 41–60. Copenhagen: Nordic Institute of Asian Studies Press, 2010.

———. *"Green Peony" and the Rise of the Chinese Martial Arts Novel*. Albany: State University of New York Press, 2009.

Wang, David Der-wei. *Fin de Siecle Splendor: Repressed Modernities of Late Qing Fiction, 1849–1911*. Stanford: Stanford University Press, 1997.

Xia Jinan 下济南 [Going to Jinan], a.k.a., *Na Guotai* 拿国太[泰] [Nabbing Guotai]. Beijing: Jukuitang, n.d.

Xiuxiang Liu Gong an quanzhuan 绣像刘公案全传 [The Illustrated Cases of Judge Liu]. Shanghai: Zhangfuju, 1908.

Xiuxiang shuochang Liu Gong an 绣像说唱刘公案 [The Illustrated Telling-and-Singing Cases of Judge Liu]. Shanghai: Zhuji shuju, 1911.

Xuanfeng an 旋风案 [The Case of the Whirlwind]. Shandong, 1894.

Xuanfeng an 旋风案 [The Case of the Whirlwind]. Tianjin, n.d.

Xuanfeng an 旋风案 [The Case of the Whirlwind]. Wannan, n.d.

Xu, Xiaoqun. *Trial of Modernity: Judicial Reform in Early Twentieth-Century China, 1901–1937*. Stanford: Stanford University Press, 2008.

Yan Qi 燕琦, ed. *Liu Gong an: Chewangfu quben* 劉公案: 車王府曲本 [Cases of Judge Liu: The Songbook from the Chewangfu Collection]. Beijing: Renmin wenxue chubanshe, 1990.

Zelin, Madeline. *The Magistrate's Tael: Rationalizing Fiscal Reform in Eighteenth-Century Ch'ing China*. Berkeley: University of California Press, 1984.

Zuben dazi Xiuxiang quantu Liu Gong an 足本大字绣像全图刘公案 [The Original, Large-print, Fully Illustrated Cases of Judge Liu]. (Shanghai: Guangyi shuju, n.d.).

CHAPTER 11

Old Forensics in Practice: Investigating Suspicious Deaths and Administering Justice in Republican Beijing

Daniel Asen

In May 1923 high judicial officials requested that the Beijing local procuracy send one of its coroners to Fengtian Province to perform an examination of skeletal remains. An accusation had been made with authorities in Shenyang that a man named Zhao Fukui had kicked a woman named Liu Guangju to death.[1] The aunt of the deceased did not accept the findings of an earlier inquest, which exonerated Zhao, and was requesting another examination of the body. Authorities in Fengtian wanted a coroner from Beijing to persuade the aunt by conducting another examination of Liu's skeletal remains. Ultimately, a Beijing coroner named Yu Yuan was sent to settle the case. Yu was one of the most senior coroners in Beijing and had performed skeletal examinations for courts in north China on many other occasions. Since the fall of the Qing empire, the Beijing procuracy had received a number of similar requests from regional officials faced with the disputed forensics of entrenched cases. These authorities valued coroners' skills in the "steaming" technique for examining skeletal remains, one element in the sophisticated repertoire of forensic practices that had developed under the Qing.

During a period in which state and society increasingly valorized modern forms of professional expertise and scientific knowledge, it is striking that successive regimes of the Beiyang period (1912–27) and Nanjing Decade (1927–37) relied on a form of specialist knowledge that had originated under the late imperial order. Those who advocated the replacement of coroners with experts in legal medicine, the branch of scientific medicine that addressed problems

1 Beijing Municipal Archives (BMA), No. J174-1-184, "Zongjiantingdeng guanyu linpai jianyan li fu Fengtian jianyan shigu ji yuyou jianyan zhi shi ying xunchi jianguan dutong jianyan li xiangshen congshi de xunling 总检厅等关于遴派检验吏赴奉天检验尸骨及遇有检验之事应迅饬检官督同检验吏祥慎从事的训令 [Orders of General Procuracy Pertaining to Selecting and Dispatching Coroners to Go to Fengtian to Inspect Skeletal Remains and that when Matters Pertaining to Inquests Are Encountered One Must Swiftly Order Officials to Supervise Coroners and Proceed Carefully]," 1923, 36–97.

© KONINKLIJKE BRILL NV, LEIDEN, 2015 | DOI 10.1163/9789004288492_013

encountered in the law, were quick to portray the continuing use of coroners as anathema to the establishment of a modern legal system of the kind that existed in Japan or Western countries. Yet, amid uneven access to physicians of scientific medicine and few specialized medico-legal laboratories, the Republican judiciary's adoption of the Qing state's forensic practices served the project of what Xiaoqun Xu has called "judicial modernity" in unexpected ways.[2] The centralized forensic techniques of the Qing furthered the goals of "formalization, standardization, and bureaucratization," which had been on the legal reform agenda since the New Policy reforms (1901–11).[3] Moreover, the corpse examination services that coroners rendered to procuratorial officials (*jiancha guan*) consolidated these new legal professionals' authority over forensic evidence in criminal investigations. Rather than impeding the modernity of the Republican judiciary, coroners facilitated the rise of the "judicial" (*sifa*) as a distinct and highly specialized area of professional activity. In this sense, they furthered the modern transformation of Chinese law.

The story of coroners like Yu Yuan demonstrates that the emergence of modern legal practices in China took place in dialogue with older institutions and precedents.[4] It also illuminates one aspect of the process through which the older conceptions of legal knowledge and expertise that had developed over the Ming and Qing were negotiated, reworked, or abandoned amid the challenges of modernity. Scholars have persuasively argued for the incipient "professionalization" of communities of Ming-Qing officials and legal specialists on the basis of the development of specialized legal knowledge, notions of shared identity and ethics, and recognized expert authority.[5] The early twentieth century saw the emergence of increasingly specialized forms of training, new mechanisms for regulating legal practitioners, and new conceptions of legal knowledge.[6] Coroners found a place in this new order not by

---

2 Xiaoqun Xu, *Trial of Modernity: Judicial Reform in Early Twentieth-Century China, 1901–1937* (Stanford: Stanford University Press, 2008).

3 Ibid., 5.

4 I.e. Jennifer M. Neighbors, "The Long Arm of Qing Law? Qing Dynasty Homicide Rulings in Republican Courts," *Modern China* 35, no. 1 (2009): 3–37.

5 Li Chen, "Legal Specialists and Judicial Administration in Late Imperial China, 1651–1911," *Late Imperial China* 33, no. 1 (2012): 1–54; Yanhong Wu, "The Community of Legal Experts in Sixteenth- and Seventeenth-Century China," chapter 7 in this volume.

6 These changes can be followed in Xiaoqun Xu, *Chinese Professionals and the Republican State: The Rise of Professional Associations in Shanghai, 1912–1937* (Cambridge: Cambridge University Press, 2001); Glenn D. Tiffert, "The Chinese Judge: From Literatus to Cadre (1906–1949)," in *Knowledge Acts in Modern China: Ideas, Institutions, and Identities*, ed. Robert Culp et al. (Berkeley: Institute for East Asian Studies Publications, forthcoming); Michael Hoi-kit Ng,

emulating models of legal or medical professionalization, but by remaining as subordinate functionaries in a judiciary that, much like that of the Qing, was interested in maintaining forensics as a technical activity supervised by legal officials. This chapter examines some of the possibilities and challenges that this process presented for the coroners of Beijing. It suggests that even as coroners remained essential functionaries within the Republican judiciary, their professional status was inherently precarious in the modern occupational marketplace in which they found themselves.

Remaking the Coroner at the Beginning of the Modern Chinese State

The forensic inspection of dead bodies was a crucial element of local judicial procedure under the Qing. The goal of such examinations was to find out what had happened in a criminally-suspicious death and produce a written record of the body to serve as evidence. Officials overseeing these examinations relied on highly formalized procedures for examining the body and documenting wounds, a reflection of the routinization of judicial procedure more generally, the formalization of case narratives and associated language, and the bureaucratization of judicial decision-making.[7] Local functionaries called *wuzuo* (coroners) were the ones who actually examined the body under supervision of a county magistrate or other local official, almost invariably assisted by legal specialists.[8] The techniques that coroners used to find cause of death and solve forensic problems were based largely on the written tradition of forensic knowledge contained in the *Records on the Washing Away of Wrongs* (*Xiyuanlu*), a bureaucratic standard according to which forensic inspections were assessed during judicial review.[9] While numerous officials,

---

"Attorney on Trial: When Lawyers Met Phony Lawyers in Republican Beijing," *International Journal of Asian Studies* 8, no. 1 (2011): 25–39.

7 Thomas M. Buoye, "Suddenly Murderous Intent Arose: Bureaucratization and Benevolence in Eighteenth-century Qing Homicide Reports," *Late Imperial China* 16, no. 2 (1995): 62–97.

8 For the essential role that legal specialists played at all levels of Qing administration of justice, see Li Chen, "Regulating Private Legal Specialists and the Limits of Imperial Power in Qing China," chaper 9 in this volume.

9 The official four-*juan* text was titled *Records on the Washing Away of Wrongs, edited by the Codification Office* (Lüliguan jiaozheng Xiyuanlu). Various government and private publishers produced editions, often in annotated and expanded form, over the course of the late eighteenth- and nineteenth centuries. For discussion of important critical editions, see Pierre-Étienne Will, "Developing Forensic Knowledge through Cases in the Qing Dynasty,"

legal specialists, and coroners scrutinized the received knowledge contained in this official text,[10] following its techniques remained a necessity under the Qing empire's bureaucratized judicial system.

Under the Qing, forensic investigation was not organized as a specialized task falling under the exclusive jurisdiction of a particular professional group.[11] The late imperial bureaucracy's primary concern was that the proper examination procedures had been followed, an outcome that would be apparent as the completed case file passed through the system of mandatory judicial review. Even as late imperial forensics developed into a field of scholarly knowledge through specialist treatises, the most routine forms of forensic practice were more akin to a regime of discipline that bestowed legitimacy on the basis of examiners' conformity with official procedure.[12] With some exceptions (discussed below), the identity or social affiliation of individual examiners was a relatively unimportant consideration in the authority of forensic claims. This notion of forensic authority is different from modern conceptions of forensics as a practice carried out by highly specialized "experts" rather than, in modern parlance, "technicians." Yet, the notion of a "technician" is, in fact, closer to

---

in *Thinking with Cases: Specialist Knowledge in Chinese Cultural History*, ed. Charlotte Furth et al. (Honolulu: University of Hawai'i Press, 2007). For a compelling argument that the official *Washing Away of Wrongs* was completed in the early 1740s (not 1694, as usually claimed), see Chen Chongfang 陈重方, "Qing 'Lüliguan jiaozheng xiyuanlu' xiangguan wenti kaozheng 清 '律例馆校正洗冤录'相关问题考证 [A Textual Study of Questions Pertaining to the Qing *Records on the Washing Away of Wrongs, Edited by the Codification Office*]," *Youfeng chuming niankan* 有凤初鸣年刊 6 (2010): 441–55. For the considerable impact of private commercial publishing on the circulation of legal knowledge during the Qing, see Ting Zhang, "Marketing Legal Information: Commercial Publications of the Great Qing Code, 1644–1911," chapter 8 in this volume.

10 See Will, "Developing Forensic Knowledge," and Catherine Despeux, "The Body Revealed: The Contribution of Forensic Medicine to Knowledge and Representation of the Skeleton in China," in *Graphics and Text in the Production of Technical Knowledge in China*, ed. Francesca Bray et al. (Leiden: Brill, 2007).

11 Chang Che-chia has argued compellingly that forensic authority lay in use of the *Washing Away of Wrongs* and that forensic knowledge "was not monopolized by members of a specific kind of group." See Chang Che-chia张哲嘉, " 'Zhongguo chuantong fayixue' de zhishi xingge yu caozuo mailuo '中国传统法医学'的知识性格与操作脉络 [English Title: Knowledge and Practice in 'Traditional Chinese Forensic Medicine']," *Zhongyang yanjiuyuan jindaishi yanjiusuo jikan* 中央研究院近代史研究所集刊 [Journal of Institute of Modern History of the Academia Sinica] 44 (2004): 1–30, esp. 14.

12 Daniel Asen, "Dead Bodies and Forensic Science: Cultures of Expertise in China, 1800–1949" (PhD diss., Columbia University, 2012).

what coroners were supposed to be under the forensic regime implemented by the late imperial state.[13]

During the second half of the New Policy reforms, officials began to reorganize the Qing empire's legal institutions along the lines of those of continental Europe and Japan, drafting new criminal and civil codes and setting the foundations for what was initially a four-level court system. As part of this project officials also turned their attention to the forensic institutions of the Qing. In 1908 the Governor-General of the newly established Three Eastern Provinces Xu Shichang (1858–1939), along with Zhu Jiabao (1864–1928) who had been appointed acting Governor of Jilin Province at the time of its creation, passed on to the court a proposal from Jilin's provincial justice department (*tifa si*).[14] The proposal was to establish in Jilin's High Court a Forensic Inspection Training School that would enroll literate coroners as well as youth over the age of 20 *sui* to complete a year-long training program based on the *Washing Away of Wrongs* and Western physiology and anatomy, undoubtedly from Japanese translation. More radically, renamed "inspection clerks" (*jianyan li*), these personnel would be eligible for the procedures already in place for clerks to obtain low-level ranked positions through competitive testing. This was an unprecedented change in the occupational and social status of coroners who, like other functionaries performing services within the yamen perceived as menial or debased, had been of "mean" status and unable to pursue an official career.[15]

This proposal, which was soon endorsed by an imperial edict, represented an accommodation between a new vision of forensics as a global field of modern science and older models of forensic practice that had developed under the late imperial state. Officials had long been concerned with the difficulties of finding competent examiners, the low quality of most coroners, and the unenforced regulations on coroner quotas and training. The idea that raising the status of coroners would solve these problems was not new. In 1877 the Governor-General of Liangjiang Shen Baozhen (1820–1879) had suggested that

13 For a critical assessment of the idea of the "technician" in seventeenth-century science in the West, see Steven Shapin, *A Social History of Truth: Civility and Science in Seventeenth-Century England* (Chicago: The University of Chicago Press, 1994), 355–407. Shapin's discussion of the tension between the low status and indispensable role of the "technician" is one which informs this study's treatment of coroners in China.

14 *Da Qing fagui daquan* 大清法规大全 [Compendium of Laws and Regulations of the Great Qing] (Zhengxue she, n.d.), falü bu, 8: 1b–2b.

15 For more on the "mean" status of yamen runners, see Jing Junjian 经君健. *Qingdai shehui de jianmin dengji* 清代社会的贱民等级 [The "Mean" Social Stratum in Qing Society] (Beijing: Zhongguo renmin daxue chubanshe, 2009), 95–105.

revoking coroners' "mean" status and granting them an occupational status equivalent to clerks of punishments (*xingke shuli*) would improve their quality and encourage more people to become coroners.[16] Coroners' low status was viewed as causing the interconnected problems of the incompetence of existing coroners, the difficulties of finding persons to fill the local quotas, and the morally debased nature that made coroners (much like other yamen runners) seem prone to corruption. Raising the status of yamen functionaries was a way of improving the "quality" of candidates who filled the ranks and encouraging the development of their technical skill and moral virtue.[17]

Yet, this reform largely left the forensic institutions of the Qing empire intact: forensic examinations were not delegated to physicians of Western medicine. At a time when there were few physicians of "scientific" medicine in China, it is hard to imagine alternatives to keeping existing institutions in place. In the end, the reform ensured that forensic examinations would, by default, remain within the professional purview of state officials who handled the administration of justice.[18] Giving coroners the status of clerks would have raised their status while keeping them subordinate to the procuratorial officials and county magistrates who investigated criminal cases. In a legal system for which county administrative authorities continued to handle judicial affairs in areas without reformed courts, maintaining older forensic practices made it possible for an institutionally heterogeneous judiciary to implement a consistent forensic system.[19] In Beijing, coroners inspected the corpses that procurators investigated as part of their involve-

16 These were the clerks (referred to as *xingshu*) tasked with explaining the *Washing Away of Wrongs* to local contingents of coroners. See Wu Yuanbing 吴元炳, ed. *Shen Wensu gong zhengshu* 沈文肃公政书 [Official Writings of Shen Wensu] (Taibei: Wenhai chubanshe, 1967 [1880]), 7: 41a–42b.

17 Cf. Rowe's discussion of Chen Hongmou's (1696–1771) mid-eighteenth-century proposal to offer clerks opportunities to improve their status through examination, a proposal which rested on these basic assumptions, refracted through Chen's own views of individuality and moral capacity. See William T. Rowe, *Saving the World: Chen Hongmou and Elite Consciousness in Eighteenth-Century China* (Stanford: Stanford University Press, 2001), 339–44.

18 Physicians of Western medicine and experts in legal medicine did become involved in legal cases in subsequent decades, but on terms shaped by judicial officials' claims over forensics. Asen, "Dead Bodies," 214–289.

19 After the fall of the Qing, the number of courts would actually decrease along with the formalization of judicial functions of administrative officials in areas without courts. This would become a major target of reform throughout this period. See Xu, *Trial of Modernity*, 43, 64–65.

ment in the city's sudden and suspicious death cases, thereby facilitating the work of a group of highly specialized legal professionals who played an essential role in the project of "judicial modernity."[20] Yet, by integrating coroners into a modern court system without changing the bureaucratic model of forensic practice on which their authority was based, the New Policy reform left their status as "experts" an unresolved question that would be negotiated for decades after the collapse of the Qing.

Coroners of Beijing

By the early 1920s there were about a dozen coroners and coroners-in-training working for the Capital Local Procuracy and its two branch offices in Beijing.[21] In an oral history compiled during the early decades of the People's Republic, Song Qixing, one of the coroners trained during this period, discussed the importance of clan affiliation for the city's coroners:

> The ancestral home of our clan, the Song, is Qihe County, Jinan Prefecture, in Shandong. We have pursued the occupation of coroner since the Ming Dynasty. At the beginning of the Qing, we moved from Shandong to Beijing, and still did the old business, serving in the Board of Punishments and passing down this work from generation to generation. By the period of the Beiyang government and GMD rule, we served in the Board of Justice and later Beiping High Court. After Liberation, one of my nephews and I served in People's Courts in Beijing, Hebei, and Shanxi.
>
> Because the members of our clan had the status of a "mean occupation," the level of cultural attainment was not high, and we relied on the classic work of our occupation, the *Washing Away of Wrongs*, as the theoretical grounds [of our work] while depending on the work experience that has been privately passed on by our forebears to maintain this work as the purview of our clan. Consequently there are no written records of the family history. Now in discussing the old occupation of "coroner,"

20 By the mid-1920s, the officers who staffed procuracies and courts had to meet unprecedentedly high standards of professional training and experience. See Xu, *Trial of Modernity*, 61–62. As Tiffert ("The Chinese Judge") has noted, the professional requirements and training that judicial officers underwent distinguished them from other legal practitioners, a group already distinguished by its professional education.

21 BMA, No. J181-18-13978. "Fatingjianyan lijijianyanjianxisheng mingce 法庭检验吏及检验见习生名册 [Register of Court Coroners and Coroners-in-Training]," 1922.

> I can only rely upon that which was orally transmitted by my elders, and which I myself can recall of what I have experienced since the age of 14 *sui*.[22]

Aside from members of the Song, those of the Yu and Fu (who, according to Song Qixing's account, were relative latecomers to the occupation) provided many of the coroners serving in Beijing procuratorial organs during the Republican period. In the late 1910s, there were at least six coroners working for local procuratorial authorities in Beijing.[23] Aside from Yu Yuan was Yu Tao, another highly experienced senior coroner, and Yu Tao's son Yu Depei. Two members of the Song, Song Ze and Song Duo, were also coroners at this time. The last coroner was Fu Shun, who had reportedly been the disciple of another member of the Song.[24] Formal drives to recruit and train new coroners were carried out in 1919 and 1942 and the effect of both was to bring in new members of these three clans alongside other unrelated recruits.[25] Several female forensic examiners, referred to as "midwives" (*wenpo*), also worked for procuratorial and police authorities, examining the genitals of female victims in forensic cases and investigating wounded victims and the anonymous dead of the city.[26]

---

22 The only information provided about Song's oral history was that it was "put in order" (*zhengli*) by Zhang Gongliang in January 1965. While I have been unable to corroborate many of the details in Song's account, claims pertaining to the Republican era are generally substantiated by court and police files. See Song Qixing 宋启兴, "Yitan wuzuo hangdang 忆谈仵作行当 [Reminiscing about the Occupation of Coroner]," in *Wenshi ziliao cungao xuanbian: shehui* 文史资料存稿选编: 社会 [Selection of Preserved Manuscripts of Literary and Historical Materials. Volume 25: Society], ed. Quanguo zhengxie wenshi ziliao weiyuanhui 全国政协文史资料委员会 (Beijing: Zhongguo wenshi chubanshe, 2002), 395–8.

23 See list of names on a March 1918 written response to the Board of Justice regarding forensic questions. BMA, No. J174-1-156, "Jingshi dijianting… Sifabu xingshisi xunwen zhenggu jianyan banfa de han 京师地检厅… 司法部刑事司询问蒸骨检验办法的函 [Letters of Capital Local Procuracy Pertaining to the Criminal Office of the Board of Justice Asking about the Methods of Bone Steaming Inquests, etc.]," 1918–1924, 51.

24 Song, "Yitan wuzuo hangdang," 395.

25 See BMA, No. J174-1-27, "Jingshi difang jianchating guanyu jianyan li de cheng 京师地方检察厅关于检验吏的呈 [Petition of Capital Local Procuracy regarding Coroners]," 1919–20, 1–11; J174-2-52. "Beijing dijianchu Yu Yuan guanyu peiyang jianyan rencai cheng 北京地检处俞源关于培养检验人才呈 [Petition of Yu Yuan of Beijing Local Procuracy regarding the Training of Inquest Personnel]," 1942–1943, 1–4.

26 Song Qixing wrote of them, "At that time the Beijing courts had over 10 coroners. Among them were two 50–60 *sui* female coroners named Ms. Xue (Xue shi) and Ms. Wang (Wang shi). Court officials called them 'midwives' (*wenpo*). They had been transferred from

The forms that coroner training took in China during the last years of the New Policy reforms and over the Republican period varied greatly, ranging from formal instruction of dozens of recruits to small programs based on personal instruction by particularly experienced coroners.[27] The training carried out in Beijing in 1919 was a kind of discipleship in which each of the four senior coroners was to accept two students for formal instruction in techniques for examining wounds and skeletal remains, many of which were drawn from the *Washing Away of Wrongs*, as well as practical training that involved accompanying them on forensic examinations. Song Qixing suggested in his oral history that this form of training was an established practice within the clan,

> Our clan has for generations let boys, starting from the age of 13 or 14 *sui*, follow the older generation out to the site of the examination of the corpse to come into contact with frightening corpses that had undergone all kinds of different deaths. In my own experience, it was from having frequent contact with the dead from a young age that later on I came to be without any misgivings when performing my work.[28]

Those who served as "coroners" in Republican China would have been a diverse group, trained in different ways, and serving in different kinds of judicial institutions. Information regarding the occupational background of those trained in Beijing in 1919 suggests that the majority had been engaged in some kind of commercial enterprise, a background that might have provided a practical

---

guard work at the prison, and did not have much knowledge of forensic examination." See Song, "Yitan wuzuo hangdang," 396. Also, for example, see BMA J181-20-653. "Jingshi jingchating Xingshisuo guanyu tisong anfan jianyan li jianyan daobi dengxiang chefei shumu de cheng 京师警察厅刑事所关于提送案犯检验吏检验倒毙等项车费数目的呈 [Report of Criminal Affairs Center of the Metropolitan Police Board regarding amounts of travel costs for transporting criminals and coroners performing inquests for those who fall dead, etc.]," 1927. This list of costs incurred by police and judicial personnel indicates that two "midwives," Ms. Sun and Ms. Chen investigated wounding cases as well as anonymous corpses for police authorities. Song Qixing's description aside, the work of "midwives" was just as important as that of (male) coroners.

27 For example, by the fall of the Qing, authorities in Fengtian had been through two iterations of forensic training institutions. After 1912 they continued their efforts, resigning themselves to a small training program within the Shenyang Local Procuracy. See "Zhunshe jianyan jiangxisuo ling 准设检验讲习所令 [Order regarding Authorization to Establish a Forensic Inspection Training Institute]," *Sifa gongbao* 司法公报 [*Judicial Bulletin*] 114 (1919): 70–1.

28 Song, "Yitan wuzuo hangdang," 395.

source of literacy of use in their forensic work.[29] None were of the ranks of "professional" workers studied by Xiaoqun Xu, for whom higher education was usually a prerequisite for occupational expertise.[30] As for their reasons for becoming coroners, several noted that they could "make a living by performing inquests" or be able to "provide for my family and make a living."[31] About a quarter of the recruits reported having no job at the moment of their enrollment in training.

Coroners were, foremost, subordinate judicial functionaries. They were not organized through associations of the kind that lawyers, physicians, and other groups used to promote their professional interests.[32] If kinship ties informed the recruitment and training of coroners in Beijing, these social relations operated within the context of the procuratorial institutions that actually employed coroners, supported their training, and established the conditions in which they worked. Coroners provided procuratorial authorities with essential services, facilitating their investigations of sudden and suspicious death cases as well as the gathering of evidence. Yet, they did so not as members of an autonomous profession distinct from the judiciary. For example, coroners rarely presented evidence through the new legal mechanism of the *jianding* (expert opinion), which provided a way for groups and individuals with special knowledge or skill not possessed by judicial authorities to participate in legal proceedings.[33] While some coroners had recognized expertise and were valued for it, the role that coroners more often played was that of a kind of procuratorial assistant who applied standardized examination techniques to make the dead body intelligible and accessible to their superiors' judicial investigations.

29 Cf. Rawski's discussion of the different kinds of and motives for literacy in late imperial China. Evelyn S. Rawski, *Education and Popular Literacy in Ch'ing China* (Ann Arbor: The University of Michigan Press, 1979).

30 Xu, *Chinese Professionals*, 65–6.

31 BMA J174-1-67, "Jingshi difang jianchating jianyan xuexisuo shijuan 京师地方检察厅检验学习所试卷 [Testing Papers of the Capital Local Procuracy Inquest School]," 1919.

32 Cf. Xu, *Chinese Professionals*.

33 Physicians and medico-legal specialists submitted evidence through this mechanism, making them roughly equivalent to Anglo-American "expert witnesses." See Asen, "Dead Bodies."

Investigating Deaths

Procurators in Republican China personally investigated crimes and gathered evidence used for trial, often in conjunction with judicial police (*sifa jingcha*) who worked under their direction. Because of the requirement in Beijing that procurators issue burial permits for deaths occurring in public, including anonymous bodies discovered on city streets, forensic inspections constituted an important area of their work. Coroners worked closely with procurators and judicial police, inspecting and documenting the dead bodies that fell under their professional purview. In many cases, coroners simply played an adjunct role to procuratorial investigation. The forensic examination of a body could be largely redundant when information about the death could be obtained from a broader investigation that included questioning of witnesses, a confession, or examination of a crime scene. For sudden deaths that occurred in public without criminal suspicion, one of the most routine kinds of cases that procurators and coroners handled in Beijing, the forensic examination often simply confirmed cause of death. Police had usually gathered the facts even before the procurator and coroner arrived at the scene.[34]

The newspaper account of a forensic inquest following a double homicide in May 1926 can give a sense of the role that coroners commonly played in judicial investigations.[35] In this case, judicial officials were called to a crowded compound near Xuanwu Gate in the southwest corner of the Inner City. A neighbor had seen a blood-soaked man, who would be identified as a rickshaw puller named Jing Tai, fleeing the residence of Wang Yu, another rickshaw puller, and his wife, Mrs. Cao. After the neighbor alerted district police, Jing was almost immediately apprehended. The police soon notified procuratorial authorities and requested that they examine the bodies of Wang and Mrs. Cao, both of whom had died from the wounds inflicted by Jing Tai. Procurator Luo Zhenqiu was sent to oversee the inquest, arriving with a secretary, a coroner named Zhao Fuhai, and the midwife Ms. Sun (Sun Shi), as well as judicial policemen and other police officers.

Luo first interrogated Jing Tai, asking about his relationship with the victims and his reasons for committing the crime. This established that Wang had owed money to Jing Tai and that the two had fought several days before the killing. According to Jing's confession, he went to collect the money from Wang,

34 For more on death investigation procedures in Republican Beijing, see Asen, "Dead Bodies," 143–87.

35 "Youfang hutong liang tiao ming'an 油房胡同两条命案 [Double Homicide at Youfang Hutong]," *Chenbao* 晨报 [Morning Post], May 10, 1926, 6/326.

bringing a dagger that he had purchased after receiving additional threats from Wang. When Wang attempted to hack Jing with a knife, he returned the attack, leading to the violence that left Wang and Mrs. Cao dead. After this round of questioning concluded, the examination of Wang's body proceeded in the presence of Jing, family, and neighbors. After enumerating the knife wounds on Wang's body, the coroner Zhao proclaimed to the procurator that they had in fact caused Wang's death, a point already established by questioning. The body of Mrs. Cao was then examined first by Zhao, who enumerated the wounds on the upper part of the body, and then by the midwife, Ms. Sun, who examined the lower body in another room, out of sight of those attending the inquest. With the inquest concluded, Jing, along with everyone else involved in the case, was released to the procuracy.

In cases such as this one, the role of the coroner was mainly to confirm cause of death and produce a record of the body. A substantial form, called a *yanduan shu*, had to be filled out and this record became part of the case file and could be used as evidence in a trial.[36] The completed form from the October 1933 examination of a female prisoner found dead at Hebei No. 1 Branch Prison illustrates the kinds of information that were recorded.[37] In this case, the investigating official and accompanying coroner, Song Chunzhi, described the body as yellow in color with eyes closed, fingers "slightly bent," the belly "slightly sunken," and with a minor wound on the left knee. Illness was recorded as cause of death with no further explanation of how this finding was ascertained. For parts of the body that did not have hand-written comments in the form, a stamp was applied indicating that there were no significant findings, thus constituting supporting evidence that the death had not been caused by violence. This kind of highly formulaic document was commonly used in legal cases in China throughout the Republican period and in Beijing well into the 1940s.[38]

36 This official form, issued in 1918, was an adaptation of forms used under the Qing. For more on the Qing-era forms, see Daniel Asen, "Vital Spots, Mortal Wounds, and Forensic Practice: Finding Cause of Death in Nineteenth-Century China," *East Asian Science, Technology and Society* 3, no. 4 (2009): 453–474. For the updated form, see *Sifa ligui bubian* 司法例规补编 [Supplementary Collection of Judicial Regulations] (Beijing: Sifa gongbao faxingsuo, 1919), 239–61.

37 BMA, No. J191-2-15648, "Beiping xiehe yiyuan lingqu shiti de qingqiu, zhixiehan ji yanduanshu 北平协和医院领取尸体的请求，致谢函及验断书 [Requests of Beiping Union Medical College Hospital for Corpses for Dissection, Letters of Gratitude, and *yanduan shu*]," 1933, 9–30.

38 When in 1947 hygiene authorities in Beijing asked procuratorial officials to record their inquest findings in a way more compatible with their own regime of public health death registration, they received the following response: "In the inquest cases handled by our

One of the most important functions that coroners performed was to literally "encode" wounds and other signs into an official forensic discourse established by the Republican judiciary on the basis of Qing precedents.[39] In a case such as Jing Tai's double homicide, coroners were not meant to implement a form of expertise professionally or epistemologically distinct from judicial officials' own fact-finding activities. As in this case, interrogation and forensic examination could be carried out in sequence, making wounds intelligible not simply as evidence of corporeal trauma but of the actions for which particular agents would be held legally responsible. The benefits of this arrangement would not have been insignificant for the practice of judicial investigation. Even the most specialized forms of forensic expertise are only useful when used in conjunction with contextualizing facts.[40] Coroners supported procurators' work by making forensic evidence immediately accessible to them and, more than this, establishing forensics as an area of the investigation already under their professional authority. Yet, coroners' utility depended on their subordination both to the judicial officials with whom they worked and to the court system that dictated the form of their examination practices.

The Search for Expert Coroners

Aside from the routine and by all accounts grinding work of investigating sudden and suspicious deaths in the city, the Beijing local procuracy also supplied examiners to regional authorities faced with disputed forensic cases. The

office [the local procuracy], we fill in *yanduan shu* that are appended to the file in all cases. Separate booklets with tables have not been made, and we have no way to fill in such information. If your bureau requires this kind of material, you can send staff to come to the procuracy, assemble the files and copy them." See BMA, No. J5-1-1278, "Weishengju guanyu tingshou chusheng siwang zhengshu ji chubin zhizhao fei de chengwen ji shizhengfu de zhiling yiji qing fa chusheng, siwang zhengmingshudeng de laiwang gonghan, xinjian 卫生局关于停收出生死亡证书及出殡执照费的呈文及市政府的指令以及请发出生,死亡证明书等的来往公函,信件 [Report of the Bureau of Hygiene Regarding Ceasing Collection of Fees for Birth and Death Certificates and Funeral Permits and Municipal Government's Instructions as well as Correspondence regarding Requests to Issue Birth and Death Certificates]," 1947, 175–179.

39 For this usage of "encode," see Francesca Bray, "Science, Technique, Technology: Passages between Matter and Knowledge in Imperial Chinese Agriculture," *The British Journal for the History of Science* 41, no. 3 (2008): 319–44.

40 I.e. Stefan Timmermans, *Postmortem: How Medical Examiners Explain Suspicious Deaths* (Chicago: University of Chicago Press, 2006).

coroners of the Beijing local procuracy were recognized by regional authorities as well as central judicial institutions as experts in this kind of examination. Given that these were cases for which there were conflicting interpretations of evidence, much depended on an authoritative forensic examination. Because the body had invariably decomposed if not skeletonized by this point, these cases required a set of forensic techniques different from those used on "fresh" bodies. The examination of decomposed remains was an area of forensic practice understood to be particularly difficult, one for which examiners with special expertise were necessary. In these cases, the forensic evidence emerged as a central issue and coroners with recognized expertise were made to take center stage in the handling of the case.

In late imperial times coroners could be transferred from other counties and even provinces to assist in these kinds of examinations.[41] For example, during his time as Surveillance Commissioner in Jiangsu in the mid-1820s, Lin Zexu (1785–1850) urged provincial officials to train additional coroners, noting that a small number of experienced coroners were repeatedly tapped for the province's skeletal examination cases:

> There are many cases involving loss of life in Jiangsu and oftentimes there are cases involving examination of skeletal remains, but coroners who are particularly adept are very few in number. Several times now, in cases involving the opening of a coffin and examination of remains, officials compete to summon the coroner Jing Qikun of Dantu. It is truly astounding that in a province this big, forensic inspections rely exclusively on one person. Given that Jing Qikun is more than 80 *sui*, how can he possibly be employed for long?[42]

---

41 Expanded editions of the *Washing Away of Wrongs* and case collections provide glimpses of this practice. For example, see the 1791 case of an "old coroner" named Tang Ming explaining the skeletal remains of a woman named Zhang Fulian, which was discussed in the specialist forensic literature as an example of the challenges of skeletal examinations. Tang was a coroner from Chenxi County (Chenzhou Prefecture), directly northeast of Yuanzhou Prefecture, where the case originated in western Hunan. The brief information included in the case suggests that Tang was tapped for the case from within the province. See *Chongkan buzhu Xiyuanlu jizheng* 重刊补注洗冤录集证 [Records on the Washing Away of Wrongs with Collected Evidence, with Supplements and Annotation, Reprinted] (Yuedong shengshu, 1865), 1: 41a–b.

42 Lin Zexu 林则徐, *Lin Zexu ji: gongdu* 林则徐集: 公牍 [Collected Writings of Lin Zexu: Administrative Documents] (Beijing: Zhonghua shuju, 1963), *gongdu* 2: 11–2.

In cases involving skeletal remains, the expertise of the individual examiner emerged as an explicit question in a way that it did not in more routine forensic inspections involving uncontested cases or deaths unrelated to criminal acts. When seeking coroners for skeletal examinations, it was conventional for officials to request coroners who were "skilled" (*anlian*) by virtue of experience, a term that appears often in the administrative discourse surrounding forensics in late imperial China.[43] These examinations could involve finding cause of death on the basis of skeletal remains without surrounding tissue, identifying signs on old and washed out bones, and accounting for long lost bone fragments and incomplete remains, questions discussed at length in the specialist literature produced by legal specialists and officials.[44] These examinations were also difficult because they required examiners to reconcile the remains before them with the Qing state's incomplete and heavily criticized official knowledge of the skeleton.[45]

The local procuracy in Beijing seems to have been a well-known source for this kind of expertise among authorities in north China. The case of Liu Guangju was one of many skeletal examination cases handled by Yu Yuan and other Beijing-based coroners during the first decades of the twentieth century.[46] In this case the dispute revolved around discolorations on Liu Guangju's

43 Wang Youhuai mentioned the practice in his *Important Points for Handling Cases* (Ban'an yaolüe 办案要略, n.d.). See Zhang Tingxiang 张廷骧, *Rumu xuzhi wuzhong* 入幕须知五种 [Five Works on the Essentials of Entering the Muyou Profession] (Zhejiang shuju. Reprinted by Taibei: Wenhai chubanshe, 1968 [1892]), 35b/500. Also see discussion of the practice in *Essentials of Trying Lawsuits* (Tingsong qieyao 听讼挈要), judicial precepts included in the 1890–91 regulations (nie, guangxu 17, 5a) appended to *Jiangsu shengli sibian* 江苏省例四编 [Provincial Regulations of Jiangsu, Fourth Collection] (Jiangsu shuju, 1890).

44 For discussion of some of the difficulties, see Xu Lian 许梿, *Xiyuanlu xiangyi* 洗冤录详义 [Detailed Explanations of the Meaning of the Washing Away of Wrongs] (Hubei guanshu chu, 1890 [1854]), 1.86b–87a. In his *Xiyuanlu jie* (1831), Yao Deyu 姚德豫 characterized skeletal examination as "especially difficult" when compared with inspecting the wounds of the living, which was "easy," and examining those of (non-skeletonized) corpses, which was "difficult." See *Xiyuanlu jie* 洗冤录解 [Explanations of the Washing Away of Wrongs], 3a, appended to *Chongkan buzhu Xiyuanlu jizheng*.

45 Despeux, "The Body Revealed," 641–44; Will, "Developing Forensic Knowledge," 90–91.

46 For additional cases, see files contained in BMA, No. J174-1-184, 1923; J174-2-279, "Hebei gaojianchu guanyu chaming youwu you jingyan xueshi jianyan renyuan xunling 河北高检处关于查明有无有经验学识检验人员训令 [Orders of Hebei High Procuracy regarding finding out whether there are inquest personnel with experience and learning]," 1929; BMA, No. J174-1-156, 1918–1924, 37–51.

bones made visible during an earlier skeletal examination conducted locally.[47] Despite the finding that there was no evidence that Liu Guangju had been kicked to death, the aunt of the deceased, Mrs. Liu née Li, identified slight discolorations on four of the ribs as "suspicious." Liu also claimed that, at the time of the examination, she had seen purple, red, and blue discolorations on the bones, thus constituting additional evidence of wounds. This too was refuted by the examiners, who all affirmed that the bones were pale yellow. On the basis of these claims, Liu accused the examiners of having been bribed to conceal wounds and refused to claim the remains for burial.

In order to resolve the case, authorities in Fengtian raised the possibility of an examination that would exclusively address the disputed issues, not another examination of the entire set of Liu Guangju's remains. Such a procedure was not uncommon. In response to the Fengtian authorities' queries, the coroner Yu Yuan composed a report citing five cases that he had personally handled in which a single part of the skeleton—for example the skull or a rib—had been the focus of the examination.[48] In these cases, the dispute had come down to a single bone, and focusing on that part in the examination was a way of resolving the case, implicitly by limiting the issues that were in dispute. Yu noted, however, that it was essential to put into place a mechanism through which the disputants would be forced to accept the legitimacy of the re-examination as well as its final outcome. This could be accomplished by having the disputant, Liu Guangju's aunt, complete a written statement beforehand, indicating that she herself sanctioned the re-examination.

In cases involving intractable disputes over evidence, a successful resolution required that a coroner make relatives or other disputants accept a new set of forensic claims, in the process eschewing their interests and reasons for rejecting the original inquest findings. How to "bring (people) into submission" (*zhefu*), as it was commonly called, had been a long-standing question in the late imperial literature on forensics and judicial investigation.[49] In his oral history, Song Qixing described vividly the techniques that he used to make an accused defendant submit to an unfavorable forensic interpretation in a case that he handled in the early 1950s. While Song's account was meant to show the relevance of the "mass line" (*qunzhong luxian*) to forensic inquests, it also constitutes a valuable description of the techniques that could be used to achieve resolution in disputed cases and the very public sources of legitimacy in inquest proceedings:

47 BMA, No. J174-1-184, 61–2.

48 Ibid., No. J174-1-184, 72–3.

49 See Xu Lian, *Xiyuanlu xiangyi*, 1: 1b.

> In 1953 there was a murder case in Shanxi's Hejin County in which a woman named Li Yueying was strangled and then made to look like she hung herself. The murderer was her divorced ex-husband. The details of the case were evident, but the accused firmly persisted in not acknowledging his guilt and it stalled for two years with no way to settle the case. In the end all that was left was to open the coffin and re-examine the body. The area had no suitable personnel, so I was sent to handle the case. After the news went out, the masses that came to the scene numbered in the several thousands. In line with past experience, before the inquest I wrote on a blackboard in the form of a big-character poster the different signs that are left on the body from being strangled and hanging oneself. I let the masses read it for reference. Then I opened the coffin and examined the bones, discovering signs of being strangled. With approval of the judge, I let all of the masses line up and take turns viewing the body, explaining it to one after another, and thereby receiving their enthusiastic support. Then the killer was brought to the scene and the proceedings and outcome of the inquest were explained to him. He had no alternative but to sigh "I didn't think it would be discovered! I am the killer!" After he signed the confession then and there, the judge sentenced him to death and it was carried out immediately, thus closing a long pending murder case to the great satisfaction of the people.[50]

In this account, Song Qixing described the process through which he deftly manipulated the social environment of the inquest to create the level of social pressure necessary to make the accused acknowledge his guilt. As he described, this process involved actions that went beyond simply distinguishing the signs of suicide versus strangulation, a question that often emerged in these kinds of cases. It was engaging the crowd present at the inquest, showing them what to look for, and then convincing them ("one after another") that the remains in front of them indicated strangulation that made the inquest successful. It is not a coincidence that in this account the coroner is the center of attention. In contrast with the case of Jing Tai, in which the procurator played the central role of investigator and relied on the coroner to confirm facts already obtained by a confession, in the case of Li Yueying, the judge (*faguan*) played a peripheral role, only exercising authority after the forensic dispute at the heart of the case was resolved by an expert coroner.

50 Song, "Yitan wuzuo hangdang," 397–98.

A Liminal Profession

This chapter has explored the role that coroners played in Republican Beijing. It has identified several sources of coroners' authority: the institutionally-sanctioned role that they played in judicial procedure, their association with procurators' professional authority, and accumulated experience and skill. While coroners were a mainstay of judicial practice throughout the Republican period, their authority was nonetheless precarious if not vulnerable. Reaching a high point in the 1920s and 1930s, proponents of legal medicine criticized the *Washing Away of Wrongs* for its perceived lack of grounding in the methods of experimental science and Western anatomical knowledge of the body.[51] Various techniques in coroners' forensic repertoire came under criticism during this period, including the official examination forms that were used to record wounds and methods of testing for poisons included in the *Washing Away of Wrongs*. Yet, unlike physicians of Chinese medicine, who faced comparable criticism yet inhabited a much more ambivalent position vis-à-vis the modern state, coroners had official sanction to participate extensively in an area of modern statecraft.[52] They did so throughout the Republican period, despite the challenges of medico-legal reformers.

Examining the professional status of coroners under modernity can reveal much about the living yet liminal fate of a highly sophisticated field of late imperial expertise that survived the fall of the Qing. While the "survival" of these practices might be explained by the lack of alternatives—for example, the paucity of trained medico-legal examiners—this chapter has suggested other explanations as well. It has suggested that the Republican state found something useful in late imperial forensic practices and the social organization of knowledge on which they were based. One explanation for the continuing use of these practices might simply have been that they were already integrated into local judicial practice and were supported by higher-level judicial authorities. This chapter has suggested that, for various reasons, these practices facilitated productive relations between coroners and judicial officials and between those who became implicated in disputed cases and the state. Coroners supported particular ways of solving cases, producing authoritative evidence, and resolving disputes. And their uncertain status—their imperfect ownership over the knowledge that they were expected to use—was ultimately a product of the modern state's adoption of forensic technologies predicated

51 Medico-legal experts' attempts to criticize and delegitimate coroners' knowledge and techniques can be followed in Asen, "Dead Bodies," 221, 281–9.

52 Cf. Xu, "Chinese Professionals," 190–214.

on the social subordination of those who actually examined the body to the legal professionals tasked with administering justice.

Glossary

faguan	法官
Fu Shun	傅顺
jiancha guan	检察官
jianding	鉴定
jianyan li	检验吏
Lüliguan jiaozheng Xiyuanlu	律例馆校正洗冤录
Luo Zhenqiu	罗镇球
qunzhong luxian	群众路线
Shen Baozhen	沈葆桢
sifa	司法
sifa jingcha	司法警察
Song Chunzhi	宋纯智
Song Duo	宋铎
Song Qixing	宋启兴
Song Ze	宋泽
Sun shi	孙氏
tifa si	提法司
Wang shi	王氏
Wang Youhuai	王又槐
wenpo	稳婆
wuzuo	仵作
Xiyuanlu	洗冤录
xingke shuli	刑科书吏
xingshu	刑书
Xu Shichang	徐世昌
Xue shi	薛氏
yanduan shu	验断书
Yu Depei	俞德霈
Yu Tao	俞涛
Yu Yuan	俞源
Zhao Fuhai	赵福海
Zhang Gongliang	张功良
zhefu	折服
zhengli	整理
Zhu Jiabao	朱家寶

Bibliography

Asen, Daniel. "Dead Bodies and Forensic Science: Cultures of Expertise in China, 1800–1949." PhD diss., Columbia University, 2012.

———. "Vital Spots, Mortal Wounds, and Forensic Practice: Finding Cause of Death in Nineteenth-Century China." *East Asian Science, Technology and Society* 3, no. 4 (2009): 453–74.

Bray, Francesca. "Science, Technique, Technology: Passages between Matter and Knowledge in Imperial Chinese Agriculture." *The British Journal for the History of Science* 41, no. 3 (2008): 319–44.

Buoye, Thomas M. "Suddenly Murderous Intent Arose: Bureaucratization and Benevolence in Eighteenth-century Qing Homicide Reports." *Late Imperial China* 16, no. 2 (1995): 62–97.

Chang Che-chia 张哲嘉. "'Zhongguo chuantong fayixue' de zhishi xingge yu caozuo mailuo '中国传统法医学'的知识性格与操作脉络 [English Title: Knowledge and Practice in 'Traditional Chinese Forensic Medicine']." *Zhongyang yanjiuyuan jindaishi yanjiusuo jikan* 中央研究院近代史研究所集刊 [Journal of Institute of Modern History of the Academia Sinica] 44 (2004): 1–30.

Chen Chongfang 陈重方. "Qing 'Lüliguan jiaozheng xiyuanlu' xiangguan wenti kaozheng 清 '律例馆校正洗冤录' 相关问题考证 [A Textual Study of Questions Pertaining to the Qing *Records on the Washing Away of Wrongs, Edited by the Codification Office*]." *Youfeng chuming niankan* 有凤初鸣年刊 6 (2010): 441–55.

Chen, Li. "Regulating Private Legal Specialists and the Limits of Imperial Power in Qing China." Chapter 9 in this volume.

———. "Legal Specialists and Judicial Administration in Late Imperial China, 1651–1911." *Late Imperial China* 33, no. 1 (June 2012): 1–54.

Chongkan buzhu Xiyuanlu jizheng 重刊补注洗冤录集证 [Records on the Washing Away of Wrongs with Collected Evidence, with Supplements and Annotation, Reprinted]. Yuedong shengshu, 1865.

Da Qing fagui daquan 大清法规大全 [Compendium of Laws and Regulations of the Great Qing]. Zhengxue she, n.d.

Despeux, Catherine. "The Body Revealed: The Contribution of Forensic Medicine to Knowledge and Representation of the Skeleton in China." In *Graphics and Text in the Production of Technical Knowledge in China*, edited by Francesca Bray, Vera Dorofeeva-Lichtmann, and Georges Métailié. Leiden: Brill, 2007.

Jiangsu shengli sibian 江苏省例四编 [Provincial Regulations of Jiangsu, Fourth Collection]. Jiangsu shuju, 1890.

Jing Junjian 经君健. *Qingdai shehui de jianmin dengji* 清代社会的贱民等级 [The "Mean" Social Stratum in Qing Society]. Beijing: Zhongguo renmin daxue chubanshe, 2009.

Lin Zexu 林则徐. *Lin Zexu ji: gongdu* 林则徐集: 公牍 [Collected Writings of Lin Zexu: Administrative Documents]. Beijing: Zhonghua shuju, 1963.

Neighbors, Jennifer M. "The Long Arm of Qing Law? Qing Dynasty Homicide Rulings in Republican Courts." *Modern China* 35, no. 1 (2009): 3–37.

Ng, Michael Hoi-kit. "Attorney on Trial: When Lawyers Met Phony Lawyers in Republican Beijing." *International Journal of Asian Studies* 8, no. 1 (2011): 25–39.

Rawski, Evelyn S. *Education and Popular Literacy in Ch'ing China*. Ann Arbor: The University of Michigan Press, 1979.

Rowe, William T. *Saving the World: Chen Hongmou and Elite Consciousness in Eighteenth-Century China*. Stanford: Stanford University Press, 2001.

Shapin, Steven. *A Social History of Truth: Civility and Science in Seventeenth-Century England*. Chicago: The University of Chicago Press, 1994.

Sifa ligui bubian 司法例规补编 [Supplementary Collection of Judicial Regulations]. Beijing: Sifa gongbao faxingsuo, 1919.

Song Qixing 宋启兴. "Yitan wuzuo hangdang 忆谈仵作行当 [Reminiscing about the occupation of coroner]." In *Wenshi ziliao cungao xuanbian: shehui* 文史资料存稿选编: 社会 [Selection of Preserved Manuscripts of Literary and Historical Materials], Vol. 25, edited by Quanguo zhengxie wenshi ziliao weiyuanhui 全国政协文史资料委员会. Beijing: Zhongguo wenshi chubanshe, 2002.

Tiffert, Glenn D. "The Chinese Judge: From Literatus to Cadre (1906–1949)." In *Knowledge Acts in Modern China: Ideas, Institutions, and Identities*, edited by Robert Culp, Eddy U, and Wen-hsin Yeh. Berkeley: Institute for East Asian Studies Publications, forthcoming.

Timmermans, Stefan. *Postmortem: How Medical Examiners Explain Suspicious Deaths*. Chicago: University of Chicago Press, 2006.

Will, Pierre-Étienne. "Developing Forensic Knowledge through Cases in the Qing Dynasty." In *Thinking with Cases: Specialist Knowledge in Chinese Cultural History*, edited by Charlotte Furth, Judith T. Zeitlin, and Ping-chen Hsiung. Honolulu: University of Hawai'i Press, 2007.

Wu, Yanhong. "The Community of Legal Experts in 16th- and 17th-Century China." In this volume.

Wu Yuanbing 吴元炳, ed. *Shen Wensu gong zhengshu* 沈文肃公政书 [Official Writings of Shen Wensu]. Taibei: Wenhai chubanshe, 1967 (1880).

Xu Lian 许梿. *Xiyuanlu xiangyi* 洗冤录详义 [Detailed Explanations of the Meaning of the Washing Away of Wrongs]. Hubei guanshu chu, 1890 (1854).

Xu, Xiaoqun. *Chinese Professionals and the Republican State: The Rise of Professional Associations in Shanghai, 1912–1937*. Cambridge: Cambridge University Press, 2001.

———. *Trial of Modernity: Judicial Reform in Early Twentieth-Century China, 1901–1937*. Stanford: Stanford University Press, 2008.

Zhang, Ting. "Marketing Legal Information: Commercial Publications of the Great Qing Code, 1644–1911." Chapter 8 in this volume.

Zhang Tingxiang 张廷骧. *Rumu xuzhi wuzhong* 入幕须知五种 [Five Works on the Essentials of Entering the Muyou Profession]. Zhejiang shuju, 1892. Reprinted by Taibei: Wenhai chubanshe, 1968.

CHAPTER 12

Simplified Legal Knowledge in the Early PRC: Explaining and Publishing the Marriage Law

*Jennifer Altehenger**

In late April 1950, Wang Feiran (1904–1994), president of the Beijing Municipal People's Court, commented on the upcoming promulgation of the PRC's first Marriage Law in a broadcast of the Central People's Broadcasting Station.[1] Trying to familiarize listeners with the new law and its role in the making of a New China under New Democracy, Wang explained that the Marriage Law was special because it was the first law to adopt the mass line as a legislative principle (*lifa fangfa*).[2] With the help of the mass line, the new law had been drafted to reflect the needs of the masses. Popular education that explained the law to people would now help create and consolidate the new society under CCP rule.

Implementation of the Marriage Law, however, proved more complicated than Wang had perhaps anticipated. New laws did not sui generis prompt people across the newly established People's Republic to act in accordance. Neither did everyone independently sit down to read this law that the new government claimed belonged to the people. Many were reluctant to go along with the social changes that the reform of the Marriage Law brought about, and others resisted.[3] As a result, between 1951 and 1952, legal reformers and high-level government officials began to explore the option of implementing

* I would like to thank Henrietta Harrison, Rana Mitter, Nicolai Volland, the members of the 'China's War with Japan' reading group at the University of Oxford, and the editors of this volume for their helpful comments. Research was kindly funded by the British Academy and the Cusanuswerk.

1 Wang Feiran 王斐然, "Youguan hunyinfa de wenti 有关婚姻法的问题 [Issues concerning the Marriage Law]," *Xin jianshe* 新建设 [New Construction], 2 (1950): 16–17.

2 Ibid., 16.

3 Some of the classic works on the Marriage Law, which also discuss local resistance to the law, include Delia Davin, *Woman-Work. Women and the Party in Revolutionary China* (Oxford: Clarendon Press, 1976); Kay Ann Johnson, *Women, the Family and Peasant Revolution in China* (Chicago: University of Chicago Press, 1983); Judith Stacey, *Patriarchy and Socialist Revolution in China* (Berkeley: University of California Press, 1983); and Neil J. Diamant, *Revolutionizing the Family: Politics, Love, and Divorce in Urban and Rural China, 1949–1968* (Berkeley: University of California Press, 2000).

© KONINKLIJKE BRILL NV, LEIDEN, 2015 | DOI 10.1163/9789004288492_014

and disseminating laws via mass mobilization campaigns. Campaigns were an all-pervasive feature of regime consolidation in the early 1950s and had been common even before the Communist takeover. Yet they had not previously been used for law dissemination. First pilot tests were carried out in 1951 and in early 1953 ideological campaigning and legal reform were joined in a nationwide legal education campaign: the Marriage Law Implementation Campaign (*guanche hunyinfa yundong*).[4]

By the logic of the mass line, the campaign would help educate citizens to understand, appreciate, and learn to live by the Marriage Law in particular and PRC law in general. Mass legal education was to contribute to linking state and society through knowledge, boost popular legitimacy for the young regime, and create the "new" socialist masses that abided by policies, laws, and party doctrine. To this end, the national, provincial, and municipal governments commissioned editors, artists, authors, and playwrights to design educational materials that could be employed in this project to generate mass legal knowledge.

Legal education of the general population, within the terminological confines outlined by government propaganda, formed part of the Communist project of regime building after the Civil War. The efforts to produce materials that could enable people to understand something about the Marriage Law and adhere to it contributed to the creation of a legal culture in the first years of the PRC. This legal culture was based on a politically shaped and controlled set of terms, intended to alter the way people talked about and referred to law. In this process, as this chapter suggests, the propaganda department was far from a cohesive body that could exert top-down pressure and dominate the production of legal education materials. More often than not, officials in the department found that they had to criticize and try to control legal language after materials had been published. These efforts amounted to rescue actions more than they did display a powerful institution of control that guided propaganda.

---

4 For an examination of legal education campaigns in post-Mao China, see Ronald Troyer, "Publicizing the New Laws: The Public Legal Education Campaign," in *Social Control in the People's Republic of China*, ed. Ronald J. Troyer, John P. Clark, and Dean G. Rojek (New York: Praeger, 1989), 70–83; Benjamin Liebman, "A Return to Populist Legality? Historical Legacies and Legal Reform," in *Mao's Invisible Hand: The Political Foundations of Adaptive Governance in China*, ed. Sebastian Heilmann and Elizabeth J. Perry (Cambridge: Harvard University Asia Center, 2011), 165–200; Mechthild Exner, "Die Verbreitung der Gesetzeserkenntnis unter den Bürgern in der VR China," *Zeitschrift für Gesetzgebung* 1 (1995): 54–79. For a political history analysis of campaigns refer to Julia Strauss, "Morality, Coercion and State Building by Campaigns in the Early PRC: Regime Consolidation and After, 1949–1956," in *The History of the PRC (1949–1976)*, ed. Julia Strauss (Cambridge: Cambridge University Press, 2007), 37–58.

Rather than address the many different aspects of the legal education campaign at national and local level, this chapter focuses on the simplification and popularization (*tongsuhua*) of the Marriage Law in print publications as both a technique to disseminate political interpretations of law and a strategy to gain legitimacy for the young party-state.[5] It explores how the government's cultural authorities, the party propaganda department, urban publishing houses, and writers dealt with the challenging task of producing and monitoring such materials. Cultural processes of simplification and popularization of law are important to understanding the legal history of the early PRC. Although not discussed in this chapter, they formed some of the basis on which judicial reforms as well as public trials and mediation techniques were built. Ideal conceptions of socialist modernity and subjectivity, at least in the first years of Communist rule, encompassed some basic knowledge of the new laws in order to enable people to participate in the construction of New China.

Simplification and Its Republican Precedents

Concerns for the need to compose a law accessible to literate and illiterate readers guided the drafting process of the Marriage Law. In the autumn of 1948, at the first conference on women work in the liberated areas, Liu Shaoqi approached Deng Yingchao, a prolific women's activist and Zhou Enlai's wife, with a request to set up a Marriage Law Drafting Small Group (*hunyinfa qicao xiaozu*) and compose a new Marriage Law in preparation of national takeover. Within days, Deng recruited a diverse group of women activists: Shuai Mengqi (1897–1987), Kang Keqing (1912–1992), Yang Zhihua (1900–1973), Li Peizhi (1904–1994), Luo Qiong, and Wang Ruqi (1912–1990).[6]

The group began regular work on the draft in the winter of the same year. Wang Ruqi, a graduate of Fudan University Law School, had a background

5 This paper thus joins those who have advocated the need to write legal histories of the early PRC, see, e.g., Dong Jieying 董节英, "Dui xin zhongguo chengli chuqi fazhi jianshe yanjiu 对新中国成立初期法制建设研究书评 [A Review of Research on the Construction of the Legal System in the Founding Period of New China]," *Zhonggong dangshi yanjiu* 中共党史研究 [Research on CCP History] 2 (2006): 110–17; Glenn Tiffert, "Epistrophy: Chinese Constitutionalism in the 1950s," in *Building Constitutionalism in China*, ed. Stéphanie Balme and Michael W. Dowdle (London: Palgrave Macmillan, 2009), 59–76; Klaus Mühlhahn, *Criminal Justice in China: A History* (Cambridge: Harvard University Press, 2009). See also Jennifer Altehenger, *Law, Propaganda, and Mass Education in Communist China, 1949–1989* (book manuscript in preparation).

6 The conference took place from 20 September until 5 October 1948 in Xibaipo.

in jurisprudence and was put in charge of writing the draft. She would listen to the group members' ideas and then incorporate these into a legal text. During the writing process, Wang made sure that the text employed clear and simple language, such that the law would be intelligible to specialists and lay readers alike. Once she had finished a new draft, it was distributed among the group members for the next round of revisions. After several months, most regulations had been laid out.[7] Article 1, 2, 3 and 8 of the law contained several simplified terms, many of which were phrased in four-character phrases, to describe the most crucial legal norms.[8] These phrases included the terms freedom of marriage (*hunyin ziyou*), monogamy (*yifu yiqi*), gender equality (*nannü quanli pingdeng*), mutual love and respect (*hu'ai hujing*), and family happiness (*jiating xingfu*). These phrases would eventually be used to create cohesion among legal education materials and simplify abstract legal notions into catchy slogans that could serve the production of character posters, cartoons, plays and short stories.

The drafting group's preoccupation with simplification was not new. Since late imperial times there had been a widespread notion that the most basic principles of law should be accessible, in some form, to the entire population if only in order to control society and public morals. This included publications that featured phrases of only a few characters that abbreviated more complicated legal stipulations and functioned as memory aids to legal

7 For an eyewitness account published by one of the drafting group members, see Luo Qiong 罗琼, "*Zasui fengjian hunyin jiasuo de zhongyao falü—yi diyibu hunyinfa dansheng qianhou* 砸碎封建婚姻枷锁的重要法律一忆第一部婚姻法诞生前后 [An Important Law to Smash the Shackles of Feudal Marriage—Remembering the Birth of the First Marriage Law]," *Renmin ribao* 人民日報 [People's Daily], May 3, 1990. See also *Renmin ribao* (Overseas Edition), October 22, 2001, reprinted in Huang Chuanhui 黄传会, *Tianxia hunyin: gongheguo san bu hunyinfa jishi* 天下婚姻: 共和国三部婚姻法纪事 [Chinese Marriage: A Chronicle of the People's Republic's Three Marriage Laws] (Shanghai: Wenhui chubanshe, 2004), 15ff and 45–49.

8 "Article 1: The feudal marriage system based on the arbitrary and compulsory arrangements and supremacy of man over woman, and in the disregard of the interests of children, is abolished"; "Article 2: Bigamy, concubinage, child betrothal, interference in re-marriage of widows, and the extraction of money or gifts in connection with marriages, are prohibited"; "Article 3: Marriage is based upon the complete willingness of the two parties. Neither party shall use compulsion and no third party is allowed to interfere"; "Article 7: Husband and wife are companions living together and enjoy equal status in the home"; "Article 8: Husband and wife are in duty bound to love, respect, assist and look after each other, to live in harmony, to engage in productive work, to care for their children and strive jointly for the welfare of the family and for the building up the new society." These translations are taken from *The Marriage Law of the People's Republic of China* (Beijing: Foreign Languages Press, 1950).

specialists and the more general readership.[9] From the late 19th- and the early 20th-century onwards, rendering laws accessible was particularly important to advocates of constitutional reform and supporters of the women's movement. They all argued that legal modernization should include the creation of legally informed citizens, male and female, who would be able to contribute to the construction of a better society.[10] Calls for the dissemination of legal knowledge accompanied the reinvigorated attempts to develop a modern legal system that could enforce and support the nation-building project at large after the collapse of the Qing dynasty in 1911.

Increasingly influential mass media became important mediators of legal knowledge. Magazines, especially women's publications, featured "General Legal Knowledge" articles (*falü changshi*) as part of their "General Knowledge" columns. As Bryna Goodman's chapter in this volume demonstrates, reportage of sensational court cases merged the world of mass media and entertainment culture with the world of law.[11] Newspapers and magazines featured reports and pictures of such proceedings thus involving a wide public in the debate over justice and law. Novels, short stories and drum ballads, such as those examined by Margaret Wan, entertained readers with tales of justice and its judges.[12] Drama brought the most popular historical and contemporary court cases onto local theatre stages. Audiences thus consumed law stories in similar

---

9 See, e.g., *Xinke fabi xinchun* 新刻法笔新春 [Reprint of a New Spring under the Legal Brush], Vol. 2, Undated; and Liang Tashan 梁他山, *Dulü guanlang* 读律琯琅 [The Wisdom-Star of Code-Readers], Xiaoyuan cangban, 1879 preface. I am grateful to Li Chen for calling my attention to this legacy and for providing these references.

10 On legal culture and law in popular culture in imperial China, see, e.g., Paul Heng-chao Ch'en, *Chinese Legal Tradition Under the Mongols: The Code of 1291 as Reconstructed* (Princeton: Princeton University Press, 1979), 89–93; Nicolai Volland, "The Control of the Media in the People's Republic of China," PhD diss., University of Heidelberg, 2003, 150–55; Xiao Zhang, "The Making of Modern Chinese Politics. Popular Culture, Protest Repertoires and Nationalism in the Sichuan Railway Protection Movement," PhD diss., University of California San Diego, 2009, 305; Harriet Zurndorfer, "Contracts, Property and Litigation: Intermediation and Adjudication in the Huizhou Region (Anhui) in Sixteenth-Century China," in *Law and Long-Term Economic Change: A Eurasian Perspective*, ed. Debin Ma and Jan van Zanden (Stanford: Stanford University Press, 2011), 91–114, at 92.

11 Bryna Goodman, " 'Law is One Thing, and Virtue is Another': Vernacular Readings of Law and Legal Process in 1920s Shanghai," at Chapter 5 of this volume. On court trials, law, and media, see also Eugenia Lean, *Public Passions: The Trial of Shi Jianqiao and the Rise of Popular Sympathy in Republican China* (Berkeley: University of California Press, 2007), 207.

12 Margaret Wan, "Court Case Ballads: Popular Ideals of Justice in Late Qing and Republican China," at Chapter 10 of this volume.

ways as previous generations had in imperial China when people flocked to see plays that featured trials, murder cases and mysteries.[13]

In the flourishing publishing industry of Republican and Nationalist China, legal education guidebooks for a general readership were included as one segment of popular education publishing (*tongsu jiaoyu*). Major publishing houses, such as the Commercial Press, printed general legal knowledge handbooks to accompany the promulgation of the Republican Civil Code and Criminal Codes in the early 1930s.[14] Snippets of legal education featured in a range of publications from teaching and study materials to self-help guides, everyday encyclopedias, and home-study books.

Despite this variety, however, and even though authors claimed to transmit legal knowledge in the most accessible manner possible, the content of many publications was still complex and not easily intelligible to anyone without further education. Some authors acknowledged this problem publicly. A 1931 booklet on *Marriage Law and Marriage Problems* written by Li Yizhen, for instance, identified two common approaches to the popularization of law: one favored the legal education of a limited group of professionals who would then use this knowledge to serve society, and the other advocated legal education of the wider population so that the law may benefit everyone directly. Li supported the broad dissemination of legal knowledge and added that the language used in writing about law should be as popular (*tongsu*) as possible.[15] Lamenting that this approach was not yet widespread enough, Li blamed politics and the legal professional sphere's disdain for any kind of popular readings (*tongsu duwu*) for the insufficient dissemination of law. Li opined that many materials published to promote general legal knowledge were of poor quality because their authors often did not know enough about law, were too opinionated, or plainly made too many mistakes.[16]

---

13 On court drama in late imperial China, cf. Melissa Macauley, *Social Power and Legal Culture. Litigation Masters in Late Imperial China* (Stanford: Stanford University Press, 1999), 33; Jeffrey C. Kinkley, *Chinese Justice, the Fiction: Law and Literature in Modern China* (Stanford: Stanford University Press, 2000), 29.

14 See Bryna Goodman, "Law is One Thing, and Virtue is Another," 67–68. See also Christopher A. Reed, *Gutenberg in Shanghai: Chinese Print Capitalism, 1876–1937* (Honolulu: University of Hawaii Press, 2004), 207.

15 Li Yizhen 李宜珍, *Hunyinfa yu hunyin wenti* 婚姻法与婚姻问题 [Marriage Law and Marriage Problems] (Shanghai: Zhengzhong shuju, 1931).

16 Ibid. For a similar example of popularization, see Zhu Caizhen 朱采真, *Falü xue ABC* 法律学 ABC [Jurisprudence ABC] (Shanghai: ABC Congshu she, 1929), and Wang Bo 汪波, *Qinshufa ABC* 亲属法 [Family Law ABC] (Shanghai: Shijie shuju, 1931). For publications on the civil code that contributed to general legal education but were written in

Examples such as this illustrate a growing awareness that at least some publications should help to make laws accessible to citizens. In Republican China, the question though was how much popular legal knowledge was necessary given the increased availability of trained legal professionals who could act as intermediaries and explain laws to the untrained. Members of the Marriage Law drafting group in 1948 were familiar with debates about citizenship, constitutional rights, women's rights, law and education. For them the answer was clear: people should have full knowledge of laws. Their efforts to compose an accessible law and promote the vernacularization of legal texts laid the groundwork for a much larger popularization effort—the Marriage Law mass campaign—that followed a couple of years later.

Popular Legal Education and Regime Transition

With the Communist takeover in 1949, sensational media reportage of flashy court trials subsided or was curtailed by the local authorities. State publishers and local branches of the party propaganda department increasingly gained control of media coverage of law implementation. Reports now focused on the propagandistic depiction of mass struggle sessions and local trials against counterrevolutionaries and landlords. These types of reports illustrated the party-state's willingness to employ coercive and violent techniques to control society.

The Marriage Law was passed in April 1950 and went into effect on 1 May. In the following months, newspapers and periodicals reported on the new law and described its core principles, most notably the stipulation for monogamy, gender equality, divorce, the abrogation of the foster daughter-in-law system, and the ban on 'mercenary marriages', coerced marriages, and matchmakers. However, by comparison to other propaganda efforts of the time—for the conflict unfolding on the Korean Peninsula and in the fight against 'counterrevolutionaries,—Marriage Law education was rather thin.

By the summer of 1951, the central government determined that the implementation of the Marriage Law was poor and demanded further attention. First investigations into the law's dissemination and enforcement began in the autumn of 1951. Municipal and district governments were instructed to

a much less accessible manner see, e.g., Gao Deming 高德明, ed., *Jiating falü changshi* 家庭法律常识 [Family Law General Knowledge] (Shanghai: Zhonghua shudian, 1948); Xu Zhixin 徐志欣, *Hunyinfa qianlun* 婚姻法浅论 [Light Discussion of the Marriage Law] (Shanghai: Zhonghua shuju, 1936).

set up Marriage Law bureaus (*hunyinfa bangongshi*). Their task was to send out investigation teams to gather data about people's marriages and families. Team members interviewed citizens and conducted public trials for Marriage Law offenders, which also illustrated to onlookers the importance of not acting in violation of the law.[17] Emphasis was on enforcing the law. Educating people in their rights and duties was part of this yet at that point the publishing authorities and propaganda department were not fully involved in the effort. Investigation teams concluded that the initial attempts to disseminate the Marriage Law since 1950 had produced adverse results: a sharp increase in divorces, suicides, and homicides as well as widespread resistance. Instead of rallying support for the party-state as vanguard legislator, the initial implementation of the Marriage Law had contributed to undermine the government's legitimacy.[18]

The central government concluded that a national education campaign could help correct what it saw as erroneous understandings of the law. A campaign could explain to people how the law fit in with the CCP's political ideology and visions for a socialist society. In late 1952, the government began to circulate internal plans for the Marriage Law education campaign scheduled for March of the next year. If mass legal education was to be successful, it would require careful coordination of production and distribution of readings. As in imperial China, the case discussed in Ting Zhang's chapter, private commercial publishers and state publishers produced law publications in the early 1950s and both required instructions.[19] Advance preparations were needed to organize and instruct writers, editors, and publishers, assemble legal education materials and booklets, have illustrations drawn and everything shipped to the printers and then on to the bookshops, work units and neighborhoods.

Preparations thus began several months before the campaign. In early December 1952, the government's Central Publishing Administration in Beijing notified all state-owned and private publishers, presses and distributing bookshops and instructed them to begin writing and editing propaganda materials.[20]

---

17 Diamant, *Revolutionizing the Family*, Chapter 2.

18 Ibid.

19 Ting Zhang, "Marketing Legal Information: Commercial Publications of the Great Qing Code, 1644–1911," at Chapter 8 of this volume.

20 The Beijing Municipal Archives (cited hereinafter as BMA), No. 8-2-699, "Zhongyang renmin zhengfu chuban zongshu guanyu zuo hao xuanchuan hunyinfa de shukan he chuban faxing gongzuo de tongzhi 中央人民政府出版总署关于做好宣传婚姻法的书刊和出版发行工作的通知 [Notification of the Central People's Government Publishing Administration on Completing the Task of Publishing and Distributing Books and Periodicals to Propagate the Marriage Law]," December 8, 1952.

To assist local publishers in their selection, the Central People's Press and the Youth Press had already started to gather materials on the Marriage Law for cadres and general mass propaganda. These materials included lesson books and introductory explanations as well as revised editions of the Marriage Law with relevant decrees and regulations. Publishers were encouraged to reprint radio broadcasts from 1950 and 1951, including Wang Feiran's deliberations on the Marriage Law and the mass line. Prefaces were added to these reprints explaining the broadcasts as part of the campaign's emphasis on education.[21]

Publishing authorities seemed to presume that many addressees of popular readings did not command more than a 'functional' literacy, if at all, and most were not going to read the entire text of the Marriage Law.[22] Officials and cadres would have to engage with the full law, but at this point the administration was more focused on ensuring that publishers prepared popular materials for a general audience because this had been one of the shortcomings of earlier implementation efforts. The circular singled out one publication, the *Illustrated Explanations of the Marriage Law* (*Hunyinfa tujie tongsu ben*) published by East China People's Press in late 1951, and instructed authors and editors to study it carefully.[23] More publications with easily accessible explanations of the law were needed. This included short stories, question and answer booklets, primers, comics, cartoons, poems, and songbooks.[24] These could then be used in regular discussion sessions and reading groups organized by local work units and neighborhood committees.[25] The standard of most publications had to be raised in order for people to pick up and engage with pamphlets and booklets.

---

21 BMA, No. 8-2-699.

22 On the difficulty of differentiating actual literacy levels from the idea of illiteracy promoted in CCP propaganda cf. Glen Peterson, *The Power of Words: Literacy and Revolution in South China, 1949–95* (Toronto: University of British Columbia Press, 1997).

23 BMA, No. 8-2-699.

24 Some of the final publications included, for example, Zhongnan minzhu fulian chouweihui bian 中南民主妇联筹委会编 [Preparatory Committee of the South-central China Women's Federation], ed., *Hunyin wenti wenda* 婚姻问题问答 [Marriage Law Questions and Answers] (Hankou: Zhongnan renmin chubanshe, 1952); Shi Shouyun 史守云 and Ge Xiumin 葛修敏, *Hunyinfa tongsu jiangben* 婚姻法通俗讲话 [Popular Introduction to the Marriage Law] (Shanghai: Huadong qingnian chubanshe, 1953); Shu Bo 舒波, *Dajia lai shixing hunyinfa* 大家来实行婚姻法 [Everyone Come Help Implement the Marriage Law] (Nanchang: Jiangsu renmin chubanshe, 1952); Huadong wenhuabu yishu shiye guanlichu 华东文化部艺术事业管理处 [East China Cultural Bureau Arts Administration Office], *Hunyinfa gequ ji* 婚姻法歌曲集 [Anthology of Marriage Law Songs] (Shanghai: Wanye shudian, 1953).

25 The Shanghai Municipal Archives (cited hereinafter as SMA), No. B1-2-3591-010/011, Letter from the East China Publishing Committee [华东出版委员会] to all shop owners across the East China region, January 15, 1950.

The administration instructed authors and publishers to make sure they incorporated different popular local art forms in order to increase the efficiency of legal education. Diversity of genres was desired, but all should communicate the same basic legal knowledge and explain that the Marriage Law forged a connection between the party, the country's government, and 'the masses.' Popular storylines were especially useful. They easily worked as illustrated serial comics (*lianhuanhua*), short stories or broadcasts, play scripts or they could be performed on local theatre stages. For the Marriage Law campaign this included well-known romance pieces such as *Liang Shanbo and Zhu Yingtai* and *The Legend of the White Snake* (*Baishe zhuan*) and newer productions such as Zhao Shuli's plays *Registration* (*Dengji*) and *Little Erhei Marries* (*Xiao Erhei jiehun*).[26]

As they assembled publications, publishers had to ensure that they adhered to the official legal terminology outlined by previous government directives. The circular carefully confined the topics to which publishers were supposed to limit themselves: free marriage, happiness, gender equality and how these factors contributed to increasing the efficiency of production. Divorce should only be mentioned in the context of local marriage dispute mediations or regulated divorce registration at court and further detailed discussions should be avoided entirely. The consistent message of all legal education was to be that the Marriage Law, legislated by the party-state, was the guarantor of a new society marked by harmonious families, gender equality and free marriages. Fearing that a variety of interpretations of the law might confuse the readers, authors were reminded to produce easily accessible stories and not to get caught up in the intricacies of individual experiences. The publishing administration feared that assembling narratives of how individuals coped under the new law, with little control from the propaganda department, could easily lead to exactly the kind of multiplicity of legal interpretations that the campaign was to prevent. To ensure that publishers, especially private businesses, were correctly instructed, all editors were told to work closely with the leading

---

26 There were multiple versions of each of these pieces, including: Zhao Shuli, "Dengji 登记 [Registration]," *Shuoshuo changchang* 说说唱唱 [Chat and Sing] 6 (1950): 27–45; Juben yuekan bianjibu, *Liang Shanbo yu Zhu Yingtai* 梁山伯与祝英台 [Liang Shanbo and Zhu Yingtai] (Beijing: Renmin wenxue chubanshe, 1953); Zhao Shuli, *Xiao Erhei jiehun* 小二黑结婚 [Little Erhei Marries] [Beijing: Renmin wenxue chubanshe, 1953); Huadong xiqu yanjiuyuan chuangzuoshi, ed., *Baishe zhuan: yueju* 白蛇传: 越剧 [The Tale of the White Snake: Yue Opera] (Shanghai, unknown publisher, 1952).

governmental and party cadres in their municipality or district, who would help publishers develop materials.[27]

The publishing administration's efforts helped carry the simplified content of the Marriage Law over into propaganda materials that strove to be equally accessible and that were based on simplified vocabulary embedded in vernacular text types. Popularizing this law in such a manner was necessary because it was the only way to try and garner people's acceptance for the new legal norms or at least, and more likely, impress on them the need to obey the law. Through popular law propaganda, the central government made popular legal knowledge one of the cornerstones of its mass line-inspired concept of law implementation. At the same time, the legal education campaign opened important opportunities for the party-state to disseminate not merely the plain stipulations of the Marriage Law, but also promote state-sponsored legal interpretations. What might have seemed like liberal legal norms—freedom of marriage and gender equality—was tied firmly into a socio-political framework in which the party-state politicized the law and sought hegemony for its blueprint of marriage, family, and a society governed by socialist law and morality.[28] A paradox was therefore inherent to mass legal education: By logic of the mass line, people had to know about and were expected to make active use of their rights and duties; but this was only permissible within a carefully defined scope of socialist language and imagery.

Producing Legal Education Primers

Instructions for the 1953 campaign emphasized that all publications should take as their main structure the juxtaposition of the "new marriage system" and the "old marriage system." Conveniently, this collocation also allowed the cultural authorities to integrate the Marriage Law campaign into the language and iconography of China's revolution. Publications were thus couched in the

27 Ibid. On the dissemination of materials published by the Xinhua bookstore, and the problems state-run publishers experienced in preparing materials, see also "Xinhua shudian yi chuban daliang peihe xuanchuan hunyinfa yundong de shuji 新华书店已出版大量配合宣传婚姻法运动的书籍 [The Xinhua Bookstore Has Already Published a Large Amount of Books to Accompany the Marriage Law Propaganda Campaign]," *Renmin ribao* 人民日报 [People's Daily], April 1, 1953.

28 On politicization for propaganda use, cf. Marina Svensson, *Debating Human Rights in China: A Conceptual and Political History* (Lanham/Oxford: Rowman & Littlefield, 2002), 308.

contrastive rhetoric advocated by the Propaganda Department. Most constructed chapters around the dichotomies between old society and new society, feudalism and new democracy, socialist and feudal, lawful and unlawful.[29] Marriage Law implementation was firmly established as part of "the last battle between light and dark," between old society and new China.[30] Harking back to Wang Feiran's discussion of the law's role in creating order, legal education materials depicted the law as the cure to disorder. This fit neatly into the CCP's claims that national unification had brought about a new society which, under the aegis of the legitimate government, would allegedly for the first time in Chinese history guarantee stability, safety and peace.

Concise and memorable terms made it possible to popularize the law's norms without having to force people to read the full law. In order to match the simplified phrases that the drafting committee had introduced into the law in 1948, some of the law's stipulations were also abbreviated in order to make them more accessible to the public. Gender equality, for instances, was reduced from a six to a four-character phrase (*nannü pingdeng*). In the publications, these phrases were then collocated with established idioms and set-phrases, often also in four characters, that epitomized "old China" and, very often, the Confucian family traditions. The "new marriage system" was described in phrases such as freedom of marriage, monogamy, gender equality, mutual love and respect, mutual support, harmonious unity, and family happiness. In addition, marriage registration was soon known as the process of "doing new things in a new way" (*xinshi xinban*). The "old marriage system," which was to be denounced and abolished, revealed itself in classical idioms and set-phrases such as: "the three subjections and four virtues" (*sancong side*), "the husband sings and the wife follows" (*fuchang fusui*), "treat females as inferior to males" (*nanzun nübei*), bigamy (*yifu duoqi*), matchmakers (*sanmei liuzheng*), "formal marriage" (denoting the Confucian marriage rites, *mingmei zhengqu*), "parents determine marriage" (*fumu zhuhun*), "those who oblige are filial" (*shunzhe weixiao*), and "exemplary chastity" (*zhenjie kefeng*).[31] The authoritative language of the law challenged the formerly authoritative language of Confucian customs.

---

29 See, e.g., Niu Zhi 牛志, *Hunyin dageming* 婚姻大革命 [The Great Revolution of Marriage] (Guangzhou: Nanfang tongsu duwu lianhe chubanshe, 1951), 9.

30 James Z. Gao, *The Communist Takeover of Hangzhou: The Transformation of City and Cadre, 1949–1954* (Honolulu: University of Hawaii Press, 2004), 201.

31 BMA, No. 196-2-473-003, "Hunyinfa xuanchuan cankao cailiao 婚姻法宣传参考材料 [Marriage Law Propaganda Reference Materials]," May 19, 1950.

This technique of centering Marriage Law implementation around a fixed set of terms allowed for some of the conformity in national, provincial and local publications that the government sought. A range of popular textbooks repackaged this message. Within a short amount of time, the Confucian classics were reconfigured as legal education handbooks in three-character classics, four-character classics, five-characters classics, textbooks, seven-character songs, and one-thousand character lessons. But the Marriage Law was also included in more general textbooks, mostly composed for female audiences such as the *Women's Three-Character Classic* (*funü sanzijing*), *Rural Women's Three-Character Classic* (*nongcun funü sanzijing*), *Women's Textbook* (*funü keben*). Some of these legal education lessons combined pictures and texts in order to help visualize the stipulations for the target group of semi-literate or illiterate readers. These pictures then also served to contextualize those explanations provided in the simplified lessons into a carefully constructed imagery of socialist marital and family life.

Variations on Confucian educational primers, especially the three-character classic, were widespread in the young People's Republic and had already been extremely popular readings for all sorts of educational purposes in late imperial and Republican China.[32] Three-, four- and five-character classics and illustrated explanatory booklets were mostly structured according to a similar pattern: the first one or two sections explain the Marriage Law in the larger context of the CCP's history, national liberation, and the fight for freedom of marriage and gender equality. The latter sections then turn to the law's individual stipulations, giving concrete—often hypothetical—examples, or explaining what the articles of the law meant. Examples and accompanying pictures were always modeled on the ideal socialist nuclear family.[33]

The *Illustrated Explanations of the Marriage Law*, which the Central Publishing Administration had recommended in its circular in December 1952, became one of the campaign's model booklets. The East China People's Press first issued the booklet in late 1951. Because the government promoted this booklet widely and because it was said to have achieved a print-run of ten million copies by spring 1953, the booklet's editors were asked to write up for national circulation in the *People's Daily* what they had experienced while

32 Barbara Mittler, *A Continuous Revolution: Making Sense of Cultural Revolution Culture* (Cambridge: Harvard University Asia Center, 2013), 141–56.

33 Susan L. Glosser, *Chinese Visions of Family and State, 1915–1953* (Berkeley: University of California Press, 2003), 186–91.

editing and publishing the volume.[34] According to the editors' account, first editorial work began in early August 1951. A similar booklet to accompany the Campaign to Suppress Counterrevolutionaries called *Illustrated Explanations of the Articles on Punishing Counterrevolutionaries* (*Chengzhi fan'geming tiaoli tujie tongsu ben*) had been published in the spring of 1951 with a print-run above a million copies.[35] Hoping to continue this success, editors decided to publish a volume to explain the Marriage Law. As they soon found out, however, assembling explanations on the punishment of counterrevolutionaries was easier than explaining the Marriage Law.

Actions against counterrevolutionaries could be based on concrete penalties, the problems were clear and did not require much additional explanation. Editors thought it was clear how to describe the process of detecting and punishing counterrevolutionaries. Explaining the Marriage Law was far more difficult because the Marriage Law mostly involved—to quote Mao—ideological contradictions among the people. Marriage Law implementation was supposed to curb the influences of "feudalism" across society. The adversaries could not be staked out as easily. A mother-in-law who treated her daughter-in-law poorly was to be reformed through education, unless she had committed a clear crime punishable by law.

In other cases, the general nature of the law's stipulations was difficult to translate into concrete examples. Article 2 of the Marriage Law, for instance, had abolished the foster daughter-in-law system, arranged marriages, coercion and other "feudal" customs. But the Marriage Law did not specify what to do with all those foster daughter-in-laws who had been married before the law was promulgated. It did not explain what would happen to children and property out of a first marriage if a widow chose to marry a second time. Such problems could not be easily addressed in pictures, even though they were highly relevant to the readership of popular materials. To circumvent the

34 The print run is discussed in "Chuban gongzuo wei guangda renmin qunzhong fuwu 出版工作为广大人民群众服务 [Publishing Work Is in Service to the Broad Masses]," in *Zhonghua renmin gongheguo chuban shiliao* 中华人民共和国出版史料 [Historical Materials on Publishing in the People's Republic of China] ed. *Zhongyang dang'anguan* 中央档案馆 et al., Vol. 4 (Beijing: Zhongguo shuji chubanshe, 2001), 228. For the description of the booklet's making, see Huadong renmin chubanshe, " 'Hunyinfa tujie tongsu ben' de bianxie jingyan 婚姻法图解通俗本的编写经验 [The Experiences of Writing and Editing the *Illustrated Explanations of the Marriage Law*]," *Renmin ribao* 人民日报 [People's Daily], February 1, 1953.

35 Zhu Jinping 朱晋平, *1949–1956 Zhongguo gongchandang dui siying chubanye de gaizao* 中国共产党对私营出版业的改造 [The CCP's Transformation of the Private Publishing Industry, 1949–1956] (Beijing: Zhongyang dangxiao chubanshe, 2008), 126.

problem, editors therefore decided to explain the individual articles of the law one-by-one, adding one picture to each article, rather than trying to tell longer human-interest stories. In addition, the booklet contained several specific examples addressing some of the above problems individually, thus avoiding generalization.[36]

By late August 1951, the first draft was ready for revision. It was submitted to the local Office for the Popularization of Current Affairs and Politics, to the East China cultural authorities, the People's Press and to the relevant central authorities under the Ministry of Culture in Beijing. The editors then contacted the Shanghai Association of Art Workers and commissioned several prominent artists to draw pictures for each article. Between September and October, the suggestions and criticisms from the authorities arrived. These emphasized that any explanation of the Marriage Law should be based on socialist political doctrine rather than personal experiences. In less abstract terms, this meant that all explanations and interpretations of the Marriage Law should be based on a comparison with the "feudal" marriage system in particular and "feudalism" in general, instead of associating "feudal" traits with individual persons. For example, the first draft of the booklet had not contained any explanation of the relationship between the custom of foster daughters-in-law and feudalism. It merely stated that the custom was bad and had therefore been abolished by the Marriage Law. Accordingly, the editors revised this and linked each example closely to the "spirit of the Marriage Law" (*hunyinfa de jingshen*) and "old society's feudalism." In mid-October, when the artists had finished their illustrations, these were printed successively in Shanghai's *Liberation Daily* with an explicit request for readers to comment. Once the comments had been received and processed by late October, the final proof was completed and submitted to the East China Party Propaganda Department and the East China People's Press. On 19 November, the first print-run was delivered to bookstores in Shanghai.[37]

After the booklet appeared on bookstore shelves, fourteen national newspapers and magazines serialized and reprinted it. Cadres and local branches of mass organizations used the volume as group reading material. Several local branches of the women's federation and party propaganda offices contacted the editors, asking for permission to reprint some of the pictures as posters. These posters were hung up in factories, neighborhoods, roadsides and shop windows. Within a few months, the East China People's Press received dozens of reader's letters from bookstore owners, housewives, propagandists, and factory workers. The owner of a bookstore in a village in Fujian province, for

36 Huadong renmin chubanshe, " 'Hunyinfa tujie tongsuben' de bianxie jingyan."

37 Ibid.

example, wrote that 70% of the customers buying the book were women. Of these women, he was sure that several had spent the money they had earned by catching fish or planting vegetables.[38]

Because it was published in the *People's Daily* and was supposed to serve as a model story, this was not a critical report of the booklet's production. It nonetheless explained the publication process of a booklet issued by a state-run publisher and it also illustrated how central authorities envisaged the publication of similar volumes modeled on the *Illustrated Explanations of the Marriage Law*.[39] Marriage Law primers should not link to individual plights and personal histories of China's people. These were described in model stories and the discussion of personal fortunes and misfortunes in local study groups. Educational primers, conversely, were to help situate the Marriage Law in the binary of political ideology and PRC law versus feudalism and old customs. Only in a second step could some of this conflict then be related to everyday experiences. One of the many consequences of this approach, however, was that the editors of many legal education publications then erred on the side of caution and issued materials that replicated each other, thus become repetitive and bland; hardly the kind of propaganda that might spark readers' attention and interest in legal knowledge.

The Propaganda Department Intervenes

The story of the People's Press' booklet was a facet of the campaign cultural authorities were keen to advertise. A perhaps more common facet, though less often addressed publicly, was the problem of how to control the appropriate use of the legal terms throughout the campaign across a wide spectrum of publications nationally. Most newspapers and publishers had dutifully printed articles or booklets about the Marriage Law in preparation of the campaign. Yet many of these did not meet the expectations of the central propaganda department in Beijing. In mid-March 1953, in the midst of the ongoing local Marriage Law campaign work, the propaganda department made an attempt to control legal education and propaganda language through internal (*neibu*) communication.[40]

---

38 Ibid.

39 For further details of the history of this model booklet, see Altehenger, *Law, Propaganda, and Mass Education in Communist China, 1949–1989*, chapter 3.

40 For the central supplementary directive that had set the tone for the campaign, cf. "Zhongguo gongchandang zhongyang weiyuanhui guanyu guanche hunyinfa yundong yue gongzuo de buchong zhishi 中国共产党中央委员会关于贯彻婚姻法运动月工

On 18 March, the department dispatched an internal circular to all provincial and municipal propaganda departments, the *People's Daily*, Xinhua News Agencies, and national broadcasting stations.[41] The memo reprimanded newspapers and other publications for failing to stick to the campaign goals and language. For some four months, from early December 1952 until mid-March 1953, the department had surveyed several provincial and municipal newspapers in search for mistakes and shortcomings in the way they contributed to the legal education of the general population. Although the memo focused on newspapers, its broad circulation underlined its relevance for everyone involved in the production of legal education media.

To begin with, the department admonished a number of newspapers for failing to propagate the Marriage Law. Publications singled out for criticism included the *Jilin Daily, Changjiang Daily, Yunnan Daily, Xikang Daily*, and *Gansu Daily*. These newspapers had not published enough, or even any, articles about the new law, its implementation, and its role in society. Then the examples became more concrete. Some newspapers were accused of having grossly misrepresented the meaning and scope of the new campaign and thus violated the central government's directives. Political language from other campaigns had been used during the Marriage Law campaign.[42] This was an easy way to avoid having to pay attention to using new terms in the correct way. *Inner Mongolia Daily*, for example, had claimed in an article published on January 18, 1953, that the upcoming campaign was meant to "criticize capitalist thinking" (*pipan ziben jieji sixiang*) and "oppose bourgeois thinking" (*fandui zichan jieji sixiang*). This kind of language was common during the Three Anti, Five Anti and Suppress Counterrevolutionaries Campaigns. The propaganda department considered it harmful to Marriage Law implementation.

作的补充指示 [Supplementary Directive of the Chinese Communist Party's Central Committee on Work during the Campaign to Implement the Marriage Law Month]", *Renmin ribao* 人民日报 [People's Daily], February 19, 1953.

41 Unless otherwise stated, the descriptions of the Propaganda Department's criticisms are taken from "Zhongyang xuanchuanbu guanyu gedi baozhi zai xuanchuan guanche hunyinfa de quedian he cuowu de tongbao 中央宣传部关于各地报纸在宣传贯彻婚姻法的缺点和错误的通报 [Circular by the Central Propaganda Department on Shortcomings and Mistakes of Newspapers across the Country in Propagating and Implementing the Marriage Law], March 18, 1953," in *Zhongguo gongchandang xuanchuan gongzuo wenxian xuanbian* 中国共产党宣传工作文献选编 [Selected Documents of the Chinese Communist Party's Propaganda Work], 521–24.

42 On the overlap between different campaigns see also: Neil J. Diamant, "Policy Blending, Fuzzy Chronology and Local Understandings of National Initiatives in Early 1950s China," *Frontiers of History in China* 9, No. 1 (2014): 83–101.

Much of the political language and terminology that the cultural authorities had been keen to disseminate in earlier years, and which many people had accustomed to, was thus to be avoided during legal education. On 19 February, for example, the *North-Eastern Daily* had stated in one article that, during the Marriage Law campaign, "all powers should be concentrated on abolishing oppression, coercion, and the feudal system." The propaganda department was quick to point out that this was the wrong formulation in the context of legal education. It might lead readers to believe that these old customs could be fully abolished within only a month's time, a goal that the slow process of implementing a new law could not achieve. Luring readers into false hopes or expectations regarding the results of a month-long legal education campaign was considered dangerous and potentially disruptive to the campaign. The propaganda department was trying to manage people's expectations. The precise formulation (*tifa*) mattered greatly and the association to previous political mass campaigns was to be avoided.[43] Campaigns to implement laws were supposed to be different from mass agitation campaigns and legal education propaganda should reflect this. The new formulation for legal education would bring about a linguistic separation from past campaigns, which, in turn, was supposed to ensure a separation in practice as well. It was therefore of utmost importance that all established phrases of mass agitation and mass accusation were dropped from the vocabulary available to propagandists carrying out legal education.

Evidently, however, this had not been accomplished as yet. Some newspapers, such as the *Hubei Daily*, had advocated the use of class struggle techniques calling for "mutual comparisons" (*huxiang pingbi*) and mobilizing people to speak bitterness (*fadong suku*). *Guangxi Daily* had advocated the practice of "denouncing husbands, mothers-in-law, and mothers" (*kongsu zhangfu, popo, muqin*). *Masses Daily* (*Qunzhong ribao*) had called for "self-criticism" (*ziwo jiantao*) and "mutual criticisms" (*huxiang piping*). The *Jiangxi Daily*, in an article of 30 January, had advocated "training women to speak bitterness" (*peiyang funü suku*). This call had quickly resulted in a full attack on husbands and mothers-in-law, an outcome certainly not welcomed by the propaganda department. But what angered the department most was that these newspapers had all made these mistakes despite the central government's previous

43 As Michael Schoenhals demonstrated, "appropriate ones [formulations] contribute[d] to the attainment of specific goals. Conversely, inappropriate formulations [were] 'factors' that may create ideological confusion among 'the masses.'" Cf. Michael Schoenhals, *Doing Things With Words in Chinese Politics: Five Studies* (Berkeley: University of California Press, 1992), 8.

efforts to explain campaign goals. The previous directives had all stressed that the above terms should not be used and had condemned these practices as unsuitable for law implementation. Many criticized articles were written after the directive was disseminated. The department therefore resolved that those journalists and editors in question had either not read the directives carefully enough, had decided to disregard their contents, or that they had not bothered to read them at all.

The attention given to precise wordings and terminology overestimated the ability of those implementing the campaign at the local level. The ideal that people would implement the law themselves, once educated about it, meant that the party would merely have to assist by providing and controlling education and the correct terminology which framed the new law as an achievement of the new society. The propaganda department's circular, the discussions about individual terms and phrases, and the process by which legal education publications were produced and criticized, however, illustrated state authorities worries that simplification and accessibility would not solve problems of dissemination. Implementation could not be left up to the people because people did not intuitively know how to appreciate the new law in the way envisaged by those who had promulgated it. The interpretation and 'correct' implementation of the law required continuous attention not merely by legal but by political authorities.

Conclusion

This chapter has illustrated some of the processes and difficulties that shaped the simplification of the Marriage Law for educational and propaganda purposes between 1950 and 1953. To the PRC government in its first years, simplification of law meant accessibility but also control as basic legal knowledge could help create law-abiding citizens. A study of the production of legal education materials can help understand one of the techniques by which agents in the party-state thought they could get people to learn about the law and also control what people learned about that law. Legal education campaigns in the early PRC, and the particular example of the campaign to implement the Marriage Law discussed here, were therefore an important facet of early PRC legal history, and indeed social and cultural history as well. Because legal education propaganda was considered vital to the way in which the new regime configured law and to the way in which law served to link state and society, the history of propaganda publications for these campaigns is central to understanding the role of law under early state socialism. The few laws of the early PRC, as many scholars have argued, were highly politicized and an instrument of party-state control.[44] Analyzing these campaigns and the legal education materials disseminated during the campaigns therefore enables a better understanding of a brief phase in Maoist China during which the politics of simplified legal language and legal knowledge mattered to the formation of a 'new society.'

Glossary

fadong suku	发动诉苦	*lianhuanhua*	连环画
fandui zichan jieji sixiang	反对资产阶级思想	*mingmei zhengqu*	明媒正娶
falü changshi	法律常识	*nan-nü pingdeng*	男女平等
fuchang fusui	夫唱妇随	*nanzun nübei*	男尊女卑
fumu zhuhun	父母主婚	*neibu*	内部
funü keben	《妇女课本》	*nongcun funü sanzijing*	《农村妇女三字经》
funü sanzijing	《妇女三字经》	*peiyang funü suku*	培养妇女诉苦
guanche hunyinfa yundong	贯彻婚姻法运动	*pipan ziben jieji sixiang*	批判资本阶级思想
hemu tuanjie	和睦团结	*sancong side*	三从四德
hunyinfa bangongshi	婚姻法办公室	*sanmei liuzheng*	三媒六证
hunyinfa qicao xiaozu	婚姻法起草小组	*shehui zhuyi fazhi*	社会主义法制
hunyinfa de jingshen	婚姻法的精神	*shunzhe weixiao*	顺者为孝
hunyin ziyou	婚姻自由	*tifa*	提法
hu'ai hujing	互爱互敬	*tongsu duwu*	通俗读物
huxiang bangzhu	互相帮助	*tongsu jiaoyu*	通俗教育
huxiang pingbi	互相评比	*xinshi xinban*	新事新办
huxiang piping	互相批评	*yifu duoqi*	一夫多妻
jiating xingfu	家庭幸福	*yifu yiqi*	一夫一妻
kongsu zhangfu, popo, muqin	控诉丈夫、婆婆、母亲	*zhenjie kefeng*	贞节可风
		ziwo jiantao	自我检讨

44 For some representative studies, cf. Stanley Lubman, *Bird in a Cage: Legal Reform in China after Mao* (Stanford: Stanford University Press, 1999); Mühlhahn, *Criminal Justice in China*; Pitman Potter, *From Leninist Discipline to Socialist Legality: Peng Zhen on Law and Political Authority in the PRC* (Stanford: Stanford University Press, 2003).

Bibliography

Balme, Stéphanie, and Michael W. Dowdle. "Introduction: Exploring for Constitutionalism in 21st Century China." In *Building Constitutionalism in China*, edited by Stéphanie Barme and Michael W. Dowdle, 1–20. London: Palgrave Macmillan, 2009.

Beijing Municipal Archives, BMA 8-2-699. "Zhongyang renmin zhengfu chuban zongshu guanyu zuo hao xuanchuan hunyinfa de shukan he chuban faxing gongzuo de tongzhi 中央人民政府出版总署关于做好宣传婚姻法的书刊和出版发行工作的通知 [Notification of the Central People's Government Publishing Administration on Completing the Task of Publishing and Distributing Books and Periodicals to Propagate the Marriage Law]." December 8, 1952.

Beijing Municipal Archives, BMA 196-2-473-003. "*Hunyinfa xuanchuan cankao cailiao* 婚姻法宣传参考材料 [Marriage Law Propaganda Reference Materials]." May 19, 1950.

Ch'en, Paul Heng-chao. *Chinese Legal Tradition under the Mongols: The Code of 1291 as Reconstructed*. Princeton: Princeton University Press, 1979.

"Chuban gongzuo wei guangda renmin qunzhong fuwu 出版工作为广大人民群众服务 [Publishing Work Is in Service to the Broad Masses]." In *Zhonghua renmin gongheguo chuban shiliao* 中华人民共和国出版史料 [Historical Materials on Publishing in the People's Republic of China] edited by *Zhongyang dang'anguan* 中央档案馆 et al., Vol. 4. Beijing: Zhongguo shuji chubanshe, 2001.

Cook, Alexander C. "Unsettling Accounts: The Trial of the 'Gang of Four': Narratives of Justice and Humanity in the Aftermath of China's Cultural Revolution." PhD diss., Columbia University, 2007.

Davin, Delia. *Woman-Work: Women and the Party in Revolutionary China*. Oxford: Clarendon Press, 1976.

Diamant, Neil J. *Revolutionizing the Family: Politics, Love and Divorce in Urban and Rural China, 1949–1968*. Berkeley: University of California Press, 2000.

Diestelkamp, Bernhard. *Rechtsgeschichte als Zeitgeschichte: Beiträge zur Rechtsgeschichte des 20. Jahrhunderts*. Baden-Baden: Nomos, 2001.

Dong Jieying 董节英. "Dui xin Zhongguo chengli chuqi fazhi jianshe yanjiu shuping 对新中国成立初期法制建设研究书评 [A Review of Research on the Construction of the Legal System in the Founding Period of New China]." *Zhonggong dangshi yanjiu* 中国党史研究 [History of the CCP] 2 (2006): 110–17.

Exner, Mechthild. "Die Verbreitung der Gesetzeserkenntnis unter den Bürgern in der VR China." *Zeitschrift für Gesetzgebung* 1 (1995): 54–79.

Gao Deming 高德明, ed. *Jiating falü changshi* 家庭法律常识 [Family Law General Knowledge]. Shanghai: Zhonghua shudian, 1948.

Gao, James Z. *The Communist Takeover of Hangzhou: The Transformation of City and Cadre, 1949–1954*. Honolulu: University of Hawaii Press, 2004.

Glosser, Susan L. *Chinese Visions of Family and State, 1915–1953*. Berkeley: University of California Press, 2003.

Goodman, Bryna. " 'Law is One Thing, and Virtue is Another': Vernacular Readings of Law and Legal Process in 1920s Shanghai." Chapter 5 of this volume.

Huadong renmin chubanshe 华东人民出版社 [East China People's Press]. " '*Hunyinfa tujie tongsuben*' *de bianxie jingyan* '婚姻法图解通俗本'的编写经验 [The Experiences of Writing and Editing the *Illustrated Explanations of the Marriage Law*]." *Renmin ribao* 人民日报 [People's Daily], February 1, 1953.

Huadong wenhuabu yishu shiye guanlichu 华东文化部艺术事业管理处 [East China Cultural Bureau Arts Administration Office]. *Hunyinfa gequ ji* 婚姻法歌曲集 [Anthology of Marriage Law Songs]. Shanghai: Wanye shudian, 1953.

Huadong xiqu yanjiuyuan chuangzuoshi 华东戏曲研究院创作室, ed. *Baishe zhuan: yueju* 白蛇传:越剧 [The Tale of the White Snake: Yue Opera]. Shanghai: (unknown publisher), 1952.

Huang Chuanhui 黄传会. *Tianxia hunyin: gongheguo san bu hunyinfa jishi* 天下婚姻:共和国三部婚姻法纪事 [Chinese Marriage: A Chronicle of the People's Republic's Three Marriage Laws]. Shanghai: Wenhui chubanshe, 2004.

Johnson, Kay Ann. *Women, the Family and Peasant Revolution in China*. Chicago: University of Chicago Press, 1983.

Juben yuekan bianjibu 剧本月刊编辑部 [*Juben* editorial board]. *Liang Shanbo yu Zhu Yingtai* 梁山伯与祝英台 [Liang Shanbo and Zhu Yingtai]. Beijing: Renmin wenxue chubanshe, 1953.

Kinkley, Jeffrey C. *Chinese Justice, The Fiction: Law and Literature in Modern China*. Stanford: Stanford University Press, 2000.

Lean, Eugenia. *Public Passions: The Trial of Shi Jianqiao and the Rise of Popular Sympathy in Republican China*. Berkeley: University of California Press, 2007.

Li Yizhen 李宜珍. *Hunyinfa yu hunyin wenti* 婚姻法与婚姻问题 [Marriage Law and Marriage Problems]. Shanghai: Zhengzhong shuju, 1931.

Liang Tashan 梁他山. *Dulü guanlang* 读律琯琅 [The Wisdom-Star of Code-Readers]. Xiaoyuan cangban, 1879.

Liebman, Benjamin. "A Return to Populist Legality? Historical Legacies and Legal Reform." In *Mao's Invisible Hand: The Political Foundations of Adaptive Governance in China*, edited by Sebastian Heilmann and Elizabeth J. Perry, 165–200. Cambridge: Harvard University Asia Center, 2011.

Lipinsky, Astrid. *Der Chinesische Frauenverband*. Münster: Verlag, 2006.

Lubman, Stanley. *Bird in a Cage: Legal Reform in China after Mao*. Stanford: Stanford University Press, 1999.

Luo Qiong 罗琼. "*Zasui fengjian hunyin jiasuo de zhongyao falü—yi diyibu hunyinfa dansheng qianhou* 砸碎封建婚姻枷锁的重要法律一忆第一部婚姻法诞生前后 [An Important Law to Smash the Shackles of Feudal Marriage—Remembering the Birth of the First Marriage Law]." *Renmin ribao* 人民日报 [People's Daily], May 3, 1990.

Macauley, Melissa. *Social Power and Legal Culture: Litigation Masters in Late Imperial China*. Stanford: Stanford University Press, 1999.

The Marriage Law of the People's Republic of China. Beijing: Foreign Languages Press, 1950.

Mittler, Barbara. *A Continuous Revolution: Making Sense of Cultural Revolution Culture*. Cambridge, MA.: Harvard University Asia Center, 2013.

Mühlhahn, Klaus. *Criminal Justice in China: A History*. Cambridge: Harvard University Press, 2009.

Niu Zhi 牛志. *Hunyin dageming* 婚姻大革命 [The Great Revolution of Marriage]. Guangzhou: Nanfang tongsu duwu lianhe chubanshe, 1951.

Pendas, Devin. *The Frankfurt Auschwitz Trial, 1963–1965: History, Genocide and the Limits of the Law*. Cambridge: Cambridge University Press, 2006.

Potter, Pitman B. *From Leninist Discipline to Socialist Legality*: Peng Zhen on Law and Political Authority in the PRC. Stanford: Stanford University Press, 2003.

Reed, Christopher A. *Gutenberg in Shanghai: Chinese Print Capitalism, 1876–1937*. Honolulu: University of Hawaii Press, 2004.

Requate, Jörg. *Recht und Justiz im gesellschaftlichen Aufbruch (1960–1975). Bundesrepublik, Frankreich und Italien im Vergleich*. Baden-Baden: Nomos, 2003.

Schoenhals, Michael. *Doing Things with Words in Chinese Politics: Five Studies*. Berkeley: University of California Press, 1992.

Shanghai Municipal Archives, SMA B1-2-3591-010/011. "Letter from the *Huadong chuban weiyuanhui* 华东出版委员会 [East China Publishing Committee] to All Shop Owners across the East China Region." January 15, 1950.

Shi Shouyun 史守云, and Ge Xiumin 葛修敏. *Hunyinfa tongsu jiangben* 婚姻法通俗讲话 [Popular Introduction to the Marriage Law]. Shanghai: Huadong qingnian chubanshe, 1953.

Shu Bo 舒波. *Dajia lai shixing hunyinfa* 大家来实行婚姻法 [Everyone Come Help Implement the Marriage Law]. Nanchang: Jiangsu renmin chubanshe, 1952.

Svensson, Marina. *Debating Human Rights in China: A Conceptual and Political History*. Lanham/Oxford: Rowman & Littlefield, 2002.

Stacey, Judith. *Patriarchy and Socialist Revolution in China*. Berkeley: University of California Press, 1983.

Stolleis, Michael. *The Law under the Swastika: Studies on Legal History in Nazi Germany*. Chicago: University of Chicago Press, 1998.

Strauss, Julia. "Morality, Coercion and State Building by Campaigns in the Early PRC: Regime Consolidation and After, 1949–1956." In *The History of the PRC (1949–1976)*, edited by Julia Strauss, 37–58. Cambridge: Cambridge University Press, 2007.

Tiffert, Glenn. "Epistrophy: Chinese Constitutionalism in the 1950s." In *Building Constitutionalism in China*, edited by Stéphanie Balme and Michael W. Dowdle, 59–76. London: Palgrave Macmillan, 2009.

Ting Zhang. "Marketing Legal Information: Commercial Publications of the Great Qing Code, 1644–1911." Chapter 8 of This Volume.

Troyer, Ronald. "Publicizing the New Laws: The Public Legal Education Campaign." In *Social Control in the People's Republic of China*, edited by Ronald J. Troyer, John P. Clark, and Dean G. Rojek, 70–83. New York: Praeger, 1989.

Volland, Nicolai. "The Control of the Media in the People's Republic of China." PhD diss., University of Heidelberg, 2003.

Wan, Margaret. "Court Case Ballads: Popular Ideals of Justice in Late Qing and Republican China." Chapter 10 of This Volume.

Wang Bo 汪波. *Qinshufa ABC* 亲属法 [Family Law ABC]. Shanghai: Shijie shuju, 1931.

Wang Feiran 王斐然. "Youguan hunyinfa de wenti 有关婚姻法的问题 [Issues Concerning the Marriage Law]." *Xin jianshe* 新建设 [New Construction], 2 (1950): 16–17.

Xiao Zhang. "The Making of Modern Chinese Politics. Popular Culture, Protest Repertoires and Nationalism in the Sichuan Railway Protection Movement." PhD diss., University of California San Diego, 2009.

"Xinhua shudian yi chuban daliang peihe xuanchuan hunyinfa yundong de shuji 新华书店已出版大量配合宣传婚姻法运动的书籍 [The Xinhua Bookstore Has Already Published a Large Amount of Books to Accompany the Marriage Law Propaganda Campaign]." *Renmin ribao* [People's Daily], April 1, 1953.

Xinke fabi xinchun 新刻法笔新春 [Reprint of a New Spring under the Legal Brush], Vol. 2. Undated.

Xu Zhixin 徐志欣. *Hunyinfa qianlun* 婚姻法浅论 [Light Discussion of the Marriage Law]. Shanghai: Zhonghua shuju, 1936.

Zhao Shuli 赵树立. "Dengji 登記 [Registration]." *Shuoshuo changchang* 说说唱唱 [Chat and Sing] 6 (1950): 27–45.

———. "*Xiao Erhei jiehun* 小二黑结婚 [Little Erhei Marries]." Beijing: Renmin wenxue chubanshe, 1953.

"Zhongguo gongchandang zhongyang weiyuanhui guanyu guanche hunyinfa yundong yue gongzuo de buchong zhishi 中国共产党中央委员会关于贯彻婚姻法运动月工作的补充指示 [Supplementary Directive of the Chinese Communist Party's Central Committee on Work during the Campaign to Implement the Marriage Law Month]." *Renmin ribao* 人民日报 [People's Daily], February 19, 1953.

Zhongnan minzhu fulian chouweihui bian 中南民主妇联筹委会编 [Preparatory Committee of the South-central China Women's Federation], ed. *Hunyin wenti wenda* 婚姻问题问答 [Marriage Law Questions and Answers]. Hankou: Zhongnan renmin chubanshe, 1952.

"Zhongyang xuanchuanbu guanyu gedi baozhi zai xuanchuan guanche hunyinfa de quedian he cuowu de tongbao 中央宣传部关于各地报纸在宣传贯彻婚姻法的缺点和错误的通报 [Circular by the Central Propaganda Department on Shortcomings and Mistakes of Newspapers across the Country in Propagating and Implementing the Marriage Law], March 18, 1953." In *Zhongguo gongchandang xuanchuan gongzuo wenxian xuanbian* 中国共产党宣传工作文献选编 [Selected Documents of the Chinese Communist Party's Propaganda Work], 521–24.

Zhu Caizhen 朱采真. *Falü xue ABC* 法律学 ABC [Jurisprudence ABC]. Shanghai: ABC Congshu she, 1929.

Zhu Jinping 朱晋平. *1949–1956 Zhongguo gongchandang dui siying chubanye de gaizao* 中国共产党对私营出版业的改造, 1949–1956 [The CCP's Transformation of the Private Publishing Industry, 1949–1956]. Beijing: Zhongyang dangxiao chubanshe, 2008.

Zurndorfer, Harriet. "Contracts, Property and Litigation: Intermediation and Adjudication in the Huizhou Region (Anhui) in Sixteenth-Century China." In *Law and Long-Term Economic Change: A Eurasian Perspective*, edited by Debin Ma and Jan van Zanden, 91–114. Stanford: Stanford University Press, 2011.

Index

Page numbers followed by f indicate figures; numbers followed by t indicate tables.

www.ingramcontent.com/pod-product-compliance
Lightning Source LLC
LaVergne TN
LVHW011107300926
849160LV00008B/299
* 9 7 8 9 0 0 4 3 6 2 8 3 3 *